The Passage
of the REPUBLIC

An Interdisciplinary History of Nineteenth-Century America

WILLIAM L. BARNEY
*University of North Carolina
at Chapel Hill*

D0060813

D. C. HEATH AND COMPANY
Lexington, Massachusetts · Toronto

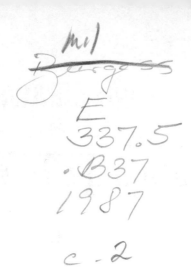
Cover art: *The Battery, New York, 1855,* by Samuel B. Waugh
(The Museum of the City of New York)

For Elaine

In more ways than I can say

Preface

The Passage of the Republic is about Americans in the nineteenth century and the ways in which they made their history. The text is based on the belief that the study of history, like the *making* of history, is an active process of engagement. It invites students to approach history not as a series of disconnected events and dates to be memorized but as an essential means of coming to know ourselves better by learning how the past has shaped our present. My hope is that the text will add texture and dimension to the study and teaching of courses in nineteenth-century United States history, in survey courses, and in courses on social history.

Two novel features of the text should be stressed at the outset:

1. *It treats nineteenth-century United States history as a conceptual whole.* There is presently no text that covers the nineteenth century in the comprehensive manner in which several texts explore the twentieth century. Of the many reasons for this omission, none looms as large as the way in which the Civil War has dominated our view of the nineteenth century. Rather than viewing the war as contemporaries did—that is, as the critical midpoint of an entire generational experience—historians conventionally have treated it as a kind of impenetrable barrier through which little of what preceded it could pass. This intellectual division of the nineteenth century has been perpetuated by the usual practice of breaking introductory-level courses in American history at the Civil War. In this setting, the division increasingly makes less sense as the sheer amount of material to be covered in the post-1865 survey grows year by year. More importantly, the division obscures the fact that nineteenth-century American history *was* a conceptual whole, especially in the years from 1815 to 1896, when Americans made the important transition from the colonial-revolutionary era to the foundations of modern America.

The title of the text, *The Passage of the Republic,* thus suggests the way in which the nineteenth century represents the major transitional phase in the American experience. During this period the republic was torn between its commitment to a republican ideology (which originally defined freedom in terms of economic independence and public virtue) and its transformation into a market society (which redefined freedom in terms of economic mobility and private gain). This passage of the republic from its eighteenth-century roots to its twentieth-century outcomes provides the conceptual core of the text.

2. *It integrates the many perspectives of history into a strong social-history narrative*. Most texts treat economic development, social relations, ideology, and politics as discrete and unconnected phenomena; *The Passage of the Republic* shows how these different aspects of the human experience are part of an interconnected whole. In this approach, social history is not simply history with the politics left out but rather is the story of how people try to find meaning in both their private and public lives. In the context of their economic and physical environments, people make countless individual decisions that, in the aggregate, form patterns of continuity and change—the core of social history. By studying these patterns we can better understand the impact of economic change on individuals and communities, how cultural values shift both to explain and to shape social change, and how politics serves as the public expression of the private needs and values of the social order.

In writing such a history I responded to what many historians and other critics have decried as the chief failure of modern American historiography—the lack of a coherent account of how America changed over time and evolved into the world we know today. A welter of specialized and technically sophisticated studies, especially in what has been dubbed "the new social history," has appeared in the last twenty years. This new literature has shared three general characteristics:

1. Much of it has relied on precise quantitative measurements based on computer ordering and manipulation of a vast array of numerical data.
2. It has borrowed heavily from the theoretical constructs of the social sciences. For example, from demography, sociology, and economics have come concepts of biological and cultural cycles of birth, marriage, and death, and their relationship to population pressure and natural resources in rural, preindustrial societies. Social psychology and cultural anthropology have given us a greater appreciation of the complexity of individual motivations and the way in which politics reflects the symbolic universe of family and community life.
3. Because these methodological and conceptual breakthroughs coincided with social activism in the 1960s and with disillusionment with public institutions of power in the 1970s, much of the energy in recent American historiography has gone into discovering the history of groups previously glossed over or ignored in traditional historical accounts.

A major result of these trends has been a tremendous increase in the amount of information available about particular groups at specific points in time. Most significantly, we have rediscovered the history of women, blacks, workers, immigrants, native Americans, and other groups who left few written records. Our view of history is no longer limited to the public actions and statements of male politicians and military figures. In short, the range and concerns of American history have been enormously enriched, even democratized. Nonetheless, a sense of the overall picture has been lost amid the technical brilliance and narrow specialization of so much of the recent work. *The Passage of the Republic* attempts to provide such an overall picture for the nineteenth century. It offers a synthesis of recent research in American social history and incorporates the insights of political, economic, intellectual, and cultural history. Through this integrated approach, the text explains the patterns that evolved in America during the nineteenth century.

The history that students can expect to find here has no heroes and villains, no simple lessons and answers. It is a history that stresses conflict as much as consensus, inequality as well as equality. The text takes students seriously and, wherever possible, permits individuals and groups to speak for themselves, so that students can gain an appreciation for the diversity of values and lifestyles that made up the various cultures of nineteenth-century America. I have tried to show by example that history does not "just happen" but rather is created through a complex process in which individuals struggle to impose their wills on impersonal circumstances that are not entirely of their own making.

The debts that I have incurred in writing this text are many. My greatest intellectual debt is to those hundreds of scholars upon whose works I have drawn. Their research and data, especially as found in the outpouring of works in social history over the past twenty years, made this text possible. The insightful comments and criticisms of outside readers—Ronald P. Formisano, Lawrence B. Goodheart, Maurine W. Greenwald, Walter Licht, and Joel H. Silbey—greatly improved the text in its earlier drafts. I am also grateful to Linda Halvorson, my editor at D. C. Heath, for her patient confidence in the project. Rosalie Radcliffe, of the Department of History in Chapel Hill, deserves special thanks for her contribution of superb typing skills and her strong interest in the progress of the project. For the support of my family—Elaine, Kristina, and Jeremy—any acknowledgement now must seem like a pittance after my having been closeted away for so long in writing this text. My debt to them can be repaid, if at all, only in the form of future gratitude and love.

W. L. B.

Contents

Maps

Tables

THE PASSAGE OF THE REPUBLIC

An Overview

The unifying theme that ties together the narrative in *The Passage of the Republic* is the transformation of late-eighteenth-century republican ideology through a continuous interaction with an expanding market economy. The market and reactions to it were the dynamic elements in the passage of nineteenth-century America from an agrarian society of largely self-sufficient farmers to an industrial society of wage laborers and salaried employees.

The market—the sum total of decisions relative to the allocation and control of capital and labor in the production of goods for sale at a profit—was a revolutionary agent of change. On the one hand, economic development greatly expanded production and the range of goods available for consumption. On the other hand, this very material abundance was made possible only by disrupting the social lives of common Americans and subordinating their social relations to economic activities. The market offered the freedom to compete and raise one's living standard, but it simultaneously took away the freedom of economic independence and self-employment. Increasingly, Americans were free to respond to market opportunities but not free from the pressure of having to respond. Responses to the market gradually broke down older dependencies rooted in the personalized ties of communities and replaced them with newer, depersonalized ones geared to market prices and the law of supply and demand.

Throughout the nineteenth century, Americans engaged in an ongoing debate over how best to reconcile the emerging market society with their political culture of republicanism. Simultaneously a political ideology and a cultural vision of what might be termed the good society, republicanism comprised a dominant cluster of attitudes and beliefs that was at the core of national self-expression in the nineteenth century.

Republicanism took shape as a coherent body of thought in the mid-eighteenth century and was the ideological basis for America's Revolutionary War against England. Freedom from economic and political dependency upon the will of another was the most cherished value in republican thought. In turn, it was believed, this fundamental liberty had to be protected at all times from encroaching centers of outside power. Only civic virtue—the willingness of citizens to participate in politics and place the public good above private interest—could provide that protection for the local autonomy of communities and the economic independence of individuals. Such civic virtue could be expected only as long as property was relatively evenly distributed

1

in a society of economically independent propertyholders. Otherwise, the propertyless, dependent poor would fall prey to the political corruption of the power-hungry rich who controlled most of the property.

Eighteenth-century republicanism was not, it must be stressed, synonymous with democracy. Unchecked power, whether from above or below in the social order, was the great enemy of republicanism; and democracy—direct rule by the people—was equated with mob rule. Thus, the Constitution set up a republic, a system of government based upon the representation of the people through elected officials. And significantly, of all the federal officials, only members of the House of Representatives were originally to be elected directly by the people. Nonetheless, the inherent egalitarian strain in American republicanism, the desire to be free from the control of others, provided a powerful impetus for the democratic currents in American society that emerged by the 1820s with the rise of a mass political culture, the expansion of voting rights for white males, and the opening up of economic choices for individuals. Captured in the name, ideology, and organization of the Jacksonian Democratic party, this upsurge of interest in the common man blurred the earlier distinction between a republic and a democracy. By the mid-nineteenth century Americans, like their contemporaries in western Europe, were beginning to use republicanism and democracy as interchangeable terms for a representative form of government marked by a broad franchise and respect for individual rights.

Although initially biased against commerce as a source of corrupting wealth, corporations as undemocratic centers of tyrannical power, and wage labor as a degraded state of dependency, republicanism also valued the right of the individual to pursue self-interest, free from external restraints. Thus, republicanism could be used either to attack or praise the spread of a market society in the nineteenth century, a society that simultaneously expanded opportunities for self-advancement and produced great inequalities in wealth and power. Defenders of community cohesiveness and promoters of competitive individualism each drew on separate strands of republican thought. In the antebellum North, republicanism blended with liberal capitalism, a social ideology that stressed the progressive development of individual freedoms and self-improvement through unrestricted access to economic gain. Meanwhile, in the antebellum South, republicanism became inseparable from cultural codes of white male honor and provided the ideological basis for a white man's democracy of slaveholders. In short, republicanism could be mobilized for quite different social purposes, because it offered a common language and symbols with which diverse groups of Americans could articulate their perceptions of reality.

At two points in the nineteenth century, conflicting republican interpretations of market change produced two major crises:

1. The first marked the end of the antebellum period. The flashpoint of the Civil War was reached when a political majority in the North and South identified the social system and market economy of the other as an immediate threat to their republican liberties. The war followed when each section fought for its own version of republicanism.
2. The second crisis was triggered by the depression of the 1890s. Dissident farmers, supported by a smaller number of workers, presented a cooperative vision of America that would curb, if not eliminate, the concentrated centers of economic

power that, they argued, made a mockery of democracy. This challenge to the corporate order, which had emerged in the post–Civil War years, was decisively defeated in the McKinley-Bryan election of 1896.

Each of these crises was a major watershed in nineteenth-century American history. Northern victory in the Civil War preserved the Union, destroyed slavery, and maintained the national boundaries of the market economy. That victory, by crushing the ideological and political barrier of planter opposition to free-labor capitalism, was an essential prelude to the new political order of industrial capitalism. The dominance of that order in American history was finalized by the failure of agrarian revolt in the 1890s.

The timing of these two crises, in conjunction with the prolonged and violent sectional debate over the inclusion of Afro-Americans in the core culture of republicanism during the Civil War–Reconstruction era, 1860–1877, is the reason for dividing the text into three Parts. Within each Part, the chapters are organized chronologically around different, but interrelated, themes in the transformation of nineteenth-century American society.

Part I deals with antebellum America, 1815–1860. The War of 1812, though a military and diplomatic stalemate, freed the young republic from its entangling involvement in European affairs and convinced the generation that had fought the Revolution that the gains of the Revolution had finally been secured. Energy now released for internal development led to a process of accelerating market change, which in turn generated a variety of ideological and organizational responses for coping with a pervasive sense of dislocation. By the 1850s, these responses had polarized into two competing but mutually reinforcing sectional ideologies: one based on the threat of slavery to a free-labor society and the other on the threat of antislavery to a slavery society. These ideologies were immensely popular precisely because they enabled Northern and Southern whites to blame the values of the other group for the disturbing changes within their respective social orders. It is in this context—the dialectic between social change and ideological response—that the narrative places the coming of the Civil War.

Part I begins with the economic and cultural meaning of land for early-nineteenth-century Americans. It then moves on to demographic pressures in the East and an explanation of how the consequences of those pressures are crucial to understanding both the settlement of the Jacksonian West and the rise of early manufacturing in the East. Chapters 2 and 3 examine the relationship between this process of material change and shifts in social attitudes and class formation. Chapter 2 is structured around native Americans, free blacks, and women. At its conceptual center is an explanation of how culture was blended with biology in popular ideologies that assigned all three of these groups to positions of social subordination. The rise of a new middle class, a crucial theme that is still neglected in most textbooks, is highlighted in Chapter 3. The evolution of this class and its formative role in the North in promoting evangelicalism, reform, and a social vision of competitive, self-disciplined individualism are the dominant themes in this chapter. Chapters 4 and 5 focus on the political response to the socioeconomic and ideological changes that were redefining the meaning and significance of public (i.e., white male) participation in political life. Chapter 4, which covers up to 1840, traces out the creation of the first mass-based party system in

American history and the way in which the parties mobilized contrasting ethnic and class responses to the market revolution. Chapter 5 deals with the 1840s and 1850s and the story of how that party system of Democrats and Whigs broke down in a seemingly irreversible cycle that set the stage for sectionalized politics and the Civil War.

Part II interprets the Civil War–Reconstruction era, 1860–1877, as a prolonged crisis of republican order. The first stage of crisis involved the existence of the Union itself and the second the social meaning and constitutional limits of the Union that had been militarily restored by 1865. By 1860 a Northern majority believed that the chief threat to republicanism was an aggressive Slave Power, a conspiratorial bloc of slaveholders who trampled upon individual freedoms in order to defend and expand slavery. For Lincoln's Republican party, born in the sectional turmoil of the 1850s, the Confederacy represented the Slave Power in its most blatant and threatening form. In their successful waging of the war for the Union, the Republicans tremendously enlarged federal powers, the most striking example of which was Lincoln's decision to make emancipation a war aim. Northern Democrats and, after the war, defeated Southern whites denounced Republican policies as a revolutionary and tyrannical infringement of states' rights and the constitutional liberties of local white majorities. By 1870 the Republican program, including its critical Southern component, congressional Reconstruction, was in place. That program embraced an indivisible Union, an end to slavery, citizenship and voting rights for the freedmen, and governmental promotion of a free-market economy.

The postwar Republican coalition of Southern freedmen and Northern businessmen, farmers, and workers splintered after 1870. The refusal of Republicans to support an eight-hour day for workers and an economic depression that began in 1873 cost the party labor support. Most importantly, the Northern middle classes, the core of Republican support, concluded that congressional Reconstruction was a failure. In 1877, the same year that the Republicans formally abandoned Reconstruction in the South, a massive wave of industrial unrest in the rail centers of the North heralded a pronounced shift in the debate over republican order. Propertied classes throughout the nation now felt that the greatest threat to republican liberties came from labor, whether white industrial workers in the North or black agricultural workers in the South. Former Confederates were welcomed back into the republican fold. The Civil War era was over.

Chapter 6 covers the Civil War. It opens with the secession crisis and then emphasizes why so many Northern and Southern whites were eager to fight each other by the spring of 1861. The second half of the chapter examines the connections between the ebb and flow on the battlefields and the domestic legislation and social change on the home fronts. The war generated its own pace of revolutionary change, the most dramatic evidence of which was the momentum toward black emancipation. Reconstruction, covered in Chapter 7, centered around efforts to contain or extend this momentum. Whites in both sections agreed that the war had destroyed slavery as an institution, but there was no agreement on the postwar status of the freed population or on whether the states or the federal government had the constitutional right to define that status. Caught in the middle of what became a bitter debate among whites were the freedmen, who had their own agenda for freedom. Chapter 7, after first showing how congressional Reconstruction evolved out of the confrontation between President

Johnson and Congress, concentrates on the class and racial conditions that cut short so much of the promise that Reconstruction held for a biracial democracy in the South.

Part III covers essentially the last quarter of the nineteenth century, 1870–1896. Often referred to as the Gilded Age, after the title of a satirical novel co-authored in 1873 by Mark Twain and Charles Dudley Warner, this was a period of fundamental, structural shifts within the economy and society at large. Massive industrialization, explosive urbanization, huge numbers of immigrants, and the intensification of commercialized agriculture all combined to produce a turbulent pattern of uneven economic growth and social unrest. Concerns over public order grew sharper because of the cultural division that had arisen between an industrial workforce that was predominately foreign-born and Catholic and a business class that was overwhelmingly native-born and Protestant. Despite widespread fears over the potential for a violent clash between labor and capital, efforts at reform centered on cultural, rather than political, solutions. Gilded Age reformers believed that poverty and unemployment were individual failings traceable to moral defects in character. Thus, the purpose of reform was to teach immigrants, the poor, and the working classes how to acquire the middle-class values of thrift, diligence, and self-discipline that they supposedly lacked.

National politics after the end of Reconstruction in 1877 settled into an equilibrium between the major parties, the Republicans and the Democrats. Both parties accepted the reigning laissez-faire orthodoxy that only the so-called natural workings of the marketplace could alleviate social injustices or poverty. Dissenting third parties of farmers and laborers challenged this orthodoxy, but they were unable to break the hold of the major parties on the loyalties of the voters. The stability and equilibrium of Gilded Age politics held until the 1890s, a decade in which the worst depression of the nineteenth century polarized Americans into political and cultural divisions that were as bitter as those of the 1850s.

In the 1890s the debate over the economic transformation of post–Civil War America came to a climax. This debate was triggered by the Populists, a major third party of insurgent farmers who politically organized in the midst of a long agricultural depression in the South and West. The Populists believed that the republican promise of economic independence and security had been betrayed by political corruption and the undemocratic concentration of economic power in business corporations. The corporate leaders, who engineered the economic changes of the Gilded Age, and those who benefited from these changes, particularly the urbanized middle classes, rallied behind the Republican party to turn back what they saw as the ungodly assault of the Populists on the rights of private property. In the climactic election of 1896, the Republicans, the party of Protestant respectability and business stability, won decisively. Henceforth American republicanism would be anchored not in economic independence and self-reliance but in the corporate values of profit, productivity, and hierarchical control. For twentieth-century Americans, a democratic consumption of goods replaced a democratic distribution of power as the touchstone of republican freedom.

Part III follows the same organizational format as Part I. Chapter 8 sets forth demographic and economic patterns of change that were keyed to the spread of a national rail network and the development of steam power. The chapter concentrates on western expansion; the postwar Southern economy; the linkage of factories, immi grants, and cities; and the growth of the corporate form of business management. Chapter 9 examines the social and cultural consequences of these patterns of change and is organized around the middle-class quest for public orderliness. Despite an increasing reliance by reformers on a newly professionalized ethic of expertise and efficiency, a wide variety of groups—Indians, blacks, women, immigrants, and workers—continued to resist crusades of cultural uplift. These groups carved out their own cultural space in what remained a highly pluralistic society. Chapter 10 shows how American politics in the Gilded Age simultaneously embodied and deflected ethnic and class pluralism in the evenly balanced competition between Republicans and Democrats. Only the jarring economic distress of the 1890s upset that balance. Centered around the rise and fall of the Populists, Chapter 11 ties together the political and cultural repercussions of the depression of the 1890s. The text concludes by showing how the Republican victory in 1896 set in place the foundations of twentieth-century corporate America.

Part I

ANTEBELLUM AMERICA

The Sweep of Economic Change

The America of 1815 was an overwhelmingly agrarian society. Four-fifths of the population lived and worked on farms. The relationship between the people and the land was direct and fundamental. It shaped the rhythms of life from the promise of birth to the finality of death. In the context of what human labor could yield and sustain from the land were fashioned the fundamental choices and actions of daily lives—decisions as to when to marry and conceive, how many children to have, how to allocate labor within the household, how to divide up the family estate upon the death of its head, and whether to stay or move on. The ratio of land to people also provided the structure of opportunities, the felt sense of what was attainable and how, in which families pursued traditional goals of independence, security, and the perpetuation of the familial lineage through male heirs.

Apart from England, where the industrial revolution had begun in the mid-eighteenth century, the preindustrial nature of America was the norm throughout the world in 1815. American society, however, was a uniquely favored one. Throughout most of the colonial period land, labor, and markets had interacted in such a way as to create extremely favorable material circumstances for the establishment in America of that family-centered independence that was increasingly being stifled in early Modern Europe by the uprooting of the peasantry from the land and the advent of wage labor. In sharp contrast to Europe, land was cheaper, more accessible, and comparatively widely owned in the colonies. Consequently, labor was relatively scarce and expensive, because most colonial males had neither the incentive nor the need to offer themselves as wage earners. Many of them controlled their own means of production and hence were free of dependence upon an employer for their livelihood. Quite limited markets for most agricultural commodities, and the lack of labor to produce larger surpluses in any event, resulted in a semisubsistence rural economy, most notably in the Northern colonies and the Southern backcountry.

More commercialized and stratified societies had emerged in the port cities, but the major, indeed the glaring, exception to the social pattern of independence and semisubsistence was in the low-country South. Here, in the absence of any alternative exploitable source, slaves imported from Africa provided the labor needed to produce the cash crops of tobacco and rice for a world market. On the eve of the Revolution, 20 percent of the colonial population, and 40 percent of the Southern, were slaves. Still, at least for the free white majority, America made possible on a scale unimaginable in the Old World a land-based security and autonomy.

Americans believed that the ownership and cultivation of land made an individual free and independent. In the moral vision of Thomas Jefferson farmers were "the chosen people of God, if ever he had a chosen people, whose breasts he has made his peculiar deposit for substantial and genuine virtue."[1] The farmer was virtuous because he did not depend upon others for the subsistence needs of his family. Because he was economically independent, he could politically pursue the public good rather than the private, selfish interests of those who made the landless beholden to them for their economic survival. The independent farmer was thus at the core of the original vision of America and its republican liberties.

The greatest threat to those liberties, it was believed, would come from the dependent and the nonpropertied. It was this class that most Americans associated with manufacturing. Drawing upon the English example, Americans equated the establishment of factories with poverty, overpopulation, and political servility. Only in a densely packed society in which land was in short supply or access to it was blocked by the legal privileges of a landlord class of aristocrats could manufacturing take root. In such a society, in which the masses were cut off from the land and forced to sell their labor for their survival, corruption and poverty would feed on one another. It would be here, in Jefferson's words, that "Dependance begets subservience and venality, suffocates the germ of virtue and prepares fit tools for the designs of ambition."[2]

As long as land remained plentiful, Jefferson believed, Americans could escape such dependency. Others agreed; as Benjamin Franklin had observed in 1760:[3]

> No man, who can have a piece of land of his own, sufficient by his labor to subsist his family in plenty, is poor enough to be a manufacturer, and work for a master. Hence, when there is land enough in America for our people, there can never be manufacturers to any amount of value.

Thus, despite Jefferson's doubts regarding the constitutionality of an acquisition of foreign territory, he completed the Louisiana Purchase of 1803 from France. At a single stroke he had doubled the land area of what he called the "empire for liberty." The nation's population density of 4.3 persons per square mile in 1810 was but one-sixth the density that Europe had reached three centuries earlier. Surely, Americans had more than enough land to fulfill their hopes for landed independence and to forestall indefinitely their fears of becoming economically dependent upon others.

From 1815 to the Civil War Americans poured into the trans-Appalachian West. On average 60,000 people a year migrated to the West. The sheer amount of land offered the opportunity to achieve the traditional goal of agrarian and familial independence. The American's "love of independence," noted an Irish emigrant society in 1817, led him "to purchase a piece of land as soon as he can, and cultivate his own farm, rather than live on wages."[4] Yet, in a seeming contradiction of the Jeffersonian vision, this mass movement to the West happened at the same time that more and more Americans moved off the land and into cities and factories. The greatest relative increase in urbanization over a forty-year period in American history occurred between 1820 and 1860. The percentage of Americans living in urban areas (defined by the census as places with a population of 2,500 and over) tripled from 7 percent in 1820 to 20 percent in 1860. During these same years America emerged as a major industrial power. Manufacturing accounted for one third of all commodity output in 1859. In the half-century after 1810, farm employment dropped from 81 percent of the total work force to 53 percent, while manufacturing employment increased from 3 percent to 14 percent.

In a process of economic change that neither Franklin, Jefferson, nor any American of the Revolutionary generation could have foreseen, the settlement of the West acted as a catalyst for, not a deterrent against, urban and industrial development. The nature of this unexpected economic transformation will be the theme of this opening chapter. The transformation began with demographic pressures in the East, the region that provided the migrants to both Western farms and Eastern cities and factories. After then tracing the settlement and market growth of the West, the northern area of which was devoted to free labor and the southern to slave labor, the chapter will turn to economic adjustments in the East. Out of these adjustments, a response to the opportunities and challenges posed by Western settlement, came the shifts in capital and labor that resulted in an ongoing pattern of urbanization and manufacturing growth. This pattern, like the settlement of the West, was also one that became sectionalized between a free North and a slave South.

Demographic Pressure in the East

Land scarcity is a relative term. In the eastern United States in the early nineteenth century, land was scarce not in an absolute sense but in a cultural one. That is, given the meaning that rural American society placed on the ownership and transmission of land as the indispensable link in the continuation of the lineal family, land was scarce relative to the number of sons making claims upon it.

The colonists were incredibly fertile. At the time of the Revolution the birth rate of 50 to 55 per 1,000 of population easily surpassed that of European countries for which comparable data exists. This fertility, which also exceeds that of any nation in the world today, was the prime factor in a veritable demographic explosion. Around 1720 the colonial population began increasing by about 35 percent per decade. This rate, three-fourths of which was attributable to natural increase as opposed to immigration from Europe, meant that the population was doubling every twenty-five years. By 1820 an original total of 651,000 white immigrants to the colonies and then the United States had multiplied to 7.9 million.

The availability of fertile, cheap land, and hence the means for a young couple to support a family, explains this very high fertility of the eighteenth century. Fertility was highest in the newly opened frontier regions, which attracted an influx of young migrants from more densely settled areas. The children of this first generation of migrants married very young because of the easy accessibility to inexpensive and plentiful land. Possession of land promised not only an independent livelihood but, equally important, security in one's old age. Because early marriage gave young American wives an average of three to five more childbearing years than their European counterparts, the number of children per family was high. As labor on the family farm, children were a decided economic asset. When settled nearby or on part of the subdivided family estate passed on to the sons, they thickened a network of kin relationships that assisted their parents in times of misfortune. Although high by modern standards, infant mortality in rural areas was low compared to that of American cities and to that of Europe. Two factors accounted for twice as many American children surviving to adulthood as in rural Europe: the scattered distribution of the farmsteads, which checked the spread of epidemic diseases, and a farm diet nutritionally superior to that of most Europeans, particularly in meat and animal proteins. Indeed, before the end of the eighteenth century, American-born whites averaged two to four inches taller than their English counterparts.

By the end of the second generation demographic pressure had built up. The family could no longer so easily balance its two fundamental but conflicting goals of maintaining the farm as a viable, efficient whole and of establishing the male heirs on part of that farm. Limits were being reached beyond which further divisions of the farm could reduce it to economic failure. Compounding the difficulties was a rise in land prices in the surrounding area as population grew and more land was brought under cultivation. Thus, it was more costly to provide a son with a neighboring farm. By this point a new demographic phase of population stability and eventual out-migration had set in. Couples married later, and this in turn reduced the fertility rate. Land-hungry migrants were no longer attracted to the area. Within two generations the former frontier region "aged," or demographically and economically matured, the land-to-population ratio shrank, and the stage was set for a population shift to another farming frontier.

The population history of Vermont is illustrative of this demographic cycle of rapid growth, stability, and slow decline. Young migrants from western Connecticut and Massachusetts first settled Vermont in the 1760s. From 1770 to 1810 the combination of heavy immigration and a high fertility rate resulted in an annual population increase of 9 percent. By the 1790s emigration was under way. Cheaper, more fertile land was available in western New York, and the sons of the first generation began leaving. Most of these migrants came out of the earliest settled regions in the southern part of the state, and three-fourths of them were under the age of thirty. Then, between 1810 and 1850, the birth rate in Vermont fell sharply, and the state's annual increase in population was reduced to 0.9 percent, or one-tenth the level of the previous forty-year period, during which Vermont had been a frontier region.

By 1815, at the end of hostilities with Britain in the War of 1812, the settled areas in the East were poised for a massive out-migration. Cultivable land was in short supply, notably in New England, where virtually all of it had been taken up by 1812. In 1820, when the population per square mile in the United States as a whole was 5.5, the three New England states of Rhode Island, Massachusetts, and Connecticut easily led the nation with population densities of 77.8, 65.1, and 57.1 respectively. Elsewhere in the East more land was available, but not nearly enough for the young men who wanted farms of their own. In York County, Pennsylvania, out of a sample of 135 wills and testaments between 1749 and 1820, 68 passed on no land at all. Of those that did, 76 percent excluded at least one child from any share. In Lancaster County, also in southeastern Pennsylvania, 30 percent of the married taxpayers were landless by the late eighteenth century, and another 30 percent were tenants, some probably sharecroppers.

In the South Atlantic states, where 40 percent of the population in 1810 were slaves, farms were larger, landholdings more concentrated, and soil erosion more extensive than in the Northeast. Here, despite a population density that was just two-thirds of that in New England, the pressure to move West was strongest. Among the

Table 1.1   Eastern Migration Rates
            (percentage of mid-decade population)

Unlike the Northeast, in which population losses were reversed after 1820, the slave states of the Southeast continued to be net exporters of population throughout the antebellum period.

	1810–1820	1820–1830	1830–1840	1840–1850	1850–1860[a]
Northeast	− 2.0	0.7	1.0	4.0	3.7
Middle Atlantic	0.5	1.6	1.0	3.3	− 0.8
South Atlantic	− 5.1	− 3.6	− 5.3	− 2.6	− 1.7

Source: Compiled from Stanley Lebergott, *The Americans: An Economic Record* (New York: W. W. Norton, 1984), Table 8.1, p. 82. Reprinted by permission of the publisher.
[a] Native Whites.

older eastern regions the South Atlantic states, as shown in Table 1.1, experienced the greatest net losses of population throughout the antebellum period. The 5 percent of white families who owned ten or more slaves had the labor supply needed to overcome the size limitations of Northern farms, which depended primarily upon family labor. Extensive acreage, in turn, permitted Southern planters to expand production to meet world demand for their chief export crops of tobacco and, after the 1790s, cotton. Repeated plantings of these crops, however, quickly leached the soil of its nutrients. The search for fresh land resulted in the gradual spread of the plantation system from its original base in the tidewater (the low-lying coastal area) to the piedmont (a broad plateau in the Southeast that runs between the coast and the foothills of the Appalachian Mountains). As planters added to their holdings to replace their worn-out soil, they pushed tenants off the land and bought out the surrounding small farmers. These displaced farmers in the tidewater, along with the upland families of young people who wanted land of their own, led the Southern exodus to the West after 1815. They were soon joined by the sons of the planters and their slaves. Despite marriages that were arranged to keep land within the wealthy families, there was no longer enough good land in the tidewater and piedmont to satisfy the ambitions of the sons for a plantation of their own.

Indicative of the growing impatience of the young, forced to wait longer and longer for their hoped-for share of the dwindling family estate, premarital pregnancies crested around 1800. From a trough of under 10 percent of first marriages in the late seventeenth century, the rate steadily rose to a peak of around 30 percent by 1800. By their actions young couples had defied their parents and forced the hand of the bride's father. Rather than have the family shamed by the birth of a child out of wedlock, the father provided the means—land or cash—for the marriage to be established. In the reproachful words of an Anglican observer, these young couples did "not repent but if they were again in the same circumstances, they would do the same again, because otherwise they could not obtain their parent's consent to marry."[5]

Especially after the end of the War of 1812, the West served as the major outlet for the accumulated strains that had built up in the East throughout the eighteenth century as population pressed upon agricultural resources. The impatient and extraordinarily young population in the East—the median age of whites in 1800 and 1810 was 16.0— had every incentive to move West. With frontier prices in 1819 at $2 to $3 an acre, as compared to $30 or $40 for average Eastern land of lesser fertility, the economic motivation for migrating was obvious. The West also offered a chance for more rapid upward mobility than was possible in the rural social structure of the East, which was sharply stratified by age and wealth. In settled farm areas of the Northeast, the richest 10 percent of the population owned 40 percent to 50 percent of the wealth; in the slaveholding areas of the Southeast the comparable figure for the upper tenth was between 50 percent and 60 percent. This wealth inequality was also highly correlated with age. Young men could not expect to accumulate much property until they were in their mid-thirties. Property, and the political and social power that accompanied it, came only after receipt of the family inheritance or many years of agricultural labor. Yet, though driven by the desire for material self-improvement, the migrants were also trying to achieve traditional cultural goals. Foremost among these goals was the acquisition of enough land for economic independence and a family inheritance. The collective security of the family, not the economic advancement of its individual members, was the measurement of rural status. In order to attain that status, one that was increasingly closed off in older regions, the surplus farm population of the East headed West.

Moving West

In 1800 fewer than one in ten Americans lived west of the Appalachian mountains; by 1860 more than half did. On specially bought wagons, canal boats, flatboats, vessels on the Great Lakes, and on foot, the population steadily shifted westward. This shift, in combination with birth rates in the West that were 50 percent higher than those in the East, enabled states that were admitted to the Union after 1815 to grow at a rate fourteen times faster than the older states during the antebellum period (see Table 1.2.).

Families and cooperatively organized groups, rather than single, footloose men, comprised the majority of the migrants. Within the families the decision to move West rested with the husbands and was often carried out against the wishes of wives. Desirous of holding onto ties of home and kindred, and anxious to avoid the dangers of childbirth while on a long journey, women were usually reluctant migrants. But wives had little choice save resigning themselves to leaving the farm and holding together the family as it plunged westward. Husbands had absolute legal authority to determine the domicile of their families, controlled all family property, and could commit the family

Table 1.2 Population in Old and New States
    (in thousands)

Americans surged westward after 1815 into the trans-Appalachian territories that became the newer states in the antebellum Union.

	1820	1860	PERCENTAGE OF CHANGE
Old[a]	9118	21058	+131
New	472	9307	+1872

Source: Compiled from *Historical Statistics of the United States,* Series A-195–209.
[a]Entered the Union before 1815.

to a move without consulting their wives. As Sarah Cummins recalled of a childhood move from Illinois to Missouri:[6]

> I came in one evening to see a look on dear mother's face that I had never seen before. . . . After a time her voice strengthened and she said, "What do you think your father has done? . . . He has sold the farm and as soon as school closes we are to move to Missouri."

Once husbands had exercised their patriarchal authority in terms of moving, American families did not scatter in a pell-mell movement across the landscape. Instead, families moved along familiar ecological paths. That is, they moved into zones of climate, soil type, and landscape that most closely approximated the region they had left. This not only enabled them to create under more favorable conditions the traditional rural economy of their parents but was also the safest and most common-sensical approach. Eventual success, perhaps even survival, was heavily dependent upon agricultural skills learned in a specific ecological setting. To move out of that setting was to risk a loss of acquired knowledge concerning the length of the growing season, the kinds of crops to be planted, and the proper mix of livestock.

At the same time, migrants sought to transpose to the West regional, and often quite localized, folk identities rooted in ethnic, religious, and linguistic bonds. Some 400,000 immigrants, mostly German and Scotch-Irish, had entered the colonies after

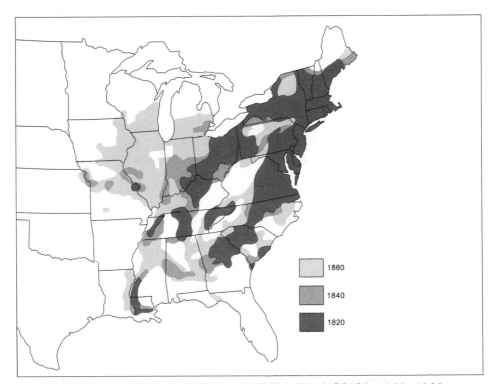

1860
1840
1820

THE SPREAD OF SETTLEMENT IN ANTEBELLUM AMERICA, 1820–1860
As the population of the United States tripled between 1820 and 1860, Americans moved steadily westward into the great heartlands of the Ohio and Mississippi River Valleys.

The National Road. Covered wagons and stage coaches carried Americans to the West during the Jacksonian era. This ca. 1840 scene on the National Road, which connected Baltimore to the Ohio Valley, shows its eastern extremity, near Cumberland, Maryland. (Brown Brothers)

1720. These immigrants and the native English stock sorted themselves out into distinct ethnocultural enclaves. The ties of religion, kinship, and community mores that developed within these enclaves were in turn transplanted to the West. Groups of neighbors collectively agreed to move, decided where to go, and traveled together to the West. Thus migration was broadly patterned by the flow of self-selected groups transplanting themselves on land that was economically and culturally evocative of the past.

One flow passed from the hills of western New England through the Mohawk and Genesee Valleys of central New York and curved along the southern rim of the Great Lakes. At its southern border in the Midwest, this Yankee-Protestant belt of migration merged with the more diverse stream of Germans, Scotch-Irish, and Quakers who pushed westward out of Pennsylvania. In turn, these Mid-Atlantic migrants abutted upland Southern whites in the hill country of the Ohio Valley westward to central Missouri. In the deep South, planters and their slaves trekked from tidewater to piedmont and on westward to the fertile prairies of Alabama and Mississippi.

The transcontinental journey to the Oregon Territory in the 1840s and 1850s represented the furthest branch of these flows before the Civil War. Here, because of the very audacity of the undertaking, family-centered networks of like-minded groups were especially evident. A striking example of these networks was the clustering in Oregon of sixteen families who had lived within twelve miles of each other in Morgan County, Ohio. In 1850, less than ten years after the territory was settled in any numbers, 69 percent of the 11,873 individuals south of the Columbia River were part of family units. In the same year, 45 percent of the 1,500 rural households in the Willamette Valley had blood connections with at least one other residence. These clusters of family and kin were the same groupings that had passed on word-of-mouth information about Oregon before the move. Reformed on the wagon trains as messmates, these neighborhood units remained intact on the open grasslands of the Willamette Valley, the location of 90 percent of the original farms.

Even as Oregon was filling up, some states in the older West had already passed through a complete demographic cycle. During Jefferson's presidency, Ohio and Indiana were raw frontier areas. Net migration into Ohio totaled over 742,000 from 1800 through 1840; it then reversed and the state had a net out-migration in the 1840s and 1850s. Just to the west, and with a lag of a decade, Indiana followed a similar pattern; by the 1850s, its migration rate had reversed and was a negative 4 percent. As Ohio became an agriculturally mature region, population density rose and agricultural opportunity, defined as the balance between supply and demand for new farmland on the county level, declined. Predictably, fertility fell: in Ohio it dropped from a mean of 2312 (ratio of children under 10 to women aged 15–44) in 1810 to 1416 in 1860. As the scarcity of cultivable land resulted in higher and higher costs of setting up their children nearby, parents increasingly limited the number of children they produced. Although the Old Northwest, the region north of the Ohio and east of the Mississippi, was still attracting a surplus of migrants in the 1850s, many of its rural areas had clearly "aged." By 1860 over 350,000 of those born in the Old Northwest had already left for the newer frontiers of Minnesota, Iowa, Kansas, and Oregon.

The socioeconomic equivalent of this demographic cycle also evolved within two to three generations. In the early stages of settlement, once speculators had sold out their holdings, land was relatively equally distributed: the wealthiest 10 percent held about 25 percent to 30 percent of the property. However, by the 1850s the richest tenth in rural townships of Ohio owned close to one-half of all the property. This wealth inequality was virtually identical to that which had prevailed in the rural Northeast by the 1770s. Also comparable were the inequality of wealth holdings by age: the Wisconsin tax lists of 1860, for example, reveal that for every additional year of age up to the mid-fifties a man would average 7.8 percent more wealth than his younger counterpart.

Thus the demographic and economic pressures that found an outlet in migration to the next frontier were continually recreated in rural America as frontier areas passed through stages of development. Young adults and the economically marginal, often one and the same group, felt these pressures most intensely and made up a majority of the migrants. Not just one, but several, moves characterized their lives. Four-fifths of the families in the overland emigration to the Pacific coast had made at least one prior move. In the most typical pattern the first move to the west occurred in the early twenties or in the first year of a marriage, followed by a second move after eight to ten years of marriage—the point at which crop yields from a newly cleared farm of average size typically began to decline. Subsequent moves also often became necessary for those who arrived too late in a farm frontier to stake out enough land for their family needs. The Shelly family of Benton County, Oregon, for example, had made at least four major moves by 1850. The father, age 35, was born in Kentucky, his wife in Tennessee, the three oldest children in Illinois, the next three in Iowa, and the youngest in Oregon.

The lure of cheap, fertile land was always there to draw the Shellys and other

Americans ever westward. Nearly all of this land was originally owned by the federal government—that is, it was in the public domain. From the adoption of the Constitution in 1787 through the 1850s the federal government acquired over 1400 million acres of land. Cessions by the states of claims dating back to colonial charters accounted for 283 million acres; the Louisiana Purchase of 1803 added 433 million; and purchases and annexations, notably from Indian tribes and the Mexican government, added another 700 million. In legislation that was gradually liberalized during the antebellum period as the political influence of the Western states steadily increased, Congress promoted rapid settlement of the public domain at the lowest possible cost.

The Land Ordinance of 1785 provided the model for the rectangular, grid pattern of surveying the public lands. Prior to being offered for sale at a public auction, the land was surveyed into townships six miles square that in turn were divided into thirty-six sections one mile square. This grid pattern ignored the natural contours of the land, but it was a quick, cheap method which produced a uniformly accurate survey. It speeded up settlement by minimizing future disputes over the correct boundaries of the land purchases. The policy of setting a uniform, minimum price for the land ignored the immense disparities in its quality and hence market value, but this was more than counterbalanced by an administrative simplicity that enabled the land to be sold in the shortest possible time. The minimum price of $2.00 an acre and the minimum purchase of 640 acres, which had been set by the Federalists in the 1790s, were reduced in stages. By the 1830s the price was down to $1.25 and the minimum purchase to 40 acres. In the Preemption Act of 1841 Congress made permanent a policy that it had first temporarily approved in 1831. Squatters, those who had settled on public land before it was surveyed, were guaranteed the right to purchase up to 160 acres at the minimum price of $1.25 when the public auction was held.

A variety of goals motivated congressional land policy. The promotion of American outposts in the interior enhanced national security while simultaneously accelerating economic development. Despite sectional and partisan bickerings over how low land prices should be reduced, Congress wanted to use the public lands as a source of revenue, either through the sale of the land or the increase in its taxable worth once it was privately developed. Most importantly, however, Congress continued to act on the Jeffersonian belief that general access to landed property was indispensable to the preservation of republican liberties. In what was a common refrain in the debates over land, Representative James B. Bowlin of Missouri argued in 1844: "If you wish to preserve and perpetuate its democratic form, you must pursue a policy tending to disseminate the lands amongst the largest possible number of people in the state."[7] This was the basic premise of the republic's political economy.

Abundant land was America's safety valve. It continually renewed the frustrated ambitions of farm families and offered the hope that Americans could preserve indefinitely their economic independence and political sovereignty. In moving West, it was believed, Americans maintained their equality.

Development in the Old Northwest

The beauty, fertility, and seemingly inexhaustible lushness of the Midwest in 1815 would have staggered modern sensibilities inured to its despoilation. Floating down the Ohio, one would see "Dense forests, far-away blue hills, green islands, the rarest color shadings, graceful and fertile areas. . . ."[8] In the river valley of the lower Missouri in the 1820s one could "travel hundreds of miles between gigantic tree trunks without a single ray of sunlight falling upon one's head."[9] North and east of the lower Missouri where the Indiana and Illinois prairies open out from the Appalachian woodlands were

> great stretches of flat land, covered with wild meadows that are hemmed by thin forests. The prairies are covered all summer long with flowers that change color every month— . yellow, blue, then red. . . . one encounters a series of surprises. Huge green surfaces of unbelievably high grass that waves in the wind like the sea, against a wooden background, more beautiful than the English parks.[10]

Where some saw beauty, the majority of the pioneers saw only obstacles and dangers to be overcome. The frontiersmen, noted a French traveler in 1831, were "insensible to the wonders of inanimate nature, and they may be said not to perceive the mighty forests that surround them till they fall beneath their hatchet."[11] Few doubted that in transforming the land they were doing what God willed, bringing forth plenty from an untamed wilderness.

The first step was to clear the land. By 1850, 114 million acres of forest had been cleared or improved. Another 40 million acres were cleared in the 1850s. Without any power machinery the quickest and cheapest method of clearing was girdling, the cutting of deep notches with an axe around a tree so as to kill it. Within two weeks the girdled trees lost nourishment and leaves, and more light filtered down to patches of the forest floor cleared of underbrush by burnings. Now the first planting of corn, the universal frontier crop because of its hardiness, high yields, and low seed requirements per acre, could begin. Pioneer families, by slowly strangling the forest cover, cleared the land at an average rate of five to ten acres per year. The visual result during the first generation of settlement—ugly stumps and shriveled and scorched trees—was anything but picturesque.

About ten years of backbreaking labor were required to make a forest farm. Labor, the greatest expense on the farm, was very scarce and expensive, so frontier communities pooled their labor resources. As observed by an Englishman on the Ohio frontier in 1818,[12] when a newcomer arrived,

> the neighbors unite in assisting him to erect a cabin for the reception of his family. Some of them cut down the trees, others drag them to the spot with oxen, and the rest build up the logs. In this way a house is commonly reared in one day. For this well-timed assistance, no immediate payment is made, and he acquits himself by working to his neighbors.

Communities also acted as a cooperative unit on the day of the public land auction. This was especially the case when settlement had preceded the government's survey and sale of the land. By the time of the auction, land values, largely because of the improvements already made by the squatters, were likely to be much higher than the minimum price set by Congress. In order to minimize bidding on the land they had improved and to sort out claims amongst themselves, the squatters organized claims clubs, many of which had formal constitutions and bylaws. Working through these local associations, the squatters entered noncompetitive bids on the land and warned outsiders to wait until local settlers had acquired what they wanted. In the consensus of the community, occupancy of the land with one's family, or tangible improvements such as a cabin, entitled settlers to protection from the uncertainties of the market price for land. Sometimes force was used against speculators who violated that consensus, but more often the speculators, who stood to profit in any event by extending credit to the farmers, cooperated with the squatters.

Whether in sharing their labor or banding together to secure land for the actual use of families, frontier settlers acted on egalitarian principles of community self-help that were central to the rural culture of the North in the early nineteenth century. The fundamental economic characteristic of that culture was its relative self-sufficiency. Because of the prohibitively high cost of moving bulky agricultural goods overland to outside markets, commercial agriculture was possible only for that small minority of farmers who had fertile land near urban centers or within a short distance of river transportation. As late as 1820, only 20 percent of all farm goods were sold in nonfarm markets. Unable to produce for a market, most farmers practiced a diversified agriculture geared to the subsistence needs of their families. Any produce left over was aptly termed a "surplus" and was used in a barter exchange with local storekeepers for those consumer staples, such as tea, coffee, sugar, and metalwares, that could not be manufactured at home or acquired from neighbors. By swapping goods and labor in local networks of rural exchanges, farm communities maintained a semisubsistence economy based on the values of household independence and public cooperation. Land was valued not for the income that it could generate (which was small), but for the family independence and security it could sustain. Cash was valued not for the consumer goods it could purchase (which were expensive and often unobtainable) but as a tool for accumulating more land. Thus, the status of the farmer was measured by his ability to do "everything within himself"[13] and to provide land for his sons.

It was not at all surprising that the migrants transplanted this traditional rural culture to the Old Northwest. Not only were these the values with which they had been raised, but the struggle to carve out forest farms consigned most of them to crude self-sufficiency for the first decade of settlement. Moreover, unless their farms were within thirty or forty miles of a navigable river or lake, the commercial sale of crops was out of the question. What was surprising was the speed with which a market agriculture spread in the Old Northwest. As it did, a competing set of more individualistic, entrepreneurial, and profit-oriented values made gradual inroads on the traditional culture.

Western soils were much more fertile than those in the East. Yields per acre were about twice as great. This fertility, combined with a series of continuous improvements in transportation, produced huge surpluses of foodstuffs that found expanding market outlets, first in the South and then in the Northeast. After the initial subsistence period of farm-making, Western farmers were steadily drawn into a market economy.

The first breakthrough in transportation came with the introduction of steamboats on Western rivers. In 1815, eight years after the steamboat's technical feasibility was established by Robert Fulton on the Hudson, the *Enterprise* ushered in a new era of transportation by successfully carrying a cargo upriver from New Orleans. By 1820, 69 steamboats, totaling 14,000 tons were operating on Western rivers; by 1855 these figures had grown to 727 and 170,000. As they became more numerous and larger, steamboats also became faster. A trip from New Orleans to Louisville that required 30–35 days in 1820 was reduced to six days by the 1850s. A keelboat or barge needed five to six months for the same trip in 1815. By increasing the speed of upriver traffic and especially by drastically lowering its costs, the steamboat was pivotal in raising the

Lockport, New York, 1836. A tiny village of two houses in 1821, Lockport became a flourishing community with the opening of the Erie Canal. The town took its name from the double set of five locks that were installed to raise or lower canal boats as they passed through. (The Bettmann Archive)

purchasing power of the Western farmer. The price of freightage rates for upriver traffic fell by a factor of ten and those for downriver traffic by a factor of three to four between 1815 and 1860. Thus, a given amount of Western produce could purchase substantially more outside goods as the antebellum period progressed.

Steamboats were instrumental in swelling the volume of Western trade, but that trade in foodstuffs, mostly corn and hogs, still flowed south. The river system of the West—the Ohio, Mississippi, and their tributaries—channeled Western goods down-river to New Orleans. Until the mid-1830s, nearly all Western corn and two-thirds of its flour went to the South. Some of the foodstuffs were sold to planters who special-ized in cotton production. The rest was exported from New Orleans to markets in the East and Europe. After the 1830s, however, canals and railroads, transportation inno-vations that followed an east-west axis, reoriented Western trade to the burgeoning urban markets of the Northeast. By the 1850s, over 60 percent of Western foodstuffs were shipped to the East.

The single most important transportation improvement for the antebellum West was the Erie Canal. When this 364-mile link between the Hudson and Lake Erie was completed in 1825, a direct water route was opened up for interregional trade between lake ports in the Old Northwest and New York City, some 200 miles down the Hudson from Albany. The Erie drastically lowered transportation costs between Buffalo, its western terminus, and New York. Wagon transport from New York to Buffalo cost $100 a ton in 1817; canal transport via the Erie reduced it to $8. The cost of eastbound freight likewise fell from 19¢ a ton-mile in 1817 to about a penny by 1860. Simultaneously, east-west trade boomed. The tonnage of Western produce shipped eastward over the Erie increased ten times over from 1840 to 1860, and the westward flow of imports and manufactured goods grew proportionately.

The Erie was so successful that other Eastern states scrambled to protect their share of the Western trade from the threat of monopolization by New York. Pennsylvania and Maryland built competing canals to the West. But the Erie, aside from being the first, had one unique advantage. The only sizable break in the Appalachian mountains from Maine to Georgia was through central New York's Mohawk Valley, the flat corridor followed by the Erie to the west. The other canals were much more difficult and expensive to construct, and they never equaled the Erie's success. When Western states in the 1830s built a series of feeder canals that linked the interiors of Ohio and Indiana with ports on the Great Lakes, the Erie benefited the most from the increased shipments of grain and meat.

The development of the steam locomotive made possible the railroads, the last chain in what aptly has been called the transportation revolution of the nineteenth century. The first lines, the Baltimore and Ohio, Boston and Worcester, and Charleston and Hamburg, tentatively pushed westward in the late 1820s. They were promoted by urban mercantile groups fearful of being bypassed in tapping Western markets by the Erie and its imitators. Over the next thirty years, the railroads relegated the canals to technological obsolescence. The railroads were faster, more dependable and regular in their service, and capable of penetrating landlocked areas that canals could not reach. Most basically, the railroads were more efficient. Compared to canals as of 1840, railroads could move four times as much freight for the same cost in labor and capital.

After drawing even with canals by 1840, rail mileage outdistanced that of canals by eight to one in 1860. Two-thirds of the nation's 31,000 miles of track in 1860 had been built in the 1850s, the decade in which rails pulled ahead of canals in total freightage shipped. Most of that freightage came from Western farmers who quickly responded to the marketing opportunities presented by the through-rail connections that tied together the Mississippi Valley and the Atlantic seaboard in the 1850s. No comparable trunk lines ran north-south.

The cumulative impact of first steamboats, then canals, and lastly railroads tremendously expanded the marketing range of Western produce. At the same time, these transportation changes also helped improve the Western farmers' balance of trade. A unit of mixed Western produce by the late 1850s purchased three times as many Eastern goods as it did forty years earlier. This interplay of transportation outlets, market sales, and rising cash income acted as an ongoing stimulus for the spread of commercial farming.

Involvement in this expanding market agriculture resulted from a process of self-selection. As frontier populations shifted and settled, a continuous winnowing-out occurred. Over time, the backwoodsmen and many of the first-generation farmers filtered out. The former were comfortable only in remote wilderness areas. The latter took advantage of the spread of settlement, as registered by higher land prices, by selling out at a propitious time. These farmers produced a small surplus of dairy items, poultry, and some fruits and vegetables, but they lacked the capital to hire laborers and were satisfied with a casual, semisubsistence agriculture. They let their livestock forage in the woods and manured their fields infrequently, if at all. Rather than making a whole series of adjustments in their lifestyles, including the development of more disciplined work habits needed to compete with their more ambitious neighbors, they sold their land at a profit when population increased and more extensive markets developed. Perhaps in search of, as one commentator noted, that "everlasting range they would have for their cattle and horses [and] of the wild game and fish that would be sufficient for them, and their sons, and their sons' sons,"[14] they bought land further west with the proceeds of the sale. These farmers in effect used the market as a means of escaping from it.

The persisters and wealthy newcomers were those who were willing to make the adjustments to advance in the market economy. It was these farmers who practiced an intensive agriculture that specialized in cash crops and who limited family size so as to increase the proportion of the family's capital assets that could be passed on to their heirs. They built large barns and permanent homes, erected grist mills and distilleries, experimented with new seeds, improved the livestock, fenced the land, sowed the pasturage, and practiced careful, planned farm strategies aimed at maximizing income by seizing upon market opportunities. Their material rewards were ample. Per-capita wealth, for example, grew at an annual rate of 5.5 percent in Ohio from 1826 to 1860. Wealth throughout the state varied in proportion to population density and was held in the greatest amounts by men who had arrived early and had remained the longest.

The most typical response to widening marketing opportunities might well have been represented by the individual whose route to the market began with the traditional goal of a competency. This was the contemporary phrase for the comfortable existence of independence and self-sufficiency that an individual could achieve with a sufficient amount of income-producing property. A competency, not ever-increasing wealth, was the original goal of most of the settlers.

To acquire a competency, John Fisher left England for America in 1830. Following the path of friends and relatives who had emigrated earlier, he went to the Michigan frontier, where he bought 80 acres in Lenawee County. The county's population boom from 1,500 in 1830 to 18,000 in 1840, and access to Lake Erie, forty miles to the south, assured Fisher an immediate market for any surpluses he could produce on his farm. The major commercial outlet was for wheat, and Fisher responded to every opportunity. He quickly added 80 acres of open prairie land to his holdings, cleared 100 acres within eight years, and borrowed and paid back money at 30 percent interest. He poured all his profits back into his expanding farm operations. By 1833 he was able to write home proudly that "I raise my own living and live as independent as your richest farmers though not in such great style." His farm land was soon valuable and productive enough that it could be let out for a handsome annual rent. "I could live without work now,"[15] he told his English kin in 1836. Fischer had surely succeeded, but his initial goal of independence and security faded or perhaps was no longer satisfying. Now the meaning of his life, as he admitted in his last letters home, consisted of a seemingly endless desire to improve his farm and capital assets. These market goals consumed all his time and income as he worked harder and harder; even his penchant for writing poetry had to be abandoned.

As more and more individuals pursued and realized similar market goals, the Old Northwest increasingly became a wealthier and more individualistic and acquisitive society. Avenues to wealth took one of two paths. The first was followed by the speculator and local booster. The basic strategy was to raise the value of land by attracting settlers to it. Towns in the Old Northwest did not just happen; they were laid out, promoted, and touted to all listeners, particularly to the legislators who would decide on the location of county seats, canals, and railroads. Town entrepreneurs actively recruited settlers and welcomed their skills and capital. Virtually everyone stood to benefit from the rise in land values and local purchasing power. Consequently, the Old Northwest, even in its formative years, supported an extraordinary number of small towns. How extraordinary can be seen in a contrast with the Old Southwest, the region south of the Ohio and east of the Mississippi. Indiana, Illinois, Alabama, and Mississippi were all settled at about the same time, and all joined the Union just after the War of 1812. On a per-capita basis, Indiana and Illinois in the early 1830s already had five times as many towns as Alabama and Mississippi in the early 1850s. Accompanying numerous towns came economic diversification. Again the contrast between these two sets of states is striking: in 1840, for every 1,000 people, 34 were engaged in commerce, trade, and manufacturing in Indiana, 33 in Illinois, 16 in Alabama, and 14 in Mississippi.

The second avenue to prosperity was followed by market-minded farmers. As a direct consequence of the Northwest Ordinance of 1787, in which Congress prohibited the introduction of slavery north of the Ohio, the family farm operated without slave labor was always the norm in the Old Northwest. Northern farmers, as opposed to Southern slaveholders, were always constrained in the acreage they could cultivate by the limits of family labor. Thus, in expanding cultivation and raising farm productivity, they followed a strategy of mechanization. They purchased a continuous sequence of labor-saving machinery, John Deere's steel plow for breaking up prairie sod and the McCormick reaper for harvesting grain being the most notable. Patented in 1837, the steel plow had the strength needed to work the exceptionally heavy and damp soils of the prairie Midwest. The reaper broke the harvest bottleneck that had sharply limited the acreage that could be devoted to wheat.

Wheat, because of its ready marketability for milling into flour, was the major cash crop in Northern agriculture. However, as long as outside help was too scarce and expensive to be hired, the acreage allotted to wheat had to be restricted to the amount of wheat that could be harvested within ten days by family labor and a few hired hands. The time limit was critical because ripened wheat quickly shed its grain. Because an experienced worker using a scythe equipped with a cradle frame could harvest no more than two acres a day, the uppermost limit on wheat production for most Northern farmers was about fifteen acres. Contrary to the situation in Europe, where small plots of land were farmed intensively with relatively cheap agricultural labor, farmers in the Midwest had more land than they could cultivate and an abundance of cheap power in the form of horses. The potential northern market for mechanical, horse-drawn reapers was huge because farmers had a positive incentive to invest in new, horse-powered machinery.

The breakthrough in reaper sales came in the 1850s. High wheat prices, spurred by European and urban demand and through rail service to the East, induced farmers to tap underutilized land. Sales of mechanical harvesters, first patented in the early 1830s, shot up from a total of 3,400 in the period before 1850 to 70,000 between 1850 and 1858. With a self-rake reaper, a farmer could harvest 10–12 acres a day, about a 500 percent increase in labor productivity over the cradle method. Labor costs were cut by 50¢ an acre. Wheat production increased by 72 percent in the 1850s, and nearly all the increase came in the Mississippi Valley. Leading the way in shifting out of corn into wheat were Illinois prairie farmers connected by rail to Chicago and points east.

By stimulating manufacturing, with its demand for agricultural implements, and by releasing labor from the land with the rise in productivity, the commercial sector of Midwestern agriculture dynamically interacted with surrounding villages and towns. Cities grew out of towns that were aggressively promoted and favorably situated by water or rail transport. By 1860 the Old Northwest was as urbanized (14 percent of the population) as the Northeast had been in 1830. There was still room for subsistence farming, but the West north of the Ohio was now characterized by economic specialization and social diversification.

Growth in the Old Southwest

Another American West took shape south of the Ohio between 1815 and 1860. Divergent social development keyed to slavery, not geography alone, warrants the use of the descriptive label "the Old Southwest" to distinguish this region from the Old Northwest.

Over 600,000 whites born in Maryland, Virginia, and the Carolinas lived in slave states to the south and west by 1850. Pushed by the press of population upon land that was either too costly or too poor for all those who wanted it, Southern whites, like their Northern counterparts, were also pulled by the lure of new and better land in the West. It was hard to argue with the logic of a settler in the Alabama Territory who wrote a friend back east in 1817: "Why will you stay in franklin and work them poor stony ridges when one half of the labor and one third of the ground heare will bring you more and not a stone nor hill in the way."[16]

Southern whites moved to the West for the same basic demographic and economic reasons that Northerners did, but the consequences of that move were quite different because of the presence of slaves among the Southern migrants. From 1790 to 1860, over 800,000 slaves were moved from the South Atlantic region into the Old Southwest. During this same period, Southern cotton production exploded from 3,000 bales to 4,500,000, and most of this vast increase came from the slave plantations of the Old Southwest. It was this fusion of the spread of plantation agriculture and expanding cotton production that indelibly stamped the Old Southwest as more Southern than Western.

In 1790 the slaves were heavily concentrated in the tobacco belt of the Chesapeake tidewater and in rice and sea-island cotton plantations along the Carolina and Georgia coasts. Although slavery was still profitable after the Revolution, it appeared that the institution would remain penned up in this narrow strip along the South Atlantic seacoast. Tobacco prices were depressed, and the other major slave-produced exports—rice and long-staple sea-island cotton—could be grown only in the very humid, hot climates of the Carolina and Georgia low country. In the late eighteenth century, however, world demand for cotton started to spiral upward. The mechanization of English textile factories accelerated a shift out of woolens and linens into cotton goods, and demand for the raw fiber took off. At virtually the same time, Eli Whitney patented a cotton gin in 1793, which eliminated the chief economic barrier to the spread of upland cotton throughout the South. Coarser but hardier than the long-staple variety, short-staple, or upland, cotton could be grown in most of the South. Yet, until the

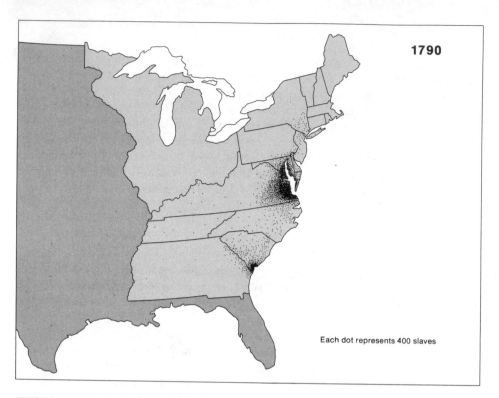

1790

Each dot represents 400 slaves

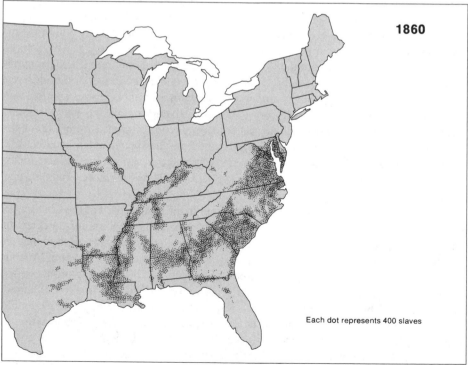

1860

Each dot represents 400 slaves

THE SPREAD OF SLAVERY, 1790–1860
Contrary to the expectations of the Founding Fathers, slavery was a dynamic, expansive institution that spread throughout the Southeast in response to a rising world demand for cotton.

Operating a Cotton Gin. Simple in design and easy to operate, the cotton gin made slavery and cotton synonymous in the antebellum South. (Library of Congress)

cotton gin appeared, it was not a major cash crop because of the time and expense needed to clean it for market, that is, remove its sticky green seeds from the fiber. The cotton gin solved that problem by increasing fifty times over the speed with which a worker could remove the seeds. Cotton was about to become king in the antebellum South.

Throughout the first half of the nineteenth century, planters and small slaveholders abandoned the light sandy soils of the Eastern tobacco belts for the far richer and higher-yielding alluvial and prairie lands of the West. When foreign demand for cotton increased drastically at the end of the Napoleonic Wars in Europe, spectacular rises in cotton prices between 1815 and 1819 were the catalyst for spreading the cotton belt from the Georgia-Carolina uplands into central Alabama and Mississippi. Successive waves of cotton prosperity pulled the cotton belt into eastern Texas and Arkansas by the 1850s. World markets, and especially British textile manufacturers, demanded cotton, and the South had the climate, soil, river transportation, and slave labor with which to supply it. The cotton frontiers of the Old Southwest, where production costs were lowest, met more and more of the demand.

Southern whites responded in one of two general ways to the booming market in cotton. Many, probably most, avoided heavy involvement in the cotton economy. These were the Southerners who were in the vanguard of the westward migration and who numerically typified the settlement of the Old Southwest. Owners of land, and of perhaps a few slaves, they had moved west to have room for a family oriented, safety-first agriculture. Often pushed out of older areas by planters desirous of their land, and unable to compete with planters for the better soil in newer areas, these farmers usually steered clear of the fertile lowlands. Instead they sought out land up in the valleys, on the ridges, and in the hill country. One such group of nonslaveholders in Montgomery County, Alabama, explained in 1817 that they had settled "the poor Broken & remote parts [because] being generally of the poorer Class we doubted Success in Settling in the richer Soil below."[17]

Exploitation of the bottomlands required credit and, above all, labor resources beyond the means of nonslaveholding families. Their wealth was in their land, not in slaves, and the safest way to protect that wealth was by assuring self-sufficiency in the form of corn and hogs. Production of a sizable surplus of cotton necessitated labor beyond what the immediate family could provide. Hired hands, as in the North, were scarce and too expensive, and the purchase of slaves meant incurring a large debt, which carried the real risk of financial ruin if market prices for cotton turned downward, as they did in the 1820s and 1840s. Thus one-quarter of Southern farmers grew no cotton. Another quarter were small producers who devoted acreage to cotton only after the food requirements of their families had been met. As for the labor resources needed for a commercial operation, 75 percent of Southern families in 1860 owned no slaves.

Preferences in lifestyle, as well as economic prudence, explain much of the behavior of the Southern yeomanry, the small, independent farmers. In the Arkansas highlands of 1860, Hardy Banks owned 200 acres of land and 8 slaves. His property was an inheritance from his father, who had brought his free and slave families westward from the Tennessee mountains in 1852. Banks' farm was valued at $2,000, and he had the land *and* the labor to produce 20 to 30 bales of cotton; instead, he settled for an occasional few bales. As his great-grandson recalled, he valued wealth in terms of "a full smokehouse and a full corn crib."[18] Self-sufficiency and leisure time for hunting and fishing were his goals. In pursuit of them, he and his slaves practiced slash-and-burn cultivation, a technique common on the Southern frontier. Partial clearing with an axe, girdling, and burning opened up small patches in the woods. Enriched by the fertilizing ash that was released, such patches often produced higher yields than completely cleared land. Once the fertility of a patch was exhausted through repeated plantings, it was then fallowed, or left unseeded for several years, while new patches were created. The fields, not the crops, were rotated. All the while, plenty of room existed for open-range herding of the livestock. Land-extensive rather than labor-intensive, this frontier agriculture was ideally suited for Banks' needs. He and his family enjoyed an annual surplus of small grains, root crops, and pork, and he could always swap his excess for store goods and cash for taxes. Here was a small slaveholder who used his bound labor for protection from the vagaries of the market economy. His family was secure, and he carried no debt. Above all, he had plenty of free time that was his own.

The second response to market incentives for cotton production was that taken by most of the planters, their sons, and ambitious slaveholders. This was the entrepreneurial response to those who sought to maximize their income as quickly as possible. In the Old Northwest, entrepreneurs and commercial farmers had likewise responded positively to market opportunities; but in the Old Southwest, where the market economy was based upon slavery, the strategies for accumulating wealth were fundamentally different. So also were the social consequences.

The ownership of slaves removed the labor restraints faced by family farmers in the North and by the yeomanry in the South. The cultivable acreage of the plantation slaveholder was limited only by the number of slaves owned. Therefore, south of the Ohio, local prosperity and individual wealth rose in proportion to the size of plantations and the number of slaves, which enabled those plantations to expand. Land speculation offered the chance for a quick fortune, but the ongoing incentive to promote towns and attract settlers and immigrants, as in the Old Northwest, was absent. An influx of newcomers did not enhance the value of slaves, the primary form of local wealth, and always carried the political threat of opposition to slavery itself. Nor was the desire for publicly funded internal improvements, so central to Midwestern town growth, as strong in the Old Southwest. Steamboats plying an extensive river system provided a market outlet for the chief cash crop, cotton. Moreover, the ratio of cotton's price to its bulk and weight made it a cheaper crop to transport than Northern grains, and hence it could be commercially produced at greater distances from navigable rivers.

Consequently, the slaveholder had little incentive to invest in labor-saving machinery. He already had a cost-effective substitute—the slave. Having capitalized not so much his land but his labor, he had a positive incentive to keep that labor working at all times. As opposed to the labor costs of the factory owner, those of the slaveholder were fixed. He could hardly fire his workers during an economic downturn or adjust their numbers to seasonal demands. Denied the labor flexibility of the industrial capitalist, the slaveholder also dreaded the time flexibility that the family farmer welcomed. Whereas a slack period for the one was a desired time of leisure, it was an inefficient use of capital for the other. Because slaves represented a conversion of labor into capital, efficient management required that their employment be maximized. The labor demands of cotton simplified the planter's task. From preparing the land in January and February through spring planting, summer thinning and cropping, and the long fall harvest, cotton needed fairly continuous care. In a contrast shown in Table 1.3, the small grains and fodder crops of Northern agriculture had very different, fluctuating labor requirements. These crops needed intensive labor at planting and during the short harvest; in between, the work load was minimal. The result was a highly irregular labor demand, which favored a free labor system. Conversely, the rationale for plantation slave labor in the South was compelling. In a climate, terrain, and market setting conducive to the profitable production of cash staples that required the continuous labor that free workers, ensconced on their own land, were loathe to

Table 1.3   Labor-Hours Per Acre for Staple Crops, 1840

The long, continuous labor demands of cotton made it a very adaptable crop for slave labor.

	BEFORE HARVEST	HARVEST	TOTAL
Wheat	12	23	35
Corn	44	25	69
Cotton	90	45	135

Source: Compiled from *Historical Statistics*, Series K-445–485.

provide, commercial farmers responded with a slave labor system that was most economically efficient when employed continuously.

In an extension of this logic, slaveholders devised work schedules for food crops and farm maintenance to complement the time demands of cotton. Nearly all cotton producers also grew corn, and most met their own needs for meat. The long growing season permitted labor diversification in different crops, and the effective management of labor made such diversification profitable. By extracting an agricultural work year of 280 to 290 days from their slaves and 3,000 hours from a prime hand, slaveholders simultaneously achieved marketing success and a high degree of economic self-sufficiency in foodstuffs. In addition, a well-run plantation could meet its normal manufacturing needs with slaves trained in artisan skills.

Because slaveholding farmers in the Old Southwest, as well as the yeomanry, did not have to import their food supplies from the outside, they comprised relatively independent economic units. What significant economic exchange that did occur—the sale of cash staples—took place in international markets and did little to foster local economic development. Unlike the Old Northwest, town-country interaction was negligible. The Southern countryside absorbed labor, free and unfree, in a self-contained cycle that balanced production and consumption from within. The isolated country store, not the bustling town at the hub of a diversified regional economy, was its hallmark.

Economic growth in the Old Southwest was substantial. Between 1840 and 1860 per-capita income in the four core states of the region—Kentucky, Tennessee, Alabama, and Mississippi—rose from $69 to $89 while the population was expanding from 2.6 million to 4.0 million. Measured by per-capita income in 1860, these states were as prosperous as those in the Midwest. But Southern prosperity was not accompanied by economic development and social change. Compared to the slave West in 1860, the free West, with 14 percent of its population in cities, was twice as urbanized, and the 46 percent of its workforce no longer engaged in agriculture was twice as great.

The social and economic mold of the Old Southwest was cast early, and it did not change. Opportunity was always directly tied to land and slaves. Once the land was initially settled, the children of the first generation of slaveholders and yeomen preferred to move west to the next frontier rather than stay and compete among themselves for the land that was left. Relatively few newcomers arrived to take their place. Before the Civil War, every core state in the Old Southwest began to experience negative migration rates; that is, discounting for natural increase, more people left the state than entered it. In the Old Northwest, where nonfarm opportunities developed in a diversifying economy, a positive migration rate still held in the 1850s (see Table 1.4).

Both of the antebellum Wests, however, played an indispensable role in national economic development. The free West became a major market for Eastern manufactured goods and provided the cheap foodstuffs that fed the growing numbers of nonfarm workers in the Northeast who were moving into cities and factories. Cotton, the preeminent crop of the slave West, accounted for over one-half of the value of the all American exports after the mid-1830s. More so than any other commodity, cotton paid for American imports and served as the basis for national credit. Simultaneously, investment capital was continually being generated from the Northern income derived from marketing cotton abroad and processing it in textile factories, the leading industry in the Northeast. The Western and Eastern economies were interlocked in the spread of the market, and it is the latter to which we will now turn.

Table 1.4 Western Migration Rates
(percentage of mid-decade population)

In the absence of economic diversification, the slave states of the Old Southwest quickly began to lose population to newly opened agricultural regions.

	1820–30	1830–40	1840–50	1850–60[a]
East North Central				
Ohio	3.8	5.8	0.0	−8.6
Ind.	17.5	10.9	1.4	1.6
Ill.	—[b]	—	9.6	18.9
Mich.	—	—	14.6	18.6
East South Central				
Ky.	−4.9	−5.8	−2.1	−6.0
Tenn.	2.7	−5.2	−4.3	−10.5
Ala.	—	−8.4	−3.1	−6.4
Miss.	7.9	—	4.8	−9.8

Source: Compiled from Stanley Lebergott, "Migration within the U.S., 1800–1960: Some Estimates," *Journal of Economic History* 30 (1970): 846–847. Reprinted by permission.

Note: These rates were estimated by a slightly different method than those cited earlier in the text for Ohio and Indiana.

[a]Native Whites.

[b]Line indicates a migration rate of over 100 percent.

Commercial Capitalism in the Northeast

In the early nineteenth century, America was, as the French diplomat Talleyrand put it in 1796, "but in her infancy with regard to manufacturers."[19] Household manufacturers furnished about two-thirds of all the clothing worn in the United States and a sizable percentage of such consumer items as shoes and hats. Artisans—skilled craftsmen working in their own shops and using their own tools—produced small batches of a wide variety of finished goods. Foreign imports, principally British textiles and iron goods, were the main source for bulk supplies of manufactured items. The British seemingly had no reason to doubt the prediction made by Lord Sheffield at the end of the Revolution that America would not turn to manufacturing because of "the high price of labor, and the more pleasing and profitable employment of agriculture."[20]

Sheffield was soon proved wrong. After 1809 the value of American manufactured goods increased by an average of 59 percent in the next three decades. During the same period, manufacturing began a pronounced shift out of homes and artisan shops and into factories. By 1840 America had joined Britain as a world leader in industrialization. Both had forged ahead in the production of textiles, coal, steel, and machinery—the building blocks of early industrialization.

What had made possible such a sustained manufacturing advance in the United States? The most direct cause was the enlargement of home markets, which occurred as internal barriers to the movement of raw materials and finished goods fell drastically as a consequence of the transportation revolution. For example, by the mid-1830s, textiles could be shipped 100 miles westward on the Erie Canal for the same cost of transporting them eight miles by wagon freight in 1815. Lower transportation costs also opened up new markets for coal, the basic fuel of heavy industrialization. After a network of coal canals built in the late 1820s permitted high-volume shipments of anthracite (hard, dense coal) from the mines of northeastern Pennsylvania, the price of anthracite fell 50 percent from 1829 to 1852. Per ton of pig iron produced, anthracite was now twice as cheap to use as charcoal, the fuel used in early American iron furnaces. Uncontaminated with sulphur and phosphorus impurities, as was bituminous (soft, porous) coal, anthracite more than equalled charcoal in producing a superior pig iron was malleable enough to be worked into axes and scythes by local blacksmiths and farmers. After 1835, anthracite was the preferred fuel of the newer, larger iron works. Meanwhile, all industries that required intensive heat energy—glass, paper, and metal processing—benefited from the ready availability of anthracite. Largely for this reason, the 1840s registered the highest rate of expansion in the manufacturing sector during the nineteenth century. Manufacturing's share of national output nearly doubled from 17 percent to 30 percent between 1839 and 1849.

Annual population increases of 3 percent and per-capita gains in real income of 1.1 percent a year in the first half of the nineteenth century provided the underlying impetus for market expansion, once the transportation revolution had allowed economic specialization to occur. Just meeting the growing demand of American farmers for iron accounted for half of the nation's output of pig iron in the 1830s. Access to markets and heightened demand stimulated the entire economy, but the Northeast was the only region in a position to foment a revolutionary economic transformation. It was here that were concentrated the essential factors of economic change—capital, labor, markets, mechanical skills, and the entrepreneurial urge to organize and manage economic risk. The greatest concentration was in the port cities, the focal points of change. Here, in the economic partnership between merchants—those who could furnish the credit and find the markets—and the artisans—those who could produce the goods and create new technologies—was the seedbed of the industrial revolution.

Merchant capitalists in the cities of the Northeast assumed the lead in organizing production for the expanding home market. Prior to 1808, these men had specialized in the exchange of goods, imported manufactured items from Europe for exported raw materials from America. This trade was a very profitable one in the early national period because of America's ability to carry goods to and from a Europe locked into the wars spawned by the French Revolution. In 1808 the trade received a blow from which it never fully recovered. At the request of President Jefferson, who was trying to pressure England and France to lift economic sanctions that each had imposed to deprive the other of benefits of trading with the United States, Congress passed the Embargo Act in late 1807. The Embargo shut off the export trade by prohibiting American vessels from clearing for foreign ports. As a consequence, mercantile capital began to shift out of foreign trade and into domestic manufacturing. Before 1808, only fifteen cotton mills had been built; in 1809 alone, eighty-seven more were added. The Embargo was repealed in 1809, but trade with Europe continued to be interrupted until the War of 1812, which closed off British imports and served as another stimulus for investing in manufacturing.

At the end of the war in 1815 and the restoration of peace in Europe, merchants were confronted, on the one hand, with an end to boom conditions in overseas trade and, on the other, with large internal markets opening up, a result of the transportation revolution. They had a strong incentive to continue their move into the production of manufactured goods, which formerly they had merely exchanged. The rationale was persuasive: the profits to be gained by transferring finished goods out of the East for the fiber, grains, and meat of the South and West would be even greater if the share earned by the independent craftsmen were reduced.

The merchants were risk-takers experienced in sensing market possibilities. The complex exchange world of trans-Atlantic commerce had taught them that markets were not simply fixed locations in which a sale took place, but ever-changing opportunities that had to be sought out and expanded. Dynamic, innovative, and backed up by credit facilities, working capital, widespread personal contacts, and organizational skills, they were in a far better position than the artisans to respond to the new domestic markets after 1815.

Nonetheless, in order to enter the system of production the merchant capitalists needed the assistance of artisans, the independent craftsmen who controlled and understood the actual process of production within their separate crafts. In 1815 artisans, about 40 percent of the urban work force, still enjoyed a high degree of autonomy. They owned their own tools (the equivalent of the farmer's ownership of land); trained their own labor in a traditionally regulated hierarchy in which one advanced from apprentice to journeyman to master craftsman; were generally able to set prices for the products they fashioned from start to finish; sold their goods directly to the consumer; and above all, were self-employed.

A driving feature of the market revolution was the constant pressure to raise the volume and lower the price of production. The only way in which manufacturing output could be significantly enlarged and cheapened in an economy that rested upon unmechanized household and shop production was by outside entrepreneurs reshaping that production. This was the revolutionary role of the merchant capitalists. At first they capitalized part of the old production process by supplying credit and raw materials to artisans. Master craftsmen, who had contracted with merchants to deliver finished goods, enlarged shop production by taking on more journeymen and apprentices. Costs were kept down by slashing piece rates below the customary scale agreed upon in the individual crafts. The apprentice system quickly lost its mutual set of obligations between master and trainee and became synonymous with cheap child labor. Some of the masters rose into the ranks of small manufacturers; others lost their independent status and became, in effect, foremen supervising semiskilled laborers.

In crafts producing finished consumer goods, and especially in clothing, the outwork system was the first step in expanding production. Processing work formerly done in the shop was distributed to outsiders working in their homes or in city lofts rented by a subcontractor. At each step in the outwork system, piece rates were driven down in order to protect the profit margins of all the subcontractors involved. After the low-priced competition of enlarged shops and outwork had weakened and splintered the crafts, the merchant (now the manufacturer) was in a position, where technologically feasible, to transfer the production process into the factory. The greater profits now realized through standardizing and mechanizing production with low-skilled labor were, in part, returned to consumers in still-cheaper goods that further undercut the surviving crafts.

In its timing and pace, this cycle varied greatly among the various crafts, but the general tendency was clear. Within a generation artisan labor, formerly an integrated whole, was bastardized into ever-more-specialized and simplified tasks. No one summarized better the economic rationale underlying this capitalist division of labor than Charles Babbage, an English promoter of industrialization. In 1832[21] he stressed that the master manufacturer, by dividing the work to be executed into different processes, each requiring different degrees of skill or of force, can purchase exactly that precise quantity of both which is necessary for each process; whereas, if the whole work were executed by one workman, that person must possess sufficient skill to perform the most difficult, and sufficient strength to execute the most laborious, of the operations with which the art is divided.

In short, per unit of production the cost of divided labor was less than the craftsman's whole labor. Gradually, the artisans lost control of the productive process.

Changes in shoe and boot manufacturing illustrate both the multiple pressures exerted on the crafts and the evolution in one major trade of a wage-earning class well in advance of the coming of the factory. In 1860 the shoe and boot industry, measured by value of product, was the fourth largest in the United States. Half a century earlier it had been a classic example of artisan production on a small capital budget in household and family shops. The men who transformed production came from both within the craft and from outside it. Village and city merchants in New England, anxious to supply the Southern market in cheap shoes for slaves, began to provide leather and credit to family producers in the early 1800s. The unified technique of shoe production began to break down with the spread of the outwork system. Meanwhile, a class of manufacturers evolved from those master shoemakers clever enough to reduce costs and increase output by hiring many journeymen at reduced rates. By the 1840s these masters were operating central shops, a forerunner of factories, and selling directly to urban wholesalers. In Randolph, Massachusetts, over 60 percent of the town's shoe and boot manufacturers in 1850 had risen directly from the ranks of shoemakers. The manufacturers in Lynn, Massachusetts, a much larger center of shoe production, were a similar amalgam of former artisans and well-to-do merchants tied by family connections to the shoemakers. It was these men, with their expanded base of production, who benefited from the introduction of the sewing machine in 1854, the technological breakthrough that wedded wage labor to mechanization in shoe factories after the Civil War.

Shoemaking represented but one of the patterns in the dissolution of the crafts. Some trades, such as carpentry and blacksmithing, barely changed before the Civil War. These artisans still worked with hand tools, shaped raw materials into a finished product, and exerted some control over their wages. Leather- and saddle-making relied on human-powered machines by 1860, while workers in hatting and trunk making were already in factories using power machinery. The impact of industrialization varied from trade to trade, and this very unevenness meant that the crafts were detached piecemeal from traditional production techniques.

With few exceptions the position of journeymen declined in all the trades. These artisans-in-training were always wage earners but prior to the post-1815 market revolution, they also had realistic expectations of opening their own shop as a master craftsman. The goal, in the contemporary phraseology, was to become ''a man for himself.'' The severe price competition in the crafts turned this goal of independent proprietorship into a mirage. In Eastern cities the number of shops run by masters shrank after 1820, and masters increasingly bypassed journeymen in favor of cheaper apprentices. Outwork in tenement garrets and factory production grew much faster than the specialized crafts. At the same time, displaced craftsmen from the British Isles swelled the ranks of artisans. About one-third of the English, Welsh, and Scottish emigrants to America in the first half of the nineteenth century were craftsmen and industrial workers. The artisans came primarily out of the older, preindustrial sector of the British economy, and they brought with them skills that were already abundant in Eastern cities. In this sense, Britain exported to the United States its own intensified craft competition. American journeymen responded by ignoring the established hierarchy of their crafts. Many moved to new areas and simply passed themselves off as masters. Others, probably the majority, accepted work in factories, where they joined former masters who were employed as foremen. Few made it to the ownership of their own shops.

Master craftsmen declined from 34 percent of Philadelphia's work force in 1820 to 16 percent by 1860. In the Philadelphia of 1860, journeymen outnumbered masters by two to one; forty years earlier, masters had been in the majority by a factor of three to two. Constricted opportunities for journeymen were part of a broader employment pattern. As the merchant-capitalist economy matured in Philadelphia, opportunities for advancement declined and lower-status jobs increased. In 1820 the city's labor force included roughly equal numbers of manual, wage-earning laborers (39 percent) and independent proprietors (34 percent). By 1860 the wage group had jumped to 55 percent and the proprietors had plunged to 16 percent of those employed.

The manufacturer could take for granted the existence of a large and permanent class of Northeastern wage earners by the mid-nineteenth century. This was an extraordinary reversal from the Jeffersonian period. In 1800 the total number of wage earners in the only two industries of any size, cotton textiles and iron manufacturing, amounted to under 0.2 percent of the nonslave labor force. The decline of the crafts had helped to create the new wage-earning class but, as we shall now see, most of the wage earners came straight off the farms.

From Farm to Factory

Economic pressure on farm populations, both in the eastern United States and in Europe, pulled labor off the land and into American factories. This pressure first directly affected the pace of American manufacturing in New England.

The development of the trans-Appalachian West put Eastern farmers at a severe competitive disadvantage. The fertility of Western soil, when combined with transportation innovations, allowed and encouraged Western farmers to flood Eastern markets with cheap wheat and corn. This economic squeeze was felt most intensely in New England, where the farms were smallest, the soil least fertile, and fresh expanses of cultivable land were in shortest supply. One response was to join the migration to the West. By 1860 more than half a million of the 3.1 million Americans born in New England had left the region. Just over half of the migrants flowed west into the Midwest and a sizable minority, 38 percent, went south and west into the Mid-Atlantic states.

Most New Englanders, those who remained in the region, had to devise responses that would enable them to balance the family's production and consumption so that the traditional goal of passing on the farm to the children could be realized. One strategy consisted of having fewer children, thereby reducing the claimants upon the family land and decreasing consumption from within. Fertility decline in rural New England dates from the mid-eighteenth century, and by 1820 New England's fertility rate was

25 percent under the national average. It declined another third by 1860. What distinguished the downward trend in the nineteenth century from that of the eighteenth was what seems to have been an increasingly deliberate decision to limit family size. Families in the eighteenth century became smaller primarily because couples, awaiting their share of a shrinking supply of cultivable land, delayed marriage. Hence, the child-bearing years of the wives were shortened. By the nineteenth century, however, fertility within marriage itself declined because women stopped having children at an earlier age. The distribution of ages at last birth ranged from 40 to 44 before 1800 and from 35 to 39 thereafter.

The positive side of family responses consisted of raising income and production. Those farmers who had enough fertile land and access to transportation and credit facilities turned to a more specialized agriculture that concentrated on income-producing crops that were relatively neglected by Western farmers. The most important ones before 1840 were oats, hay, and forage crops. The growing urban population of New England, and the horses that transported its people and goods, provided a ready market for the cereal and grass crops. Farmers also responded to urban energy demands by exploiting wood as a cash crop. After 1840 the same thickening rail network that exposed New England agriculture to yet more Western competition also carved out marketing niches in perishable goods that, without refrigeration, only farmers in the East could meet. Rail links between urban consumers and suburban producers stimulated a marked shift into dairy products and fresh fruits and vegetables.

The more isolated and poorer farmers were the least successful in making the switch to a land-intensive agriculture. Their economic survival depended on a shift of family labor to nonfarm activities. As revealed in their inventories and probate records, these families did not have the wherewithal for self-sufficiency. Far more so than their wealthier neighbors, they lacked the household and agricultural implements essential for economic independence. Without spinning wheels, looms, plows, and oxen, they were heavily dependent on outside exchange networks to provide for their needs. By trading their labor and farm surpluses for the use of equipment or the purchase of finished goods, they made do. By 1815 these community exchange networks in services and kind had already started to break down. Increased mobility, the growing commercialization of agriculture, and a persistent rise in the number of landless all contributed after 1815 to the spread of a system in which cash progressively replaced agricultural services as the medium of exchange. Cash had to be raised, not just to pay off debts or borrow for farm improvements, but most critically to maintain control over the family farm, the basis of rural independence. Thus, fathers put their wives and children to work in the household finishing of goods supplied to them by outside merchant-capitalists. The result was the rural outwork or putting-out system, a halfway station to the factory system.

By perceiving the putting-out system as an extension of the customary household production performed by women and children, farm families did not experience it as a radical change. Instead of processing the food and fiber produced on the farm for home consumption, women and children now worked up raw materials and semifinished goods provided by local merchants and manufacturers. Outwork complemented the rural family's traditional division of labor by gender, converted to cash the children's obligation to contribute to the family's upkeep until they established their own households, and filled in seasonal slack time with profitable employment. It had the additional advantage of relieving the father of some of the pressure to find odd jobs to compensate for the family's lack of self-sufficiency. The father readily accepted a system that supplemented his patriarchal authority. Work and its scheduling were still under his control, and all wages were for family, not individual, use.

As for the actual laborers in the system—the wives and children—it is likely that they welcomed their new tasks compared to what they had known before. Under the outwork form of production, their work pace may have intensified but the physical demands were lessened. Processing wool into cloth, for example, had been an incredibly demanding chore in the prefactory period. Just the daily movement required to guide the yarn (after the raw wool had been painstakingly cleaned, greased, and combed) through a spinning wheel amounted to a twenty-mile walk. Weaving factory-prepared yarn on a home loom and receiving wages for the effort lessened household labor in two ways: it lightened the drudgery and provided income to purchase commodities that no longer had to be produced at home.

Domestic manufacturing under outwork arrangements enabled manufacturers to meet the rising consumer demand for clothing, shoes, and hats. In a society without a large, preexisting pool of wage labor—that is, individuals separated from the land and utterly dependent on wages for their economic survival—farm families filled the labor void. In the aggregate the putting-out system was the largest employer of nonslave labor in the generation after the War of 1812. Outworkers wove yarn, stitched the upper part of shoes with cut leather supplied to them, and braided into hats palm leaves imported from Cuba and distributed to them by local merchants. Their labor was cheap, and it could be exploited by outsiders who had no need to make large commitments of capital to machinery.

The putting-out system grafted itself onto the precapitalist relations of family labor. Aside from the cost advantage of so doing, this utilization of the family was a socially acceptable way of undermining cultural resistance to the loss of independence and free time that Americans identified with factory labor. Farm families gradually blurred the distinctions between manufacturing for home use, working at home for a merchant, and producing the same goods outside the home in a factory. Economically innovative but culturally conservative, the putting-out system eased the transition to factory employment.

The New England textile factory was another offspring of the marriage of economic convenience between the manufacturer and the farmer. From the viewpoint of the manufacturer, outwork had one crippling disadvantage: he had no control over the actual production process. He could slash piece rates, penalize late work, or withhold payment, but the workers were on their own. As one cynic observed of outworkers in Philadelphia: "They work at such hours as they choose in their own homes, and their industry is mainly regulated by the state of the larder."[22] Concentrating production in one place under the supervision of an overseer increased the even flow of finished goods and lowered costs by reducing wastage. Moses Brown, a mill owner, well understood the rationale: "We have 100 people now at weaving, but 100 looms in families will not weave so much cloth as 30, at least, constantly employed under the immediate inspection of a workman."[23]

Until massive numbers of immigrants began entering the Northeast in the 1840s, manufacturers had no choice but to seek out labor from farm families. Their task was simplified by the fact that most factories had to be built in the countryside near cheap sources of water power. Textiles, the leading manufacturing industry by 1840, used two systems of labor recruitment. The earliest, and the one that remained dominant in smaller mills, involved recruiting entire families. Because Yankee mothers generally refused to enter the mills and fathers were loathe to become factory dependents, normally only the children worked in the mills. In 1820 children constituted 55 percent of the mill workers in Rhode Island, 54 percent in Connecticut, and 45 percent in Massachusetts. Widows, adolescents, and skilled male supervisors made up the rest of the labor force. In order to attract families and hence gain access to their children, the mill owners hired the fathers to work company farms and furnished housing. Mothers, in addition to their usual household duties, took in boarders and did piecework on mill yarn given out to be woven into cloth.

These mill families were the rural poor, those without land or the means of raising the $500 minimum in cash needed to establish a farm in the Midwest. Rather than gambling on a very risky move to the West, these families went into the mill villages. Not only were they able to find employment for the entire family but, at least initially, they were able to maintain customary patterns of work and authority. The family lived in a separate house, the father still worked the land, the mother had full domestic responsibilities, and the children still labored in the interests of the family. Factory dependency surely existed but only for the family members who had always been ordered about—the children.

From the 1820s onward, the owners and their foremen chipped away at the family's authority. Because the textile industry was extremely competitive and prone to booms and busts, owners were under incessant pressure to raise productivity by speeding up work and running the machinery at full capacity. By ordering overtime and Sunday work, eliminating morning and afternoon work breaks, and stripping skilled operatives of their former authority to hire kin, the owners both maximized their profits and shifted power away from the household to the factory. The critical step was taken in the 1840s when factory owners began paying wages directly to the individual worker. Children now had the basis for their own economic independence. Many seized their new options by moving to a boarding house or leaving the area entirely.

Another, somewhat later, group of textile manufacturers avoided the problem of undermining familial authority by not hiring families in the first place. Their method of recruitment, known as the Waltham System as opposed to the family Rhode Island System, characterized the larger, more mechanized mills that were constructed after the War of 1812. These mills completely mechanized cotton production (earlier ones had mechanized only through the spinning process) and equaled their British counterparts in the use of the most technologically advanced equipment. Built with Boston mercantile capital, the first of these mills opened in 1814 in Waltham, Massachusetts. If these heavily capitalized mills were to be profitable, the owners had to find a cheap and steady stream of mostly unskilled labor to operate the machines. In particular, they needed more workers than family recruitment could provide, as it tended to be limited by the number of families in the locality surrounding the mill. The owners turned instead to the most expendable members of the family, the single, adolescent farm daughters who could be recruited from all over New England.

The demographic consequences of migration to the West and the inroads of early factories into household manufacturing rendered the daughters expendable. Heavy male-dominated migration in the first third of the nineteenth century left New England with a surplus of women, especially young ones. In 1820 only four states had a female majority: all were in New England, the region that became the center of the textile industry. Meanwhile, factories were taking over household production, for which daughters had always borne a heavy responsibility. In the East from 1810 to 1840 per-capita household output of manufactures fell from $5.60 to $0.91. The price of factory coarse cloth dropped 80 percent, and families were quick to abandon homespun. Farmers were losing the occasional income from the sale of home manufactures at the same time that they were spending more for store-bought goods. Under these conditions many farmers concluded that they could no longer afford to keep daughters in the household while their productive and marriageable value was steadily declining. It was far better to send them to the mills and add to the family income the wages they sent back.

In order to assuage parental fears over the removal of their daughters from the protective privacy of the home, the textile companies assumed parental responsibilities over them. The model was set by the Lowell, Massachusetts, mills in the mid-1820s. The mill owners required their single female operatives to live in company-subsidized boarding houses and paternalistically supervised their activities. Curfews, strict control over visitors, reporting of improper conduct, and mandatory church attendance were the key elements in a system of moral policing that complemented supervision within the factory. As for the time-regulated factory regimen, a textile operative put it succinctly in 1844:[24]

> We go in at five o'clock'; at seven we come out to breakfast; at half-past seven we return to our work, and stay until half-past twelve. At one, or quarter-past one four months in the year, we return to our work, and stay until seven at night.

Boarding mills spread throughout southern New England, and until the 1850s three-quarters of their hands were women. The bulk of the recruits, women between the ages of 15 and 25, came from large farm families under economic duress. These families had property, about half that of their non-mill neighbors, but not enough for their size. In the words of one of the mill daughters, Sarah Bagley, these families experienced economic need as "a father's debts . . . to be paid, an aged mother to be supported, a brother's ambition to aided."[25]

Many of the daughters left with a sense of relief. However much some of their parents may have pushed them, these young women were also pulled by reasons of their own. The mills offered a much higher wage than any other employment open to antebellum women. Even though their hourly wage was under a nickel, a female mill hand could earn six to seven times as much on an annual basis as teaching school, one of the few other occupations that was open to them. Mill work also offered an opportunity for independence and self-expression that was virtually shut off at home. The chance to open a savings account, shop in stores with one's money, borrow books at the library, listen to regularly scheduled lectures, and simply to live free from constant parental supervision was for many an exhilarating experience. Motivated by a desire to be their own person, many had no intention of ever returning home. As Sally Rice, writing to her parents from a Connecticut mill, explained:[26]

> I am now most 19 years old. I must of course have something of my own before many more years have passed over my head and where is that something coming from if I go home and earn nothing. . . . You may think me unkind but how can you blame me for

wanting to stay here. I have but one life to live and I want to enjoy myself as well as I can while I live.

The daughters left and they changed. In contrast to the normal European pattern, in which daughters working outside of the home were expected to send home all their earnings, these young women weaned themselves earlier from the family economy. They spent their wages on their own needs, saved the rest, and sent home only what they felt they could afford. They used the factories to help plan their futures. After staying in the mills for about four years, the typical female operative left and married. Relative to rural women who did not migrate to the mills, these women married later, chose spouses half as likely to be farmers, and had fewer children. About one-third settled permanently with their husbands in urban areas. Thus the boarding mills, like the family mills, transformed rural culture while drawing upon it. By feeding labor into the factories through kin networks and sending daughters and younger sons off to textile jobs while the older sons stayed at home to look after the farm and aging kin, farm families acted upon defensive strategies of preservation that, ironically, contributed to the destruction of the very rural way of life the families were seeking to save.

South of New England in the Mid-Atlantic states, immigrants played a larger role in the formative stages of industrialization. Competing with a more prosperous agricultural hinterland than their factory counterparts in New England, and one without a surplus of young farm women, New York and Pennsylvania capitalists were forced to turn much earlier to immigrants as they sought to create a wage-labor pool. In 1820 immigrants comprised at least half of the factory labor in the Middle States. America's first large milling center, the Brandywine Valley near Wilmington, Delaware, drew its labor chiefly from Irish immigrants, many of whom drifted into the mills after construction work on canals. In the skilled positions were British textile operatives who provided invaluable technical knowledge that permitted American manufacturers to circumvent British prohibitions on the exporting of trade secrets.

Although immigrants were proportionately much more likely than native-born Americans to be engaged in industrial labor, their numbers, under 5 percent of the total population in 1820, were simply insufficient for the creation of a large factory force. This changed in the 1840s, the decade in which mass emigration to America began (see Table 1.5). In the midst of a series of crop failures, Europe, and particularly Ireland, southwestern Germany, and parts of Scandinavia, disgorged hundreds of thousands of peasants who had been forced off the land.

Table 1.5 Antebellum Immigration
(in thousands)

Triggered by the potato famine in Ireland and economic and political unrest on the Continent, European emigration to the U.S. skyrocketed in the 1840s and 1850s.

DECADE	TOTAL	IRISH	GERMAN
1820–29	129.5	51.7	5.7
1830–39	538.3	170.7	124.8
1840–49	1427.3	656.1	385.4
1850–59	2814.5	1029.5	976.1

Source: Compiled from *Historical Statistics,* Series C-89–119.

Certainly in the case of the Irish, the result was more of a flight than a migration. The potato famine struck in 1846. In the next eight years, over one million Irish, or about one-sixth of the 1840 population on the island, went to America. Their concentration in the port cities, lack of skills and capital, and sheer destitution left them little choice as to employment. All they had to sell was their labor power. Manufacturers and contractors were eager purchasers, because these displaced peasants, who accounted for nearly half of the increase in the nonslave labor force from 1830 to 1850, resolved their persistent problem of a shortage in unskilled labor. One factory worker recalled that her employer turned to immigrants because "not coming from country homes, but living as the Irish do, in the town, they take no vacations, and can be relied on at the mill all year round."[27] Desperate for wages, the Irish sent their children into the mills at an earlier age than their Yankee predecessors and stayed at their jobs longer. They soon replaced the Yankee women in the mills. In the mid-1830s over 95 percent of the textile operatives in New England were native born, and mostly women; by the early 1850s over half of them were foreign born, and mostly Irish.

Up and down the Eastern seaboard and in the interior towns where they were stranded when construction contracts expired, the Irish had the same unenviable economic role—tending machines at entry-level factory jobs and hauling, ditching, and shoving in seasonal urban labor. Typical of their employment patterns was the situation in Philadelphia in 1850. Comprising 27 percent of the city's male work force, the Irish held 77 percent of the factory jobs in textiles. About one-third were day laborers, and another 12 percent were hand-loom weavers. Wives and daughters brought the family income up to a survival level by working as domestics.

In certain industries, such as textiles, and in certain cities, notably Boston, the mass arrival of immigrants after 1845 was crucial in converting a labor shortage into a surplus. Confident that the army of immigrants would have to come to him, a factory agent in Fall River, Massachusetts, could declare in 1855: "I regard people just as I regard my machinery. . . . When my machines get old and useless, I reject them and get new, and these people are part of my machinery."[28] The labor surplus, nonetheless, was also fed by a less visible but numerically more significant source of wage labor that was gradually created after 1815. It was the merging of this source, young men without land who did not migrate West, with the immigrants in the 1850s that decisively and permanently enlarged labor markets.

Even in Massachusetts, a state in which Irish immigration was unusually heavy and short-term female labor was essential for textile factories, male in-migrants and landless native sons were crucial to industrialization. Males dominated the production of boots and shoes, an industry that employed twice as many workers as cotton textiles in the 1850s. In 1860 the state's 185,000 foreign-born Irish were nearly balanced by 165,000 migrants from other New England states and New York. These newcomers flowed to the eastern countries around Boston in which commercial and manufacturing jobs could be found. There they intermingled with the rural sons of Massachusetts who had been rendered superfluous in the countryside. In Concord, for example, the percentage of landless taxpayers rose from 42 percent in 1801 to 59 percent in 1840 and 69 percent by 1850. During the same period, the number of farms stabilized and local jobs in the trades and crafts showed little growth. Those unable or unwilling to secure a farm in the West moved to the factories in the East.

The demographic pressures on limited agricultural sources that characterized New

England in the early 1800s spread to the Mid-Atlantic states a generation later. South-eastern Pennsylvania and other rural areas settled in the eighteenth century became exporters of population, especially in the 1820s and 1830s. By 1850, 13 percent of native Pennsylvanians were living in the Old Northwest. Although most sons stayed, they did not remain on the family farm. Instead, they moved short distances into surrounding towns and small cities, where they made up the largest component of the new industrial labor force.

The unusual diligence of one census taker, Charles Neidly, who listed precise birth information on residents in Reading, Pennsylvania, in 1850, makes it possible to trace out these local moves for one area. Reading, the county seat of Berks County, is about fifty miles up the Schuylkill River from Philadelphia. The center of a prosperous agricultural-manufacturing area and the transportation hub for regional trade, Reading exemplified the rapidly growing mid-sized city in which most antebellum manufacturing occurred. In the 1840s Reading's population doubled, to 15,000. The city drew on the countryside of Berks and contiguous counties for most of this increase. In Spruce Ward, the most working class of the city's five wards, over 70 percent of the work force was native born in 1850. Of particular note was the predominance of local rural migrants among unskilled laborers, those who had the worst-paying jobs with the least security. Nearly half of the laborers, 48 percent, came from a circle within a twenty-five-mile radius of Reading. The rural locales they had left within this radius were disproportionately those with the lowest land values and highest fertility rates in 1830. The young left at home after their siblings were cycled out of the family economy into neighboring households as apprentices, servants, and farm hands made their way to Reading. Undoubtedly, they were willing to take jobs on the lowest rungs of the urban economy, because the pressure that had driven them off the land had been so strong.

The labor sources we have discussed—women and children, immigrants, and native-born males—came straight off the land and entered the wage-labor pool with little or no manufacturing experience. They were far more likely than the artisans to hold unskilled or semiskilled industrial jobs. By the 1850s the sheer increase in the number of all manufacturing workers had accounted for at least two-thirds of all gains in manufacturing output. To be sure, American manufacturers, because labor costs were higher than in England, had an incentive from the very beginning to substitute machines for labor. One result became famous in the 1850s as the American system of manufacturing—low cost and standardized mass production, built around the use of interchangeable parts. Nonetheless, this system was not characteristic of American industry in the antebellum period. Before 1860 it was limited to about twenty industries, mostly those in metal cutting. More workers, not gains in productivity per worker, were responsible for most of the expansion in antebellum manufacturing.

Urbanization and Manufacturing

Manufacturing and urbanization reinforced each other in their patterns of growth. Between 1820 and 1860, the same period in which manufacturing more than tripled its share of commodity output, the urban population grew five times as fast as the rural. The pace of urbanization, as shown in Table 1.6, accelerated after 1840, in step with the late-antebellum surge in heavy industry tied to sources of coal. Clearly, manufacturing and urbanization were related, but the connection was not necessarily a direct

Table 1.6 Urbanization

Especially in large cities, the rate of antebellum urbanization quickened after 1840.

	PERCENTAGE OF POPULATION IN SETTLEMENTS OVER:	
	2,500	**50,000**
1820	7.2	2.6
1830	8.8	3.3
1840	10.8	4.1
1850	15.3	6.2
1860	19.8	9.9

Source: Compiled from *Historical Statistics*, Series A-57–72.

one. The correlation between urban size and manufacturing was weak. Less than one-third of the labor force in the largest cities held manufacturing jobs in 1860, and cities of all sizes contained similar numbers of factories.

The major barrier to industrialization in antebellum cities was a technological one. Most industrial power was generated by the flow of water around a submerged tub-wheel attached to a wooden rod that drove the machinery. Water power was generally twice as cheap as stream, and not until the 1870s did the steam engine replace the waterwheel as the main source of industrial power. Thus, antebellum manufacturing was limited to sites near rivers and, with the exception of textiles, metal working, and machine building, remained widely scattered in small towns with cheap water power.

Apart from this technological limitation of reliance upon a fixed power source in the countryside, the largest cities were slow to industrialize because of the very success of their traditional mercantile functions. The great port cities—Boston, New York, Philadelphia, Baltimore, and New Orleans—were huge trading marts exchanging foreign and domestic goods. These five ports accounted for 56 percent of all American exports in 1815 and 68 percent by 1840; their share of imports grew from 84 percent to 92 percent in the same period. A trend toward investing in manufacturing set in after 1815, but for most merchants it was a third choice after reinvesting in retailing and speculating in urban property. In 1840 retailing was still favored two to one over manufacturing as a capital investment in the five dominant port cities. Speculation in building lots and construction, triggered by rising urban population, offered a chance for incredible capital gains. The boom in Manhattan carried real estate values from $5 million in 1823 to $253 million by 1836. Consequently, although commercial capital flowed into turnpike, canal, and railroad construction as each group of urban merchants jockeyed to protect or expand its share of hinterland trade, urban manufacturers had to depend on their own capital resources. "I am inclined to think," noted a Bostonian in 1832, "that few manufacturers rely upon permanent loans from banks or individuals, the capital invested being their own property."[29]

Much as they had done in the eighteenth century, urban merchants limited their manufacturing investment to concerns that were adjuncts of their commercial economy. The resultant industry was of two sorts. One branch, such as the milling of flour, refining of sugar, and tanning of leather, processed raw materials shipped through the city. The óther was a response to direct demands for commercial related services through the proliferation of the shipbuilding, printing, and cooperage trades. Urban manufacturing as a whole remained in the handicraft stage of production, and its growth resulted more from a rise in consumer demand than from any infusions of commercial capital. Before 1840 the bulk of that demand, as well as the labor which supplied it, originated within the surrounding countryside.

The demographic pattern already noted for Berks County and the growth of an industrial labor force in Reading differed only in scale from that repeated in other Eastern cities. Philadelphia, for example, attracted about 30 percent of all who left its surrounding hinterland during the 1820s. In the same decade, Boston's population growth of 40 percent was more than twice the rate in the rest of Massachusetts. If those who left farming but remained in the East became day laborers and semiskilled workers in the urban economy, those who remained on farms with access to transportation outlets increasingly specialized in market production. Economically, both groups were mutually part of an interaction between a city and its hinterland. The city produced goods for rural consumption with displaced rural labor fed by the food surpluses produced by those still left on the farms. Two events were critical for setting off this interaction: demographic pressure in the countryside and improved transportation facilities. The former generated a surplus of underemployed rural labor exportable to cities, and the latter increased the disposable income of farmers by reducing the cost of what they imported and raising the profit on what they sold.

This access to a pool of cheap rural labor was a major stimulant to urban manufacturing. Economic change in the Delaware Valley in the 1820s illustrates the advantages of utilizing that labor. In the wake of a sharp recession in 1819 and a temporary saturation of European demand for American foodstuffs, the export of agricultural commodities out of Philadelphia stagnated. Farm wages fell 15 to 20 percent in the ensuing decade. Farm laborers, the harvest hands and tenants who comprised one-third of the rural work force, migrated to Philadelphia, where the same recession had lowered urban living costs back to 1790 levels. The city and its manufacturers offered slightly higher wages and significantly more regular employment than the depressed rural economy. Under these conditions the attraction of mill work must have been considerable. "I know that," reported a Delaware Valley manufacturer in 1832, "in consequence of our men losing no time from bad weather, want of jobs, and at fifty cents per day, the old men and youths thrived better than on a farm or at laboring work and job work."[30] The recession mobilized in an urban and manufacturing setting the surplus and seasonal labor of the rural hinterland and thus was a boon to local manufacturers. The wage differential between skilled and unskilled labor in textile factories was now so large that it made sound economic sense to rely increasingly on mechanization. By using the cheap labor uprooted from the countryside, the manufacturer realized capital savings, which then were invested in the latest technology. In this way unskilled labor, in effect, was converted to skilled labor, for the combination of machinery and low-priced operatives produced the same output at lower cost than production that formerly had relied more heavily on skilled artisans. In the Philadelphia region this combination led to cost savings of $120 to $142 per operative.

As a result of similar urban-rural feedback interactions, early industrialization and urbanization were increasingly centered in the Northeast. On a scale in which 100 equals the national average, in 1840 urbanization in New England stood at 180 and in the Middle Atlantic states at 176. On a comparable scale for the percentage of the labor force engaged in nonagricultural activities New England's level was 185 and that of the Middle Atlantic states 154. Its own cities and countryside generated most of the manufacturing demand within the Northeastern economy. Per-capita income was one-third higher in the Northeast than the rest of the nation, and less than 20 percent of the Northeast's manufacturing output left the region before 1840.

Within the Northeast, economic development first occurred within subregions, such as that of Philadelphia and its hinterland of 45 counties in the surrounding area that made up a marketing cluster serviced by the city. Within the subregion, the major impetus for economic development came from rural demand. Manufacturing output in Philadelphia increased by 88 percent between 1810 and 1840, and the bulk of it went to the rural hinterland. In turn, exports from the hinterland to Philadelphia tripled in the quarter-century after the War of 1812. Philadelphia County directly consumed 60 to 70 percent of the exports. In a cycle of economic development fueled by rising incomes, improved transportation, and the reciprocity of urban and rural needs, the per-capita value of commerce rose 60 percent in the 1820s and 1830s. It was through this expanding subregional trade that the advantages of economic specialization were realized. The western hinterland diversified its economy by developing its coal and iron resources and by changing its crop mix to meet the urban demand for grain and meat. The eastern hinterland in New Jersey and Delaware specialized in corn, lumber, and diversified manufacturing for the Philadelphia market. After the mid-1830s, this subregional development gradually merged into the regional economy of the Northeast as a whole. Eastern markets took an increasingly large share of Philadelphia's goods. By mid-century this intraregional market accounted for 63 percent of Philadelphia's nonlocal exports, more than twice as much as the combined Southern and Western markets.

Within the Northeastern regional economy that formed in the last two antebellum decades, manufacturing and urbanization began to mesh more closely. The development of stationary steam engines, fired by coal, removed the major technological barrier in urban industrialization. The new technology, coupled with another drop in transportation costs with through rail service to the Midwest, heightened the attraction of locating manufacturing in old commercial cities. Inherent urban advantages for manufacturing now came into play. High population density meant a compact, easily accessible market that spent three times as much of its income on consumer goods as did rural households. The city provided a large, diversified labor supply, and one that was augmented tremendously by mass immigration after the mid-1840s. By placing capital and labor in close physical proximity, the urban environment permitted workers to live within walking distance of the factories, and it facilitated the communication of information for making economic decisions.

The Southern Exception

As the Northeastern economy continued to develop, the economy in the Southeast remained pretty much what it had always been—overwhelmingly agricultural, with a small commercial and manufacturing sector. The dimensions of this contrast can be seen in Table 1.7. This divergence had grown ever wider during the antebellum

Table 1.7 Developmental Contrast of Northeast and Southeast, 1860

As measured by the key indices of urbanization and manufacturing, economic development in the Southeast lagged far behind that in the free states of the antebellum East.

	PERCENTAGE OF POPULATION URBANIZED	MANUFACTURING WAGES PER CAPITA
New England	36.6	33.23
Middle Atlantic	35.4	19.05
South Atlantic	11.5	4.74

Source: Douglas C. North, *The Economic Growth of the United States. 1790–1860* (New York: W. W. Norton, 1966), p. 258, for urban data; Earle and Hoffman, op. cit., p. 1078, for wages; *Historical Statistics,* Series A-195–209.

period, despite the fact that the agricultural societies in both regions had faced very similar problems after 1815. Soil exhaustion, Western competition, demographic pressures, and outflows of migrants were as characteristic of the South Atlantic states as of those north of the Potomac. Yet, whereas the Northeast was able to reverse its negative migration rates of the early nineteenth century and attract newcomers after 1820, the South Atlantic states continued to lose population to other regions in every decade before the Civil War. The Northeast met the economic and demographic challenge of the West by adjusting along paths of agricultural diversification, urbanization, and industrialization that converged into a process of economic development; by 1860, only 30 percent of its labor force was still employed in agriculture. The Southeast made no similar adjustments; the bulk of its labor, free and slave, was still working the land in 1860.

The road to economic development began in the countryside, and it was there that the regional contrasts had their origin. Sharply dissimilar climatic and soil conditions left farmers in the Northeast and Southeast with quite different agricultural options. In the North there were no ecological barriers against the adoption of agricultural methods pioneered in the eighteenth century by the English and Dutch. These methods were based on an efficient blend of mixed crop and livestock farming. In place of the former land-extensive agriculture, which mined the soil through successive plantings and then relied upon long periods of fallow to restore fertility, Northeastern farmers, especially after 1815, switched to the land-intensive English methods. They carefully rotated food crops with soil-conserving grasses and legumes that returned nitrogen to the soil. They fenced their livestock, fed them the fodder crops, collected their manure to fertilize the fields, milked them for urban dairy products, and slaughtered them for meat and leather. Made possible by transportation improvements and the cash income of producing for urban markets, this diversified agriculture was essential for the urban-rural exchange of goods and capital that drove so much of the Northeastern economy.

With the exception of parts of the upper South, climate and soil conditions prevented this agricultural shift in most of the slave states. The central Appalachian highlands of the mountainous South were too rough and isolated for commercial agriculture to be feasible on a large scale. From the southern Virginia piedmont through the lower South, farmers faced disadvantages absent in the North. In general, Southern soils were less fertile than the Northern average. Leached by heavy summer rains, they were predominately sandy, thin, and acidic. They produced poorer and less nutritious yields of corn, wheat, small grains, and fodder. High humidity and thunderstorms made the mowing and curing of hay crops particularly difficult, and most Southern farmers did not even try to grow these grasses. The absence of long, killing winter frosts, which act to conserve the mineral and moisture content of soil, further exacerbated the poor soil conditions. By not killing off animal parasites and other disease carriers, the same mild winters also left Southern agriculture vulnerable to pest infestations that drastically reduced livestock quality. Swine kidney worm and the Texas fever, spread by the cattle tick, often reached epidemic proportions.

Unable to rely upon fodder crops and to improve significantly the quality of livestock, the two critical components of the shift in Northern agriculture, lower South farmers continued their former practices. Slaveowners produced a cash staple for the market, and most nonslaveowners stayed with a shifting, land-extensive agriculture that produced a sustenance with a minimum amount of work. Because the former were self-sufficient in food supplies, their market involvement, as we saw in the case of the Old Southwest, did not generate high levels of urban-rural interaction. Because the latter only rarely entered the market, the demand coming from the Southern rural masses was hardly sufficient to generate much manufacturing activity. The manufactured items that slaves consumed in large quantities, shoes and clothing, were usually produced in the Northeast. In addition, this self-sufficient rural population was so scattered that 95 percent of all Southern counties in 1860 had a population density under the Northern-county median of 32 persons per square mile.

After 1815 the Southeastern agricultural economy remained locked within the same narrow range of commercial crops. The economic need to maximize the use of slave labor, as well as ecological factors, provided no incentives to shift out of tobacco and cotton or to mechanize production. The eight- to twelve-month labor demands of cotton or tobacco, combined with corn, meshed neatly with a long growing season and the continuous employment of slaves. Because the agricultural work year in the South was so much longer than the four months of heavy labor required in the mixed grain-livestock economy of the Northeast, annualized rural wages were correspondingly higher. As a result, the wages that a manufacturer in the South had to offer in order to entice unskilled labor to leave the countryside were higher than in the North. By the 1850s free unskilled labor could command about $400 a year in Southern cities; this was twice the cost of comparable labor in the North. Even at these wages Southern manufacturers had difficulty in attracting labor. Through their lifestyles of easy self-sufficiency, the nonslaveholding majority in the rural South gave every indication that they preferred leisure time to wage labor.

Agricultural recessions, notably those in the 1820s and 1840s, did lead to demands for economic diversification, and farmers in the upper South gradually put more emphasis on wheat and less on tobacco. Nonetheless, economic adjustments in the Southeast usually did not go beyond exporting population to the Old Southwest. Slaveholders either migrated with their slaves or, if they stayed, sold off slaves at the high market price set by the fertile Southwest. Nonslaveholding farmers were even more likely to migrate, but if they stayed they were not especially hurt by Western competition in foodstuffs, because few of them specialized in the commercial production of wheat, corn, and meat. Unlike the recession of the 1820s in the Delaware Valley, no stream of women, children, and rural poor moved into urban factories.

Itinerant farm labor was rare in the Southern hinterland, and without this source of cheap and displacable rural labor, the Southeast lacked one of the major structural preconditions for industrialization.

Finally, and undoubtedly decisively, the Southeastern economy did not significantly change, because returns on agricultural slave capital averaged about 10 percent. Because this was a profit level comparable to New England textile firms or other capital investments, there was no economic reason for slaveowners to shift out of agriculture into industry. Some planters and merchants did invest in factories, and Southern manufacturing returns have been estimated at over 20 percent in the 1850s. Such high profits, however, were limited to small, localized markets that were ignored by Northern industry. High volume, low profit markets, where they existed in the South, were dominated by Northern concerns. Rather than risk their comparative advantage in the international marketplace in cotton production, most slaveowners took their accustomed profits and continued to base their lifestyle and social structure on land and cash staples.

What was economically and socially rational for individual planters was not the most efficient economic course for the South as a whole. Given undeniable ecological constraints, the production of foodstuffs in the lower South was an inefficient use of labor resources. Yet, rather than industrializing and importing its food from outside, the lower South continued to produce inferior corn and livestock. The existing system was profitable, and changing it would have endangered not only profits but also the racial discipline and segregation imposed by plantation units.

Southern whites did not change their economy, and the paradoxical result was the juxtaposition of high per-capita income with an economic structure that was closer to that of modern underdeveloped nations than that of the antebellum North. In 1860 only Australia, the North (if treated as a separate nation), and Great Britain exceeded the South in per-capita income. Still, in the only politically relevant comparison, Northern per-capita income was 40 percent higher than the Southern in 1860 and had grown faster in each of its subregions since 1840. In fact growth in the Southern economy masked the lack of development. The South's weak service and manufacturing sectors were less than half the size of those in the Midwest in 1860. Immigrants were ten times as likely to settle in the North as in the South. For all the economic growth the rural population of the South remained scattered, isolated, and wrapped in a cocoon of economic self-sufficiency that only the Civil War began to unravel.

In the first half of the nineteenth century, the United States entered the era of modern economic development. The reality of economic change was readily apparent but the meaning that Americans placed on that change was not. On one hand, there were the obvious benefits. The growth rate in per-capita income was two to three times as fast as in the eighteenth century. Americans were earning more and spending their incomes on a wide variety of consumer goods, which raised their standard of living. On the other hand, Americans were working longer and harder and becoming increasingly stratified by wealth.

The industrial work year in the nineteenth century was about 3,000 hours, or 50 percent longer than the 2,000 hours of agricultural labor. The steady drop in agriculture's share of labor force employment after 1810 meant that a growing number of Americans were subjected to the longer working hours. The productivity of an industrial worker was three times that of one in agriculture, but clearly a price had to be paid in reduced leisure time. Manufacturing work was also more intensive. In human terms the phrase "labor-saving machinery" is a misnomer. Machines powered by inanimate sources save labor costs relative to those of capital for the manufacturer, but they do so by extracting more human effort per worker. By one contemporary estimate, for example, the introduction of newer and larger continuous-motion machines in British textiles tripled the labor done by the workers between 1800 and 1850. American textile manufacturers ran their machines at even higher speeds than the British. After all, the whole point of concentrating workers in a factory setting under centralized discipline was to increase the amount and rate at which work was done.

At the same time that Americans began to assume a heavier work burden, work that made them economically dependent on somebody else, the economic distance between themselves was widening. Wealth inequality increased markedly after 1815. In the rural Northeast the upper 10 percent increased their share of total wealth from 40 percent to over 50 percent. By 1860 inequality in the Midwest had reached the Eastern levels of 1800. In the Cotton South the top 10 percent owned nearly 60 percent of the agricultural wealth in 1860. Inequality was greatest in the cities. As Brooklyn grew from a village of 5,000 in 1810 to a city of 41,000 in 1841, the richest 1 percent doubled their share of noncorporate wealth from 22 percent to 42 percent. Throughout the nation, 85 percent to 90 percent of urban wealth was held by one-tenth of the urban population in 1860. In areas as disparate as Stonington, Connecticut, and Chicago, Illinois, two-thirds to three-fourths of all households were propertyless. In short, economic development meant cumulative inequality. Owners of capital and income-producing property were able to generate returns that disproportionately enlarged their share of wealth over and above that of Americans who had only their labor power to produce income.

More work, more inequality, and, above all, a dislocating sense of social change accompanied the economic transformation. How and why Americans turned to categories of race and gender to cope with this change will be the themes of Chapter 2.

SUGGESTED READING

To conserve space, the following abbreviations are used in lieu of the complete names of professional journals in all of the end-of-chapter Notes in this book.

AAAG	*Annals of the Association of Amer-ican Geographers*	HCQ	*History of Childhood Quarterly*
		HEQ	*History of Education Quarterly*
AGH	*Agricultural History*	HM	*Historical Methods*
AHR	*American Historical Review*	JAC	*Journal of American Culture*
AJS	*American Journal of Sociology*	JAH	*Journal of American History*
APSR	*American Political Science Review*	JAS	*Journal of American Studies*
AQ	*American Quarterly*	JEH	*Journal of Economic History*
AS	*American Studies*	JER	*Journal of the Early Republic*
AW	*Annals of Wyoming*	JFH	*Journal of Family History*
BHR	*Business History Review*	JHG	*Journal of Historical Geography*
CWH	*Civil War History*	JIH	*Journal of Interdisciplinary History*
EEH	*Explorations in Economic History*		
FS	*Feminist Studies*	JSH	*Journal of Southern History*
GR	*Geographical Review*	JSOH	*Journal of Social History*

JUH	*Journal of Urban History*	PAH	*Perspectives in American History*
KHQ	*Kansas Historical Quarterly*	PH	*Pennsylvania History*
LH	*Labor History*	PS	*Population Studies*
MASJ	*Midcontinent American Studies Journal*	PSQ	*Political Science Quarterly*
		RAH	*Reviews in American History*
MP	*Marxist Perspectives*	SAQ	*South Atlantic Quarterly*
MVHR	*Mississippi Valley Historical Review*	SH	*Social History*
		WMQ	*William and Mary Quarterly*
NLR	*New Left Review*		

The colonial and late eighteenth-century background to the themes discussed in the opening chapter is superbly covered in James A. Henretta, *The Evolution of American Society, 1700–1815* (1973). His "Families and Farms: *Mentalité* in Pre-Industrial America," WMQ 35 (1978), is the most significant statement of the dominance of premarket, family values among rural Americans in the early 1800s, but it should be read in conjunction with James T. Lemon, *The Best Poor Man's Country* (1972), for an opposing view that stresses early market responses to individualism and economic self-gain.

For a very readable introduction to demographic patterns of change in American history, see Walter Nugent, *Structures of American Social History* (1981). Another helpful synthesis in historical demography, though with a different emphasis, is Robert V. Wells, *Revolutions in Americans' Lives* (1982). J. Potter provides a useful statistical survey for the colonial and antebellum periods in "The Growth of Population in America, 1700–1860," in D. C. Glass and D. E. C. Eversley, eds., *Population in History* (1965). For a more detailed treatment of the causes and consequences of demographic pressure in the East, see Colin Forster and G. S. L. Tucker, *Economic Opportunity and White American Fertility Ratios, 1800–1860* (1972); Nancy Osterud and John Fulton, "Family Limitation and Age at Marriage: Fertility Decline in Sturbridge, Massachusetts, 1730–1850," PS 30 (1976); H. Temkin-Greener and A. C. Swedlund, "Fertility Transition in the Connecticut Valley: 1740–1850," PS 32 (1978); and Gary L. Laidig et al., "Agricultural Variation and Human Fertility in Antebellum Pennsylvania," JFH 6 (1981). Demographic patterns in the antebellum West can be traced in James E. David, *Frontier America, 1800–1840* (1977); Jack E. Eblen, "An Analysis of Nineteenth-Century Frontier Populations," *Demography* 2 (1965); and Richard A. Easterlin, "Factors in the Decline of Farm Family Fertility in the United States," JAH 63 (1976). Maris A. Vinovskis, *Fertility in Massachusetts from the Revolution to the Civil War* (1981), is the most thorough study of fertility transition for a single state.

The classic work on the significance of the frontier in American history remains Frederick Jackson Turner, *The Frontier in American History* (1921). Turner interpreted the frontier experience as a unique source of individualism and democratic renewal in American culture, and this approach also characterizes Ray Allen Billington, *Westward Expansion* (1974). For two works that challenge the Turnerian interpretation by placing the American frontier in a comparative perspective, see Richard Hofstadter and Seymour Martin Lipset, eds., *Turner and the Sociology of the Frontier* (1967), and Howard Lamar and Leonard Thompson, eds., *The Frontier in History: North America and South Africa Compared* (1981). Richard A. Bartlett, *The New Country: A Social History of the American Frontier, 1796–1890* (1974), provides a synthesis of the settlement process, and Malcolm J. Rohrbough, *The Trans-Appalachian Frontier* (1979) is especially strong on the Jacksonian West. The actual process of migration, and what it meant for women as well as men, is covered in John Mack Faragher, *Women and Men on the Overland Trail* (1979). For the extraordinary cooperation required of migrants on the long overland trek to the West Coast, as well as a revisionist critique of stereotypes of Indian attacks, see John D. Unruh, *The Plains Across* (1979). William H. Bowen, *The Willamette Valley: Migration and Settlement on the Oregon Frontier* (1978), is unrivalled for establishing the importance of kinship ties in migration, and Michael J. O'Brien, et al., *Grassland, Forest, and Historical Settlement: An Analysis of Dynamics in Northeast Missouri* (1984), stands out for its close attention to the ecological consequences of settlement.

The best survey of antebellum agriculture is Paul W. Gates, *The Farmer's Age: Agriculture, 1815–1860* (1960), and his "An Overview of American Land Policy," AGH 50 (1976), is a useful introduction to public land policy. Percy W. Bidwell and John I. Falconer, *History of Agriculture in the Northern United States, 1620–1860* (1925); Clarence H. Danhof, *Change in Agriculture in the Northern United States, 1820–1870* (1969); and Lewis C. Gray, *History of Agriculture in the Southern United States to 1860* (2 vols., 1933), remain the standard treatments of agriculture in the North and South respectively. The techniques and extent of land clearing can be found in Michael Williams, "Clearing the United States Forests: Pivotal Years, 1810–1860," JHG (1982), and, in a beautifully written book, John R. Stilgoe, *Common Landscape of America, 1580–1845* (1982), describes how the landscape and attitudes toward it changed. The economics of creating a farm are laid out in Jeremy Atack, "Farm and Farm-Making Costs Revisited," AGH 56 (1984). Paul P. Christensen, "Land Abundance and Cheap Horsepower in the Mechanization of the Antebellum United States Economy," EEH 18 (1981), is excellent for showing why Northern farmers were world leaders in agricultural mechanization.

For specialized studies on the Old Northwest, see David C. Klingaman and Richard K. Vedder, eds., *Essays in Nineteenth Century Economic History: The Old Northwest* (1975); Allan G. Bogue, *From Prairie to Corn Belt* (1963); and Richard L. Power, *Planting Corn Belt Culture: The Impress of the Upland South and the Yankee in the Old Northwest* (1953). On the Old Southwest, see W. H. Yarbrough, *Economic Aspects of Slavery in Relation to Southern and Southwestern Migration* (1932); Ulrich B. Phillips, "The Origin and Growth of the Southern Black Belts," AHR 11 (1906); and John Solomon Otto, "The Migration of the Southern Plain Folk: An Interdisciplinary Synthesis," JSH 51 (1985). On the striking contrast in town development between the free and the slave Wests, see Stanley Elkins and Eric McKitrick, "A Meaning for Turner's Frontier: Democracy in the Old Northwest" and "The Southwest Frontier and New England," PSQ 69 (1954). The different ecological and labor requirements of wheat and cotton are set forth by Carville V. Earle, "A Staple Interpretation of Slavery and Free Labor," GR 68 (1978).

Economic surveys that are excellent on the antebellum period include Stanley Lebergott, *The Americans: An Economic Record* (1984), and W. Elliot Brownlee, *Dynamics of Ascent* (1979). More detailed overviews can be found in Stuart Bruchey, *The Roots of American Economic Growth, 1607–1861;* the seminal study on regional specialization by Douglas C. North, *The Economic Growth of the United States, 1790–1860* (1961); and the concise monetary analysis of Peter Temin, *The Jacksonian Economy* (1969). Diane Lindstrom, *Economic Development in the Philadelphia Region, 1810–1850* (1978), is a superb regional study that persuasively challenges some of North's conclusions. Lindstrom, "Macroeconomic Growth: The United States in the Nineteenth Century," JIH 13 (1983), provides a recent summary of the statistical findings on the economy. Despite its age, Victor S. Clark, *History of Manufactures in the United States, 1607–1860* (3 vols., 1929), remains indispensable.

Transportation changes were fundamental to economic growth, and George R. Taylor, *The Transportation Revolution, 1815–1860* (1951), is the best guide. Governmental assistance to the transportation projects is the theme of Carter Goodrich, *Government Promotion of Canals and Railroads* (1960). The links between transportation and industrialization are examined in Alfred D. Chandler, "Anthracite Coal and the Beginnings of the Industrial Revolution in the United States," BHR 45 (1972). For the cultural impetus behind industrialization, see Thomas C. Cochran, *Frontiers of Change: Early Industrialism in America* (1981). On the critically important, but often neglected, development of a labor market for industrialization, see David M. Gordon, et al., *Segmented Work, Divided Laborers* (1982), esp. pp. 48–99; Alexander James Field, "Sectoral Shift in Antebellum Massachusetts," EEH 15 (1978); John Modell, "The

Peopling of a Working-Class Ward: Reading, Pennsylvania, 1850," 5 (1971); and Carville Earle and Ronald Hoffman, "The Foundation of the Modern Economy," AHR 85 (1980). The best study of the impact of immigration on a regional labor market is Oscar Handlin, *Boston's Immigrants* (1959). For antebellum immigration in general, see Marcus L. Hansen, *The Atlantic Migration, 1607–1860* (1940). Excellent local studies include Robert Ernst, *Immigrant Life in New York City, 1825–1863* (1949), and Kathleen N. Conzen, *Immigrant Milwaukee, 1836–1860* (1977). Charlotte Erickson, *Invisible Immigrants: The Adaptation of English and Scottish Immigrants in Nineteenth-Century America* (1972), provides a fascinating collection of immigrant letters.

A host of recent studies approach the early industrial revolution in the U.S. from the perspective of workers. Among the most stimulating are: Paul G. Faler, *Mechanics and Manufacturers in the Early Industrial Revolution: Lynn, Massachusetts, 1780–1860* (1981); Jonathan Prude, *The Coming of Industrial Order: Town and Factory Life in Rural Massachusetts, 1810–1860* (1983); Alan Dawley, *Class and Community: The Industrial Revolution in Lynn* (1977); Bruce Laurie, *Working People of Philadelphia, 1800–1850* (1980); Thomas Dublin, *Women at Work: The Transformation of Work and Community in Lowell, Massachusetts, 1826–1860* (1980); and Susan Hirsch, *Roots of the American Working Class: The Industrialization of Crafts in Newark, 1800–1860* (1978). Less analytical, but still useful, is Norman Ware, *The Industrial Worker, 1840–1860* (1924). Two excellent studies on the transition from a rural family economy to involvement in an industrializing market economy are Richard L. Bushman, "Family Security in the Transition from Farm to City, 1750–1850," JFH 6 (1981), and Christopher Clark, "The Household Economy, Market Exchange, and the Rise of Capitalism in the Connecticut Valley, 1800–1860," JSOH 4 (1984). For a comprehensive treatment of this transition in a rural community, see Anthony F. C. Wallace, *Rockdale* (1978).

Sam Bass Warner, Jr., *The Urban Wilderness* (1972), and Howard P. Chudacoff, *The Evolution of American Urban Society* (1981), provide a good introduction to antebellum urbanization. Richard C. Wade, *The Urban Frontier* (1964), focuses on urbanization in the West, and Allan R. Pred, *Urban Growth and the Circulation of Information* (1973), correlates urban size in the Northeast with communication networks of business news. Blake McKelvey, *Rochester,* Vol. 1, *The Water-Power City, 1812–54* (1945), and Edward K. Spann, *The New Metropolis: New York, 1840–1857* (1981), are exemplary studies of individual cities. Stuart M. Blumin, *The Urban Threshold* (1976), examines Kingston, New York, to recreate the experiences of a rural village as it evolves into a small city. On the relationship between economic growth and the preindustrial city, see Allan R. Pred, "Manufacturing in the American Mercantile City, 1800–1840," AAAG 56 (1966), and Jeffrey A. Williamson, "Antebellum Urbanization in the American Northeast," JEH 25 (1965).

Robert W. Fogel and Stanley Engerman, *Time on the Cross: The Economics of American Negro Slavery* (1974), and Gavin Wright, *The Political Economy of the Cotton South* (1978), two works with markedly different methodologies and conclusions, present the basic reference points for understanding the economy of the slave South. *Time on the Cross* is a controversial work, and the response of the critics, as well as much additional research, can be found in Herbert G. Gutman, *Slavery and the Numbers Game* (1974), and Paul A. David, et al., *Reckoning with Slavery* (1976). The commercial system that marketed cotton and handled the accounts of planters is explained in Harold Woodman, *King Cotton and His Retainers* (1968). The latest study on the relative failure of the antebellum South to industrialize is Fred Bateman and Thomas Weiss, *A Deplorable Scarcity* (1981). Robert G. Starobin, *Industrial Slavery in the Old South* (1970), remains the standard source on the limited industrial use of slaves. Ulrich B. Phillips, *Life and Labor in the Old South* (1929), and Eugene Genovese, *The World the Slaveholders Made* (1969), both make the case for the economic and cultural dominance of planters. There is no satisfactory account of the economic role of the yeomanry, but Frank L. Owsley, *Plain Folk of the South* (1949), remains the point of departure. Recent works that should be consulted include: John Solomon Otto, "Slaveholding General Farmers in a 'Cotton County'," AGH 55 (1981); Donald Schaefer, "Yeoman Farmers and Economic Democracy," EEH 15 (1978); Harry L. Watson, "Conflict and Collaboration: Yeomen, Slaveholders, and Politics in the Antebellum South," SH 10 (1985); and the early chapters in Steven Hahn, *The Roots of Southern Populism* (1983). For an account of the ecological limits confronting Southern agriculture, see Julius Rubin, "The Limits of Agricultural Reform in the Nineteenth-Century South," AGH 49 (1975).

Estimates for wealth distribution in antebellum America can be found in Jeffrey G. Williamson and Peter H. Lindert, *American Inequality: A Macroeconomic History* (1981), and, for the mid-nineteenth century, Lee Soltow, *Men and Wealth in the United States, 1850–1870* (1975). Albert W. Niemi, Jr., "Inequality in the Distribution of Slave Wealth," JEH 37 (1977), covers the South, and Edward Pessen, *Riches, Class, and Power before the Civil War* (1973), is especially useful for the concentration of wealth in the urbanized Northeast.

NOTES

1. Thomas Jefferson, *Notes on the State of Virginia*, ed. William Peden (Chapel Hill: University of North Carolina Press, 1955), p. 164.
2. Ibid., p. 165.
3. Quoted in Alexander James Field, "Sectoral Shift in Antebellum Massachusetts: A Reconsideration," *Explorations in Economic History* 15 (1978): 152.
4. Quoted in Stanley Lebergott, *Manpower in Economic Growth: The American Record since 1800* (New York: McGraw-Hill, 1964), p. 38.
5. Quoted in Daniel Scott Smith and Michael S. Hinders, "Premarital Pregnancy in America 1640–1971: An Overview and Interpretation," *The Journal of Interdisciplinary History* 5 (1975): 557.
6. Quoted in John Mack Faragher, *Women and Men on the Overland Trail* (New Haven: Yale University Press, 1979), p. 164.
7. Quoted in Mary E. Young, "Congress Looks West: Liberal Ideology and Public Land Policy in the Nineteenth Century," in David M. Ellis, ed., *The Frontier in American Development* (Ithaca: Cornell University Press, 1969), p. 93.
8. Fred Gustorf, ed., *The Uncorrupted Heart: Journal and Letters of Frederick Julius Gustorf, 1800–1845* (Columbia, Missouri: University of Missouri Press, 1969), pp. 19–20.
9. Gottfried Duden, *Report on a Journey to the Western States of America*, ed. and trans. by George H. Kellner et al. (Columbia, Missouri: The State Historical Society of Missouri and University of Missouri Press, 1980), p. 56.
10. Gustorf, op cit., pp. 52–53.
11. Alexis de Tocqueville, *Democracy in America*, 2 vols., ed. by Phillips Bradley (New York: Vintage Books, 1945), II, p. 78.
12. James Flint, cited in Wayne D. Rasmussen, ed., *Agriculture in the United States: A Documentary History*, 4 vols. (New York: Random House, 1975), Vol. 1, p. 443.
13. This contemporary phrase is cited in Clarence H. Danhof, *Change in Agriculture: The Northern United States, 1820–1870* (Cambridge: Harvard University Press, 1969), p. 16.
14. Rasmussen, Vol. 1, op. cit., p. 464.
15. The quotes are from Charlotte Erickson, *Invisible Immigrants: The Adaptation of English and Scottish Immigrants in Nineteenth-Century America* (Coral Gables, Florida: University of Miami Press, 1972), pp. 120, 123.
16. Quoted in Malcolm J. Rohrbough, *The Trans-Appalachian Frontier: People, Societies, and Institutions, 1775–1850* (New York: Oxford University Press, 1978), p. 196.
17. Ibid., p. 196.
18. Quoted in John Solomon Otto, "Slaveholding General Farmers in a 'Cotton County'," *Agricultural History* 55 (1981): 177.
19. Quoted in Stanley Lebergott, *The Americans: An Economic Record* (New York: W. W. Norton, 1984), p. 124.
20. Quoted in Robert L. Heilbroner, *The Economic Transformation of America* (New York: Harcourt Brace Jovanovich, 1977), p. 19.
21. Quoted in Harry Braverman, *Labor and Monopoly Capital: The Degradation of Work in the Twentieth Century* (New York: Monthly Review Press, 1974), pp. 79–80.
22. Quoted in Bruce Laurie and Mark Schmitz, "Manufacture and Productivity: The Making of an Indus-

trial Base, Philadelphia, 1850–1880,'' in Theodore Hershberg, ed., *Philadelphia: Work, Space, Family, and Group Experience in the 19th Century* (New York: Oxford University Galaxy Book, 1981), pp. 63–64.

23. Quoted in Victor S. Clark, *History of Manufactures in the United States,* 3 vols. (Washington, D.C.: Carnegie Institution, 1939), Vol. I, p. 432.
24. Benita Eisler, ed., *The Lowell Offering: Writings by New England Mill Women, 1840–1845* (New York: Harper Culophon Book, 1977), p. 53.
25. Quoted in David M. Gordon, Richard Edward, and Michael Reich, *Segmented Work, Divided Workers: The Historical Transformation of Labor in the United States* (New York: Cambridge University Press, 1982), p. 72.
26. Quoted in Thomas Dublin, ed., *Farm to Factory: Women's Letters, 1830–1860* (New York: Columbia University Press, 1981), p. 20.
27. Quoted in Herbert Gutman, ''Work, Culture, and Society in Industrializing America, 1815–1919,'' *American Historical Review* 78 (1973): 545.
28. Quoted in Heilbroner, op. cit., p. 41.
29. Quoted in Allan Pred, ''Manufacturing in the American Mercantile City, 1800–1840,'' in Kenneth T. Jackson and Stanley K. Schultz, eds., *Cities in American History* (New York: Alfred A. Knopf, 1972), p. 119.
30. Quoted in Carville Earle and Ronald Hoffman, ''The Foundation of the Modern Economy: Agriculture and the Cost of Labor in the United States and England, 1800–1860,'' *American Historical Review* 85 (1980): 1085, fn.

2

Culture and Social Order

A sense of change, of a sharp and uncontrollable break with the past, galvanized and shaped antebellum American culture. Change was everywhere—in the departure of sons to the West, the growth of cities, the spread of factories, the inundation by immigrants, and the new steam-driven technology—and it was simultaneously exhilarating and frightening.

On the one hand, all restraints on individual progress seemed to have been lifted. An expanding range of personal choices held out the promise of unbounded individual advancement. An advice book to young men could unabashedly proclaim in 1826 that *"you may be whatever you resolve to be."*[1] On the other hand, the very openness and materialism of antebellum society—its geographic mobility and economic acquisitiveness—seemingly removed precisely those restraints formerly imposed by church, community, and family that had curbed individual behavior in the interests of social harmony and public morality. The result for the Baptist missionary, the Reverend James L. Scott, was the sin of a "world, deluged in inequity with its millions floating down the current of time, and plunging over the cataract into the burning billows below. . . ."[2]

Whether experienced as liberating individualism or unbridled sin, social change in Jacksonian America necessitated cultural shifts in how Americans defined themselves and their society. An interlocking system of norms and beliefs that gives meaning to the outside world and integrates individual expectations and behavior into the maintenance of society as a whole, culture is inseparable from its material surroundings but not determined by them. By serving as a bridge between ideas and action, culture provides the signposts, the cluster of meanings and guiding principles, by which individuals simultaneously transform the very reality to which they are reacting. Out of this transformation comes a new reality, which is in turn acted upon.

Most notably, Americans were now reacting to an economic environment that offered new opportunities for material self-advancement. As the transportation revolution brought more and more Americans into the marketplace of economic exchange, expectations rose along with per-capita income. More individuals could now realize what one newspaper editor in 1815 described as the "almost universal ambition to get forward."[3] The public ethic of egalitarianism, a social vision that held that individuals were of equal moral worth and should have an equal opportunity to better themselves economically, developed in tandem with the new dynamism of the economy. Egalitarianism and its atomistic image of freely competing individuals eclipsed older, more hierarchical notions of deference, place, order, and status that were grounded in an earlier America of limited economic horizons and rural isolation.

To be sure, egalitarianism did not suddenly emerge full-blown in Jacksonian America. "All men are created equal." Thus did the Declaration of Independence announce to the world the legitimating ideology of the American Revolution. And, at least since the Revolution, Americans had prided themselves on their political equality and the openness of their society. What was new about the doctrine of equality in the early nineteenth century was the aggressive insistence that all barriers to individual advancement had to be removed. Anything that smacked of legal privilege that stacked the odds in favor of one group over another was vulnerable to attacks of public outcry. The right to vote, still tied in the state constitutions of 1800 to the possession of a minimum amount of property, was extended in most of the states to virtually all adult white males by 1824. Credit, once a privilege conferred by the wealthy, was demanded by the 1830s as the democratic right of all men of good character. Egalitarian rhetoric proclaimed that all could advance, if only given an equal chance. Much more so than in the eighteenth century, egalitarianism was now an optimistic and liberating expression of faith in the drive, hopes, and potential of the common man.

Egalitarianism, for all its limitless optimism, exposed central contradictions in the American experience and produced its own anxieties. Wealth, as we have seen, became more concentrated during the market revolution, and the upward mobility that egalitarianism held out often proved to be illusory. As explained by Alexis de Tocqueville in his classic commentary on Jacksonian society:[4]

> The same equality which allows every citizen to conceive these lofty hopes, renders all the citizens less able to realize them. . . . They have swept away the privileges of some of their fellow-creatures which stood in their way; but they have opened the door to universal competition: the barrier has changed its shape rather than its position.

If economic competition that was equally open to all generated frustrations through the sheer numbers of competitors, it also threatened to unleash vice and immorality as individuals placed private gain above public good. Antebellum reformers warned that selfish acquisitiveness endangered the virtue and order that were indispensable to the survival of republican freedoms. "The licentiousness of a lawless democracy, without virtue or intelligence, is," wrote Sarah Hale, the editor of *Ladies' Magazine*, "more terrible than the oppressions of despotism." The improved transportation and communications that stimulated the economy were, for Henry Clarke Wright, the "very things" that "will be our destruction—by inflaming the passion for prosperity & giving it tenfold more activity & power."[5]

Fears of both competition and disorder provoked a generalized cultural response that amounted to a doctrine of biological determinism. This doctrine was expressly linked to the ideology of equality, so that egalitarianism applied only to white males. If, as most white Americans came to believe, biology rendered certain groups incapable of competing, then these groups—Indians, blacks, and women—could be assigned subordinate social positions outside the marketplace without violating the ideology of equality. By making a distinction between artificial and natural inequalities, between those that were reversible because they resulted from undemocratic political privileges and those that were irreversible because they were rooted in allegedly immutable conditions of race and sex, the doctrine of biological determinism was powerfully appealing to most white males. Here was a way to sanction policies and attitudes that both expanded the size of the marketplace for white males and excluded from it potential competitors. Here also was a way to offer white males an assured and permanent status of superiority that was independent of their own economic fortunes. Finally, by postulating that woman's preeminent role was in the home as a guardian of moral virtue, the doctrine provided a scheme of social classification that reconciled material gain with moral order.

This fusion of biology and egalitarianism was all the more persuasive because it developed out of prior cultural prejudices and attitudes. This chapter will deal with the history of that development and its impact on the subordinated majority in antebellum America—Indians, free blacks, and women.

Indian Removal

Between 1820 and 1844 white Americans pushed Native Americans off their remaining tribal lands east of the Mississippi. The Indian population in the East dropped from 125,000 to 30,000, and whites laid claim to Indian cessions of 3 million acres in the Midwest and some 25 million acres in the Old Southwest. Indian removal was part of a long prior pattern of Indian-white relations characterized by white aggressiveness and Indian response, economic competition, and violent conflict. Certainly much of these relations can be explained by the simple fact that Indians had land and whites wanted it. White attitudes were more complex and ambivalent, however, than a sheer hunger for land might suggest. These attitudes and the hardening of anti-Indian racial thought after 1815 were intimately bound up with the emergence of a liberal capitalist society and the process by which white America forged its self-identity.

The world view of Native Americans was diametrically opposite that of whites. For Native Americans the land, the people and life on it, and the spiritual world flowed together in a sense of oneness with being. It followed, in perhaps the most obvious contrast seized upon by white culture, that this unity of space and the individual's personal, continuous oneness with it could not admit of any division of land into private property. The tribal land belonged to all or none, and it was to be shared by its temporary trustees. To share was to survive, to establish one's right to leadership, and to mourn for the dead through the communal distribution of the deceased's possessions. Gifts freely given, not goods avidly accumulated, were the measurement of status.

Whites understood little of this and cared less. It is hard to imagine how it could have been otherwise. Nature for white Americans was despiritualized, and their world view was linear and compartmentalized into quantifiable units of time and space. For them, the ownership of private property was what freedom was all about. Whites were professed Christians, and their religious convictions were at the center of their cultural identity. Seen from this perspective as ungoldy savages, the Indians were all the more alien.

Largely because Indian economies, based on a mixture of hunting, fishing, and farming, were much more land-extensive than those of whites, the Indians were stigmatized as nomads who failed to use the land productively. Yet, the Eastern tribes had originally lived within settled communities bounded by definite ecological zones. These tribes had taught the early colonists the basic techniques of farming in the New World and had produced the agricultural surpluses that enabled many of the first settlers to survive. Because they had no written laws and formalized institutions that whites could recognize as evidence of civilization, the Indians were denigrated as lawless savages. Yet, as described by a white captive of the Indians in the early nineteenth century, the Indians

> live under an implied social compact; have chiefs and other superior officers, and traditionary laws for their government; but, nevertheless, they surrender comparatively no portion of their personal liberty: they chastise offences, and revenge insults . . . and neither yield obedience nor acknowledge fealty to any other.[6]

The tribes were social and political organizations in which kin groupings and standards of shame regulated individual behavior. Though denounced as barbarians, the Indians enforced unwritten criminal codes that were tolerant of a much wider variety of personal behavior than those of whites, especially in sexual and religious matters. Their herbal healing remedies, the basis for modern pharmacology, were far more sophisticated and effective than the techniques of white medicine until quite late in the nineteenth century. Damned as heathens in the minds of whites, the Indians' greatest sin might simply have been viewing the earth as their mother.

Whites lacked the self-confidence to recognize the right of Native Americans to interpret the world as they saw fit through legitimate cultures of their own, and they were interested in Indians primarily out of a desire to acquire their land for farming and speculation. The economic dependencies of the marketplace and the ravages of disease, both introduced into Indian culture by whites, provided the leverage by which whites pried loose land from Native Americans.

In a repetitive cycle initiated by the colonists in the seventeenth century, whites offered the Indians textiles, guns, liquor, and metal goods in return for furs and other forest products. Indians acquired a taste for the goods but not the means of reproducing them. As they grew more dependent on European supplies, and tastes became needs, they transformed their economies in an effort to pay for the supplies. Subsistence hunting became commercial overkilling, and craft traditions withered as tribal labor grew more intensive and specialized in exploiting the goods, such as herbal medicines and dyes, that the white market demanded. Intertribal warfare increased as competition for dwindling forest resources became endemic. Meanwhile, whites clearly understood that it was to their advantage to reduce the Indians to economic dependency. The following Machiavellian strategy was proposed by President Jefferson to the governor of the Indiana Territory:[7]

> To promote this disposition to exchange lands, which they have to spare and we want, for necessaries, which we have to spare and they want, we shall push our trading uses, and be glad to see the good and influential individuals among them run in debt, because we observe that when these debts get beyond what the individuals can pay, they become willing to lop them off by a cession of lands.

Economic dependency was accompanied by biological disaster. Lacking any natural immunity to white diseases, Indian populations were decimated. What an army officer observed in the Oregon Territory of 1850 had been occurring for many years all over the Western Hemisphere:[8]

It is melancholy indeed to witness the tremendous devastation which has here so rapidly followed in the footsteps of the [white] strangers. Death and destruction has been dealt out to the Aborigines with an unsparing hand, even those diseases which we are accustomed to consider the most trifling extending to the indians have been fearful epidemics sweeping off whole tribes. It is but a few years since that the measles swept off thousands of the poor natives.

Everywhere in the Americas the indigenous native population declined by 90 percent within a century of the first contact with whites.

Thus, individual tribes were scarcely in a position to bargain from strength when an offer was made for their land. After decades in which their population shrank, their wants increased, and their resources dwindled, they often reached the treaty grounds, in the words of a Congressional report of 1829, "poor, and almost naked." There, goods were readily available in return for a cession of land. The price paid was a bargain because, as the House Committee on Indian Affairs candidly admitted in 1830, "certain causes" had succeeded "first in diminishing the value of forest lands to the Indians, and secondly, in disposing them to sell readily. . . ."[9] The game had fled or been destroyed, and survival was a bitter contest against famine and encroaching whites. "Half convinced and half compelled." as de Tocqueville expressed it, "they go to inhabit new deserts, where the importunate whites will not let them remain ten years in peace."[10]

More than the dangling of goods, however, was required to dislodge the great tribes of the Southeast after the War of 1812. These tribes—the Chickasaws, Choctaws, Cherokees, Creeks, and Seminoles—numbered about 50,000 in 1815 and held some 33 million acres. These lands were an incredibly lucrative prize, and not just because of real estate killings to be made by insiders. These lands became the marketplace just as fast as whites could acquire them. The tactics and rationales used in the acquisition of what became the great cotton frontiers of southwestern Georgia, Alabama, and Mississippi highlight the aggressive shifts in Indian policy during the Jacksonian period.

Three sets of conditions had weakened the position of the Southeastern tribes by 1815:

1. Imperial competition in the eighteenth century between the French, Spanish, British, and, after 1783, the Americans had enabled the interior tribes to play off one nation against another and gain some living space for themselves. After 1803 and the sale of the Louisiana Territory the French dropped out of the race, and Spain's sickly economic and military condition made it a feeble partner for any Indian tribe. Alliance with the British proved disastrous for the tribes virtually annihilated by Andrew Jackson's victorious American armies in the War of 1812. In the climactic 1814 battle of Horseshoe Bend in Alabama, all but 70 of the 900 Red Sticks (pro-British Creeks) were killed. The victories were bittersweet for the pro-American tribes. Now the Federal government had no use for them as buffers against scheming Europeans, for there were no Europeans left to scheme.
2. Isolated and alone against the new American monopoly of power, the tribes also had to contend with an upsurge of economic interest in their lands touched off by exploding European demand for cotton.
3. The rapid post-1815 settlement of the West quickly produced political channels

through which demands for a more forceful Indian policy were carried to state and Federal officials.

Counterbalancing these external pressures was the resiliency of tribal organizations toughened by a century of coping with white probes. In particular, despite cessions of some land, what did not crack was the commitment to remaining in the East on land held in the name of the tribe as a whole. Federal policy, based since Jefferson's first administration on the voluntary removal of tribes to west of the Mississippi, had failed. Impatient with the Federal government and furious over what they deemed the blind intransigence of the tribes, the state governments of Georgia, Alabama, and Mississippi passed legislation in the 1820s and 1830s that stripped the Indians in their borders of any protection under tribal laws. Whites were encouraged to move onto Indian lands, debts owed to Indians were voided, and Indians were denied the right to testify in legal cases involving whites. All of these state actions directly violated prior Federal treaties that promised the Indians perpetual ownership and control over their tribal lands and recognized the rights of tribal law independent of state jurisdiction. The Supreme Court reaffirmed the sanctity of these Federal treaties in *Worchester* vs. *Georgia,* a decision in 1832 that defined the tribes as "domestic dependent nations" subject only to Federal jurisdiction. President Jackson made it clear that he had no intention of enforcing the decision, and the states stepped up the pressure.

Still, the tribes held out until their ranks were broken by the enticement of allotments, grants of land to be held under white definitions of private property that were parceled out to individual Indians who chose to remain. As unity began to disintegrate, many decided to leave rather than surrender their tribal life. Ironically, this tactic of divide and conquer worked because of the very success the Southeastern tribes had in adopting to white efforts at acculturation. Values based on competition and profits gradually infused traditional cultural patterns shaped by cooperation and subsistence. Personified by the racially mixed half-bloods, the resultant tension separated from tribal norms a significant minority who were eager for the wealth and prestige that their white benefactors could bestow upon them. Thus in the case of the Cherokees, the strongest support for removal came from the 20 percent of the tribe who were part white. As a group, these racially mixed Cherokees were wealthier than the full-bloods and had the economic resources, including slaves, to establish themselves in the Indian Territory of the West. As individuals, in return for supporting treaties of removal, they could expect governmental favors for themselves and their children. The full-bloods, poorer and with fewer linguistic and occupational skills, fought the longest against deculturation and removal. Eventually, the fraudulent 1835 Treaty of New Echota, a treaty opposed by over 90 percent of the Cherokees, was maneuvered through the Senate, and in 1838 the U.S. Army enforced it.

The Cherokees resisted the longest, and their reward was the agony of the "Trail of Tears." Rounded up by the army and herded into detention camps, they were moved West under military guard in contingents of about 1,000 each. About one-fourth of the 15,000 who started died along the way, victims of disease, malnutrition, and bureaucratic bungling. Although their trauma was the worst of the 100,000 Eastern Indians who were relocated in the West, death and misery stalked all of the removals. The Choctaws had been forced out of Mississippi in the winter of 1831–1832. Major Francis W. Armstrong, a friend of President Jackson's, had been appointed as the

Choctaw Agent and given $50,000 in funds to hire private contractors to supervise the removal. He and the money never arrived in the Arkansas Territory on the west bank of the Mississippi until the end of February. He spent most of the winter in Nashville because the weather was so cold. Meanwhile, uncounted Choctaws died from the bitter cold and cholera. During the Creek removal in 1836, 300 lives were lost when an overloaded steamboat sank in the Mississippi. Others met a slower death from spoiled rations and white harassments along the way. Federal officials at the top blandly insisted that all had gone well. The Cherokee debacle of 1838 moved President Van Buren to report to Congress that the government's "efforts for their civilization [had been] constant, and directed by the best feelings of humanity. . . ."[11] Regarding this kind of moral posturing, de Tocqueville concluded: "It is impossible to destroy men with more respect for the laws of humanity."[12]

Resistance to removal ultimately meant war. The Second Seminole War of 1835–1842 was the longest and costliest Indian war in American history. Occupying a swamp terrain in central Florida perfectly adaptable to the hit-and-run tactics of guerrilla warfare, and steeled in their resistance by a tribal leadership laced with remnants of the Red Creeks and fugitive slaves, who rightfully feared reenslavement if they allowed themselves to be rounded up for removal, the Seminoles officially held out for seven years. It was a vicious, dirty little war. Even Jackson admitted it was "disgraceful . . . to the American character."[13] Seminole women killed their children to keep them out of the hands of whites and to free themselves to fight with the men in the resistance. Malaria and yellow fever sapped American troops. A turning point came when Osceola, a Seminole chief of Red Creek ancestry, was captured by General Jesup under a white flag of truce. Although the resistance smoldered into the 1850s, President Tyler simply declared that the war was over in 1842. Most of the Seminoles and their black allies, assured as a precondition of their surrender that they would not be turned over to Southern slaveowners, were removed to the West. As for Osceola, he had died of malaria in a Charlestown prison fort in 1838. His attending physician cut off his head and subsequently posted it at the foot of his sons' beds as a way of punishing them for unruly behavior.

In the Midwest the tribes were smaller and more scattered. The battles and outcome of the War of 1812 decisively removed any lingering threat of unified tribal retaliation against whites. After the war most tribes were forced to undergo a series of short moves, each of which left them progressively weaker, before they were placed west of the Mississippi. Here, as in the Southeast, removal was commercialized. Business firms, many of which had their origin in the fur trade, profited in a number of ways. The House of Ewing, for example, supplied goods to Indians enriched by the sale of their lands, by Federal annuities written into the removal treaties, and by government payments to support removal. The Ewings also contracted out to move tribes and diverted into their own pockets a good part of the annuities because, according to their records, many of the Indians were in debt to them. Nonetheless, the weight of the evidence indicates that the Midwestern Indians were reliable customers in the 1820s and 1830s. At Solon Robinson's general store in northwestern Indiana, the Potawatomies were his best customers until 1840. Whites ran up large debts and tried to default on them, but the Potawatomies regularly paid for their store goods with cranberries and furs that were then shipped on to markets in Detroit and Chicago. "They are by no means unpleasant neighbors," concluded Robinson of the Indians

that he knew.[14] Whites and Indians could and did intermingle on a basis of cooperation, though not one of mutual respect. Still, as the so-called Black Hawk War tragi-
cally illustrates, beneath the surface of white attitudes simmered fears, ambitions, and
frustrations that all too easily could burst forth in a sudden rage against Indians.

In April 1832, the Sauk chief, Black Hawk, led a band of his people, including
women and children, from the Iowa Territory back across the Mississippi into their
former tribal lands in Illinois. Unrelenting white pressure that had culminated in the
burning of forty lodges at the Sauk and Fox village of Rock Island, Illinois, in 1827
had left the Indians no alternative but removal. In part a protest against promised corn
supplies that never arrived for the first winter, and in part a show of support for the
Fox, an allied tribe embroiled in a dispute with Federal authorities, Black Hawk's
return was not intended to be a belligerent act. Nonetheless it touched off a white
panic. Frontier fears and political machinations manufactured a war. From Governor
John Reynolds downward to local officials politicans grasped the benefits of proclaiming an invasion of the state. An influx of Federal monies, an excuse to extinguish
remaining Indian land claims, and military glory to be converted into future political
accolades were opportunities too tempting to pass by. Drunken militia slaughtered
most of the emissaries sent out by Black Hawk to head off a conflict, and the "war"
was on. Desperately trying to get back to safety across the Mississippi, Black Hawk's
band was finally cornered at the mouth of the Bad Axe River on the Wisconsin side of
the Mississippi. What followed was a massacre. In the midst of the raping of Indian
women and the crazed violence of the American troops one soldier, John House,
wantonly killed an Indian baby left tied to a cottonwood bark and shouted: "Kill the
nits, and you'll have no lice."[15] In a postscript to the affair an American general wrote:
"The Inds. were pushed literally into the Mississippi, the current of which was at one
time perceptibly tinged with the blood of Indians who were shot on its margin & in the
stream."[16]

The Battle of Bad Axe,
1832. Cornered and
massacred while trying to
cross the Mississippi
back into the Iowa
Territory, Black Hawk's
band was reduced to
fleeing women and
children. (The Granger
Collection)

As with Osceola, whites contrived a way to make Black Hawk useful even in death. Black Hawk survived the Bad Axe, was imprisoned, and died in 1838. Grave robbers stole his bones, and they were displayed in an Iowa museum until a fire destroyed the building in 1855.

Few whites mourned Black Hawk, but many had favored removal out of a sincere belief that it offered Indians a chance for survival in the West where presumably they would be isolated from the land-hungry whites who were dooming them to certain destruction in the East. A vocal minority of whites were morally disgusted over the slaughter at the Bad Axe and other spectacles of anti-Indian violence. And, for all their condescending paternalism, white missionaries believed that the Indians were capable of becoming their religious equals in Christ and of learning the whites' civilization. There can be no doubt of the good intentions of at least a minority of white Americans in their dealings with Indians. In the end, however, the good intentions made little difference.

Sincerity, unless accompanied by compassion and understanding, can often lead to blatant forms of injustice. Such injustice defined the tragedy of Indian-white relations in the Jacksonian period because of the refusal of white Americans, humanitarian reformers or not, to accept Indians as fully adult humans. In a psychological process that began with the initial contacts, whites projected onto Indians the fears and desires that they were culturally bound from recognizing in themselves. The Indian that was acted upon, whether out of hostility or sympathy, was the product of a white culture that could never accept the Indian as an Indian.

In the seventeenth century, the archetypical Indian was the heathenish anti-Christ whose presence confirmed the Puritans' Christianity. In the eighteenth and on into the nineteenth century, the Indian also became the barbarian, an uncivilized impediment that had to be brushed aside like any other natural barrier in the advancement of secular progress. It was intolerable, as Lewis Cass, a Jacksonian politician, put it, that "a few naked wandering barbarians should stay the march of cultivation and improvement."[17] Heathenish, uncivilized, and so savage as to take delight in the slaying of defenseless women and children—this was the white composite of the bad Indian who had to be removed.

It mattered little whether or not Indians acted contrary to this image. The Cherokees, to cite the most notable example, had a written alphabet, churches, and schools, and by the time of their removal had developed a socioeconomic structure with an upper-class gentry and a growing middle class. All this was dismissed. White Americans now turned to doctrines of permanent racial inferiority that took root in the nineteenth century as both a rationale for, and a rationalization of, exploitation of nonwhites. Governor George Troup of Georgia, for example, argued that it was immaterial whether or not the Chrokees farmed the land because God had destined the earth "to be tilled by the white man and not by the Indian."[18]

The other Indian, the good one in the white imagination, was free and innocent, literally a child of nature. In the phrase of a nineteenth-century American historian this Indian was "the irreclaimable son of the wilderness, the child who will not be weaned from the breast of his rugged mother."[19] This Indian, one described from the very beginning by Columbus, was as intolerable as the bad one, especially by the nineteenth century.

As American society entered more fully into market relations after 1815, self-control, the inner discipline necessary to repress immediate gratification for the efficient and orderly accumulation of material wealth, became the core value of the emerging middle class. The mythical Indian of childlike bliss, a projection of the free enjoyment of life that some whites felt they had to repress in themselves, had no self-control because nature supplied all wants. Such an Indian, like any child, had to be controlled and disciplined by mature adults. To do otherwise would be an avoidance of responsibility on a grand scale. To leave the Indian undisturbed would be to foster the wasting of economic resources that whites could efficiently develop; to encourage a shameful cultural escape for those whites who would flee their responsibilities by joining the Indians in the wilderness; and to sanction behavior that was the very antithesis of the acquisitive, inner-controlled values that drove American progress.

By convincing themselves that Indians naturally lacked self-control, whites also absolved themselves of any responsibility for Indian destruction. If Indians failed to advance, the reason was clear. "Their improvidence is habitual and unconquerable," declared a Congressional report in 1829. "The gratification of his immediate wants and desires is the ruling passion of an Indian."[20] The destruction of such an Indian was preordained. One could be melancholy, said President Jackson, "but true philanthropy reconciles the mind to those vicissitudes, as it does to the extinction of one generation to make room for another."[21]

The Free Blacks

Free blacks constituted 13 percent of America's black population in 1820; the rest were slaves. As with red Americans, black Americans had been assigned a subordinate position well before the Jacksonian era. Free blacks, James Madison wrote General Lafayette in 1820, "are every where regarded as a nuisance, and must really be such as long as they are under the degradation which public sentiment inflicts on them."[22] Congressional legislation registered this public sentiment by limiting naturalization to white resident aliens (1790) and by barring blacks from serving in the militia (1792) and carrying the U.S. mail (1810). Exclusionary legislation and antiblack prejudice at the state and local levels left free blacks in the anomalous position of being treated with even more contempt than Native Americans, despite the fact that their acceptance of Christianity and norms of private property placed them squarely within the mainstream of white culture.

The degraded status of free blacks made it all the easier for Southern whites to argue that slavery for blacks was preferable to exposing them to the poverty and misery of those blacks who were already freed. The fact that the position of free blacks deteriorated even further after 1815 made it all the easier for Northern whites to argue that blacks were unable to compete in an open marketplace. Yet that very marketplace, by generating economic insecurities and ruthless competition, produced conditions that made it more likely that whites would continue to deny equality to blacks.

White prejudice and control over capital and jobs segregated free blacks in an economic and social straitjacket that grew progressively tighter in the antebellum years. In their efforts to loosen the constraints, blacks used tactics and options that varied according to the timing, background, and social conditions of their emancipation. Three distinct free black societies evolved between 1800 and the Civil War, and each struggled for greater freedom and opportunities with a different set of resources.

Prior to the Revolution, slavery was legal in all the colonies, and over 90 percent of all blacks were slaves. North of Delaware, slavery was profitable, but the slaves constituted less than 5 percent of the total population, and their labor did not support an entire class nor produce the region's main source of wealth, as it did further south. Without the sustained support of a ruling class and entrenched economic interests, slavery was susceptible in the new Northern states to the egalitarian thrust inherent in the natural-rights ideology of the Revolution. Many Northern whites took the phrase "life, liberty, and the pursuit of happiness" seriously enough to apply it to slavery. In an emancipation movement that spanned about a quarter of a century and was led by Quakers, Federalists, and their black allies, all the Northern states provided for the eventual freedom of their slaves.

The qualifier *eventual* is crucial because, with the exception of New Hampshire and Massachusetts, the two states with the fewest slaves, Northern legislatures passed programs for gradual emancipation. The last state to do so (in 1804) was New Jersey, the state with the highest percentage of blacks—about 8 percent of the population in the 1790s. In other words, the timing and pace of Northern emancipation correlated very closely with the numbers of blacks and with white fears concerning the alleged negative impact of freeing them. These fears were allayed by conservative state programs that freed no current slaves but stipulated that future blacks born into slavery were to be emancipated upon reaching adulthood. In effect, masters received an indirect and partial compensation for the loss of their slave property by having access to its labor up through adolescence. For this reason, 16 percent of Northern blacks were still slaves as late as 1820.

The same overwhelming white majorities that eventually made emancipation possible also virtually assured that freed blacks would be shut out of any meaningful economic opportunity. The Northern economy did not need black labor; indeed, this was one of the prime reasons that the emancipation forces prevailed in their appeals to Revolutionary ideology. As they were released piecemeal into freedom, blacks gravitated toward the expanding coastal cities. Here, native and immigrant craftsmen kept them out of the better jobs and prevented many blacks from practicing any skills they had learned in slavery. Blacks were forced to begin at the bottom and their position there was frozen. In the late 1850s, only 12 percent of the free blacks in New York City worked at skilled trades; in the slave cities of Richmond, Virginia, and Charleston, South Carolina, the percentages for free blacks were far higher, at 32 percent and 75 percent respectively.

Denied the right to compete economically, Northern free blacks nonetheless had access to a greater range of civic and political expression than their Southern counterparts. The same enforced isolation that pushed most Northern blacks to the outskirts of cities, where they lived in the cheapest and least desirable dwellings, also bound the black community together. Out of this shared sense of community came a plethora of mutual aid societies, communication networks, newspapers, and petition campaigns against white discrimination and in favor of emancipation for the remaining 90 percent of the nation's black population. The black convention movement of the 1830s sprang from these community sources. Northern free blacks could and did organize in their own behalf; they had to. The constant pressure they brought against white authorities was essential in preserving the civil liberties they were allowed to enjoy.

Just over half of all antebellum free blacks lived in the South, and most of these blacks, over 80 percent, were in the Upper South. After rapid growth between 1790 and 1810, the number of free blacks in this region remained fairly constant relative to the slave population. From a jump of 5.5 percent of the black population in 1790 to 10.4 percent in 1810, free blacks leveled off to 12.8 percent of all blacks in the Upper South by 1860. The ideological and economic repercussions of the Revolution accounted for the early spurt in the size of the free black caste.

Responses of conscience to the natural rights doctrine, disruptions to tobacco markets, and the conversion from tobacco to wheat farming by many planters in the Chesapeake region resulted in a sizable rise in manumissions by individual slaveholders. The more sporadic labor demands of wheat production, as opposed to tobacco, provided an economic incentive to free favored slaves. In addition, the growth of towns and light manufacturing after 1790 induced planters to hire out more of their slaves for annual rents. Some of these slaves, by saving their wages, were able to purchase their freedom. Still, however much the bars of slavery were partially pried open, no state-sponsored emancipation plans were passed that would have forced them open for the overwhelming majority of blacks. Delaware's population was 22 percent black in 1800, and that figure represented a threshold of the black presence beyond which whites were unwilling to countenance emancipation. Revived anxieties over slave uprisings, spawned by the bloody success of the revolt on the French island of Santo Domingo in the 1790s and, closer to home, Gabriel Prosser's conspiracy in Richmond in 1800, convinced whites to pull back from even the limited emancipation that had occurred. Legislation was passed making individual manumissions more difficult, and laws against runaway slaves were tightened.

Free blacks in the Upper South were better off materially than in the North. They entered freedom with a wider diversity of artisan skills and found a job market that at least allowed them to carve out niches of limited economic security. As a consequence of living in a society that labeled certain kinds of work as degrading because performed by servile black slaves, Southern whites were less likely than Northerners to feel threatened by free blacks in the workplace. Although free blacks still faced overt job discrimination, especially from urban immigrant labor, they were more than mere common laborers. Half of the plasterers and one-sixth of the blacksmiths and brick masons in antebellum Richmond were free blacks. The fourfold increase in real property holdings of the free blacks in the city from 1830 to 1860 far outstripped the growth of their population. Just as the mores of a slave society paradoxically offered freed blacks more economic opportunity than the free North, so also did white attitudes conditioned by slavery permit more integrated residential patterns to develop in slave cities. Viewing free blacks as the natural allies of the slaves, whites in the Upper South were leery of concentrated blocs of urban blacks. Consequently, the urban black population was scattered and lived within walking distance of where they worked.

In return for relatively greater economic freedom, these free blacks were forced to accept limitations on the social and political liberties that were available to Northern blacks. White statutes and surveillance restricted rights of assembly and the press. Mobility was checked by the requirement for travel passes and the constant need to be able to establish one's legal freedom. These barriers, when added to the dispersed nature of the black community, stunted the development of any vigorous organizational expression of black grievances comparable to that which occurred in the North.

The economic dependency of the small black middle class on whites further buttressed white precautions against the formation of a subversive alliance between free and enslaved blacks. In order to practice a trade or open a shop, blacks needed the approval of white patrons. Subsequent economic success required white customers. The tensions between acting in one's economic self-interest by courting white approval and risking that white support by forging active racial ties with the enslaved were often excruciating for the leaders of the free black community. Trapped between two worlds that alternately attracted and repelled them, successful free blacks in the Upper South had no easy escape from their dilemma of race and class.

The small free-black caste of the Lower South was by far the lightest skinned, wealthiest, and best educated in the antebellum United States. Nearly 70 percent of this caste were of mixed racial ancestry in 1860; in the Upper South only 38 percent of the free blacks were mulattoes, and in the North but 29 percent. The origins of free blacks in the Lower South were unique. In contrast to areas further north, very few slaves here were manumitted as a result of the Revolution. Blacks were an absolute majority in the plantation belts of South Carolina and Georgia, and their labor was in great demand in the low country for the production of rice and then, after the cotton gin ensured the expansion of slavery, in the upcountry districts of the booming cotton culture. Racial fears and economic considerations overwhelmed Revolutionary egalitarianism. However, a revolution that occurred elsewhere, on Santo Domingo in the French West Indies, unleashed a stream of black émigrés who moved across the Caribbean to the cities of the Lower South in the 1790s. Artisans, shopkeepers, farmers, and other servicing agents of the island's plantation economy, these émigrés brought enough capital to secure an economic foothold from the start. They were well-educated compared to most American freed blacks, and they were considerably lighter. Often fathered by French planters who availed themselves of female slaves in the absence of white women on Santo Domingo, many of them had received their freedom and other special favors from their wealthy male parents. The American incorporation of the French-speaking creole population of New Orleans in the Louisiana Purchase of 1803 soon more than doubled the size of the free-black caste in the Lower South. In the future most of its increase came from within. Manumissions were few and generally resulted from planters freeing their offspring.

A majority of the free blacks in the Lower South lived in Charleston and New Orleans. Their position in the skilled trades was nearly the reverse of that of free blacks in Northern cities. In Charleston, for example, free blacks constituted 15 percent of the city's nonslave male labor force, but they comprised 75 percent of the millwrights and 50 percent of the tailors. Three-quarters of the city's free blacks practiced a skilled craft. In part because they had so much to lose, and in part because of their relatively close connection to a white power structure that included many of their blood kin, these urbanized mulattoes tended to set themselves apart from the black slave majority. They founded their own exclusive cultural and fraternal organizations and relied on their lighter skin, and the greater status that whites attached to it, as a way of distancing themselves from full-blooded blacks, free or slave. Their white patrons were careful to give them enough extralegal privileges to keep them well above the black majority but not enough to endanger white supremacy. A three-tiered hierarchy emerged in New Orleans, Mobile, and Charleston, and nowhere else in the United States. Although similar to the social structures of race relations in the Caribbean and Latin America, this Southern version was constructed on a much more limited demographic base. In this three-caste system, in contrast to the situation elsewhere, most mulattoes had no reasonable expectation of ever being freed. In 1850 over 93 percent of all mulattoes in the Lower South were slaves. There were distinct limits to the benefits that even white parentage could bestow on blacks.

In all regions, distinctions of class and color acted as barriers to a united black front. Denied industrial jobs and generally shut out of economic opportunity, Northern free blacks were not nearly as diversified by wealth and occupation as were whites. What diversification did occur fell along a color line between mulatto and full black. As a result of the general cultural association between freedom and light skin, and the comparative advantages in literacy and skills that many manumitted mulattoes had over full blacks, the Northern black community was stratified by color. Mulattoes were disproportionately wealthier, more skilled, and more involved in leadership positions within black associational life. To the extent that rates of intermarriage measure internalized notions of separateness, blacks were sharply divided. Among black marriages in Philadelphia in 1850, only 8 percent involved a union between black and mulatto spouses. The urban black middle class in the North was largely mulatto, and in its struggle for acceptance by whites it increasingly committed itself to the same white bourgeois values of individual self-help that blamed poverty on flaws of character. What the middle class, regardless of race, ignored in this self-serving rationalization were the systemic forces of racial prejudice and economic discrimination that made a mockery of the self-help ethic for most free blacks.

Egalitarianism and Racism

Egalitarian doctrine after 1815 proclaimed an explicit linkage between the moral and economic self-worth of the individual. Assigned ranks of status anchored in tradition, legal distinctions, and tightly knit community life had no place in this ideology. Contrary to the more hierarchical and less democratic societies of Europe and Latin America, status here was to be earned in theoretically free and open competition. Eighteenth-century remnants of assigned rankings, notably property qualifications for voting, collapsed among white males in the more mobile society of Jacksonian America as they maneuvered to take advantage of the expanding marketplace. It was every white man for himself, and much was expected of him. The generalized high aspirations were summarized by de Tocqueville:[23]

> When all the privileges of birth and fortune are abolished, when all professions are accessible to all, and a man's own energies may place him at the top of any one of them, an easy and unbounded career seems open to his ambition, and he will readily persuade himself that he is born to no common destinies.

But what of those who failed by these standards? By mid-century 59 percent of all adult white men held no landed property. The wealthiest 23 percent owned 92 percent of all real estate value. Even accounting for the increase of wealth with age, 20 percent to 40 percent of white males never accumulated any wealth throughout their lifetimes. This fact of inequality, itself a product of the marketplace, placed a tremendous burden on the growing number of white males who were forced into the job market as wage

Minstrel Shows. As graphically illustrated by this sheet-music cover of 1847, minstrel shows presented a stereotyped, Jim Crow image of the American blacks of that era. (The Granger Collection)

earners. If they were really the architects of their own destiny, who else but themselves could be blamed for their low or uncertain status? These men understandably recoiled from defining themselves as morally unfit, as deficient in the ambition, thrift, and inner drive necessary for success. Instead they took refuge in a culturally sanctioned refuge for their threatened self-esteem. They only had to look at blacks—slaves in the South and an impoverished, degraded caste in the North—to find a group whose color provided a visual contrast in which the moral fitness of all whites was fixed and certain.

For the many Northern whites who rarely or never actually saw blacks, popular entertainment in the form of blackface minstrelsy implanted and reinforced racial stereotypes of black inferiority. White performers in blackface demeaned blacks by portraying them in the shuffling and ridiculous poses of those who were comically incapable of upward mobility. A part of the common man's culture, the minstrel show packed in urban crowds starting in the 1830s. Its message in racial matters was unmistakable and played for laughs: no matter how inept whites might feel in reacting to the chaotic urban environment, blacks were even worse.

Thus egalitarianism, by way of its direct link with individualism, also forged an indirect link with racism. America's public and political culture fervently denied the existence of class divisions and advantages. Without acknowledged classes to serve as status rankings, whites substituted racial rankings, which guaranteed all whites a measure of superiority. So intense was the search for race as an ordering device that earlier eighteenth-century ideas that explained black inferiority by the temporary, debilitating impact of environmental factors gave way to formal doctrines of permanent, biological inferiority that were legitimated by the new science of ethnology. Simultaneously, the states created a body of legislative enactments that systematically defined free blacks as an inferior caste under the law. The cumulative impact on blacks came close to being crushing. In 1854 the free black Charlotte Forten wrote in her journal:[24]

> At times I feel it almost impossible not to dispond entirely of there ever being a better, brighter day for us. None but those who experience it can know what it is—this constant, galling sense of cruel injustice and wrong.

Much of this anguish was in response to the fact that equality of opportunity declined for Northern free blacks in antebellum America at the same time it legally rose for white males. In both absolute and symbolic terms, advances in the status of whites were often made at the expense of blacks. From 1819 to the outbreak of the Civil War not a single new state passed legislation permitting blacks to vote. Several states that had permitted blacks to vote, in changing their constitutions to allow for universal adult white male suffrage, retained or added property qualifications that disfranchised a majority of blacks. In New York the constitutional convention of 1821 was a hallmark in establishing white political equality, but it restricted the black vote to those with a freehold estate of $250. Practical disfranchisement was achieved. "To be worth two hundred and fifty dollars is not a trifle for a man doomed to toil in the lowest stations," observed an English traveler to New York in 1832; "few Negroes are in consequence competent to vote. They are in fact very little better than slaves, although called free."[25] Proponents of white democracy in Pennsylvania eliminated entirely the black vote in the new constitution of 1837. Thus, only 6 percent of Northern blacks could vote on equal terms with whites by 1860. With the exception of Massachusetts, public opinion or law barred blacks from jury service. In most of the western states, black legal testimony was prohibited in cases in which a white was involved.

The Northern job market also excluded blacks. The only jobs open to blacks were those in the service trades as cooks and barbers, domestic work as servants, daywork as common laborers, and seamen jobs as sailors. An occupational census published by the Pennsylvania Abolition Society in 1838 revealed that 80 percent of employed black males in Philadelphia worked as unskilled laborers. In the 1830s and 1840s, three out of five black households in the city had less than $60 in total wealth. The exclusionary practices of white artisans contributed to the blacks' precarious economic position, and the impact worsened over time. Whereas 23 percent of black artisans in Philadelphia could not practice their craft in 1838 because of white prejudice, 38 percent could not do so by 1847. Blacks, 5 percent of the city's male workforce in 1850, held barely over 1 percent of the jobs in industry, the fastest-growing sector of the urban economy.

Only unskilled jobs were open to blacks and in filling them blacks unwittingly fed the white ego by conforming to white stereotypes of being fit only for menial labor. Such work tended to push whites higher up in the labor market and generally posed no threat to white fears that blacks were aspiring to equality. One group of urban workers, however, was threatened by even this kind of lowly black labor. It was the lot of the

Irish to be thrown into the pit of labor competition at the very bottom with blacks. The poorest of all the immigrants, and unable to escape port cities like the British and Germans, the Irish had to take jobs away from blacks in order to survive economically. Subjected themselves to job discrimination and ethnic slurs, the Irish viewed blacks as their worst economic enemies. The antagonism between the two groups was in turn played upon by businessmen who used blacks to break Irish-led strikes in the mines and construction. The greater numbers, if not desperation, of the Irish displaced black labor and deprived blacks of what little economic security they had. In New York City blacks dominated domestic service in 1830. Twenty years later, the number of Irish servants alone was ten times the total black population. A letter of 1849 in the Philadelphia *Daily Sun* summarized the plight of blacks in construction and on the docks: "Where a few years ago we saw none but blacks, we now see nothing but Irish."[26]

The story was the same in the area of social and educational rights. Rigid segregation was the rule everywhere in the North with, again, Massachusetts being the lone legal exception. Even the right of free blacks to move into many Northern states was restricted. Three states—Indiana, Illinois, and Oregon—had outright constitutional bans on black immigration. Commonplace in the Midwest were black codes that required incoming blacks to post bonds for "good behavior." The bonds, ranging from $500 to $1000, were prohibitively expensive. Although not strictly enforced, this legislation did provide a legal cover for antiblack riots that periodically swept Northern cities. One half of Cincinnati's black population left after such a riot in 1829. The largest contingent moved to Canada, where they founded the town of Wilberforce.

Comparative demographic data confirm the harsh living conditions confronting antebellum blacks. The crude death rate for blacks was about twice as high as any that has been recorded in the modern world since World War II. By one estimate black mortality in the mid-nineteenth century was 80 percent higher than for whites. As shown in Table 2.1, there was a substantial difference by race in life expectancies at birth. Although mortality estimates do not distinguish between free blacks and slaves, the evidence indicates that free blacks were worse off. From 1820 to 1860 the number of male slaves increased 41 percent faster than free black males; among female slaves the increase was 48 percent higher. In these forty years the free black percentage of the Afro-American population fell from 13.2 percent to 11.0 percent. Migration to Liberia, Haiti, and Canada held down the free black increase, but the numbers involved were much too small to markedly effect the discrepancy in the growth rates.

Extreme poverty and frightening mortality placed a terrible strain on black family life in the cities. As shown in Table 2.2, black families in Philadelphia in 1850, relative to immigrant and native white families were more likely to be headed by

Table 2.1   Life Expectancies at Birth, 1850

The life expectancy of antebellum blacks was substantially shorter than that of whites.

	MALES	FEMALES
Whites	40	43
Blacks	33	34

Source: Compiled from Jack Eblen, "New Estimates of the Vital Rates of the United States Black Population During the Nineteenth Century," *Demography* 11(1974): 307–308. Reprinted by permission of the author.

Table 2.2 Family Composition by Race in Philadelphia, 1850
             (in percentages)

*As a result of their poverty, antebellum black families in the North were disproportionately
headed by females.*

	BLACK	IRISH	GERMAN	NATIVE WHITE
Female Head	22.5	13.4	3.3	13.3
Male Head	6.0	7.2	3.2	4.0
Couple Head	71.5	79.4	93.5	82.6

Source: Compiled from Hershberg, op. cit., Table 3, p. 441.

females. Abject poverty explains most of this disparity in family composition. Husbands, regardless of race or ethnicity, who are unable to provide for their families are those most likely to desert or move out in search of better-paying jobs elsewhere. And, as we have seen, black males were restricted to the worst-paying jobs in the cities. If the wealth holdings among all Philadelphia families are held constant, family composition becomes very similar among all groups. Adding to the pressures on black urban families was the difficulty in remarrying experienced by black widows with children. Throughout the antebellum period, free black women outnumbered men; for every 100 females there were 93 males. Because black males suffered higher mortality than females, this sex imbalance was especially pronounced in the prime marriageable years. In 1860, for example, among free blacks age 20 to 29, there were but 84 men for every 100 women; for those in their thirties, the sex ratio was still low: 89 men per 100 women. Moreover, black women outnumbered men even more disproportionately in cities, because women could more easily find work, usually as seamstresses or domestics, in the restricted urban job market. In Philadelphia in the 1850s, the sex ratio of about 70 was extremely unbalanced. Thus black widows, especially poor ones with little bargaining power, literally could not find a suitable urban mate for remarriage.

In Philadelphia and elsewhere the free blacks were undeniably poor. According to an egalitarian logic that held that moral virtue determined economic success, it followed that they also must have been immoral. The free blacks, like the Indians, were labeled as being too idle and vicious to better themselves economically. For wealthy and economically secure whites, such racist attitudes amounted to an act of moral self-congratulation. For poorer and less secure whites, those who displaced the anxieties and frustration of their lowly material status onto blacks, racism was a psychological counterweight to their own lack of self-esteem and a means toward social mobility and economic advancement. Blacks, of course, were trapped either way. Racism served the needs of all white classes, and it functioned as a self-fulfilling myth that prevented most blacks from improving their position. Blacks were told that to remove prejudice, they must rise by their own efforts; but as long as prejudice existed, most could not.

The fear and mistreatment that free blacks elicited from whites were inseparable from both their poverty and their race. The idleness, laziness, debauchery, viciousness, and instinctual passions that whites ascribed to them were the same pejorative attributes whites used when describing Indians, the Irish, and the poor in general. The Irish could hardly be sent back, but the Indians could be removed and their land taken—and perhaps the free blacks could be removed as well. During its heyday between 1817 and 1830, the American Colonization Society certainly tried. By 1832, with its encouragement and financial assistance, some 2,500 blacks had been sent back to Africa and established a colony that became present-day Liberia. The rationale behind colonization was summarized by Henry Clay in 1827. He described free blacks as "the most vicious" of all Americans. "It is the inevitable result of their moral, political, and civic degradation. Contaminated themselves, they extend their vices to all around them, to the slaves and to the whites."[27] Once rid of free blacks, it was argued, white America would be purer and safer.

Colonization failed as a solution to the white-created racial "problem." It neither made America all white, as its Northern supporters hoped, nor all free, as its Southern supporters feared. While a few thousand blacks were being colonized in Africa in the 1820s, the natural increase of America's slave population was 700,000. The staggering economic cost of colonizing truly large numbers of blacks was sufficient to defeat the movement. Still, most important in its failure was the adamant opposition of the free black community. The preamble of a black petition in 1817 eloquently states their reasons:[28]

> Whereas, our ancestors (not of choice) were the first successful cultivators of the wilds of America, we, their descendants, feel ourselves entitled to participate in the blessings of her luxuriant soil, which their blood and sweat enriched; and that any measure or system of measures, having a tendency to banish us from her bosom, would not only be cruel, but in direct violation of those principles, which have been the boast of this republic.

Not physical separation, but the social and psychic distance created by white prejudice would continue to shape antebellum race relations.

Toward the Cult of Domesticity

The largest increments of land and labor that fueled the market economy after 1815 were extracted from the two groups, Indians and enslaved blacks, who were consigned by biological determinism to a natural position of subordination that made their exploitation inevitable and justifiable. In parallel fashion, the dependent status of women also played a central role in market expansion. Egalitarianism was applied only to white males because this was the only way of reconciling two dominant themes in American popular thought—the individualism that expanded opportunities for self-fulfillment and the cult of domesticity that limited women to the home and family.

Sex is a biological fact, but gender is a cultural construct, the social meaning that culture places upon sex. Historically, gender provides a way of socially assigning and organizing roles by sex in a hierarchical pattern that replicates the division of labor on which a given culture is based. Experiencing and living within a particular gender hierarchy convinces individuals that a social pattern that is a cultural product in fact represents natural, immutable differences between the sexes. For example, sex determines the link between womanhood and possible childbearing, but culture determines the link between womanhood and full-time childrearing. Motherhood, as an act of reproduction, is a function of sex; as a social responsibility and labor demand, it is a function of gender as defined by a specific culture. Culture, not sex, keeps women at home with the children.

In America prior to the market revolution of the Jacksonian period, the family was overwhelmingly the basic unit of economic production. Family labor on the farms was interdependent. Although males performed most of the heavy work in the fields, women's labor was still responsible for one-third to one-half of all food production. The actual preparation of the food, manufacturing of clothing, and caring of the children were women's labor alone. Despite the general scarcity of labor, which enhanced the importance of women's labor, and a surplus of males, especially in the seventeenth century, which gave women more leverage in marriage contracts than in Europe, the preindustrial period was not a golden age for American women. They did more than an equal amount of the physical work but received in turn a much less than equal share of the power. In marriage virtually no one questioned that, as one colonial male put it, "the Husband is ever to be esteem'd the Superior, the Head, and to be reverenc'd and obey'd as such."[29] In law the doctrine of coverture held sway, that is, a wife's legal identity was covered by her husband's. She could not hold property, earn her own wages, or enter into contracts.

Patriarchal family government was the model for all civil authority. Firmly entrenched in the Judeo-Christian tradition, the starting point for Western political thought, male rule in domestic politics preceded the rise of state power and reinforced it as the latter developed historically. Men monopolized the public spheres of politics and economic exchange. Men had the time for politics, because women's domestic labor freed the husband to leave the home and assume a role that culture defined as an exclusively male one.

The very traditional sexual imbalance of power in eighteenth-century America was only slightly altered by the Revolution and its republican ideas of freedom and natural rights. Patriarchal authority held firm as ballast against the currents of republican individualism. Moreover, because the republican polity mandated the possession of property as a prerequisite for political participation, the denial of political rights to women, a propertyless class in general, could easily be reconciled by men with the Revolutionary ideology. Efforts to grant property rights to married women and to liberalize divorce were rebuffed. Many women, however, were politicized by the Revolution. In a war of fluid military zones that penetrated throughout the countryside, most women were personally exposed to the war's violence. In an economy of decentralized home production, their labor in the absence of soldier-husbands was indispensable for patriot success. Out of this wartime role came the notion of republican motherhood. This notion represented an ambivalent step toward recognizing a broader role for women in civic affairs. The republican mother was charged with the politically vital task of rearing virtuous, liberty-loving sons who would willingly sacrifice themselves for the good of the new nation. The family itself was not threatened by this extension of the mother's influence. Rather, through the patriotism and intelligence of the republican mother, herself still a second-class citizen, it would become a nursery for the future guardians of the republic.

Another revolution, the economic one after 1815, created conditions and responses that had the potential to unleash the potential for the self-enhancement of women implicit in republican motherhood. Liberation for women, as for any group, involves a matter of choices. Individuals can truly shape their own lives only when meaningful alternatives that can be freely acted upon are available. For the vast majority of women in eighteenth-century America, as in all preindustrial societies, the choices to shape individual lives beyond very narrow confines simply did not exist. Spinsterhood was shameful because it represented an abnegation of woman's duty to marry and bear the children that an agricultural, semisubsistence economy needed for farm work, and that males needed to perpetuate the familial line. Marriage, if the husband were successful, was about the only avenue to economic security. The price was high. Marriage meant, above and beyond hard farm labor, the physical pain, danger, and all-encompassing time demands of bearing and rearing children— pregnancy, birth, nursing, weaning, and pregnancy again. This cycle repeated itself every two years, and fifteen to twenty years of a married woman's life were consumed by it. When menopause finally arrived, she was old beyond her years. These women had few illusions about how they could control their lives. Listen to Lucinda Casteen, a young woman who moved with her husband and five children from Kentucky to Illinois in the early 1830s, as she writes her mother back home:[30]

> I have but little time for Settled work but less oppertunity to write as i cant have mi mind composed with as many around me. So that you eccuse all my mistakes of Scrabling if you can only make out to read it. I find it difficult to write with my noisy Children around me & my babe in my lap part of the time which must be sufficient apology.

Although Lucinda Casteen and her family had temporarily moved beyond its reach, the spread of commercial capitalism after 1815 began to offer some women of her generation a new range of choices with which to shape their lives. This market revolution undoubtedly offered more hope for women's self-fulfillment than any earlier social system. This hope was only partially realized. It was no coincidence that the cult of domesticity, which culturally anchored women in the home and defined individualism in male terms, arose precisely when the possibility first existed that women might leave the home.

A necessary, though not a sufficient, condition for individual autonomy is time that is one's own. American middle-class women began to acquire such time in the nineteenth century. Few dry sets of data encapsulate so much social change as those that track the decline of white fertility in the nineteenth century. In what amounted to a quiet, incremental revolution, women bore progressively fewer children throughout the century. Expressed as a statistical average, the average number of children borne by a white women declined from 7.04 in 1800 to 5.42 in 1850 and 3.56 by 1900. Changes in marital fertility accounted for 60 percent to 75 percent of this decline. By lengthening the interval between children and terminating childbirth at an earlier age for women, married couples reduced the size of their families.

Several features of the American decline stand out:

1. It preceded any large-scale urbanization and industrialization. A majority of the white population still worked on the land in 1860, and even as late as 1900, most American families lived on farms.
2. It occurred earlier in Europe. In 1800 the United States had the highest fertility rate in the West; by 1860 it had fallen so rapidly that only Sweden's was slightly lower. In Western Europe in the nineteenth century, France alone experienced substantial fertility decline and then not until the 1860s and 1870s.
3. The American decline was not the result of any technological breakthrough. Condoms, spermicidal douches, and a primitive diaphragm (the "sponge

method'') were available, but abstinence and male withdrawal appear to have been the major means of birth control.

4. This decline was clearly related to the spread of a commercialized economy. The most commercialized and urbanized regions, New England and the Middle Atlantic States, had fertility rates 25 percent and 4 percent respectively below the national average in 1820. As their fertility continued to drop, the rates in other regions declined even faster after 1820 as their economies passed out of semisubsistence. The decline between 1820 and 1860 was 38 percent in the East North Central states (the Old Northwest) and 33 percent in New England. Farmers in areas outside or on the periphery of the market persistently had the highest fertility among native groups. Within the social structure of the marketplace, family limitation was mainly a phenomenon of the business class. The working class and immigrants, two groups that were virtually synonymous in the nineteenth century, continued to have large numbers of children.

During the eighteenth century, farm families began delaying marriage and limiting fertility as a way of protecting their landed resources by reducing the numbers of male heirs laying claim to it. For those families of marginal economic assets who did not curb their fertility, excessive subdivision of their land destroyed the functional unity of family labor. Sons left for the West or for unskilled urban jobs, and daughters turned to outwork and the mills. No longer was work defined solely in terms of a patriarchally controlled task, the value of which rested in production that could actually be used by the family. Work now meant wage labor, paid time owed to an outsider, and its value rested in producing goods that returned a profit to the outsider through their value in being exchanged for other goods or cash.

Once the meaning of work changed and production began to be taken out of the household, the logic of reproducing a paternalistic system through large numbers of children was weakened. But fertility did not decline uniformly in all classes. The alternatives of outwork and the factory partially reestablished much of the old paternalistic logic by bringing families back together as an economic unit in which children's labor for the family was now monetized. Consequently, wage-earning families, native and immigrant alike, had higher fertility than the middle and upper classes. In the working class the role of women and attitudes toward them barely changed. Wives continued to supply domestic services within the home that were not paid for in the market. Their labor enabled employers to obtain their family's labor at a cheaper rate than if the family had been dependent on the market for all its needs.

Through limiting the size of their families and producing goods for which there was strong market demand, many rural families with ample land reserves made a successful transition to the middle class. The birth control they practiced was part of a new orientation toward both the family and the economy. The spread of the market created an expanding range of choices for families. Actions and roles that had been taken for granted now became more deliberative choices. The particular crop mix for anticipated market conditions, the type of work the children would perform or how much education they should receive, and, most especially, the number of children to have all involved a growing rationalization of family life that the traditional, semisubsistence economy had not required. In short, although the degree of consciousness is difficult to measure, couples apparently perceived that reduced fertility would enhance economic options for themselves and the children they did have. This perception was part of a cluster of attitudinal changes in which planning for the market replaced passivity and improvisation.

The demographic change of a decline in fertility was accompanied economically by a shift of production out of the home. Both of these changes meant that middle-class women had more time to devote to fewer children, each of whom assumed greater individual importance. The woman's motherly role was further enhanced by the absence of the father, who increasingly did not work near the home on the farm, but left the home for work in a nonfarm occupation. All the while, the dominance of women in the churches and the more favorable religious imagery of women continually reinforced this rise in the status of the mother.

The preponderance of women in the churches had increased markedly after the mid-eighteenth century. In the Congregational churches of Massachusetts and Connecticut, women comprised 69 percent of new converts from 1800 to 1835. Throughout the nation in the antebellum years, women were about twice as likely as men to be church members. As churches became women's domain, theology shifted. The traditional Christian view of woman as an Eve-like temptress who snared and corrupted man through the power of her sexuality was radically altered to that of a self-sacrificing and passionless agent of moral redemption. By turning their Christian love outward, women would now spirtually save their families and society as a whole.

As the mother became sanctified, so also did her children. Calvinist notions of infant damnation for children who died before baptism gradually gave way to a conception of children as pure and innocent, though potentially corruptible. Their souls were now to be nurtured by the love of a Christian mother. God, though still viewed as a Him, was feminized into a more forgiving and reachable figure who, like the moral mother, beckoned sinners to Salvation. The father left the home and the Father-God left the church. The smaller, child-centered middle-class family entrusted its spiritual care to figures of moral authority who expressed the greater centrality and accessibility of women in both the home and the church.

In middle-class families the roles of women and the values attached to those roles did change. By the 1830s these changes were expressed culturally in what has been called the cult of domesticity. From the pulpit, popular literature, and women's groups themselves came an interrelated set of ideas that placed women, by virtue of their sex, firmly within the home. Because women, it was argued, were uniquely pious, pure, and submissive, their proper and naturally ordained social role was to remain in the home morally training and uplifting their families. The cult of domesticity sharply divided life into public and private spheres segregated by sex. In so doing, it offered a social explanation and justification for the changes that defined the middle-class family as it emerged in the first half of the nineteenth century.

For those families in which the earnings of the husband were sufficient to support the family, separate and distinct spheres of work did in fact evolve. Work itself did not actually leave the home but rather was redefined. No longer was work defined as the task-oriented labor of farm life in which both sexes performed an acknowledged productive role. Now, in a society in which the word *spinster* meant first and foremost "an unmarried woman" and not, as formerly, "a farm daughter spinning at home," work became defined as salaried or wage labor. Work, precisely measured and disciplined by time controls, was now valued only when it was monetized. Among middle-

Middle-Class Domesticity. The mother was at the center of the sentimentalized, middle-class family of the mid-nineteenth century. The family, under her moral guidance, was now conceived as a spiritual retreat from the competitive world of economic production. (Historical Pictures Service, Chicago)

class Americans, this expansion of market-defined work was almost exclusively a male sphere of activity. Throughout the nineteenth century, fewer than 3 percent of married women worked outside the home. The one-third of single women who did so were drawn predominately from the black and immigrant working classes. To be sure, middle-class women continued to work inside the home but, because they received no wages, their work was not valued as such. Services such as cleaning and child rearing were defined as domestic duties, not as work. Only the husbands produced goods that had an exchange value in the marketplace. The market thus determined what work was deemed valuable, and women's domestic work was devalued.

The cult of domesticity, like the new work patterns in the marketplace, was class and sex specific. A cultural formulation for and by the middle class that emerged in the commercializing Northeast after 1815, it converted the sexual division of labor into a social ideology that sanctioned male power and in return held out to women the promise of greatly expanded influence. Because it offered each sex a convincing and mutually rewarding set of values by which to understand their new class roles, the cult of true womanhood became a vehicle for both class and sexual self-identification.

Women and Social Order

At its core, the cult of domesticity expressed a profound fear of the marketplace revolution. On one hand, the split between work and home implicitly threatened the patriarchal foundations of family government. Ideally, as an early nineteenth-century guidebook for families phrased it, "Every family is a little state, an empire within itself, bound together by the most endearing emotions, and governed by its patriarchal head, with whose prerogative no power on earth has a right to interfere."[31] The daily absence of the male ruler of this "little state" weakened his authority as a role model and moral preceptor. Most fundamentally, without a landed inheritance to pass on, most middle-class fathers had lost the traditional material basis for their familial power. On the other hand, the father's quest for material success outside the home required bold self-assertiveness and an unceasing pursuit of economic self-interest that, it was feared, would undermine social stability and commitments to the public good. The public arena of economic competition became more threatening at the same time as the private foundation of social order, the family, was being weakened.

By ascribing to each sex specialized attributes that were the mirror image of each other, the cult of domesticity recast the frightening dualism of marketplace involvement into a psychologically comforting classification scheme based upon presumedly natural sexual differences. The scheme was comforting not only because it seemed to describe and explain what was actually happening, but also because it created moral and social order out of complementary sexual divisions. Every male attribute that was needed for economic success—cold calculation, ambition, aggression, and self-centeredness—had its opposite female counterpart within the home—warm emotion, passivity, submissiveness, and self-sacrifice. Values, like work, were sexually divided, and the resultant whole functioned as a psychological flywheel that stabilized otherwise conflicting demands and needs. Cultural unity was achieved out of sexual opposites.

On the surface, the gender politics of the cult of domesticity established a reciprocal balance between the powers and status allotted to each sex. What was denied women in the public sphere was reserved for them in the private sphere. Women lacked political rights, and their disfranchisement seemed all the more galling when the vote was no longer limited by property qualifications but was granted to all adult white males, including recently arrived immigrants. In return, however, the family, woman's domain, was infused with heightened political importance. It was here, under the mother's tutelage, that citizens more virtuous than the immigrants would be trained. Middle-class women's exclusion from economic opportunities was balanced by the effort to elevate household work into a profession of its own. This was the central theme of Catherine Beecher's immensely popular *Treatise on Domestic Economy,* first printed in 1841. Both sexes, Beecher argued, were co-partners in sacrificing for the sake of the family.

Most women apparently accepted their domestic role or at least did not openly protest against it. Because the cult of domesticity was class specific, women of the upper class could bask in the status of refined ladyhood while looking down upon "loose girls" of working-class origin. It was often the labor of Irish domestics, young women whom native-born ladies would never dream of including under the rubric of true womanhood, who provided the leisure time in which ladies could display their husband's wealth in the form of the latest fashions. Nor did the physical frailty of women, a central rationalization for keeping middle-class women out of the job market, extend to the 10,000 women in New York City who lived by their needlework in the 1840s. By working twelve to fourteen hours a day, they could expect to earn 12½ cents. Class, in other words, revealed the sham of the biological rationalizations for the cult of domesticity. Quite apart from the class hierarchy built into the cultural image of women were the overriding considerations that over 90 percent of women married, the house in fact was their social turf, and public participation in politics and business was closed off. Thus, the cult of true womanhood addressed itself to the objective conditions—marriage, the home, and domesticity—under which most middle-class women lived. Given the reality of their daily existence, most of these women took comfort in the venerated role that domesticity assigned them.

A distinct minority of women, many of whom came out of the abolitionist movement in the 1830s, found little comfort in confusing the promise of influence with the reality of power. These women, led by Susan B. Anthony and Elizabeth Cady Stanton, organized America's first women's-rights movement in the 1840s, a call for the extension of political and economic equality to women. They stressed that the cult of domesticity offered women false and empty promises, because women's alleged moral superiority proved illusionary when it conflicted with male needs. Stanton stated the double standard:[32]

> So long as woman labors to second man's endeavors and exalt his sex above her own, her virtues pass unquestioned; but when she dares to demand rights and privileges for herself, her motives, manners, dress, personal appearance, and character are subjects for ridicule and detraction.

The boundaries between the private sphere of influence and the public sphere of power were real, and they were designed to restrict women. The issue, as the early feminists clearly saw, was the question of self-autonomy for women. The cult of domesticity held out the promise of influence but only at the price of a loss of self. Women were enjoined to submerge their own selves into prescribed social roles of self-sacrifice for the sake of others. As the *Young Lady's Own Book* put it in 1833: "There is, indeed, something unfeminine in independence. . . . A really sensible woman feels her dependence."[33]

Thus, the balance within gender politics was not so reciprocal after all. Disfranchisement meant that politically, as well as legally, woman's identity was encompassed by that of her husband's. The political importance of the mother's role was heightened, but only the males in her family would be the direct beneficiaries of her political virtue. The only professional fields open to women, nursing and teaching, accepted them as surrogate mothers, not as career-minded individuals in their own right. Even here, openings occurred primarily because of an economic fit between the social demand for cheap labor in a new field, particularly teaching, and cultural conceptions as to the nurturing sort of work women were capable of performing. Viewed as temporary help who were working to save up a small dowry, women teachers were hired at wages 30 percent to 50 percent lower than what males commanded. Housework, despite the efforts of Beecher, failed to gain recognition as a respectable profession.

Like any widely acknowledged system of social classification in which options are effectively foreclosed, the cult of domesticity offered the minimal security of knowing one's place. Undoubtedly, many women shared with Elizabeth Cady Stanton the shock of first recognizing at an early age just how inferior their place would be. The moment of recognition for Stanton came when she was four. At the birth of a sister she began to realize that "girls were considered an inferior order of beings" when family friends gathered around the birthing bed and remarked, "What a pity it is she's a girl." The lesson was driven home seven years later upon the death of her only brother. Her father's grief expressed itself in the exclamation: "Oh, my daughter, I wish you were a boy!"[34]

Stanton's response of political activism was too extreme for the vast majority of women. Nor would they have agreed with her blunt statement of 1860 that "The Negro's skin and the woman's sex are both *prima facie* evidence that they were intended to be in subjection to the white Saxon man."[35] Instead, most women tried to take advantage of whatever opportunities the system did allow. These openings emerged from the very logic of the classification scheme and the historical way in which it developed.

The separation of work and home reduced the productive function of the middle-class family but heightened its emotional importance. Arranged marriages that set up economic partnerships based on land declined, and marriage increasingly became viewed as a companionship voluntarily entered into by loving couples. By the 1800s husband and wife were also likely to be living together longer. One study of marriages among the Philadelphia gentry revealed a marked rise from the colonial period in completed families—that is, marriages not broken by the death of one of the partners before the wife completed her childbearing years. The rise in Philadelphia was from 57 percent of all marriages contracted in the period 1700–1775 to 72 percent of those in the next half-century. With family limitation resulting in fewer children and an earlier end to childbirth, these couples also had more time for each other.

Women were the moral rulers of the companionate marriage and its smaller, more privatized families. Her moral status rose as that of her husband fell, and she was recognized as having a far greater capacity to do good than had been the case in the eighteenth century. Above all, she now had the responsibility to preserve the home as a refuge from the strains of the marketplace. However much her husband may have been mistreated in the marketplace, his wife, the reason and reward for his hard work, was always waiting "to calm the tumult of his passions, and bid him struggle on, and find his reward in her sweet tones, and soothing kindness. . . ."[36] Through a variety of mutually reinforcing roles—soothing a husband's ego battered by economic competition, reading the new advice manuals on child rearing, or participating in church activities—the middle-class mother found some room for personal dignity and self-enhancement.

In quite an unintentional way, the very rationale by which the cult of domesticity sought to segregate women within the home also provided them with an ideological justification that many women used to take themselves out of the home. As mothers, wives, and spiritual leaders, middle-class women discovered after 1815 that they were a class apart. Isolated as they were within the same specialized social space, women became conscious of the common bonds between themselves. They developed extensive social networks of female kins and friends. Through these networks of sisterhood, they expressed and shared their concerns and common plight. Ironically, therefore, the very social system that restricted women also united them. What bound them together was their cultural status, which placed them in the home and proclaimed their moral superiority over men. Over time, and building upon their sisterly ties, some women began to turn the logic of domesticity inside out. In a natural extension of this logic they argued that women should not limit their moral domain only to the privatized home. Without ever straying beyond the limits of their assigned role, middle-class women left the home and became active in social reform movements. In effect, they claimed the public sphere as their home. Any social ill that threatened the sanctity of the family could legitimately be included in their benevolent efforts. By enlisting in temperance, antislavery, antiprostitution, and missionary reform, these women were able to critique their male-dominated society and raise their own self-esteem.

As long as the reformers stopped short of asserting their own individual rights and self-interests, their efforts were welcomed by most middle-class males. Most of the reformers did not try to breach the limits of their role as social mothers. With but few exceptions, they did not commit themselves to a full-fledged political drive to secure the vote and legal equality. By not so doing, they tacitly admitted they had made a virtue out of necessity. Operating from a position of political inferiority and still dependent upon male power for their sources of income, these reformers only pushed as far as they thought they could. In the end they did not so much change their society as they contributed through their unpaid voluntary labor to the consolidation of middle-class values and institutions.

In a political and economic arena cleared of Indians, free blacks, and women, politics and business were reserved for white males. Male success, and the standards by which it was achieved, came to be measured by the values of a new middle class. The creation of this middle class was the most significant social development in antebellum America and will be the focal point of the next chapter.

SUGGESTED READING

Robert F. Berkhofer, Jr., *The White Man's Indian* (1978); Richard Drinnon, *Facing West: The Metaphysics of Indian-Hating and Empire-Building* (1980); and Roy H. Pearce, *The Savages of America* (1965), are excellent sources on white attitudes toward Indians. The intellectual and cultural reactions of whites to Indians and the wilderness are covered in Richard Slotkin, *Regeneration Through Violence* (1973), and Roderick Nash, *Wilderness in the American Mind* (1967). For broad surveys of Indian-white history, see Wilcomb E. Washburn, *The Indian in America* (1975), and William Brandon, *The Last Americans* (1974), a work that emphasizes white injustices. Virgil J. Vogel, ed., *This Country Was Ours* (1972), provides a superb set of documents on this history. Vogel is also an excellent source for understanding the belief systems of Indians, a topic that is sensitively covered for one tribe in George W. Linden, "Dakota Philosophy," AS 18 (1977). The clash between these beliefs and those of white missionaries is covered in Henry Warner Bowden, *American Indians and Christian Missions* (1981).

Francis Paul Prucha, *The Great Father: The United States Government and the American Indians*, Vol. 1 (1984), surveys the policies of the federal government in the nineteenth century. The Jeffersonian period is detailed in Bernard Sheehan, *Seeds of Extinction: Jeffersonian Philanthropy and the American Indian* (1973). Three works that carry the story up to the 1850s are:

Herman J. Viola, *Thomas L. McKenney, Architect of America's Early Indian Policy, 1816–1830*; Ronald H. Satz, *American Indian Policy in the Jacksonian Era* (1975); and Robert A. Trennert, Jr., *Alternative to Extinction: Federal Indian Policy and the Beginnings of the Reservation System, 1846–1851* (1975). Trading patterns with Indians and the spread of white economic values on the frontier are treated in Robert A. Trennert, Jr., *Indian Traders in the Middle Border* (1981), and Daniel H. Usner, Jr., "American Indians on the Cotton Frontier," JAH 72 (1985). Cecil Eby, *"That Disgraceful Affair," the Black Hawk War* (1973), stresses the role played by white political ambitions. On the removal of the Indians in the Southeast, see Michael Paul Rogin, *Fathers and Children: Andrew Jackson and the Subjugation of the American Indian* (1975); Charles Hudson, *The Removal of the Southeastern Indians* (1978); and Arthur D. De Rosier, Jr., *The Removal of the Choctaw Indians* (1970). Political and cultural rivalries that divided individual tribes are examined in Richard P. Metcalf, "Who Should Rule at Home? Native American Politics and Indian-White Relations," JAH 61 (1974), and William G. McLoughlin and Walter H. Conser, Jr., "The Cherokees in Transition," JAH 64 (1977). Tribal resistance to removal is highlighted in Alvin M. Josephy, Jr., *The Patriot Chiefs* (1969), and the special case of the Seminole War and the role played in it by fugitive slaves is handled in Kenneth W. Porter, "Negroes and the Seminole War, 1835–1842," JSH 30 (1964).

The two basic studies on free blacks in antebellum America are Ira Berlin, *Slaves without Masters: The Free Negro in the Antebellum South* (1974), and Leon F. Litwack, *North of Slavery* (1961). On urban blacks, see Leonard P. Curry, *The Free Black in Urban America, 1800–1850* (1981); Jean Riblett Wilkie, "Urbanization and De-Urbanization of the Black Population Before the Civil War," *Demography* 13 (1976); and Theodore Hershberg, "Free Blacks in Antebellum Philadelphia," in Theodore Hershberg, ed., *Philadelphia: Work, Space, Family, and Group Experience in the Nineteenth Century* (1981). The best study on the small black middle class is William A. Murashkin, *Middle-Class Blacks in a White Society: Prince Hall Freemasonry in America* (1975). For a demographic overview, see Jack E. Eblen, "Growth of the Black Population in *antebellum* America, 1820–1860," PS 26 (1972).

George M. Fredrickson, *The Black Image in the White Mind* (1971), has a brilliant analysis of the connection between egalitarianism and racism in the Jacksonian period. Also useful on this issue are Reginald Horseman, *Race and Manifest Destiny* (1981), and Ronald T. Takaki, *Iron Cages: Race and Culture in Nineteenth-Century America* (1979). On the ways in which popular culture fostered a belief in white supremacy, see Robert C. Toll, *Blacking Up: The Minstrel Show in Nineteenth-Century America* (1974), and Alexander Saxton, "Blackface Minstrelsy and Jacksonian Ideology," AQ 28 (1975). The hardening of white attitudes on race and attempts to ground them in science are explained in William Stanton, *The Leopard's Spots: Scientific Attitudes Toward Race in America, 1815–59* (1960). P. J. Staudenraus, *The African Colonization Movement, 1816–65* (1961), is a solid treatment, and David M. Streifford, "The American Colonization Society," JSH 45 (1979), shows how the poverty of free blacks made them a social and political threat to the tenets of republican ideology. For the black response to white racism, see Leonard I. Sweet, *Black Images of America, 1784–1870* (1976), and Floyd J. Miller, *The Search for a Black Nationality* (1975). A revealing contemporary account is Ray Allen Billington, ed., *The Journal of Charlotte L. Forten: A Free Negro in the Slave Era* (1981).

Work in women's history has exploded in the last generation, and much of it is surveyed in Carl Degler, *At Odds: Women and the Family in America from the Revolution to the Present* (1980). For an overview of the nineteenth century, see Catherine Clinton, *The Other Civil War: American Women in the Nineteenth Century* (1984). Linda Kerber, *Women of the Republic* (1980), and Mary Beth Norton, *Liberty's Daughters* (1980), both stress that the egalitarian implications of the Revolution did not extend to women, but Norton detects a heightened importance for white women through their portrayal as republican mothers. Pioneering articles by Barbara Welter, "The Cult of True Womanhood: 1820–1860," AQ 18 (1966), and Gerda Lerner, "The Lady and the Mill Girl: Changes in the Status of Women in the Age of Jackson,"

MASJ 10 (1969), set the agenda for much of the subsequent research on antebellum women. Both emphasized the oppressiveness of the new ideology of domesticity. In a work of sparkling originality, Nancy F. Cott, *The Bonds of Womanhood: 'Woman's Sphere' in New England, 1780–1835* (1977), argued that the rise of separate spheres for men and women was an essential step in elevating the esteem of women within marriage and the home. A similar argument tied to the decline in family size is set forth by Daniel Scott Smith, "Family Limitation, Sexual Control, and Domestic Feminism in Victorian America," FS 1 (1973). Important works that show the tensions between domesticity and civic activism for white women include: Keith M. Melder, *Beginnings of Sisterhood: The American Women's Rights Movement, 1800–1850* (1977); Barbara J. Berg, *The Remembered Gate: Origins of American Feminism—The Woman and the City, 1800–1860* (1978); and Ellen C. Dubois, *Feminism and Suffrage: The Emergence of an Independent Women's Movement in America, 1848–1869* (1978). The changing legal status of women is reviewed in Norma Basch, "Equity vs. Equality: Emerging Concepts of Women's Political Status in the Age of Jackson," JER 3 (1983).

On the growing dominance of women in churches, see Richard D. Shiels, "The Feminization of American Congregationalism, 1730–1835," AQ 33 (1981). Ann Douglas, *The Feminization of American Culture* (1977), and Kathryn Kish Sklar, *Catharine Beecher: A Study in American Domesticity* (1973), present different interpretations of the impact of this trend on popular culture and women's status. For the relationship between evangelicalism, reform, and women, see Barbara Epstein, *The Politics of Domesticity: Women, Evangelism, and Temperance in Nineteenth-Century America* (1981); Ian R. Tyrrell, "Women and Temperance in Antebellum America, 1830–1860," CWH 28 (1982); and Anne M. Boylan, "Women in Groups: An Analysis of Women's Benevolent Organizations in New York and Boston, 1799–1840," JAH 71 (1984). Blanche G. Hersh, *The Slavery of Sex: Feminist Abolitionists in America* (1978), looks at women and the antislavery crusade. A provocative study that relates the class position of women to the types of reform they favored is Nancy A. Hewitt, *Women's Activism and Social Change: Rochester, New York, 1822–1872* (1984).

Much of the recent literature has tended to neglect farm women, working-class women, and slave mothers. For a look at the promising start that has been made for the antebellum period, see John Mack Faragher, "History From the Inside-Out: Writing the History of Women in Rural America," AQ 33 (1981); Julie Roy Jeffrey, *Frontier Women: The Trans-Mississippi West, 1840–1880* (1979); Carol Groneman, "Working-Class Immigrant Women in Mid-Nineteenth-Century New York: The Irish Woman's Experience," JUH 4 (1978); and Jacquelin Jones, "'My Mother Was Much of a Woman': Black Women, Work, and the Family Under Slavery," FS 8 (1982).

NOTES

1. Quoted in Robert H. Wiebe, *The Opening of American Society: From the Adoption of the Constitution to the Eve of Disunion* (New York: Alfred A. Knopf, 1984), p. 165.
2. James L. Scott, *A Journal of a Missionary Tour. . . .* (Readix Microprint Corporation, 1966 [1842]), p. 2.
3. *Niles' Weekly Register,* December 2, 1815, cited in George Rogers Taylor, *The Transportation Revolution, 1815–1860* (New York: Harper Torchbooks, 1968), p. 4.
4. Alexis de Tocqueville, *Democracy in America,* 2 vols., ed. by Phillips Bradley (New York: Vintage Books, 1945), Vol. II, p. 146.
5. Quoted in Nancy F. Cott, *The Bonds of Womanhood: "Woman's Sphere" in New England, 1780–1835* (New Haven: Yale University Press, 1977), p. 95 and fn.
6. John D. Hunter, *Memoirs of a Captivity among the Indians of North America* (London: Longman, Hurst, et al., 1823), in Virgil J. Vogel, ed., *This Country War Ours: A Documentary History of the American Indian* (New York: Harper & Row, 1972), p. 262.
7. Quoted in Richard Drinnon, *Facing West: The Metaphysics of Indian-Hating and Empire-Building* (New York: New American Library, 1980), p. 87.

8. Robert V. Hine and Savoie Lottinville, eds., *Soldier in the West: Letters of Theodore Talbot During His Services in California, Mexico, and Oregon, 1845–53* (Norman: University of Oklahoma Press, 1972), p. 141.
9. Cited in de Tocqueville, op. cit., I, fn., pp. 353–354.
10. De Tocqueville, op. cit., I, p. 354.
11. Martin Van Buren, "Second Annual Message," Dec. 3, 1838, in Fred L. Israel, ed., *The State of the Union Messages of the Presidents, 1790–1966* 3 vols. (New York: Chelsea House, 1967), I, p. 510.
12. De Tocqueville, op. cit., II, p. 369.
13. Quoted in Alvin M. Josephy, Jr., *The Patriot Chiefs* (New York: Viking Compass, 1961), p. 177.
14. Herbert Anthony Kellar, ed., *Solon Robinson, Pioneer and Agriculturist* 2 vols. (New York: Da Capo Press, 1968 reprint), I, p. 55.
15. Cecil Eby, *"That Disgraceful Affair," the Black Hawk War* (New York: Norton, 1973), cited in Drinnon, op cit., p. 199.
16. Quoted in Josephy, op. cit., p. 252.
17. Quoted in William Brandon, *The Last Americans: The Indian in American Culture* (New York: McGraw-Hill, 1974), p. 268.
18. Quoted in Blanche Wiesen Cook, "In Pursuit of Property: The Dispossession of the American Indian," in *Past Imperfect: Alternative Essays in American History*, ed. by Blanche Wiesen Cook, Alice Kessler Harris, and Ronald Radosh, 2 vols. (New York: Alfred A. Knopf, 1973), I, p. 200.
19. Francis Parkman, quoted in Michael Paul Rogin, *Fathers and Children: Andrew Jackson and the Subjugation of the American Indian* (New York: Alfred A. Knopf, 1975), p. 115.
20. Cited in de Tocqueville, op. cit., I, fn. p. 353.
21. Quoted in Rogin, op. cit., p. 248.
22. Quoted in Drinnon, op. cit., p. 113.
23. De Toqueville, op. cit., II, p. 146.
24. Ray Allen Billington, ed., *The Journal of Charlotte L. Forten: A Free Negro in the Slave Era* (New York: Norton Paperback, 1981), p. 64.
25. Quoted in Leon F. Litwack, *North of Slavery: The Negro in the Free States, 1790–1860* (Chicago: Phoenix Books, 1965), pp. 83–84.
26. Quoted in Theodore Hershberg, "Free Blacks in Antebellum Philadelphia: A Study of Ex-Slaves, Freeborn, and Socioeconomic Decline," in Hershberg, ed., *Philadelphia: Work, Space, Family, and Group Experience in the Nineteenth Century* (New York: Oxford University Press, 1981), p. 376.
27. Quoted in David M. Streifford, "The American Colonization Society: An Application of Republican Ideology to Early Antebellum Reform," *Journal of Southern History* 45 (1979): 201.
28. Billington, ed., op. cit., p. 15.
29. Quoted in John Mack Faragher, "History From the Inside-Out: Writing the History of Women in Rural America," *American Quarterly* 33 (1981): 541.
30. Ibid., 542.
31. Quoted in Barbara Leslie Epstein, *The Politics of Domesticity: Women, Evangelism, and Temperance in Nineteenth-Century America* (Middletown, Conn.: Wesleyan University Press, 1981), p. 80.
32. Quoted in Barbara J. Harris, *Beyond Her Sphere: Women and the Professions in American History* (Westport, Conn.: Greenwood Press, 1978), p. 96.
33. David Brion Davis, ed., *Antebellum American Culture: An Interpretive Anthology* (Lexington, Mass.: D. C. Heath, 1979), p. 75.
34. Donald M. Scott and Bernard Wishy, eds., *America's Families: A Documentary History* (New York: Harper & Row, 1982), p. 208.
35. Quoted in Willie Lee Rose, "The Emergence of American Women," *The New York Review of Books*, September 13, 1977, p. 24.
36. "Essay on Marriage," *Universalist and Ladies' Repository* 2 (1834): 371, cited in Cott, op. cit., p. 70.

3

The New Middle Class and Reform

Americans and foreign observers alike viewed the United States as virtually a classless society at the start of the nineteenth century. They recognized the existence of classes—that is, social groups defined by their differing relations to the means of production (ownership or nonownership being the most critical ones)—but denied their importance because of the absence of a rigid class structure. The major class division of European society—an aristocracy of hereditary nobility at the top who owned the land and a peasantry at the bottom who were tied to the land and the aristocracy through the burden of traditional rents and personal obligations—never took root in colonial America. There was always too much land and too many opportunities to acquire it in the colonies. Speaking for white males, a delegate to the Constitutional Convention in 1787 could justifiably declare: "There is more equality of rank and fortune in America than in any other country under the sun."[1]

America skipped the feudal age, and this basic fact had profound consequences for class formation during the market revolution of the antebellum years. There was a conservative upper class of wealthy merchants, lawyers, and landed gentry, but America never had a conservative class in the European mold of an entrenched aristocracy that fought a rearguard action to defend the social forms and legal prerogatives of the past. America had its rural poor but, aside from the slaves who were legally denied liberty, no impoverished peasantry who would join a European-style proletariat favoring socialistic programs to gain political rights and economic opportunities.

Instead of this polarity between the top and bottom, class lines in the antebellum United States merged into the bulging ranks of the middle class. Free to pursue opportunity and abundance unchecked by personal and legal restraints on market involvement, property-holding groups in the middle set the tone for society as a whole. Wealth, not aristocratic privilege, was the measure of one's status, and the desire for physical gratification channeled ambitions into a seemingly democratic quest for money and goods. De Tocqueville provided the best clue as to what was happening:

> When . . . the distinctions of ranks are obliterated and privileges are destroyed, when hereditary property is subdivided and education and freedom are widely diffused, the desire of acquiring the comforts of the world haunts the imagination of the poor, and the dread of losing them that of the rich.

The result was a "passion for physical comforts" which, above all, was "a passion of the middle classes."[2]

Much more so than in Europe, *democracy* and *capitalism* very nearly became synonymous terms in the United States. As long as white males apparently had an equal chance to compete, making money and pursuing liberty meant the same thing, and most Americans continued to believe that they lived in a classless society. Classes in the sense of fixed, hierarchical differences in status were associated with the tyranny of the Old World. As summarized in 1848 by the educational reformer Horace Mann,[3]

> According to the European theory, men are divided into classes—some to toil and earn, others to seize and enjoy. According to the Massachusetts theory, all are to have an equal chance for earning, and equal security in the enjoyment of what they earn. The latter tends to equality of condition; the former to the grossest inequalities.

What then could explain the growing extremes in wealth and poverty after 1815 or the emergence of a new working class of wage earners who had but little chance of becoming independent proprietors? If permanent classes did not exist in America, the answer had to rest with individual character. An expanding economy produced enough avenues of upward mobility to make plausible the claim of the propertied classes that economic success was a measure of moral worth. In America, declared a journalist in 1844, "one has as good a chance as another according to his talents, prudence, and personal exertions."[4] Poverty or permanent wage-earning status was, in the words of Abraham Lincoln, not "the fault of the system" but the result either of "a dependent nature which prefers it, or improvidence, folly, or singular misfortune."[5]

Thus, character was substituted for class as the great dividing line in American society. This was preeminently the social outlook of the economic winners who had a stake in preserving the status quo. Most of these winners came out of the middle class of commercial farmers, businessmen, and professionals. Their America was one of self-made men in which morality and productivity were interchangeable. This image was so successfully promulgated that it is still the most common way in which Americans today define their society.

An ethic of self-restraint was central to the middle-class vision of antebellum America. The middle class first fashioned this ethic in the family world of their domestic lives and then tried to universalize it throughout society in their reform activities. This chapter will examine the development of that ethic and its relation to the economic and cultural changes discussed in Chapters 1 and 2. De Tocqueville was right. The ascendancy of middle-class values and institutions was the most dynamic feature of antebellum society. As we shall see, the evolution of these values and institutions was largely a Northern phenomenon, and hence the rise of the middle class was itself a major factor in the growing tensions between a free North and a slave South.

The Revolutionary Middle Class

The middle class, especially in America, has never lent itself to a precise definition. The term *middle class* was not used before 1812, and for the remainder of the century it was commonly associated with the eighteenth-century notion of the middling ranks or interests of American society. Because America lacked an aristocracy and peasantry, "middle class" simply connoted a moderate position between extremes of wealth and poverty. By the mid-nineteenth century, however, a distinctive middle-class culture was forming in the North. What made it distinctive was a new and more explicit definition of what it meant to be middle class. Now, the term referred to the aggregate of self-made individuals who had learned to discipline their ambitions. More moral than economic, this definition was the key to the way in which the middle class responded to the growing division in American society between the economic haves and the have-nots.

Half of the adult white males were propertyless by the 1850s, and a wealthy elite at the top, 5 percent of the population, owned close to 60 percent of all property. In between was the middle class—the farmers, businessmen, professionals, and independent artisans who held property and who were involved in the market economy. This one-third of the population controlled most of the businesses, the churches, the schools, and the press, and their spokesmen were the cultural leaders of the nation. The philosopher Ralph Waldo Emerson summarized their creed when he wrote: "A dollar is not value, but representative of values, and, at last, of moral values."[6]

This marriage of moralism and materialism was the distinguishing characteristic of the Northern middle class. Unlike the European bourgeoisie, the American middle class did not have to free itself from an aristocratic system of rank and privilege. However, precisely because the legal and social barriers to the individual pursuit of economic self-interest were so weak in America, the fears of disorder which that pursuit engendered were correspondingly more intense. In response to these fears, anxieties that were inseparable from the very opportunities they were grasping, the middle class reordered its social world in a radically new way. They abandoned the eighteenth-century belief in the need for external social controls and replaced it with a call for internalized controls, which made the individual solely responsible for his moral and economic fate.

By turning inward for its sources of authority and control, the middle class developed an ethic of self-restraint. This ethic, when applied to society as a whole, provided a means of class self-identification and simultaneously promised moral and social order through inner controls. Just as the belief in biological determinism justified the elimination of Indians, blacks, and women from the marketplace, so also did the new bourgeois conception of the self-regulated individual create a classification scheme that sorted out economic competitors and naturally explained why some white males were winners in the marketplace and others were losers. Because their own lives embodied a split between work and home, and because they feared that political controls over the economy would be in the interests of the privileged wealthy, the middle class came to view the economy in abstract terms, as a naturally self-regulating mechanism.

The roots of this market conception were in late-seventeenth-century England, but the American middle class of the nineteenth century was the first to have the political authority and social legitimacy to elevate that conception into a generalized social construction of reality. As perceived by the middle class, the public world of economic competition, the marketplace, automatically rewarded moral fitness and self-restraint and punished those of weak moral character. No one could be blamed for the plight of economic losers. As freely consenting individuals, winners and losers alike agreed to contractual relations that were inherently fair because of their voluntary nature. All that could be expected of the middle class in dealing with poverty was the attempt on their part to help others to control themselves. This was the source of the reform energies of the middle class during the antebellum period. These reform efforts could narrow, but never eliminate, the natural division of society as viewed by the middle class. There would always be the industrious (those who were in control of themselves) and the idle (those who were slaves to their passions).

This new conception of reality was the basis for the revolutionary role of the American middle class. It was a view of reality that became persuasive as the middle class sought to make sense of the new social territory they were occupying. They had abandoned the old territory, the rural world of patriarchal farm families in which economic activity and social organization were daily experienced as part of the same unified whole. In this world land was the basis both for class divisions and for the subsistence and security that were the primary goals of most adults. The institutions of family and church reinforced one another, especially in New England, to curb the pursuit of private economic gain and to create at least the semblance of an organic sense of social community. What influence these institutions did have was related to an economy of low expectations in which most rural Americans more or less knew their place. Economically, that place was within the confines of the corporate family economy. Socially and politically, that place was first one of submission to patriarchal authority, and then, after economic independence was achieved, one of deference to the consensual agreements reached by men who personally knew one another and shared local positions of authority.

The rural youth who left this world freed themselves both from its restraints and its sense of belonging. Those who did not move West became pioneers in the new social space of America's growing towns and cities. Perhaps most characteristic of these cities was the literal newness of the people who inhabited them. In a typical ward of Syracuse, New York, in 1855, 42 percent of the population was foreign-born. Of the native-born, 45 percent were migrants from counties outside the one in which Syracuse was located. In the Boston of the 1830s and 1840s only 10 percent to 15 percent of household heads were natives of the city, and by one estimate the annual population turnover in the city was 30 percent. In most antebellum cities and towns over half of the population, predominantly the lower, poorer half, moved on within a decade. In Rochester, New York, a booming milling center once the Erie Canal was completed, five out of every six wage earners left between 1827 and 1833. Rochester also illustrates two of the other central features of the urban social environment. In 1830 three-fourths of its population was under the age of thirty, and four-fifths of the adult males were not self-employed but worked for others.

This was a world in which the institutions of the past that bound individual to place seemed either irrelevant or hopelessly weak. Gone were the face-to-face ties, ethnic homogeneity, and comparative population stability of the rural, village past. In their place was a kaleidoscopic scene of ever-changing, youthful, strangers, most of whom lacked the economic independence that Americans traditionally associated with political equality. In the eighteenth-century New England town, strangers without visible means of support were legally warned out of town. In the nineteenth-century

Moving Day in the City, ca. 1850. The frenzied mobility of urban life is captured in this drawing of moving day in New York City. On May 1, the day that yearly leases expired, about one-third of the city's population changed residences. (Historical Pictures Service, Chicago)

city, such strangers came close to being the city. These wage-earning strangers appeared all the more threatening because, in contrast to household production in the past, they no longer lived with and worked under the supervision of a master craftsman. Residential segregation by class separated employers from employees in Rochester by the mid-1830s. At the workplace, discipline was increasingly exercised by managers and foremen on behalf of the owner. Both in the home and at work the intimacy of the personal ties that conferred legitimacy upon patriarchal power was lost.

In reacting against and as part of this highly mobile and seemingly unstructured world, certain Americans who were successful in staying above the level of wage earners began to define themselves as a middle class. These men and their families—professionals, shopkeepers, and clerks—no longer perceived themselves as simply being in the middle of a fixed social continuum in which some families happened to own more land than others. They saw themselves as a class apart with interests and values distinct from the rest of society.

The middle class, like any class, was formed in repeated conflicts with groups having opposing interests. These conflicts, many of which were fought over reform issues, gave cultural expression to the very real differences that had emerged between the middle class and the rest of society. These differences were most obvious in American cities. On the one side were the business and middle classes, the primary owners of capital and income-producing property. On the other side, and in the majority, were the wage earners, those who sold their labor. In turn, the visible contrast in economic lifestyles, one expressed in different types of residential accommodations and consumption patterns, was reinforced after the 1830s by an ethnic division in which most immigrants were in the working class.

To those native born with enough capital to stay above wage labor but not enough to assure themselves that they would not slip into it and join the ethnic poor, the economic polarization of their urban world was as threatening as what they believed was the city's lack of social cohesion. By convincing themselves that the fundamental class division around them was in reality a moral division between the industrious and the idle, the middle class insulated themselves from the social and economic fears that the city held for them. Social order would be maintained by the same inner-controlled class who had the ambition and moral fortitude to take advantage of freely available economic opportunities. Their code of self-restraint, by setting an example for others, would bring self-regulating order to both the economy and society. The same code differentiated the middle class from the classes above and below them. In contrast to the wealthy, whose riches were largely inherited and ostentatiously displayed, the middle class earned their property through hard work and self-denial. In contrast to the poor, the code of self-restraint explained away the disturbing presence of poverty by the same logic with which it accounted for the greater economic success of the middle class. In either case, the middle class was in a position of moral superiority.

Sexuality and the Middle Class

Self-control began with one of the most basic drives of all—sex. By the 1830s, a stream of advice literature directed at the middle class prescribed an ideology of sexual repression. Male abstinence and female purity were its defining characteristics. Men were enjoined to curb their natural lust and women were assumed to be passionless. This literature often drew on metaphors of closed energy systems. The human body, it was argued, contained only a finite amount of energy. It followed that men, the culturally appointed agents of progress in the public sphere, would fail at their economic tasks if their energy were depleted in private acts of sexual passion. In a metaphor saturated with sexual imagery, the abolitionist Henry Clarke Wright compared the man who wasted his semen with "him who was ever toiling for wealth, but who could derive no enjoyment from it, except by throwing it as fast as he earned it, into the fire or the sea."[7] Sperm, like capital, had to be saved through an accumulating process of self-denial.

As strained, if not farcical, as these analogies of the spermatic economy might strike us, the connection between the spread of a market economy, the rise of a middle class, and the promulgation of a new sexual ideology is unmistakable. Before the 1830s, sex was a matter of no particular concern. When written about, it was described as a natural and intensely pleasurable fact of human life. Clerical and medical opinion praised marital moderation as the ideal, but no one issued dire warnings against excessive sexual intercourse within marriage or thundered against the unspeakable evils of masturbation. Sex, in other words, was viewed as part of the natural order of things. By the mid-nineteenth century, that natural order had been upset by the market revolution. Uprooted, urbanized male reformers, those who wrote the sexually prescriptive literature after they had left the rural Protestantism of New England and upstate New York, were acutely aware of that disruption. And so was their urban middle-class audience. Of all the symbols of uncontrollable, overpowering desire that had to be held in check if individual achievement was not to result in social anarchy, none was as all encompassing as the sexual drive. Here, at the most intimate level of human existence, the unfathomable boundary between self and loss of self, was an instinctual urge that the middle class struggled to master. Not the inherited blue blood of an aristocratic lineage, but the self-willed bodily control of the reformed individual became the basis for the social superiority of the middle class.

Undoubtedly a gap existed between the sexual behavior prescribed by the advice literature and the actual practices of the middle class. Prostitution, the flourishing of underground pornography that depersonalized female sexuality in graphic, mechanical imagery, and a sharp rise of abortions among middle-class women by the 1850s were all indicative of behavior that fell far short of the cultural ideal. On a more positive note, diaries and letters reveal that middle-class women did enjoy sex, although a majority felt that sexual pleasure should be associated only with procreation. Still, the middle class was not being hypocritical in its espousal of sexual continence. They did build psychological cages to suppress their sexuality. More so than any other group, the middle class consciously limited its family size. In Buffalo, New York, fertility was lowest in 1855 among the new middle class of professionals, accountants, and sales personnel. As a group, laborers had the most children, and their fertility was 44 percent greater than that of the new middle class. Moreover, within all age groupings, native-born women bore fewer children than the foreign-born, most of whom were in the working class. In antebellum Utica, New York, for example, immigrant women on average had two more children than did the natives, and they experienced shorter intervals between births. (See Tables 3.1 and 3.2.)

Table 3.1 Fertility Ratios by Class in Buffalo, 1855

Fertility was lowest in the new business class of white-collar workers, who rarely owned their own businesses. They attempted to raise their standard of living and ensure their children's future by limiting the size of their families and by passing on an inheritance, not of capital, but of education. Fertility was highest among laborers who, faced with low wages and sporadic employment, viewed children as an economic asset who could go to work at an early age for the support of the family.

	CHILDREN UNDER 5 PER 1,000 MARRIED WOMEN
Old Business Class[a]	1,220
New Business Class[b]	927
Skilled Workers	1,271
Laborers	1,332

[a] Primarily merchants, manufacturers, and clerks.
[b] Primarily professionals and white collar.
Source: Adapted from Michael B. Katz and Mark J. Stern, "Fertility, Class, and Industrial Capitalism: Erie County, New York, 1855–1951," *American Quarterly* 33 (1981): Table 1, p. 77.

Table 3.2   Average Number of Children by Age Group and Nativity of Mothers, Utica, New York, 1865

As a result of ethnic customs and religious traditions that had encouraged large families in the peasant economies of Europe, immigrants consistently had more children than native-born Americans throughout the nineteenth century. This pattern was also reinforced by the working-class status of most immigrants.

	AGE				
	20s	*30s*	*40s*	*50s*	*60s*
Nativity					
Native-born	0.6	2.3	3.3	3.6	5.1
Foreign-born	1.0	3.7	5.2	5.2	6.5

Source: Adapted from Mary P. Ryan, *Cradle of the Middle Class: The Family in Oneida County, New York, 1790–1865* (New York: Cambridge University Press, 1981), Table E.1, p. 267.

In the absence of widely used birth control devices, the family limitation of the middle class can be explained only by a decline in the frequency of sexual intercourse during marriage or, and more likely, by male withdrawal. In either case the sexual experience was voluntarily restricted. Husband and wife mutually benefited from this restriction. As the birth rate fell, women came to value the additional time and independence that caring for fewer children gave them. Men appreciated the economic benefits of being responsible for fewer children to support. Both realized that the rising living standards and familial privacy they had come to value in their middle-class lifestyle were jeopardized by too many children.

Children and Self-control

Detached from the land, the material basis of the old family economy, and the traditional mode of child rearing that it supported, the middle class pioneered in new strategies for raising children and providing for them as adults. Without a family farm, children were no longer economic assets valued for their labor. To send the children into the factories, as the working class did out of the necessity to raise the family income to the level of economic survival, would have been tantamount to dropping out of the middle class. But keeping them at home as consumers, and foregoing the wages they could have brought in, raised the cost of having children. In compensation, a strict Christian regimen under the mother's care at home and extended years of schooling outside the home could equip children with a moral and intellectual inheritance to take the place of the former landed inheritance. At a basic economic level, patterns of inheritance were simplified. Most middle-class families, to say nothing of the working class, had very little tangible, productive property to transfer to their children. In Utica, New York, only 2 percent of the wills in the generation after 1825 passed on any productive business—a store, shop, or farm. Most commonly after 1825, fathers divided up what little cash they had in equal shares among the children. Moral capital, not real property, was now their legacy. Thus, in fashioning responses to their material circumstances, the middle class was instrumental in creating the modern conception of childhood. The stress on fewer children, egalitarianism, character molding, deferred expectations, and education set it apart from the childhood experiences of farm families in the past and working-class families in the antebellum present.

Middle-class parents were told, and presumably many believed, that their primary responsibility was to teach their children self-control. Bronson Alcott, a teacher noted for his reform ideas, stated the ideal in the 1830s:

> The *child* must be *treated* as a *free*, *self-guiding, self-controlling being*. He must be allowed to feel that he is under his own guidance, and that all external guidance is an injustice which is done to his nature unless his own will is intelligently submissive to it.

Such a child could meet parental expectations only through demonstrated acts of self-denial. As Alcott later told Anna, one of his daughters, "by and by you will love me well enough to give up your wants always."[8] Alcott, and the other purveyors of child-rearing advice, magnified the normal tensions that parents brought to their task. The child's nature was now presented as infinitely malleable and deeply, even irreversibly, impressionable. One wrong parental step, one false infliction, could, the advice literature warned, permanently set the child on a road to self-destruction.

What middle-class parents were told to avoid, and what conservatives most feared, was the morally lax family that would reflect and reproduce the social disorder of a rapidly changing America. If democracy were not to run amuck, obedience had to start in the family. Francis Wayland, a Baptist minister and president of Brown University, vented the fears of his generation in 1835:[9]

> The notion that a family is a society, and that a society must be governed, and that the right and duty of governing this society rests with the parent, seems to be rapidly vanishing from the minds of men. In the place of it, it seems to be the prevalent opinion that children may grow up as they please, and that the exertion of parental restraint is an infringement upon the personal liberty of the child.

Although physical punishment was still used (even Alcott succumbed), increasingly it became a last resort, a virtual admission of failure on the part of the middle-class parent. "Speak gently—it is better by far to rule by love than fear,"[10] advised Lydia Child in *The Mother's Book* in 1831. Withdrawal of love and the inculcation of guilt were the preferred disciplinary techniques. Training could not start too early. One couple wrote in to *Mother's Magazine* in 1834 that they had begun to "correct" their infant daughter for crying before she was a year old. "This has been a severe but wholesome discipline. It has taught her a command over her feelings, which we trust may be of great service in her subsequent life."[11] When necessary, some children had to be jolted, even broken, into self-governance. In a letter anonymously published in 1831 Wayland described his technique. When his son of fifteen months refused to take food offered to him, Wayland starved the child for thirty-six hours until the boy willingly submitted to his father. In a classic example of blaming the victim, Wayland concluded: "I am right and he was wrong. He might at any moment have put an end to the controversy. He was therefore inflicting all this misery voluntarily upon himself."[12]

If advice manuals, occasional medical survey literature, and the surviving diaries are reliable guides to actual behavior, the scheduling of feeding, toilet training, religious instruction, play, and school work became more regimented in middle-class homes. Constant surveillance, especially in sexual matters as the child grew older, had its obvious limits. Self-repression, assisted by the channeling of sexual drives into education and work, had no such limits.

Privatization

In the generation before the Civil War, the middle class began to segregate itself from the rest of society. This process, often referred to as privatization, can be seen in the distinctive class neighborhoods that emerged in antebellum cities by the 1850s. In Milwaukee, to cite one case, the upper and eastern half of the first ward was known as Yankee Hill. Protestant business leaders and the successful native-born middle class lived there. The lower half of the ward was populated by the predominately German-born shopkeepers and artisans. South of the hill was the Irish and unmistakable lower-class third ward. Suburbanization reflected the same process of separation rooted in class. Because they could afford to live beyond walking distance to work and wanted to escape the noise, congestion, and exposed class divisions of the central business district, the middle class led the shift to the newer, more countrylike areas that were annexed to cities. By about mid-century, a move to outlying districts began to serve as a certification of rising status. In Philadelphia's Penn District, an area in the midst of the northwesterly flow of the city's expanding population, the middle class moved in during the 1850s at a rate twice as fast as artisans and five times as fast as unskilled laborers.

The use of living space within middle-class homes also registered a quest for privatization. Domestic arrangements for the middling ranks of the eighteenth and early nineteenth centuries were cramped and crowded. There was literally no room for much privacy or differentiated space for family functions. Rising affluence, combined with the technological innovation of balloon frame construction, enabled the middle class to have domestic privacy. Pre-cut, standardized lumber, held together in a frame by factory-produced nails, gave the balloon frame its name. It was first widely used in Chicago in 1839. Much quicker and cheaper than former housebuilding techniques, balloon frame construction provided the middle class with affordable, single-dwelling residences with enough room for an ordered, specialized environment. In the pattern books of model homes put out by architects, ministers' sermons, and the domestic literature in general, the middle-class home was portrayed by the 1840s as a moral statement of a disciplined and progressive set of values.

In the 1820s the Yale theological professor, Timothy Dwight, argued that "the mode of living sensibly affects the taste, manners, and even the morals, of the inhabitants. If a poor man builds a poor house, without any design or hope of possessing better, he will . . . conform his aims and expectations to the style of his house."[13] The middle-class homes of the next generation were designed and used to show that no class of poor lived within them. The order, specialization, respectability, and privacy that the middle class valued were embodied in the layout of rooms, each of which was associated with a particular function. Domestic space, like social interaction, was to be compartmentalized and controlled. In the rear, and often in a separate wing, were the kitchen and pantry; outsiders were to be entertained in the parlor; the family met socially in the sitting room; eating was done in the dining room; parents now had marital privacy in their own bedroom; children, though not yet individually assigned bedrooms of their own, were to be isolated for moral self-examination in a separate

Constructing a Balloon Frame House. By eliminating the need for skilled carpentry, balloon frame construction produced significant savings of time and labor in the building of homes. It has remained the standard form of home construction since it was introduced in the late 1830s. (The Bettmann Archive)

room when they misbehaved. In cities, where horizontal frontage for construction was at a costly premium, the upper middle class achieved the same specialized privacy in their multi-level row houses. Bedrooms were on the second floor and servants' quarters in the attic.

Privacy from other classes and among themselves was a fundamental expression of both class and individual self-identity. But privacy carried one grave and obvious risk: If the middle class retreated within itself, the rest of society would go its own way. The rich would continue to be irresponsible and greedy, the poor licentious and lazy, and the city's youth dissolute and uncontrollable. The 1840 exhortation from the religious writer Horace Bushnell for ''a place of quiet, and some quiet minds which the den of our public war never embroils''[14] could easily have become a rationale for a dangerous retreat into domesticity from the outer world of amoral economic competition and divisions between the rich and poor. To control a world from which they were retreating or, more accurately, to reshape that world in their own image, the middle class sought to universalize the ethic of self-restraint, to make it the standard by which society measured itself. One of its great allies would be evangelical religion.

Evangelicalism

The Second Great Awakening is the name given to cyclical bursts of religious revivals and conversions between 1800 and the early 1830s, which resulted in a doubling of the percentage of the churched population in America. By 1835 about one in eight Americans belonged to a church. A host of new sects sprang up. Among them was Mormonism, the most native of all American religions, with the exception of the Indian belief systems. Founded in 1830 (in a region of upstate New York known as the Burned-Over District because of the fire of its religious zeal), Mormonism was the most controver-

A Frontier Revival. Before they were refined and institutionalized in an urban setting by the middle class, revivals were associated with the frontier and the anguished release of pent-up emotions. (The Whaling Museum, New Bedford, Massachusetts)

sial of the dissenting sects. Mormons eventually were able to escape persecution only by migrating in the 1840s to the desert fastness of the Far West.

The impulses behind the revivals and conversions cannot be reduced to a formula. All social classes and geographic sections were at least partially caught up in them. Still, a definite pattern did emerge. Associated in its early phases with the hunger for community and social discipline on the part of isolated, trans-Appalachian migrants, the revivals by the 1820s began to acquire a decidedly middle-class imprint. By mid-century the core ideas of evangelicalism—the individual as a moral agent capable of accepting or rejecting salvation, the perfectionist urge to cleanse society of sin, and the postmillennialist conviction that saved Christians, through their own efforts, could usher in a thousand years of peace and progress before Christ physically returned to the earth—were claimed by the middle class as their own.

Viewed as an ideology, as a way of constructing the world and providing a coherent, satisfying explanation of one's place in it, evangelicalism met the most basic needs of the middle class. By embracing the value structure of evangelicalism, with its emphasis on moral self-determination, the male middle class was able to confirm and sanctify its pursuit of economic self-interest, that inner drive by which males were convinced that they created their own fortunes. For the middle class, religious and secular notions of success were fused into an image of the self-advancing individual. In religion, as in worldly affairs, the individual rose through an act of self-will. There were no artificial barriers. The "full weight of [Christ's] atonement is offered to all men," preached the Reverend Albert Barnes of Philadelphia's evangelical First Presbyterian Church in the 1830s; "All that *will*, may be saved."[15]

The middle class, acting on its need to believe that the successful businessman, like the saved Christian, was self-made, was especially attracted to the urban revivals of the early 1830s. In Rochester, New York, an instant city whose population exploded by 512 percent in the 1820s, Charles G. Finney led a revival in 1830–1831. Only certain kinds of men were attracted to it. Businessmen, master craftsmen, clerks, and professionals composed about 55 percent of his converts. Only 12 percent came from the ranks of semiskilled or common labor. The same pattern occurred in Philadelphia; merchants, gentlemen, and professionals comprised 61 percent of the church admissions under the evangelical pastorship of the Reverend Albert Barnes from 1830 to 1837.

In his sermons and writings, Barnes identified the inner grace of regeneration with the outer signs of middle-class respectability and economic success. As he wrote in his *Choice of a Profession,* "success in any calling . . . depends probably more than on anything else, on stability of purpose and settled intention." National and individual virtues were equated with "the pursuits of honest and sober industry." Quite different was the emphasis of the Reverend C. C. Cuyler, the leader of the Old School, or nonevangelical, Presbyterians in Philadelphia. Cuyler preached a more conservative Calvinism, one that underlined God's omnipotence and inscrutability and the individual's impotence and depravity. Whereas Barnes' or Finney's God made each person a moral free agent, Cuyler's God exercised "a controlling influence over the affairs of men." And Cuyler, with a finality that the evangelicals shunned, insisted that "the highest degree of worldly prosperity does not prove the favour of God or the good estate of men."[16]

As we might expect from the contrasting religious perspectives of their respective ministers, New School and Old School Presbyterians in Philadelphia sorted themselves out along definite class lines. Men of entrepreneurial or professional status, those who saw themselves as economically ascendant through their own efforts, comprised 57 percent of New School numbers and but 22 percent of the Old School in 1838. The proportions for artisans and laborers were reversed, 23 percent in the New School and 63 percent in the Old School. Most of these men were experiencing declining, not rising, status in the 1830s. The tensions and pessimism of traditional Calvinist doctrine, which refused to put a moral gloss on economic change, had more appeal for those who saw no liberating self-advancement in their status.

Evangelicalism meant far more than the sanctification of individualistic economic behavior. If this were its only value or purpose, ambitious Americans, such as planters or merchants, would have adopted a version of it much earlier than the nineteenth century. Not acquisitiveness per se, but the control of self and society through a guilt-releasing submission to a supreme authority, characterized the evangelicalized middle class.

Dissenting Protestantism, of which American Puritanism is a leading example, had traditionally condemned private economic gain that appeared to be acquired at the expense of others in the community. In seventeenth-century New England, the courts fined merchants, and ministers censured them, for economic behavior that would be necessary for success in a profit-maximizing, market society. Among the practices that the Puritans sought to limit and punish were: buying as cheap and selling as dear as possible; raising prices in one part of the market to make up for losses in another; and, as a Boston minister in 1639 phrased it, acting on the assumption that "as a man may take the advantage of his own skill or ability, so he may of another's ignorance or necessity.''[17] Although Puritan constraints were gradually lowered as the colonial economy grew, cultural and religious fears over the economically unrestrained individual were still strong in the early nineteenth century. The model of success held up to American males in the pre-1815 period was one of social usefulness and moderation in all pursuits. Service for the public good was both a virtue and a standard of success. Thus, ambitious men, those who had foresaken community for what became an endless quest for economic advancement, often experienced their materialistic single-mindedness as guilt. As exemplified in the case of John Fisher, the farmer we met in the first chapter, evangelical conversion offered these men a deliverance from their guilt.

"Pray for me," Fisher wrote his English kin in 1837, "that the acquireing of the things of this life may not engage the whole of my attention but that I may seek first the kingdom of God. . . . I am afraid that business is gradually [turning my] thoughts from God and religion." In the spring of 1838, Fisher found the spiritual release that he was seeking and the replacement for community that he needed. Urged on by his wife and brother-in-law, he joined the Methodist church. His guilt had been overpowering. At a prayer meeting he "found that I had sinned against God all my life long & that I deserved to be sent to hell. This brought me deep and lasting conviction." Within three weeks he could "rejoice in a sin-pardoning God. My load of guilt was gone. . . ." With the enthusiasm of the newly converted, he now spent his evenings proselytizing among neighbors in prayer meetings. He knew "such rejoicing as I never saw or felt before."[18]

Evangelicalism meant many things to John Fisher. At the most fundamental level, his embracing of evangelicalism meant that he was literally worthy of himself. Now that he no longer felt self-alienation, his life had a new sense of wholeness. He found a model of committed discipline in which his economic and religious lives were simultaneously ordered around self-directed goals. The same fusion of outer and inner worlds occurred for other male converts. John Crozer was a textile magnate in the Delaware Valley. For Crozer, the continual need of the evangelical Christian to seek spiritual self-improvement in a testing of personal salvation produced a moral activism that complemented his entrepreneurial need to be ever responsive to fluid market conditions. In order to be economically competitive, Crozer repeatedly had to improve his mill machinery. He invested 40 percent of his profits in new equipment. By using the latest power technology and increasing production in his Chester Creek mills, he was able to meet his severe price competition. But the efficiency of that technology contributed to an industrywide overproduction of textiles that drove down his profit margins. Crozer could take nothing for granted. He was always operating on the thin edge between prosperity and failure. In his religious and business lives, the same model of reality was at work. Moral and economic success required unstinting self-effort, an ability to respond to ever-changing conditions that tested one's resolve and inner worth.

The Reform Impulse

The individual dynamics of evangelicalism—alienation, guilt, conviction of sin, fear of damnation, submission, salvation, rejoicing, and proselytizing—spilled over into an outer surge of social reform in antebellum America. Most evangelicals did not become reformers, but the drive for social betterment drew most of its membership from the ranks of the evangelicals. Revival spokesmen made explicit the dynamics of reform that were implicit in the conversion process. For Finney the truly converted should "aim at being useful in the highest degree possible."[19] Just as conversion was an active process, a seeking-out of God, a public confession of a sinful life, and a call for forgiving assistance, so also was the Christian life of the converted one of voluntary benevolent action. By submitting their lives to God's will, the saved also agreed to combat sin everywhere by rooting it out and leading lives of right behavior for others to emulate. A Christian identity could never be assumed; it had to be sustained through daily denials of self-gratification. Virtue, far from being a quiet piety, was a continuous acting out of moral choices in society at large. The greatest virtue was to work for the liberation of the damned, those enslaved by their own passions. All barriers between the unsaved and their acceptance of God were fit subjects for moral reform.

In establishing Sunday schools, Bible-tract societies, and missionary endeavors, the evangelicals sought to create a benevolent empire. Although often supported by more theologically conservative Protestant denominations, the evangelicals nonetheless infused the effort with their own particular urgency. Fisher prayed that the word would be spread "till all shall know the Lord from the least to the greatest."[20] Finney told his audience in Rochester's Third Presbyterian Church in 1830 that committed and disciplined Christians could bring about the millennium within three months. Because the millennium was imminent, Christians should redouble their efforts to usher it in. The evangelicals were convinced that they were marching in step with history. Progress and Christianity were one and the same. A writer in the *New Englander* magazine flatly declared in 1847 that "the progress of man has been directly proportional to the influences of Christianity." And, as he hastened to add: "The influence of Christianity is essential to prevent popular progress from being purely selfish, and consequently cruel and tyrannical."[21]

By transforming liberation into control and secular progress into the coming of the millennium, evangelicalism exerted a powerful appeal on the middle class. For all its boundless optimism, evangelicalism promised a society of self-regulating individuals who, by submitting to God's moral authority, set limits on their own lust for power. Here was a doctrine that assured middle-class parents, so concerned over molding their children's personalities, that self-control could be internalized. *Mother's Magazine* in 1862 softly but chillingly hammered home the point:[22]

> Remember, children of the earth,
> Each house is in its way
> Bearing its own report to heaven,
> Of all you do and say.

The children of evangelical households learned at an early age how proper adults divided the world. They also recognized that a line of shame cut through that division. On Communion Sunday in 1858, fifteen-year-old Carolyn Richards of Canandaigua, New York, wrote in her diary:

> Dr. Daggett always asks all the communicants to sit in the body pews and the non-communicants in the side pews. We always feel like the goats on the left when we leave Grandfather and Grandmother and go on the side, but we won't have to always.

So that she would not "have to always," Carolyn experienced guilt on the rare occasions when she defied parental authority. One such occurrence was a forbidden sleigh ride in February of 1856. She did not enjoy herself at all. "I had no idea that sleigh rides could make any one feel so bad. It was not very cold, but I just shivered all the time."[23]

Fathers as businessmen also found evangelicalism reassuring. Temporary debt was a fact of life in an economy whose principal activity was the seasonal movement of crops to market. Established, institutional sources of credit, such as banks and insurance companies, were too few or too localized to offer a steady and reliable source of capital. Consequently, entrepreneurs turned to family and kin for venture and operating capital. Some 42 percent of the wealthiest tenth of Rochester propertyholders in 1827 were in business with relatives. However, as the geographic scope of business credit expanded in pace with the economy, a substitute for the personalized, blood ties of family capitalism had to be found. The notion of moral character, a secular version of the evangelical virtue of individual worthiness, served as that substitute.

The Mercantile Agency, the first formalized business vehicle for reporting on individual credit worthiness, was founded in 1841 by two evangelical merchants, the Tappan brothers of New York City. In order to qualify for credit an individual had to meet subjective criteria that corresponded to the evangelical definition of the re-generated, disciplined Christian. Marital status, reputation as a father, drinking habits, leisure-time activities, and religious affiliation, if any, were the standards that determined whether a credit applicant received a positive rating from the reporting agent in the field. The evangelicalization of business leaders in the 1820s and 1830s brought together men who could trust each other in economic affairs because of their common commitment to the same strict moral code. By the 1840s the Mercantile Agency extended that code into the enlarged market economy by screening out the moral sheep from the untrustworthy goats among those who sought credit from these leaders.

Of course, if evangelicalism spread throughout society, a Mercantile Agency would not be needed for moral policing, nor would businessmen have to be concerned with controlling their workforce. In a sense, businessmen had brought this problem of control upon themselves. As noted earlier, in the preindustrial, household-centered economy, masters and laborers had worked together and often lived together. The factory system dissolved that arrangement, which had bonded the master's economic control with his social responsibility. The dilemma of the manufacturer was a real one: the economic distance between himself and his workers widened when the progression of apprentice to journeyman to master jelled into the more rigid division between employer and employee. The social gap widened simultaneously with the master's abdication of his patriarchal authority in daily life. Evangelicalism potentially could close both of these gaps: if the workers turned to evangelicalism, external controls embodied in the person of the master would no longer be necessary. The internal controls of evangelicalism would dedicate workers to self-improvement and guarantee social harmony and a motivated labor force. As Christian benefactors, and as shrewd businessmen, manufacturers built churches for their workers. There is even some evidence that in Rochester in the 1830s an evangelical affiliation helped workers keep their jobs.

Christian businessmen put up the money for reform organizations staffed by their wives and daughters. This gender-based division of labor within the business class was a logical one. Men had the capital and women the time to devote to the reform causes of evangelicalism. For example, in an expression of their commitment to evangelicalism and their motherly devotion to raising good children, women contributed the unpaid labor that made possible the Protestant Sunday school. By 1832 nearly one in ten American children between the ages of 5 and 14 was attending one of the 8,000 Sunday schools.

Women comprised the rank and file of antebellum reform. In general, they came from a middle-class, evangelical background. Reform activity offered them a respectable career at a time when they were shut out of most professional outlets. It also gave them an opportunity to continue a critique of male society that many of them had begun through their evangelical fervor. In effect, evangelicalism sanctioned their resentment of male dominance. It allowed them to appeal to an authority higher than that of a husband or father. Lyman Beecher, a minister and advocate of revivals, warned of how "religion disturbs the families of the religious." He empathized with the woman who defied male authority by attending a revival and returned home where "she is reproached, chided, scolded, and it may be *beaten,* by the hands of her husband or father."[24] To openly protest her submission was a terrifying and lonely act of cultural betrayal for a woman; but to submerge that protest in the legitimating language of evangelicalism was a more subtle, and perhaps more effective, way of establishing her sense of autonomy. The tables were turned when a female convert, as recalled by a minister, could turn to her unconverted husband and proclaim in a revival meeting: "O my dear husband, you *must submit,* you must submit."[25]

Temperance

The link between evangelicalism, middle-class benevolence, and women's self-assertion was most evident in the temperance movement, the largest single reform effort in antebellum America. Males apparently went on something of a drinking binge in the early nineteenth century. Liquor was very cheap because many Western farmers in the precanal age could market their grain only by reducing its bulk and shipping it as whiskey. Alcoholic consumption more than doubled between 1790 and 1830, to over 5 gallons per capita annually. It then sharply declined, and since 1850 has fluctuated between one and two gallons per capita. The interest of women in this antebellum decline was starkly summarized in 1846 by the New York *Pearl,* a temperance newspaper edited by women: "a drunkard is a deliberate, voluntary savage, and he treats his wife accordingly."[26] The evangelicalized middle class as a whole would have agreed with this harsh indictment. For them the drinker was a moral and social rebel in need of self-mastery.

Drinking, like sex, was a casually accepted activity in pre-1830 America, which produced no prescriptive movement seeking to control it. More particularly, the imbibing of distilled spirits was an integral part of social behavior that cut across all class lines. As a bond of male fellowship, alcohol was found wherever men gathered in groups. Heavy drinking was a matter of course on public occasions such as elections, court days, and militia musters. A less feverish use of liquor characterized the easy sociability between master and workers and their relaxed, pre-modern attitudes toward work and leisure. These men worked hard but irregularly, set their own pace, and interspersed periods of intense labor with conversation and shared drinks. The line between work and leisure was as fluid in the countryside. Peter Cartwright, a Methodist circuit rider on the Southern frontier, recalled that "if a man would not have it [whiskey] in his family, his harvest, his house-raising, log-rollings, weddings, and so on, he was considered parsimonious and unsociable. . . ."[27] Rural and urban workers alike expected part of their wages to be paid in whiskey. The lack of suitable alternatives to alcoholic beverages reinforced the commonality of rural and urban drinking. Before refrigeration and modern water systems, milk spoiled quickly, and water in cities and low-lying areas was often unsafe to drink. Coffee and tea were available, but relatively expensive. Rum, hard cider, and whiskey were not only cheap and plentiful but also, according to popular lore, were nutritious and helped cut the grease in the usual diet of fried pork and corncakes.

Temperance, which by the 1820s was being defined as total abstinence, brought together the evangelicals, the middle class, and women in a mass reform movement. The basic issue for all three was the securing of self-control. Unless men learned to master themselves, the Christian millennium would never come to pass, social order and economic efficiency would never be achieved, and domestic discord would continue to victimize women. The problem of drinking was a real one, and some evidence suggests that it was reaching pathological proportions by the 1820s, but what highlighted temperance reform was the immense symbolic weight placed upon the issue of drinking.

Indulgence in alcohol, much like indulgence in sex, was for the reformers a violation of natural law, a willful wasting of one's self, family, work, and community. Alcohol clouded men's minds and blocked them from being receptive to God's grace; it produced unreliable workers; it enticed them into squandering their wages and throwing upon society the cost of welfare for their impoverished families; it made them easy prey for demagogues; and it turned them into brutes who beat their wives and children. In short, the problem of drinking became a way of telescoping and explaining a host of unsettling social ills that were magnified by the advent of a market economy. The intemperate, said Lyman Beecher in 1826, were in "a state of internal sensation." The imagery of constant agitation in Beecher's mechanical metaphor evoked the reformers' fears of a social order unhinged by too-rapid change and too few restraints. America was plunging out of control into a future fraught with danger. Intemperance, "the sin of our land," according to Beecher,[28]

> is coming in upon us like a flood; and if anything shall defeat the hopes of the world, which hang upon our experiment of civil liberty, it is that river of fire, which is rolling through the land, destroying the vital air, and extending around an atmosphere of death.

Organized temperance reform began just after the War of 1812. At first it was nonevangelical and upper class in its leadership. The evangelicals assumed control of the movement with the founding of the American Temperance Society in Boston in 1826. The proliferation of state and local societies, most of them in the North, resulted in upwards of 5,000 temperance organizations with a million members by 1835. Women made up 35 percent to 60 percent of the membership in the local societies. Although women sometimes founded their own chapters, most proselytized within male-led societies. The Protestant clergy sought out evangelical women as allies. Without a strong-enough political base to win passage of coercive legislation, the male reformers had to rely on women's moral suasion in the crusade for converts. Women responded, because temperance was directly relevant to their daily lives as wives and mothers. In their homes they read sentimental novels centered on heart-rending themes of the brutality and sexual abuse of the drunken husband; in their local communities they passed by grog shops and taverns that doubled as places of prostitution; and, in the area of family finances, they were hampered by a legal system that denied them property of their own and left them doubly exposed to the economic costs of alcoholism.

The use of alcohol came to represent the very antithesis of that controlled interior that was the essence of the bourgeois self-identity. Duty, usefulness, frugality, and progress itself were all negated by giving in to the temptation to drink. Not surprisingly, young, upwardly mobile, entrepreneurial groups supported temperance. Not backward-looking farmers, but a forward-looking, middle-class coalition based in growing towns and commercialized agricultural areas, was the backbone of temperance. In Rowan County, North Carolina, for example, where farming employed more than 90 percent of all white males, 90 percent of the members of the Salisbury Sons of Temperance were manufacturing proprietors, independent artisans, professionals, merchants, and clerks. Where farmers did support temperance, they were wealthier and more committed to market production and the latest techniques of cultivation than their rural neighbors.

The professional, manufacturer, small businessman, and commercial farmer all tried to live the same ethic of frugality and thrift. These men saw themselves as economic innovators who harbored their moral and material resources in the cause of individual and social progress. For them, the drinker was a lazy sinner and the source of crime, pauperism, and shiftless work habits. Unless controlled and reformed, he was a threat to himself and a well-ordered society.

By mid-century the temperance forces in the North had the political clout to secure passage of state-wide prohibition laws. Already, liquor had been banished from the middle-class home, and a generation of teetotalers raised in these homes was coming of voting age. Valuable allies were found in the Washingtonians, temperance advocates from the Protestant working class who had turned to the self-help ethic during the economic depression of 1837 to 1843. The Maine Law of 1851, banning the sale and manufacture of intoxicating beverages, provided the basic model for state prohibition. By 1855 thirteen other states, only one of which, Delaware, was marginally in the slave South, followed suit with similar legislation. Although court challenges quickly overturned most of these laws outside New England, reform had nonetheless taken an ominous, new turn. Gone was the earlier optimism that all individuals could ultimately control themselves. Now, an outside agency, the state, was being enlisted in a coercive attempt to force that mastery that some individuals were too weak to will upon themselves. The precedent had already been set with state intervention in schooling. In an extension of the same logic, reformers now approached adults in moral matters much as they earlier viewed children in educational matters—as subjects for mandatory reform in spite of themselves.

School, Prisons, and Other Institutions

Public schooling as we know it—"free," tax-supported schools, compulsory attendance, age-graded classes, and administrative layers of bureaucratic officials—originated in Jacksonian America. In 1820 the common school was an uncommon responsibility of the state. By 1850 the establishing and maintenance of schools was widely accepted as one of the prime duties of public authorities. Additional centralization and standardization would occur after the Civil War, but the basic system of public schooling was an antebellum creation.

Education in pre-1815 America was centered in the family and the church. Most children learned to read at home. The Puritan insistence on literacy for understanding the Bible did result in public support for common schools in New England, but attendance was spotty and the very brief schooling was primarily a supplement to religious training by the family. Independent schools, staffed with private teachers, and tutors for the wealthy were available for those who wanted more than a modicum of formal education for their children. The only urban schools in which parents were not expected to pay a fee were charitable ones intended for the children of paupers. Both teachers and students were transient and unregulated. These haphazard and mostly private means of education met community needs, in large part because no one placed heavy demands or high expectations on formal education. Job training for the minority of adolescent males not going into farming was done by apprenticing them out. Everyone held that moral education, what nineteenth-century Americans would call character building, was the responsibility of the family, not the state. Children were effectively socialized into their adult roles, and literacy rates of 70 percent to 80 percent for adult white males in 1800 were quite high by contemporary European standards.

What changed in the first half of the nineteenth century were perceptions of just what schooling should accomplish. Enhanced mobility, the uprooting of rural youth and their migration into cities, the rise of a class of wage earners, including child labor in factories, and growing ethnic diversity and economic polarization were all visible signs of the more fragmented, complex social relations that accompanied the rise of commercial capitalism. The educational reformers and their middle-class allies interpreted these new relations as evidence of a breakdown in the cultural equilibrium and community consensus that formerly had assured civic order and virtue. What was at stake for the reformers, aside from the professional careers in education that state funding would subsidize, was the very future of the republic. Compulsory, systematized schooling run by the state with public tax dollars was their solution for restoring what they were convinced was the shattered social equilibrium of Jacksonian America.

If the social fabric was splitting, then by definition the former agencies of socialization, the family and the church, must have failed in their traditional functions. The church could be partially excused because so many of the unchurched were moving West beyond its reach, but parents were regularly castigated by the reformers for their alleged ignorance and dereliction of duty. In dramatizing the consequences of such parental irresponsibility, the reformers, much like the revival ministers, used the apocalyptic language of impending social collapse. Horace Mann, the first secretary of the Massachusetts State Board of Education, accused lax parents of "degrading the human race. They who refuse to train up children in the way they should go are training up incendiaries and madmen to destroy property and life, and to invade and pollute the sanctuaries of society." Any society capable of maintaining a government, argued Mann, invited "the certain vengeance of Heaven" if it did not support free schools for all children. Mann's listing of the divine retributions that could be expected read like a reformer's catalogue of the evils besetting American society: "squalid forms of poverty and destitution," "scourges of violence and misrule," "corruptions of licentiousness and debauchery," and "political profligacy and legalized perfidy."[29] The unschooled child, like the unchurched, the intemperate, and the sexually unrestrained, was a horrible social danger.

The promoters of more systematized education achieved their greatest success in Massachusetts. Here, because of the influx of the Irish Catholics and early industrialization and urbanization, the social consequences of economic change were apparent sooner than in other states. Thus, the fears that Horace Mann earnestly expressed and exploited led rather quickly to political action. In 1830 a coalition of academy teachers, clergymen, and philanthropic leaders formed the American Institute of Instruction in Boston. Their republic, a somewhat idealized New England village of social harmony and Puritan virtues, was under attack on all sides. Native sons were leaving, rural poverty was on the rise, New England's voice was being ignored in national councils, Congregationalism no longer had the special legal status of an established church, and Boston was becoming poverty-ridden and congested with newcomers. To arrest what they saw as a decline into irreligion and disorder, and to counteract the effects of universal suffrage, which now gave the vote to even the most ignorant males, the reformers worked for the restitution of moral order by trying to centralize state control over the schools of Massachusetts. They were convinced that a properly ordered school system could "sway the public sentiment, the public morals and the public religion more powerfully than any agency in the possession of the government." The goal, said the Reverend Elipha White in 1837, was to produce "patriots and Christians, loyal and obedient subjects of civil authority and moral government."[30]

The type of schooling the reformers wanted to replace was, it must be stressed, one that was already meeting the needs of the Massachusetts citizenry. In 1800 the legislature had given school districts the right to tax and in 1817 recognized them as legal entities. Parents responded by fashioning a flexible, localistic, and highly practical educational format. Each district, and there were over a thousand (rural Berkshire County alone had 225), created schooling to meet its own needs. About the only uniform feature was that all of the districts violated state law by not keeping their schools open for the full school year. Wealthier districts supported schools in the winter and summer, poorer ones only in the summer. The teachers were an assortment of male college students, hired in the winter while on their long vacation break; young, single women, hired usually in the summer; and various townspeople earning extra income during the slack time of their trades. The teachers, if outsiders, boarded in local households. Classes were ungraded and mixed children of all ages. Clearly, the schools did not try to compete with the planting and harvesting seasons. They were there for the intermittent use of farm youth who set their own schedules for learning the rudimentary skills that would assist them in a farming economy. Open, cheap, and very equitable in their use of tax monies, the district schools absorbed rising enrollments after 1810. As the traditional agricultural economy and household production gave way to more commercialized pursuits off the farm, education began to assume greater importance for rural youth.

Control by local communities and the lack of structure were the features of district schooling that most rankled the reformers. Standardization, centralization, professionalism, and compulsory attendance were the governing principles in their notion of reform. What they wanted was a system, a hierarchical structure of relationships between students and teachers within the classroom and between local communities and a state school board outside the classroom. All schools should have the same uniform standards; attendance should be compulsory and enforced; teachers should be properly trained in normal schools; and students should be segregated by age in order to instill more consistent behavior and improve discipline and efficiency. What the American Institute of Instruction meant by education can perhaps be gleaned from their choice of the ideal school house. In a competition sponsored by the Institute the winning design was for a rural school house in which the windows were placed above eye level so as "to make it more difficult to look out." Education, the root meaning of which is "to lead out," was confused with a regimen designed to shut in. Minds were not to be stretched so much as they were to be drilled in the Protestantized middle-class values of obedience, punctuality, and steady work habits. Educational reformers, like James Carter of Worcester County, Massachusetts, were quite frank in acknowledging that state power, exercised through outside experts, should oversee this form of educa- tion. He wrote in 1826 that "the strong arm of the government should *make* children learn." He added, apparently unaware of the irony, that in the area of popular educa- tion "a *free* government must be arbitrary."[31]

School reformers, by simultaneously appealing to the hopes and fears of the middle class, were remarkably successful in transforming education, especially in the Northeast. The creation by the Massachusetts legislature of the first state board of education in 1837, and the passage in the same state of the first compulsory-attendance law in the early 1850s, stand out in this transformation. Education, in the rhetoric of a skillful promoter like Mann, promised a secular millennium in which social order would be restored and economic inequalities leveled. In his *Twelfth Annual Report* of 1848, Mann portrayed education as a panacea for the growing imbalance in class power. He admitted that in Massachusetts "the fatal extremes of overgrown wealth and desperate poverty" contradicted the egalitarian creed of a society in which economic opportunities were to be equally open to all. The potential risk was obvious:[32]

> Are we not in danger of naturalizing and domesticating among ourselves those hideous evils which are always engendered between capital and labor, when all the capital is in the hands of one class, and all the labor is thrown upon another?

As a counterweight to the fears that extremes of poverty triggered among holders of capital, Mann offered "universal education." Because, he argued, property would eventually follow education, the diffusion of knowledge would more equalize the possession of property. The hostility of the poor toward the rich would always be there, but education would eliminate poverty: "It prevents being poor."

Public education promised more than a classless society. It also promised to produce youth with the self-control necessary to take advantage of economic opportu- nities and the moral character essential for the responsibilities of citizenship and the preservation of the republic. As applied first to the urban poor and then to school children in general by the 1840s, the school, in the words of Philadelphia officials in 1819, provided a "wholesome discipline" through which "the minds of youth may be impressed with those great principles of morality and virtue so conducive to their own happiness and the welfare of our country."[34]

The increasing emphasis on centralizing uniformity easily merged after the 1840s with the concerns of the Protestant middle class over Americanizing the flood of Catholic immigrants. Because crime, proverty, and vice were in fact fostered by the slum conditions in which too many of the immigrants were consigned to live, the middle class viewed immigrants as desperately in need of lessons in Protestant morality and civic virtue. *Putnam's Monthly,* in a rather visceral metaphor of the school as a purifying device, felt in 1853 that "Our readers will agree with us that for the effectual defecation of the stream of life in a great city, there is but one rectifying agent—one infallible filter—the SCHOOL."[35] This perceived need to use the schools for socializing immigrants explains why, in a state such as Massachusetts, high concentrations of Irish Catholics densely packed into multi-family housing correlated quite strongly in 1855 with the length of the school session. Local Protestant business elites had the political power to determine the length of the school sessions in the various districts. They used that power to promote schooling as social insurance for community protection against the anticipated disorder of the Irish.

In the crushing burden of responsibilities placed upon schools, it is easy to lose sight of the positive way in which education was starting to reinforce and institutionalize the middle class conception of itself. The reformers pushed for a certain kind of school. It was one that rigidly structured classroom space, disciplined by rewarding punctuality and conformity, promoted sequentially through grades, and defined, in its choice of reading materials, habitualized self-restraint as virtue. Such a school, the reformer's ideal, was far from a reality in most school districts before the Civil War. But in attempting to create it, the reformers could count on the growing support of the middle class who saw in such a school an environmental model for socializing their children. He who could control himself would rise on his own merit. This was the creed of the middle class, what they tried to socialize in their children at home, and what they hoped the schools would internalize in their children away from home. "Selfish passions eradicated as much as possible." "Attainment, not *place,* made the standard of merit."[36] In setting forth these pedagogical principles in 1826, the school board of Cheshire, Connecticut, like the reformers in general, articulated the cardinal tenets of the middle-class faith. By structuring a school system around these tenets, assuring parents that teachers were second only to mothers as moral preceptors for children, and stressing the economic practicality of a system designed not to overeducate children for idle, intellectual pursuits, the reformers addressed themselves directly to the value system of the middle class. In so doing, they were instrumental in moving education toward the center of middle-class culture.

Not surprisingly, the school attendance of older children varied by class. As Table 3.3 illustrates for Boston, white-collar and professional families kept their children in school the longest. These parents were investing in the future mobility of their children. They were betting that the generalized educational skills their children were receiving, in addition to socializing them in good work habits, would best equip them for the uncertainties of an unpredictable job market. In contrast, working-class parents, in inverse proportion to the job security and income of the father, pulled their children out of school earlier. These families could not afford the luxury of foregoing the wages their older children could bring home. The Boston pattern held throughout the North. Within families worth $10,000 and over in 1860, 57 percent of children age 15 to 19 attended school. Of the children of the same age from families worth under $100, only 25 percent attended school.

Table 3.3   School Attendance in Boston, 1850

The class status of the household head markedly affected the school attendance of children after the age of twelve. The poorer the family, the greater was the likelihood that young teenage children would be taken out of school and put to work.

| | AGE GROUP | | | |
	4–5	*6–12*	*13–16*	*All Ages*
Occupation of Household Head				
Professional/White Collar	44.7	86.9	57.6	74.6
Artisans	52.7	88.9	53.7	72.9
Specified Unskilled	58.2	88.4	43.6	72.0
Unskilled	50.3	85.1	39.3	68.3
Unemployed	53.6	85.0	34.2	64.0

Source: Adapted from Janet Riblett Wilkie, "Social Status, Acculturation and School Attendance in 1850 Boston," *Journal of Social History* 11 (1977): Table 1, p. 181.

The transformation of schools in the North was the best known and most visible of a whole system of specialized institutions that were established after 1820. State legislatures, prodded by Protestant charitable groups and secular reformers, committed extensive public funds for housing criminals in penitentiaries, the mentally ill in asylums, the delinquent in reformatories, and the poor in almshouses. In the most common pattern, states replaced or superseded the earlier reliance upon voluntarism with official state institutions. The nation's first mental hospital, McLean's, was private and was opened in Massachusetts in 1818. Seventeen years later Massachusetts established the first state mental hospital in Worcester. By 1860 all but five of the thirty-three states had public institutions for the insane. The first juvenile reformatory, the New York House of Refuge, was privately organized in 1825. The first state reformatory appeared in 1848. The penitentiary system built in New York (Auburn and Ossining) and Pennsylvania (Philadelphia and Pittsburgh) in the 1820s served as models for other states. The new institutions tended to be massive brick structures of fortresslike dimensions. Their very appearance emphatically expressed the determination of their founders to resort to institutionalization for the management of the deviant and dependent.

The simultaneous appearance of so many new public institutions—schools, prisons, hospitals, orphanages, reformatories, and poorhouses—suggests a generalized perception on the part of reformers that Jacksonian America was plagued with common social problems that had a common public solution. Clearly, the reformers rejected the former methods of dealing with youth, criminals, the poor, and the insane. These methods had been informal, indiscriminate, and, depending upon one's perspective, either realistic or fatalistic.

Care of dependents and the ill in the eighteenth century, like children's education, was entrusted to families who could count on networks of kin for assistance. Because crime and poverty were viewed as a natural part of the social order, their presence did not elicit any extraordinary efforts to eliminate them. The poor were always there, but work was generally available for all who wanted it in an unspecialized rural economy whose members regularly exchanged labor for goods and services. Outdoor work relief or a temporary stay in the almshouse took care of the truly desperate. Criminals and dependent strangers were treated more harshly. The latter were warned out of town and the former were dealt with swiftly. No one entertained the possibility of rehabilitating criminals. They were briefly detained before trial in a jail that looked like nothing more than a rather sturdy colonial house. Depending upon the severity or repetitiveness of their crimes, they were fined and expelled, whipped, mutilated, or executed. Punishment was a public act of humiliation with the local community as the audience.

Beginning in the 1820s, institutional reformers redefined the existence of dependency and deviancy as a grave social problem in need of state correction. What had formerly been seen as inevitable and unthreatening was now labeled preventable and dangerous. The reformers, and the middle class in general, believed that family, church, and community, when detached from the hierarchy and localism of the eighteenth century, could no longer safely control crime and poverty or care for dependents. Counterbalancing these fears was an exuberant faith in the potential for human betterment. As inheritors of secular ideas of individual progress associated with the Enlightenment and the American Revolution, and often as proponents of the religious espousal of human perfectionism, they offered a philosophy of reform that promised to restore self-dignity and social usefulness to the misfortunate.

Sincere, humanitarian impulses motivated the reformers. The treatment of dependents in the eighteenth century was often cruel and arbitrary. If not assisted by family, the insane were thrown together with criminals in filthy workhouses. Connecticut kept its prisoners in an abandoned copper mine. The reformers were also reacting to real problems. The social costs of commercial capitalism had first become apparent in the mid-eighteenth century when New England towns became alarmed over the problem of the wandering poor. Transient, landless males trekked from town to town in search of work. Their presence foreshadowed the ceaseless mobility of the laboring poor in antebellum cities. Cut off from the security of land ownership or the regulated activity of a craft trade, more and more men were simply laborers, available for seasonal work wherever it could be found. The number of men who identified themselves as such leaped from 5 percent to 27 percent of the workforce in New York City between 1796 and 1855. Poverty, worsened by periodic economic depressions, was on the rise, and traditional mechanisms for coping with it were inadequate.

In two reports of the 1820s, Josiah Quincy of Massachusetts and John Yates of New York recommended that their states take over responsibility for poorhouses. The men were surprised by the amount of poverty they discovered. There were more poor, and they were more mobile than in the past. The state stepped in because the earlier town practice of sending the poor back to their county of origin no longer made any sense when so many were uprooted. Such intervention also held out the hope of alleviating class tensions. Joseph Tuckerman, who worked with Boston's poor in the 1820s, described why those tensions had risen. "Men are not only divided and separated by great inequalities of their condition in respect to property, but by the very fact of the extent of their numbers."[37]

In order to contain and then eliminate the disorder they sensed in American society, especially in the cities, the reformers argued that the self-reliant traits of the ideal bourgeois citizen had to be universalized throughout society. Everyone had to be the same, and all had to be self-reliant; if they were not, then the reformers initially blamed the environment. In the case of the insane, they were literally overexcited by the strain of too much freedom and mobility. They lacked the internal guidelines to cope with excessive expectations of worldly success. The family was pinpointed as the culprit for poverty and crime. In a report of 1844, William H. Channing, a Unitarian minister and one of the founders of the New York Prison Association, explained that crime began at home: "The first and most obvious cause is an evil organization derived from evil parents. Bad germs bear bad fruit."[38] Given their interpretation of the sources of dependency and deviancy, the reformers concluded that a properly ordered environment could redeem the misfortunate. The criminal could be taught social responsibility, the poor inculcated in habits of thrift, and the insane cured of their disorderly sensibilities. The very optimism of the reformers led them to adopt the asylum as a tool.

As with the school, only a certain kind of asylum would do. Whether a prison, hospital, poorhouse, or reformatory, the model antebellum institution implemented the same blueprint of reform. State power was used to segregate and supervise individuals who had succumbed to the corrupting temptations of the outside world. Within the walls of the institution, a strict moral regimen minutely governed the lives of the inmates. Designed as a mirror image of the outside environment, daily repetitive, standardized routines ordered and controlled behavior through rigidly enforced schedules. The vigilance that individuals had failed to provide for themselves was forced upon them. To assist them in internalizing this vigilance, manual labor was made the core of the routine. Inmates were considered cured once they demonstrated by their behavior that they had learned to equate work discipline with self-worth.

Here was a model, proclaimed the reformers, that society should emulate. In commenting on the need for strict supervision to prevent prisons from becoming "nurseries of vice," the directors of the Prison Discipline Society in Boston drew this lesson in 1829: "This brings into view a principle of very extensive application to families, schools, academies, colleges, factories, mechanics' shops; i.e., the importance of unceasing vigilance." Directors of the Society for the Reformation of Juvenile Delinquents in New York fully agreed: "In almost every case . . . the discipline of the institution works a reformation." The same officials claimed that their inmates experienced "a new birth."[39] Those that could not be reached by evangelical ministers would be saved by asylum officials. The institution, as a forced, involuntary revival, would serve as a moral incubator for future additions to the middle class. Their inmates, said the directors of the orphanage in Charleston, South Carolina, would leave with transformed characters that made them morally fit for becoming "practical men of business and good citizens, in the middle classes of society."[40] Thus, the same message was repeated over and over. Americans had to internalize a respect for authority, and the institutional reformers would show them how. If the message were rejected, if parents continued to fail in their duty of instilling moral discipline within their family governments, then the state had the right to create surrogate families in the new asylums. "Massachusetts," Horace Mann proudly wrote in 1846, "is *parental* in her government."[41]

In the end, asylums, like schools, succeeded more in classifying and standardizing their inmates than in reforming them. Freedom was identified with tractability and conformity. Confinement turned out not to be a cure. After some early successes, especially in mental hospitals, rates of recovery dropped. Schools, reformatories, and prisons did not eliminate or even demonstrably check poverty, crime, and vice. Rather than admitting that their initial premises may have been wrong, that individuals cannot be taught to act as morally responsible citizens by subjecting them to authoritarian regimentation that deprives them of exercising any responsibility, the reformers by mid-century began to abandon their earlier environmental explanations. Increasingly they viewed deviants and dependents as a natural class of outsiders formed by in-grained defects of character. The walls remained, only now they restrained the incur-able, those labeled as permanent misfits. In disproportionate numbers the native and immigrant poor, those categorized as guilty of a willful lack of productivity, were kept behind the walls. The asylum was now the custodian of the unproductive. Even the best of humanitarian intentions turned out to have its repressive side.

The Unreformed South

In the above discussion of the middle class and reform the antebellum South dropped out of view. The reason for this was quite obvious to contemporaries. The South was largely untouched by the social and ideological consequences of the market revolution that spawned a middle class and its reforming zeal in the North after 1815. As we saw in Chapter 1, economic diversification, ethnic pluralism, and urbanization were pre-dominately Northern phenomena. By 1860 a Southern white was only one-third as likely as a Northerner to work at a nonfarm job, live in a city, or be foreign born. Because the South, relative to the North, remained much more rural and agricultural, Southern class formation and folkways changed little after 1815. Moreover, the need to protect slavery always muted any reform impulses.

Of all the Northern reforms, only temperance found much of a following in the South. Even here the reformers did not have broad community support; the South had 35 percent of the nation's free population in 1831 but registered less than 10 percent of the temperance pledges. Most of the Southern states had a semblance of public school-ing by 1860, but the Southern educational system lagged far behind that of the North. Only 35 percent of the white population between the ages of five and nineteen in the slave states were enrolled in school in 1860; in the free states, 72 percent were. The Southern school year was shorter and, on average, Southern children spent only one-fifth as much time in school as Northern ones. Not surprisingly, illiteracy among Southern whites (17 percent) was three times that of Northerners (6 percent).

Northerners, especially middle-class ones, interpreted the South's lack of en-thusiasm for reform as a sign of moral backwardness. What else could be expected, they asked, in a slave society divided between rich nabobs and poor whites? "In the slave states," said a Republican congressman in the 1850s, "there is in substance no middle class. Great wealth or hopeless poverty is the settled condition."[42] According to this indictment, the absence of a Southern middle class was proof that an individual could not improve his position in a slave society and that hence there could be no reform movements for economic and moral progress.

To be sure, this critique overlooked the existence of an ambitious, middle group of Southern whites. This group, the 24 percent of whites in 1860 who owned fewer than forty slaves, ranged across the social spectrum from village merchants, trades-men, and professionals to aspiring planters on-the-make. These Southerners were upwardly mobile and clearly not adverse to making money. Many of them undoubtedly met Northern standards of middle-class behavior and beliefs. Yet, for all its exaggeration, the Northern view was not that far off the mark. The Southern middle class was too small and too closely tied to land and slaves, or the goal of obtaining them, to mount a challenge to the reigning values of Southern culture. These values—manly self-assertiveness, the defense of one's honor, and the enjoyment of the physical pleasures of leisure time—were those of an agricultural slave society that continued to reject the bourgeois ethic of self-control, delayed gratification, and the glorification of work for its own sake.

Throughout the antebellum years, Southern culture remained rooted in isolated farms and plantations. Work underwent no change of meaning as it did in the North. Most Southern whites did not have to answer to the time demands of a market economy, and work meant what it always had—something that had to be done at one's own pace in order to enjoy one's leisure time. Because so much of it was done by the despised slaves, work could hardly be infused with the moral purpose that the Northern middle class gave it. Leisure remained highly valued, but styles differed by class. Planters favored the conspicuous consumption of lavish parties, extended hospitality, and stables of blooded horses for racing. The pleasures of the plain folk were simpler—hunting, fishing, cockfights, and rough-and-tumble games in which physical strength and the ability to give and take a beating counted the most. In either case, the liberal use of alcohol was commonplace. Sober restraint was not high on the list of Southern virtues.

Authority in the South flowed outward from localized webs of kin-centered dependencies headed by paternal authority. Formal, written law, an ordering device that lays down impersonal rules of consensus in a society undergoing rapid change, was always less influential in regulating behavior in the South than in the North. Economically undiversified and ethically homogeneous, Southern communities were small, localized, and personalized. Oral customs and traditions, enforced by one's word and public opinion, set the boundaries of permissible behavior. Compared to the rural North, the scope of the law was narrow. Blacks were not permitted to testify in court cases involving whites. Planters had wide discretionary powers in their private rule over the slaves, and rural nonslaveholders, as one Northerner put it, were "habitually a law to themselves, while they are accustomed, from childhood, to the use of the most certain deadly weapon."[43]

Socially recognized honor, not inner dignity, was the basis of one's character in the South. Status, far from being associated with an internalized conscience, had to be publicly asserted in the face-to-face encounters of daily life. Emotions were displayed, not controlled, and the slightest challenge to one's honor touched them off. Southern white males were notoriously quick to sense a personal insult because a loss of honor carried the shame of being treated like the dishonored caste of slaves. A loss of face for a planter meant an end to his claim for righteous leadership over both blacks and poorer whites. As one of them simply noted: "Reputation is everything."[44] For the nonslaveholding majority, ever fearful of falling into the personalized subordination of the slave, dishonor meant a loss of that individual independence that made them the social equal of even the haughtiest planter.

Honor, vengeance, and violence were interwoven in Southern culture. Issues of personal honor were kept outside the legal system, and private justice revenged alleged public slights to honor. Because honor consisted of winning the esteem of others, Southerners literally fought to gain and hold that esteem. Gentlemen fought duels, and the common folk disfigured each other in knife-wielding and eye-gouging brawls. Northerners were more prone to commit suicide, but the Southern homicide rate was four times that of the Northeast in the mid-nineteenth century.

Southern evangelicals, supported by the small middle class, denounced the culture of honor and its strain of violence. After 1830 evangelicalism made heavy inroads in the planter class, and the South's new men of wealth increasingly substituted the inner strength of religion for the outer show of character. Although the cult of honor survived, public attitudes by 1860 were much more ambivalent. As summarized by a commentator in the *Southern Presbyterian Review* of 1857: "The mass of our intelligent community do not approve of duelling, but neither do they positively and earnestly disapprove it, nor speak out boldly and loudly against it."[45]

Southern culture was changing but not nearly fast enough to meet the approval of the Northern middle class. To the extent that the South clung to its traditional and highly personalized values, many Northerners viewed the region as primitive, threatening, and in need of reform. Southern honor, for these Northerners, was simply a loss of self-control.

The Northern middle class, by restricting their family size, working steadily, saving their capital, submitting to God's will, and looking and acting as if they were in control of themselves, was certain that they lived by a code of self-restraint. They attributed their success to it, and the failure of others to its absence. The growing poverty and menace of disorder that so concerned them were explained as evidence of a natural human tendency to be lazy and morally enslaved to passions. Otherwise, as the English biologist Charles Darwin put it, "If the misery of our poor be caused not by the laws of nature, but by our institutions, great is our sin."[46]

Reformers tried to help these poorer Americans to be productive and morally free. The impulse was sincere, but it was also grounded in the belief that the morally unfit, those who could not govern themselves, were a threat to the middle-class conception of order and prosperity. At best, the productive would ultimately have to support the unproductive; at worst, the idle would attack the property rights of the industrious. Thus when moral suasion apparently had reached all it could, by mid-century the reformers turned to coercion. But coercion carried its own risks, especially when the nation's political culture was polarizing in the minds of the Northern middle class between the worthy and the unworthy, between the North and the South.

The story of that polarization is inseparable from the history of antebellum politics. The next two chapters will look at that history and the eventual failure of national politics to contain the sectionalism that was dividing the nation into two hostile camps.

SUGGESTED READING

There is no adequate history or theory of the antebellum middle class. Stuart M. Blumin, "The Hypothesis of Middle-Class Formation in Nineteenth-Century America: A Critique and Some Proposals," AHR 90 (1985), provides an excellent summary of the theoretical literature and advances an hypothesis that links the middle class to common areas of social experience. For a sweeping interpretation of the bourgeois world view as it developed in Western culture, see Donald M. Lowe, *History of Bourgeois Perception* (1982). Louis Hartz, *The Liberal Tradition in America* (1955), remains the classic expression of the argument that, in the absence of a feudal past, Americans did not develop distinctive classes but instead evolved a consensus on individualistic, entrepreneurial values.

Brilliantly suggestive insights on the social psychology of the middle class, especially its anxieties, individualism, and economic acquisitiveness, can be found in Alexis de Tocqueville, *Democracy in America*, ed. by Phillips Bradley (2 vols., 1942). Mary P. Ryan, *Cradle of the Middle Class: The Family in Oneida County, New York, 1790–1865* (1981); Paul Boyer, *Urban Masses and Moral Order in America: 1820–1920* (1978); and Paul E. Johnson, *A Shopkeeper's Millennium: Society and Revivals in Rochester, New York, 1815–1837* (1978), are major works that show how the middle class used the issue of moral reform to define itself. E. Anthony Rotundo, "Body and Soul: Changing Ideals of American Middle-Class Manhood," JSOH 16 (1983); Donald M. Scott, "The Popular Lecture and the Creation of a Public in Mid-Nineteenth Century America," JAH 66 (1980); and Karen Halttunen, *Confidence Men and Painted Women: A Study of Middle-Class Culture in America, 1830–1870* (1982), also place the middle class within a cultural framework. For interpretations more grounded in marketplace relations, see Michael B. Katz, et al., *The Social Organization of Early Industrial Capitalism* (1982), and David A. Gerber, "Cutting Out Shylock: Elite Anti-Semitism and the Quest for Moral Order in the Mid-Nineteenth-Century American Market Place," JAH 69 (1982).

On rural mobility, see Michael B. Katz, et al., "Migration and the Social Order in Erie County, New York: 1855," JIH 8 (1978), and on the very high urban mobility that structured so much of the middle-class experience, see Stephen Thernstrom and Peter R. Knights, "Men in Motion," JIH 1 (1970), and Peter R. Knights, *The Plain People of Boston, 1830–1860* (1971). Carroll Smith-Rosenberg, "Sex as Symbol in Victorian Purity," AJS 84 (1978), shows how fears over the socialization of the single, young men in the cities were central to new codes of sexual conduct. On sex and the middle class, Peter Gay, *Education of the Senses, Vol. 1: The Bourgeois Experience, Victoria to Freud* (1984), is a landmark study. Dense, but ultimately rewarding, is Michael Foucault, *The History of Sexuality*, vol. 1 (1978). Especially helpful for the late antebellum period are: Charles E. Rosenberg, "Sexuality, Class and Role in Nineteenth-Century America," AQ 25 (1973); Stephen Nissenbaum, *Sex, Diet, and Debility in Jacksonian America* (1980); and Ronald G. Walters, ed., *Primers for Prudery: Sexual Advice to Victorian America* (1974).

Lawrence Stone, "Family History in the 1980s," JIH 12 (1981), is a good guide to the literature on the emergence of the privatized, nuclear family. On nineteenth-century shifts in attitudes toward children, see Bernard Wishy, *The Child and the Republic* (1968). For the child-rearing practices that became identified with the middle class and evangelicalism, see Daniel T. Rodgers, "Socializing Middle-Class Children," JSOH 13 (1980); Charles Strickland, "A Transcendentalist Father: The Child-rearing Practices of Bronson Alcott," HCQ 1 (1973); William G. McLoughlin, "Evangelical Child-Rearing in the Age of Jackson," JSOH 9 (1975); and Glenn Davis, *Childhood and History in America* (1976). Clifford E. Clark, Jr., "Domestic Architecture as an Index to Social History," JIH 7 (1976), examines how architectual patterns for private homes in the mid-nineteenth century embodied an idealized vision of the middle-class family.

The insights offered by Perry Miller, *The Life of the Mind in America* (1965), have informed much of the literature on evangelicalism. Martin E. Marty, *Righteous Empire: The Protestant Experience in America* (1970), and William G. McLoughlin, *Revivals, Awakenings, and Reform* (1978), provide provocative overviews. For revivalism on the frontier, see Charles A. Johnson, *The Frontier Camp Meeting* (1955), and, for the cities, Richard Carwardine, "The Second Great Awakening in the Urban Centers," JAH 59 (1972). Donald G. Mathews, *Religion in the Old South* (1977), is unsurpassed for Southern evangelicalism, and his "The Second Great Awakening as an Organizing Process, 1780–1830," AQ 21 (1969), remains critical for understanding how the evangelical churches helped individuals organize their lives. For the special case of Mormonism, see Klaus J. Hansen, *Mormonism and the American Experience* (1981).

Alice Felt Tyler, *Freedom's Ferment* (1944), provides the fullest panorama of antebellum reform, but it should be supplemented by Ronald G. Walters, *American Reformers, 1815–1860* (1978). On the connection between revivalism and reform, consult Carroll Smith-Rosenberg, *Religion and the Rise of the American City* (1971); Timothy L. Smith, *Revivalism and Social Reform* (1957); and Clifford S. Griffin, *Their Brothers' Keepers: Moral Stewardship in the United States* (1960). The special attention that religious reformers placed on the young can be seen in Lois W. Banner, "Religion and Reform in the Early Republic: The Role of Youth," AQ 23 (1971), and Anne M. Boylan, "The Role of Conversion in Nineteenth-Century Sunday Schools," AS 20 (1979). Two of the best attempts at explaining the social basis of reform and revivalism are Whitney R. Cross, *The Burned-Over District: The Social and Intellectual History of Enthusiastic Religion in Western New York, 1800–1850* (1950), and Robert W. Doherty, "Social Bases for the Presbyterian Schism of 1837–1838: The Philadelphia Case," JSOH 2 (1968). William G. McLoughlin, *The Meaning of Henry Ward Beecher* (1970), is superb at showing why a softened, sentimentalized evangelicalism appealed to the mid-nineteenth-century middle class in the cities. James H. Moorhead, "Between Progress and Apocalopse," JAH 71 (1984), explains the centrality of millennialism in American Protestant thought.

Temperance, the great mass reform in antebellum America, is treated in Ian R. Tyrrell, *Sobering Up: From Temperance to Prohibition in Antebellum America* (1979); Jed Dannenbaum, *Drink and Disorder: Temperance Reform in Cincinnati from the Washington Revival to the WCTU* (1984); and William J. Rorabaugh, *The Alcoholic Republic* (1979). Jill Siegel Dodd, "The Working Classes and the Temperance Movement in Ante-bellum Boston," LH 19 (1979), and William J. Rorabaugh, "Prohibition and Progress: New York State's License Elections, 1846," JSOH 14 (1981), show how temperance was used to promote notions of progress based on internalized codes of self-control.

The literature on antebellum education is extensive and controversial. For the traditional view that stresses the commitment of the educational reformers to democratic participation in public life, see Lawrence A. Cremin, *American Education: The National Experience, 1783–1876* (1980). More critical assessments that stress the theme of social control are Michael Katz, *The Irony of Early School Reform* (1968); Stanley K. Schultz, *The Culture Factory: Boston Public Schools, 1789–1860* (1973); and Mary McDougall Gordon, "Patriots and Christians: A Reassessment of Nineteenth-Century School Reformers," JSOH 11 (1978). Very thorough studies that try to strike a middle ground are Carl F. Kaestle, *The Evolution of an Urban School System: New York City, 1750–1850* (1973), and Carl K. Kaestle and Maris A. Vinovskis, *Education and Social Change in Nineteenth-Century Massachusetts* (1980). For good discussions of how class affected educational policy and school attendance, see Alexander James Field, "Economic and Demographic Determinants of Educational Commitment: Massachusetts, 1855," JEH 39 (1979), and Jean Riblett Wilkie, "Social Status, Acculturation and School Attendance in 1850 Boston," JSOH 11 (1977). Lee Soltow and Edward Stevens, *The Rise of Literacy and the Common School in the United States* (1981), is the best source on literacy and schooling.

The major interpretive account of reformatory institutions in Jacksonian America is David S. Rothman, *The Discovery of the Asylum* (1971). Whereas Rothman traces the asylum to fears over social order, Gerald N. Grob, *Mental Institutions in America* (1973), stresses humanitarian impulses aroused by the Second Great Awakening. Michael B. Katz, "Origins of the Institutional State," MP 4 (1978), offers a third interpretation that links the rise of public institutions to economic changes that led to increases in the numbers of transient dependents. For specific institutions see W. David Lewis, *From Newgate to Dannemora: The Rise of the Penitentiary in New York* (1965); Steven L. Schlossman, *Love and the American Delinquent: The Theory and Practice of "Progressive" Juvenile Justice, 1825–1920* (1977); and Glenn C. Altschuler and Jan M. Saltzgaber, "Clearinghouse for Paupers: The Poor Farm of Seneca County, New York, 1830–1860," JSOH 17 (1984).

118   *The New Middle Class and Reform*

On the distinctiveness of the antebellum South relative to the North by the mid-nineteenth century, see the succinct argument of James M. McPherson, "Antebellum Southern Exceptionalism," CWH 29 (1983). Bertram Wyatt-Brown, *Southern Honor: Ethics and Behavior in the Old South* (1982), provides the fullest treatment of why honor, not self-control, was at the center of the value system of Southern whites. For the Southern violence that concerned many Northerners, see Dickson D. Bruce, *Violence and Culture in the Antebellum South* (1979), and Edward L. Ayers, *Vengeance and Justice: Crime and Punishment in the 19th-Century South* (1984). Elliott J. Gorn, " 'Gouge and Bite, Pull Hair and Scratch': The Social Significance of Fighting in the Southern Backcountry," AHR 90 (1985), shows the persistence of physical aggression in the public self-assertiveness of common whites in the South. The absence of an extensive Southern middle class, and hence of a strong temperance movement, is stressed in Ian R. Tyrrell, "Drink and Temperance in the Antebellum South," JSH 48 (1982). Michael Stephen Hindus, *Prison and Plantation* (1980), uses South Carolina and Massachusetts as case studies and finds striking contrasts in the sectional patterns of criminal justice and institutional response to criminal deviance.

NOTES

1. Charles Pinckney, quoted in Carl N. Degler, *Out of Our Past: The Forces That Shaped Modern America* (New York: Harper Colophon Books, 1962), p. 99.
2. Alexis de Tocqueville, *Democracy in America,* 2 vols., ed. by Phillips Bradley (New York: Vintage Books, 1945), Vol. II, p. 137.
3. David J. Rothman and Sheila M. Rothman, eds., *Sources of the American Social Tradition* (New York: Basic Books, 1975), p. 169.
4. David Brion Davis, ed., *Antebellum American Culture: An Interpretive Anthology* (Lexington, Mass.: D. C. Heath, 1979), p. 97.
5. Roy P. Basler, ed., *The Collected Works of Abraham Lincoln* (New Brunswick, N.J.: Rutgers University Press, 1953), Vol. III, p. 479.
6. Quoted in Burton J. Bledstein, *The Culture of Professionalism: The Middle Class and the Development of Higher Education in America* (New York: W. W. Norton, 1976), p. 21.
7. Quoted in Lewis Perry, " 'Progress, Not Pleasure, Is Our Aim': The Sexual Advice of an Antebellum Radical," *Journal of Social History* 12 (1979): 362.
8. Quoted in Charles Strickland, "A Transcendentalist Father: The Child-rearing Practices of Bronson Alcott," *History of Childhood Quarterly: The Journal of Psychohistory* 1 (1973): 15, 43.
9. Quoted in William G. McLoughlin, "Evangelical Child-Rearing in the Age of Jackson: Francis Wayland's View on When and How to Subdue the Willfulness of Children," *Journal of Social History* 9 (1975): 22.
10. Quoted in Glenn Davis, *Childhood and History in America* (New York: The Psychohistory Press, 1976), p. 65.
11. Ibid., p. 38.
12. Quoted in McLoughlin, op. cit., p. 37.
13. Timothy Dwight, *Travels in New England and New York,* 4 vols. (Cambridge: Harvard University Press, 1969 [1822]), vol. 4, p. 73.
14. Quoted in Ronald W. Hogeland, " 'The Female Appendage': Feminine Life-Styles in America, 1820–1860," *Civil War History* 17 (1971): 197.
15. Quoted in Robert W. Doherty, "Social Basis for the Presbyterian Schism of 1837–1838: The Philadelphia Case," *Journal of Social History* 2 (1968): 76.
16. Ibid., pp. 77, 79.
17. Quoted in Barbara Leslie Epstein, *The Politics of Domesticity: Women, Evangelism, and Temperance in Nineteenth-Century America* (Middletown, Conn.: Wesleyan University Press, 1981), p. 25.
18. Charlotte Erickson, *Invisible Immigrants: The Adaptation of English and Scottish Immigrants in Nineteenth-Century America* (Coral Gables, Fla.: University of Miami Press, 1972), pp. 125, 127, 128.
19. Quoted in James David Essig, "The Lord's Free Man: Charles G. Ginney and His Abolitionism," *Civil War History* 24 (1978): 27.
20. Erickson, op. cit., p. 128.
21. David Brion Davis, op. cit., p. 369.
22. Cited in Glenn Davis, op. cit., p. 40.

23. Caroline Cowles Richard, *Village Life in America, 1852–1872* (Williamstown, Mass.: Corner House Publishers, 1972), pp. 100, 55.
24. Quoted in Epstein, op. cit., p. 61.
25. Ibid., p. 61.
26. Quoted in Ian R. Tyrrell, "Women and Temperance in Antebellum America, 1830–1860," *Civil War History* 28 (1982): 131.
27. Quoted in Ian R. Tyrrell, "Drink and Temperance in the Antebellum South: An Overview and Interpretation," *Journal of Southern History* 48 (1982): 506–507.
28. David Brion Davis, op. cit., p. 395.
29. Joyce O. Appleby, ed., *Materialism and Morality in the American Past: Themes and Sources, 1600–1860* (Reading, Mass.: Addison-Wesley, 1974), p. 390.
30. Quoted in Mary McDougall Gordon, "Patriots and Christians: A Reassessment of Nineteenth-Century School Reformers," *Journal of Social History* 11 (1979): 559, 562.
31. Ibid., pp. 561, 565.
32. Rothman, op. cit., pp. 169–170.
33. Quoted in Ronald G. Walters, *American Reformers, 1816–1860* (New York: Hill and Wang, 1978), p. 209.
34. Rothman, op. cit., p. 173.
35. Quoted in Carl F. Kaestle, *The Evolution of an Urban School System: New York City, 1750–1850* (Cambridge: Harvard University Press, 1973), p. 141.
36. Rothman, op. cit., p. 178.
37. Quoted in David J. Rothman, *The Discovery of the Asylum: Social Order and Disorder in the New Republic* (Boston: Little, Brown, 1971), p. 178.
38. Ibid., p. 73.
39. David Brion Davis, op. cit., pp. 31, 32.
40. Quoted in Rothman, *The Discovery of the Asylum*, op. cit., p. 214.
41. David Brion Davis, op. cit., p. 42.
42. Timothy Jenkins, quoted in Eric Foner, *Free Soil, Free Labor, Free Men: The Ideology of the Republican Party before the Civil War* (New York: Oxford University Press, 1970), p. 47.
43. Frederick Law Olmsted, quoted in Edward L. Ayers, *Vengeance and Justice: Crime and Punishment in the 19th-Century American South* (New York: Oxford University Press, 1984), p. 32.
44. James H. Hammond, quoted in Drew Gilpin Faust, *A Sacred Circle: the Dilemma of the Intellectual in the Old South, 1840–1860* (Baltimore: The Johns Hopkins University Press, 1977), p. 39.
45. Quoted in Ayers, op. cit., p. 31.
46. Quoted in R. C. Lewontin, "The Inferiority Complex," *The New York Review of Books*, Oct. 22, 1981, p. 16.

4

The Creation of a Party System

Politics is about power in the public sphere and how it is organized, exercised, and distributed. What distinguishes *political* power from other types of power is its recognized monopoly on the right to use force to compel obedience in public matters. Authority, the ability to elicit voluntary compliance, legitimizes political power and prevents it from degenerating into brute coercion. The extent to which authority is conferred rests upon a consensus over the shared values that are confirmed through political action. These values, and the symbols associated with them, make up a political culture. Embedded within a particular political culture is a vision of the good and proper society, a sense of ultimate goals and purposes. The dominant political culture of nineteenth-century America was republicanism, a linked set of ideas, values, and symbols that justified the revolutionary break from England and articulated the kind of society Americans wanted to protect with their independence.

Republicanism meant, above all, opposition to monarchy and aristocracy. Once the Tories, about 20 percent of the colonial free population, had left or been driven out during the Revolution, nearly all Americans were republicans in this sense. They believed that sovereign power should be derived from the people and that individual liberties (for white males) should be preserved and expanded. These beliefs, in an age of rule by divine right and rigid social distinctions based upon birth, made republicanism a revolutionary ideology.

The key positive concepts in the political vocabulary of republicanism were property, equality, freedom, and virtue. The right to property was identified with the acquisition of a sufficient amount of land, or artisan skills and tools, to ensure independence and a decent, or competent, existence. Equality meant lack of dependence upon others; freedom, the ownership of productive property; and virtue, sacrifice of self for the public good. Disinterested service to the *res publica*, public affairs, and not the pursuit of private ends, was the measure of the virtuous citizen.

The major enemy of republicanism was the privileged aristocrat. Although America had no titled nobility, it had its share of men of wealth, birth, and social distinction who, as one opponent of the Constitution phrased it, wanted "to lord it over the rest of their fellow citizens, to trample the poorer part of the people under their feet, that they may be rendered their servants and slaves."[1] An aristocrat, in the language of republicanism, was privileged because his status did not rest on his own productive

121

labor. His wealth was either inherited, conferred in favors by politicians, or wrung from the real labor of others through the conniving manipulation of credit and speculation. The aristocrat, like the politician beyond the control of local majorities, was a source of corruption. Both used wealth not honestly earned to build up a personal following of sycophants, fawning dependents from the overly ambitious and the unpropertied poor. Such corruption, if unchecked by a virtuous citizenry, would lead to enslavement, the enforced dependence upon others that was the opposite of republican freedom.

American republicanism drew on a classical body of political thought that was revived in the Italian city-states of the Renaissance. It also borrowed heavily from the writings of radical English Whigs in the eighteenth century who opposed monarchical power. Nonetheless, American republicanism was much more than a disembodied set of political theories. The hopes and fears expressed in its ideas and values were the lived experiences of the majority of white males in a semisubsistence agrarian economy in which land was widely distributed. These Americans of the late eighteenth century were as nearly equal in their political, economic, and social conditions as any large social group before or since. The basis of their equality and freedom was their economic independence. Their property was the foundation of their political rights. Because they were self-supporting, they were freed from the corruption of those dependent upon the favors of the economically privileged. Control over their own property enabled them to withstand economic coercion and left them independent and fiercely self-assertive. When they spoke of the public good, they were referring to that which had been fashioned through the direct, personal involvement of themselves, their kin, and their neighbors.

Republicanism established a core consensus of values that Americans carried into their politics. Yet, as indicated by the rapid and unexpected rise of political parties in the young nation, that consensus was sufficiently broad to permit quite diverse groups to use the common language of republicanism to articulate their own distinctive version of republican ideology. By the early nineteenth century, there were four basic types of republicanism. Each was expressive of a particular blend of ethnic, religious, class, and regional interests.

1. New England was the home of *Yankee* republicanism, a vision of the good society propounded by Congregationalist ministers, farmers, and merchants anxious to use the power of government and the churches to regulate public morality and promote economic growth.
2. At the opposite extreme was the *individualistic* republicanism of most Southerners. Baptists and Methodists, mostly nonslaveholding farmers, insisted on the right of the individual to be left alone in matters of religious conscience. This stand ideologically reinforced the economic self-interest of the planters who abhorred the thought of governmental interference with their slave property.
3. In the Mid-Atlantic states, the *egalitarian* republicanism of Scotch-Irish Presbyterians and German Lutherans, farmers who harbored Old World resentments of the snobbery and privileges of European landlords, merged with that of urban artisans to reject programs of government aid for business as signs of aristocratic exploitation.
4. Favoring such programs in the name of *nationalist* republicanism were the Quaker

and Episcopalian urban elites of financiers and merchants. These elites had a cosmopolitan vision of an economically expanding America organized and directed by centralized authority at the top.

Republicanism was thus not a binding faith that precluded political dissent and conflict. On the contrary, its basic values encompassed a variety of meanings that in turn provided the ideological basis for political divisions between competitive parties. The first such parties in American history were the Federalists and Republicans. After sketching out of the origins of these parties and their collapse after the War of 1812, this chapter will focus on the development of what is known as the Second Party System of the Democrats and Whigs. The first mass political parties in history, the Democrats and Whigs represented an organized political response to the market revolution in antebellum America. They constituted broad social divisions within which Americans debated the meaning of that revolution and their response to it.

The First Parties: 1787–1815

Prior to the War of 1812, Americans surprised themselves by building a party structure more developed than any in the Western world. They were surprised because republican doctrine was intensely suspicious of any organized party behavior. By parties eighteenth-century Americans meant factions, temporary coalitions of self-serving aristocrats and notables who were scheming against the public good. Once independence had been achieved, it seemed as if the only meaningful political distinction, that between Patriots and Tories, republicans and monarchists, had been erased. Now that power was in the hands of the people, politics could have but one legitimate purpose, the consensual expression of the public interest. Party division would factionalize that interest and hence by its very nature was a threat to the public good.

This antiparty bias rested on the assumption that a corporate, organic community really existed. Indeed, such a community, one that was geographically small and ethnically homogeneous, was believed to be the only one in which republicanism could ever flourish. A diverse society spread over a large area would have no unified sense of civic purpose. Inevitably, as the historical record confirmed, republicanism in such a setting would degenerate into monarchy or anarchy. The republic of ancient Rome became an empire as it expanded, and the only contemporary models of republics in Europe were to be found in the compact Netherlands and the small city-states of Italy and Switzerland. The largely self-sufficient, agricultural communities of eighteenth-century America, however, met all the presumed preconditions for a successful experiment in republican government. Yet, because these communities were also part of a larger polity that included more commercialized and cosmopolitan social groupings in the port cities and areas of export agriculture, Americans soon discovered that a common social purpose was elusive at best. American society was simply too fluid and the opportunities to pursue economic self-interest too great for the survival of a corporate sense of an identifiable common good.

The Founding Fathers, the architects of the Constitution in 1787, had little faith in the disinterested civic virtue of classical republicanism. Fearful over what they viewed as the selfish and potentially tyrannical behavior of ignorant majorities in the state governments under the Articles of Confederation, they created a new edifice of government specifically designed to counterbalance and checkmate the ceaseless competition of self-interest groups. They also, most notably in the writings of James Madison of Virginia, turned on its head traditional republican doctrine by arguing that individual liberties and property rights could best be protected in a large republic. An extensive, expanding republic, reasoned Madison, by constantly adding new interest groups and making it more difficult for any given set of interests to coalesce into a majority, would check the tyranny of the majority over the rights of minorities.

Madison's political economy was grounded in a market vision of society, one divided into innumerable, competing interest groups of propertyholders. This vision implicitly overturned the central tenet of classical republicanism, the belief in a common social purpose as an organic outgrowth of a small, homogeneous community. If such a community, splintered by the social consequences of the market, could not coexist with the market, then Madison, however unwittingly, had made a compelling case for political parties. Some mechanism was needed not only to find leaders and formulate policy for the new national government but also to represent and harmonize the diverse social groupings of economic interests generated by market activity. Much to their surprise, the Founding Fathers ushered in the age of parties.

Virtually all of the Founding Fathers would have agreed with Alexander Hamilton that an underlying premise behind the Constitution was the imperative need for "one great American system, superior to the control of all trans-Atlantic forces or influence, and able to dictate the terms of the connection between the old and the new world."[2] However, they differed over how to implement such a system and over how much centralized power should be entrusted to the federal government. Out of these differences emerged two distinct political parties in the 1790s.

The Federalists, the party of Washington and Hamilton, wanted to build a commercial empire based on an informal alliance with England. Hamilton's economic program was the heart of its domestic policies. Economically, the program intended to create fluid capital for internal development out of a nearly worthless national debt. Politically, its purpose was to ally leading capitalists with the still-fragile central government. The funding of the old continental war debt at par through the issuance of federal bonds; the assumption by the federal government of state debts incurred during the Revolution that were still unpaid by 1790 (most of which were in the North); and the chartering of a quasi-public Bank of the United States, capitalized on a scale to be the most powerful financial institution in the country, were the cornerstones of the program. Hamilton was masterful. His program passed, and he succeeded in putting the nation's credit on a sound footing. However, there was no denying that his fiscal policies catered to the shippers, merchants, and creditors of the Northeast, the nation's financial elite, and were paid for by the small propertied masses.

Thanks in no small measure to Washington's prestige, the Federalists were the majority party in the 1790s. The party was pro-British in orientation and elitist in its political assumptions. Its programs and ideology blended the national republicanism of the Mid-Atlantic states with the moralistic republicanism of New England. Established economic groups and higher-status Americans, predominately the old English stock that was Congregationalist or Episcopalian in religion, were its staunchest supporters. Those who felt shut out of or threatened by the Federalists' economic program, as well as those who were outside the cultural circle of the party—recently arrived non-English immigrants and religious dissenters, such as Baptists and Methodists— gravitated toward the opposition party of Republicans led by Jefferson and Madison.

The Republicans won control of the federal government in 1800. The Federalists had made the fatal mistake in 1798 and 1799 of levying heavy taxes for an expected war with France that America never fought. Vulnerable to the charges of being a pro-British party of tyranny, militarism, and taxation, the Federalists lost their majority support and were never to regain it. The key defection occurred in the Mid-Atlantic states where German farmers, angered by the Direct Tax of 1798 on land and homes, switched to the Republicans.

Although definitely tilted toward the South and the petty producing class of small farmers and artisans, the Republican coalition cut across class and sectional lines. Southern planters resented an economic program that favored the Northeast at the expense of the landed interests. They also feared for the future safety of slavery in the wake of Federalist precedents that read broad, nationalistic powers into the Constitution—powers that someday could be directed against slavery. Backwoods farmers, most of whom were Scotch-Irish, equated Hamilton's policies with the hated English system of economic privilege and social prestige that they had hoped to escape by coming to America. The same farmers chaffed under taxes on whiskey that, as far as they were concerned, took money from them and put it in the pockets of the paper aristocracy of bondholders. Urban artisans, in competition with cheap English imports, were angered by a Federalist tariff policy that encouraged the raising of revenue rather than the erection of barriers to keep out English goods. Small producers of all sorts, unable to break into the tight Federalist controlled circle of finance and credit, joined in the outcry against, in Jefferson's phrase, the "Anglican monarchical aristocratical party."[3]

Republican ideology told the Jeffersonians what had gone wrong under Federalist rule. The nonproducers, the parasitical class of paper aristocrats, following the lead of the English titled nobility, were conspiring to centralize federal power and unfairly tax the real producers of wealth. Once in control, the Republicans pared federal expenses to the bone and eliminated the Federalist taxes. Fiscal stringency, however, should not be confused with a stance against economic development. What the Republicans had objected to were the specific economic policies of the Federalists, and the openly elitist way in which Federalists such as Hamilton sought to build up the coercive power of the Federal government.

Republican objectives were all the more effective with voters because of the contradiction in the Federalist approach to the political economy. On the one hand, the Federalists fostered a commercialized type of economic growth that challenged the agrarian bias of republican doctrine and promoted social diversity. On the other hand, fearful of such diversity and its political expression in an opposition party, the Federalists favored political controls, such as the Alien and Sedition Acts of 1798, to shore up the social order that their economic program was undermining. These acts were clearly aimed at the Republican opposition. The Alien Act lengthened the time of naturalization (and hence the waiting period for voting rights) for immigrants from five to fourteen years, and the Sedition Act declared virtually any criticism of the federal government to be a crime punishable by stiff penalties.

In short, the Federalists tried to have it both ways—a commercialized economy combined with what they felt was the proper deference owed to one's social betters. Still, whether in promoting economic growth or checking its social consequences, the Federalists were politically vulnerable. The Republicans did not make the same mistake. They favored only economic change that would benefit primarily farmers producing for an export market. They avoided coercive controls out of the conviction that in a nation of farmers the collectivized self-interest of private economic motivations was the same thing as the public good.

The Jeffersonian vision of republican America was rooted in the land. It was best summarized by Jefferson in 1787:

> I think our governments will remain virtuous for many centuries; as long as they remain chiefly agricultural; and this will be as long as there shall be vacant lands in any part of America. When they get piled upon one another in large cities, as in Europe, they will become corrupt as in Europe.

Only the propertied farmer had the economic independence, the sturdy self-sufficiency, the organic ties to nature, and the intrinsic honesty—in a word, the virtue—with which to resist the speculative excesses and corrupting offers of material favors and political rewards that had destroyed earlier republics. Once in debt, once enticed or driven off the land, the American citizenry would degenerate into the black beast of republican ideology, the city mob, "the panders of vice and the instruments by which the liberties of a country are generally overturned."[4]

Had the Jeffersonians been able, they would have frozen America's agrarian society as it existed in the late eighteenth century. As it was, they tried to do the next best thing. They sought to escape the past, to keep one step ahead of history, by recreating the present in the future. They would use federal power, not to ensnare the individual in controls that were unwanted and unnecessary, as the Federalists had attempted, but to acquire land that would permit and encourage individuals to recreate indefinitely the social conditions of true republicanism. The same power would insist on open and free access to world markets for the bounty of American farmers. The outlets secured through this access were indispensible to the maintenance of republican virtue. Without the profits from the sale of his surplus, the farmer would have little incentive for frugality or diligence. He would lapse into sloth and indolence. Assured, however, that his efforts would be rewarded, he would strive to raise his family's standard of living. Agrarian profits would be spent on imported manufactured goods, the purchase of which would be made possible by America's role as food producer for the world. Neatly balanced between the fears of the nasty brutishness of agrarian isolation and self-sufficiency, on the one hand, and the corruption of a society divided by sharp inequalities of wealth and the presence of the laboring poor, on the other, the agrarian republic of the Jeffersonians used space, not time, to define America's political economy.

The quest of the Jeffersonians for a particular type of agrarian society committed the party to both a commercial and landed conception of empire. In seeking to create their "empire for Liberty," to use Jefferson's phrase, the Republicans are best known for the Louisiana Purchase of 1803 and the War of 1812. Both resulted from the same premises. The former clearly represented a tremendous expansion of the agrarian frontier. For that very reason, the Federalists, fretting over how the controls of the federal government and New England Congregationalism could be extended over so wide an area, opposed the purchase. Controls, political or religious, were the last thing the Republicans wanted. The inducements of producing for the world market would soon enough act as a civilizing force in the new West. But that market had to be open on the basis of free trade. Otherwise, the United States would become economically

The Battle of New Orleans. This battle catapulted Jackson to national fame. He is shown here directing the fortified center of the American line and pointing in the direction of the attacking British troops, which were supported by the fire of British ships in the background. (Brown Brothers)

dependent on any foreign power that had the naval capability of controlling the flow of international commerce. Britain, locked in a death struggle with Napoleonic France, was just such a power. Both England and France tried to keep American goods out of the hands of the other, but the English had the navy to make good on that effort. Unless the Jeffersonians were willing to surrender the keystone of party policy—that is, admit that their claim of economic independence, and hence real national sovereignty, was a charade—they had to resist British interference with America's markets in Europe. The acquisition of land and the sale abroad of what virtuous farmers produced on that land were two sides of the same Republican coin. Without free markets in Europe, the American ability to finance imported manufactured goods with exported agricultural goods would be hampered. Faced with that eventuality, the Republicans might just as well have fostered the factories and cities they so hated.

After a series of conflicting and confusing economic sanctions directed against Britain and France, and finally only against Britain, the United States fought its second war for independence against the British. The War of 1812 was the Republicans' war and everyone knew it. Not a single Federalist in the Senate voted for the war. Primarily because of Andrew Jackson's utter rout of the British forces at the Battle of New Orleans in January, 1815, Americans convinced themselves that they had won the war. The fact that Jackson's victory was won after the war had formally ended with the

Treaty of Ghent, signed on Christmas Eve, 1814, was a fitting conclusion to this strange and chaotic war. Massive strategic blunders and pathetic communications prolonged a war that neither side seemed able or willing to win. The Treaty of Ghent, in ignoring the issues that had fueled the conflict and establishing no clear victor, seemed to cast doubt on whether the war ever should have been fought.

Yet, "Mr. Madison's War" marked a major watershed in American history. Americans, by interpreting the war as a victory, felt that for the first time they had truly established their sovereignty vis-à-vis the rest of the world. Now, their economy was no longer a pawn in European diplomacy. Turning inward to the development of the continent, Americans discovered that their first party organizations, the Federalists and Republicans, had outlived their usefulness. As governing structures designed to secure the Revolution by showing that the Constitution could work, that a republican order could survive and evolve in a hostile world of monarchical despotism, the parties had accomplished their fundamental purpose. The Revolutionary generation of leadership began to move off the center stage of the political arena, and new leaders in the 1820s started to build a party system that they hoped would be capable of expressing and channeling the restless dynamism of post-1815 American society.

The Collapse of Parties: 1815–1824

With the War of 1812, and its alleged success, foreign policy was removed as a divisive issue in American politics. Debates over whether the United States should be pro- or anti-British in what amounted to a European civil war spawned by the French Revolution had kept party divisions alive after 1800. In these debates conservative Britain and revolutionary France represented the extremes of order and equality that Americans were willing to sanction within their own society. Thus, apart from the economic issues, the debates pitted Federalist values of social hierarchy versus Republican values of individual freedom.

The Federalists, much to the alarm of the Republicans, had made a real comeback in the political fallout of Jefferson's embargo policy of 1807. The comeback was short-lived. Bitterly opposed to a war that they felt should have been fought against Napolean, a veritable Antichrist in the minds of New England Congregationalists, and stung by the loss of a very lucrative prewar trade with Britain, the Federalists resisted Republican calls for national unity. In New England, Federalist governors refused to order their state militia into national service, and merchants boycotted subscriptions for war loans. In the fall of 1814, a minority wing of the party met in Hartford, Connecticut, and made what the Republicans denounced as thinly veiled threats of disunion. These Federalists wanted constitutional changes to protect the beleagured minority status of New England. In their demands for constitutional amendments that would have required a two-thirds vote in Congress for a declaration of war and for the imposition of an economic embargo, they sought a constitutional veto over the power of the detested Republican majority. In their call for the removal of the three-fifths clause, the constitutional stipulation by which slave states received additional federal representation and electoral votes through a formula that counted a slave as three-fifths of a free person, they vented their frustration over the dominance of the federal government since 1800 by Virginia slaveholders.

The timing of the Hartford Convention could not have been worse. Within a few months the war was over, the public deemed it a victory, and the Federalists were permanently stigmatized as disloyal Americans prepared to abandon the country at its hour of greatest need. Beyond pockets of continuing strength in New England and Delaware, the collapse of the Federalists was swift. Their share of seats in Congress fell by half between 1814 and 1816, to about 20 percent. Their presidential nominee in 1816, Rufus King of New York, received a paltry 16 percent of the electoral vote. By 1820 the Federalists abandoned even the formality of nominating a presidential candidate.

Although the War of 1812 seemed to confirm the Republican view on foreign policy—the British were the real enemy and had to be fought—it ironically also corroborated the Federalist insistence on the need for centralized national power. The near economic, political, and military collapse of the United States under the strains of waging a major war for which the Republicans had ill prepared it threw into bold relief the inadequacy of the Republican stand on limited government. Republican reliance upon an armed citizenry, the militia, and its naval equivalent of cheap, defensive gunboats had proved woefully deficient in defending America's coastal regions. The burning of Washington by the British in August 1814 (in retaliation for an earlier American burning of the capital of Canada) epitomized the Republicans' failure in military strategy. The Republicans had allowed the charter of the First Bank of the United States to expire in 1811, and the absence of any centralized financial controls during the war was a key factor in driving the nation to the brink of bankruptcy. Indicative of the financial problems was the sorry record of the Treasury Department in raising hard cash for the war effort. Confidence in the federal government was so low that state banks and private investors would subscribe to Treasury paper only at a huge discount. Out of war loans totaling $80 million in currency, the Treasury received only $34 million in specie (coin). Chastened by such experiences, the Republicans quickly enacted postwar measures of economic nationalism that looked suspiciously like the old Federalist program.

In 1815 funds for a permanent navy base on frigates, not gunboats, were appropriated. A standing regular army of 10,000, about quadruple the prewar size, was authorized. Then, in 1816, the Republicans rechartered a national bank, the Second Bank of the United States. Given the chaos of the nation's finances, the need was obvious. Where the economic demand and need for a uniform paper currency and sound system of agricultural credit were most urgent, in the South and West, the support for the Bank was the strongest. In New England and the Middle Atlantic states, already well served by state banks and an ample supply of credit, support for the Bank was lukewarm.

The Republicans also passed a tariff in 1816 that was more protective than anything Hamilton had ever wanted. The party, anxious to protect the small manufacturing nucleus that Jefferson's embargo and the ensuing war against Britain had fostered, was unwilling to give cheap British goods ready access once again to the American market. The Federalists split over the higher tariff; Republicans backed it by a vote of two to one. New England, just beginning its transition out of a maritime, commercial economy, opposed the tariff. Also in opposition was the old tobacco belt of Virginia, the original heartland of Republican agrarianism. Somewhat surprisingly, in light of the tremendous hue and cry that the South was soon to raise over high tariffs, Southern congressmen were rather evenly divided over the Tariff of 1816. There was as yet nothing particularly threatening to Southern interests in the rise of manufacturing. As long as the small industrial work force was composed primarily of women, children, and slaves, the South was fully competitive with the North in manufacturing. As late as 1810, Georgia produced more cotton cloth than Rhode Island. Only when manufacturing became capital intensive, not labor intensive, a conversion that got underway in the 1820s, was the slave South at a real competitive disadvantage, because its strength lay in its slave labor.

Although vetoed by President Madison on strict constitutional grounds, a bill providing federal subsidies for internal improvements was passed by this same Republican Congress. John Calhoun of South Carolina, the Secretary of War, strongly favored the bill. Pointing to the primitive conditions of interior transportation that had resulted in disastrous delays in moving soldiers and supplies during the war, Calhoun rested his case on national security. Others, particularly a nearly solid phalanx of congressmen from the Mid-Atlantic region through the Ohio Valley, stressed the economic benefits. In 1815 the only profitable way to move bulky, trans-Appalachian agricultural goods to Eastern markets was by floating them down the Ohio-Mississippi river systems and then transloading them in New Orleans for water shipment around Florida and up the Atlantic coast. Federal funds for macadam roads, canals, and improved river transportation, by establishing a series of rapid, cheap links between the East and the West, could reverse this slow, expensive, counterclockwise flow of internal trade and accelerate the economic development of the West. The demand for federal action increased after the war because of the vast market potential of land rendered secure from British interference north of the Ohio and seized from pro-British Indians south of the Ohio. Precisely because the West stood to gain the most from federal subsidies, New England was in opposition. Yankee congressmen had no desire to enhance the attractiveness of the West. New England was already suffering from a heavy outflow of its rural population. This population drain translated into fewer seats in Congress and added to the costs of Yankee businessmen by reducing the potential pool of cheap, surplus laborers available for hire.

Under Madison the Republicans had, in the words of Josiah Quincy, a Federalist from Massachusetts, "out-Federalized Federalism."[5] For a brief period between 1816 and 1819, dubbed "The Era of Good Feelings" by a Federalist newspaper editor, it seemed as if it made no difference who was out-Federalizing whom. The Federalists were dead as a national force, and nearly every politician called himself a Republican.

The national consensus of the immediate postwar years, the basis for whatever "good feelings" there were, collapsed in 1819 and 1820. The effectiveness and harmony of one-party rule rested on the burst of patriotic unity after the war and the booming agricultural prosperity during James Monroe's first term. Both conditions proved to be temporary when class and sectional tensions returned with a vengeance in 1819.

In response to postwar economic dislocations in Europe, American exports of foodstuffs soared in volume and price from 1815 to 1818. Meanwhile, British textile manufacturers were rebuilding inventories of raw cotton that had been depleted by the disruption of trade during the war years. The price of cotton shot up from 15¢ to 30¢ a pound, and American cotton production more than doubled between 1815 and 1819. Incentives for Americans to buy land and enter the market were tremendous. In 1817 the federal government made it easier to act on these incentives by dropping to 80 acres the minimum amount of public land that could be purchased on credit. Annual sales of public land, which had averaged 360,000 acres from 1800 through 1813, climbed to over one million acres starting in 1814 and peaked at over three million in 1818. In the speculative frenzy, it was easy to ignore the growing mountain of debt that was being created, especially among farmers. By 1818 some $21 million was owed to the federal government for payment of public lands, a sum that was a third again greater than the annual value of farm goods west of the Appalachians.

The speculative bubble burst in the fall of 1818. The European harvest was a good one, the extraordinary demand for cotton subsided, and agricultural prices sank. News of these developments reached the United States in early 1819 and touched off a financial panic. In the East, the values of real estate, rents, and commercial capital plunged. In the West, land values fell on the average 50 percent to 75 percent. Thousands of farmers who had mortgaged their land on the assumption that high export prices would easily permit them to pay off their debts were financially ruined. The value of American exports, nearly all of which were agricultural goods, declined 41 percent between 1818 and 1821.

Given the speculative excesses that had occurred, some sort of sharp and painful deflationary contraction was inevitable. But the actual contraction that took place was exacerbated by the policies of the Second Bank of the United States. Under its first president, William Jones of Philadelphia, the Bank was extremely lax in policing the loose financial policies of its branches. Largely because of a flood of bank notes (interest-bearing loans in the form of paper certificates that issuing banks were pledged to redeem on demand in gold or silver specie) from its Southern and Western branches, the Bank of the United States faced a situation by the summer of 1818 in which demands against its specie stood at ten to one—that is, it had issued ten times the amount of notes that it could actually redeem in coin. A five-to-one ratio of notes to reserves was the rough standard that well-run banks tried to maintain. Jones, by not periodically returning notes to the issuing banks for redemption, but allowing them to accumulate, had made the postwar speculation even worse.

Before the financial markets collapsed in 1819, Jones was replaced by Langdon Cheves of South Carolina. Cheves stopped any further issuance of notes, refused to collect or purchase bank drafts on the Southern and Western branches, and demanded immediate repayment of all outstanding debts to the Bank. What to Cheves was an absolutely necessary policy of strict retrenchment was seen as the vindictive, ruthless greed of a monstrous conspiracy of paper aristocrats by the agrarian debtors of the Bank. The Bank as Monster entered the lexicon of American politics. A Missouri politician, Thomas Benton, spoke for his region: "All the flourishing cities of the West are mortgaged to this money power. They may be devoured by it at any moment. They are in the jaws of a monster!"[6] The economy turned up in 1821 but the memory of the Monster remained.

As the nation was being polarized between debtor West and creditor East, the fault line of free North versus slave South ominously widened at the same time. The Congressional sessions of 1819 and 1820 were nearly monopolized by the Missouri crisis. The request of the Missouri Territory to enter the Union as slave state triggered debates on slavery and its extension that were longer and shriller than any heard up to that time in national politics. What was truly new and ominous about these debates, however, was the appearance for the first time of a bipartisan Northern majority determined to stop the spread of slavery. The opportunity for such a majority to form had been there in the past. Congress had to decide on the status of slavery when it organized the Mississippi Territory in 1798 and the Louisiana Territory in 1804. Both times, despite efforts by some Federalists to keep it out, slavery was permitted with relatively little debate or opposition. Most Northern congressmen had been willing to let slavery spread into areas in which the climate and geography favored plantation agriculture and the production of cash staples by slave labor. By 1819 that willingness was gone. Something had clearly changed.

That something was a combination of Northern resentment and frustration, a mixture made all the more combustible by the breakdown of the Federalist party. As foreshadowed in the Hartford Convention of 1814, many Northerners were becoming angry over what they considered the overweening political power of the South. For these Northerners the presidency had become the private preserve of Virginia slaveholders—Jefferson and Madison for sixteen years and, after 1816, James Monroe. Certainly the Federalists felt that Southern political control, aided and abetted by the unfair advantage of the three-fifths clause, had resulted in such disastrous policies as Jefferson's embargo and the War of 1812. Most of these Federalists and their sympathizers were out of politics by 1819. Instead, they channeled their thwarted ambitions for political leadership into reform organizations of private exhortation after 1815. Many of these organizations, in providing a correspondence network that applied constant pressure on Northern congressmen not to give in on the Missouri issue, created an antislavery link between congressmen and their constituencies that had earlier been absent.

Northern frustration over slavery gradually built up when it became apparent that previous expectations of slavery dying a natural death were quite unrealistic. When slavery was confined, as it had been in the 1780s, to a narrow coastal strip of Virginia and the Carolinas and was not yet locked into an ever-growing world demand for cotton, such expectations were not completely unreasonable; but by 1819 they were. As an institution, slavery was healthy, prosperous, and expanding. In Kentucky, Tennessee, Alabama, and Mississippi, all states added since 1787, slaves made up one-third of the population in 1820. Nor were expectations of a decrease in the slave population borne out when Congress prohibited the African Slave Trade in 1808. Unlike other slave populations in the Western Hemisphere, which needed continual imports to maintain their size, American slaves continued to increase by natural means. In the West Indies and Latin America, on the other hand, the profits from slavery were higher, especially for sugar planters, and these profits financed the huge imports needed to replenish a labor supply of predominately young, male slaves who died off rapidly from disease and brutal working conditions.

The Missouri issue brought Northern frustrations over slavery to a climax. Slavery seemed to be moving aggressively into both the South and the West. Florida, long an objective of the Republican presidents, was about to be added to the United States under the terms of the Adams-Onís Treaty of 1819. Everyone knew that the territory would eventually enter the Union as another slave state. Moreover, the South was ready to push slavery across the Mississippi into the Louisiana Purchase territory. The North could dismiss the admission of Louisiana as a slave state in 1812 because slavery had already been established there under the Spanish and French. But Missouri was different; it was Americans who were responsible for slavery there. In vote after vote a Northern majority in Congress, prompted by a core of staunch old Federalists, tried to make gradual emancipation a precondition for the admission of Missouri. By 87 to 16, Northern congressmen also voted to keep slavery out of the newly organized Arkansas Territory. What few Federalists were left in Congress could now vote their antislavery feelings because there was no longer any Southern wing of their party left to be damaged. Northern Republicans could do likewise, secure in the knowledge that their party could not be damaged because the South, in the absence of an opposition party, had no political alternative to the Republicans.

By the narrowest of margins, the Northern majority fell short of its objectives. Just enough Northern Republicans voted with a nearly solid South to allow slavery into Arkansas and to pass what became canonized as the Missouri Compromise. The admission of Missouri as a slave state was linked with the admission of Maine as a free state, thus maintaining the happy coincidence of an even balance of slave and free states in the Senate. The southern boundary of Missouri, the famous 36° 30′ line, was extended westward through the remainder of the Louisiana Purchase territory. North of the line slavery was to be prohibited when territories were politically organized by Congress. South of the line slavery was to be permitted, although not mandated. The crisis was over. Or, to put it more precisely, Jefferson's "fire bell in the night," his metaphor for the terrifying spectre of disunion, was temporarily stilled.

Badly split along an East-West axis by the divergent economic responses to the Panic of 1819, and along a North-South axis by the divisiveness of the Missouri Compromise debates, the Republican party fractured into a politics of personalities in the early 1820s. The party had collapsed as an effective vehicle for resolving the policy differences that divided Americans. That collapse, accompanied as it was by a tendency toward sectionalized political allegiances, carried an implicit threat of disunion. That was the message of the Missouri issue in 1820 and of the confused election of 1824.

The dangerous irrelevancy of the empty shell of the Republican party to the nation's political life was starkly evident in 1824. Four candidates, all claiming to be Republicans, and each associated with a different section, vied for the Presidency. Differences over the desirability of federal funding for internal improvements between the West, which generally favored it, and the East, which opposed it, when superimposed on the North-South divisions over slavery, had the effect of sectionalizing the electorate into geographical quadrants. Identified most strongly with the Northeast was John Quincy Adams of Massachusetts; with the Southeast, William Henry Crawford of Georgia; with the Northwest, Henry Clay of Kentucky; and with the Southwest, Andrew Jackson of Tennessee. In the absence of any opposition party capable of winning office, the Republicans had no incentive with which to discipline the party into a coherent whole. The party was unable to agree upon a candidate, let alone a unified stand on the issues. Worse than useless in 1824 was the old, informal mechanism by which Republican congressmen met every four years and conferred the presidential nomination upon the incumbent Republican president or his hand-picked successor. Crawford did receive the approval of the congressional caucus, but it was a mixed blessing. His opponents charged him with being the tool of King Caucus, an aristocratic conspiracy of secretive power-seekers. As it was, only 66 out of 218 Republican congressmen even bothered to attend the meeting of the caucus in February of 1824.

With no party mechanisms to channel and focus voter identification, the rival candidates cancelled each other out in 1824. Jackson, with 43 percent of the nationwide

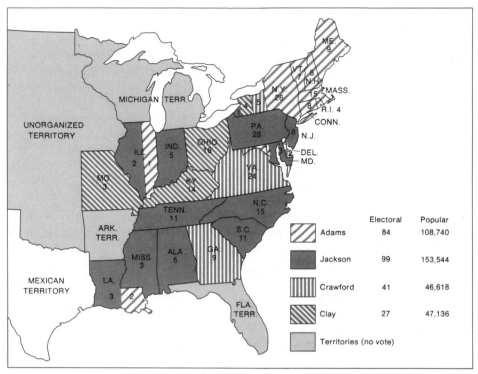

THE ELECTION OF 1824

In the four-cornered election of 1824, each of the major sections tended to identify with its own regional candidate. Aside from his poor showing in New England, Jackson was the only candidate who came close to having national appeal.

vote, was the most popular of the four candidates. But because no one received a majority of the electoral votes, as mandated by the Constitution, the election was thrown into the House of Representatives. Now, only the top three vote-getters were eligible for possible election. Clay, the low man on the totem pole, dropped out of the race. Crawford had suffered a debilitating stroke and was effectively out of the running. In choosing between Jackson and Adams, the House was influenced by an alliance between the Clay and Adams forces. As Speaker of the House and a veteran political insider, Clay was in a position to swing some key votes. In agreement with Adams' ideas on the need for centralizing federal authority, anxious to undercut his chief rival for the political favor of the West, Jackson, and enticed by a promise that he would be appointed Secretary of State, the unofficial stepping stone to the presidency in previous Republican administrations, Clay backed Adams. The result was the ill-fated Adams presidency.

Adams and the Jacksonian Democrats: 1824–1828

Probably no individual ever brought so much intellectual talent to the presidency and produced so little in his administration as did John Quincy Adams. An absolutely brilliant Secretary of State, almost single-handedly responsible for the transcontinental dimensions of the Adams-Onis Treaty of 1819 which gave the United States an undisputed window on the Pacific, and the lone voice in the Monroe cabinet in favor of the United States issuing a unilateral declaration that declared the Western Hemisphere off limits to future European colonization, the Monroe Doctrine of 1823, Adams was nonetheless an undeniable failure as president. It is hard to see how he could have succeeded. He started off with no independent base of support, be it among the voters, Congress, or his nominal party, the Republicans. He was a minority president who held office only because of a tainted, though legal, set of political dealings. What made the agreement with Clay all the more extraordinary, and undoubtedly painful for Adams, was the fact that he was generally loathe to use power for personal political ends. In this regard he was by temperament, if not age, the last of the generation of Revolutionary leaders.

Adams was a throwback to a social type of politician—the cultivated gentleman— who was now being shunted aside in the coarser politics of the 1820s. Superbly trained and educated, he viewed politics as a matter of statesmanship, the principled duty and social responsibility of those who belonged to a natural aristocracy of birth, refinement, and talent. Bargaining for political support or treating politics as a job was, at best, a distasteful necessity; at worst, it was dishonest. Thus, like his father during his administration, Adams was slow to ferret out political opponents from within his own cabinet. His party opponents gained strength as his administration dragged on. Again, much of the blame rests with Adams himself. In his first annual message to Congress in 1825, he outlined a bold vision of a positive use of federal power in a coordinated program of tariffs, internal improvements, credit, and scientific exploration. The vision was stillborn. It aroused the jealousies of too many interest groups and too many states. In it the South saw the specter of federal interference with slavery, and the West feared that it was all a cover for class legislation that would be manipulated by the creditor East.

Still, for all of Adams's weaknesses as a political leader, the failure of his presidency also represented the most obvious failure of the Republican conception of the presidency. Twenty-eight years of Republican rule from 1800 to 1828 produced only one brief period of effective presidential leadership, Jefferson's first term. Jefferson in his second term, after Congress rebelled against his embargo policy, and his three successors were all hamstrung by the isolation of their office. Viewed as the leading gentleman among a coterie of gentlemanly statesmen, the Republican president was expected to be above mere politics, not part of it. The antipower bias of republican ideology, much stronger among the Jeffersonians than the Hamiltonians, made the office of president especially suspect as a source of monarchical designs. In an effort to ensure that the office would not encroach upon the liberties of the people, the Republicans kept the president dependent upon Congress. Chosen by the party caucus in Congress, facing little, if any, Federalist opposition, the Republican president owed little to the voters at large. In turn, the voters showed little interest in the president. Prior to 1828, gubernatorial and state legislative elections almost invariably drew larger turnouts than the presidential elections. Unable to make any claim of representing all the people as a weapon in dealing with a recalcitrant Congress, the Republican president was also constrained in using what limited power he did have. The veto was resorted to rarely, and then only for very precise constitutional reasons. Patronage, the appointment of nonelected federal officials who fell under the executive's jurisdiction, was primarily a device for selecting those local notables who had the wealth, social standing, and presumed civic virtue that entitled them to serve the people. The notion of bartering patronage for legislative support or partisan purposes was viewed as an unethical affront to republicanism, a lusting after personal power.

Thus, the office that Adams inherited was one deliberately conceived and designed to be weak. Ironically, by unmistakably revealing that no organized power existed at the nation's center, the Adams presidency did have one positive result. It reinforced the growing impression among a new generation of politicians that a revived presidency with a mass electoral base structured through a new party was needed as a counterweight against the sectional drift of political loyalties in the 1820s.

The key to the successful building of any new, intersectional party in the 1820s was an open recognition that first the Federalists and then the Republicans had outlived the social order that spawned them. In the first quarter of the nineteenth century, a new political and socioeconomic environment evolved that made demands in terms of organization, voter mobilization, and issues that neither of the old parties was capable of meeting.

As compared to 1800, a politically unorganized, mass electorate had gradually formed by 1824. The number of states increased by 50 percent, from 16 to 24. The Federalists never gained a foothold in these new states, and Republican party organizations in them were hardly worthy of the name. In these new states, political life was governed by marriage alliances between landholding oligarchs who competed amongst themselves and friends for a personal following. The potential importance and size of the electorate also increased in these twenty-four years. In 1800 only two states chose presidential electors by a straight popular vote. By 1824 a majority did so, and by 1832 only one, South Carolina, still clung to the old method of having the state legislature select the electors. Property qualifications for voting in 1800 were sufficiently high to limit the suffrage to about 70 percent of the adult white males. In their constitutions the newer states set no property restrictions on voting, and the older states liberalized or abandoned their restrictions after 1800, partly to reduce voting fraud and partly in response to the rise of new classes divorced from the ownership of land. Consequently, suffrage was all but universal by 1824 for adult white males. Largely unstructured by party discipline or competition, especially at the national level, the mass electorate was an immense prize for any party that could mobilize it. The dimensions of what could be gained were quite evident in 1824. Only 25 percent of the eligible electorate bothered to vote in that presidential election.

During the same quarter of a century, rapid economic growth and social change had generated a host of new issues and interest groups. Jefferson's Embargo of 1807 and the War of 1812, by keeping out British goods, marked the real beginning of American industrialization. The political response was the heightened demand for protective tariffs after the war. The spread of the market into the West after 1815 and the Panic of 1819 politicized internal improvements, land policy, credit, and banks. The undisciplined and bloated postwar Republican party lacked the internal cohesion to resolve the policy differences or set up compromises among the clashing interests. Organized, as were the Federalists, around the eighteenth-century notion of deference, the belief that the citizenry should defer to the leadership of a natural, sociopolitical elite, the Republicans disintegrated as a functioning party once confronted with the conflicting demands of the more individualistic, acquisitive Americans of the nineteenth-century marketplace.

Out of the party chaos of 1824 emerged a new and victorious mass-based party by 1828, the Jacksonian Democrats. It was more than fitting that the new party was associated from the very beginning with Jackson's name. His incredible popularity and charisma, that rare gift of personal magnetism that can attract uncommonly devoted followers, gave his party managers the first indispensable element that was needed to restructure American politics—a leader with mass appeal. As a military hero, Jackson was already visible and popular. His stature in the Old Southwest amounted to that of a folk hero. He had met and slain the region's worst enemies —the Spanish, British, and Indians—and had opened up millions of acres for white settlement in the Southwest with his victories in the War of 1812. His political strength in the region was such that in 1828 Jackson outpolled his presidential opponent, Adams, by the astounding margins of 94 percent, 90 percent, 80 percent, and 60 percent respectively in Georgia, Tennessee, Alabama, and Mississippi. Beyond his military reputation, Jackson's career was a dramatic and colorful personification of those social traits so valued by the restless, mobile Americans of his generation. Voters identified with Jackson because he seemed like one of their own. Jackson, a brawling and poorly educated product of the Carolina back country, had risen to planter status in Tennessee through his own wits and physical strength. He was the first president who could be portrayed as having made it on his own, with no formal training, education, or family connections. A self-made product of the frontier, with an immense will power that would stare down death to take advantage of an opportunity, Jackson was anything but a privileged aristocrat in the minds of the public.

After his defeat in 1824, Jackson vowed to win the presidency. He was outraged when what he called "aristocratical influence"[7] cost him the election in the House. Comparing Clay to Judas in his treachery, Jackson pledged to undo the "corrupt bargain," the "unholy alliance" between Adams and Clay.

This alliance inadvertently presented the Jacksonians with the second element for forging a new party in the face of an unorganized electorate. In the hands of the Jacksonians, the Corrupt Bargain became the archetypical symbol for the popular discontent of the 1820s. It personified the hatred of the old political order that had brought the economy crashing down in the Panic of 1819 and that had disregarded the People's Will as expressed in the election of 1824. As a symbolic issue that cut across class and sectional lines, the Corrupt Bargain had the immense virtue of fuzziness. In their efforts to mobilize the greatest number of voters, the Jacksonians were shrewd enough to avoid any specific stand on issues. Specificity entailed the likelihood of alienating as many voters as were attracted by a clear-cut stance on sectional or economic questions. It was no way to build a mass-based party.

Jackson's popularity and the political salability of the Corrupt Bargain gave the anti-Adams forces a great edge, but the magnitude of Jackson's victory in 1828 owed at least as much to sophisticated techniques of party organization and voter mobilization developed by a new breed of state politicians who jumped onto the Jacksonian bandwagon. These were men who saw a virtue in parties that their republican predecessors could not. Middle-class or lower in social origin, anonymous and manipulative in the eyes of their social superiors, most of whom were their political opponents, the new party professionals redefined parties as good things in and of themselves. The permanence and discipline of party organization offered these men real advantages as they competed against the prestige and wealth of local notables. For Jacksonian state leaders like Martin Van Buren of New York and Amos Kendall of Kentucky, the party itself, not social connections that they never had, was the source of political power.

Van Buren, for example, was the son of a tavernkeeper. Born in the old Dutch village of Kinderhook, New York, in 1782, he had no ties to the patrician political families of the Hudson Valley. But, by converting politics into a career, by viewing it as a business and being ever quick to label his patrician opponents as a privileged aristocracy, he was able to work his way up through the ranks of the Bucktails, the rival party to the more socially prominent Clintonians. By the 1820s the discipline and party regularity of the Bucktails had paid off. With Van Buren as their leader, they ruled New York politics through a party organization known as the Albany Regency.

In Van Buren's New York, and throughout the Mid-Atlantic region as a whole, a semblance of two-party competition was always the norm after the 1790s. The region lacked the South's intense fear of a strong centralized government and New England's cultural homogeneity and rigid elites who fused Congregationalism with mercantile interests. This part of the East also had a more diverse social and economic mix than the newer states in the West. As a result, the republican ideal of an organic, harmonious community quickly gave way after 1800 to a more fragmented, pluralistic conception of the social order. A variety of political ideas competed for public attention, and politicians such as Van Buren pioneered in arguing that only a permanent party could adequately and fairly sift through these ideas to find and express the will of the majority. Allegiance to party now became a virtue, a means of ensuring that a demo-

THE ELECTION OF 1828

As in 1824, Adams was still the regional favorite of New England, but elsewhere Jackson's vote-getting appeal and the superior organization of his party carried the Democrats to a sweeping victory.

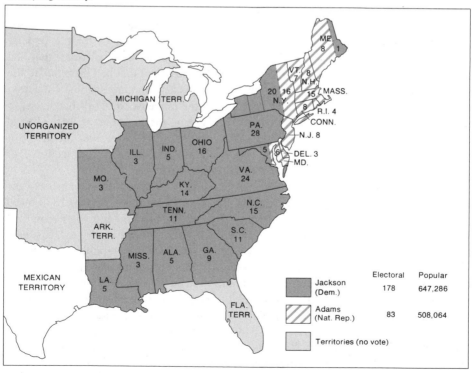

cratically run organization would successfully fight the people's battles against the aristocracy. The same arguments were heard in the West of the 1820s. Here, the impact of the Panic of 1819 telescoped party development. Demands for debtor relief catapulted hitherto obscure men such as Kendall into positions of leadership in state politics. Kendall's party in Kentucky and similar organizations in the depressed West all proclaimed the same principle: the common people had to turn to the disciplined and egalitarian structure of their own parties in order to break the oppressive link between creditors and local elites.

The Kendalls and Van Burens, on a scale not seen before in American politics, built up grassroots organizations that called out the voters in support of a presidential candidate. Beginning with the election of 1828, the Jacksonian party managers used newspaper chains for publicity, campaign workers to get out the vote, county and district conventions to nominate candidates, physical symbols, such as Old Hickory sticks and buttons, to familiarize the ties between the party faithful and their leader, and massive rallies and barbecues to entertain the public while instructing them. The result was a surge in voter turnout and a victory of sweeping proportions. Not only did Jackson carry every state west and south of Pennsylvania, but the percentage of eligible voters who participated in the 1828 election (56 percent) more than doubled the figure for 1824 (26 percent).

The Bank War and Nullification

The leader, issue, and organization had come together in 1828 to put the Jacksonians into power. Over the next twelve years, two more elements were added that trans-formed what might otherwise have been the temporary victory of pro-Jackson men into a national party system structured around close two-party competition in all the sec-tions. First, out of the political struggles over the Bank of the United States and Nullification in 1832–1833, the Jacksonians acquired a permanent party image, a combination of style, tone, and rhetoric, that stamped the party in the minds of the public as the friend of the Union and the common man. With this image the party became something more than just the personal followers of Jackson; it became a lasting institution known as the Democratic party. The Bank War and Nullification were also, as a consequence both of the Democratic victories and the very way in which they achieved those victories, the catalysts for the formation of an effective opposition party to the Democrats. By raising the constant threat of electoral defeat, this party, called the Whigs, reinforced internal discipline and party zeal among the Democrats. With the first major national victories of the Whigs in 1840, the party system of Democrats and Whigs was firmly in place.

Apart from a real, though quite amorphous, identification with reform and loud demands for restoring the federal government to the republican simplicity of Jefferson's years in office, the Jacksonians had no particular program in 1828. To the extent that the party had any definite orientation toward the use of federal power, the states'-rights philosophy of Van Buren came closest to summarizing party attitudes. In an insight that was brilliant in its simplicity, Van Buren realized that any attempt to formulate a national program to deal with sectional issues and the economy was bound to fail. At bottom, slavery was a question of morality not susceptible to the compromis-ing skills of a politician. As for the political economy, there was no way to satisfy everyone. Far better, argued Van Buren, to turn the problem over to the states and localities and rationalize the decision in constitutional terms.

Once in power, the Jacksonians discovered that even a loose coalition of state and local interests needed some ideological cement to keep the party from flying apart. Talk of reform was one thing, but the record of Jacksonian appointees to federal office left the party exposed to the same charges of corruption it had leveled against the Adams forces. Corruption probably did increase under the Jacksonians. Party loyalty, not social standing, now became the criterion for appointment. As one appointee, William T. Barry, told another: "[You] received the appt. . . . under the full impression that you were ready and willing to take upon yourself the entire responsibility of cooperating with the administration in its measures."[8] Turnovers in office became more frequent, and each group of partisans accused the others of milking the offices for all they were worth. Secondly, the nascent federal bureaucracy grew very rapidly under the Jacksonians, in part because the party paid the costs of mass electioneering by creating jobs for its campaign workers. This was especially true in the post office and the land office, in both of which the number of positions doubled in the 1830s. Although administrators like Kendall, postmaster general under Jackson, began to implement such bureaucratic controls as frequent audits, close supervision, and routinization of duties, unprecedentedly spectacular corruption did occur. In the mid-1830s Samuel Swartwout, Jackson's appointee as collector of customs for the port of New York, left the country with $1,225,706 in embezzled customhouse funds. That sum represented about 8 percent of all federal expenditures in an average year in the late 1820s.

The call for fiscal retrenchment, with its implied promise to restore the government to a purer republican simplicity, conflicted with the institutional needs of the party. During Jackson's two terms, from 1828 to 1836, federal spending doubled, and most of the increase went toward internal improvements. Despite the much-publicized Maysville Road Veto of 1830, in which Jackson vetoed a federal subsidy for a local road within Kentucky, the home state of his most bitter enemy, Clay, Congress under Jackson spent more money on internal improvements than had all of its predecessors combined. Congress became the conduit through which the party, as a servicing agent, met the needs of the local constituents who had voted the party into power.

Drift and disarray characterized most of Jackson's first term. Jackson himself was obsessively preoccupied with the Eaton Affair. A close friend of Jackson's and his choice for Secretary of War, John Eaton, was engaged to Peggy Timberlake. To official Washington society, led by the wife of Jackson's vice-president, John Calhoun, the engagement was scandalous, because Peggy's former husband was rumored to have committed suicide upon receiving news that, while he was away on naval duty, his wife was having an affair with Eaton. Quite the contrary, insisted Jackson; he declared the future Mrs. Eaton to be chaste and pure and made it clear that anyone who disagreed was now his political enemy. Having been unable to defend his wife Rachel from the slanders of the 1828 campaign, Jackson was convinced that Rachel's death shortly after his election resulted from a heart broken by the filth slung at her by his enemies, including, of course, Clay. Now, through Peggy, he could vindicate Rachel's memory and lash out at those cowardly enough to defame a woman's honor in an effort to break up his political family. Van Buren, who happened to be a widower, went out of his way to ingratiate himself with Jackson by openly siding with the Eatons. Meanwhile, Calhoun's political stock sank lower and lower in Jackson's estimation.

The political repercussions of the affair climaxed in the spring of 1831 when five of the six members of Jackson's cabinet resigned. The divided Jacksonians, reduced almost to the point of brawling, were hardly a cohesive party as yet. In the spring of 1832, Henry Clay, quite an unexpected source, set the stage for the rebuilding of Jacksonian unity around a clear ideological position. The Bank War was about to begin.

After Adams' miserable showing in 1828, Clay assumed the leadership of the anti-Jackson forces, a group known as the National Republicans. As part of his bid for the presidency in 1832 and his search for a winning issue, Clay, with the approval of Nicholas Biddle, the Bank's president since 1822, pushed a bill through Congress for the early rechartering of the Bank. The Bank's federal charter was not scheduled to expire until 1836. In early 1832 the Bank was about as popular as it ever became with Americans. The country was in the midst of a renewed cycle of economic expansion, and the Bank, under Biddle's adroit control, was superbly meeting its responsibilities. It provided a stable national currency through its bank notes, accounted for one-fifth of the nation's loans, chiefly bills of exchange (IOUs drawn against crops in transit between producers and purchasers), and safely handled one-third of all bank deposits and specie through its legal role as the official depository for the funds of the federal government. Clay, assuming that the Bank would be approached on its economic merits, felt that he had Jackson trapped. An early rechartering would highlight Clay's economic foresight; Jackson's attempt to block the new charter would expose him as an economic fool. Clay's strategy was clever, but it backfired when Jackson converted the issue from an economic one to a symbolic one of outraged public morality.

The Bank was politically vulnerable, because in fact it did occupy a privileged economic position. Only the Bank of the United States could ignore the objections of states and establish branches within their borders; the Bank was by law the only depository of federal funds; and its leadership, both at Philadelphia and the two dozen branches, came from established social elites. Jackson used the privileges and sheer economic power of the Bank as a springboard to depict the Bank as a monster, an unnatural monopoly of government-granted privilege that violated republican liberties and corrupted public morality. With words that suggested to Biddle "all the fury of a chained panther biting the bars of his cage," Jackson called upon all the real producers of wealth to support him in his Bank Veto of July 10, 1832:[9]

> When the laws undertake to add . . . artificial distinctions, to grant titles, gratuities, and exclusive privileges, to make the rich richer and the potent more powerful, the humble members of society—the farmers, mechanics, and laborers—who have neither the time nor the means of securing like favors to themselves, have a right to complain of the injustices of their Government.

On two separate occasions, the Clay forces in Congress failed to override Jackson's vetoes. Government deposits, the lifeblood of the Bank, were removed in 1833 at Jackson's insistence. Although there is no evidence that the Bank War enhanced the Jacksonians' popularity, it did cement their claim to represent the common man. In a society in which political consciousness and economic expectations were rising in unison, the Jacksonians could now proclaim that only they had the courage to defend the right of the common man to rise unimpeded by the grants of unfair privileges to others. Moreover, the Jacksonians offered common Americans a symbolic resolution for the disturbing changes that accompanied the spread of the market—the hectic mobility, social dislocation, breakup of families, and loss of individual autonomy. All these social costs of economic change, the Jacksonians argued, were magnified and worsened by the unrepublican speculation produced by the paper-money system of banks. By first destroying the most loathsome bank, the Bank of the United States, and then trying to require other banks to rely primarily upon the honest value of hard coinage, the Jacksonians promised to weed out paper money and restore hard work and stability to the social order. Such measures, said Jackson, would "do more to revive and perpetuate those habits of economy and simplicity which are so congenial to the character of republicans than all the legislation which has yet been attempted."[10]

Jackson forced the Bank issue once Clay and Biddle presented him with it. The other crisis that came to a head in 1832–1833, Nullification, was forced on Jackson by South Carolina planters. Elaborating on precedents first set forth by Jefferson and Madison in the Virginia and Kentucky Resolutions of 1798, statements of Republican opposition against what they saw as tyrannical Federalist centralization, Calhoun worked out a full-blown constitutional theory by which an individual state could nullify, or declare void within its borders, a federal law.

Calhoun started from the premise that the Union was a compact of states in which final sovereignty continued to rest with the states. In his secretly written *South Carolina Exposition* of 1828 he reasoned that a state, if confronted with a federal law it held to be unconstitutional, had the right to demand the passage of a constitutional amendment to grant the specific federal power in dispute. Because any constitutional amendment required first a two-thirds approval in Congress, and then a three-fourths approval by the states, Calhoun in effect was seeking the same minority veto over majority power that the Hartford Federalists had proposed in 1814. Calhoun, however, went considerably further. If all constitutional remedies failed, he concluded that a state could resort to nullification and, as a final measure, secession.

In the fall of 1832, a special South Carolina convention nullified the tariffs of 1828 and 1832 and declared that as of February 1, 1833, they would no longer be enforceable within the state. The key to Jackson's subsequent victory over the Nullifiers was the fact that South Carolina stood virtually alone in its open defiance of federal authority. A unique racial demography and a very conservative political structure distinguished the Palmetto State from its slaveholding neighbors. In 1830 South Carolina was the only state with an absolute majority of blacks. Its 56 percent black majority, mostly slaves, was concentrated on the sea-islands and tidal flats south of Charleston. In this plantation district, the black majority approached 95 percent in the summer months, when wealthy whites fled from malaria and yellow fever. In addition, South Carolina had been the only state that kept open the African slave trade until 1808. As a result, the sea-islands harbored a sizable minority of African-born, unassimilated slaves who appeared especially threatening to white security. The same low-country planters who lived surrounded by the overwhelming presence of black slaves also controlled state politics. After 1810 all adult white males could vote, but very high property qualifications for officeholding kept power in the hands of the planter elite. The state legislature appointed most officials, including the presidential electors. Thus, once the elite decided on a maverick role, it had tremendous leverage with which to influence public opinion in the state.

In playing the maverick role of Nullifiers, the elite orchestrated a stunning political campaign in which federal tariffs, much like the Bank for Jacksonians as a whole, symbolized both corrupting outside power and painful socioeconomic changes. By the 1820s, South Carolina was already an old cotton state: the collapse of cotton prices in the Panic of 1819, soil erosion, competition from cotton produced on cheaper, more fertile western lands, and an outflow of whites totaling 200,000 between 1820 and 1860 left the state reeling under the problems of economic adjustment. Up-country slaveholders incurred heavy losses when upland cotton prices fell by 72 percent between 1818 and 1829, and they were receptive to the Nullifiers' argument, which blamed the tariff for their plight. The average import duties under federal tariffs had increased from 20 percent in 1816 to 30 percent in 1824, and then leaped to 50 percent in 1828 before a downward revision to 33 percent in 1832. These duties, argued the Nullifiers, were an unfair and unconstitutional tax on farmers. By raising prices for domestic manufactured goods and potentially limiting export markets for agricultural products, the tariffs penalized one class for the profits of another. But a protective tariff, which nowhere was specifically authorized in the Constitution, was not the main issue for the Nullifiers. An editorial in 1830 stressed that "the Tariff is only one of the subjects of complaint. . . . The Internal Improvements, the general bribery system, and the interference with our domestic policy—most particularly the latter—are things which . . . will, if necessary be met with more than words."[11] Stripped of its bland euphemism, "domestic policy" meant slavery. The leaders of Nullification were rice and sea-island cotton planters whose economic fortunes had held up quite well during the 1820s. The fear of losing control over their black majority, not concern over losing cotton profits, drove these men into political radicalism.

The 1820s began with the bitter debates over the Missouri Compromise and the temporary formation in Congress of a Northern majority against the spread of slavery. Two years later, Charleston was rocked by the Denmark Vesey Plot, a well-planned slave uprising that was betrayed at the last minute. The Ohio Resolutions of 1824, which would have emancipated slaves at the age of 21 if they agreed to be colonized in Africa, touched off annual debates in Congress over a variety of proposals for federal subsidies to underwrite African colonization of freed slaves. The decade ended with the publication of David Walker's *Appeal to the Colored Citizens of the World*. Written by a North Carolina free black living in Boston, the *Appeal* was a scathing, vitriolic indictment of white greed and a call for revolutionary resistance by the enslaved. Nat Turner's bloody slave uprising in Southampton County, Virginia, in the summer of 1831 served to confirm the Nullifiers' worst fears. Before Turner and his followers were captured and executed, about 60 whites had been killed. Uncounted blacks were massacred by vengeful white mobs.

In all of these episodes the Nullifiers saw a common pattern. Dark, malevolent, and conspiratorial forces were encircling the local world of the farm and plantation. Encroaching, uncontrollable outside power that expressed itself in unconstitutional tariffs, schemes for federal internal improvements, and meddling with slavery had to be checked by the manly independence of South Carolina's native sons. In a culture in which power was based on the open, personal display of patriarchal authority over slaves, wives, and children, any challenge to the autonomy of white males was an attack on the core of male self-esteem. The horror of losing independence could not be escaped; it was daily evidenced in the presence of the black slaves. Submission to the tariff, preached the Nullifiers, would mean shame and degradation that was fully equivalent to being enslaved. To Robert Barnwell Rhett, it meant being "destitute of

From Nullification to Despotism. This cartoon, which appeared at the height of the
Nullification Crisis in 1833, depicts Calhoun as the archenemy of the republic, intent on
seizing the crown of despotism. Jackson, at lower right, is uttering his famous warning that he
would hang a few traitors in order to save the Union. (Historical Pictures Service, Chicago)

every principle of manhood.'' Another Nullifier, Waddy Thompson, put the issue of
submission more graphically. Anyone who so dishonored himself by failing to resist
the tariff should adopt as his national emblem ''a spaniel kissing the rod''[12] of his
master.

By merging concern over economic decline with the phobia over slave uprisings in
a stirring rhetoric that demanded actions befitting free men, the Nullifiers tapped into
the generalized fear of South Carolina whites over the menace of outside power.
Superheated, as it were, by the rural isolation of a slaveholding society, this very
traditional republican ideology was instrumental in making the Nullifiers the majority
party in South Carolina by the early 1830s. They had grown so strong so swiftly that
Calhoun had no choice but to assume public leadership of the movement.

Jackson decisively met the Nullification crisis. The Nullifiers, from his perspective, were led by a spiteful, personal enemy, Calhoun; they had refused to accept
Jackson at his word when he repeatedly pledged to work for a lowering of the tariff;
and, to add insult to injury, South Carolina had not even backed Jackson in his

reelection in 1832. Congress passed a Force Bill in January, 1833, which gave Jackson explicit military power and authorization to put down Nullification by force, if necessary. Civil war was a real possibility, because the Nullifiers had announced that they would meet federal coercion with armed resistance. To forestall this possibility, as well as to win Southern backing for the Force Bill, Congress also passed a new tariff, the Compromise Tariff of 1833, which ostensibly met South Carolina's demand for economic relief. Put together by Clay, Calhoun, and Daniel Webster of Massachusetts, this tariff lowered duties to a maximum rate of 20 percent, but the reductions were spread over a decade, and most of them were sandwiched into the two years from 1840 to 1842. The Nullifiers backed down, and the Jacksonians won their image as defenders of the Union.

The Rise of the Whigs: 1832–1840

In defeating the Bank and the Nullifiers, Jackson redefined the presidency as the only federal office representing all of the people. His bold and strident proclamations of executive power were unprecedented. Earlier presidents had resorted to the veto a total of nine times; Jackson alone used it a dozen times. He also used the hitherto unheard of, but constitutionally valid, argument that the president could veto legislation on any grounds he so chose. In dominating his administration, Jackson left no doubts that cabinet members served only at his pleasure. He summarily dismissed two Secretarys of the Treasury before he found one, Roger Taney, who would sign the legal order for the removal of deposits from the Bank. And, unlike any of his predecessors, he took his case directly to the people with an egalitarian rhetoric that his opponents labeled as demagoguery designed to incite mob fury.

Jackson's defiance of established procedures, his willingness to ignore congressional opinion, which he could neither shape nor control, and the very aggressiveness of his style of leadership set off shock waves that brought together the unlikely triumvirate of Clay and Webster, the nationalists, and Calhoun, the Nullifier. Tempermentally and philosophically at odds with each other, these men, like the early Whig party as a whole, were united in the beginning only by their opposition to Jackson. They spoke for an earlier, more elitist tradition of republicanism that insisted that the will of the people should be filtered through the leadership of a small group of cultivated and confidential gentlemen. That was the very leadership that Jackson was now bypassing in his direct appeals to the people. The issue, as the new Whig party saw it, was the executive tyranny of King Andrew. Thus, the party named itself the Whigs in reference to the parliamentary opponents of monarchial despotism in eighteenth-century England.

The Clay-Adams faction of the Old National Republicans, Southern states'-righters shocked by the nationalistic implications of Jackson's Force Bill, and conservative pro-Bank Democrats from the Northeast comprised the original nucleus of the Whig party. Rounding out their initial public support were converts from the Antimasonic Party. Organized as a party in 1827, the Antimasons combined evangelical intensity with egalitarian impatience. They were the first popularly based party that insisted that equal access to power necessitated a leveling attack on all forms of special privilege. By linking their egalitarian demands with traditional republican themes, they introduced new forms of appealing to voters that party professionals in the Democratic and Whig parties would subsequently follow.

Western New York, a region undergoing rapid economic growth and social change with the opening of the Erie Canal, and a fertile source of recruits for Finney's revivals, was the seed bed of Antimasonry. William Morgan, an artisan and Freemason in Batavia, New York, was on the verge of publicly exposing the fraternal secrets of the Order of Freemasons when he was kidnapped and presumably murdered in 1826. Morgan's disappearance (no trace of him was ever found) triggered a public outcry for a full investigation. When it appeared that the truth was being covered up, antimasonic sentiment spilled over into a full-fledged political party. In 1830 the party won nearly half the vote in New York. In scattered regions of New England and the Mid-Atlantic states, the Antimasons became the major opposition party to the Jacksonians.

The appeal of Antimasonry was persuasive because, much like the Jacksonian's attack on the Bank and the Nullifiers' indictment of the tariff, it pinpointed and personalized threatening change. In this instance, the conspiracy against individual autonomy and public liberties, the fountain of corrupting, special privilege, was the fraternal order of Freemasons. Because Masons tended to monopolize political and economic power in western New York, public resentment against landlords and local creditors could effectively be fused with popular suspicions about a secret organization that seemed to offer its members unfair advantages in the race for wealth and distinction. Moreover, many who were troubled by the disintegration of village consensus in the highly competitive and commercially oriented economy of western New York sensed that the old social order was literally being subverted from within. Again the Masons, secret and powerful, were a ready target for popular anxieties. In their pointedly named Anti Masonic Declaration of Independence, the citizens of Le Roy, New York, attacked the Masons for belonging to an aristocratic, unchristian, intemperate, and unpatriotic institution "unfit to exist among a free people."[13] By bestowing special favors on its members, Masonry violated equal opportunity and was aristocratic; by hiding itself from public view and access, it was unrepublican; and, by entrapping individual consciences in ritual and dogma, it was unchristian. Here, in other words, was another monster.

Initially, the affinity between Antimasonry and Whiggery was something of an accident. In western New York, the original home of the Antimasons, power at the local level was wielded by insiders close to the Albany Regency of Martin Van Buren. In their espousal of equal justice and social equality, the Antimasons naturally focused on local Democrats as the entrenched, aristocratic elite who had to be tossed out of office. Because the most obvious example of a licensed monopoly of aristocratic privilege in western New York was the Safety-Fund system of state banks controlled by the Albany Regency, the Antimasons had another reason to be anti-Jacksonians. Realizing the potential of Antimasonry for shaping a mass electorate organized in opposition to the Democrats, future Whigs such as Thurlow Weed and William Seward of New York, and Thaddeus Stevens of Pennsylvania, used the extraordinary, but somewhat ephemeral, appeal of Antimasonry as the basis for building a permanent, anti-Jacksonian party. Thus, despite the fact that the elitism of a Webster was quite obvious when he criticized Jackson's Bank veto, Webster found himself in the same Whig party as the Antimasons who saw elitism and favoritism in the Albany Regency.

Before the Whigs could win a national election, the diverse and often contradictory elements in the party had to coalesce into an ongoing, functional unit held together by group discipline and driven by the need to appeal to a mass electorate. The Whigs were slower than the Democrats in learning how to win in an age of mass electioneering. Grassroots organization of the electorate, something the Democrats had a firm grasp on by 1828, was a critical weakness for the Whigs until the late 1830s. The crux of the Whigs' hatred of Jackson was the fact that he appealed directly to the people for support. Understandably, with their emphasis on the need for natural deference to the rule of an enlightened elite, the Whigs saw Jackson as a demagogue and reasoned that the people should come to them. This attitude practically guaranteed Whig failure when the opposition was as skilled as the Democrats in getting out the vote.

The turning point in the maturing of the Whigs as a party came with the election of 1836. Up to then, the Whigs and their Clay-Adams nucleus had been virtually paralyzed by their inability as a party to compete against Jackson's personal popularity. This election, a presidential victory for Van Buren over the four regional candidates of the Whigs, revealed to the Whigs that party organization and electioneering techniques were the real keys to national success. Jackson had not run, and yet the Democrats still held the presidency with a candidate who had nowhere near Jackson's appeal to the electorate. In particular, the election results gave the Whigs an incentive to organize in the South. A measure of the drop-off in Democratic support in the South was their sharply reduced margin of victory in 1836 as compared to 1832. Jackson bested Clay by an average margin of 46 percent in the slave states, but Van Buren led his Whig opponents by only 9 percent. In addition, Georgia and Tennessee went to the Whigs in 1836. The Democrats, without Jackson heading the ticket, were clearly vulnerable to further Whig inroads. Of a more immediate consequence, however, was the good fortune of the Whigs in having a Democratic administration in power when the Panic of 1837 hit.

In a cycle of boom and bust similar to what had happened from 1815 to 1819, the buoyant economy crashed in 1837. The long boom that had started in 1821 ended when the Bank of England raised interest rates and curtailed the flow of British capital into the American economy. Cotton, the main security for the American credit system, fell in price. Because British credit had been fundamental in financing the American boom, and because high cotton prices were essential for confidence in the ability of Americans to carry a foreign debt and finance imports, the result of the British action was a financial panic in which American banks suspended redemption of their notes in specie. After a brief recovery in 1838, a replay of the same events in 1839 drove the economy into a prolonged deflation. Americans were riding quite an economic roller coaster. The index of wholesale commodity prices, measured at the start of the year, climbed by 51 percent from 1830 to 1837 and then plunged by 46 percent before it bottomed out in 1843. The plentiful investment capital of the 1830s dried up and then fell by 23 percent between 1838 and 1843.

Complex shifts in the international flow of specie, not the economic policies of the Democrats, were the most immediate cause of the Panic of 1837. Nonetheless, the most commonsensical explanation of what happened, and certainly the most politically expedient one for the Whigs, appeared to be that Jackson's destruction of the Bank and shifting of federal deposits to selected state banks, the so-called Pet Banks, had unleashed a flood of bank notes and speculative credit that inevitably led to a day of deflationary reckoning. In fact, state banks did not change their lending policies; the ratio of reserves to liabilities stayed fairly constant from 1833 to 1836. Yet the Democrats, the party that had so dramatized banking as a moral issue between the people and the paper aristocrats, could hardly avoid popular blame for the Panic. The Democrats had politicized banks, and these banks, with deposits put there by the Jacksonians, had violated the public trust by reneging on their promise to honor redemptions in specie. Unable to protect themselves from their own rhetoric, the Democrats were thus impaled on the same antibank stake that they had driven into the public consciousness.

A final shuffling of party lines occurred during Van Buren's administration. Calhoun and most of his following of Southern states'-righters returned to the Democrats, the party in which they were always most ideologically comfortable. Crossing over in the opposite direction were conservative, soft-money Democrats. Many of these men had favored the destruction of the Bank, because they felt it would result in expanding opportunities for entrepreneurs denied credit by Biddle's Bank; they were not opposed to banks per se. But hard-money Democrats, poorer farmers and disgruntled laborers who were suspicious of paper money as a cause of inflation and who hated all banks, not just the Bank of the United States, were the backbone of Jackson's support on the Bank issue. As a result, the Democrats moved toward a hard-money position. The Treasury attempted to regulate the Pet Banks by limiting the amount of small-denomination bank notes they could issue. Decrying this policy as unwarranted government interference with the interests of the state bankers, entrepreneurial Democrats began to leave for the Whig party.

The departures of soft-money Democrats became a stampede with the introduction of the Independent Treasury System with Van Buren's backing in 1837. This Democratic measure set up government receivers, or subtreasuries, for federal funds. Because it was designed to phase out private credit in the form of bank notes, the plan met with the nearly unanimous opposition of state bankers and their political allies. This was of minor concern to the Democrats, compared to the immense political benefits of the Independent Treasury System. The party could now proclaim that it had prevented the paper aristocracy from speculating with the people's money. No longer would federal deposits serve as the backing for private bank notes. The Democrats restored ideological purity by at last divorcing themselves from their incestuous and politically damaging relationship with state banks.

In an election that reversed the roles and symbolism of the campaign of 1828, the Whigs defeated the Democrats in 1840. Now it was Van Buren, not John Quincy Adams, who was portrayed as an aristocrat sneering at the popular will, and it was William Henry Harrison, the Whig candidate who had been a general in the War of 1812, who played Jackson's role of the military hero who rose from humble origins to become the friend of the common man. The Whigs had learned their lessons well. They passed over their most prominent leader, Clay, blurred the issues, and put together a frolicking campaign of slogans, pomp, and parades. The *Democratic Review* ironically muttered, ''We have taught them to conquer us!''[14]

Party Appeals and Voters

The campaign of 1840 capstoned the party revolution that had begun in 1824. Grassroots party organizations tripled voter turnout, from 25 percent of those eligible in 1824 to 78 percent in 1840. What the Democrats started between 1824 and 1828, in

The Whig Campaign in 1840. Emotional appeals to the common man were essential to successful campaigning in the new age of mass politics. Although Harrison was a member of the Virginia slaveholding aristocracy, the Whigs used the log cabin symbol to link him to the common man and won the election. (Historical Pictures Service, Chicago)

terms of fashioning an active, mass electorate, the Whigs completed between 1836 and 1840. The personalized and sectional political factions of 1824 were molded into evenly balanced, trans-sectional political parties by 1840. As this revolution in organization and involvement gathered momentum, politics emerged as a cultural form all its own, a public forum for identifying, debating, and displaying the conflicting attitudes that Americans held regarding the massive, often sudden, shifts in their material environment.

The underlying issue was change—how Americans reacted to it and how it was to be ordered. Because the change was so pervasive, and because the market revolution generated anxieties over how social order was to be maintained and individual autonomy preserved, the parties competed with each other in offering the voters outlets for these anxieties and proposals for maintaining order. This competition fed on itself, because each party mobilized its supporters by identifying threats to republicanism, such as the Monster Bank or King Andrew, and then promising to eliminate that threat if elected. In this sense, politics provided a language invested with symbolic meanings that enabled the voters, by relating to the symbols that best reinforced their own values, to place themselves in one of the two great partisan camps.

The Whigs appealed to those who favored the positive use of governmental power to promote more economic change and simultaneously to control and regulate the social consequences of that change. The class and ethnic identity of these Americans tended to merge. Native-born Protestants who were at the top of the class structure, the old mercantile elite, and those on the way up—aspiring and prosperous farmers, artisan-businessmen, and the new middle class—comprised the rank and file of Whig supporters. These were the winners in the marketplace, or those who sensed they were

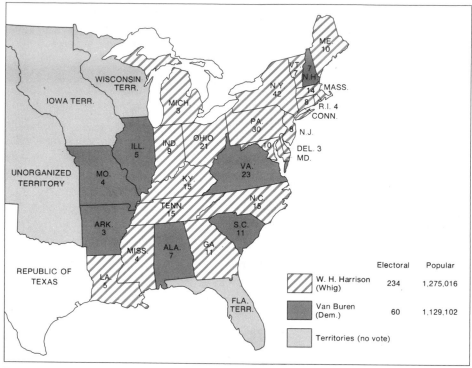

THE ELECTION OF 1840

In 1840 the Whigs arrived as a major national party. The Harrison ticket ran well in all sections of the country and, in particular, made major inroads in formerly Democratic states in the South and West.

going to be. They welcomed the Whig program of banks, protective tariffs, internal improvements, and the freer and more general use of a new form of business organization, the corporation, because all of these measures promised to promote more of the change that had benefited them. As long as this change was ordered according to the Protestant cultural norms with which these Americans had been raised, and which defined for them the moral guidelines of the good society, further economic change was not to be feared.

The threat to order came from the poor and those outside the mainstream of evangelicalized Yankee culture. Thus, working-class Catholic immigrants were immediately suspect as potential subversives of republican order. The Whigs offered these Americans, as well as the poor in general, a program of economic incentives and moral guidance. With an egalitarian emphasis brought to the party by the Antimasons, the Whigs argued that the incentives would flow from an expanding economy that would promote real equality by giving all men the opportunity to improve their material conditions. In particular, the use of government funds for a transportation network would equalize opportunities by drawing into the market those previously denied access to it. Moral guidance, on the other hand, was to be imposed by the Protestant guardians of republican virtue. Wherever possible, the Whigs relied on the voluntary efforts of reform societies. Where private initiatives were insufficient, as in education, the use of alcohol, and, from their perspective, the desecration of the Protestant Sabbath, the Whigs turned to state coercion. Far more so than the Democrats, the Whigs supported state-run common schools, prohibition, and Sabbatarian legislation, which decreed what business and social activities had to be curtailed or abandoned on Sundays. In all of these areas, the Whigs insisted that their goal was a virtuous, egalitarian society. The schools, for example, by equalizing knowledge and teaching morality, would promote the growth of the Christian middle class. Still, coercion was just below the surface, and its presence was a prime reason why other Americans were Democrats.

In contrast to the Whigs, who expressed Americans' fear of disorder, the Democrats reflected fears about the loss of personal independence. The Democrats appealed to those who favored a weak or negative use of governmental power. The party sanctioned the use of a strong executive for the removal of artificial barriers to the equality of opportunity, the destruction of the Bank being the prime example; but the crux of its republicanism was the demand that the government leave the individual alone in both economic matters and issues of morality. Drawing their mass support from the economically marginal—farmers who were on the periphery of the market, or whose local trade was disrupted by the intrusion of the market in the form of outside farm produce, and laborers forced out of artisan production when they could no longer compete against factory goods—the Democrats spoke to the victims of the market. Whereas the Whig farmer saw higher profits in more internal improvements, his Democratic counterpart saw higher taxes, more expensive land, and unwanted competition. For the Whig businessman, paper money was a convenient form of credit for expanding production. For the Democratic laborer, it was the cause of wild fluctuations in prices and wages that profited only the monied corporations. As Jackson explained in his final presidential address:[15]

> The mischief springs from the power which the moneyed interest derives from a paper currency which they are able to control, from the multitude of corporations with exclusive privileges which they have succeeded in obtaining in the different states, and which are employed altogether for their benefit.

The market meant liberating prosperity for the Whigs but crushing dependency for the Democrats. Beware the banks, cautioned Van Buren, for they "produce throughout society a chain of dependence;" they "nourish, in preference to the manly virtues that give dignity to human nature, a craving desire for luxurious enjoyment and sudden wealth, which renders those who seek them dependent on those who supply them. . . ."[16] Democratic ideology was thus a political message of resentment, an argument that the market meant pain and loss.

The non-English immigrants, who equated a strong government with an overbearing aristocracy similar to that which had oppressed them in Europe, and states'-rights Southerners, who saw in the Whig program a subterfuge by which the federal government would gain the power to interfere with slavery, were also in the Democratic fold. The urban Catholic immigrant and the rural Protestant slaveholder were political allies because of their common fear that governmental power would be used against them. Both as Catholics and as workers, the immigrants resented the support their Protestant employers gave to temperance and Sabbatarian legislation. The Whig reformers, by trying to change the drinking habits of the Irish and Germans, dictating to them how their time should be spent on Sundays, and using the common schools for the dissemination of Protestant beliefs, reinforced the immigrants' conviction that the Democrats were the party of individual conscience.

The two-party system achieved a synthesis that was beautifully balanced by 1840. Americans were almost exactly divided numerically between the two parties. In an ideological sense, as well, the parties had an equal share of the electorate. Each party spoke to different fears that were rooted in traditional republican doctrine and that registered one's place in the class and ethnic hierarchy. The emerging market produced anxieties; as an outlet for these anxieties, the parties offered a choice of competing ideologies. Cutting across sectional lines, these ideologies were presented to the voters in powerful, cultural symbols of greed, tyranny, disorder, and dependency. In the 1840s Americans began to reshape these ideologies in very direct and explicit sectional terms. Once this process started, the political synthesis of 1840 began to crack along sectional lines as well.

SUGGESTED READING

The best introduction to the literature on early American republicanism is Robert E. Shallope, "Toward a Republican Synthesis," WMQ 29 (1972), and "Republicanism and Early American Historiography," WMQ 39 (1982). J. G. A. Pocock, *The Machiavellian Moment: Florentine Political Thought and the Atlantic Republican Tradition* (1975), traces the transmission of classical republican ideas to eighteenth-century America. Picking up where Bernard Bailyn, *The Ideological Origins of the American Revolution* (1967), leaves off, Gordon S. Wood, *The Creation of the American Republic, 1776–1787* (1969), masterfully shows how republicanism changed in the social and political context of revolutionary America. Whereas Pocock and Wood see a tension in republicanism between civic virtue and private commerce, Joyce Appleby, "The Social Origins of American Revolutionary Ideology," JAH 64 (1978), and Isaac Kramnick, "Republican Revisionism Revisited," AHR 87 (1982), argue that republicanism was predominately an ideology of economic individualism and material self-interest. This is also the position of John P. Diggins, *The Lost Soul of American Politics* (1984). Robert Kelley, "Ideology and Political Culture from Jefferson to Nixon," AHR 82 (1977), makes a persuasive çase for the existence of four distinct variations of republicanism in the early nineteenth century.

Robert H. Wiebe, *The Opening of American Society* (1984), is a provocative, new interpretation of the period from the Constitution to the Civil War. John C. Miller, *The Federalist Era, 1789–1801* (1960), and Marshall Smelser, *The Democratic Republic, 1801–1815* (1968), are solid political narratives on the early national period. Though clearly outdated in some areas, Henry Adams, *History of the United States During the Administration of Jefferson and Madison* (9 vols., 1889–91), is often brilliant in its insights and is still the most comprehensive treatment of the first Republican administrations. The most recent interpretation of the Federalists and Republicans is Joyce Appleby, *Capitalism and a New Social Order* (1984), a stimulating work that connects the market expansion of commercial agriculture to the democratic aspirations of the Jeffersonians. Seymour Martin Lipset, *The First New Nation* (1963), and William N. Chambers, *Political Parties in a New Nation* (1963), provide a comparative and sociological context in which to approach the early American parties. Paul Goodman, "The First American Party System," in William N. Chambers and Walter D. Burnham, eds., *The American Party Systems: Stages of Political Development* (1967) is a stunning piece of social and political synthesis. For understanding why the very legitimacy of political parties was not initially taken for granted, see Richard Hofstadter, *The Idea of a Party System* (1969). Three excellent sources on political culture in the early nineteenth century are: James S. Young, *The Washington Community, 1800–*

1828 (1966); Ralph Ketcham, *Presidents above Party. The First American Presidency, 1789–1829* (1984); and Ronald P. Formisano, "Deferential-Participant Politics: The Early Republic's Political Culture, 1789–1840," APSR 68 (1974).

The close connection between Republican ideas on political economy and the coming of the War of 1812 is explained in Drew R. McCoy, *The Elusive Republic* (1980), and J. C. A. Stagg, *Mr. Madison's War* (1983). Republican party fears over the future of free government are stressed in Roger H. Brown, *The Republic in Peril* (1964), and Bradford Perkins, *Prologue to War: England and the United States, 1805–1812* (1961), is thorough on the diplomatic background to the war. James M. Banner, *To the Hartford Convention: The Federalists and the Origins of Party Politics in Massachusetts, 1789–1815* (1970), is the best source on the Hartford Convention, and Shaw Livermore, Jr., *The Twilight of Federalism* (1962), relates the rapid collapse of the Federalists after 1815. Charles S. Sydnor, "The One-Party Period of American History," AHR 51 (1946), is a helpful overview of postwar politics, but for full accounts grounded in the economic consequences of the war, see George Dangerfield, *The Era of Good Feelings* (1952), and *The Awakening of American Nationalism, 1815–1828* (1965). On the end of postwar prosperity, see Murray N. Rothbard, *The Panic of 1819* (1951). Glover Moore, *The Missouri Controversy, 1819–1821* (1953), and Donald L. Robinson, *Slavery in the Structure of American Politics, 1765–1820*, Ch. 10 (1971), are the best sources on the Missouri Compromise. Richard H. Brown, "The Missouri Crisis, Slavery, and the Politics of Jacksonianism," SAQ 65 (1966), locates the origins of the future Jacksonian party in the political reaction to that crisis. On the expansion of suffrage by the 1820s, see Chilton Williamson, *American Suffrage: From Property to Democracy* (1960), and on the growing political power of the West, see Frederick Jackson Turner, *Rise of the New West, 1819–1829* (1906). There is no adequate work on the election of 1824, but two useful studies are Paul C. Nagel, "The Election of 1824: A Reconsideration Based on Newspaper Opinion," JSH 26 (1960), and Donald J. Ratcliffe, "The Role of Voters and Issues in Party Formation, Ohio, 1824," JAH 59 (1973).

Arthur M. Schlesinger, Jr., *The Age of Jackson* (1945), is the classic liberal interpretation of the Jacksonian Democrats as the champions of the common man against conservative vested interests. However, ever since the publication of Lee Benson, *The Concept of Jacksonian Democracy: New York as a Test Case* (1961), which emphatically argued that the Jacksonians were not a party of reform, the historiography on the second party system has been in flux. Important works that differ widely in their interpretations are: Richard P. McCormick, *The Second American Party System: Party Formation in the Jacksonian Era* (1966); Harry Watson, *Jacksonian Politics and Community Conflict: The Emergence of the Second Party System in Cumberland County, North Carolina* (1981); Ronald P. Formisano, *The Transformation of Political Culture: Massachusetts Politics, 1780s–1840s* (1983); and Amy Bridges, *A City in the Republic: Antebellum New York and the Origins of Machine Politics* (1984). Edward Pessen, *Jacksonian America: Society, Personality, and Politics* (1978), and William G. Shade, "Political Pluralism and Party Development: The Creation of a Modern Party System, 1815–1852," in Paul Kleppner et al., *The Evolution of American Electoral Systems* (1981), are efforts at a synthesis. The ideological and cultural side of Jacksonian Democracy is especially well treated in John William Ward, *Andrew Jackson: Symbol for an Age* (1955), and Marvin Meyers, *The Jacksonian Persuasion: Politics and Beliefs* (1957). On Jackson's career, see Robert V. Remini, *Andrew Jackson and the Course of American Empire* (1977); James C. Curtis, *Andrew Jackson and the Search for Vindication* (1976); and Richard B. Latner, *The Presidency of Andrew Jackson* (1979). Robert V. Remini, *Martin Van Buren and the Making of the Democratic Party* (1959), and Donald B. Cole, *Martin Van Buren and the American Political System* (1984), cover his key party role.

The Bank War, the catalyst for the crystallization of the Jacksonians as a party, can be followed in Bray Hammond, *Banks and Politics in America from the Revolution to the Civil War* (1957). Robert V. Remini, *Andrew Jackson and the Bank War* (1967), presents Jackson's side, while Thomas P. Govan, *Nicholas Biddle: Nationalist and Public Banker* (1959), defends the Bank's position. An important, but neglected, study of the role of the state bankers in the controversy is Jean Alexander Wilburn, *Biddle's Bank: The Crucial Years* (1967). John M. McFaul, *The Politics of Jacksonian Finance* (1972), is superb on the political consequences of the Bank War and the hard-money philosophies of most Democrats. The continuing importance of the banking issue in state politics is shown in James Roger Sharp, *The Jacksonians versus the Banks: Politics in the States after the Panic of 1837* (1970), and William G. Shade, *The Money Question in the Western States, 1832–1865* (1973). Nullification, the other great formative crisis for the Jacksonians, is deftly treated in William W. Freehling, *Prelude to Civil War* (1966). Two other important sources are James Brewer Stewart, " 'A Great Talking and Eating Machine': Patriarchy, Mobilization and the Dynamics of Nullification in South Carolina,'' CWH 27 (1981), and Jane H. Pease and William H. Pease, "The Economics and Politics of Charleston's Nullification Crisis,'' JSH 47 (1981). The utter centrality of slavery in Southern politics is the focal point in William J. Cooper, *The South and the Politics of Slavery, 1828–1856* (1978).

The long formative period of the Whig party from 1824 to 1840 is not adequately covered in any single work. Essential studies for any synthesis are: Samuel F. Bemis, *John Quincy Adams and the Union* (1956); George R. Poage, *Henry Clay and the Whig Party* (1946); Charles G. Sellers, Jr., "Who Were the Southern Whigs?,'' AHR 59 (1954); Lynn Marshall, "The Strange Stillbirth of the Whig Party,'' AHR 72 (1967); and Glyndon G. Van Deusen, *William Henry Seward* (1967). For Whig ideology, see Glyndon G. Van Deusen, "Some Aspects of Whig Theory and Thought in the Jacksonian Period,'' AHR 63 (1958), and Daniel W. Howe, *The Political Culture of the American Whigs* (1980). A comprehensive, interpretive study of the Antimasonic Party has also not been done. A sound, but somewhat thin, narrative history is William Preston Vaughn, *The Antimasonic Party in the United States, 1826–1843* (1983), and Kathleen Smith Kutolowski, "Antimasonry Reexamined: Social Basis of the Grass-Roots Party,'' JAH 71 (1984), suggests the direction that future research will take.

Many of the works cited above deal with the issue of party appeals and voter mobilization, but studies that are particularly insightful on the partisan divisions within the mass electorate by 1840 are: Robert Kelley, *The Cultural Pattern in American Politics: The First Century* (1979); Joel H. Silbey, *The Partisan Imperative: The Dynamics of American Politics Before the Civil War* (1985); and Herbert Ershkowitz and William G. Shade, "Consensus or Conflict? Political Behavior in the State Legislatures During the Jacksonian Era,'' JAH 53 (1971). The divergent responses of Democrats and Whigs to the market revolution is stressed in John Ashworth, *'Agrarians' and Aristocrats: Party Political Ideology in the United States, 1837–1846* (1983), and Michael A. Lebowitz, "The Jacksonians: Paradox Lost?,'' in Barton J. Bernstein, ed., *Towards a New Past: Dissenting Essays in American History* (1968). Sean Wilentz, "On Class and Politics in Jacksonian America,'' RAH 10 (1982), is the best discussion of the unresolved issue of how class affected party development.

NOTES

1. Quoted in Gordon S. Wood, *The Creation of the American Republic, 1776–1787* (Chapel Hill: University of North Carolina Press, 1969), p. 488.
2. Quoted in Sheldon S. Wolin, "The People's Two Bodies,'' democracy 1 (1981): 16.
3. Quoted in Michael Paul Rogin, *Fathers and Children: Andrew Jackson and the Subjugation of the American Indian* (New York: Alfred A. Knopf, 1975), p. 36.
4. Quoted in Richard Hofstadter, *The American Political Tradition* (New York: Vintage Books, 1961), fn. pp. 27, 31.
5. Ibid., p. 42.
6. Quoted in Rogin, op. cit., p. 291.
7. Ibid., p. 257.
8. Quoted in William E. Nelson, *The Roots of American Bureaucracy, 1840–1900* (Cambridge: Harvard University Press, 1982), p. 24.

9. Quotes are from Frank Otto Gatell and John M. McFaul, eds., *Jacksonian America, 1815–1840: New Society, Changing Politics* (Englewood Cliffs, N.J.: Prentice-Hall, 1970), pp. 151, 145.

10. Quoted in Marvin Meyers, *The Jacksonian Persuasion: Politics & Belief* (New York: Vintage Books, 1960), p. 27.

11. Georgetown (S.C.) *Winyaw Intelligencer*, May 12, 1830, cited in James Brewer Stewart, " 'A Great Talking and Eating Machine': Patriarchy, Mobilization and the Dynamics of Nullification in South Carolina," *Civil War History* 27 (1981): 210.

12. Quoted in ibid., pp. 210, 209.

13. David Brion Davis, ed., *Antebellum American Culture: An Interpretive Anthology* (Lexington, Mass.: D. C. Heath, 1979), p. 187.

14. Quoted in Glyndon G. Van Deusen, *The Jacksonian Era, 1828–1848* (New York: Harper Torchbooks, 1963), p. 148.

15. David Brion Davis, ed., op. cit., p. 193.

16. Quoted in Meyers, op. cit., p. 161.

5

The Breakdown of a Party System

American republicanism faced a basic dilemma in the antebellum period. That dilemma is summarized in the observation that whereas 83 percent of the free workforce was self-employed in 1800, only 48 percent was by 1860. By the middle of the nineteenth century, the spread of market relations had reduced a majority of free labor to a status of economic dependency that contradicted the original definition of republican freedom.

Eighteenth-century republicanism envisioned the good society as one materially grounded in structures of opportunity that would enable succeeding generations of males to lead lives of economic and political self-sufficiency on family farms. But the advance of the market created structures of opportunity that required men to leave the farms of their fathers whether they wanted to or not. The market offered economic incentives but at the cost of personal independence. In order to advance, a man had to become dependent, be it on the uncertainties of market conditions, on bankers or lenders who granted him the credit necessary to expand production, or an employer whose self-interest was to get the most labor for the cheapest price. The result was a profound tension in American culture that expressed itself in conflicting definitions of freedom, which competed in the political arena.

The Democrats were the primary spokesmen for the original definition of freedom, one based on the ownership of productive property in an agrarian society of independent farmers and artisans. It was this freedom, and the equal right of individuals to be economically and culturally independent, that the Democrats claimed was being threatened by the political privileges and cultural arrogance of a monied aristocracy of Yankee evangelicals.

Rank-and-file Democrats, as we have seen, were farmers and workers who benefited the least from the market revolution or were economically injured by it. For these men and their families, the market meant violent swings in business conditions, which undermined the security and stability of the household economy; a decline in the status of artisan skills; an erosion of the traditional authority of the patriarchal farmer; and a proliferation of paper money, which fluctuated in value. Farmers and small producers were exposed to new competition when their former monopolies in local markets were broken by canals and railroads, which shipped in foodstuffs and finished goods from the outside. Most artisans were unable to compete with the merchant capitalists, and the economically marginal were driven into the class of wage earners, where they joined the Irish Catholic immigrants.

At the same time that economic independence was being undermined, the cultural freedom to live one's life as one saw fit was threatened by the political moralism of reformers in such areas as drinking, behavior on the Sabbath, and parental control over schooling. There was a close and visible fit between wealth, Whiggery, evangelical-ism, and reform. Thus, poorer, nonevangelical voters had all the more reason to respond to a Democratic ideology that linked a cultural defense of individual freedoms with an economic attack on the monied aristocracy.

The Democrats, especially outside of the South, appealed to economically declin-ing groups, who saw corruption and loss in the market, and to religious and ethnic outsiders, who saw cultural coercion in reform. The Whigs and their successors in the 1850s, the Republicans, attracted economically rising groups, who saw virtue and opportunity in the market, and the cultural insiders of English-stock Americans, who equated reform with individual liberation. These Americans—the manufacturers, pros-perous townspeople, and commercial farmers whose status and material well-being were enhanced by the spread of the market—redefined freedom. This new definition—possession of self, achieved through inner restraint—spoke to the ambitions of the entrepreneur, the needs of the middle class, and the logic of evangelicalism. It empha-sized not the right to be left alone, but the duty to do good for others.

The Whigs, the beneficiaries of the market revolution, came to view property as something earned in competition divorced from the precapitalist household. Having experienced in their own lives a separation of work from home, they realized that the links had been broken between landed property, on the one hand, and personal inde-pendence, patriarchal authority, and the perpetuation of the family lineage, on the other. Just as their capital was now likely to be intangible, a particular skill or talent that could be parlayed into economic advancement and social mobility, so also did their conception of freedom become more abstract. Freedom could no longer be grounded in the possession of land and the reality of economic self-sufficiency. It came to represent an intangible inner being, a measure of self-control. Only through freedom defined in this way could one be prosperous, respectable, and saved. Without such freedom, one would squander economic and moral resources and be doomed to poverty and damnation.

Whig ideology stressed economic self-interest, moral duty, and the class harmony that would result from the economic and moral guidance of an activist government. Whigs did not place much credence in the Democratic notion of a rapacious Money Power, an all-powerful group of paper aristocrats who corrupted politics as they conspired to rob individuals of their independence. Wage labor, as the permanently dependent victims of the Money Power, simply could not exist for the Whigs or Republicans. "There is no such thing as a man being bound down in a free country through his life as a laborer,"[1] stated Lincoln in a classic expression of Republican ideology. What the adherents of the new definition of freedom feared most was the loss of self-restraint, not economic or cultural dependency. Beginning in the 1840s, the South, as a section, came to represent such a loss of self-governance in the minds of middle-class, entrepreneurial Northerners.

By the 1850s the newly formed Republican party identified slaveholders as the masterminds of a vast, conspiratorial force that was seeking to subvert the liberties of the republic. According to the Republican indictment, slaveholders, unable to restrain their greed and lust for power, were now plotting to extend slavery, extinguish equality of opportunity, and degrade all forms of labor throughout the nation. Because the institution of Southern slavery was in fact the very antithesis of freedom, however defined, the Republican concept of the Slave Power overshadowed the Democratic concept of the Money Power as the rallying cry for Northern defenders of the republic. As part of the same process of cultural polarization, Southerners were now arguing that a conspiracy of abolitionists, Republicans, and Northern reformers was plotting to take away their liberties. The most sensitive of these liberties was, of course, the right to own slaves, a right that slaveowners shrilly insisted was the foundation of all white freedoms. As they interpreted republicanism, only the presence of black slaves saved the bulk of Southern whites from that degradation of wage labor that Northern workers tellingly denounced as wage slavery.

The fear of conspiracies against individual liberties haunted many Americans in the generation before the Civil War. They expressed these fears of power in the traditional language of republicanism. But now, rather than communicating a shared set of values, republicanism itself was a source of division, because its vocabulary and its core definition of freedom meant different things to different classes and sections. In the bitter, emotionally charged debates of the 1850s, Americans searched for a common center that no longer existed in their political culture. Such a center had been eroded away by the accelerated pace of material change after 1815, and by the reactions of Americans to that change as a series of threatening conspiracies.

Before the search for the nonexistent center collapsed in the disaster of a fratricidal war, antebellum Americans tried to contain social and ideological change through their political institutions and values. The first significant loss of confidence in this political solution occurred in the 1840s. After looking at why this happened, the chapter moves on to the 1850s and the breakdown of the second party system. When that breakdown led to a Republican victory in the presidential election of 1860, the stage was set for the Civil War.

Tyler and the Frustrated Whigs

The election of Harrison in 1840 gave some Whigs the opportunity they had been waiting for since 1824. Here, finally, was a chance for the original Clay nucleus of the party to establish their claim on leadership by translating into legislation the economic program dubbed by Clay "the American system." The Clay Whigs had all the urgency to act of any new party that gained power for the first time. This impatience was compounded by Clay's suspicion, understandable enough in light of Jackson's use of presidential power, that the executive inevitably held the trump card in American politics. Confident that he could control the aged, pliable Harrison, Clay convinced the president to call Congress into special session in the spring of 1841. Clay wanted to move quickly before the temporary, election-induced unity of the party dissipated into petty factionalism.

Clay's political instincts were all too correct. Harrison suddenly died on April 4, 1841, a month to the day after assuming office. His successor, John Tyler of Virginia, repeatedly demonstrated to the Whigs the negative power of the presidency. Clay's party program—the repeal of the Independent Treasury and its replacement by a new

Bank of the United States, a protective tariff, and the distribution of proceeds of public land sales to the states as funds for internal improvements—was gutted beyond recognition by Tyler. Clay wound up with no national bank, no distribution, and but a slightly higher tariff. Through his use of the presidential veto, Tyler had stolen victory from the Whigs, his nominal party.

At stake in the Tyler-Clay struggle were competing definitions of federal power and the unspoken assumptions of American politics. Tyler, an ex-Nullifying Democrat, was on the Whig ticket as a vice-presidential candidate in 1840 because he balanced the ticket ideologically and geographically. He represented a distinct minority wing of the party, Southern states'-righters who had broken with Jackson over the Force Bill. Scenting victory in 1840, the Whigs, for the most obvious of partisan reasons, took the contradictory position of arguing simultaneously that the federal government was sovereign in its own right (the Clay position), and that it was but an agent of the states with strictly limited powers (the Tyler position). Of course, no one expected that the contradiction would be exposed. No president had ever died in office, and hence the Whigs utterly failed to see the vice-presidency as a real office with potentially great power. Once Tyler, who flinched whenever the Whigs called him "His Accidency," became president, the situation was still salvageable. Party morality, the placing of the needs of the party as an institution above the needs of its members as individuals, dictated that Tyler owed his prime loyalty to the party that had nominated him. Yes, candidates stood for certain principles, but those principles were subject to modification or redefinition if they conflicted with the sentiments and needs of the party as a whole. The unspoken assumption was that candidates were accepted by the party with the unsuspecting confidence that they could be trusted to work with the party. This was Tyler's apostasy in the minds of most Whigs. He was a traitor to his party and was dealt with accordingly. He was expelled from the party. By the fall of 1842, Clay controlled the party, but Tyler still had the presidency—and the power that went with it.

As a president without a party who was also anxious to vindicate his principles by winning the presidency in his own right, Tyler clearly had to create a power base for the election of 1844. He most obviously needed an issue around which to rebuild his bridges back to his former Democratic party. The perfect issue for Tyler's purposes would have national appeal, the support of Jackson, and the potential to force a break between Jackson and his successor at the head of the Democrats, Van Buren. The immediate annexation of Texas was just such an issue.

By 1836 some 30,000 Americans were living in the Mexican province of Texas. Fifteen years earlier the newly formed republic of Mexico had invited the first Americans into the province. Reasoning that American penetration of their northern province was inevitable in any event, the Mexicans hoped to control and limit that penetration by offering liberal land grants in return for allegiance to the authorities in Mexico City. The Mexicans miscalculated badly. The Americans arrived faster, in greater numbers, and with more slaves than the Mexicans had anticipated. The situation was inherently unstable. The Americans were Protestants in a Catholic culture that they equated with bigoted superstition, and they were Anglo-Saxons under the formal rule of a race they believed was a degraded, inferior mixture of black, Indian, and Spanish blood. As slaveholders and commercial farmers, the leaders of the Anglo-Texan community knew only too well that their economic future lay to the north. Slavery was illegal in

Mexico, and Americans held their slaves only by the sufferance of Mexican authorities who temporarily accepted the legal fiction that black indentured servitude did not constitute slavery. The United States, the source of imports (on which a foreign duty had to be paid) and the chief market for exports, was the natural economic partner for Texas. The predictable War of Independence, precipitated by belated Mexican efforts to reestablish control, erupted in 1836.

Assisted by the none-too-subtle presence of an American army in southwestern Louisiana poised to intervene if needed, the Texans won their independence. The new republic was officially recognized by Jackson once the election of 1836 was safely past and the Texas issue could no longer damage Van Buren's chances in the North. Jackson's caution in delaying recognition was warranted. Texas was a politically explosive issue because the rise of an abolitionist movement in the 1830s had made politicians in both parties acutely sensitive to any intrusion of slavery into national politics. For that reason, neither party wanted to touch the question of the annexation of Texas. But, in his search for an issue, Tyler rushed in where even Jackson had feared to tread.

Resurrected by Tyler in the spring of 1843, the Texas issue enabled Tyler to ingratiate himself back into the good graces of the Southern and Western wings of the Democratic party. Southern Democrats, led by Calhoun, appointed Secretary of State by Tyler, did not trust Van Buren on slavery. Western Democrats, eager to challenge the eastern wing for control of the party, doubted that Van Buren could win the election in 1844. Texas, if handled carefully, suited the needs of both groups perfectly. By rallying behind annexation, the party could heal the rift of 1840 and welcome back the Nullifying Democrats who had bolted. Tyler, needing Democratic support to get Texas, could be convinced to back off from his threat of heading a third party in 1844. And, most important, Van Buren could be maneuvered into a position that would cost him the party's presidential nomination.

Personified by James A. Polk of Tennessee and Stephen A. Douglas of Illinois, the new breed of Democrats had their way. They led Tyler to believe that he would get the nomination in 1844, only to dump him; they used Van Buren's expected stand against the immediate annexation to unify the Southern and Western wings against his nomination; and, at the last minute, and with Jackson's blessing of his Tennessee protégé, they brought forward Polk's name to a deadlocked convention. Their power play was neatly timed and developed, but in its very execution it brought back into national politics what the party system was designed to keep out—slavery and all the fears of disunion that it engendered. A terrifying new conspiracy began to form in the minds of the Northern opposition. In denouncing the annexation of Texas, Senator Thomas Benton of Missouri, an earlier proponent of expansion and a stalwart Jacksonian in the 1830s, proclaimed:[2]

> Disunion is at the bottom of this long-concealed Texas machination. Intrigue and specu-
> lation cooperate; but disunion is at the bottom; and I denounce it to the American people.
> Under the pretext of getting Texas into the Union, the scheme is to get the South out of it.

Initial opposition to acquiring Texas was so strong that the first treaty of annexation was defeated in the Senate by a margin of two to one in June of 1844. Just before Tyler left office, a second treaty passed in March of 1845. Reversing their usual roles as strict constructionists, Tyler and the Southern Democrats now stretched the Constitution to its limits. They not only maintained that the United States could acquire an independent nation but further argued that Congress, as a committee of the whole, could annex territory by simple majority vote. This latter tactic was a clever way of sidestepping the treaty-making power of the Senate, where a two-thirds vote of approval was required. Beyond their parliamentary adeptness, however, the Polk Democrats relied upon the lure of expansion itself to quell opposition to Texas. They gambled that a coordinated program of expansion would appeal to various sections and interest groups and unite the nation behind their leadership.

Polk's narrow victory over Clay in 1844 gave the Democrats the chance to implement their program. Their solution for maintaining order in the marketplace was fundamentally different from that of the Clay Whigs. Whereas the Whigs began with the premise that governmental power should be concentrated in a limited area, the Democrats started from the assumption that governmental power should be dispersed over an ever-widening area. The Whigs' vision of America was oriented to a future in which planned and controlled change would improve the republic through time. The Democrats' image looked to the present and was deeply suspicious of social and economic change. Rather than controlling the marketplace, the Democrats hoped to expand it through space so that change would be minimized and an agrarian democracy would reproduce itself free from external controls. The Whig solution was in shambles by 1842. Now it was the Democrats' turn.

Polk and the Mexican War

The Polk Democrats ran on a platform explicitly calling for the "reannexation" of Texas and the "reoccupation" of Oregon. Both were spurious claims. The United States had given up all rights to Texas in the Adams-Onis Treaty of 1819 (hence we could hardly reannex what was never ours) and had occupied the Pacific Northwest only up to the 46th parallel, a boundary far south of that claimed in the Democratic slogan, "Fifty-four forty or fight." Shaky, if not nonexistent, in international law, the Democratic demands nonetheless made superb political sense. The linkage of Oregon with Texas promised to unite Northern and Southern Democrats behind a balanced program of expansion that would close the party rift opened up by Van Buren's hard-money policies and his subsequent defeat in 1840. If, as expected, the Whigs opposed expansion, then Democratic unity would be all the greater.

The greatest expansionist prize was one that Polk never publicly admitted that he wanted—California. A land of unsurpassed beauty and fine, natural harbors, this Mexican province, reasoned Polk, surely offered something to all sections. Northern and Southern agrarians would rush in to stake out farms, eastern businessmen would be excited by the prospect of anchoring the western terminus of a transcontinental railroad on the California shore, and New England Whigs could be expected to agree with Webster that the economic potential of the port of San Francisco made it worth Texas several times over. In private, Polk admitted his interest in California; in the fall of 1845, he told Senator Benton, "I had California and the fine bay of San Francisco as much in view as Oregon."[3] In public, however, Polk was silent on California. The Mexican government was understandably quite sensitive about American designs on its territory, especially after the national humiliation of losing Texas to the hated "gringos." Hopeful of purchasing California, Polk avoided any public statement that might cause the Mexicans to reject a sale out-of-hand. And, because he was prepared as a last resort to go to war to get California, he was careful not to tip his hand in advance to the Whig opposition at home.

Polk presided over a radical redrawing of the map of the United States. During his single term, the acquisition of Texas was finalized, Britain ceded sovereignty in the Pacific Northwest up to the 49th parallel, and the United States added some half a million square miles in the Mexican Cession of 1848. The physical size of the Union grew by 51 percent with these three additions. Polk's program of artfully balanced expansion was, on the surface at least, one of the greatest successes in presidential history. Yet, measured by its purpose of securing order and reducing tensions within the Union, the program was a failure. It failed because Polk, in order to acquire California, manufactured a war with Mexico that was widely interpreted in the North as an immoral act of aggression committed in the interests of the slave South.

By January 1846, Polk was convinced that he had run out of peaceful options for acquiring California. The last attempt at purchase, the Slidell mission in December 1845, was a total failure. Polk used the American consul at Monterey, Thomas Larkin, as a secret agent to encourage a Texas-style revolt against Mexico, but then he grew tired of waiting. Despite the lack of any real evidence, he was certain that the British were plotting to gain control over California, and he wanted to act before the British could move in.

The ostensible issue that provoked the Mexican War was a boundary dispute that the United States inherited when it annexed Texas. Santa Anna, when captured by Texas troops in 1836, agreed to the Rio Grande river as the boundary between Texas and Mexico. As an administrative unit of Mexico, Texas had its southern boundary set at the Nueces river, considerably north of the Rio Grande. Neither by governance nor settlement did the Republic of Texas ever actually control the area south of the Nueces. Both historical precedent and the illegality of a boundary that was dictated to a prisoner of war, and that was quickly repudiated by his government, conclusively undercut the claims of the Texans. Legalities aside, the issue was vital because a boundary on the Rio Grande, the headwaters of which were in northern New Mexico, more than doubled the size of Texas.

It was a safe assumption that the Mexicans would fight to keep American troops out of the Rio Grande valley. Polk acted on that assumption when he ordered Zachary Taylor in January, 1846, to move his army to the mouth of the Rio Grande. Even before receiving news of the expected Mexican counter-attack, Polk announced to his cabinet on May 9 that he would send a war message to Congress because "in my opinion we had ample cause of war." Among the causes cited was the failure of Mexico to keep up with payments on old debts and claims it had agreed to pay to Texan-Americans. Because the sum involved was much less than the amount lost by British creditors when states in the South and West repudiated their bonds in the crash of the late 1830s, it is easy to see why James Buchanan, the Secretary of State, would have been "better satisfied"[4] had the Mexicans attacked American troops. As it turned out, news of just such an attack in late April reached Washington later on the 9th. In his war message Polk announced, rather disingenuously, to put it mildly, that Mexico "has invaded our territory, and shed American blood upon the American soil."[5] Nonetheless, by a vote of 174 to 14 in the House and 40 to 2 in the Senate, Polk had his war.

Polk knew what he wanted and he got it quickly and cheaply. Concerning a cabinet meeting on May 30, 1846, he wrote in his diary: "I declared my purpose to be to acquire for the United States, California, New Mexico, and perhaps some others of the Northern Provinces of Mexico whenever a peace was made."[6] Before the year was out, U.S. armies, aided by the Bear Flag Rebellion, conquered California, secured the New Mexico corridor between Texas and California, and made good on the American claim to the Rio Grande as a boundary. At an original cost of $73 million, some $20 million less than the War of 1812, the war was a bargain compared to that stalemated affair. If an additional $64 million in veterans' pensions are figured in, the United States gained half a million square miles at a cost of 48¢ per acre.

A stunning military and economic success, the Mexican War was also the catalyst for the ultimate collapse of the party system put together by the Democrats and Whigs. The war produced and brought to the surface an interrelated set of political, sectional, and moral tensions which that party system was eventually incapable of containing. It also raised the issue of slavery's expansion, which led directly to the Civil War.

The Democrats could not escape the political impact of the Northern condemnation of the war and its origins. Speaking for the Whigs, John Sherman of Ohio claimed that "there is no doubt but that a large majority of the people consider it an unjust aggression upon a weak republic, excused by false reasons, and continued solely for the acquisitions of slave territory."[7] Sherman may have exaggerated, but many Northern Democrats were politically vulnerable to the charge that they supported a war whose purpose was to expand slavery. The Wilmot Proviso, attached as a rider to a $2 million war bill of August 1846, offered these Democrats a way out of their dilemma. Proposed by a Northern Democrat, David Wilmot of Pennsylvania, the proviso prohibited slavery in any territory that might be acquired as a result of the Mexican War. Although the Proviso never passed the Senate and would surely have been blocked by Polk, it nevertheless revived the slavery issue, which the parties had tried to bury for a quarter of a century. Once again, as in 1819 and 1820, a Northern antislavery majority formed in Congress.

Joining the Northern Democrats in opposition to the spread of slavery were the Conscience Whigs. A label loosely attached to a minority of Whigs who believed that if the origins of the war were highly suspect, its prosecution was downright unconscionable, "Conscience Whigs" applied more specifically to a dissenting faction within the Whig party in Massachusetts. Young men outside the inner circles of political and economic power, many of these Whigs came from the former ruling families of Massachusetts and deeply resented being shunted aside by the rise of the cotton manufacturers to party dominance. Bound up with this sense of loss was the belief that moral decline had set in. Mammon, the false god of worldly gain, had blunted moral sensibilities. These young Whigs contemptuously labeled as Cotton Whigs the ruling alliance in the party between textile manufacturers and merchants. The Cotton Whigs, supposedly concerned only with tariffs and dividends, supported an iniquitous war and thus implicated the entire party in their guilt.

Further complicating the strains within the parties was the resurgence of sectional tensions. Much as the Missouri issue had done, the Wilmot Proviso was an outlet for long-simmering Northern sentiments against Southern political power. In the half-century the republic had existed, the presidency had been held by Northerners for only

An Antislavery View of General Taylor. This cartoon expresses the moral outrage felt by many antislavery Northerners over the Mexican War and the Whig presidential nomination of Zachary Taylor, one of the military heroes of the war. (Courtesy of the New York Historical Society, New York City)

twelve years. None of these Presidents—the Adamses, father and son, and Van Buren—had been a stirring success. All the others, with the very brief exception of Harrison, had been slaveholders. Furthermore, Southerners also tended to control committee assignments in Congress. Most galling was the pattern Northerners saw in which federal arms aligned with Southern interests to expand slavery, first in Florida in the 1830s and then in Texas and the Southwest in the 1840s.

The special grievances of the West against the Polk administration intensified this anti-Southern resentment. Polk agreed to a compromise with Britain on the boundary dispute in the Pacific Northwest. The nub of the compromise was the extension of the preexisting 49° boundary between Canada and the United States westward to the Pacific. The compromise was eminently sensible to both sides, neither of which wanted a war over Oregon. The British had skimmed the cream off the fur trade, were on the verge of widening their home market for American grain, and realistically figured that the flow of American settlers would soon give the United States control of the territory up to the 49th parallel, anyway. Polk, though an intense Anglophobe, welcomed the prospect of an enlarged British market for American farmers and did not want to endanger congressional support for his proposed lowering of the tariff. Most important, hostilities with Britain, closely following the war with Mexico, would likely be economically and militarily disastrous for his administration.

For all its prudent statesmanship, however, Polk's handling of Oregon struck Western Democrats as a sellout. After their hopes had been raised by visions of "Fifty-four forty or fight", and after they had backed Polk on Mexico, these Democrats now felt that they had been cynically manipulated. When Polk also vetoed several internal improvements bills, and particularly the Rivers and Harbors Bill of 1846, which was enthusiastically supported in the West, cries of pro-Southern favoritism became even louder. It was the votes of Southern Democrats that sustained Polk's vetoes.

This growing anti-Southern sentiment confused and angered Southern politicians. In vain, they pointed out that the South did not present a united front behind Polk's war. Most conspicuously, Calhoun was an early and persistent opponent of the war. He accused Polk of recklessly plunging the nation into a war that was unnecessary and unconstitutional. Like his fellow South Carolinians and the Whig party in general, Calhoun was convinced that slavery would not move into the arid Southwest. The danger, as he predicted, was that the sudden acquisition of territory would reopen the Pandora's box of slavery, and the Wilmot Proviso proved that he was right. Party lines broke in the South, as well as the North, over the Proviso. Southerners now rallied behind what to them was the overriding constitutional and moral issue, the right of Southerners to have equal opportunity to share in territories that Southern blood and treasure had helped to acquire.

Finally, there were the moral strains imposed by the war. In a development that was both ominous and prophetic for the future of the Union, the war symbolized for its severest moral critics the desecration of the ideals of the republic. Reports reaching the North told of American troops, largely volunteers, acting with the same uncontrollable savagery that they usually reserved for wars against Indians. General Winfield Scott, a firsthand observer, said that the troops had "committed atrocities to make Heaven weep and every American of Christian morals blush for his country. Murder, robbery and rape of mothers and daughters in the presence of tied-up males of the families have been common all along the Rio Grande."[8]

Such reports reinforced the preexisting moral anger, especially among New England reformers and intellectuals. A few of them became as alienated as Henry David Thoreau who wrote, in *Civil Disobedience,* published in 1849:[9]

> How does it become a man to behave toward this American government today? I answer, that he cannot without disgrace be associated with it. I cannot for an instant recognize that political organization as *my* government which is the *slave's* government also. . . . This people must cease to hold slaves, and to make war on Mexico, though it cost them their existence as a people.

Theodore Parker, a Boston abolitionist, said much the same thing when he proclaimed his opposition to the war: "If it be treason to speak against war, what was it to make war? . . . If my country is in the wrong, and I know it and hold my peace, then I am guilty of treason, moral treason."[10] This sense of outrage, of a terrible wrong for which the republic was collectively at fault, burned deeply in the Northern conscience. Much of it fed off a generation of abolitionist agitation and flowed into the Free Soil party of 1848, the first party that revealed the latent dynamism of political antislaveryism.

Abolitionism

The abolitionists had prepared the ground in which popular antislaveryism took root in 1848. Back in the 1830s, the same decade in which a mass-based party system was built, the abolitionists became an organized reform movement. The simultaneous appearance of the abolitionists and this party system was not coincidental. Both, though in radically different ways, were responding to the new egalitarian ethos in American public life, and both achieved organizational success by innovatively responding to the same breakthroughs in transportation and communication that were instrumental in the emergence of that egalitarian ethos. Thirdly, and most ironically, given their diametrically opposite solutions for preserving the Union, both were a response to the growing fears of disunion in the 1820s.

Whereas the Jacksonians adroitly rode egalitarian currents into political office, the abolitionists followed those currents to their logical end. By viewing society in egalitarian terms along a horizontal axis of freely competing individuals, the abolitionists argued that slavery stood out as a glaring and hideous barrier to economic progress and moral justice. In this way, the abolitionists grasped that the advent of a competitive market society destroyed what had traditionally sanctioned slavery. As long as society was seen as an organic hierarchy structured around natural social dependencies, and as long as work was conceived as something to be extracted and coerced from a naturally idle, lazy population, then slavery was buffered from direct attack. In such a premarket society, slavery, however personally objectionable to some individuals, did not contradict the ethical and ideological basis of social order. Quite the contrary: slavery could be accepted and defended as part of the natural order. Slaves were simply the most dependent of entire classes of social dependents, and slavery represented an unfortunate, but understandable, extreme use of external coercion to extract productive work. Thus in seventeenth- and eighteenth-century England, slavery could be proposed as a permanent cure for the idleness of those poor who failed to respond to treatment in a public poorhouse. The market revolution, as manifested in a bourgeois ideology that redefined work as the self-motivated virtue of economically rational individuals striving to improve themselves in open competition, gradually exposed slavery as an unnatural, and unnecessary, system of unfree labor. The bourgeois definition of itself and its society was based on the internalized controls of individuals who literally possessed themselves free from external restraints. In direct opposition to that bourgeois world view was slavery, the extreme example of individuals who had lost self-possession.

Slavery was vulnerable in a market society in a way in which it had not been previously. This was the first fundamental insight of the abolitionists. In acting upon that insight, the abolitionists defined an ideological position that set them apart from earlier antislavery movements. Central to that ideology was the doctrine of immediatism. By this the abolitionists meant an immediate, moral commitment by individuals to work toward the end of slavery. Immediate emancipation, though it would have been welcomed with joy, was not necessarily the goal. Instead, what was essential was that the work of emancipation should immediately *begin*. Immediatism did not imply a rejection of gradual programs of emancipation. Indeed, as the abolitionists emphasized, such programs had already been rejected by the South in the 1820s. However, the abolitionists were astute enough to realize that gradualism could not serve as an effective organizing philosophy for the movement. As a practical alternative, it had failed; as an ideological goal, it reinforced preexisting prejudice and complacency and made it all too easy to postpone any action; and, as a moral statement, it was flawed by its suggestion that the establishment of Christian freedom for all could be delayed. Gradualism also contradicted the logic of evangelical ideology. Although there was no one-to-one relationship between evangelicalism and abolitionism, both movements in the North shared a common concern with the unfettered right of the individual to work for self-achievement. In either religious or secular terms, slavery directly violated that right. As Charles Finney put it: "To enslave a man is to treat a man as a thing—to set aside moral agency; and to treat a moral agent as a mere piece of property."[11] Consequently, for Finney and many other evangelicals, abolitionism and revivalism were part of the same holy process of achieving human redemption. The abolitionists, like the revival ministers, insisted that sin could be vanquished only through a total and immediate commitment to its eradication.

The other defining characteristic of abolitionist ideology was its stand on racial equality. If slavery were ever to be ended without massive violence, then slaveholders had to see that freeing their slaves was a Christian duty they owed to those equal to whites in the sight of God. If this freedom were to be meaningful, and not the mockery imposed on free blacks by white prejudice, then all whites had to accept black equality before the law as a goal that would hasten the end of slavery. By working for racial justice in the free states, Northern whites would undermine the racial defense of slavery by showing Southerners that an egalitarian, biracial society was a living reality.

In their second critical insight, the abolitionists realized that their success was dependent on their skill in performing their self-appointed role as social agitators. Unlike the politician, whose task was to *reflect* public opinion, the reformer in an unpopular moral cause had to *change* public opinion. The core problem was public apathy, the moral numbness by which most whites isolated themselves from the plight of the slave. To break through that apathy, to reach individual consciences and make whites identify with the horrors of bondage, the abolitionists used blunt, uncompromising language. As William Lloyd Garrison, the firebrand who provided the early, driving leadership for the abolitionists, said of his moral indignation, "I have need to be *all on fire,* for I have mountains of ice about me to melt."[12] Wendell Phillips, a Boston lawyer who became the best-known abolitionist orator, articulated a brilliant defense of agitation, which he anchored in classic republican ideology:[13]

> Each man . . . holds his property and his life dependent on the constant presence of an agitation like this of antislavery. Eternal vigilance is the price of liberty: power is ever stealing from the many to the few. . . . Only by continual oversight can the democrat in office be prevented from hardening into a despot: only by unintermitted agitation can a people be kept sufficiently awake to principle not to let liberty be smothered in material prosperity.

Much to the dismay of his critics, Garrison proved correct when he proclaimed in the first issue of the *Liberator* in January 1831 that "I WILL BE HEARD."[14] In making sure that they were heard, the abolitionists were as adept as the party professionals in developing techniques to reach the people. Public rallies, revivalistic exhortations, speakers' series, bureaucratic agencies, and, above all, the printing press were all exploited by the abolitionists in spreading their message. The application of steam power to the printing press in the early 1830s dramatically lowered the cost and raised

The Slave Trade. One of the worst features of the domestic slave trade was its breaking up of black families. Following a slave auction in Richmond, Virginia, recently sold slaves are saying goodbye to relatives. (Chicago Historical Society)

the output of printed material. The abolitionists could now reach a huge audience for a relatively small capital investment. In 1835 they flooded the nation with over a million pieces of literature, a ten-fold increase over 1834.

The voluntary work of women supplemented this reliance on printing technology. First drawn to abolitionism as just one of many reforms, women soon identified particularly strongly with the movement. In the slaves they came to see fellow victims of social injustice. The slave, like the wife, was legally dependent upon the will of another and was discriminated against on grounds of inherent, biological inferiority. "In striving to strike his irons off," Abby Kelley wrote in 1838, "we found most surely that *we* were manacled *ourselves*."[15] Often operating out of local church societies, these women were the grassroots organizers of the massive effort in the mid-1830s to inundate Congress with antislavery petitions. By 1838 Congress had received petitions with over 400,000 signatures.

The abolitionists were so loud and so persistent that they provoked a concerted effort to silence them. In the North they were met with mob violence. There were four times as many riots resulting in significant property losses in the 1830s as there had been in the preceding two decades combined. Many of them were triggered by hatred of the abolitionists, a hatred that often spilled over into antiblack violence. In the South, abolitionist literature was burned, and local postmasters, in direct defiance of federal authority, censured the mails to keep out antislavery materials. Slave codes were tightened, and a series of state laws abridging the freedom of speech and the press were speedily passed. In 1836, Congress adopted the so-called Gag Rule, by which antislavery petitions were automatically tabled without a reading.

The intensity of the reactions to the abolitionists was the best indication of how contemporaries perceived them as dangerous radicals. The abolitionists attacked as unsound and impure the critical public institutions that bound together the nation—the churches, political parties, and the Union. All sanctioned slavery, either through their active support or their silence. They were radical in reminding white Americans of what they did not want to hear—that slavery was a national institution and its guilt was shared by all whites. In demanding an end to slavery, they were calling for the destruction of the cornerstone of the American economy in the 1830s. Without slavery and what it produced in export earnings, the national growth of the economy would have been far slower. They bypassed local elites in molding public opinion and heightened lower-class anxieties over black competition for jobs. And, in pushing for racial equality, the abolitionists rejected the almost universal racist assumptions of white Americans. It was no wonder that they aroused such intense fears.

In the South the abolitionists struck at the very roots of the social order. The issue here was as basic as it could be. It was not so much a question of what the abolitionists actually said, which usually consisted of appeals to the Christian consciences of slaveholders, but whether any opponent of slavery should say anything at all. Slaveholders were easily outnumbered by the nonslaveholding Southern majority. They had far too much at stake to permit any public debate on slavery. In admitting this in 1835 Governor Wilson Lumpkin of Georgia argued:[16]

> Should, however, the abolitionists be permitted to proceed without molestation or only
> have to encounter the weapons of reason and argument, have we not reason to fear, that
> their untiring efforts may succeed in misleading the majority of a people who have no
> direct interest in the great question at issue, and finally produce interference with the
> constitutional rights of the slaveholders.

Partly as a result of the sheer violence and anger directed against them, the abolitionists divided internally. In the 1830s the abolitionists were at least formally united under the leadership of the American Anti-Slavery Society, founded in Philadelphia in 1833. A rival organization, the American and Foreign Anti-Slavery Society, was established in 1840. The Garrisonians, those who remained in control of the AAAS, interpreted the violence to mean that American institutions and values were fundamentally impure and immoral. A complete regeneration, one based on the renunciation of force in all human relationships, be it in the patriarchal family, black slavery, the churches, or government, was necessary if America were ever to return to its revolutionary ideals. Expressed in an ideology of nonresistance, pacifism, and Christian anarchism, the Garrisonian position provoked opposition from more moderate abolitionists. They felt that the Garrisonians, by rashly identifying the movement with radical attacks on all traditional centers of authority, had helped isolate abolitionism from the public at large. The last straw for the moderates was the election of a woman, Abby Kelley, to the Executive Committee of the AAAS in 1840. American institutions were certainly flawed, said the anti-Garrisonians, but the best way to redeem them would be through the political pressure of a third political party devoted exclusively to the single issue of emancipation. Out of this conviction was born the Liberty party.

Entrenched external opposition, combined with the internal split of 1840, did not, however, significantly weaken abolitionism. The fervor of individual members remained high. To many, perhaps most, of the original converts, abolitionism was a commitment to a lifelong career that was only intensified by the repression of the 1830s. Although we are far from having an adequate explanation or theory for what motivated individual abolitionists, their commitment does seem to have represented in an intensified form a generational revolt of the sons and daughters of New England against the crumbling patriarchal authority of their elders. Abolitionism was especially appealing to young Yankee evangelicals struggling with difficult career choices in a commercializing society of dislocating mobility and seemingly unchristian materialism. Set adrift in an America in which the family farm and God-fearing village community, the world of the fathers, could no longer be taken for granted, and alienated from that America by the righteous standards of their parental upbringing, these evangelicals resolved their conflicts of career and conscience in the holy vocation of abolitionism. The struggle against slavery, the institution that personified in a horrifying, magnified form all the greed, lust, and unchecked power that they saw as rampant in America, established their worth in the eyes of God. "Never were men called on to die in a holier cause,"[17] wrote the abolitionist Amos Phillips in 1835. As Christians and as Unionists, the abolitionists strode into battle. If the Union were ever to be saved from the bloodbath portended by Nat Turner's rebellion or the breakup portended by the Nullification movement, then no less was demanded than the immediatist solutions of God's secular missionaries to a fallen people.

Despite, and in many cases because of, the opposition, the original core kept the faith in the 1830s. Meanwhile, the abolitionists could point to impressive growth. At the end of the decade some 2,000 local societies claimed a membership of up to 250,000. The nucleus of a popular constituency had been built. In the cities it was organized around artisans, shopkeepers, and manufacturers; the greatest support came from artisans. Heirs to the radical republicanism of Thomas Paine, skilled craftsmen, much more so than the preindustrial elites, were prone to see slavery as a threat to economic independence and political equality. The abolitionists appealed to this antislavery antipathy; James G. Birney of the Liberty party wrote, "The large slaveholder wants no free mechanics about him: he has mechanics among his own slaves: nor does he need the shop-keeper; because he can go to the place where the shop-keeper now purchases, and buy for himself."[18] In rural areas, pockets of abolitionist strength overlapped prosperous, evangelicalized settlements of Yankee farmers. Here, slavery was vulnerable for its denial of the right to self-improvement and its degradation of the moral benefits of labor.

The split of 1840 did not lead to a fragmentation of this constituency. If anything, by fostering a variety of immediatist positions consistent with the makeup of local societies, the split promoted a healthy, democratic pluralism. By the same token, the decision by more conservative abolitionists to engage in direct political action through the Liberty party widened the appeal of the movement. Scattered evidence from western New York suggests that the Liberty party began mobilizing for antislavery a new constituency, mostly journeymen mechanics and laborers. Men without land who never quite established themselves in their new communities, they were responsive to the warnings of the Liberty party that Northern aristocrats, in alliance with slaveholders, were conspiring to reduce all white workers "to the condition of serfs."[19] To be sure, and as predicted by Garrison, the political abolitionists diluted moral suasion in an effort to attract followers. Voting for the Liberty party, a political act, did not require the revolution in moral values that was at the core of the original conversion to abolitionism. Nonetheless, in several Congressional districts Whig politicians, who no longer had a monopoly on the Yankee evangelical vote, were forced into stronger antislavery positions. And simply by being in the political arena with a stand on slavery deemed extremist by the public, the Liberty party made any antislavery stance in the major parties appear more moderate and respectable in comparison.

The Politics of Antislavery and Free Soil

Any success of political antislaveryism in the 1840s was ultimately grounded in the Northern reaction to the cycle of agitation and repression set off in the first decade of abolitionism. This cycle steadily revealed the slaveholders as that most hated enemy of republicanism, the privileged aristocrat. It was on this point, not on the moral issue of the plight of the slave, that slaveholders were most vulnerable to political attack. As portrayed by the abolitionists, the slaveholders were privileged politically by the three-fifths clause and economically by their use of unpaid, compulsory labor. The result was an unrepublican arrogance in which slaveholders dictated to the public on matters of individual conscience. Confronted with an abolitionist onslaught they dared not ignore for fear it would provoke a general debate *within the South* over the merits of slavery, slaveholders used their political power to confirm all the unrepublican things the abolitionists were saying about them. Censorship by Southern postmasters not only looked like the slaveholders were telling the public what to read and believe, it also negated the constitutional right of Northern whites to the use of the federal mails. Even closer to home for Northerners was the Gag Rule, a repudiation of the constitutional right to petition Congress for redress of grievances. Thus, as the 1840s began, the civil rights of Northern whites were starting to become entangled with the original issue of the immorality of slavery.

The consequences of Southern political power, as expressed in the Tyler and Polk administrations, firmly riveted the links between antislavery and the self-interests of Northern whites. Again, as in the 1830s, Southern politicians were their own worst enemies. Tyler and Calhoun dramatically politicized the issue of slavery in Texas, and their efforts intensified Northern fears of an encroaching Slave Power. John Quincy Adams, who had a long career as an antislavery congressman after he left the presidency, tapped these fears when he warned in a public address that the objectives behind the annexation of Texas were *"the perpetuation of slavery and the continued ascendency of the slave power."*[20]

The Polk administration never grasped the transcendent importance the Northern majority now placed on the status of the territories. What was at stake was a cluster of issues and values that the Free Soil party crystallized in one of the great slogans of American political history: "Free soil, free labor, free men." The backbone of Northern society, its farmers and artisans, felt that their economic future, and that of their sons, was hanging in the balance. All the aspirations and values they held dear—the freedom to compete, economic advancement, social mobility, the dignity of free labor, and a chance to stay one step ahead of economic dependency by leaving an Eastern social order divided into permanent classes—were challenged by the spectre of slavery advancing into the territories.

Predisposed to believe in the reality of the Slave Power by over a decade of abolitionist agitation and the Southern repression that it provoked, proponents of free soil were certain that nothing less than republicanism itself was on trial. "If the schemes of the South succeed, farewell to liberty,'' predicted Martin Grover, a New York Free Soiler. ''The crisis has come for the trial of our fidelity,'' proclaimed a Free Soil tract in 1848. Whether or not American republicanism would continue ''as a model of government to the world''[21] would be decided in the fate of the territories.

The party system held in 1848. The Whigs, abandoning any effort at ideological consistency, ran General Zachary Taylor for the presidency. A war hero and Louisiana slaveholder, Taylor avoided any stand on the Wilmot Proviso. The Democrats, in a strategy they used until 1860, nominated a Northerner, Lewis Cass, deemed safe by Southerners on the slavery issue. An opponent of the Wilmot Proviso, Cass offered instead popular sovereignty—that is, leaving the decision on slavery up to the actual settlers in the territories. Taylor was elected in a close race that Cass would have won had he carried New York. The election was a tribute to the ability of the major parties to retain voter allegiances in the crosscurrents of sectional tensions. But the showing of a third party, the Free Soilers, was a better gauge of what the future would soon bring.

The Free Soilers were a coalition of three groups: Van Buren Democrats, Conscience Whigs, and former members of the Liberty party. A mixture of antislavery convictions and a desire for political revenge motivated the Van Buren Democrats, or Barnburners as they were known in New York. They did support the exclusion of slavery from the territories, but they also had never forgiven Polk (with the help of Cass) from maneuvering Van Buren out of the Democratic nomination in 1844. They exacted their revenge in 1848 by costing Cass the New York electoral vote. On the other hand, the Conscience Whigs deserted their party more out of morality than political expediency. Any chance of their adhering to the Whig ticket in 1848 evaporated when Taylor, a slaveholder, received the nomination. The Free Soilers pointedly refused to endorse black suffrage and were decidedly not an abolitionist party. Still, most Liberty men could support a party that opposed the extension of slavery, demanded the abolition of slavery in the District of Columbia, and called on the federal government to divest itself of any constitutional responsibility to protect slavery. In a rousing convention in Buffalo, New York, the Free Soilers nominated Van Buren for president and Charles Francis Adams, a Conscience Whig, for the vice-presidency.

The Free Soilers failed to carry a single state in 1848, and the party was all but defunct by the next presidential election. What organizational strength the party did have came chiefly from the Barnburners, and they were back in the Democratic Party by 1850. In that same year, the issue that had brought the Free Soilers together, the status of slavery in the territories conquered from Mexico, was apparently settled. The sections were too divided for any single compromise to pass Congress in 1850. In that sense, there was no Compromise of 1850. Rather, under the leadership of Stephen Douglas, the compromise package was broken up into separate bills, which passed by attracting enough Northern Democrats who were willing to cross sectional lines. California, an even greater prize after gold was discovered in 1848, was admitted as a free state. The rest of the former Mexican lands were organized into the two large territories of Utah and New Mexico. Here, Congress placed no restrictions on slavery but, in language that was intentionally ambiguous, never specified just what powers, if any, the territorial legislatures could exercise over slavery. The best assessment of what had happened came from Salmon P. Chase, a Freesoiler: ''The question of slavery in the territories has been avoided. It has not been settled.''[22]

Chase was right; and because he was, the Free Soilers cannot be written off as of little consequence. The national Free Soil ticket of Van Buren and Adams foreshadowed the way in which the strains and protests produced by the slavery issue could dissolve old party loyalties and submerge former partisan identities in a new party. The Free soil vote in 1848 was only 10 percent of the total, but that was a much better showing than the 2.3 percent won by the Liberty party in 1844. Although organized very late in the campaign, the Free Soilers won twelve congressional races and polled over 15 percent of the presidential vote in one-third of the counties in the North. With a peak strength of 20 percent in New England, the Free Soil vote was a very sectionalized one.

In reviving sectionalized politics, the Free Soilers taught Northern politicians one fundamental lesson: slavery, if approached as both a political and a moral question, was potentially a winning issue. By first appealing to the fears of Northern whites over Southern political power depriving free labor of an equal opportunity in the territories, the Free Soil party had staged a dress rehearsal for the far more successful Republican party of the 1850s. The Republicans' turn came when the Kansas-Nebraska Act proved just how right Chase had been.

Kansas-Nebraska and Know-Nothingism

In a slower-paced, less-dynamic America of isolated, rural communities, the compromise settlements of 1850 might have held into the indefinite future. Certainly they would have lasted longer than four years. But sectionalism returned with frightening force in 1854 when the demands of market expansion again reopened the debate over the status of the territories.

Between the raw, entrepreneurial energy of Chicago in the east and the frenzied speculation in the gold fields of California in the west stretched, politically speaking, a great void in the early 1850s. The area west of the Mississippi, east of the Rockies, and north of the Missouri Compromise line of 36° 30' was still politically unorganized. As the essential first step in the building of a transcontinental railroad and the promotion of sustained white settlement, Stephen Douglas introduced a bill to organize that area in 1854. What Douglas hoped to achieve was a bisectional consensus supporting the profitable development of the trans-Mississippi West. Indians would have to be displaced and federal promises made in the removal treaties of the 1830s would have to be broken, but Indian rights seemed a small price to pay for the expected benefits of renewed national unity under the leadership of Douglas and the Democratic party. However, Douglas could not have been more wrong; like Polk, he soon discovered that the Democratic solution of expanding the marketplace highlighted the very sectional tensions it was meant to submerge.

In order to win Southern backing, Douglas was forced to state explicitly in his bill that the Missouri Compromise prohibition on slavery was "inoperative and void." In the territory north of 36° 30' the status of slavery was now to be governed by the exceedingly vague concept of popular sovereignty. The result was the Kansas-Nebraska Act, the single most explosive piece of legislation ever passed by Congress. It led directly to the formation of the Republican party and the collapse of the Whig party and was instrumental in the growth of the one-party Democratic South.

What especially put the charge in the explosive Northern response was a widely publicized statement known as "The Appeal of the Independent Democrats." Written

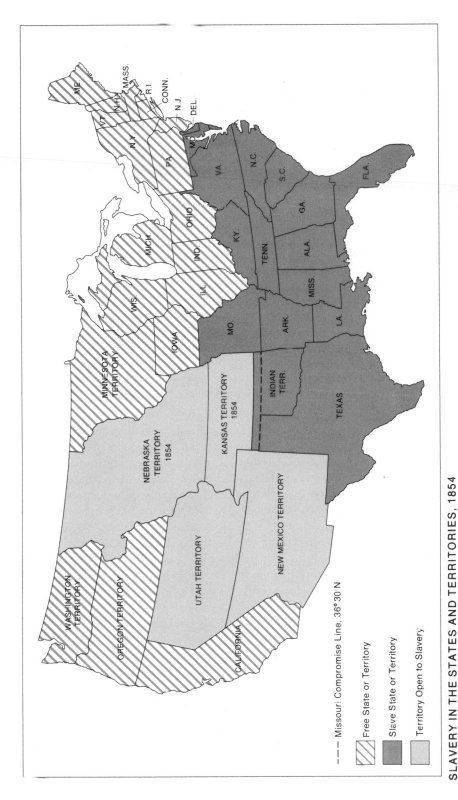

SLAVERY IN THE STATES AND TERRITORIES, 1854

Under the doctrine of popular sovereignty, the territories of Utah and New Mexico conquered from Mexico were opened to slavery by the Compromise of 1850. Far more politically explosive in its impact was the Kansas-Nebraska Act of 1854. Because it opened to slavery the area from which it had been prohibited (north of 36° 30') by the Missouri Compromise of 1820, it was interpreted by many Northerners as a betrayal of freedom.

- - - Missouri Compromise Line, 36° 30' N

Free State or Territory

Slave State or Territory

Territory Open to Slavery

by six antislavery congressmen, including two Free Soil senators, Charles Sumner of Massachusetts and Salmon P. Chase of Ohio, the Appeal branded the Kansas-Nebraska Act as the latest and most monstrous outrage by the Slave Power. With an invective that blended the egalitarian appeals of a stump-speaker with the moral absolutes of a revival minister, the Appeal succeeded in defining for the North what the Kansas-Nebraska Act meant and in serving as the rallying cry for a new antislavery party. The slave-power conspiracy was now accused of rolling back the tide of freedom in the trans-Mississippi West and completing its plan to nationalize slavery. The Appeal branded the legislation as "a criminal betrayal of precious rights" and "as part and parcel of an atrocious plot."[23]

The Kansas-Nebraska Act was the catalyst for the New Republican party, but only the disarray of party loyalties in the early 1850s permitted the Republicans to become a major political force within just two years. When the Republicans first organized at a meeting in Jackson, Michigan, on July 6, 1854, the old party system was already quite disorganized. Several political factions with active local organizations, but no firm party anchor, were ripe to be mobilized into a new party.

Four political groupings flowed into the Republican party. The largest influx came from former Whigs. A party that fused into a coherent whole during the depression of the late 1830s, the Whigs lost their chance to enact their economic program in 1841–1842 and failed to fashion an effective political response to the more buoyant economy that set in under Polk. Compounding the party's problems was the confusion projected by the inconsistent choice of presidential standard-bearers. Taylor's candidacy in 1848 alienated many Northern Whigs, and the turn in 1852 to Winfield Scott, another Mexican War hero, was unpopular with both Northern and Southern Whigs. A lukewarm supporter of the compromises of 1850, Scott was not conservative enough on slavery for the South. For the North he failed to inspire confidence from Whigs leaning towards antislavery. Thus, in Massachusetts the Whigs polled barely half of their normal presidential vote in 1852. Oriented from the beginning toward strong leaders, the party floundered when its giants, Clay and Webster, died at mid-century.

The Whigs also had always been susceptible to the virus of antipartyism. The Antimasons and evangelicals who came into Whiggery during the 1830s harbored fears of parties as unrepublican institutions of centralized authority. Parties were suspect because they demanded an allegiance that could override the duty of an individual to find moral purpose in public policy. Partisanship could easily become a secular and profane perversion of the religious impulse that should inspire political belief. Constantly hampered in their efforts to compromise differences, because compromise itself implied a violation of moral principle, the Whigs were unable to prevent the permanent defection of ideological dissidents. Following quickly after the departure of the Conscience Whigs in the late 1840s came a numerically larger defection, to Know-Nothingism.

For a brief period between 1853 and 1856, the Know-Nothing party appeared to be on the verge of replacing the Whigs as the major opposition party to the Democrats. Taking its name from the oath of secrecy sworn to by members of nativist lodges, the party surprised all seasoned politicians by the suddenness of its success in 1854. It carried scores of local elections in the Northeastern and Mid-Atlantic states, controlled both houses of the Massachusetts legislature, and sent 121 supporters to Congress. Even after the Republicans had made major inroads, the presidential candidate of the Know-Nothings still won 21 percent of the vote in 1856.

As a political phenomenon, Know-Nothingism had much in common with the rise of Jacksonian Democracy a generation earlier. Both movements appealed to those disillusioned with a standing political order that they felt did not protect them from dislocating and threatening economic change. Whereas the monster that personified and caused social disruption for the Jacksonian Democrats was the Bank, for the Know-Nothings it was the Catholic conspiracy, "the papal plot to subvert American freedom."[24]

Transmitted to the New World with the Puritan vanguard, anti-Catholic prejudice in America was older than the republic. With the increase in Catholic immigration in the Jacksonian period, this prejudice was exploited by Whig politicians in their recruitment of voters. By the 1840s new anti-Catholic parties began to mobilize native-born Protestant artisans in Northeastern port cities. For these artisans the Catholic immigrants were the symbol, and in many cases the cause of, the industrial capitalism which was undermining their crafts. The nativist artisans also blamed the new Catholic workers for the moral decline that they associated with the evolution of an urban culture of brothels, gambling dens, and secret gangs. What transformed the localized political symptoms of anti-Catholicism into a mass political movement was the conjuncture of two special conditions in the early 1850s: the proportionately heaviest immigration in American history and the significant acceleration of market change.

In the decade that ended in 1854, nearly three million immigrants arrived in the United States. These newcomers alone comprised almost 15 percent of the total population, the highest percentage registered at any time in American history. Urban immigrant communities, concentrations of slum-dwelling Catholics packed 50 to a house

An Anti-Catholic Riot, 1844. Anti-Catholic prejudices fueled much of the Know-Nothing movement. During this riot in Philadelphia, twenty-four people were killed and two Catholic churches were burned before the state militia (shown on the left) were able to restore order. (The Bettmann Archive)

in New York City and 163 per acre in the city's low-income wards, added a highly visible ethnic and religious dimension to the growing gap between the rich and the poor. By 1851, after the five-year waiting period required in most states for naturalization had passed, immigrants began to vote in large numbers. As noted earlier, most of them, predominately poor, Irish, and Catholic, voted Democratic in support of that party's stand on matters of individual conscience.

Concerns over the enhanced political power of the Catholics detached many Protestants from their old parties and sent them into the ranks of Know-Nothingism. About two-thirds of these Protestants were former Whigs who were angry and confused by the abortive Whig effort to attract Catholic voters in the presidential campaign of 1852. Former Democrats who became Know-Nothings tended to be rural Methodists and Baptists in the Midwest who now feared Catholicism more than the Congregationalist establishment.

The Know-Nothings, like the Whigs before them, offered a politics of cultural uniformity. The Know-Nothing publicist, Samuel Busey, in a statement that echoed eighteenth-century concepts of republicanism and contemporary fears of cultural differences, declared, "A government, to be homogeneous, must preserve the homogeneity of its citizens."[25] By opposing temperance, legal restrictions on Sunday behavior, and Protestant socialization in the public schools, the immigrants resisted homogenization. Then, in the early 1850s, the archenemy of Protestant America, the Catholic Church, launched an aggressive campaign that seemingly elevated cultural pluralism to a desirable social good. The Church entered politics in an effort to eliminate Protestant Bible readings in public schools and to convince state authorities to set aside school taxes on Catholics for a separate, parochial school system. In response, membership in Know-Nothing lodges swelled.

The school issue alerted working-class Protestants, as well as the middle class, to the Catholic menace proclaimed by the Know-Nothings. Whereas the middle class valued the schools as a training ground for moral self-determination, the working classes associated them with vehicles for social mobility. In either case, the Catholic offensive had to be stopped. The Church, so it was argued, was aiming to undermine the financial health of the public schools and to further the papist plot of spreading the subversive doctrines of superstition and ignorance that held all Catholics in intellectual slavery.

When the school issue became highly politicized in the early 1850s, Protestant workers were especially worried about their chances for social mobility because so many of them were backsliding or barely holding their own. The completion of the first trunk-line railroads connecting the Northeast with the Midwest between 1851 and 1854 produced severe economic dislocation throughout the North. Jobs that were dependent on outmoded forms of transportation, such as the handling of river freight, or on local industries, such as iron foundries, which had prospered in the absence of outside competitors, were suddenly in jeopardy. Trade routes shifted, favorably situated manufacturers enlarged and modernized their factories at the expense of others, and jobs were lost and displaced. And, just when job security was endangered, the cost of living jumped. The inflationary impact of California gold, combined with the raising of local agricultural prices by Western farmers who could now ship to enlarged Eastern and foreign markets, resulted in a 34 percent increase in wholesale commodity prices from 1849 to 1855. The cost of living for the unskilled poor in Eastern cities rose by 42 percent between 1851 and 1855. Unemployment, inflation, and sharp slumps in business activity in 1851, 1854, and 1855 exposed an increasingly angry work force to a menacing economic environment.

In struggling to defend themselves against the bewildering uncertainties of market change, American workers found refuge in the certainties of their native birth and Protestant heritage. In a self-proclaimed crusade to purify America of the Catholic conspirators who supposedly defiled the workplace with ignorant, cheap labor, the schools with superstitious bigotry, the working-class neighborhood with prostitutes and drunken criminals, and democracy itself with blocs of regimented Catholics voting under the orders of the priest and the Democratic liquor dealer, workers joined the Know-Nothings to impose their own moral order on the disruptive forces of economic change. The surge of workers and the lower middle class into Know-Nothingism accounted for the movement's explosive growth. Convinced that the major parties were unwilling to protect their jobs and Protestant republicanism, many shed their former political ties. Others were jolted into political activity for the first time by the shock of economic disruption. The result was a party led by politicians who were younger and more likely to be artisans and clerks than their counterparts among the Democrats and Whigs.

Despite their stunning successes in the early 1850s, the Know-Nothings were unable to establish themselves as a permanent national party. Membership in the lodges was very volatile, and the party was unable to escape charges of bigotry and negativism. Although the Know-Nothings were skillful at exploiting specific, local grievances, their position as a national party boiled down to little more than a demand for an extension of the naturalization period for immigrants and a prohibition on the foreign-born holding political office. Consequently, the party could offer no positive solutions to a national electorate. Then, in 1856, the party split on sectional lines over what stand it should take on slavery. Know-Nothings now filtered into a Republican party that successfully submerged fears over the Catholic plot into those of the Slave Power conspiracy.

Political abolitionists and a minority of Northern Democrats outraged by the Kansas-Nebraska Act filled out the Whiggish core of the Republicans. The former viewed the Republicans as a necessary, though flawed, political weapon in the struggle against slavery. The latter, known as the anti-Nebraska Democrats, invoked the imagery of the Slave Power to justify their party break. The national party, charged Democratic bolters in New York, now no longer "spoke and acted for Freedom" but had "fallen into the Hands of office holders and political adventurers, serving as the tools of a slave-holding oligarchy."[26] In the Northeast, often after passing through Know-Nothingism first, 20 percent to 25 percent of the Democratic voters of 1852 defected to the Republicans by 1856. In the Midwest, some 10 percent to 15 percent of the Democrats made the same journey.

The defection of Northern Democrats sealed the fate of the Whig party. Antislavery and nativist Whigs in the North now had a compelling reason to drop their old party name and form a new party that could embrace their former political enemies. Once this fusion began, Northern Democratic strength in Congress suddenly fell and, as shown in Table 5.1, the House Democrats were predominately Southerners after 1854. The sectionalized Republican party fed off the loss of sectional balance within the Democracy.

Table 5.1   Sectional Balance of House Democrats

The ability of House Democrats to serve as a counterweight to sectionalism dropped markedly in the 1850s. As a result of the unpopularity of the Kansas-Nebraska Act in the North, the sectional balance among Democratic representatives swung decisively to the Southern wing of the party.

YEAR ELECTED	NORTHERN	SOUTHERN	PERCENTAGE OF NORTHERN
1846	54	54	50
1848	55	61	47
1850	81	60	57
1852	91	67	58
1854	25	63	28
1856	53	75	41
1858	34	68	33

Source: Compiled from figures in David M. Potter, *The Impending Crisis, 1848–1861* (New York: Harper Colophon Books, 1976), pp. 174–175, 238–239.

The Republican Synthesis

By 1856 the Republicans were the new political home for Conscience Whigs, many former Know-Nothings, anti-Nebraska Democrats, and former Liberty men and Free Soilers. The party carried 11 of the 16 free states in the presidential election of 1856. Had the Republicans also won Pennsylvania and Indiana or Illinois, they would have captured the presidency. That the party came as close as it did was the overriding message of the campaign.

The Republicans revealed just how ripe was the timing for a major new party. The Polk administration had simultaneously politicized the expansion of slavery and laid to rest the old economic issues around which Democrats and Whigs had formed their enduring identities. The low Democratic tariff of 1847 and the reestablishment of the Independent Treasury under Polk coincided with a return of prosperity financed by California gold and British investments shifted out of a Europe wracked by fears of revolution in 1848. Banks and tariffs receded as reference points for partisan division just as the slavery issue came to the forefront. Then, the Democrats and Whigs mutually pledged themselves to honor the slavery settlements of 1850. As had happened after the War of 1812, the parties no longer seemed to offer voters clear and distinct choices. Consequently, politicians in the early 1850s, especially the younger ones and those without a secure power base in one of the major parties, based much of their appeal on the argument that change was long overdue. Illustrative of the argument was a speech in Cincinnati in 1852 by George Julian, an Indiana Free Soiler and a founder of the Republican party:[27]

> There was once a time when the Whig and Democratic parties were arrayed against each other upon certain tolerably well defined political issues. That time is past. . . . They are at this time pitted against each other in a mere scramble for place and power. . . . But if I am right in this, then I have been wrong in dignifying these organizations as *parties.* They are *factions,* the great bane of republics, and every lover of his country should labor for their overthrow.

A Democratic Satire of the Republicans. This cartoon from the Presidential campaign of 1856 shows how the Democrats tried to portray the Republicans as a motley collection of cranky reformers who threatened the personal liberties of white, male Americans. Incidentally, although Frémont was an Episcopalian, the cartoonist included a priest in order to pin the charge of Popery on the Republicans. (Museum of the City of New York)

Young men, those who were most vulnerable to sudden economic reversals in the 1850s and least attached, if at all, to a major party, were the voters most likely to be persuaded by this argument. The Know-Nothings had shown the way. Their appeal to young Pennsylvanians in 1854 was such that a voter in his twenties was twice as likely to support the Know-Nothings as was one over the age of thirty. Throughout the 1850s the largest age cohort of voters, 36 percent to 38 percent of the total, were those under the age of thirty, and the Republicans followed the Know-Nothings' lead in mobilizing these newer, younger voters.

The most popular slogan of the Republicans in the campaign of 1856 was "Free Soil, Free Labor, Free Men, Free Speech, and Frémont." The last alliteration in this expanded refrain of the Free Soil party referred to John C. Frémont, the Republicans' presidential nominee. An adventurer, military explorer, and highly publicized figure in the American conquest of California, Frémont was a political newcomer who was accepted by all party factions. He offered the familiar symbolic appeal of the soldier unsullied by partisan corruption. Frémont would soon fade as a national figure in the party, but the themes in the slogan that his name so neatly rounded off continued to hold and attract voters to the Republicans. It was those themes, set off in bold relief against the menacing backdrop of the Slave Power, that fused material ambitions and moral discomforts into an ideology that spoke to the new political majority in the North.

The Republican economic platform represented an updated and politically viable version of Clay's American System. What now provided a majority backing in the

North for Whiggish economic ideas was the maturation of the complementary market needs of the East and West. As prefigured by the Erie Canal, and as hammered into place by the trunk-line railroads of the 1850s, all of which ran east-west, not north-south, the economic interests of the North had coalesced into one common market by 1860. The development of iron-ore deposits in the upper Midwest, the growth of local industries, and the accumulation of manufacturing capital, all of which were accelerated by the railroads, now made the West more receptive to the high tariffs long favored by Eastern manufacturers. In turn, the East now supported a more liberal land policy. By the time Webster's generation had passed, Eastern conservatives had lost their fear that the rapid growth of the West represented an economic and political drag on Eastern progress. As a market psychology took hold, conservatives were less prone to think in terms of a static order in the East losing population, political representation, and cheap labor to the West. Now, the very expansion of the West was generating an ever-enlarging home market for industrial goods manufactured in the East. Beginning in the 1820s, a new factory population compensated in numbers for the farmers who were leaving for the West. Because both the Northeast and Midwest favored increased federal support for internal improvements, the agenda was set for the Republican commitment to a protective tariff, homestead legislation, and transportation subsidies.

In formulating their activist economic program, the Republicans were riding the crest of a tremendous market expansion in the 1850s. That expansion was temporarily interrupted in the North by the Panic of 1857, a brief but sharp downturn triggered by excessive speculation in railroads. The Panic, however, aided the Republicans by seemingly highlighting the need for the economic stimulus of their program.

Nearly half of all business corporations in America in 1860 were chartered during the 1850s. The same decade registered a near doubling of capital invested in manufacturing. Breakthroughs in communications were achieved by the spread of the commercial telegraph. Total wire miles jumped from 3,000 in 1848 to 56,000 in 1860. From the beginning, financial and commercial items dominated the new information network. Markets, the buying and selling of goods, now functioned over a greatly expanded area at a fraction of the time and cost needed before electronic communication.

One unmistakable result of the demographic and social consequences of more business being conducted more cheaply and quickly was a surge in the growth of small and medium-sized towns, the nerve centers of market transactions in the countryside. These towns, ranging from 2,500 to 25,000 in population, grew by 67 percent during the 1850s. The increase was twice the national average. Far more prevalent in the North than the South, these local marketing centers were the economic heartland of Republicanism. Leadership in these towns spoke for upwardly mobile, middle-class Protestants who readily identified with the Republicans' economic program.

Evangelical in religious outlook and entrepreneurial in economic orientation, the Republicans were the favored party of the Protestant middle class. By secularizing the evangelical millennium, the Northern middle class came to believe that moral progress and material self-improvement were mutually reinforcing in a republican society dedicated to Christian capitalism. Moral order and economic progress were inseparable. This convergence of evangelicalism and capitalism solved the problem of how to maintain order and virtue in an individualistic, materialistic society. Starting from the assumption that human nature was naturally lazy, savage, and sinful, the middle class saw the market operating as an essential civilizing force. By offering the hope of a tangible reward, the market would elicit that self-discipline necessary for productive work. The virtuous citizen of the mid-nineteenth century was now the economically successful man, and his virtue consisted precisely in his success at self-centered economic activity. This success demonstrated a capacity for self-control and set an example of private gain that, when followed by others, would automatically contribute to the public good.

As success was redefined from service to others to gain for oneself, evangelicalism began to merge with market values. From its eighteenth-century origins as a movement of the underprivileged who attacked their social betters for their ungodly worldliness and arrogant displays of wealth and power, evangelicalism in the North was slowly transformed in the first half of the nineteenth century into a respectable movement of the middle class. The key to this transformation, as we saw in Chapter 3, was the interchangeability of the notions of moral and economic self-determination. Both served the same ends of social order and individual virtue.

Once middle-class evangelicalism found a sectionalized political vehicle in the Republican party, America's political culture became moralized in a dangerously new way. The Whigs, for all their politicizing of moral issues, were a national party. Moreover, the Whigs were always limited in their egalitarian appeals by the party's identification with the restrictive aspects of evangelicalism. By using the concept of the Slave Power as the linchpin of their ideology, the sectionalized Republicans were able to combine evangelical fervor with a broadened egalitarian appeal.

As anti-Southern as it was antislavery, the Slave Power construct was a master symbol that functioned on a variety of levels to promote Republican unity and the party's sense of moral purpose. On the most basic level the symbol identified the common enemy against which all egalitarian Christians should unite. Conservatives were warned that Constitutional safeguards were being trampled by Southern political power; radicals were told that the very brazenness of the Slave-Power Conspiracy required a rededication to the principles of the Declaration of Independence. Evangelicals were assured that the millennium was still realizable if only the ungodly barrier of the Slave Power was faced and overcome. Nonevangelicals and the irreligious were promised economic prosperity if the Slave Power could be stopped from blocking Republican legislation aimed at promoting economic opportunity. White supremacists heard that the Republicans would safeguard the territories for free, *white* labor. Racial egalitarians saw the containment of Slave Power as the first step toward emancipation and the ultimate acceptance of blacks as legal equals.

The Republicans' use of the Slave Power concept did more than identify the common enemy. It also offered an explanation for what was wrong with America. If the old parties were corrupt and unresponsive to the people's needs, then, as Julian argued, it was because the Slave Power "has maintained its supremacy for years past through the agency of these heartless factions." If, as the abolitionist Theodore Parker charged, "Wealth is the great object of American desire" and "Covetousness is the American passion,"[28] then the debasement of Christian ideals by the Slave Power's control of the Churches was to blame. In this way, the Slave Power came to symbolize Northern anxieties and doubts over the direction of social change in their own society. Rather than directly attacking the economic exploitation and social dislocation in the North, an attack that would have called into question the assumptions on which economic growth was predicated, Northerners indirectly critiqued the commercialization of their society by equating the Slave Power with the source of unchristian greed and arbitrary power.

In a parallel fashion, *Uncle Tom's Cabin* became a form of moral therapy for the Northern middle class. By far the best selling novel in antebellum America, and one that was serialized in magazines and presented on the stage, Harriet Beecher Stowe's classic brought the antislavery message into the bourgeois parlor. The book both titillated and reassured its readers. It sentimentally dramatized the central concerns of the Protestant middle class—the breakup of families, male sexual lust, the degradation of Christian motherhood, and the dangers of unrestrained power—and then confronted the reader with the message that such excesses were possible only in a society polluted by slavery. Stowe knew her audience well; her most unforgettable villain was the Yankee, Simon Legree.

Appearing in the midst of the Northern uproar over the Fugitive Slave Act of 1850, federal legislation that legally obligated all citizens to assist, if requested, in the capture of a fugitive slave, *Uncle Tom's Cabin* drove home the point that the Slave Power corrupted all that it touched. Thus, the South became important for the North as a reference point for what would happen if economic power were unrestrained by Christian morality. As described first by the abolitionists, and then the Republicans, Southern whites typically drank too much, gambled away their money, and assaulted one another in brawls. Stereotyped very much like their party colleagues in the Northern slums, the Irish Catholics, Southern whites were depicted as slothful, savage heathens. They were presented as what Northerners would become if the Slave Power remained unchecked.

The core demand, the minimum stand that the Republicans said had to be taken against the Slave Power, was the prohibition of slavery in the territories. Here was a constitutional way in which all those morally troubled by slavery could combat the institution. Here as well, argued the Republicans, was the way to guarantee economic opportunity and independence in a market society that was becoming overcrowded with competitors. The Republicans always denied that permanent class lines were forming in the North. However, they also recognized that economic power was becoming concentrated and that poverty was on the rise. They reconciled these positions by arguing that any class imbalance was a temporary one that would be eliminated by the safety valve of the territories. This argument, one that was steeped in Jeffersonian overtones, was hardly a new one. Caleb Cushing, a Whig, had classically expressed it in 1839:[29]

> Emigration to the West is the great safety-valve of our population, and frees us from all the dangers of the poverty, and discontent, and consequent disorders, which always spring up in a community when the number of its inhabitants has outrun its capacity to afford due recompense to honest industry and ambition.

What was new in the 1850s was the Northern perception of a deliberate Southern plot to deny free labor fair and equal opportunity in the territories. This is what the Free Soilers had proclaimed in 1848 and what apparently had been confirmed by the Kansas-Nebraska Act in 1854. Because Northerners believed that slavery degraded all labor by associating it with the despised slave, any effort to establish slavery in a territory was interpreted as a move to keep out free labor. Similarly, Southern opposition to homestead legislation in the 1850s was viewed as an attack on free labor. This legislation would have granted 160 acres of public land to any citizen who made a commitment to work it. By blocking free homesteads, Southern politicians were accused of locking into poverty those Northerners who otherwise would seek to econom-ically better themselves in the West. In fact, the laboring poor lacked the capital, skills, and perhaps the desire to stake out farms in the West. But land-hungry farmers and their sons had the resources and were eager to make the move. They did perceive the Slave Power as a real threat to their dreams of economic independence. Thus, the Republican commitment to free soil was simultaneously an effort to expand the market and to escape its consequences. In time the territories, if settled by free labor, would become part of the home market. But the very process of their settlement would reduce class pressures in the East and offer another generation of Americans the hope of escaping economic dependency.

The Democratic Party Splits

The national structure of the Democratic party kept the Republicans out of the White House in 1856. Still, the Democrats had clearly lost their sectional balance. Their nominee was James Buchanan of Pennsylvania. Like his predecessor, Franklin Pierce of New Hampshire, he was a Northerner whom Southern Democrats trusted. Two-thirds of the Buchanan electoral vote came from the slave states. In the South the Democrats lost only Maryland, a state carried by the Know-Nothing nominee, Millard Fillmore, the Whig president from 1850 to 1852 after the death of Zachary Taylor.

The issue of the territories was so central to the future of the republic and had become so politicized that the Buchanan presidency, fated to be the last antebellum administration, could hardly avoid becoming enmeshed in it. A cautious man, with a lawyer's faith in the efficacy of procedure, Buchanan nonetheless uncautiously com-mitted his party to two measures that were disastrous to party unity. Both measures were attempts to undercut the Republican opposition by eliminating the territorial issue that had fueled Republican growth. But, as quickly became apparent, neither the Dred Scott decision nor the administration's handling of statehood for Kansas removed the issue. Indeed, the very opposite occurred. The issue became more explosive than ever.

At least indirectly, Buchanan encouraged the Supreme Court to take a definite stand on the status of slavery in the territories. The Court took such a stand in the Dred Scott case. In a long legal battle financed by antislavery money, Dred Scott, a slave, claimed his freedom on the grounds that a former owner had taken him into free territory north of the Missouri Compromise line of 30° 30'. In a decision announced in the spring of 1857, just after Buchanan had called attention to its importance in his inaugural address, a divided Court ruled that Congress had no constitutional authority to prohibit slavery in the territories. Slavery, as a form of property recognized in the Constitution, fell under the protection of the Fifth Amendment, which stated that no citizen could be deprived of life, liberty, or property without due process of law. A slaveholder was a citizen and, said the Court, Congress had no right to single out slave property for prohibition in the territories. As a black, Dred Scott was not a citizen, whether free or slave, according to Chief Justice Roger Taney. Blacks were entitled only to those rights of citizenship that a given state might decide to grant them. They were not citizens of the United States as defined in the Constitution.

Slaveholders were elated. The Northern reaction was epitomized by an editorial in the Cincinnati *Commercial,* which stated "It is now demonstrated that there is such a thing as the Slave Power."[30] Contrary to Buchanan's expectations, a legal decision, especially a sectionalized one supported by five of the six Southerners sitting on the Court and opposed by three of the four Northerners, could not settle a decisive issue that was more moral than judicial in content.

The *Dred Scott* decision, if enforced, would have destroyed Douglas' position that the settlers in a territory acting under the right of self-government had the legal authority to decide the question of slavery. It was hard, if not impossible, to see how a territorial legislature could now exercise a veto over slavery when the Supreme Court had denied that power to Congress, the constitutional superior of the legislature and the source of its legal existence. Anxious to avoid an open confrontation with Douglas, and influenced by the Southern Democrats to whom he owed his election, Buchanan threw the full weight of his administration behind the Lecompton Constitution in 1857.

Named after the Kansas town where a proslavery constitutional convention met, the Lecompton Constitution legalized slavery in Kansas. It offered the voters a choice as to whether they favored the admission of additional slaves, but slave property already in the territory was recognized and protected. The North in general, and Douglas in particular, blasted Lecompton as a travesty of majority rule. In an emotionally charged setting in which popular sovereignty was reduced to a race between free-soilers and proslavery men to gain formal control of the territorial government, the proslavery forces won by resorting to fraud and violence. There was no doubt that the free-soilers were in the majority and had been deprived of a fair vote for or against slavery. Still, from Buchanan's perspective, Lecompton had one great virtue. It was a legal state constitution which, once approved by Congress, would put the status of slavery under the authority of a state government. That government could subsequently make any decision on slavery it wanted to without any constitutional issues being raised. If Lecompton were accepted, Buchanan could sidestep the clash between popular sovereignty and the *Dred Scott* issue.

Buchanan's reasoning made legal sense, but the result was that he had to sacrifice political sense. Douglas, already damaged by his association with the Slave Power by Northern voters after the Kansas-Nebraska Act, had to oppose Lecompton in order to save his political career. After a complicated battle in Congress, a coalition of Northern Democrats and Republicans sent Lecompton back to Kansas with the stipulation that a new ratifying election be held. Kansas eventually entered the Union in 1861 as a free state.

The Lecompton Constitution, on top of the *Dred Scott* case, completed the sectionalization of the Democratic party. Each wing of the party now accused the other of betraying them. Northern Democrats still held, *Dred Scott* to the contrary, that slavery could not be established in any territory unless the settlers supported it by passing the police legislation necessary to protect it. Popular sovereignty, they insisted, would have worked in Kansas had not the collusion of Buchanan with the proslavery forces turned it into a shameful deception. According to the Southern Democrats, the deceit rested with the other side. In an act of bad faith, the Douglas Democrats refused to abide by the *Dred Scott* decision. Only the enemies of the South would have harped on popular sovereignty as a pretext to deprive the Union of another slave state. In addition, the Southern Democrats held that any honest implementation of the decision required Congress to pass legislation protecting the rights of slaveholders in the territories. This was their answer to Douglas' attempt to salvage popular sovereignty.

A Divided Culture and the Election of 1860

By 1860 the institutional centers binding together the sections were greatly weakened, in some cases gone. In religion, as in politics, institutional affiliations now drove Americans apart. The major Protestant denominations had split in the 1840s and 1850s over the issue of religiously sanctioning slavery. Church members were still overwhelmingly Protestant, but they worshipped an antislavery God in the North and a proslavery one in the South. Faith in republicanism, which often has been compared to a civil religion, was likewise sectionalized. Although Americans still used the vocabulary and concepts of republicanism as their common political language, the words now had a far different meaning for Northerners and Southerners. There was no better example than the sectionalized reaction to the caning of Charles Sumner in May 1856.

In the midst of a blistering attack on the Kansas policy of the Pierce administration, Sumner, a Republican senator from Massachusetts, viciously maligned a Southern senator, Andrew Butler of South Carolina. Preston Brooks, a nephew of Butler's and a representative from South Carolina, retaliated by beating Sumner senseless, leaving him slumped over his Senate desk. In the South Brooks was hailed as a hero who had upheld civilized standards and personal codes of honor by giving a foulmouthed, fanatical abolitionist the only punishment he was worthy of, a physical thrashing. In the North Brooks was vilified as a beast out of control, a savage, bloodthirsty animal whose behavior was just what one could expect from a society cursed by slavery. Sumner, a "Damn Rascal liar tory and Traitor," in the eyes of John Lawson of Columbia, South Carolina, was a "Christian, a gentleman, a statesman, and a scholar"[31] to the Reverend Henry Ward Beecher of New York City.

The Brooks Caning of Sumner. The caning occurred at a critical point in the history of the still-young Republican party. It spurred recruitment of new members to the party by fixing in the Northern mind the image of a violent South that favored force over reason in settling political disputes. (The Boston Public Library)

Both sets of antagonists in the debate claimed to be defending republican standards of civility, restraint, honor, and individual liberty. Yet, depending on the sectional origin, the meaning of these concepts was reversed. Most frightening about the debate was its stark revelation of how Northerners and Southerners could no longer agree even on what constituted civilized standards of conduct. What was bestial aggression for the one was honorable defense for the other. Such a fundamental disagreement indicated that Northerners and Southerners were using each other to define different moral identities for themselves. Once these moral dichotomies infused a political culture already obsessed with the search for conspiratorial enemies of republican independence and dignity, each section began to see the other as the enemy. In national politics this process climaxed in the presidential election of 1860 and its immediate aftermath. John Brown's raid at Harpers Ferry, Virginia, in the preceding fall had aroused the worst fears of Southern whites regarding their own personal safety. Brown was quickly captured and executed, and the Republicans, like the vast majority of Northern whites, denounced Brown's efforts to overthrow slavery by force. Nonetheless, many Southern whites now believed that the Republicans were a party of murderous abolitionists. Remaining bonds of national trust seemed about to snap.

Only the Northern Democrats stood as a political center in 1860. In an election rife with cries of disunion, four candidates jockeyed for position in what became two sets of sectional elections. The Republicans ran Abraham Lincoln of Illinois. His reputation as a moderate on the slavery issue and his regional identification were very useful assets to the Republican strategy of forging a solid Northern front by shifting states in the lower Midwest into the Republican camp. After Southern Democrats bolted the party's national convention at Charleston, South Carolina, over the refusal of the platform committee to endorse a congressional slave code for the territories, the Democrats nominated two candidates in two separate conventions—Stephen Douglas for the North and John Breckinridge of Kentucky for the South. The fourth candidate was an old-line Whig from Tennessee, John Bell. He represented the Constitutional Unionists, a new party of die-hard Know-Nothings and former Whigs from the upper South. Fearful that victory for any of the other three parties would precipitate disunion, the Constitutional Unionists campaigned as the only true defenders of the Union. They conspicuously refused to take a stand on the issue of slavery in the territories.

As shown in Table 5.2, the election was mainly a contest between Lincoln and Douglas in the North and Breckinridge and Bell in the South. The distribution of Douglas' vote revealed him as the most national of the candidates. However, aside from the Irish Catholic vote in the cities, his strength was scattered, and he won outright the electoral votes of only one state, Missouri. Bell more than held his own against Breckinridge in the upper South, but Breckinridge swept the lower South. The sweep that mattered in terms of electoral votes was in the North. The Republican coalition of rural and small-town Yankees, evangelicals, and the middle class gave Lincoln absolute majorities in well over 90 percent of the counties in the Northeast and Midwest. Although he polled only 40 percent of the total popular vote, Lincoln nonetheless had a clear electoral majority, with 180 out of 303 electoral votes.

The mere fact of Lincoln's election was enough to trigger secession in the lower South. In turn secession touched off an internal crisis of order that would keep the sections divided until 1877. The themes of Civil War and Reconstruction America will be explored in Chapters 6 and 7.

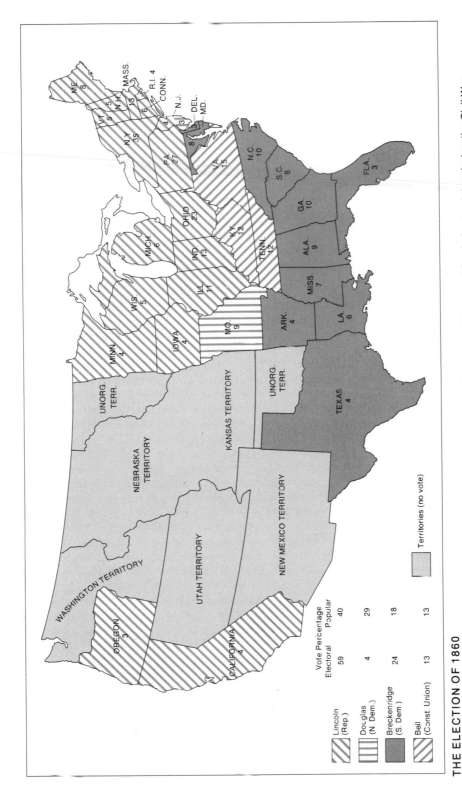

THE ELECTION OF 1860

The pattern of Lincoln and Breckinridge states comes very close to the eventual division into Union and Confederate states during the Civil War. Virginia and Tennessee, two Confederate states carried by John Bell, are the major exceptions. Also noteworthy is the disparity between the size of Douglas's popular vote (a scattered one) and his very low electoral vote.

	Vote Percentage	
	Electoral	Popular
Lincoln (Rep.)	59	40
Douglas (N. Dem.)	4	29
Breckenridge (S. Dem.)	24	18
Bell (Const. Union)	13	13

Territories (no vote)

Table 5.2   Presidential Vote by Sections, 1860
              (in percentages)

The election of 1860 amounted to a North-South contest between two different sets of candidates. Lincoln received the most sectionalized vote and most probably would have still carried the free states even had he been faced with a united opposition.

	FREE STATES	SLAVE STATES
Lincoln	54	2
Douglas	24	13
Breckinridge	3	45
Bell	2	39
Fusion	17	1

Source: Compiled from figures in Potter, op. cit., 443.

SUGGESTED READING

William R. Brock, *Parties and Political Conscience* (1979), is the best political synthesis for the 1840s. Joel H. Silbey, *The Shrine of Party: Congressional Voting Behavior, 1841–1852* (1967), by stressing the resiliency of institutional and partisan loyalties, offers quite a different political interpretation of the decade. Helpful surveys can also be found in Glyndon G. Van Deusen, *The Jacksonian Era, 1828–1848* (1959), and F. J. Turner, *The United States, 1830–1850* (1935).

There is no adequate study of the critical Tyler administration. Useful, but outdated, are Oscar D. Lambert, *Presidential Politics in the United States, 1841–1844* (1936), and Robert J. Morgan, *A Whig Embattled: The Presidency under John Tyler* (1954). Three political biographies—Clement Eaton, *Henry Clay and the Art of American Politics* (1959); James P. Shenton, *Robert John Walker: A Politician from Jackson to Lincoln* (1961); and Robert F. Dalzell, Jr., *Daniel Webster and the Trial of American Nationalism, 1843–1852* (1973)—fill in part of the story. The resurgence of expansionism under Tyler is explained in James C. N. Paul, *Rift in the Democracy* (1951), and Thomas R. Hietala, *Manifest Design: Anxious Aggrandizement in Late Jacksonian America* (1985), a penetrating study on the commercial and territorial goals of the Democrats in the 1840s. Frederick W. Merk, *Manifest Destiny and Mission in American History* (1963), and *The Monroe Doctrine and American Expansionism* (1966), are important revisionist studies on the ideology and diplomacy of expansion in the 1840s, and his *Slavery and the Annexation of Texas* (1972) provides a necessary counterpoint to J. H. Smith, *The Annexation of Texas* (1911). William C. Binkley, *The Texas Revolution* (1952), is the standard account of the Texas independence movement, and Gene M. Brack, *Mexico Views Manifest Destiny, 1821–1846* (1976), presents the Mexican side.

The best balanced and the most thorough treatment of the Polk presidency is Charles G. Sellers, *James K. Polk: Continentalist, 1843–1849* (1966). The most critical assessment of his role in the coming of the Mexican War will be found in Glenn W. Price, *Origins of the War With Mexico: The Polk-Stockton Intrigue* (1967). Otis Singletary, *The Mexican War* (1960), is a short work that is especially strong on Polk's political problems with his generals, while K. Jack Bauer, *The Mexican War, 1846–1848* (1974), concentrates on the military campaigns. The American thrust to the Pacific is detailed in Norman A. Graebner, *Empire on the Pacific* (1955). John H. Schroeder, *Mr. Polk's War* (1973), deals with antiwar dissent, and Kinley J. Brauer, *Cotton versus Conscience* (1967), chronicles the rise of the Conscience Whigs in Massachusetts politics. The politics of the Wilmot Proviso is covered in Chaplain W. Morrison, *Democratic Politics and Sectionalism* (1967). Robert W. Johannsen, *To the Halls of the Montezumas* (1985), is an imaginative cultural history of the impact of the Mexican War upon American thought. For the election of 1848 and the Free Soil Party, see Joseph G. Rayback, *Free Soil: The Election of 1848* (1970), and Frederick J. Blue, *The Free Soilers: Third Party Politics, 1848–1854* (1973).

Three magisterial studies by David Brion Davis provide a broad perspective on abolitionism: *The Problem of Slavery in Western Culture* (1966); *The Problem of Slavery in the Age of Revolution, 1770–1823* (1975); and *Slavery and Human Progress* (1984). Gilbert H. Barnes, *The Anti-Slavery Impulse* (1933), is a valuable older work that stresses the impact of evangelicalism on abolitionism. For modern surveys, see Louis Filler, *The Crusade against Slavery* (1960); Merton L. Dillon, *The Abolitionists: The Growth of a Dissenting Minority* (1974); and James B. Stewart, *Holy Warriors: The Abolitionists and American Slavery* (1976).

Particularly helpful on setting abolitionism in the cultural mainstream of Northern reform is Ronald G. Walters, *The Anti-Slavery Appeal* (1976). Lewis Perry, *Radical Abolitionism: Anarchy and the Government of God in Antislavery Thought* (1973), examines the perfectionist and anarchist strain in abolitionism, and James David Essig, "The Lord's Free Man: Charles G. Finney and His Abolitionism," CWH 24 (1978), shows how millennialism informed the abolitionist critique of the slave South. On abolitionism and the Northern churches, see John R. McKivigan, *The War against Proslavery Religion* (1984). John L. Thomas, *The Liberator: William Lloyd Garrison* (1963), and Walter M. Merrill, *Against Wind and Tide: A Biography of William Lloyd Garrison* (1963), are the best biographies of Garrison; and Aileen S. Kraditor, *Means and Ends in American Abolitionism* (1967), analyzes the role of the Garrisonians in the 1840 split of the abolitionists. Lawrence J. Friedman, *Gregarious Saints: Self and Community in American Abolitionism, 1830–1870* (1982), presents a psychological profile of the regional subgroups within abolitionism, and Robert H. Abzug, *Passionate Liberator: Theodore Dwight Weld and the Dilemma of Reform* (1980), is a superb psychological study of a leading abolitionist. On opposition to abolitionism in the North, see Leonard L. Richards, *"Gentleman of Property and Standing": Anti-Abolition Mobs in Jacksonian America* (1970), and Lorman Ratner, *Powder Keg: Northern Opposition to the Antislavery Movement, 1831–1840* (1968); for the South, see Clement Eaton, *The Freedom-of-Thought Struggle in the Old South* (1964). Martin Duberman, ed., *The Antislavery Vanguard* (1965), and Lewis Perry and Michael Fellman, eds., *Antislavery Reconsidered* (1979), are major collections of articles on abolitionism as a whole.

In demonstrating the support of artisans and shopkeepers for abolitionism, John B. Jetz, "The Antislavery Constituency in Jacksonian New York City," CWH 27 (1981), cautions against viewing abolitionism as just a movement of middle-class evangelicals. Abolitionism also had a critical black component, as was first established in the groundbreaking study by Benjamin Quarles, *Black Abolitionists* (1969). The racial prejudice that these abolitionists often encountered from their white counterparts is shown in Jane H. Pease and William H. Pease, *They Who Would Be Free: Blacks' Search for Freedom, 1830–1861* (1974). On the activities of black abolitionists in Britain, see R. J. M. Blackett, *Building an Antislavery Wall: Black Abolitionists in the Atlantic Abolitionist Movement, 1830–1860* (1974).

Dwight L. Dumond, *Antislavery: The Crusade for Freedom in America* (1961), is a very readable survey of antislavery politics, but it has been superseded by Richard H. Sewell, *Ballots for Freedom* (1976). The political linkage of civil liberties for whites with freedom for blacks is traced out in Russel B. Nye, *Fettered Freedom: Civil Liberties and the Slavery Controversy* (1963), and Thomas O. Morris, *Free Men All: The Personal Liberty Laws of the North, 1780–1861* (1974). Eugene H. Berwanger, *The Frontier Against Slavery* (1967), is a vivid reminder that many Northern whites favored political antislaveryism out of a racist desire to keep all blacks out of the territories. Biographies that are strong on the politics of antislavery in the 1840s include: Betty Fladeland, *James Gillespie Birney: Slaveholder to Abolitionist* (1955); Richard H. Sewell, *John P. Hale and the Politics of Abolition* (1965); and James B. Stewart, *Joshua R. Giddings and the Tactics of Radical Politics* (1970).

Allan Nevins, *Ordeal of the Union* (2 vols., 1947), is a very thorough political survey of the last decade of the antebellum Union, but David M. Potter, *The Impending Crisis, 1848–1861*

(1976), is unsurpassed for its subtle mastery of detail. An original and powerfully argued synthesis that is indispensable for understanding the shifts in party loyalties in the 1850s is Michael F. Holt, *The Political Crisis of the 1850s* (1978). Superb on the political infighting that led to the Compromise of 1850 is Holman Hamilton, *Prologue to Conflict* (1964). The literature on the Kansas-Nebraska Act is complex and controversial, and Roy F. Nichols, "The Kansas-Nebraska Act: A Century of Historiography," MVHR 43 (1956), is a very helpful guide. Robert W. Johannsen, *Stephen A. Douglas* (1973), provides the fullest assessment of Douglas's role. For the actual settlement of the Kansas-Nebraska territories and the local disputes over land, see James C. Malin, *The Nebraska Question, 1852–1854* (1953), and Paul W. Gates, *Fifty Million Acres: Conflicts over Kansas Land Policy, 1854–1890* (1954). Three recent studies offer the best introduction to Know-Nothingism: Michael F. Holt, "The Politics of Impatience," JAH 60 (1973); Stephen E. Maizlish, "The Meaning of Nativism and the Crisis of the Union," in Stephen E. Maizlish and John J. Kushma, eds., *Essays on American Antebellum Politics, 1840– 1860* (1982); and William E. Gienapp, "Nativism and the Creation of a Republican Majority in the North before the Civil War," JAH 72 (1985). Essential for understanding the Protestant roots of the anti-Catholic prejudice off which so much of Know-Nothingism fed is Ray Billington, *The Protestant Crusade, 1800–1860* (1938). For the South, see W. D. Overdyke, *The Know-Nothing Party in the South* (1950). Jean Gould Hales, "'Co-Laborers in the Cause': Women in the Antebellum Nativist Movement," CWH 24 (1979), explains the important role played by working-class women.

Eric Foner, *Free Soil, Free Labor, Free Men* (1970), is the best analysis of the ideology of the new Republican party in the 1850s. Allan Nevins, *The Emergence of Lincoln* (2 vols, 1950), and Hans Trefousse, *The Radical Republicans* (1969), are also important works on the Republicans. Michael F. Holt, *Forging a Majority: The Formation of the Republican Party in Pittsburgh* (1969), is an exemplary local study, and the rise of the Republicans is a central theme of two recent, excellent works: Stephen E. Maizlish, *The Triumph of Sectionalism: The Transformation of Ohio Politics, 1844–1856* (1983), and Dale Baum, *The Civil War Party System: The Case of Massachusetts, 1849–1876* (1984). The economic philosophy of the party, as exemplified by Lincoln, is outlined in G. S. Boritt, *Lincoln and the Economics of the American Dream* (1978).

Roy F. Nichols, *The Disruption of American Democracy* (1948), brilliantly tells the story of the sectionalization of the Democratic party in the late 1850s. On Democratic ideology and cultural beliefs in the North, see Bruce Collins, "The Ideology of the Ante-bellum Northern Democrats," JAS 11 (1977), and Jean H. Baker, *Affairs of Party: The Political Culture of Northern Democrats in the Mid-Nineteenth Century* (1983). For the Southern Democrats, see Avery V. Craven, *The Growth of Southern Nationalism, 1848–1861* (1953), and David M. Potter, *The South and the Sectional Conflict* (1968). On the ill-fated Buchanan administration, see Philip S. Klein, *President James Buchanan* (1962). Don E. Fehrenbacher, *The Dred Scott Case* (1978), is the definitive work on this landmark case. James A. Rawley, *Race and Politics: "Bleeding Kansas" and the Coming of the Civil War* (1969), covers the turmoil in Kansas, and David E. Meerse, "Presidential Leadership, Suffrage Qualifications, and Kansas: 1857," CWH 24 (1978) reviews the Lecompton controversy and gives Buchanan surprisingly high marks for leadership.

On the formation of the conspiratorial images that each section had of the other by the 1850s, see David Brion Davis, *The Slave Power Conspiracy and the Paranoid Style* (1969). For the critical role of Brooks' caning of Sumner in this process, see William E. Gienapp, "The Crime Against Sumner," CWH 25 (1979), and Harlen Joel Gradin, "Losing Control: The Caning of Charles Sumner and the Erosion of the 'Common Ground On Which Our Political Fabric Was Reared'" (M.A. thesis, University of North Carolina at Chapel Hill, 1981).

No single individual inflamed sectional feelings more passionately than John Brown. For the most negative portrait of Brown, see James C. Malin, *John Brown and the Legend of Fifty-Six* (1942), and, for the most positive, see Stephen B. Oates, *To Purge the Land with Blood: A Biography of John Brown* (1970). The climactic election of 1860 can be followed in Ollinger

Crenshaw, *The Slave States in the Presidential Election of 1860* (1945), and Elting Morison, "Election of 1860" in Arthur M. Schlesinger, Jr., ed., *History of American Presidential Elections, 1789–1968,* Vol. 2 (4 vols., 1971).

NOTES

1. Quoted in Bruce Collins, "The Ideology of the Ante-bellum Northern Democrats," *Journal of American Studies* 11 (1977): 117.
2. Quoted in Frederick Merk, *Slavery and the Annexation of Texas* (New York: Alfred A. Knopf, 1972), p. 93.
3. Allan Nevins, ed., *Polk: The Diary of a President, 1845–1849* (New York: Capricorn Books, 1968), p. 19.
4. Ibid., pp. 81, 82.
5. Quoted in Glyndon G. Van Deusen, *The Jacksonian Era, 1828–1848* (New York: Harper Torchbooks, 1963), p. 223.
6. Nevins, op. cit., p. 106.
7. Rachel Sherman Thorndike, ed., *The Sherman Letters: Correspondence between General and Senator Sherman from 1837 to 1891* (New York: Da Capo Press, 1969), pp. 38–39.
8. Quoted in Carey McWilliams, "'Not Counting Mexicans'," in Bruce A. Glassrud and Alan M. Smith, eds., *Promises to Keep: A Portrayal of Nonwhites in the United States* (Chicago: Rand McNally, 1972), p. 167.
9. Williard Thorp, ed., *Great Short Works of the American Renaissance* (New York: Harper and Row, 1968), pp. 288–289.
10. Quoted in William R. Brock, *Parties and Political Conscience: American Dilemmas, 1840–1850* (Millwood, N.Y.: KTO Press, 1969), p. 191.
11. Quoted in David Brion Davis, ed., *Antebellum American Culture: An Interpretive Anthology* (Lexington, Mass.: D. C. Heath, 1979), p. 34.
12. Quoted in Ralph Korngold, "'Woe if it comes with storm and blood and fire'," in Stephen B. Oates, ed., *Portrait of America,* Vol. I (Boston: Houghton Mifflin, 1978), p. 259.
13. Douglas T. Miller, ed., *The Nature of Jacksonian America* (New York: John Wiley, 1972), pp. 130–131.
14. Quoted in Korngold, op. cit., p. 257.
15. Quoted in Blanche Glassman Hersh, "'Am I Not a Woman and a Sister?' Abolitionist Beginnings of Nineteenth-Century Feminism," in Lewis Perry and Michael Fellman, eds., *Antislavery Reconsidered: New Perspectives on the Abolitionists* (Baton Rouge: Louisiana State University Press, 1979), p. 282.
16. Quoted in Clement Eaton, *The Freedom-of-Thought Struggle in the Old South* (New York: Harper Torchbook, 1964), p. 128.
17. Quoted in James Brewer Stewart, *Holy Warriors: The Abolitionists and American Slavery* (New York: Hill and Wang, 1976), p. 44.
18. Quoted in John B. Jentz, "The Antislavery Constituency in Jacksonian New York City," *Civil War History* 27 (1981): 121.
19. Quoted in Alan M. Kraut, "The Forgotten Reformers: A Profile of Third Party Abolitionists in Antebellum New York," in Perry and Fellman, op. cit., p. 144.
20. Quoted in Merk, op. cit., p. 206.
21. Quoted in Rush Welter, *The Mind of America, 1820–1860* (New York: Columbia University Press, 1975), p. 367.
22. Quoted in David Potter, *The Impending Crisis, 1848–1861* (New York: Harper Colophon Books, 1976), p. 116.
23. *Congressional Globe,* 33 Cong., 1. session., p. 282.
24. Quoted in Robert Kelley, *The Cultural Pattern in American Politics: The First Century* (New York: Alfred A. Knopf, 1979), p. 190.
25. Quoted in Carl F. Kaestle, *The Evolution of an Urban School System: New York City, 1750–1850* (Cambridge: Harvard University Press, 1973), p. 141.
26. Quoted in Welter, op. cit., p. 357.
27. David Brion Davis, ed., *The Fear of Conspiracy: Images of Un-American Subversion from the Revolution to the Present* (Ithaca: Cornell Paperbacks, 1972), p. 125.
28. Ibid., pp. 125, 129.
29. Quoted in Welter, op. cit., p. 316.
30. Quoted in Kelley, op. cit., p. 209.
31. Quoted in Harlan Joel Gradin, "Losing Control: The Caning of Charles Sumner and the Erosion of the 'Common Ground On Which Our Political Fabric Was Reared'" (M.A. thesis, University of North Carolina at Chapel Hill, 1981), pp. 48, 42.

Part II

CIVIL WAR AMERICA

6

The Crisis of Secession and War

In early 1860, Lincoln rhetorically asked in a speech in New York City what would satisfy or appease the South. His answer was: "This and only this: cease to call slavery *wrong,* and join them in calling it *right.* And this must be done thoroughly—done in *acts* as well as in *words.*"[1] In late 1860, in the midst of the secession crisis, an editorial in the New Orleans *Bee* likewise pinpointed an irreducible moral division over slavery as the crux of sectional discord. The editor ruled out any reconciliation because of

> the absolute impossibility of revolutionizing Northern opinion in relation to slavery. Without a change of heart, radical and thorough, all guarantees which might be offered are not worth the paper on which they would be inscribed. . . . The feelings, customs, modes of thought and education of the two sections, are discrepant and often antagonistic. The North and South are heterogeneous and are better apart.[2]

The moral clash was very real, and it slowly dissolved those authentic bonds of the Union that Jefferson Davis referred to as "mutual attachments and common interests."[3] Disunion, the breakdown of the mutual forebearance and trust on which the antebellum Union had rested, was a reality long before the secession winter of 1860–1861.

William Seward of New York, the best known and most visible Republican leader in the late 1850s, spoke of "an irrepressible conflict between opposing and enduring forces"[4] in the free and slave states. Others, notably Democrats in the North and former Whigs in the upper South, strongly disagreed. They saw no fundamental reason for sectional conflict. Sectional tensions were undeniable, but these they traced to the plottings of irresponsible and brazenly ambitious politicians. Nonetheless, Lincoln was right when he stated in 1858 that "this government cannot endure, permanently half *slave* and half *free.*"[5] This underlying division did fuel a sectional conflict that was seemingly "irrepressible." Paradoxically, it did so because of, and not in spite of, a set of cultural values shared by most white Americans.

Northern and Southern whites in 1860 held in common a shared cultural legacy. Both took immense pride in the Revolutionary heritage and were committed to social mobility, individual advancement, white supremacy, Protestantism, especially of the evangelical variety, and a democratic political culture based on mass participation. Both fervidly believed that the American republican form of government was providentially inspired and a priceless bequest of freedom and liberty that set white Americans apart from the rest of the world. And, most importantly, both believed that this bequest was under constant attack.

Change itself was threatening because to many it was producing a socioeconomic order that eroded individual autonomy and galvanized traditional fears of the tyrannical potential of any form of organized power. As more and more Americans were drawn into a market economy after 1815 by networks of improved communications, commercialized agriculture, industrialization, and urbanization, the enslaving potential of organized power took the form of impersonal, external forces—the invisible controls of the marketplace, monied institutions such as banks and corporations, or political centers such as the federal government or state legislatures. At the same time, a mass-based political system arose in which, though real issues were debated, the key to office was the ability to manipulate popular discontent by focusing it upon some symbolic enemy that personalized the electorate's fears.

This linkage between political culture and the tensions induced by a rapidly changing economy existed in both the North and the South. In a positive sense the linkage provided each section with a mechanism by which the citizenry could convince itself that the threatened republican values of autonomy and mobility were being protected. In a negative sense, however, the linkage became self-destructive of national unity, because each section increasingly projected onto the other anxieties generated from within. By 1860 slavery and antislavery, as symbolic constructs, had become inseparable from the self-image each section had of itself and of its own definition of republicanism. For the North, slavery, in the guise of the Slave Power, was an affront to republicanism and a threat to individual autonomy and advancement. For the South, slavery was indispensable to republicanism and a guarantor of individual freedom and mobility for whites. It was opposition to slavery, in the guise of Black Republicanism, that represented a conspiracy against white liberties. Thus, it was the very shared republican culture that provided the context for the perceptions of irreconcilable differences that emerged in the 1850s. Each section came to view the other as the betrayer of true republicanism, as heretics from America's civil religion. The Northern version of this process made possible Lincoln's election in 1860. The Southern version was instrumental in the success of secession a few months later.

The Dual Crisis of the South

Secession was an attempt to resolve a dual crisis that confronted the late antebellum South. What defined the crisis was the need to secure protection for the power, prestige, and property of slaveholders from the external threat of growing antislavery-ism in the North and the internal one of developing divisions within Southern society.

The most obvious threat was the external one posed by the increasing material power of the free states and the intensifying commitment of the North to a democratic capitalism that would expand opportunities for free white labor by shutting slavery out of the territories. This threat assumed a tangible political form in 1860 with the victory of the Republicans. For the first time, a completely sectionalized party that was openly hostile to the future of slavery as a permanent institution had gained national power.

Whites in the lower South saw sufficient cause for secession in Lincoln's election itself. The secessionists argued that Lincoln's administration was a real danger to the

institution of slavery. Viewed from a long-term perspective, the secessionists' indictment of the Republicans was perfectly rational. The Republicans were pledged to the
containment of slavery, a policy that they openly proclaimed would lead to the eventual destruction of the institution. On this point the secessionists and Republicans were
in agreement. Both well knew that American slavery was a dynamic institution. By
1860 over 50 percent of all slaves lived in areas outside the original slave states at the
nation's founding. Both were convinced that the continual expansion of slavery was
essential to the preservation of the institution, its profits, and techniques of racial
control.

The thought of containing slavery galvanized a whole cluster of fears for Southern
whites. Containment, it was believed, would result in worn-out plantation lands over-
stocked with unmarketable slaves; a growing black presence confined to a limited area
in which a white minority would be engulfed in a sea of black pillage and licentiousness; angry and resentful common whites turning against slavery once the economic mobility promised by slavery's expansion was closed off; and an ever-
decreasing Southern ability to block the free-soil majority in national politics. In the
following depiction from the Montgomery (Ala.) *Advertiser* of a South hemmed in by
free soil, one can sense the claustrophobic terrors that the secessionists exploited:[6]

> Hemmed in . . . by a chain of nonslaveholding States; fanaticism and power, hand in
> hand, preaching a crusade against her institutions; her post offices flooded with incen-
> diary documents; her by-ways crowded with emissaries sowing seeds of a servile war, in
> order to create a more plausible excuse for Congressional interference; the value of her
> property depreciated and her agricultural industry paralyzed, what would become of the
> people of the Southern States, when they would be forced at last to let loose among them,
> freed from the wholesome restraints of patriarchal authority, a population whose only
> principle of action has ever been animal appetite?

This dread of encirclement was all the more intense because of the growing
isolation of the slave South in the nineteenth century. In 1800 slavery was the dominant
form of labor organization in the Western Hemisphere. By 1860 slavery was a minority
institution attacked on all sides. Emancipation accompanied the nationalist revolutions
in Latin America that broke up the Spanish Empire. The major colonial powers, led by
England in the 1830s, freed the slaves in their overseas empires. By mid-century, only
Cuba, Brazil, and the southern United States remained as strongholds of slavery.

To be sure, both the benefits, from the Northern perspective, and the horrors, from
the Southern perspective, of containing slavery were exaggerated for political effect.
For example, the South was in no immediate danger of running out of cotton land for
slave labor. Twice as much acreage was in cotton in 1890 as at the end of the
antebellum period. In relative terms, the South had an excess of land over labor in the
1850s. The South's most pressing economic need, as registered by the sharp rise in
slave prices in that decade, was for more slaves, not more land. Still, the assumption
that in the long run slavery needed to expand in order to survive was a valid one.
Southern whites, like their Northern counterparts, identified westward migration with
upward mobility and individual advancement, as well as another chance to escape
economic dependency. The safety valve of slave territory had to be kept open by the
planters if they hoped to retain the proslavery support of the common whites.
Moreover, most Southern planters were convinced that slave labor was, as Jefferson

Davis put it, ''a wasteful labor, and it therefore requires a still more extended territory than would the same pursuits if they could be prosecuted by the more economical labor of white men.''[7] The reality that Southern whites confronted was one in which the geographical diffusion of slavery had provided successive generations of farmers and planters with the material basis for their economic power and social prestige. To shut off that diffusion meant damming up the social pressures that expansion had released. As slavery matured in a given locale, landholdings became concentrated in planter families and the yeomanry were displaced. By 1850, over 40 percent of all South Carolina–born whites were living outside the state. Most of these migrants were in the newer slave states further west. Planter hegemony in South Carolina would have been much less secure had these migrants either remained and challenged the planters for landed resources or moved to free soil and added their votes to political antislaveryism.

In addition to their quite-plausible argument that the Republican program promised a slow death for slavery, the secessionists stressed that the Republicans were now in a position to bring antislaveryism directly into the South. With the territorial issue having been apparently settled by Lincoln's election in favor of the exclusion of slavery, it seemed likely to the secessionists that the slavery controversy now would be transferred back into the South. When it was, the secessionists feared that antislaveryism would find a receptive audience.

The upper South was particularly suspect as an area in which the defense of slavery was weak and vulnerable. The northernmost tier of slave states had gradually sold off their excess slaves to the lower South. Between 1830 and 1860, the percentage of slaves in the total population dropped from 4 percent to 1 percent in Delaware, 23 percent to 13 percent in Maryland, 24 percent to 19 percent in Kentucky, and 18 percent to 10 percent in Missouri. Delaware could be written off in any general crisis affecting slavery, and the slave demography in the other three states was approaching the point at which gradual emancipation had been enacted in New York and New Jersey at the turn of the eighteenth century. Support for slavery, both as an economic investment and a means of racial control, was eroding. Although there was no immediate prospect of emancipation, antislavery agitation had begun in the urban centers. The trend was unmistakable, and it was pushed along by the increasing integration of the economy of the upper South into the marketing networks of the free states. The local capital for this integration came from the profits of exporting slaves to the cotton South. Convinced that the conditions for the victory of free labor were being created in the upper South, the secessionists isolated that region as the first one that the Republicans would detach from slavery.

While slavery was crumbling in the upper South, the secessionists predicted that the Republicans, using their control of federal patronage for political leverage, would organize a free-labor party throughout the South. Its numbers, the secessionists were certain, would come from the nonslaveholding poor. According to a writer in *De Bow's Review,* a New Orleans journal, these poor harbored ''a *feeling of deep-rooted jealousy and prejudice, of painful antagonism, if not hostility, to the institution of negro slavery, that threatens the most serious consequences, the moment Black-republicanism becomes triumphant in the Union.*''[8] If the secessionists were to be believed, the nonslaveholders were susceptible to the economic argument of the free-labor ideology and deeply resentful of the planters as an unrepublican aristocracy. They were an enemy waiting to be mobilized by the Republicans. Once they were, secessionist logic dictated that the antislavery debate would enter the slave quarters and undermine the master's authority. The climax would be the catastrophe of a massive slave rebellion.

Although the secessionists skillfully depicted the Republicans as abolitionist aggressors who had to be resisted by leaving the Union, it had been the aggressive politics of the secessionists themselves that had been largely responsible for Lincoln's election. The strategy of cotton-state Democrats at the national convention of their party at Charleston in April, 1860, was clearly one of rule or ruin. Rule meant acceptance by the Democrats as a national party of a proslavery plank in the party platform that called upon Congress to provide positive protection for the rights of slaveholders in all federal territories. Failing in that objective, the delegates from the lower South bolted the Charleston convention and nominated their own candidate. The Democratic party was irrevocably divided.

Without a doubt, some Southern Democrats supported the breakup of the party in the belief that the subsequent election would be deadlocked and thrown into Congress. In the ensuing negotiations it could be argued that a united South would be able to extract a favorable resolution of the slavery issue as its price for settling upon a president. On the other hand, there also is little doubt that the fire-eater (radical) wing of the Southern Democrats bolted at Charleston for the precise reason cited by their opponents—to split the Democracy and thereby ensure a Republican victory that could be used as immediate justification for secession from the Union. In short, regardless of external events in 1860, a strategically placed number of Southerners—the so-called fire-eaters—were committed to secession.

The cultural meaning of slavery provides an essential departure for understanding the radicalism of the fire-eaters and the internal crisis of the South that they struggled to resolve. As Southerners knew all too well, the South was not just a society with slave labor. It was a slave society in which bondage for blacks permeated the consciousness of whites, impacted on white family structure and roles, and defined the culture as a whole. What Southern whites felt compelled to defend was not just slavery as a profit-making institution, not even just as a system of racial control, but as an entire culture with values that were embedded in slavery and the tensions and the dilemmas it generated.

One dilemma posed by the existence of slavery was the inability of the South to compete with the growing political and economic power of the North. Industrialization, urbanization and an expanding population were the material foundations undergirding the Republican triumph in 1860. In all three areas the slave states were falling further behind year by year. The South's share of the nation's urbanized population decreased from 29 percent in 1820 to 17 percent in 1840 to 16 percent in 1860. Population growth, the numbers that translated into political strength in the federal system, revealed a growing disparity. In 1820, when the free and slave states were evenly balanced at twelve apiece, 116 Americans lived in the free states for every 100 in the slave states. By 1860, when the free states outnumbered the slave states by 18 to 15, the population edge had increased to 154 per 100, and it promised to get wider. The last five states added to the antebellum Union—Iowa, Wisconsin, California,

Table 6.1   Population Change in Free and Slave States
         (population shown in thousands)

Population growth in the slave states increasingly fell behind that of the free states during the antebellum period.

	1820	1860	PERCENTAGE OF CHANGE
Slave-State Population	4,448	12,240	175
Percentage of Total	46.4	39.4	—
Free-State Population	5,142	18,800	266
Percentage of Total	53.6	60.6	—

Source: Compiled from *Historical Statistics,* Series A-195–209.

Minnesota, the Oregon—were all free, and all had gone for Lincoln. As shown in Table 6.1, the Southern population was certainly growing, but the numbers in the free states were increasing much faster.

Industrialization and urbanization meant economic opportunities for the Northern rural population and the immigrants that simply were not available on the same scale in the South. Another consequence was the greater difficulty experienced by the South in holding on to its native sons and daughters. By 1860 whites born in the South Atlantic states were 35 percent more likely to have moved out of their native region than were New Englanders. In the East South Central region (Kentucky, Tennessee, Alabama, and Mississippi), the likelihood of out-migration was 48 percent greater than it was in New England. In the flow of white population between the sections, the free states by 1860 registered a net gain of 800,000 Southern born.

In this contest of economic development, the South could not hope to compete successfully with the North. The reason was not because of any intrinsic economic rationale associated with slavery, but rather because of the distinct political, ideological, and social limits in which the slaveholders had to maneuver. Slavery and sustained industrialization, for example, were incompatible. Again, the issue was not just one of making money. Industrial slavery in the antebellum South was profitable, and the tendency by the 1850s was toward the replacement of industrial free labor with slaves. Still, only about 5 percent of the slaves were used in manufacturing, and most of these worked in small rural enterprises. Among free labor, twice as high a percentage of Northerners, 41 percent, were engaged in manufacturing as were Southerners in 1860.

As we saw in Chapter 1, several factors accounted for the South's slow rate of industrialization. However, the capital, labor, and market constraints imposed by the fundamental reliance of the Southern economy on plantation slavery were in themselves an insurmountable barrier to sustained industrialization. The massive capital outlays necessary for a significant acceleration of Southern industrialization could have come only from outside sources or from a sizable liquidation of the capital already tied up in slaves. The latter, of course, would weaken the very institution Southerners were trying to protect, and the former carried the political risk of worsening the preexisting dependency of the Southern economy on the capital resources of the Yankees. Plantation profits were invested in local manufacturing but on a scale commensurate with the small size of the Southern home market. Because it was based upon slave labor, the Southern economy lacked a middle sector—that is, a portion of the economy in which consumer wants were very high and that thereby could provide a basis for the extensive development of local manufacturing. Thus, whereas per-capita income for non-slaveholding whites was only $985 per square mile in the South, it was $2,000 in the states of the Old Northwest. As long as most nonslaveholders preferred the security of community self-sufficiency to the risks of market involvement, and as long as the plantation, aided by cheap Yankee shoes and textiles, met the economic needs of the slaves, there was little reason to expect the Southern home market to grow. Meanwhile, those Southerners with capital to invest, mainly planters, would continue to put most of it into agriculture as long as the external demand for cotton made it profitable.

The industrialization that did occur was limited enough to keep manageable the politically explosive issue of the size and composition of the manufacturing work force. Most planters and manufacturers favored the use of slaves for industrial labor. Both preferred the predictability and stability of slave workers to the mobility, wage demands, and work stoppages of free labor. Both were aware that a reliance upon free labor meant uprooting Southern farmers from the land and concentrating them in a factory setting in which antislavery class consciousness was more likely to develop than among individuals scattered in the countryside. "Drive out negro mechanics and all sorts of operatives from our Cities, and who must take their place?" asked the Charleston lawyer, Christopher Memminger. His answer was "the same men who make the cry in the Northern cities against the tyranny of capital." Very soon, Memminger feared, these men would become "hot abolitionists."[9]

In opposition, a vocal minority of planters argued that industrialization would ultimately ruin slave discipline because of the incentives needed to produce efficient manufacturing labor. Moreover, if nonslaveholders were deprived of manufacturing jobs, they would have all the more reason to be economically resentful of slavery. The result was a stand-off. Through a combination of cheap slave labor and higher-priced white artisans, Southern manufacturers were able to show a profit. However, this very slave black and free white mixture produced a political backlash from those whites most economically threatened—immigrant artisans in Southern cities.

Most immigrants avoided the South because they perceived fewer economic opportunities there and had no wish to compete with slave labor. This collective decision by itself retarded Southern urbanization and industrialization, for in both the North (though in much greater numbers) and the South, immigrants were attracted into cities and factories much more easily than native-born farmers. Like their Northern counterparts, Southern immigrants tended to settle in cities in which they could practice their trades and find work as common laborers. Once in the cities, they were bitterly and persistently hostile to slave competition. In what became a rising tide of protest in the 1850s, artisans demanded that black labor be barred from the crafts or subjected to heavy taxes. These protests, in combination with a strong rural demand for slaves, were a main factor in the decline of urban slavery. From 1820 to 1860, slaves decreased from 22 percent to 10 percent of the South's urban population. The decline accelerated during the 1850s and was sharpest in those cities, mainly in the upper South, that were experiencing the heaviest influx of foreign immigrants.

As the record of industrialization and urbanization indicates, the South was caught in a bind. It could not modernize rapidly or completely enough to meet the Northern

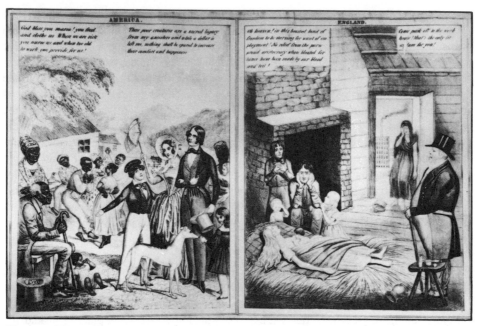

Black and White Slaves. To become like Yankees, most Southern whites and Northern Democrats believed, was to accept white slavery in the form of a degraded and impoverished factory class. This critique of free-labor society, with England as its most horrendous example, was often juxtaposed with a grotesquely romanticized defense of black slavery. (Historical Pictures Service, Chicago)

challenge. On the other hand, it is clear that many Southerners feared the consequences of modernization itself. After all, most whites did not want to Yankeeize their society. "Free society! we sicken at the name," said the Muscogee (Ga.) *Herald* in 1856. "What is it but a conglomeration of greasy mechanics, filthy operatives, small-fisted farmers, and moon-struck theorists?"[10]

Another internal dilemma generated by slavery might be termed the perils of prosperity. Higher cotton prices in the 1850s increased the demand and hence the price of slaves. By the late 1850s, a prime field hand cost over $1500. Over the decade as a whole, slave prices increased by 72 percent. Most Southern whites were now priced out of the market for slave property. Planters could use their cotton profits to expand production by purchasing more slaves. But nonslaveholders, dependent on the limited labor supply of their families, were shut out of the cotton prosperity, because they could not expand production without access to slave labor. To purchase a slave on credit meant taking a tremendous gamble. The failure rate among small slaveholders was high. In the cotton region of Dallas County, Alabama, a slaveholder with fewer than ten slaves in 1850 stood a 50 percent chance of being slaveless in 1860. The odds of dropping out of the slaveholding class were about the same in the tobacco belt of Kentucky and Tennessee. Nearly 50 percent of the small slaveholders there lost all or part of their slave assets in the 1850s. Thus, it was quite prudent for the yeomanry to continue to concentrate on subsistence crops with family labor. A financial setback with mortgaged slaves could easily result in the loss of one's land and the horror of economic dependency.

The very prosperity of the 1850s paradoxically created conditions in which a shrinking percentage of Southern whites could find real opportunities for material advancement. As of 1830, 35 percent of all Southern families owned slaves; by 1850 the percentage was down to 31 percent and, on the eve of the Civil War, it had been reduced to 25 percent. Even in the heartland of the slave economy, the cotton South, the long-range trend was working against slave ownership. Here, the percentage of farm operators who owned no slaves increased from 39 percent to nearly 50 percent in the 1850s. To be sure, the rates of slave ownership were still extraordinarily high when measured against rates of investment in productive property in the modern economy. In 1949 only 2 percent of all U.S. families owned corporate stock worth at least $5,000, a sum comparable to an investment in one slave in 1860. Nonetheless, slaveholders could not help but feel that the future safety of slavery was threatened by the steady, proportionate decline in Southern families with a direct economic stake in the institution. The logic of one slaveholder was elementary: "The minute you put it out of the power of common farmers to purchase a negro man or woman to help him in his farm, or his wife in the house, you make him an abolitionist at once."[11]

The movement in the mid-1850s to reopen the African slave trade was a political response to this concern over retaining the loyalty of nonslaveholders. By driving down slave prices, cheap imports were hailed as a way to enable more Southerners to have a vested interest in slavery. The revival of the trade also promised to reverse the growing political danger of urban economies becoming more dependent on immigrant labor, whose allegiance to slavery was doubted by most of the planters. Reopening the trade, however, directly challenged the economic self-interest of Southerners who already held slaves. As the critics of the trade noted, any policy that lowered the price of slaves invariably would erode the political commitment of individual owners to protect that form of property. Moreover, by eliminating most of the profits in the internal slave trade from the upper to the lower South, a flood of African imports would further weaken the already shaky economic position of slavery in the border states. Opposition within the South, let alone the North, was enough to defeat the movement to revive the African slave trade. In trying to resolve one internal dilemma, the movement promised only to create an even worse one.

Cotton prosperity based on slave labor also drove up the price of land, so that increasing numbers of white males were eliminated from competing for either land or slaves in the rural marketplace. By 1860 about 25 percent to 30 percent of all farm operators in the Georgia cotton belt were tenants. In Dallas County, Alabama, one of the leading cotton-producing counties in the South, the percentages of both landholding farmers and slaveholders dropped in the 1850s. The former fell from 31 percent to 20 percent of all adult white males and the latter from 48 percent to 40 percent. As part of the same linkage between the slaveholding class and economic change, plantation profits by the 1850s were being invested in local insurance companies, banks, and railroads. These investments were centered in Southern towns, and, though on a scale dwarfed by Northern urbanization, a more volatile and heterogeneous social order was emerging that contradicted the static agrarian order defended by the proslavery ideologues.

The pressure of economic change in the cotton South was felt most intensely by young males. These men experienced the change in their inability to assume traditional roles of household responsibility and economic independence. Again, Dallas County,

Alabama, is illustrative: during the 1850s the percentage of married white males in their twenties dropped from 43 percent to 26 percent, of household heads from 49 percent to 28 percent, and of landholding farmers from 29 percent to 12 percent.

The sons of planters faced special problems in establishing a cultural and personal identity. As obedient sons of patriarchal fathers, they were expected to fulfill a set of conflicting demands. The planter father demanded subordination as a necessary and just good from all his dependents—his wife, children, and slaves. The son's reward for his submissiveness was a share of the patrimonial estate, the material basis for extending patriarchy into the next generation. Especially in areas in which the plantation regime had matured, planters' sons in the late antebellum period tended to remain at home awaiting their inheritance in what amounted to a prolonged state of adolescent dependency. In Dallas County, for example, the sons of planters were twice as likely to stay in the county during the 1850s as were the sons of farmers owning no slaves or fewer than ten. One-third of these persisting sons reported no occupation in 1860 and still lived with their parents. In the families of Charleston planters in 1860, 40 percent of the co-residing sons age 15 and over were unemployed.

The conflicting demands upon the planters' sons were inescapable. They were expected to be economic successes as planters, but their socialization discouraged individual initiative and consigned them to extended periods of enforced idleness. They were to carry on the family name in the world at large, but they were tied to home by the prospect of wealth that someday would be theirs. They were to become independent patriarchs after serving a long apprenticeship as dependent sons to fathers loathe to surrender their suffocating control. Their parents and their culture offered them role models worthy of emulation, but they found few opportunities to follow those models. The preeminent models were those of the Revolutionary soldier who sired Southern liberties; the Indian fighter who advanced Christendom while protecting innocent white women and children; and the planter patriarch who established the family pedigree while "civilizing" the Africans. All these models belonged more to the past than to the present.

Southern white males could hardly help being excessively concerned with proving their manhood. Guilt and anxiety over miscegenation heightened their ambivalence over their self-identities. The slave population noticeably lightened in the 1850s. The federal census classified 7.7 percent as mulattoes (by legal definition a mulatto could have up to seven-eighths white ancestry) in 1850 and 10.4 percent in 1860, an increase of 35 percent. Racial intermixture would have been even higher had it not been for the resistance of black women and men and the gradual spread among the planter class of evangelical norms in sexual mores. Most white-black sexual unions seem to have developed out of the master-slave relationship and involved a white male and a female slave. Mary Chesnut spoke for many of the planters' wives when she scathingly noted:[12]

> Like patriarchs of old our men live all in one house with their wives and their concubines, and the mulattoes one sees in every family exactly resemble the white children—and every lady tells you who is the father of all the mulatto children in everybody's household, but those in her own she seems to think drop from the clouds, or pretends so to think.

A particularly intense form of the cult of true womanhood offered Southern white women partial compensation for the sexual transgressions of their males. In this myth white women became paragons of asexual purity and black women were converted into symbols of degraded promiscuity. Sexual passion itself became degraded because it was linked in the minds of whites with an inferior race. Hence, white women, by being above sexual passion, proved their superiority through their purity in sexual matters. However much the myth helped males cope with their guilt by enshrining their women on a pedestal, issues of self-contempt and self-hatred remained. Southern society condemned sexual irregularity generally and viewed sexual intimacy with blacks as especially shameful. In extreme cases, self-contempt led to sadism—projections of hatred onto, and violence against, the black victims. More frequently, in compensation for their sexual infidelities and to shore up their own sense of manhood, which had been contaminated, white males assumed a raucous male bravado, a shrill and violent defense of the honor and rights of Southern white women. In effect, these men had to forever proclaim to the world that their masculinity was unsullied and in the service of white womanhood.

As the antebellum period came to a close, notions of Southern womanhood and of the South itself became fused into one symbolic construct. Once this process occurred, attacks on the South simultaneously became attacks on white womanhood. Thus, for Southerners to have accepted the Northern indictment of them, expressed in the Republican policy of containment, as morally inferior citizens, would have been an open admission that the pretensions of slaveholders to power as a class were morally bankrupt and that the role of males as protectors of women was a sham. From their point of view, Southern males were being asked to ignore the potential peril to Southern womanhood implicit in the destruction of slavery, however long that destruction might be put off.

Instead, slaveholders reacted in the only way consistent with their values as a class and as males. They boldly pushed for Southern independence in an effort to morally vindicate the slave South as a culture worthy of the respect of Christians elsewhere, and they were ready to accept enthusiastically the role that the ensuing war would thrust upon them, that of defenders in practice, and not just in theory, of Southern white women. Moreover, by insisting that the hypocritical, mercenary Yankees were the aggressors, and that Southerners were struggling solely for their rights and independence, Southerners could proclaim to the world that they were morally spotless. In their view, they, unlike the Yankees, placed honor and rights above money.

Southern images of the North comprised a self-fulfilling prophecy and an emotionally satisfying release from the tensions and strains within their slave society. In particular, the Republican party became the monster upon which Southerners projected all their fears of both external and internal changes that threatened to overturn their moral and social order. For the Augusta (Ga.) *Chronicle & Sentinel*, the Republican party was

> hideous, revolting, loathesome, a menace not only to the Union of these States, but to Society, to Liberty and to Law. It has drawn to it the corrupt, the vile, the licentious, the profligate, the lawless, and is the embodiment not only of antislavery, but of communism, of agrarianism, of free-loverism, and all the abomination springing from a false society.[13]

By protecting the South from this menace and becoming Christian defenders of women, homes, and property, Southern white males found a cause worthy of their lives.

Secession

In the secession crisis, as in the earlier rehearsals for secession, Southern youth was in the forefront of political radicalism. In 1851 an upcountry Unionist, Benjamin Perry, described the secessionists in South Carolina as "mostly political novices, a set of young enthusiasts inspired with notions of personal honor to be defended and individual glory, fame and military laurels to be acquired."[14] The same was true in 1860–1861. It was the young, slaveholding professionals and planters who spearheaded the break from what was perceived as a corrupt and ineffective national government and, indeed, social value system. Further down the socioeconomic scale, young, non-slaveholding clerks, lawyers, and tradespeople rushed to join the volunteer military companies that sprang up in the late 1850s. In a generational reaction that paralleled the disillusionment of newer, younger voters in the North with the old, two-party system, Southern politics shifted in the 1850s to accommodate the impatience and anger of young men anxious to find protection from threatening change and a sense of moral purpose in public life.

Political radicalism offered this protection and moral purpose. The Breckinridge demand for congressional protection of slavery in the territories was the Southern equivalent of the Republican commitment to free soil. It appealed both to those who wanted to enter the market and those who wanted to leave it. It promised cheap land and fresh opportunities for those aspiring to planter status and economic relief for nonslaveholders unable to compete with the spread and intensification of plantation agriculture. Both a planter's son in the black belt and a hired hand in the Tennessee mountains could relate to the economic argument for slavery in the territories. Such a hand told a Yankee traveler that he hoped "Nebrisky" would be slave:[15]

> The people here all wanted it to be slave States, because they might want to move out there, and a fellow might get a nigger and have to sell him. If a man moved into a free State, he'd have to sell his niggers; if he didn't, they'd be free as soon as he took 'em in.

At least as appealing was the insistence by the Breckinridge Democrats that their territorial policies alone could vindicate the rights and liberties of all Southern whites against the moral onslaughts of the antislavery North. First the Breckinridge Democrats, and then the secessionists, effectively invoked the ethos of an agrarian republicanism that guaranteed individual autonomy and honor for all free white males. Because of slavery, Southern whites were passionately devoted to traditional republican ideals. To be economically and morally free was the very essence of an honorable self-identity in a society in which the black presence daily reminded whites of the abyss of shame and degradation that awaited those who lost their freedom. In the secessionist mindset, submission to the Republicans entailed a loss of equality tantamount to enslavement. The Republicans, for a South Carolina "Minute Man" in the crisis of 1860, were "mongrel tyrants who mean . . . to reduce you and your wives and your daughters on a level with the very slaves you buy and sell."[16]

In the cause of Southern independence, young males found a crusade in which to unburden any inner doubts over their own self-identity and the moral legitimacy of a Southern culture condemned by outsiders. For young nonslaveholders, the crusade kept alive their hopes for upward mobility and enabled them to bask in the approval of communities that allocated power and prestige to those who owned slave property or promised to defend it. For the sons of planters, many of whom were unable to break free from the constraints of paternal authority, the crusade and its open, confrontational stance against Yankee tyranny offered public liberation from private subordination. In defending Southern rights, they forged a culturally approved passage to an adult identity and status denied them by their fathers.

In hundreds of vigilance committees, military companies, and associations of "Minute Men," Southern youth mobilized for secession in the wake of Lincoln's election. Exploiting community fears already rubbed raw by John Brown's raid at Harpers Ferry in the fall of 1859, and intimidating those who would now hang back, these paramilitary units put the lower South on an emergency footing. The leaders of the majority Breckinridge party in the cotton states launched a campaign for immediate secession by separate state action that was aided immeasurably by the widely held belief that the Republicans would move quickly to instigate slave uprisings.

A series of state elections for delegates to secession conventions were held, but the results in the lower South seemed to have been a foregone conclusion. Combined voter turnout in Alabama, Mississippi, and Louisiana declined from 70 percent to 49 percent between the presidential and the secession elections. The falloff was particularly heavy among the Whig voters for Bell. Nearly 40 percent of them, either out of fear of reprisals or a sense that secession was inevitable, boycotted the elections in these three states. The rural vote of native-born Southerners, notably those in the newer cotton districts opened up for commercial agriculture by the spread of railroads in the 1850s, carried the conventions for the secessionists. Breckinridge Democrats and slaveholders took the lower South out of the Union. About two-thirds of the popular vote for immediate secession came from the Breckinridge men. Whereas the immediate secessionists won 59 percent of the counties in the lower South in which slaves comprised less than 25 percent of the population, their support soared to 80 percent of the counties in which slaves were in the majority.

The secessionist victory in the lower South was achieved at the cost of sharpening the political divisions between slaveholders and nonslaveholders. The Breckinridge Democrats, though controlled and led by slaveholding professionals and planters, cut across class lines in their appeal. As long as the choice was the traditional one between defense of individual liberties and submission to the moneyed aristocracy, the yeomanry and plain folk supported the Democratic party. But once the choice was reduced, as it was in the secession elections, to staying in the Union or joining a new polity designed primarily to serving the interests of slaveholders, party lines broke. In both Alabama and Georgia, many of the Breckinridge farmers in the mountains opted for the Union.

The perceived threat of Republicanism—its challenges to Southern social order, property interests, and racial controls—was simply not as real in the mountains as it was in the black belts. Not only were there few slaves in the highlands, but white culture in the mountains was much more cohesive than in the plantation regions. In particular, young males were more easily assimilated into traditional roles of familial responsibility and positions of economic independence. As compared to their rural

Table 6.2   Slaveholdings and Secession in the Lower South

The timing of secession in the seven original states of the Confederacy was closely correlated to the relative number of slaveholders in the white population.

	DATE OF SECESSION	PERCENTAGE OF SLAVEHOLDERS
South Carolina	Dec. 20, 1860	48.7
Mississippi	Jan. 9, 1861	48.0
Florida	Jan. 10, 1861	36.0
Alabama	Jan. 11, 1861	35.1
Georgia	Jan. 19, 1861	38.0
Louisiana	Jan. 26, 1861	32.2
Texas	Feb. 1, 1861	28.5

Source: Compiled from slaveholding data in Otto H. Olsen, "Historians and the Extent of Slave Ownership in the Southern United States," *Civil War History* 18 (1972): 111; dates of secession are given in Potter, op. cit., pp. 494, 498.

counterparts in Dallas County in 1860, men in their twenties in the Alabama mountains were twice as likely to be married and four times as likely to be landholding farmers. The urgency and energy that young males brought to secession in the plantation areas were missing in the mountains.

By early February 1861, the seven states of the lower South had seceded from the Union and formed a provisional government for the Confederate States of America. As indicated in Table 6.2, these states left the Union in almost exactly the descending order of their percentages of white families who owned slaves. In the upper South, where slave investments were relatively smaller, fears of losing racial control less intense, and economies more tightly bound in free labor markets, secession was defeated by popular vote. The greatest comparative advantage of the Unionists here over their disorganized and demoralized counterparts in the lower South was the persistence of two-party competition in the upper South. A combination of Know-Nothings, Whigs, and Constitutional Unionists kept alive a viable, non-Democratic alternative in state and local elections. In contrast, the lower South was virtually a one-party region by the mid-1850s. By 1860 the differences between these regional political cultures was such that in the presidential election the average Democratic margin of victory on a statewide basis was three times greater in the lower South (28 percent) than in the upper South (8½ percent). Because competing parties in the upper South continuously offered legitimate choices for controlling the government and protecting individual liberties, voters were confident that the normal workings of the political process would absorb and deflect the Republican challenge. Whereas mountain whites in the lower South relied on the inner strength of their folk culture as a shield to blunt the Republican threat, whites in the upper South found a comparable shield in two-party competition.

When Lincoln was inaugurated in early March 1861, the Union was in a state of suspended animation. The lower South was out, the upper South was in, and everything seemed to be in a holding pattern. It was clear to both of the new governments, Lincoln's and Davis's, that the pattern could not hold for long. The cotton Confederacy was painfully aware that its chances for economic, political, and military survival were contingent on winning over the upper South. Meanwhile, Lincoln was running out of time in which to make good on the Northern claim that the Union was indivisible. The longer his government made no overt move to counteract secession, the greater was the likelihood that the Republicans would be pilloried as do-nothing, cowardly Buchanan Democrats who sat idly back while the Union was dissolved. At a place called Fort Sumter, in the harbor of Charleston, South Carolina, Lincoln decided to take his stand on enforcing federal authority. In the chain reaction that followed, the secessionists finally gained the upper South.

The Fort Sumter Crisis

Until the firing on Fort Sumter, Southerners could still believe that peaceable secession was a real possibility. Certainly that is what they said they wanted—to depart in peace and be left alone. At the same time, many Republicans could still argue that secession was a reversible phenomenon. Once secession was arrested in the upper South, it was easy enough to conclude that the Slave Power had overextended itself, and that a latent Unionist majority, even in the lower South, was biding its time before exposing the secessionist conspiracy and restoring their states to the Union.

Yet, all the while, war preparations were under way on both sides. A naval officer's wife, Elizabeth Blair Lee, captured the buildup of war tensions that contradicted the seeming indecisiveness of the North. In late January she wrote her husband:[17]

> What strikes me in this contest is the entire supineness & noninterference of the North in every way—except when War comes—they are *keen for it*—Nine tenths of the northern men evidently only want to hear the trumpets blast.

If war came, Southerners were just as keen to fight. In the words of Mary Chesnut, South Carolinians "had exasperated and heated themselves into a fever that only bloodletting could ever cure —it was the inevitable remedy."[18] Both women read their sections well. It soon became apparent to everyone that the secessionists had lit the fuse of the powder keg of war that was detonated by the Northern reaction to the firing on Fort Sumter.

In deciding to resupply the federal garrison at Fort Sumter, a fortification that had become a symbol of Union resolve in the lower South, Lincoln acted to establish the credibility of his party's right to rule and of the Northern commitment to preserving the Union. It was a measure of the sagacity of his political judgment that the decision placed Lincoln in a no-lose situation. Lincoln knew that the federal garrison at Fort Sumter was within a few weeks of running out of essential supplies. He was also aware that an abandonment of the fort, however justifiable in a military sense, carried the risks of shattering the unity of the Republican party and destroying any Northern confidence in the willingness of his administration to take a stand against secession. Such confidence was already quite low. Many Northerners would have agreed with the humiliating assessment of the New York lawyer, George Templeton Strong: "The bird of our country is a debilitated chicken, disguised in eagle feathers."[19]

Lincoln weighed these considerations against the risk of igniting a war over Fort Sumter. Acting against the advice of his general-in-chief, Winfield Scott, he decided to order a relief expedition to the fort and to inform Confederate authorities in advance of his intentions. Aside from upholding an inaugural pledge to maintain possession of what federal property still remained within the seceded states, a successful reprovisioning of Fort Sumter would have undercut the sovereign claims of the new Confederacy. If, as seemed likely, the Confederates responded by firing upon Fort Sumter in order to lay claim to what they insisted was now theirs by sovereign right, then Lincoln had won an immense psychological advantage. The Confederacy would be blamed, rightly or wrongly, for firing the first shot of the Civil War. Lincoln won the advantage. By April 13, a day after the shelling of Fort Sumter, Strong's confidence had soared. "The Northern backbone is much stiffened already. Many who stood up for 'Southern rights' and complained of wrongs done the South now say that, since the South has fired the first gun they are ready to go all lengths in supporting the government."[20]

Going "all lengths" meant answering Lincoln's call of April 15 for 75,000 militia to put down by force what Lincoln described as "combinations too powerful to be suppressed by the ordinary course of judicial proceedings." The North rallied behind the call. The issues, as Lincoln carefully phrased them, were "the existence of our National Union, and the perpetuity of popular government."[21]

Just as secession had first replaced slavery as the focal point of the sectional controversy, now the inseparable concepts of the Union and republicanism overshadowed for Northerners any initial differences over the proper response to secession. Because Northerners fervently believed that those concepts had been attacked and defiled at Fort Sumter, they were convinced that free government itself was on trial. The Northern press, Republican and Democratic alike, reiterated in a common chorus that anarchy, lawlessness, and violence were about to dissolve all civil and social obligations. The mob violence of urban politics in the 1850s when Know-Nothings and immigrants clashed, the bloodlettings on the Kansas frontier, the beating of Sumner, John Brown's raid, and the disunion bluff and bluster of Southern politicos were all prior indications to many Northerners that disorder was reaching the threshold of social anarchy. For anxious conservatives worried over what they viewed as a growing disrespect for law and order, for frustrated reformers who increasingly felt that only coercion could teach men to curb their passions, and for an expanding middle class whose very definition of republicanism in a disruptive market economy was predicted on internalized self-control, the Confederate actions at Fort Sumter confirmed their worse fears over rampant individualism in a republican polity.

Put starkly, the issue was simple enough for Northerners. If the secessionists could flout the will of the majority through violent rebellion, what would prevent other Americans, including Northerners, from doing the same? This concern over a spiraling disintegration of the Union transcended ethnic and class boundaries in the North. In explaining to his father back in England why he had volunteered for the Union army, an immigrant weaver wrote in 1861:[22]

> If the Unionists let the South secede now the West might want to seperate next Presidential Election, & they would be justified in so doing because if one goes out the Union is broke and there would have to be another form of a constitution wrote and after it was written who would obey it?

American society was one in which, to an extent unimaginable in the twentieth century, the government was the male citizenry. White males made their local governing institutions, both on the formal level of drawing up state constitutions and on the more informal level of combining their talents and interests to form political parties, claims clubs to regulate access to public lands, reform organizations to set standards of community conduct, and an endless variety of ad hoc associations to deal with local issues as they arose. In a society organized along neither the bureaucratic lines of modern America nor the traditional, socially hierarchical lines of aristocratic Europe, but around the voluntary, associative actions of its citizenry, the armed defiance of the minority South was perceived in the North as nothing less than an invitation to anarchy. In the firing upon Fort Sumter, most Northerners saw a personal threat to their own self-respect and a direct challenge to the stability of their communities. The Chicago *Journal,* speaking for this public reaction, identified the Confederacy with "the total overthrow and annihilation of all republican liberty."[23] In the same feverish days of mid-April 1861, the New York *Tribune* pinpointed Northern fears when it proclaimed that the purpose of the upcoming war was to prove that "freedom is not another name for anarchy."[24]

Lincoln's call for troops produced quite a different reaction in the upper South. It quickly drove four states—Virginia, North Carolina, Tennessee, and Arkansas—into the Confederacy. Here, as in the North, the values of republicanism framed individual responses; but in the upper South, a different set of republican virtues was under attack. In their editorials, speeches, and private correspondence, Northerners spoke of respect, obedience, dependence, and order; they feared anarchy and its mirror image, despotism. Virginians referred to rights, honor, vindication, and duty; their fears were the more personalized ones of shame and cowardice. In their republicanism, as in their social order, Virginians harkened back to the rural, family-bound localism of an older America that had been bypassed in many areas of the North by the pace of industrialization and urbanization. The nationalism of mid-nineteenth-century Northerners, one which offered both autonomy and security to inner-directed, competing individuals in a rapidly changing, free-labor society, was abstract and uninspiring to a Virginian like Robert E. Lee. Once Lincoln issued his call for volunteers, the choice in the upper South was no longer between secession and the Union but the more elemental one of fighting with or against kin and family. Obligations to blood and locale, and the dishonor of not fulfilling those obligations, left no real choice at all. "My husband," wrote the wife of Robert E. Lee, "has wept tears of blood over this terrible war, but as a man of honor and a Virginian, he must follow the destiny of his State."[25]

By late May of 1861, the initial political map of Civil War America had been drawn. Four more states had joined the Confederacy since February, and two others, Kentucky and Missouri, seceded but were controlled by the Union military for most of the war. Only the combined commitment to slavery and local self-determination added the upper South to the cotton Confederacy. As indicated in Table 6.3 on the political divisions between the fifteen slave states of 1860, the original secessionists had quite accurately sensed that time was running out on their bid to use the slavery issue to create an independent South. Where the inroads of free labor had been greatest in the South, the willingness to break free from the Union was the weakest.

The Self-Motivated War

The Sumter crisis destroyed any hope of a peaceful separation. Then, as the war ground on for four years, one illusion of war after another was dispelled. The expecta-

Table 6.3   Demographic Change and Confederate Commitment

The willingness of slave states to join the Confederacy corresponded closely to demographic patterns within those states, which reveal whether slavery was an expanding or declining institution.

	PERCENTAGE SLAVE IN 1860	PERCENTAGE CHANGE IN WHITE POPULATION, 1850s	PERCENTAGE CHANGE IN SLAVE POPULATION, 1850s
Core Confederacy[a]	47	32	31
Post-Sumter[b]	29	19	15
Divided[c]	14	41	10
Delaware	2	28	−21

Source: Compiled from *Historical Statistics*, Series A, 195–209, and U.S. Census Bureau, *The Statistics of the Population of the United States: Ninth Census*, Volume I (Washington: Government Printing Office, 1872), p. 7.
[a] Alabama, Florida, Georgia, Louisiana, Mississippi, South Carolina, Texas
[b] Arkansas, North Carolina, Tennessee, Virginia
[c] Kentucky, Maryland, Missouri

tion of a quick and glorious little war went up in the smoke at First Bull Run in July 1861. The belief that either side could win the war without horrendous losses was one of the many casualties at Shiloh in April 1862. On sun-dappled fields of dogwood and honeysuckle, under a soft spring sky, more Americans were killed by each other at Shiloh than had died of battle wounds in the entire Mexican War. If Shiloh was bloody, Antietam was a massacre. On a single day in September 1862, 23,000 were killed or wounded. Those losses were four times what Americans sustained at D-Day in World War II. For far too many generals, especially in the Confederate armies, one illusion was never stripped away. This was the belief that one final, heroic charge could produce a climactic victory that would bring the war to an end. In charge after charge, thousands of broken and maimed bodies bore screaming, and sometimes silent, witness to the awful ability of rifled firearms to smash into agony the gallantry and selfless courage of those who began the charge. The following description of the scene at Franklin, Tennessee, the morning after a disastrous Confederate assault on a Union position in 1864, easily could have described numerous other battlefields. A surviving Confederate recalled:[26]

> We looked over the battlefield, O, my God! What did we see! It was the grand holocaust of death. . . . The dead were piled the one on the other all over the ground. I never was so horrified and appalled in my life.

Among the Confederate dead was General Patrick Cleburne. His body had been riddled with forty-nine bullets.

When it was all over, General Cleburne was one of the more than 600,000 soldiers who died in the war from combat wounds or disease. Even from the perspective of the mass destruction of the twentieth century, the Civil War still has the power to shock and numb us with the sheer magnitude of its casualties. More American soldiers died in this war than in *all* of America's other wars combined. What drove these men to face mortality rates ten times greater than those experienced by American soldiers in World

Confederates Ready for a Fight. This photograph, taken in Richmond before the Battle of First Bull Run in the summer of 1861, captures the carefree abandon and boyish enthusiasm of the Confederate soldiers early in the war. (The Valentine Museum)

War II? Quite apart from the political and constitutional issues involved in secession, what explains our fraticidal bloodbath?

Part of the answer rests with the fact that for more than a generation Americans had been mentally conditioning themselves for a sectional war. The moral consensus on which the original Union was based began crumbling in the 1820s. It was in that decade, for example, that antagonism started to replace accommodation in legal cases involving the property rights of masters who were traveling with their slaves in the free states. From then through the 1850s, Northern courts moved toward emancipating sojourning slaves, while Southern courts retaliated by ruling that residence in a free jurisdiction did not preclude a black from being reenslaved when he or she returned to the South.

The moral tensions in the legal system reflected pervasive cultural shifts in the ways in which Northerners and Southerners viewed each other. When Charles C. Jones, Jr., of Savannah, Georgia, wrote his father in late January 1861 that Northerners and Southerners were "two races which . . . have been so entirely separated by climate, by morals, by religion, and by estimates so totally opposite of all that constitutes honor, truth, and manliness, that they cannot longer coexist under the same government,"[27] he was saying no more than what many common Americans had been telling each other throughout the 1850s. Nowhere did they do so with more dehumanizing imagery than on the plains of Kansas. The proslavery forces, in the eyes of the free-soilers, were "Pukes," filthy and degenerate beasts wallowing in their own depravity. A journalist for the Chicago *Tribune* described them as "a queer-looking set, slightly resembling human beings, but more closely allied to wild beasts.'' Southerners in Kansas responded in kind. They attacked the free-soilers as either hypocritical and greedy Puritan do-gooders, who were intent on stealing slaves, having sex with them, and selling them for an easy profit, or as a subhuman underclass from Northern cities, ''the filth, scum and off-souring of the East and Europe [dispatched] to pollute our fair land.'' The free-soiler, if triumphant, would turn the Southern moral universe upside down. ''Our white men would be cowards, our black men idols, our women ama-zons,''[28] predicted a proslavery newspaper.

The reactions in Kansas represented in an extreme form how the sectional antago-nists hated most in their opponents what they feared most in themselves. Southern whites, desperate to convince a critical world that slavery was a moral good, and unable to tolerate the possibility that they might be lying, projected immorality and hypocrisy onto antislavery Northerners. Moneymaking and materialism *had* to be Yankee traits, for otherwise the profits of slavery would besmirch the South's civiliz-ing mission and expose masters as moral monsters. The simultaneous attraction and repulsion of the intimate black presence could not be faced directly. It was far more comfortable to project an uncontrollable sexual lust onto Northerners who secretly hated blacks. Conversely, Northern fears over losing self-control and giving vent to their impulses became precisely what the Yankees saw in the ''Pukes.'' The border ruffians of Missouri (and by extension most Southern white males) had regressed to a whining, primitive stage of instinctual gratification. Whether in bedding a slave woman, sucking on a bottle of whiskey, chewing on a wad of tobacco, or slashing someone for an imagined insult, the Southerner represented the repressed barbarity of the ''civilized'' Yankee.

In this deadly duet of psychological point and counterpoint, many Northerners and Southerners had created imagined personalities of each other that were so frightening, even bestial, that in order to release the pent-up anxieties, a violent resolution appeared all but inevitable. In this sense, the Civil War was an emotional reality before the first shot was ever fired.

When the actual war broke out, and the lethal potential of sectional stereotyping was realized, it came as no surprise. It was a welcome relief. Evangelicals on both sides embraced it. ''Let it come!'', intoned the *South Western Baptist*. ''In the name of God we will set up our banners: and by the blessing of Him who ruleth in the armies of Heaven the sword will never be sheathed until the last invader shall be driven from our shores.''[29] The Reverend Charles G. Jones of Georgia, one of the South's leading proponents of evangelicalizing the slaves, could find no Christianity in the soul of Republicans. ''That party is essentially *infidel!*''[30]

Northern evangelicals also saw God's hand at work. They were convinced that it was their providential duty to teach obedience to the seceders who, like spoiled chil-dren, were in defiance of God's will. Like others whom middle-class evangelicals in the North depicted as morally weak because driven by passion—Indians, blacks, and immigrants—Southerners needed to have their sinful wills broken for their own good. Moreover, in teaching moral submission to the South, Northern evangelicals would be acting out a providential design. For years antislavery ministers had warned that, in the Civil War phraseology of Julia Ward Howe in the ''Battle Hymn of the Republic,'' the ''grapes of wrath'' were being stored away for the divine retribution that would trample them out. In themes that foreshadowed the sacrificial atonement of the ''Battle

Hymn," Finney prophesized in 1853 that a bloody Christian redemption for the sin of slavery would soon come. "This is part of God's great enterprise and He will press it on to its completion. . . . How many lives and how much agony to get rid of this one sin!"[31] Because they were already marching to the stirring cadence of the "Battle Hymn" before it was written early in the Civil War, antislavery evangelicals not only expected the war as the unfolding of a divine drama, but they were also ready to judge and be judged as Christian warriors.

In both secular and religious terms, a gap existed between what Civil War Americans wanted to be and what their society permitted them to be. Nothing was more indicative of this gap than the holiday spirit that reigned as the volunteers went off to war. Especially in the South, the mustering of troops became a community celebration as Southerners relived the joy and enthusiasm with which the first news of secession had been greeted. Then, as the troops were transported to their stations of war, an adoring citizenry feted them along the way. "It was one magnificent festival from one end of the line to the other,"[32] recalled a Tennesseean of his company's railroad trip to northern Virginia in the spring of 1861. The accumulated tensions of two generations had found their outlet.

Like all holidays from the routines of daily social life, Americans went on this one because they wanted to. Volunteers, not draftees, fought the Civil War. This was especially the case before 1863. Then, as casualties mounted, the North increasingly relied on bounties to spur enlistments, and both sections drew more heavily on a military draft. Still, for the war as a whole, about 94 percent of Union forces and 82 percent of Confederate were volunteers. Another defining characteristic of Civil War armies was their youth. Half of all the soldiers were 24 or younger at the date of their enlistment, and nearly 40 percent were 21 or younger. In part the youth of the armies reflected the overall youth of American society. On the eve of the war, one-third of all white males were between the prime military ages of 20 and 39. By 1970 that proportion was down to one-quarter. In larger measure, however, the Civil War was a notably young man's war because volunteering enabled the young to act out the male roles that their culture expected them to fulfill.

This acting out of a set of assumptions about themselves applies to youth in all wars, but the community pressure and individual need to do so were particularly intense for the youth of 1861. To be a man, to pass from the uncertainties and semidependencies of adolescence into the full circle of adult manhood, meant, above all, to do one's duty. In countless Northern and Southern communities in the spring of 1861, and throughout the war, one's duty was as clear as it could be. As a patriot, Christian, republican, and husband, or husband-to-be, a male had to volunteer. Here was an instant passage to adulthood that was immensely appealing to young males. Relative to the twentieth century, adolescence, defined as a social condition and not just a biological reality, was prolonged in mid-nineteenth-century America. It often stretched from the age of thirteen to the mid-twenties. Throughout this period, young men put off firm decisions on leaving home, launching a career, and starting a family. They moved in and out of jobs, schools, and their parents' homes. The purpose of formal education was unclear, and career choices were perplexing for these youth in the midst of the long transition of the American economy from family farms and small shops to blue-collar factories and white-collar businesses. Volunteering removed many of the ambiguities of their extended adolescence and helped relieve the resultant difficulties in forging adult identities. In a process very similar to evangelical conversions, one also made disproportionately by the young, the act of volunteering fused peer pressures and loyalties into a firm commitment to resolve inner conflicts by making a choice about one's life plans. In both instances the choice involved self-sacrifice to ideals worthy enough to command one's life.

Why men enlisted and what they hoped to find in the military that had eluded them in civilian life varied, of course, with individuals. The following soldiers illustrate some of that variety, as well as the different personal meanings that young men found in the war:

For Ira Pettit, a farm boy from upstate New York who was 21 when he enlisted in May 1861, the war offered a chance to break free from the dust, dependency, and tedium that he so disliked while working on his father's farm as an unpaid helper. As he confided to his cousin Clinton (but apparently never to his father): "I'de rather soldier than to pick stone, hoe corn, taters, beans, mow, rake, pitch and mow hay, rake and bind wheat, oats and Canada thistles combined in the stifling heat of the summer."[33] By regularly sending home his army pay of $13 a month, he enhanced his self-esteem. In this role reversal with his father, Ira was now a major family provider. Pettit was ordered where to go, but he hardly minded. In return he had the opportunity to fulfill boyhood dreams of travel, sightseeing and soldiering.

For Arthur Carpenter, the son of a Massachusetts farmer, the war also offered an escape from economic drudgery. When the war broke out, the twenty-year-old Carpenter was in Indianapolis, where he was learning the shoemaker's trade from an uncle. Bored with the trade, and convinced that he was being exploited by those who "care nothing for right or wrong, but dollars + cents," Carpenter welcomed the war as a cleansing agent for the nation's morally debilitating greed. "I believe that a war of 5 or 10 years would be a good thing. It would purge our nation of some of its filth and dead heads, and then we should be ready to commence anew. . . ." After a bitter struggle to gain his parents approval, he enlisted in October 1861. He was intensely proud of the officer's commission he earned in December 1862, and he totally committed himself to a war he viewed as an immense moral drama in which men earned their redemption through their suffering. As he told his parents when he enlisted, "I have found my sphere."[34]

In contrast to Carpenter, who was estranged from his local society when he enlisted, James M. Williams, a native of Ohio, joined the Confederate army in 1861 because he identified so completely with his adopted South. Williams was 24 and a bookkeeper in Mobile, Alabama, at the start of the war. To the surprise of his father, who had sent his son south to learn a clerical trade from a family friend, Williams was utterly devoted to the Confederate cause. He had married a Mobile woman in the fall of 1860 and throughout the war always insisted that she was the reason he was fighting. "I mean to prove myself a man worthy of you my dear wife." As an outsider intent on establishing his identity as a Southerner, Williams was overjoyed with the opportunities the war offered him. "I rejoice that I am permitted to take up arms in this war," he exclaimed after a few month's service. He especially valued the military as a meritocracy in which young men like himself, one who "entered the army unknown and unfriended,"[35] could rise quickly on their own merit. A superb combat soldier, Williams rose to the rank of lieutenant colonel. By the war's end he had earned his place in his adopted South.

Theodore W. Montfort, a farmer lawyer from southwestern Georgia, already had a secure social position in the South when he went off to war in 1861 at the age of 37. For this father, husband, and slaveholder, the war was a moral test of his worthiness to shoulder the burden of Southern patriarchal responsibility. He experienced the war as a fusion of his manhood with his sense of duty and self-worth. The Yankee threat was against "the happiness of home," and he would be less than a man if he failed to meet it. As he wrote his wife, "I should be unworthy to be your husband or to be a freeman." The Yankee enemy, "the Mercenary race" of moral monsters, in Mont-fort's view, threatened in a terrifyingly personal way the Southern male's need to see himself as a defender of the honor of his women. Montfort vowed "to avenge the damning insult & outrage that has been offered & promised by them for our wives, daughters, & sisters." He admitted that the military struggle was an unequal one, but, for that very reason, the cause was all the more worth fighting. "Let life, property, Yes, every thing but our honor be given up. . . . Let them see that we value our honor, independence & rights more than money."[36]

There were hundreds of thousands of Pettits, Carpenters, Williamses, and Mont-forts. Each came to grips with the war in his own way, but nearly all were self-motivated to fight. They fought to win honor and avoid shame and to prove that they were good sons and worthy husbands. Statements that they had measured up, that they had not turned and run in battle, appeared like a litany in the soldiers' correspondence on both sides. "All I need say about the 14th," wrote James Newton to his parents about his Wisconsin regiment at Shiloh, "is that they *didn't run.*"[37] A Wisconsin soldier, his stomach ripped open by shot, was set next to a tree at Antietam to die. "He gave his name and the name of his parents and [wanted] them to know that he had done his duty,"[38] remembered a Union comrade.

The remarkable combat record of Civil War regiments, their repeatedly demon-strated ability to absorb casualties of 20 percent and higher in charges that would break a modern regiment, reflected not only the self-motivation of the soldiers but also the bonds of local communities that were reproduced at the company level within individ-ual regiments. Entire communities of men in their teens and twenties went off to war by forming themselves into military companies. Especially in the first half of the war, the soldiers fought alongside friends and neighbors and were commanded by men they knew and trusted. They were fighting with and for their communities. By the second half of the war, when community ranks had been depleted by death and injury, veteran units had the self-discipline to lead themselves. "Our officers, as usual, were nowhere and the men commanded themselves,"[39] wrote a New York sergeant of his regiment's action at Petersburg, Virginia, in June 1864.

Militarized communities and self-willed soldiers largely fought the Civil War. On an individual level, the war experience was a mosaic patterned by countless, voluntary journeys to selfhood. These journeys ended in death for one out of every six Union soldiers and an astounding one out of every three Confederates.

Social Change and the Home Fronts

Wars often cause social and political change. When the complexity of demands placed upon public authority are reduced to the simplicity of victory or defeat, peacetime restraints on the use of power are loosened or removed altogether. What was formerly unthinkable becomes acceptable if necessary for victory. In proportion to the length of the war, the level of casualties, and the involvement of civilians and the sacrifices extracted from them, the cohesion and loyalties of the warring societies are severely tested. When, in addition to these strains, one of the belligerents targets as a military objective the morale and productive capacity of the enemy's civilian society, the stage is set for revolutionary change. The Civil War reached this point with Lincoln's Emancipation Proclamation on January 1, 1863.

Lincoln, like most of his contemporaries, expected a short war. Instead the war dragged on for four years, with losses that would have been unimaginable in the spring of 1861. It was, in fact, a civil war between two highly motivated contestants. It was not, as the Republicans first thought, a plot to gain power by a fanatical minority of planters. Thus, because majorities on both sides were unwilling to recognize the legitimacy of the objectives of the other side—the preservation of the Union versus Southern independence—there was no way to negotiate an end to the war. Once mass, voluntary armies of the citizenry had been mobilized, and casualties started to mount, the rival societies, civilians and soldiers alike, insisted that there be no turning back. Very early it became their war and their cause. When the mass armies did clash, the result was a bloody stalemate. The new rifled firearms, the predominant weapons in the Civil War for the first time in military history, had far greater range and accuracy than the muskets previously used by infantrymen. These weapons enabled both sides to inflict such heavy damage on the other that, regardless of the tactical winner or loser, it was almost impossible for either side to achieve a decisive victory. The extensive network of railroads, another factor new in this war, permitted each side to quickly resupply their armies and redeploy them for yet another round of indecisive battles.

As the campaigns of 1862 wore on, Lincoln was confronted with Confederate resistance that was more massive and effective than he had thought possible, resulting in a war that seemingly had no end. He first broached the possibility of emancipation as a war measure to his cabinet in the summer of 1862. Lincoln believed that slavery was a great moral wrong, but he had been cautious in moving against the institution. Politically and strategically, he was restrained by the fear that forced emancipation would irrevocably turn the loyal border states of Missouri, Kentucky, and Maryland against the Union. He also wanted to avoid unleashing a war of total resistance in the lower South. Counterbalancing these fears was the increasing pressure from abolitionists, the black community, and antislavery Republicans for an official commitment to end slavery. The Confederate war effort that had so successfully resisted Union advances was vulnerable at one major point: it rested on an economy and social structure that depended on slave labor. Lincoln finally decided that the only way to combat it effectively was to undermine it by removing that base, thereby disrupting both the economic and social foundations of Confederate resistance. Thus, according to Gideon Welles, Lincoln's Secretary of the Navy, Lincoln argued in July of 1862 that a proclamation of emancipation "was a military necessity absolutely essential for the salvation of the Union, that we must free the slaves or be ourselves subdued."[40]

Whether Lincoln moved directly against slavery because he was convinced that he had run out of other options to save the Union, or whether he waited with the instincts of a masterful politician until the time was right to do what was morally just, are issues that cannot be definitely resolved. Lincoln was a shrewd-enough politician to provide evidence for either interpretation. Nonetheless, the Emancipation Proclamation that he

Fleeing to Freedom. Whenever a Union army was near, slaves escaped in family units to freedom behind the Union lines. This photograph shows a fugitive family crossing the Rappahannock River in Virginia. (Library of Congress)

issued on January 1, 1863, did add a real moral dimension to a war that hitherto could be criticized as a mere struggle for power. With joy, but also with understandable reservations, Charlotte Forten, a free black, could begin her journal for 1863 by exclaiming, "The most glorious day this nation has yet seen, I think."[41] Although the proclamation, consistent with Lincoln's constitutional scruples that he could act only under his war powers as Commander-in-Chief, applied only to slaves within areas still controlled by the Confederacy, it became fixed in the public mind as a call for a moral crusade against slavery. In the Confederacy it was equated with a demand for unconditional surrender.

Official proclamation or not, slaves seized freedom whenever the opportunity presented itself. By the end of the war, one-quarter of the slave population had sought refuge and freedom behind Union lines. The presence of Federal forces acted like a magnet in attracting slave families from surrounding areas. This first occurred on a large scale in the low country of rice and sea-island plantations between Charleston and Savannah. In response to Union enclaves established after a successful amphibious assault in the fall of 1861, slavery collapsed along the coast. A dispatcher for the New York *Tribune* reported in December: "Everywhere the blacks hurry in droves to our lines; they crowd in small boats around our ships; they swarm upon our decks; they hurry to our officers, from the cotton-houses of their masters, in an hour or two after our guns are fired."[42]

The same scene was repeated in a ripple effect wherever Union armies pushed into new areas. The Confederate loss of New Orleans in the spring of 1862 shook the foundations of slavery throughout the lower Mississippi Valley. Thousands of blacks streamed into Union camps set up on the outskirts of the city. In the river parishes above and below New Orleans the comforting myths of black docility were blown away when the slaves saw their chance to release their accumulated anger and hostility. The slaves stopped working, drove off overseers, seized land they wanted for their own use, or fled to the Union lines.

Upriver, the pushing and prodding of Grant's army as it probed for the weaknesses of the Confederate stronghold at Vicksburg, halfway between Memphis and New Orleans, had the same effect. Between the issuing of Lincoln's preliminary emancipation proclamation in September 1862 and the Union capture of Vicksburg in July 1863, the controls of slavery crumbled in the Mississippi Valley. Whites feared an explosion of slave vengeance, but the lure of freedom acted to defuse it. The flight of slaves from the plantations became a flood with the news of Lincoln's emancipation policy. "They will not even wait until 1st January," reported a Union general from northern Mississippi in September 1862. "I do not know what we shall do with them. . . ."[43]

The recruitment of soldiers from among the former slaves was the most revolutionary use made of the fugitive population. In a major policy shift decided upon by Lincoln in the late summer of 1862, the Union began an active program of enlisting black soldiers. This was a bold step by Lincoln, almost as bold as emancipation itself. The insecurities of the white supremacist majority in the North were immediately aroused by the thought that their freedom would be somehow tainted if the blood of black soldiers were shed in its defense. Despite the political risks of a white backlash and the military danger of a drop in troop morale, Lincoln successfully implemented his new policy. Voluntary white enlistments were down in the middle of 1862, and the manpower needs of the Union military were still voracious. Abolitionists and free blacks were pleased with a program they had pushed on Lincoln from the beginning, Union generals were happy with a policy that systematically relieved them of much of their former responsibility for the black refugee population, the soldiers were mollified by the reserving of commissions in the black regiments for whites only, and conservative Unionists found it hard to fault the military rationale behind Lincoln's decision. "The colored population is the great *available* and yet *unavailed of*, force for restoring the Union,"[44] stressed Lincoln.

Eventually some 200,000 Afro-Americans served in the Union military. Four-fifths of them came from the slave states of 1860, and nearly half were recruited in the Mississippi Valley. Although the number of black soldiers was smaller in the loyal slave states of the border South, the impact of Lincoln's new policy was also revolutionary there. As noted earlier, the Emancipation Proclamation did not touch slavery in these states. Nonetheless, the institution was but a shell of its former self by 1863. An Englishman traveling on the eastern shore of Maryland in the autumn of 1863 immediately saw why. "The government is revolutionizing this district by recruiting all negroes who will go, slave or free."[45] Union steamboats picked up runaways along the eastern shore of the Chesapeake and transported them to the training camps in Baltimore. Taught in childhood by their parents to mask their intentions from whites, the slaves feigned docile loyalty right up until the moment they fled.

No battles of note were fought in eastern Maryland, but the English traveler, H. Y. Thompson, was surely correct when he wrote from there that "a social change is going on at the moment such as is rare in the life of a nation—the destruction of slavery." As to the meaning of that change, Thompson has left us with an unforgettable portrait of how one elderly black and his former master reacted to the new order. The master, a Mr. Macgruder, told Thompson in the fall of 1863 that all his slaves, save one woman, had suddenly left on June 19, 1862. Convinced that whites could not work as hard as blacks in the fields—indeed, should not even be asked to do so—Macgruder left most of his fields uncultivated in 1863. The elderly black was George, the former body-servant of Macgruder's father. Thirty years earlier, the father had saved George's life by paying for the amputation of George's frost-bitten hands and legs. Although he was economically "useless," according to Macgruder, the father and son kept George on as a cook and to help out with light chores. To Macgruder's utter amazement, George had left with the other slaves on June 19. Macgruder recaptured George after the first escape, but it was no use. George fled again and dragged himself to Washington, twelve miles away. The only explanation Macgruder could think of was "the ungratefulness of the negro." In Thompson's words:[46]

> So the white man sits in his tumble-down verandah, folding his hands and gazing on his untilled acres because he conceives that any life more active than an overseer's is incompatible with his white skin; and the mutilated old nigger so strongly yearns for liberty that he leaves cornbake and molasses and "better clothes than I have, Sir," to stump twelve miles to Washington that he may starve there but be free.

Major chunks of slavery disintegrated with an irreversible momentum during the war, but most of the slaves in the Confederacy, perhaps 75 percent, remained at least under the nominal control of Southern whites until the Confederacy collapsed in the spring of 1865. This was especially the case on interior plantations not vulnerable to the river raids of Union gunboats and in areas, such as Texas, that were strategically peripheral to the flow of Union armies. In some respects, the war made open resistance or flight more difficult and dangerous. The nervous whites that were left in the countryside redoubled their surveillance, and home guards were ready to smash any suspected insurrectionary plot. Confederate authorities and masters held down the number of runaways by the forced migration of slaves to more militarily secure regions. Caravans of slaves and much of their owners' property headed west into Texas from the lower Mississippi Valley in 1863; along the Carolina-Georgia coast the shift was into the uplands. The impressment of slave labor for military work placed thousands of slaves under direct military supervision. Most workers in Confederate war plants, and at least half the nurses in the military hospitals, were slaves. Confederates had boasted that their slave labor would be a source of great strength in the war. The Union general Ulysses S. Grant agreed that they had made good on the claim. "The 4,000,000 colored noncombatants were equal to more than three times their number in the North, age for age, sex for sex,"[47] conceded Grant.

As impressive as the Confederate utilization of its slave labor was, slavery underwent fundamental changes even in the absence of Union armies. With so many white males drawn off into the Confederate armies, the master-slave relationship weakened without masters to enforce it. Women and their young sons stood in as replacements for the departed masters, but they were no match for the guile and determination of the slaves. Typical of what occurred were the complaints of Mrs. Louticia Jackson to her older son, who was in the army. Mrs. Jackson was trying to manage the slaves with the assistance of Johnny, her teen-aged son. "They seem to feel very imdepenat [sic] as no white man comes to direct or look after them, for Willes speaks shorter to johny and orders *him* about more than any negro on the place."[48] Intimidated by Willes, Johnny gave up trying to give orders. Throughout the Confederacy, the letters and diaries of those left in charge of the slaves in the countryside indicate a steady decline in the amount of work that could be extracted from the slaves. As the war progressed, slaves were more likely to roam off plantations without passes, ignore work assignments, and test the expanding limits of the liberties they now enjoyed. By 1864, the ultimate goal of emancipation seemed all the closer for these slaves when the Confederacy began a debate over arming its slaves.

Generally favored in states in the western Confederacy already overrun by Union troops, and opposed in the older, eastern states on the Atlantic seaboard, the issue of slave soldiers ignited the long-dreaded, internal debate over slavery itself. Common sense and concern for their own safety told Southern whites that a general emancipation would have to follow, once a significant number of slaves were armed and trained for the defense of the Confederacy. Unless the slave soldiers and their families were removed from the Confederacy after the war, any effort to limit emancipation only to them would have been suicidal for whites. The security of slavery would have been irreparably breached. Black slavery or white independence, these were the stark choices as outlined in the debate. A vocal and enraged minority insisted that black soldiers and subsequent emancipation meant a base surrender of all that the Confederacy was fighting for. A bare majority, including that most influential proponent for black troops, Robert E. Lee, argued that no sacrifice was too much for Southern independence. Far too late to have any impact on the military outcome of the war, the Confederate Congress authorized President Jefferson Davis in early March, 1865, to ask the states for up to 250,000 male slaves "to perform military service in whatever capacity he may direct."[49]

Had the Confederacy preserved its independence, it most likely would have been shorn of its slaves but not its masters. If emancipation were the price of Confederate independence, many slaveholders were confident that they would still be able to control their former slaves. Judah P. Benjamin, a member of the Confederate cabinet and an advocate of slave soldiers, explained that an "intermediate stage of serfage of peonage" would emerge. The freed population would have "certain rights of property, a certain degree of personal liberty, and legal protection for the marital and parental relations."[50] In short, their status would have been very similar to that defined in the post-emancipation Southern Black Codes of 1865. Blacks would still be a legally inferior race beholden to the landed elite of former owners for access to work and a livelihood.

Mastery over whites, as well as blacks, was an issue in the debate over slave soldiers. Planters were well aware of the cry in the South of "a rich man's war, and a poor man's fight." Nonslaveholders were especially embittered by the "20-Negro law," an exemption from the Confederate draft for those whites responsible for at least twenty slaves on a plantation. The enlistment of slaves and their emancipation would have had the political advantage of demonstrating to the nonslaveholding majority that planters were willing to surrender their own property on behalf of victory. As it was, planters had good reason late in the war to be concerned about the white majority's loyalty to the Confederacy. Extraordinary demands had been placed on Confederate whites, especially the nonslaveholders and their families.

In order to be competitive in what quickly turned into a total war of both economic and military power, the Confederacy had to draw on its more limited resources earlier and more completely than the Union did. The Confederate draft of 1862 came a full year earlier than the milder Union version. The proportion of draftees in Confederate service, 18 percent, was three times that in the Union armies. In 1863 Confederate authorities were empowered to impress food supplies for the military. The prices subsequently paid to farmers were set by government arbitration boards at one-third to one-half the market value. Tax-in-kind legislation in 1863 took one-tenth of all agricultural production for the Confederacy. The inflation of paper money for which the Confederacy became notorious amounted to a hidden tax in which the purchasing power of the government's currency declined by an average of 10 percent a month. The real wages of Confederate free laborers fell by two-thirds during the war. Whether sent forth from the Confederate Congress or the state legislatures, a host of government bureaucrats fanned out in search of resources and able-bodied males.

Such direct governmental interference with their persons and property was the exact opposite of the individual liberties that most Confederates felt they were fighting to defend in 1861. The loss of their republican liberties became all the more horrifying because it was accompanied by mass poverty. The basic dividing line in white society, the one between those who had slave labor and those dependent solely upon family labor, was threatening to split into a chasm by 1864. A real labor shortage existed in the nonslaveholding rural areas of the hill South. With the men off at war, more and more wives being widowed, heavy taxation, and rapacious raids by parties clad in both the blue and the gray, the yeomanry were reaching the limits of their endurance. One-quarter of Alabama's white population was on some form of government relief in 1864. Civilian morale was on the verge of collapse, and in some regions had broken down completely. Spreading pockets of no man's land, areas fought over by roving bands of deserters and bushwackers, suggested that the Confederacy might disintegrate into near anarchy. Now, and only now, did desertion become a major problem in the Confederate armies. The men went home to protect and care for the same families they thought they were defending when they marched off to war.

The disintegration of the Confederate home front was a specific military objective of Union armies in the second half of the war. In what has aptly been called a strategy of exhaustion, Federal commanders deployed the superior size of their armies not only to gain and hold territory but also, and just as importantly, to seize and destroy everything that could be of use to Confederate armies. A federal force gouging the soft underbelly of an unprotected Confederate area was a fearsome sight. "Farms disappear, houses are burned and plundered, and every living animal killed and eaten,"[51] wrote the Union general, William Sherman, of the destruction wrought by his troops in Mississippi in 1863. A year later, on his army's march through Georgia from Atlanta to Savannah, Sherman showed why he became the most hated practitioner of the strategy of exhaustion. A young Georgia woman, Eliza Andrews, described the scene between Sparta and Gordon, a district called the "Burnt County" after Sherman's passage:[52]

> The fields were tramped down and the road was lined with carcasses of horses, hogs, and cattle that the invaders, unable either to consume or to carry away with them, had wantonly shot down to starve out the people and prevent them from making their crops. The stench in some places was unbearable. . . . Hay ricks and fodder stacks were demolished, corn cribs were empty, and every bale of cotton that could be found was burnt by the savages.

Such a strategy, one which literally exhausted the Confederacy of men and resources, recognized that the boundary between military and civilian targets was all but eliminated when an invading army was confronted with determined, popular resistance. "The South has united people and as many men as she can arm, and though our armies pass across and through the land, the war closes in behind and leaves the same enemy behind,'' noted Sherman in 1862. Simply occupying places was not enough. It was just the beginning, the establishment of launching pads for punishing raids into surrounding areas, the cumulative impact of which was instrumental in bringing the Confederacy to its knees. The Confederates, as Sherman explained, ''must be made to feel and acknowledge the power of a just and mighty nation.''[53]

The military and domestic pieces of the Union's victorious war plans fell into place in 1863. By its policy of both freeing and arming the slaves, Lincoln's government gained the double advantage of subtracting one worker from the Confederate war effort for every soldier it added to Union armies. While Lee was being held in check in the East, Union generals continued to advance in the West, where they could exploit river routes of invasion and encirclement. Meanwhile, Republicans on the Northern home front were legislating a quiet revolution in the nation's political economy and conceptions of centralized authority.

In their policies on emancipation, conscription, and economic development, the Civil War Republicans laid down the preconditions for transforming the antebellum union of states into a powerful nation-state. Spurred on by the unprecedented demands of organizing and financing a total war, the Republicans passed a sweeping program of economic nationalism over determined Democratic opposition.

In currency and banking, issues the Democrats had always felt should be left up to the individual states, the Republicans expanded federal authority. Greenbacks, treasury notes that paid no interest but that were legal tender for all debts, were issued in order to raise mass purchasing power and to resolve a banking crisis caused by a drain on specie reserves. The Legal Tender Act of 1862 created the first national currency in American history. The National Banking Act of 1863 reorganized the hodgepodge of more than 1,600 state-chartered banks into a national system under federal charters. The prewar Democratic trend toward lower tariffs was reversed, and by the end of the war average tariff rates had risen from 19 percent to 47 percent. Huge federal subsidies were provided in legislation for the Pacific land-grant railroads. The public domain was also used to subsidize agriculture and public education. The Homestead Act of 1862 granted 160 acres of public land to citizens who would live on it for five years. And, in an effort both to diffuse the benefits of public education and to train a professional elite, the Morrill Act of 1862 allotted land to states that would establish public agricultural colleges.

This burst of positive liberalism came on top of a military draft, a host of new, wartime taxes (including the nation's first income tax), and highly publicized suspensions of the writ of habeas corpus in cases involving antiwar dissidents. All of this was very threatening to most Democrats, traditionally the party of localism, individual liberties, and states' rights. They accused the Republicans of forcing individuals into a crushing dependency on forces beyond their immediate control. Thus, the Republican commitment to a more centralized republic, one often couched in the militant language of a millennial, triumphant Protestantism, provoked a bitter response from such hardcore Democrats as the Catholic immigrants in the cities and Southern-born Baptists and Methodists in the lower Midwest.

When the Republicans revealed their class bias by a draft law that permitted an individual to commute, or buy his way out of, military service for a fee of $300, the result was the worst riot of the nineteenth century, the bloody draft riots of July 1863, in New York City. The rioters poured out of the working class, Irish slums in a vengeful, insurrectionary fury that claimed over 100 lives. Unable to attack the rich directly, the rioters vented their wrath on any blacks they could lay their hands on. An English officer in New York saw at once how class tensions were displaced on blacks:[54]

> The people who can't pay $300 naturally hate being forced to fight in order to liberate the very race who they are most anxious should be slaves. It is their direct interest not only that all slaves should remain slaves, but that the free Northern Negroes who compete with them for labor should be sent to the South also.

When commutation was repealed in March 1864, draft evasion rose and spread from the immigrant cities into the rural heartland. For the combined four Union drafts, 21 percent of all those called failed to report to their draft boards.

By appealing to those fearful of a black inundation of Northern labor markets, and those resentful of such direct interference with their lives as the government's military draft, the Democrats maintained their base of popular support. Democratic voters insisted that they were still loyal Unionists, but their allegiance was to a prewar Union of local self-determination that they felt was being destroyed by the Republicans and the hateful zeal of Puritanical New England. The war, in a typical Democratic editorial, had become one "of abolition, of violation of the Constitution, a war by the Eastern oligarchy."[55] Running on such a platform, the Democrats polled 45 percent of the popular vote in the presidential election of 1864. Despite Republican charges of treason, the endorsement of Lincoln by many War Democrats, the nearly 80 percent soldier vote for Lincoln, and the absence of Democratic voters from the border South who were in Confederate armies, the Democratic party was still a powerful force in Northern public life.

The Republicans, however, remained the major political force in the North. Writing in late 1863, Senator John Sherman of Ohio pinpointed one of the main reasons; "The wonderful prosperity of all classes, especially of laborers, has a tendency to secure acquiescence in all measures demanded to carry on the war."[56] Sherman overstated his case—the real wages of Northern labor trailed inflation by about 20 percent for most of the war—but high agricultural prices and government contracts did mean prosperity for farmers and businessmen. Although labor felt that it was not receiving its fair share of the prosperity, Protestant, native-born workers remained loyal Republicans. A Union victory meant the destruction of slavery and the triumph of their free-labor principles.

Once the Union settled on its victorious strategy—hold in the east, win in the West, and grind away at the Southern social fabric—the Confederacy had already run out of enough soldiers to defeat it. Confederates fought to stay out of the Union in much the same way as they had acted in leaving it—boldly, defiantly, and recklessly. The soldiers that could have protected the Confederacy, or at least prolonged the war to the point at which Northern sentiment might well have voted an end to the stalemate, were left on the battlefields of the first twenty-seven months of the war. From First Bull Run in July 1861, through Chickamauga in September 1863, the Confederacy lost 175,000 men, dead and wounded. The bulk of these losses came in charges against Union positions. Although the Confederacy needed only to defend itself in order to win the war, its generals, spurred on by President Davis, public pressure, and their own

The Idealized War and the Real War. This romantic painting by Ole Peter Hansen Balling, *Grant and His Generals,* portrays the glorified vision of the Civil War. The photograph of Union war dead on the Gettysburg battlefield, July 1863, brings home the reality of war: the cost in human lives. (*Above:* National Portrait Gallery, Smithsonian Institution, Washington, D. C.; Gift of Mrs. Harry Newton Blue in memory of her husband, Harry Newton Blue, 1893–1925, who served as an officer of the regular U. S. Army. *Below:* Chicago Historical Society)

desire to prove their valor, ordered one hopeless charge after another. Thus the Confederates were the tactical attackers in eight of the first twelve major campaigns. In these eight battles alone, Confederate losses totaled 97,000. Southern generals were as sacrificial of themselves as they were of their soldiers. In a ratio that was triple that of the Union generals, 55 percent of the Confederate generals were killed or wounded in combat. "The rebels fight as though a mans life was not worth one sent [sic],"[57]

Richmond, Virginia, 1865. The ruins of what a few weeks before had been the capital of the Confederacy graphically illustrate the devastation all over the defeated South. (Historical Pictures Service, Chicago)

observed a Union private. Depleted Confederate armies, bled by their commanders at a rate twice as fast as their Union opponents, lacked the manpower to turn back the Federal offensives in the last year of the war.

The failure of the Confederate high command to formulate a strategy of maintenance to offset the Union's strategy of exhaustion sealed the fate of the Southern bid for political independence. Consistent with the same values and ideals they had brought to the war, Confederate leadership in the spring of 1865 decided to surrender their armies rather than continue the miliary struggle by guerrilla resistance. They gave up their armies, but not their honor. They had fought bravely, if not always wisely. Surely they had vindicated themselves and the slave culture they had headed. "I dare look any man in the face," proclaimed E. M. Boykin of South Carolina. "There is no humiliation in our position after such a struggle as we made for freedom from Yankees."[58] If nothing more was to be gained for the sake of honor, the social order in which that honor was displayed would likely be lost if the South were now racked by interminable, partisan warfare. The signs of an impending breakdown were already all too obvious. To preserve what was left of that social order, and their own preeminent position of power within it, Confederate leaders accepted defeat.

SUGGESTED READING

Clement Eaton, *A History of the Old South* (1975), provides a narrative overview of the late-antebellum South. For provocative works that reach contrasting conclusions as to the political and ideological consequences of slavery's expansion for Southern whites, see Eugene D. Genevese, *The Political Economy of Slavery* (1965); J. Mills Thornton III, *Politics and Power in a Slave Society* (1978); and James Oakes, *The Ruling Race: A History of American Slaveholders*

(1982). Otto H. Olsen, "Historians and the Extent of Slave Ownership in the Southern United States," CWH 18 (1972), stresses the widespread nature of slave ownership, while William W. Freehling, "The Founding Fathers and Slavery," AHR 77 (1972), makes a strong case for the gradual weakening of slavery in the upper South. Shearer Davis Bowman, "Antebellum Planters and *Vormarz* Junkers in Comparative Perspective," AHR 85 (1980), perceptively compares Southern planters with another powerful and conservative landholding class in the nineteenth century.

The best source on the effort to reopen the African slave trade in the 1850s is Ronald T. Takaki, *A Pro-Slavery Crusade* (1971). The tensions produced in Southern society by the maturing of its economy can be followed in Drew Gilpin Faust, "The Rhetoric and Ritual of Agriculture in Antelbellum South Carolina," JSH 45 (1979); Harold D. Woodman, "The Old South: Global and Local Perspectives on Power, Politics, and Ideology," CWH 25 (1979); William L. Barney, "The Ambivalence of Change: From Old South to New in the Alabama Black Belt, 1850–1870," Walter J. Fraser, Jr., and Winfred B. Moore, Jr., *From the Old South to the New* (1981); and James Oakes, "The Politics of Economic Development in the Antebellum South," JIH 15 (1984). Michael P. Johnson, "Planters and Patriarchy: Charleston, 1800–1860," JSH (1980), is a careful study of the dilemmas faced by the sons of planters in assuming adult roles of responsibility. On the economic position of Southern white artisans, see Ira Berlin and Herbert G. Gutman, "Natives and Immigrants, Free Men and Slaves," AHR 88 (1983), and, for the political problems that they posed for planters, see Fred Siegal, "Artisans and Immigrants in the Politics of Late Antebellum Georgia," CWH 27 (1981). Anne Firor Scott, *The Southern Lady: From Pedestal to Politics, 1830–1930* (1970), and Catherine Clinton, *The Plantation Mistress* (1982), detect among white women an undercurrent of discontent with slavery and the subordinate roles imposed upon them by the white male patriarchy. For the most thorough study of antebellum Southern women, see Suzanne Lebsock, *The Free Women of Petersburg* (1984).

The definitive study on secession has yet to be written, but several excellent studies on individual states exist. Among them are: Steven A. Channing, *Crisis of Fear: Secession in South Carolina* (1970); William L. Barney, *The Secessionist Impulse: Alabama and Mississippi in 1860* (1974); and Michael P. Johnson, *Toward a Patriarchal Republic: The Secession of Georgia* (1977). For the upper South, see Daniel W. Crofts, "The Union Party of 1861 and the Secession Crisis," PAH 11 (1978); Joseph Carlyle Sitterson, *The Secession Movement in North Carolina* (1939); Henry T. Shanks, *The Secession Movement in Virginia, 1847–1861* (1934); and the excellent analysis in Craig M. Simpson, *A Good Southerner: The Life of Henry A. Wise of Virginia* (1985). Very helpful for the South as a whole is Ralph A. Wooster, *The Secession Conventions of the South* (1962). The best source on Northern reactions to secession is Philip S. Paludan, "The American Civil War Considered as a Crisis in Law and Order," AHR 77 (1972). The policy of the Republicans during the secession crisis and the background to the Sumter crisis can be followed in David M. Potter, *Lincoln and His Party in the Secession Crisis* (1942), and Kenneth M. Stampp, *And the War Came* (1950).

Peter J. Parish, *The American Civil War* (1975), is a fine one-volume history of the war. The most recent synthesis is in James M. McPherson, *Ordeal By Fire: The Civil War and Reconstruction* (1982). For the most recent attempt to fashion a fresh synthesis of the enormous military literature on the war, see Herman Hattaway and Archer Jones, *How the North Won* (1983). Shelby Foote, *The Civil War* (3 vols., 1958–1974), is a gracefully written narrative of Confederate operations, and Thomas L. Connelly and Archer Jones, *The Politics of Command* (1977), provides a thoughtful critique of Confederate strategy. The Southern commitment to offensive warfare is the central theme of Grady McWhiney and Perry D. Jamison, *Attack and Die* (1982). The most popular and readable chronicler of the Union armies has been Bruce Catton, best known for his works on the Army of the Potomac: *Mr. Lincoln's Army* (1951), *Glory Road* (1952), and *A Stillness at Appomattox* (1953). Michael C. C. Adams, *Our Masters the Rebels* (1978), uses a psychological approach to explain the early failure of this main Union army in the East. T. Harry Williams, *Lincoln and His Generals* (1952), is still the point of departure for understanding the evolution of Union strategy. Individual battles can be studied in John T. Hubbell, ed., *Battles Lost and Won* (1975). For an especially effective re-creation of a single battle, see Wiley Sword, *Shiloh: Bloody April* (1974). The basic studies on the common soldiers are Bell I. Wiley, *The Life of Johnny Reb* (1943), and *The Life of Billy Yank* (1952).

For an imaginative interdisciplinary approach to the values and motivations of the soldiers, see Michael Barton, *Good Men: The Character of Civil War Soldiers* (1981). The growing sectionalization in the legal and popular cultures from which these values were drawn can be seen in Paul Finkelman, *An Imperfect Union: Slavery, Federalism and Comity* (1981), and Michael Fellman, "Rehearsal for the Civil War: Antislavery and Proslavery at the Fighting Point in Kansas, 1854–1856," in Lewis Perry and Michael Fellman, eds., *Antislavery Reconsidered* (1979). The bibliographical lists in Charles E. Dornbusch, *Regimental Publications and Personal Narratives of the Civil War* (3 vols., 1961–1971), are invaluable for locating the accounts and memoirs of individual soldiers.

The evolution of Lincoln's policy on emancipation is shrewdly analyzed in Richard N. Current, *The Lincoln Nobody Knows* (1958). Other important sources include: John Hope Franklin, *The Emancipation Proclamation* (1963); James McPherson, *The Struggle for Equality* (1964); and La Wanda Cox, *Lincoln and Black Freedom* (1981). Black participation in their own emancipation comes across powerfully in the remarkable documents collected in Ira Berlin et al., eds., *Freedom: A Documentary History of Emancipation, 1861–1867* (1982). Lawrence W. Levine, *Black Culture and Black Consciousness* (1977), and Leon F. Litwack, *Been in the Storm So Long* (1979), also have superb sections on the black quest for freedom. For the contemporary black reaction to the war, see the primary sources in James McPherson, ed., *The Negro's Civil War* (1965). Black military service for the Union is covered in Dudley T. Cornish, *The Sable Arm* (1966), and Benjamin Quarles, *The Negro in the Civil War* (1953). Willie Lee Rose, *Rehearsal for Reconstruction* (1964), and Louis Gerteis, *From Contraband to Freedman* (1973), are important accounts of the wartime federal policies towards blacks in the South. Though badly outdated in many areas, Bell I. Wiley, *Southern Negroes, 1861–1865* (1938), is still the most comprehensive treatment of blacks in the Confederacy. It should be supplemented with James H. Brewer, *The Confederate Negro: Virginia's Craftsmen and Negro Laborers, 1861–1865* (1969), and Clarence L. Mohr, "Before Sherman: Georgia Blacks and the Union War Effort, 1861–1864," JSH 45 (1979). The extraordinary debate over emancipation in the Confederacy is covered in Robert F. Durden, *The Gray and the Black* (1972).

Charles W. Ramsdell, *Behind the Lines in the Southern Confederacy* (1944), and Emory M. Thomas, *The Confederate Nation, 1861–1865* (1979), are the best surveys of the Confederate home front. Mary E. Massey, *Refugee Life in the Confederacy* (1964), is superb on the social disruption of the war. For a summary of resent research, see Harry P. Owens and James J. Cooke, eds., *The Old South in the Crucible of War* (1983). Various approaches to Confederate politics can be found in: Wilfred B. Yearns, *The Confederate Congress* (1960); Thomas B. Alexander and Richard E. Beringer, *The Anatomy of the Confederate Congress* (1972); and Eric L. McKitrick, "Party Politics and the Union and Confederate War Efforts," in William Nisbet Chambers and Walter Dean Burnham, eds., *The American Party Systems* (1967). The development of internal dissent in the Confederacy is treated in Frank L. Owsley, *State Rights in the Confederacy* (1925); Georgia Lee Tatum, *Disloyalty in the Confederacy* (1934); and Paul D. Escott, *After Secession: Jefferson Davis and the Failure of Confederate Nationalism* (1978). For the resistance of planters to Confederate taxation and war loans, see Stanley Lebergott, "Why the South Lost: Commercial Purpose in the Confederacy, 1861–1865," JAH 70 (1983).

The best study on the Northern home front remains Emerson D. Fite, *Social and Economic Conditions in the North During the Civil War* (1910). There is also much useful material in Allan Nevins, *The War for the Union* (4 vols., 1959–1971). Important works on Northern agriculture are Paul W. Gates, *Agriculture and the Civil War* (1965), and Wayne D. Rasmussen, "The Civil War: A Catalyst of Agricultural Revolution," AGH 39 (1965). George M. Fredrickson, *The Inner Civil War* (1965), and James H. Moorhead, *American Apocalypse: Yankee Protestants and the Civil War, 1860–1869* (1978), are excellent for the impact of the war on intellectual and religious thought. For the role of women, see Mary E. Massey, *Bonnet Brigades* (1966), and Ann Douglas Wood, "The War within a War: Women Nurses in the Union Army," CWH 18 (1972). The human and economic cost of the war for a local community is presented in Emily J. Harris, "Sons and Soldiers: Deerfield, Massachusetts, and the Civil War," CWH 30 (1984). Edward Dicey, *Spectator of America,* ed. by Herbert Mitgang (1976) is unrivalled for a contemporary account of Northern society during the war.

Wartime politics in the North are surveyed in James A. Rawley, *The Politics of Union* (1974). The essays in David Donald, *Lincoln Reconsidered* (1956), are insightful, and Allan G. Bogue, *The Earnest Men: Republicans of the Civil War Senate* (1981), takes a close, quantitative look at divisions within the Republican party. James G. Randall, *Constitutional Problems Under Lincoln* (1951), is a magisterial study, and William B. Hesseltine, *Lincoln and the War Governors* (1948), is very solid. Leonard P. Curry, *Blueprint for Modern America* (1968), is the best source on the sweeping legislative program of the Republicans that transformed the nation's political economy. For Northern Democratic opposition to the war itself, see Wood Gray, *The Hidden Civil War* (1942). The economic basis for Democratic opposition to the Republicans' wartime nationalism is emphasized in Frank L. Klement, *The Copperheads in the Middle West* (1960), and, in a recent survey, Joel Silbey, *A Respectable Minority: The Democratic Party in the Civil War Era* (1977), stresses the cultural sources of Democratic opposition. The growing resistance in the North to the draft is demonstrated in Peter Levine, "Draft Evasion in the North during the Civil War, 1863–1865," JAH 67 (1981). Adrian Cook, *The Armies in the Streets* (1974), looks at the class and racial hatreds that exploded in the New York City draft riots of 1863.

NOTES

1. Roy P. Basler, ed., *The Collected Works of Abraham Lincoln* (New Brunswick, N.J.: Rutgers University Press, 1953), Vol. III, p. 547.
2. New Orleans *Bee,* Dec. 14, 1860, cited in Kenneth M. Stampp, ed., *The Causes of the Civil War* (Englewood Cliffs, N.J.: Prentice-Hall, 1959), p. 114.
3. Quoted in William R. Brock, *Parties and Political Conscience: American Dilemmas, 1840–1850* (Millwood, N.Y.: KTO Press, 1979), p. 322.
4. Quoted in Stampp, op. cit., p. 105.
5. Basler, op. cit., II, p. 461.
6. Montgomery *Advertiser,* Nov. 21, 1849, quoted in J. Mills Thornton III, *Politics and Power in a Slave Society: Alabama, 1800–1860* (Baton Rouge: Louisiana State University Press, 1978), p. 205.
7. Quoted in William L. Barney, *The Road to Secession* (New York: Praeger Publishers, 1972), p. 11.
8. Ibid., p. 40.
9. Ibid., p. 36.
10. Cited in Stampp, op. cit., pp. 159–160.
11. Quoted in Ronald T. Takaki, *A Pro-Slavery Crusade: The Agitation to Reopen the African Slave Trade* (New York: The Free Press, 1971), p. 60.
12. C. Vann Woodward, ed., *Mary Chesnut's Civil War* (New Haven: Yale University Press, 1981), p. 29.
13. Quoted in Barney, op. cit., p. 138.
14. Quoted in John Barnwell, *Love of Order: South Carolina's First Secession Crisis* (Chapel Hill: University of North Carolina Press, 1982), p. 150.
15. Frederick Law Olmsted, *A Journey in the Back Country* (New York: Shocken Books, 1970), p. 241.
16. Quoted in Michael F. Holt, *The Political Crisis of the 1850s* (New York: John Wiley, 1978), p. 242.
17. Virginia Jeans Laas, ed., "'On the Qui Vive for the long letter': Washington Letters from a Navy Wife, 1861," *Civil War History* 29 (1983): 42.
18. Woodward, op. cit., p. 4.
19. Allan Nevins, ed., *Diary of the Civil War, 1860–1865: George Templeton Strong* (New York: Macmillan, 1962), p. 109.

20. Ibid., p. 119.
21. Basler, op. cit., IV, p. 332.
22. Charlotte Erickson, *Invisible Immigrants: The Adaptation of English and Scottish Immigrants in Nineteenth-Century America* (Coral Gables, Fla.: University of Miami Press, 1972), p. 348.
23. Chicago *Journal,* April 17, 1861, quoted in Stampp, op. cit., p. 146.
24. Quoted in Phillip S. Paludan, "The American Civil War Considered as a Crisis in Law and Order," *American Historical Review* 77 (1972): 1019.
25. Quoted in Bertram Wyatt-Brown, *Southern Honor: Ethics & Behavior in the Old South* (New York: Oxford University Press, 1982), p. 110.
26. Sam R. Watkins, *"Co. Aytch": A Side Show of the Big Show* (New York: Macmillan, 1962 reprint), pp. 234–235.
27. Robert Manson Myers, ed., *The Children of Pride: A True Story of Georgia and the Civil War* (New Haven: Yale University Press, 1972), p. 648.
28. Quoted in Michael Fellman, "Rehearsal for the Civil War: Antislavery and Proslavery at the Fighting Point in Kansas, 1854–1856," in Perry and Fellman, *Antislavery Reconsidered* (Louisiana State University Press, 1979), pp. 292, 300–301.
29. Quoted in Albert D. Kirwan, ed., *The Confederacy* (New York: Meridian Books, 1959), p. 74.
30. Quoted in Myers, op. cit., p. 667.
31. Quoted in James David Essig, "The Lord's Free Man: Charles G. Ginney and His Abolitionism," *Civil War History* 24 (1978): 42.
32. Watkins, op. cit., p. 23.
33. *The Diary of a Dead Man, 1862–1864,* compiled by J. P. Ray (n.p.: Acorn Press, 1979) p. 114.
34. Quoted in Thomas R. Bright, "Yankees in Arms: The Civil War as a Personal Experience," *Civil War History* 19 (1973): 198, 199.
35. John Kent Folmar, ed., *From That Terrible Field: Civil War Letters of James M. Williams, Twenty-First Alabama Infantry Volunteers* (University, Ala.: The University of Alabama Press, 1981), pp. 34, 30, 93.
36. Spencer B. King, Jr., ed., *Rebel Lawyer: Letters of Theodorick W. Montfort, 1861–1862* (Athens, Ga.: University of Georgia Press, 1965), pp. 49, 64–65.
37. Stephen E. Ambrose, ed., *A Wisconsin Boy in Dixie: The Selected Letters of James K. Newton* (Madison: University of Wisconsin Press, 1961), p. 13.
38. James B. Casey, ed., "The Ordeal of Adoniram Judson Warner: His Minutes of South Mountain and Antietam," *Civil War History* 28 (1982): 226.
39. Edward G. Longacre, ed., "The Roughest Kind of Campaigning: Letters of Sergeant Edward Wightman, Third New York Volunteers, May–July 1864," *Civil War History* 28 (1982): 338.
40. Quoted in Richard N. Current, *The Lincoln Nobody Knows* (New York: Hill and Wang, 1964), p. 225.
41. Ray Allen Billington, ed., *The Journal of Charlotte L. Forten: A Free Negro in the Slave Era* (New York: Norton Paperback, 1981), p. 171.
42. John W. Blassingame, ed., *Slave Testimony: Two Centuries of Letters, Speeches, Interviews, and Autobiographies* (Baton Rouge: Louisiana State University Press, 1980), p. 359.
43. Quoted in Cam Walker, "Corinth: The Story of a Contraband Camp," *Civil War History* 20 (1974): 6.
44. Basler, op. cit., VI, p. 149.
45. Christopher Chancellor, ed., *An Englishman in the American Civil War: The Diaries of Henry Yates Thompson, 1863* (New York: New York University Press, 1971), p. 91.
46. Ibid., pp. 94, 104.
47. Quoted in William L. Barney, *Flawed Victory* (New York: Praeger Publishers, 1975), p. 133.
48. Quoted in Emory M. Thomas, *The Confederate Nation: 1861–1865* (New York: Harper & Row, 1979), p. 239.
49. Quoted in Robert F. Durden, *The Gray and the Black: The Confederate Debate on Emancipation* (Baton Rouge: Louisiana State University Press, 1972), p. 202.
50. Ibid., p. 183.
51. Rachel Sherman Thorndike, ed., *The Sherman Letters: Correspondence between General and Senator Sherman from 1837 to 1891* (New York: Da Capo Press, 1969).
52. Spencer Bidwell King, Jr., ed., *The War-Time Journal of a Georgia Girl, 1864–1865* (Macon, Ga.: The Ardwain Press, 1960), pp. 32–33.
53. Thorndike, op. cit., pp. 166, 153.
54. Walter Lord, ed., *The Fremantle Diary* (New York: Capricorn Books, 1960), p. 242.
55. Quoted in Robert Kelley, *The Cultural Pattern in American Politics: The First Century* (New York: Alfred A. Knopf, 1979), p. 235.
56. Thorndike, op. cit., p. 216.
57. Quoted in Grady McWhiney and Perry D. Jamieson, *Attack and Die: Civil War Military Tactics and the Southern Heritage* (University, Ala.: University of Alabama Press, 1982), p. 18.
58. Woodward, op. cit., p. 809.

7

The Crisis of Reconstruction

What we normally refer to as Reconstruction, the new state governments created in most of the states of the former Confederacy under the provisions of the Military Reconstruction Act of 1867, was not legislated into place until a full two years had passed since the end of the war. Reconstruction under these governments did not actually begin until 1868. Thus, in the critical period just after the war, the status of the South and Northern expectations of the defeated rebels were vague and unsettled.

During this period of uncertainty before the Republicans imposed their political terms of reunion, the traditional leaders of the South had a largely free hand to stabilize the potentially revolutionary situation that flickered in the ashes of defeat. In the spring of 1865, former slaves were claiming, and sometimes seizing, the land as their own. The impoverished yeomanry, in the lament of James Chesnut of South Carolina, "were lighthearted at the ruin of the great slave owners,"[1] and, for their participation in the rebellion, the planters faced legal penalties that could have deprived them of their estates and political rights. Everything was in a state of awful suspense. Yet, although emancipation fundamentally transformed class relations, no social upheaval occurred. The planters, for all their well-grounded fears, remained in control.

Under the presidential Reconstruction of Andrew Johnson in 1865–1866, a generous program of amnesty and pardons restored political and economic rights to the planters. Land was returned that otherwise would have been forfeited under the provisions of the Confiscation Acts passed by Congress in 1861 and 1862. The bid of the freedmen for a sweeping redistribution of the land was turned back. The yeomanry, though still in debt, did not organize politically to express their demands for economic relief.

As a consequence of Johnson's program, the most propitious moment for revolutionary change in the South had already passed by the time the "radical" policy of the North was set forth in 1867. Nonetheless, the new post-1867 governments posed a real threat to traditional power relations in the South. The old planter class now faced the challenge of a biracial coalition of Southern Republicans, in which the freedmen had the reality of political rights and the yeomanry the hope of economic assistance. At this point, however, just when political reconstruction in the South was only beginning, the Republican majority in the North was concluding that the crusade for a reformed South had already been fought and won.

This basic miscalculation was implicit in the evolution of Northern ideas and policies on Reconstruction between Appomattox and the passage of the Fifteenth Amendment in 1870. After looking at how Reconstruction gradually evolved into a fixed policy, this chapter will move on to the internal dynamics of Reconstruction within the South and the reasons that so much of its promise was unfulfilled.

Prelude to Reconstruction

At the war's end, neither the Republicans as a party nor the North as a section had any blueprint for reconstruction. Undertones of competing impulses and needs pulled in different directions. Themes of restoration and regeneration intermingled in the public mood of the North. On the one hand, there was the natural urge to heal the wounds as quickly as possible and return to the security of political normalcy. On the other hand, there was an even greater need to honor the fallen heroes in blue by finding a high moral purpose and justification in the cause for which they had died. Somehow, the postwar settlement had to recognize that a regenerated and more perfect Union could be the only fitting monument to the Union war dead.

The divergent political needs and constituencies of the Republican and Democratic parties gave these themes of restoring the old and regenerating the new a decidedly partisan coloration. Somewhat surprisingly, the war had done little to recast the party allegiances of Northern voters. If anything, the loyalties that were set in the realignment of the mid-1850s were solidified. The Republicans' wartime program of centralizing nationalism had intensified all the traditional concerns of the more localistic-minded Democrats. Thus, though it was often reduced to ugly demands for white supremacy, Democratic ideology after the war was a defensive call for the protection of personal freedoms from encroaching federal power. In the case of the rebel South, this meant home rule by local whites who would have to meet but minimal conditions for the speedy restoration of their states to the Union. The Northern Democrats could expect that such an agenda would be very popular among Southern whites. With the additional support of just a few Northern states, notably New York, the Democratic party could even hope to replace the Republicans as the nation's ruling party.

The other side of the same political logic dictated that the Republicans would want to institute safeguards for the future of their party before readmitting the South. The Republicans had yet to win a national election under normal political conditions. A divided Democratic party was instrumental in Lincoln's victory in 1860, which garnered only 40 percent of the national vote. The Republicans were so concerned about their prospects in 1864 that they discarded the Republican label and ran as the Union party. In 1865 the future of the party could not be taken for granted. Unanswered was the question of how a still-young party, fused together first by antislaveryism and then the goal of preserving the Union, would maintain its unity once these organizing principles were gone. Adding to the uncertainties was the ironic fact that a readmitted South would have more representatives and electoral votes than the antebellum South, now that the three-fifths clause had been eliminated and the slaves freed.

The Republicans did enter the postwar period with two great strengths:

1. Their numerical preponderance in Congress had never been greater. The Congress that would convene in December, 1865, had a Republican margin of 145 to 40 in the House and of 42 to 10 in the Senate.
2. Of more critical importance for the future, was the popular identification of the party with the redeeming glory of the successful struggle to preserve the Union. When the Union volunteers mustered out in the spring and summer of 1865, they did so with a feeling of immense pride. Their personal commitment had been worth it. For Joel Chambers of the 89th Illinois Volunteers, "the suffering we all endured while in the army was a sacrifice not made in vain for the results of the war could not have been more triumphant, more glorious or more satisfactory than as it is."[2]

This sense of having sacrificed for a great cause was fully shared by Northern civilians. The some 3,000 Northern women who served as army nurses, and the countless thousands who staffed the 7,000 local auxiliaries of the U.S. Sanitary Commission, a volunteer relief organization to aid the soldiers, fused their roles as Christian mothers and patriotic Americans into an intense involvement with the war. As surrogate ministers and mothers, they personally experienced the war as a fulfillment of all the idealized themes of middle-class domesticity. "I am here to do my Master's work," wrote Union nurse Hannah Ropes from a Washington hospital; "the poor privates are my special children for the present."[3] Victory belonged as much to these women as it did to the soldiers. It also belonged to many of the workers who had voted against Lincoln in 1860. A mechanic told H. Y. Thompson in 1863 of the sacrifices his male kin had made. He himself had not enlisted because of his poor health, but all of the remaining six brothers and brothers-in-law in his family had fought for the Union. One had died of cholera, two others were wounded, one of whom would be bedridden for life, two had served out their enlistments, and the sixth was still in the army. The mechanic had not voted for Lincoln, noted Thompson, "yet what sacrifice he has now made and how proud he is for the sake of the Union."[4]

These sacrifices had sustained the Union, and they would have to be honored in any peace settlement. By failing to recognize that irreducible demand of the Northern public, Andrew Johnson lost the support of that public and unwittingly radicalized the peace terms. The assassination of Lincoln on April 14, 1865, a Good Friday, catapulted Johnson into the presidency and gave the Republican party its enduring martyr:[5]

> In the beauty of the lilies Christ was born across the sea,
> With a glory in his bosom that transfigures you and me;
> As he died to make men holy, let us die to make men free,
> While God is marching on.

This final stanza of the "Battle Hymn of the Republic" now had a literal application in the atonement figure of Lincoln. To make certain that no one missed the point, the Republicans sent Lincoln's body home to Springfield, Illinois, on a long, circuitous funeral trip that encouraged more than a million Northerners to view Father Abraham's casket.

Johnson Versus Congress

Johnson was a loyal War Democrat from Tennessee. As the only senator from a seceded state who remained in the U.S. Senate, and as a lifelong opponent of the planter aristocracy, he was a very valuable asset to the Republican party. Fresh from his war governorship of Union-occupied Tennessee, where he stridently proclaimed his willingness to hang unrepentant rebels, Johnson was teamed with Lincoln on the Union party ticket of 1864. Useful to the Republicans when Lincoln was alive, Johnson soon became a liability with Lincoln dead. He clashed with his nominal party for the most basic of reasons. Because he was neither a Northerner nor, in any meaningful sense of the term, a Republican, Johnson simply could not understand what the war and the Union had come to mean for the Northern majority.

Although Johnson was a successful slaveholder, lawyer, and politician by the 1850s, he never overcame the insecurities and resentments of a childhood spent in illiteracy and poverty after the death of his father, a tavern porter in Raleigh, North Carolina. He blamed the rebellion on that same "upstart, swelled headed, iron heeled, bobtailed aristocracy"[6] whom he believed had always looked down their noses at him. Johnson hated this aristocracy with a passion, and he meant it when he thundered away in the spring 1865 of the need to punish individual rebels. But once these men admitted they had made a mistake, once they were humbled by defeat and the need to apply to him, the self-made plebeian, for a pardon, Johnson received a personal satisfaction that had been missing throughout his career. He was then willing to follow through on a program of reconstruction that, while recognizing the end of slavery, seemed for all practical purposes to be turning the clock back to 1860. Victory for Johnson meant a return of the Southern white masses to loyalty. The measurement of this loyalty would be a renunciation of secession, an acceptance of emancipation in the form of the Thirteenth Amendment of 1865, and a repudiation of all Confederate war debts. Once these terms were met, Johnsonian reconstruction was over.

Johnson's program, which was implemented in the spring and summer of 1865 when Congress was not in session, initially received broad but cautious support in the North. It appealed to both the traditional republican doctrine of minimal interference by the federal government in the concerns of individual states and the core faith of antebellum republicanism, the right of local white majorities to determine their own affairs. It held out the promise of stabilizing social conditions in the South and providing Northern businessmen with the confidence they would need before committing capital to reestablish the South as the major export sector in the American economy. There also appeared to be a hardheaded realism in Johnson's approach that appealed to the Union generals. "We cannot keep the South out long," reasoned General Sherman in August 1865, "and it is a physical impossibility for us to guard the entire South by armies, nor can we change opinions by force. . . ." Because Sherman believed that the "poor whites" and freedmen were too ignorant to be entrusted with political offices, he saw no alternative to the old elite returning to power under the Johnson settlement. Thus, "for some time the marching of state Governments must be controlled by the same class of whites as went into the Rebellion against us."[7]

In the hands of a more skillful politician, the main outlines of Johnsonian Reconstruction might well have survived the inevitable counterresponse registered by the Republicans when Congress convened in December, 1865. Certainly, it is difficult to imagine Lincoln isolating himself from the centrist wing of his party as Johnson did in 1866. Whereas Lincoln had been shrewd, flexible, and pragmatic in his handling of wartime reconstruction for the Union-occupied portions of Louisiana, Arkansas, and Tennessee, Johnson was clumsy, rigid, and doctrinaire in the postwar setting. Above all, Lincoln always acted as if he already knew what a local Republican convention from New York told him in 1862: "He has no army, he has no navy, no resources of any kind except what the people give him. In a word, he is powerless unless the people stand at his side and uphold his hands."[8] By staying in touch with the public mood, leading or deferring to its cumulative weight as conditions warranted, Lincoln used the party machinery for his own ends. Johnson's greatest party achievement was the negative one of uniting the party *against* his programs. He relied for support on the tenuous alliance of Northern Democrats, conservative Republicans, and Southern moderates who rallied behind him in 1865. But this alliance was as much outside the mainstream of Northern public opinion as was Johnson himself.

By the fall of 1865 Northerners, and most particularly members of the Republican party, were convinced that Southern whites were forgetting who had won the war. A minimal expectation of the North was that the former rebels should act as if they recognized their defeat. The Northerners were the victors, and they wanted assurances and proof of their victory. Instead, the state governments set up under the Johnson guidelines seemed to embody the same arrogant white Southernism that the North believed had brought on the war in the first place.

The Southern Black Codes of 1865, state legislative enactments necessitated by the need to define the legal rights of the emancipated blacks, were attacked for returning the freed population to a status little better than slavery. Intended, as Southern whites candidly admitted, to substitute the coercive power of the state for the former legal prerogatives of the master as a means of disciplining a plantation labor force, the black codes directly challenged the free labor ideology of the Republicans. Sweeping vagrancy, apprenticeship, and contractual provisions in the codes left the blacks with virtually no economic freedom save that of agreeing to work as a landless peasantry under labor terms set by their former owners. By flagrantly denying all blacks even the pretense of equality before the law, the Black Codes also challenged the expanded Northern conception of loyalty to the Union. That conception now included the willingness to support those who had come to the aid of the Union during the war. In return for seeking the military assistance of the blacks, the Union was now obligated to protect those blacks from their former masters. "Loyal negroes must not be put down, while disloyal white men are put up,"[9] was how one moderate Republican expressed his view of it.

Who was now disloyal? The sections could not agree on an answer. In a continuation of a trend that had set in by the midpoint of the war, Southern whites turned to former Whigs and Douglas Democrats for leadership in the Johnson governments. Most of these men were antisecessionists but loyal Confederates. Where Southerners saw loyal men of principle who had stood by the Union as long as possible, Northerners saw out-and-out rebels. When Northern opinion balked at immediately accepting the Southern congressmen elected in the fall of 1865, men who included within their ranks a bevy of former Confederate generals and officials, both sections accused the other of hypocrisy.

About the only thing that was certain in the winter of 1865–1866 was that Congress eventually was going to have a say in reconstruction. The Republicans had reached no consensus on reconstruction. A few, led by Thaddeus Stevens of Pennsylvania, wanted to revolutionize Southern society by breaking up the estates of the planters and distributing the land in forty-acre freeholds to each freedman. Stevens' vision was the classic one of preindustrial republicanism, which held that political freedom could rest only on economic independence. "No people will ever be republican in spirit and practice where a few own immense manors and the masses are landless," he said. "Small independent landholders are the support and guardians of republican liberty."[10] A future middle class of black yeoman, however, could be created only by violating the most basic tenet of the present white middle class in the North—the sanctity of private property. Talk of confiscation frightened most Republicans as much as it did Southern planters.

Much more compatible with Northern middle-class liberalism was an effort led by Charles Sumner of Massachusetts to extend suffrage to the freedman. Sumner's case was straightforward: Blacks needed the vote in order to protect their freedom. By separating political liberties from the ownership of productive property, Sumner's position promised no revolutionary upheaval in the South, but it did threaten a revolutionary change in the balance of antebellum federalism. Suffrage had always been an issue left up to the individual states. Opposition on both constitutional and racist grounds kept Sumner in a minority position. The fact that three Northern states in 1865—Connecticut, Minnesota, and Wisconsin—rejected state constitutional amendments to confer suffrage on black males hardly helped the congressional case for black suffrage in the South.

While Stevens and Sumner were testing the limits of how much change would be sanctioned, the moderate majority of their party had decided on a holding action. A Joint Committee of Fifteen on Reconstruction, chaired by a respected moderate, William Pitt Fessenden of Maine, was appointed. The decision on readmitting the former Confederate states would await its recommendation.

While the Committee of Fifteen was deliberating, Johnson openly defied the Republican majority in Congress. Maybe it was because he saw a personal insult in the Republican decision against the immediate readmission of Tennessee, the state in which he had served during the war as military governor. Maybe he feared losing face in the South after he had committed his prestige to the success of presidential Reconstruction. Or, and most likely, perhaps Johnson simply could not countenance any change in the South beyond the absolute minimum demanded by his program. Certainly he reacted to black suffrage as something that was personally threatening. In early February 1866, he bluntly told a black delegation led by Frederick Douglass that he opposed extending the vote to the freedmen. When the delegation left, Johnson, according to one of his private secretaries, remarked: "Those d----d sons of b-----s thought they had me in a trap! I know that d----d Douglass; he's just like any nigger, and he would sooner cut a white man's throat than not."[11] Whatever combination of reasons motivated Johnson, he abandoned his party in the winter and spring of 1866.

Johnson first vetoed a bill to extend the life of the Freedmen's Bureau, a federal agency created in 1865 to administer emergency relief to the war refugees, black and white, in the South. Then, after publicly attacking Stevens and Sumner as "traitors" who should be punished for delaying the readmission of the South, he vetoed a major civil rights bill in March. The final break came when Johnson announced his opposition to the Fourteenth Amendment. Reported out by the Joint Committee on Reconstruction in the spring, the amendment was intended as the North's peace terms to the South. In opposing it, Johnson highlighted the immense distance between his reading of the war and that of the Republican majority.

Johnson's actions effectively obliterated the earlier distinctions between moderate Republicans and the more radical minority. The bills for the Freedmen's Bureau and civil rights were supported by nearly all congressional Republicans as reasonable measures that represented minimal guarantees for protecting the rights of the freed population. Testimony heard by the Joint Committee left little doubt that the Black Codes and white control of the Southern courts deprived the freedmen of any impartial legal justice. Accordingly, the Freedmen's Bureau was granted jurisdiction in cases in which black civil rights had been violated. The Civil Rights bill was meant to provide more permanent protection. Written in response to both the Black Codes and the *Dred Scott* decision, which had declared that blacks were not American citizens, the bill for the first time defined citizenship. Birth or naturalization in the United States conferred national and state citizenship. The principle of equality before the law was also nationalized by extending its protection to all citizens. In vetoing these two bills, Johnson virtually ruled out any hope of future cooperation between himself and Congress. He argued that any legislation on the freedmen was solely a matter for the individual states and that no legislation affecting the excluded states could be constitutional as long as these states were denied representation in Congress. The rigidity of Johnson's position forced an extraordinary unity on the Republicans. In order for the party to have any say in reconstruction, it had to close ranks almost to a man. Otherwise, without the two-thirds majority needed to override a presidential veto or to pass constitutional amendments, Johnsonian Reconstruction would be left untouched.

The Fourteenth Amendment, the last possible bridge between Johnson and his erstwhile party, contained five sections:

1. The amendment's first section was a restatement of the Civil Rights bill, now protected against the possibility of being repealed.
2. The second section was an awkward compromise on black suffrage that satisfied no one. Suffrage was still left up to the states, but congressional representation would be proportionately reduced to the extent that a state denied the vote to its eligible male citizens. In practice this meant that the former rebel states, where over 90 percent of the black population lived, would not receive the benefits of more congressmen unless they correspondingly enfranchised the former slaves. The choice was up to them.
3. The third section was politically the most important. It addressed Northern fears over a resurgence of rebel political power by disqualifying from officeholding (state and federal) all individuals who had supported the rebellion after having taken an oath to uphold the Constitution. The careful, bland language of this section barred from political office the old ruling class of the South. Prewar military, federal, state, and local officials were all disqualified if they had aided the rebellion.
4. The fourth section reaffirmed that the Union war debt would be paid, repudiated the Confederate war debt, and voided the possibility of any monetary compensation to the slaveowners for their emancipated property.
5. The fifth, and final, section granted Congress the power to enforce the amendment.

There it was, the Northern peace settlement. The passage of the amendment by Congress in June 1866, was not a victory for the radicals but a distillation of the minimum terms the Northern public demanded of the defeated South. The settlement did not force black suffrage, disfranchise former Confederates, or confiscate the land of the planters. It left intact the structure of the Johnsonian governments but insisted that loyal Southern whites, those who had upheld the Union, be entrusted with political power until Congress saw fit to lift the disqualification of former rebels.

The Republicans had built a bridge that Johnson could have crossed to reunite himself with the party. Instead, with the virtue of consistency, Johnson burned the bridge by opposing the amendment and advising the still-excluded states not to ratify it. The passage of the Thirteenth Amendment of 1865, which freed the slaves, had established the principle that all the states had to be counted for purposes of ratifying a constitutional amendment, despite the anomalous status of some of the states not being fully in the Union. The consequences of this precedent were momentous for the future course of reconstruction in 1866 and 1867. There was no way that the Fourteenth Amendment could receive the required three-fourths vote of approval from the states unless some of the former states of the Confederacy ratified it. Only Tennessee did so. The remainder (joined by Kentucky and Delaware) accepted Johnson's advice and opposed it.

Some of the Johnsonian leaders in the unreconstructed South believed, along with the president, that Northern Democrats would rally to their defense and team up with the Northern conservatives to inflict crippling losses on the Republicans in the congressional elections of 1866. Others were shrewd enough to realize that their own political careers in the postwar South would be ruined if they went on public record in favor of a constitutional change that most Southern whites felt branded the South with the stigma of war guilt. The third section was widely viewed as an unconscionable demand for a shameful surrender of honor on the part of Southern whites, an admission that they were wrong and at blame for the war. Regardless of the immediate consequences, the leaders of the Southern provisional governments, men who had risen to power after the war and who were already susceptible to charges of collaboration with the enemy, reasoned that they would ultimately be in a stronger political position among Southern whites if the Fourteenth Amendment were forced upon them. They could then hope to return to power as the spokesmen for Southern whites united in their determination to overturn congressional Reconstruction. Over time this strategy worked. As for the immediate consequences, the Republicans were now left in the frustrating and infuriating situation of having written a peace treaty that the South refused to sign. The Reconstruction Act of March 1867, provided a way out of their predicament.

The Final Peace Terms

The Republican majority in Congress that turned to military reconstruction in the spring of 1867 felt fully vindicated in their struggle with Johnson by the results of the congressional elections in the fall of 1866. The elections amounted to a referendum on the Fourteenth Amendment and the opposing position represented by Johnson. In a politically disastrous speaking tour, Johnson took his case to the people and was loudly rebuffed, first by hecklers during his speeches and then by the Republicans at the polls. With telling effect, the Republicans accused Johnson of deserting the party that had put him into power, of dishonoring the memory of the Union war dead by turning to disloyal Democrats for support, and of disgracing the office of the presidency by stooping to shouting contests with hecklers. Mob violence against freedmen and white Unionists in Memphis and New Orleans during the spring and summer confirmed for the Northern public the Republican charge that Johnson wanted to unleash unregener- ate rebels against the only true friends of the Union in the South. The emotional loyalties of the war were remobilized, and a clear Northern majority reaffirmed that the results of the war meant fundamental change. "In a word," editorialized the New York *Herald,*[12]

> Mr. Johnson forgets that we have passed through the fiery ordeal of a mighty revolution, and that the pre-existing order of things is gone and can return no more—that a great work of reconstruction is before us, and that we cannot escape it.

Nearly two years had now passed since Appomattox, and the "great work" had yet to begin. In order to get it underway, and more specifically, to make the South accept the Fourteenth Amendment, the Republicans resorted to the unprecedented measures of the Reconstruction Act of 1867. Military reconstruction was a cumber- some, almost desperate, compromise between the Johnsonian extreme of immediate, unqualified readmission and the radical extreme of declaring the excluded states to be territories subject to military rule for an indefinite period. A long and enforceable military occupation was out of the question. The army lacked the manpower and logistical support for such an occupation, and even attempting it would have been a politically unacceptable contradiction of the most basic principles of republicanism. These same principles also ruled out any large-scale disfranchisement of Southern whites. What was in accord with republicanism, however, was an enlargement of the Southern electorate by extending suffrage to the freedmen, thus creating a loyal major- ity that would accept the Fourteenth Amendment. Under the complicated provisions of the Reconstruction Act, black suffrage was now added to ratification of the Fourteenth Amendment as the price of readmission for the ten rebel states still out of the Union (Tennessee, having ratified the Fourteenth Amendment, was back in the Union). Temporarily divided into five military districts, these states had to:

1. hold elections for constitutional conventions in which all male citizens, except those disqualified by the Fourteenth Amendment, were eligible to vote
2. draft and approve new state constitutions which provided for "impartial" suffrage
3. ratify the Fourteenth Amendment.

The capstone of congressional Reconstruction was the Fifteenth Amendment, which passed Congress in early 1869. Throughout the Civil War decade, the Republi- cans had acted with remarkable consistency and integrity in expanding the concept of equality to include Afro-Americans. Rank-and-file Republicans supported black suf- frage in the referenda held in seven Northern states in the 1860s, and a mere 20 out of 1,826 Republican state legislators voted against ratification of the Fifteenth Amend- ment. There was a natural progression from freedom in the Thirteenth Amendment, to citizenship and equality before the law in the Fourteenth, and to the vote for the protection of the rights of citizenship in the Fifteenth.

Although the Republicans did not hypocritically force upon Southern whites a black vote that they themselves were unwilling to accept, there was also clearly a large

Black Voting Under Reconstruction. This scene illustrates what made Reconstruction
radical—the conferral of political rights upon the emancipated slaves. (Virginia State Library)

dose of political reality behind the Fifteenth Amendment. The best hope for the
Republicans to become a nationalized party, as opposed to the sectionalized one they
had remained from the beginning, lay in permanently securing the black vote. Before
the ratification of the Fifteenth Amendment, that vote rested primarily on the extraordinary legislation of 1867 that mandated black suffrage in ten former Confederate states.
That legislation could be repealed or declared unconstitutional. Once states had been
readmitted, revived Democratic majorities might well rewrite their state constitutions
and disfranchise the freedmen.

Outside the reconstructed South, the nation's largest concentration of blacks was
in the loyal border states. Reconstruction legislation did not apply here, and consequently there was no black suffrage. What strength the Republicans did have in the
upper South was contingent upon state legislation that temporarily disfranchised many
former Confederates. In short, if the Republicans wanted to hold on to the gains they
had made in the upper South, and to build a lasting foundation for the party in the lower
South, they needed to place black suffrage in the Constitution, where it would be
protected from the whims of white majorities in the states.

Motivated by a mutually reinforcing blend of party expediency and individual
morality, the Republicans passed a compromise amendment on suffrage that prohibited
the states from depriving its male citizens of the vote on grounds "of race, color, or
previous condition of servitude."[13] The Republicans rejected a more radical version
that stated directly and unequivocally that all male citizens had the right to vote.

When ratified in 1870, the Fifteenth Amendment registered the high-water mark of congressional Reconstruction. The Northern middle class that had supported the war effort and sustained the Republicans in their reconstruction program now concluded that a traumatic era was over. The New York *Tribune* captured the mood in the spring of 1870: "Let us have done with Reconstruction."[14] The last of the great issues raised by the war had apparently been settled. The Union dead had been honored, the rebels had been made to recognize their defeat, and a more perfect Union had arisen from the ordeal of fratricide. The egalitarian creed at the middle-class core of the Republican party was written into the Constitution and extended to those Americans whose emancipation and military sacrifices had been necessary to save the Union. This creed had always stressed legal equality, not political, social, or economic equality. By the logic of middle-class liberalism, blacks in the South now had the same chance as other Americans to make good in a competitive economy in which all had an equal opportunity to succeed. The crusade for reconstruction was over in the North. In the defeated and impoverished South, however, it had barely begun.

The Radicalism of Reconstruction

What made congressional Reconstruction radical was the conferral of political rights upon the recently freed black population. Political reconstruction was inherently radical, because it threatened to upset the traditional class relations in the rural South by which planters had enjoyed a virtual monopoly on economic resources. "Let the Negro once understand that he has an organic right to vote," Frederick Douglass told President Johnson in 1866, "and he will raise up a party in the Southern states among the poor, who will rally with him. There is this conflict that you speak of between the wealthy slave owner and the poor man."[15]

In this statement Douglass laid bare the conflict between labor and capital that was at the core of defining a new social order for the postwar South. Johnson opposed black suffrage for the same reason that Douglass favored it: Armed with the vote, blacks could forge a biracial alliance with common whites in which class would replace race as the ideological pivot of Southern politics. Once demands for equality and power were expressed by the poor of both races, the white elite rightfully feared that this process of political democratization would challenge their property rights. "First, the negro is to be invested with all political power, and then the antagonism of interest between capital and labor is to work out the result," warned Benjamin F. Perry, Johnson's choice as the provisional governor of South Carolina. Emancipation now appeared to Southern conservatives as the opening salvo in a Northern war against Southern property and the class prerogatives of those who had formerly monopolized it. "When will all this war against human inequality end?", asked a writer to *DeBow's Review* in 1866. "Why only by the attempt to equalize properties, which beget the only real inequalities of condition—the men of property being, in all save the name, the owners and masters of those without property."[16]

Southern planters immediately recognized the radical potential of congressional Reconstruction and the threat that it represented to their class interests. Their success in blunting that potential was a measure of their determination to remain masters of the South's political economy, even if they had lost their slaves.

"You will find that this question of the control of labor underlies every other question of state interest.''[17] In this prediction to the governor of South Carolina in late 1865, William H. Trescot, a planter, isolated the fundamental issue in the postwar politics of the South. Control over the labor power that slavery had reserved for the masters was now *the* issue, because most planters believed that blacks would not work without compulsion—and without black labor, the plantation economy could never be rebuilt. Slavery had been justified as a necessary, Christian system of labor that had extracted productive work from an inferior, childlike race that was naturally lazy. Unless Southern whites admitted that they had been lying to themselves and to the outside world, there was now no reason to expect the freed blacks to embrace honest labor. This belief that the former slaves would have to be forced to work resulted in the Black Codes of 1865 and 1866.

By blatantly invoking the legal power of the state in the Black Codes, the planters raised the stakes of political involvement for the other two groups most interested in controlling black labor—Northern entrepreneurs and the freedmen themselves. Whereas the planters had little faith in the ability of market forces to discipline black labor, Northern entrepreneurs were confident that the spread of market relations and free-labor values would usher in a new age of prosperity and racial harmony for the South. Divided over the issue of incentives and controls for black labor, these two groups of whites were united in their insistence that the blacks had to be brought into a market economy for the production of plantation staples. The freedmen joined the Northern entrepreneurs resident in the postwar South in an effort to convert the Republican promise of civil equality into a political reality, but most of them rejected the Yankee commitment to market involvement. The goal of the former slaves was freedom from both market controls and white supervision. What was freedom and how was it to be exercised? Who would define the new political economy of the postwar South, control access to its resources, and decide how its rewards were to be distributed? Answers to these questions broke along lines of race, class, and section. The success and durability of the new state governments set up under congressional Reconstruction would depend upon their ability to fashion answers that could forge and hold together a voting majority of freedmen and common whites.

Blacks in Reconstruction

The mass voting base of political reconstruction was the freed population. By their political activism, perceptions of their own best interests, and determination to use their labor power as a leverage to exact concessions from their former masters, Southern blacks exposed the myths of both the proslavery and the antislavery advocates. Slavery had produced neither a class of lazy, irresponsible "Sambos," the purported existence of whom was essential to the master's self-image of a beloved patriarch, nor, as the abolitionists believed, a class of uprooted, passive individuals so brutalized by slavery and so lacking in any culture of their own, that they had no choice but to turn to their Northern benefactors for guidance. To an extent that Northern and Southern whites found difficult to grasp, because each had a psychological investment in black dependency, Afro-Americans emerged from slavery with an inner strength and cultural resiliency that enabled them to set much of the reconstruction agenda. More so than whites could admit, reconstruction was a response to black demands and actions.

The goal of securing freedom for their families was the most immediate concern of blacks as slavery began to collapse during the war. In contrast to the prewar pattern, in which young males acting alone comprised most of the runaways, slave escapes during the war were organized along family lines. After the arrival of Federal troops and blockading vessels off the Georgia coast in late 1861, some 2,500 slaves reached Union lines by the fall of 1864. Despite the greater risk of detection and capture incurred by moving in large groups, over eighty percent of the slaves who organized their own escape plans were members of groups of three or more, including women and children.

Loyalty to family and group also motivated blacks to join the Union army. The military recruiters on the Georgia sea islands soon discovered that there was no greater incentive for black enlistments than the personal opportunity to help gain and protect the freedom of kin and friends. A Northern official reported of one recruitment rally on St. Simons Island:[18]

> They were asked to enlist for pay, rations and uniforms, to fight for their country, for freedom and so forth, but not a man stirred. But when it was asked them to fight for themselves, to enlist to protect their wives and children from being sold away from them, and told of the little homes which they might secure to themselves and their families in after years, they all rose to their feet, the men came forward and said "I'll go," the women shouted, and the old men said "Amen."

The commitment of these Georgia blacks to their families was just one of the many indications of the strong bonds forged within the slave community. Contrary to the expectations of the abolitionists, the black family was not demoralized and shattered by slavery. About two-thirds of the slave families were headed by both parents, a ratio that corresponded almost exactly to family patterns in preindustrial England. Although slave marriages had no legal standing in the antebellum South, slave unions did produce stable, long-lasting commitments and a supportive moral code for family members. During marriage ceremonies conducted late in the war by Federal officials in Concordia Parish, Louisiana, 454 former slaves acknowledged a previous slave marriage. Nearly 90 percent of these unions had remained intact until death or forcible separation (such as the sale of husband or wife) ended the partnership. Although, in accord with African tradition and the mores of peasant societies in general, premarital sexual intercourse was not uncommon, promiscuity was rare. Sexual fidelity in marriage was the norm, and the average age of slave women at the birth of their first child was twenty, indicating an abstention from sexual intercourse for an average of three years after they first became capable of bearing children.

The moral code of the stable, two-parent family was reinforced by a network of overlapping kin relationships that knitted the slave community together. These kin ties were fostered by the closing of the African slave trade, slave prohibitions against cousin marriages, and the bunching of more than half the slave population into holdings of twenty and more. Ties of blood and marriage were thickest on older plantations in which slaves remained at the same location for at least a generation. On the Good Hope Plantation in South Carolina, for example, 28 percent of the slaves were directly related to individuals in other slave families in the late antebellum period.

Wherever possible, blacks chose freedom as family units, and when they came into contact with Federal authorities during the war, they insisted that the interests of their families be recognized. Their most pressing demand was education for their

A Freedmen's School. Blacks eagerly grasped educational opportunities after emancipation. This scene—blacks attending a freedman's school, taught by Yankee women affiliated with a Northern missionary society—was an all-too-common one for many Southern whites. (Library of Congress)

children, and to secure it blacks used the main weapon at their disposal—their labor. In its need for black laborers and troops, the Union army showed little regard for the black family. Black soldiers were, of course, separated from their families, and in the consignment of labor gangs to work on the plantations of loyal Southerners, wives and children were often divided from husbands and fathers. Quickly grasping the import-ance of their labor to the Union war effort, as well as the urgency with which Federal officials wanted to establish that free black labor could be as profitable and disciplined as slave labor, the blacks refused to work until they were assured that their children would receive an education.

How well this tactic worked can be seen in a circular issued by General Nathaniel P. Banks, commander of the Gulf Department centered in Union-occupied southern Louisiana. In June 1864, Banks notified all parish provost marshals "that it is indis-pensable to the cultivation of the soil, that schools for colored children shall be maintained." Without such schools, he stressed, the laborers "become discontented, and will be allowed to remove to Parishes where such provisions are made." The blacks, some of whom were reported as saying "they would sooner work for nothing, than have their children deprived of learning to read,"[19] applied the initial pressure for schools. The Union army responded by establishing a well-organized system of black elementary education in Louisiana as early as 1864.

Apart from the paramount political objective of proving that plantations could be efficiently operated with a stable supply of free black labor, army commanders were motivated to provide schools by the basic tenets of Northern liberalism. Perceiving former slaves as a class of desperate poor, driven, as were all the poor, by the base passions of animal instincts, the commanders believed that education offered the best means of teaching blacks the self-control to be civilized and the self-motivation to be productive workers in a free labor system. Most of the Northern teachers in the freedmen's schools agreed. One, after working with the blacks, put it starkly: "If we do not teach them, they will be a terrible power."[20]

At the war's end, the emancipated slaves needed no whites to give them an agenda for freedom. They immediately seized freedom as the opportunity to build an autonomous black community anchored in the values and institutions that had sustained them under slavery. The core institution was the family. As the fugitives had shown so strikingly during the war, the first objective under freedom was the achievement of domestic security. Despite the prime importance of family ties under slavery, thousands of black families had to reconstitute themselves in 1865, because many had already been broken up before the war. Ownership of spouses by different masters was a main reason why women headed one-third of all slave households. A slave who reached the age of fifty stood a 50 percent chance of having been sold, and throughout the South one-fifth to one-third of slave marriages had ended with the sale or forced removal of one of the partners. The war years then brought on massive family disruptions as masters relocated their slaves to keep them away from the Yankees, and as Union and Confederate officials competed for able-bodied black labor. Throughout 1865, many blacks left the plantations in a search of family members.

By physically moving around in an effort to reunite their family units, the freedmen also were attempting to remove themselves psychologically from that direct white supervision that had been so integral to the slavery experience. They demonstrated this desire for their own cultural space by laying claim to full control over the key community institution of slave society, the black church.

Much as native Americans had done, Afro-Americans created a sacred world view of their own that fused Man, Nature, and God into a seamless whole. As revealed in their spirituals and folk beliefs, this world view combined elements of African and Euro-Christian cultures into an expression of personal self-worth and communal solidarity. The fusion of the sacred and the secular, the ecstatic style of worship, and the rhythms of the preaching were borrowed from African patterns. From the Christian Bible, blacks took the master's Jesus of the New Testament who preached deliverance in a world to come and transformed him into a Moses of the Old Testament who would lead his people to deliverance in this world of the here and now. For their spiritual ethos, they turned not to the calls to obedience in the Epistles of Paul but to the liberating messages of Exodus and Revelations. Their evangelical Christianity promised them that change would come and that ultimate justice was at hand. In the psychological warfare between master and slave, Afro-American Christianity gave the slaves the strength to accept what was inevitable, the master's power, and the inner dignity and autonomy to prevent that power from subsuming the slave's own being.

Driven by racial pride and their own sense of community, the freedmen pushed for separate black churches once deliverance came. The religion that had sustained them as slaves was now drawn on to inform their self-definition as a freed people. Blacks used the disciplinary structure of their churches as a community-controlled judiciary system that operated like a small-claims court in moral and economic matters. Here, free from white interference and prejudice, the freedmen set down and enforced the behavior they expected of each other. Here, organizational skills were learned, family disputes were settled, social gatherings were planned, labor meetings were held, and lessons in literacy were offered for children and adults. In the rural South, the freedmen made their churches synonymous with their communities.

The freedmen, by knitting together families separated by slavery and the war, sending their children to schools, usually at great economic sacrifice to the parents, and regulating their own affairs using their own institutions, largely reconstructed their own lives in the aftermath of emancipation. As eager as the freedmen were for domestic security and cultural independence, they also realized that the full measure of freedom could come only with economic independence. Possession of land offered the surest path to such independence for the freedman and his family.

When the Confederacy surrendered, the freedmen immediately pressed their moral claims to a share of the land they had always worked against the legal claims of their former masters. In the moral economy of the freedmen the land was already theirs by virtue of their uncompensated labor under slavery. "We has a right to the land where we are located," proclaimed Virginia freedman Bayley Wyat in 1866, in a protest against the expulsion of a group of blacks from a contraband camp. In an economic argument that revealed that former slaves were no fools when it came to analyzing the moral costs of wealth accumulation in antebellum America, Wyat explained:[21]

> Our wives, our children, our husbands, has been sold over and over again to purchase the lands we now locates upon; for that reason we have a divine right to the land. . . . And den didn't we clear the land, and raise de crops ob corn, ob cotton, ob tobacco, ob rice, ob sugar, ob everything. And den didn't dem large cities in de North grow up on de cotton and de sugars and de rice dat we made? . . . I say dey has grown rich, and my people is poor.

The black claims were denied. Expectations that were high in the spring and summer of 1865 were dashed in the fall when President Johnson ordered that confiscated and abandoned lands being administered by the Freedmen's Bureau would not be distributed to the freedmen but instead were to be returned to the pardoned owners. Still in control of the land were the same planters who had told their slaves during the war that Confederate defeat would mean the confiscation of their estates.

Barred from claiming the land, often at the point of federal bayonets, the freedmen nonetheless forced basic changes in plantation agriculture. The planters attempted to structure working conditions under freedom as closely as possible to the labor regime under slavery. What the planters wanted, and what they generally reconstructed in the planting seasons of 1865 and 1866, was the centralized control of the prewar years. The freedmen were organized into labor gangs, directly supervised by an overseer or resident planter, provided rations from the employer, and housed in the old slave quarters. The only difference now was the contractual obligation to pay fixed wages for the blacks' labor. Designed to minimize change and to recreate the power relations under slavery, the wage system of 1865 and 1866 did just that. It looked as if President Johnson would be proved right. As long as they retained the land, planters would continue as masters. In his words, the former slaves "without land of their own . . . will continue to work for those who have it."[22]

What Johnson overlooked, and what frustrated the intentions of the planters, was the determination of the freedmen to achieve greater control over their own lives. The freedmen rejected the personal dependency and coercive controls of the old system that had reemerged in the guise of wage labor. They hated being treated like slaves all over again. Declaring that the entire family would no longer work like slaves, they pulled their women and children from the fields. They flooded the local agents of the Freedmen's Bureau with complaints of being cheated by employers who dismissed them without their annual wages once the harvest was in. Capitalizing on the mobility that came with emancipation, they moved in search of better working conditions. Some sought out jobs in the towns and cities, but most moved to other local, rural locations. They forced the planters to bid for their services by creating temporary shortages of labor, which they then exploited for a better contract. By 1870 the typical contract was not for cash wages but for a share of the crop. Under this arrangement the planters divided their estates into small family plots that were worked by the croppers. Depending upon the amount of food and farm supplies provided by the planter, the cropper turned over one-third to one-half of the crop as rent.

For blacks as well as whites, sharecropping became an economic trap that ensnarled the tenants in a form of semipeonage. But when first instituted, sharecropping offered blacks real advantages over what the planters had originally tried to fix upon them. Unable to acquire land of their own, blacks still sought the economic independence and social autonomy that they associated with the ownership of land. In their quest, blacks did transform the plantation. Sharecropping eliminated overseers, gang labor, and daily supervision by whites. The freedmen now had more control over their time, working conditions, and family life. They had more freedom to choose between work and leisure and, in common with other emancipated labor forces in the Western Hemisphere and the white yeomanry of the antebellum South, they opted, wherever possible, for self-sufficiency, a reduced work load for the family, and more leisure time for hunting and fishing. They also had the pride of knowing that they were not wage laborers who could be ordered about by whites. If they wanted to leave the plantation to attend a political meeting, that was their business, not the planter's. "I am not working for wages," an Alabama freedman told an employer who questioned his right to leave for a political rally, "but am part owner of the crop and as I have all the rights that you or any other man has I shall not suffer them abridged."[23]

Sharecropping was in place by the end of the 1860s because blacks wanted it. Typical was the comment of D. Wyatt Aiken, a South Carolina planter: "In 1868, hands could not be hired for wages. The custom of the country was to 'give a part of the crop.' I had to yield, or lose my labor."[24] Planters surrendered a real measure of their control and lost the flexibility of a wage system. After emancipation, the planter's capital was tied up in his land, not in his labor, and he no longer had the same economic incentive to maximize his use of labor. It made good economic sense to limit his hiring and lay off laborers during the slack agricultural seasons. Black sharecroppers were hardly an independent yeomanry, but they were better off than they would have been had they not resisted being coerced into the status of an agrarian proletariat. The planters grudgingly gave in to black demands. Most of them were short on capital after the war, and the failure of the plantation economy to revive quickly left them scrambling for credit. Despite their concerns that sharecropping left the freedmen with too much independence, planters recognized the advantages for them in an economic arrangement that conserved their scarce capital by not requiring that it be spent on wages.

By the time congressional Reconstruction got under way, blacks had already made significant gains since emancipation. The earnest enthusiasm with which the freedmen registered to vote, and the speed with which a new political class of blacks arose, were the best evidence that the freedmen realized that these gains could ultimately be protected and extended only through political mobilization. If land could not be acquired, then the legal protection of their right to a share in the crops they produced became an even more vital political objective. Economic and political power in the cash-starved postwar South was a matter of controlling the crops. Agricultural credit took the form of advances secured by a lien upon the crops. In order to ensure that the sale of the crop would cover their advances, plus interest, planters and merchants vied with one another to establish a superior legal claim on the crops. The freedmen, supported by the Freedman's Bureau, insisted that their claims for wages or shares should take precedence. The struggle to gain economic justice by establishing their rights under the crop-lien system shaped much of the freedman's political experience. Other major goals included public support for schools and the recognition by Southern courts of black equality under the law. Shortly after receiving the vote, blacks put together a political program that focused on their economic, educational, and legal needs in the communities in which they lived.

Although the freedmen supplied 80 percent of the vote for the Southern Republican parties, they held only 15 percent to 20 percent of the political offices. At the upper echelon of leadership, federal offices, black politicians were literate, well-educated men drawn primarily from a Northern-born professional class of ministers, lawyers, and teachers. State and local offices were filled predominately by former slave ministers and artisans, those who had held positions of leadership and trust in the slave community. The tendency of the freedmen to turn to those who had been free before the war or had acquired some measure of literacy and independence as slave artisans was illustrated in the makeup of the 74 black delegates at the South Carolina Constitutional Convention in 1868. About one-fifth of these blacks were born in the North. Most of the native South Carolinians had had experience as tradesmen, and one-third had been antebellum free men. We still know little of the blacks who did the grassroots organizing, those who mobilized the plantation workers, spoke at meetings of the local Republican clubs, the Union Leagues, got out the vote, and led protests against white economic pressure. At this level of political activity, where the basic issue was one that all blacks could understand—the right of the freedmen to work the land free from white harassment—leadership probably came straight from the ranks of the field hands.

Blacks supplied the votes, but white politicians held the power. With the exception of South Carolina, and to a lesser extent in Mississippi, blacks did not come close to filling offices in proportion to their numbers in the population. This imbalance between black voting power and officeholding meant that the attainment of black political goals was dependent on the Northern and Southern whites who monopolized the key leadership posts within the new Republican parties. Once the unstable alliance between the Northern whites, forever stigmatized by the pejorative label "carpetbaggers," and the Southern whites, scornfully referred to as "scalawags," broke down, a major casualty was not just these black goals, but the very reality of meaningful black political participation in Southern civic life.

Whites in Reconstruction

At the state and federal levels, the Northern-born Republicans were the driving element in political reconstruction. Their voting strength was small, about 2 percent of the party total, but they held over half of the Republican governorships, half of the party seats in Congress, and one-third of the elected Republican offices in the South. During the state constitutional conventions of 1868, they controlled the committees that reported out the sweeping changes in education, civil rights, and the franchise. These changes were the cutting edge of the congressional program for the South. The party link between these Republicans and the freedmen was a direct one. When given a choice between supporting a Northern or a Southern-born Republican, the freedmen usually favored the former, a representative of that section that had given them citizenship and the vote. Consequently, the four reconstructed states with the largest percentages of blacks—South Carolina, Mississippi, Louisiana, and Florida—were those in which the party power of the Northern Republicans was the greatest.

The Northern Republicans brought many strengths to political reconstruction, and foremost, in a material sense, was their capital. Depicted by Southern whites as carpetbaggers, footloose political adventurers who crammed their scant belongings into a carpetbag and rushed to the prostrate South to loot the section, these Republicans in fact carried badly needed capital into the South. Most of them were former Union officers who remained in the South after the war. They were young, well-educated entrepreneurs who invested their modest stakes of capital in the local economies. A profile of the 159 outside whites who served in the constitutional conventions for the new state governments revealed an economically successful group of planters, farmers, professionals, and businessmen with median property holdings of $3,500.

In combination with the more apolitical Yankee missionaries and teachers who staffed the freedmen's schools, these entrepreneurial Republicans also had a clear vision of what they wanted the South to become under Northern guidance and leadership. The vision was that blend of materialism and moralism that the Republicans had always promoted as true Christian prosperity. The schools, churches, factories, internal improvements, pride in labor, and restless drive for self-improvement that supposedly had been ignored and blighted in the antebellum South by the withering force of slavery would be regenerated under the guidance of the Republican party. The South would be ushered into the modern age. With their program of legal equality, economic opportunity, and education, these Republicans were convinced that in time white Southerners, as well as the freedmen, would realize that the party offered them a newer and better world.

Well aware of how their stand on black civil rights aroused the fury of Southern whites, the so-called carpetbaggers stressed the conservative, producer side of their racial ideology. They argued that equality before the law did not mean an end to white superiority. In a free-labor society, all classes, spurred by an equal chance to enjoy the fruits of their labor, would improve themselves, and because the freedmen were starting at the bottom, they would remain below whites. Equal black access to education should be welcomed by all employers, nearly all of whom were whites. Educated labor was more productive labor. It knew the value of work and was no longer deluded into wasting time by superstitious follies. As a Republican judge explained in a speech:[25]

Education enhances the value of labor. The workman who is so ignorant that he cannot kill his pig because the moon is not of the right age, will lose two days waiting for fear the meat will shrink, or he will not set his fence at another time of the moon for fear the bottom rail will sink into the ground, and so he waits a week; or perhaps he fancies he is bewitched, wears salt in his boots, and spends much time visiting a conjuror. Such labor is not valuable.

Educated labor would also help stabilize the social order. Like the immigrants in the Northern cities, the freedmen would be taught the values of thrift, self-reliance, and temperance that would cure them of their degraded licentiousness. Black revolutionary schemes for land confiscation were labeled a product of ignorance. Schooling would replace such wild ideas with self-restrained virtues of an obedient, productive citizenry who would ask only for fair compensation for their labor.

Northern Republicans had the seed capital to establish themselves in Southern communities, and their free-labor ideology seemingly promised all Southerners a future of progress and material betterment. Yet, these very strengths also worked against them. The relative wealth of these Republicans, when measured against the precipitious drop in the wealth of Southern whites because of uncompensated emancipation and the destruction of the war, made it all the easier to depict them as the agents of Yankee economic imperialism. For example, the plunge between 1860 and 1870 in the per-capita wealth of white males in Alabama ranged from 50 percent in the mountains to almost 90 percent in the plantation counties. Ethnic Yankees were now often the wealthiest group in Southern communities. Their wealth, though usually modest, was bitterly resented. Meanwhile, their value system aroused the same hostility in most Southern whites as it had in 1860. Where a Yankee Southerner saw progress in the bridges, railroads, and schools to be built with state assistance, native Southern whites saw higher taxes and growing indebtedness. Where the Yankee praised the material benefits of industrialization, his rural Southern counterpart damned the loss of economic independence for factory labor.

The Yankees had won the war, they had the money, and now they wanted to go into Southern politics to take away what little money Southerners had left. They had killed the sons of the South and freed the slaves, and now they wanted to make the freedmen independent when most Southern whites wanted to make them dependent. All the while, they arrogantly proclaimed their cultural superiority. This was the image of the Yankees in the postwar South, and it was encapsulated in the hateful stereotype of the carpetbagger. Because this image was so pervasive and so convincing, the carpetbaggers absolutely had to create a lasting alliance with at least a minority of Southern whites if the Republican party were to remain a vital force in the former Confederacy.

This minority of Southern whites became known as scalawags, a term used for the scrawny, biologically inbred cattle and horses on the Scottish island of Scalaway. As applied by the enemies of congressional Reconstruction, the term instantly conveyed an image of sleazy, filthy, and mean poor whites who prostituted their racial pride for a chance to profit from the plight of the defeated South. The term has stuck because it was so politically valuable to the Southern Democrats in regaining and holding power in the 1870s and after, but it was as intentionally misleading as was the carpetbagger label.

Close to 20 percent of Southern whites became Republicans in the late 1860s.

They were almost as divided between themselves as they were from the majority of Southern whites. Most had been Unionists during the war. As such, they had harsh memories of being vilified and persecuted for their failure to support the Confederacy. Atrocities, such as the virtual lynching of forty-four Unionists in Gainesville, Texas, by a white mob in September 1862, and the execution-style murder of thirteen suspected Unionists guerrillas in Shelton Laurel, North Carolina, by Confederate troops in January 1863, left old scores to be settled after the war. Concentrated in the Appalachian interior of the Confederacy, a region of disloyal Confederates bounded on the north by the mountains of western Virginia and in the south by the highlands of Alabama, these Unionists had traditionally distrusted and opposed the rule of the planter elite in the black belts. The disastrous war transformed that distrust into a commitment to the Republicans. Not only had Lincoln's party smashed the power of the slaveholding aristocracy, but its emphasis on free homesteads and the dignity of labor were inherently popular in the egalitarian Appalachian society of small propertyholders.

Although most Southern white Republicans were yeomen from the mountainous and hilly counties, the leadership of these native Republicans came from their old class opponents in the plantation South, planters and businessmen. Whiggish in their politics, these conservative, upper-class Republicans had been reluctant secessionists. They supported the war effort out of a need to maintain political and civic influence, but they were concerned more with goals of economic development and social order than the quest for Southern independence. They turned to Republicanism in an effort to achieve these goals. They were vain enough to think that, as former masters, they could control the freedmen's vote, and they were ambitious enough to believe that they could emerge as the economic leaders of a New South if only they could gain access to Northern capital through the Republican party. By making an accommodation with the victors, they hoped to both unseat the Democrats in power and fulfill the economic goals of their antebellum Whiggery.

The Biracial Alliance Crumbles

The freedmen supplied the mass vote, the Northerners controlled most of the key offices, and former Southern Whigs provided the indispensable link to the native white communities. This was the basic functional division of power and influence within the Southern Republican parties. At the birth of these parties in 1867 and 1868, such a division enabled the Republicans to command real majority support. Blacks comprised about 40 percent of the population in the reconstructed South, and their solidly Republican vote, when added to the 20 percent of the native whites who joined the party, left the Republicans representing most Southerners. The majority, however, did not hold for very long. The Democrats, often just calling themselves the Conservative party, regained power by 1874 in all but four of the former Confederate states. The remaining four, not surprisingly those with the largest black populations—South Carolina, Mississippi, Louisiana, and Florida—were lost by the Republicans in 1876 and 1877. Thus, congressional Reconstruction lasted less than a decade.

It is tempting to dismiss political reconstruction as an ill-fated experiment in biracial democracy that had little, if any, chance for permanent success. Only the truly extraordinary circumstances of 1866 and 1867, and particularly the bludgeon-like way in which Johnson deprived the Republicans of any middle ground in reaching a compromise with him on a political settlement for the South, made political reconstruction possible in the first place. Its distinguishing feature—black suffrage—was anathema to most Southern whites, who, once they regrouped as the political disqualifications in the Fourteenth Amendment were quickly lifted by Congress, rallied behind the cry of racial solidarity. They then reclaimed the state governments that they felt had been unjustly taken away from them. "SHALL NEGROES or WHITE MEN RULE NORTH CAROLINA?"[26] was indicative of the Democratic campaign appeals that were used effectively against the Republicans throughout the South. Once everything was reduced to a matter of race, the Republicans were inevitably cast aside by an avalanche of white Democratic votes.

To be sure, the race issue explains much of the failure of congressional Reconstruction, but it is only part of that failure. White racism was always there; it was there at the beginning in 1867 and 1868. Moreover, however extraordinary were the political conditions that culminated in congressional Reconstruction, even more extraordinary was the temporary coalition of freedmen and white yeomen that represented the best opportunity for the survival of Republicanism in the South. Frederick Douglass was right: a class alliance between blacks and lower-class whites had the potential to transform power relations in the postwar South. It was the failure of the Republicans to solidify and extend that alliance, not the race issue alone, that doomed political reconstruction.

As in any partnership, each side had certain expectations. The freedmen were Republicans for the most obvious of reasons. The party of freedom and suffrage offered them their best, indeed their only, opportunity to protect their civil rights, educate their children, move into local offices, and perhaps acquire or rent land. The freedmen perceived the Republican party as helping them on their way up. The yeomanry, on the other hand, turned to it to help them from slipping down any further. The war had dealt a devastating blow to the subsistence family economy of the Southern yeomanry. The family was their labor, and the war losses of able-bodied males—25 percent of all white males between the ages of 20 and 40—were irreplaceable. Moreover, if the war destroyed the planters' capital in slaves, it also destroyed much of the yeoman's capital in the form of livestock. Even by 1870, five years after the fighting stopped, per-capita supplies of hogs, cattle, and horses were but half those of 1860. The consequences were less food for the family, shortages in the draft power needed for agricultural production, and a rise in economic dependency. Per-capita food production dropped by 50 percent in the Civil War decade, and a formerly independent class now had to depend on outside sources for food. Just as the capacity of the yeomen to supply their own family needs declined, claims on their property and cash rose. The public debts of the Confederacy were repudiated in the terms of readmission to the Union, but private debts, often contracted at highly inflated Confederate prices, remained legally binding. Personal bankruptcies soared after the war, and common white farmers were hard pressed to hold on to their land. Farm tenancy in Mississippi, as estimated by Governor James Alcorn in 1871, doubled among whites during the 1860s.

Blacks on the way up and whites on the way down temporarily met in the Republican party. The white farmers wanted debt-relief legislation, stay laws for the collection of back taxes, and exemption of homesteads from debt collections. The blacks, an agrarian class struggling to achieve what the whites were in danger of losing, supported this economic program, both out of their own economic interests and in return for white support for state-funded social programs, especially for education. This black-white alliance was a tenuous one, but it might well have held, had the Republicans delivered on their initial promises of economic relief for the yeomen. But no relief came. The leadership of the Southern white Republicans was too often comprised of the very planters and creditors against whom the Southern white directed his Republican vote. Unwilling to sacrifice their own economic interests in legislation for working-class agrarians, these upper-class Republicans instead preached the gospel of economic development. Northern capital, they told the voters, would unleash the untapped mineral and timber resources of the South, build railroads to haul the coal and lumber, and provide jobs for both races in cotton mills and steel factories. In the meantime, in order to attract this capital, property rights in the South had to be protected from lower-class agitation. Nonetheless, no large amounts of Yankee capital flowed South. The Republican governments in the South were then thrown back on their own war-gutted resources. When the Republicans squeezed these resources for desperately needed tax revenues, they gave common whites every reason to leave the party and join the Democrats.

The emancipation of the slaves eliminated the major source of state revenue in the South, the slave tax. About 60 percent of the revenues in South Carolina had come from the tax on slaves. In the rest of the lower South the figure was between 30 percent and 40 percent. At the same time, emancipation tremendously increased the size of the population to be served in social-service programs by the Republican governments. In South Carolina, for example, 20,000 children—all white—were enrolled in public schools in 1860. An expanded commitment to public education under congressional Reconstruction resulted in an enrollment of 120,000 children in 1870—50,000 whites and 70,000 blacks. In addition to the new fiscal burden of providing social services for both races, the Republicans also had the responsibility for rebuilding property destroyed during the war and restoring capital investment in the depleted Southern economy.

The total wealth of the South, independent of the loss of slave property, declined by some 40 percent between 1860 and 1870. Faced with a drastically reduced tax base and an immediate need of cash for large capital projects, the Republican governments borrowed money in order to raise capital. Above all, capital was needed to rebuild and expand the South's railroads, which were considered the key to reviving prosperity. More than three-fourths of the increase in the total indebtedness of the eleven states of the former Confederacy, from $175 million in 1867 to $305 million in 1871, took the form of state-endorsed bonds for railroad construction. Debt service (or interest charges) on these bonds was a huge financial drain. Northern financiers, burnt once in 1862 by Confederate repudiation of debts owed them, and half expecting to be burned again by future Democratic governments in the South who would repudiate state debts incurred by their Republican predecessors, charged annual interest of 15 percent to 20 percent on bonds issued at a large discount to their face value. South Carolina's bonds raised only thirty-three cents in cash for each dollar of bonds sold.

The daily governmental expenses for the Republicans came from taxes on land. Only about one-third of antebellum tax receipts had come from the land. Now, most of them did. Because the war had reduced land values by one-half, assessments had to be doubled just to raise the same amount of revenue. They went up even more, by an

Table 7.1   Southern Millage Rates for Land Taxes

Increases in Southern land taxes such as these, however justifiable by the new social demands placed on the Radical governments and the need to replace revenue lost after the abolition of the slave tax, were a major factor in driving the yeomanry out of the Republican party in the South.

STATE	YEAR	RATE
Mississippi	1857	1.6
Mississippi	1871	9.0
Mississippi	1873	12.5
Alabama	1860	2.0
Alabama	1870	7.5
Louisiana	1860	2.9
Louisiana	1872	20.5
Louisiana	1874	14.5
Florida	1860	1.7
Florida	1870	7.0
Florida	1874	13.0

Source: Compiled from data in J. Mills Thornton III, "Fiscal Policy and the Failure of Radical Reconstruction in the Lower South," in J. Morgan Kousser and James M. McPherson, eds., *Region, Race, and Reconstruction: Essays in Honor of C. Vann Woodward* (New York: Oxford University Press, 1982), p. 351.

average factor of three to four, to cover the enlarged demands on the Republican governments. As illustrated in Table 7.1, white farmers were hit with what seemed to them to be exorbitant increases in taxes. These farmers were steeped in a republican tradition that associated taxation with tyranny. They were accustomed to the very low taxes of the prewar years, and now they were struggling to maintain their economic independence after the war. Under these conditions, the yeomen who had broken racial ranks by joining the Republicans soon felt they had been betrayed. The Republicans, far from giving them an economic stake in the party, were giving them an economic reason to leave it.

The black-white alliance quickly cracked open from the economic tensions inherent in the demands of white farmers for relief from taxation and the desire of the freedmen for revenue from taxation. In an obvious legacy of slavery, the vast majority of freedmen entered political reconstruction with no property. Consequently, the black 40 percent of the population paid less than 10 percent of the state taxes. Yet, if the freedmen were to acquire property, they had to overcome another legacy of slavery— their own and their children's illiteracy. This goal could be achieved only through the support of public monies derived from taxes on whites who owned property. In order to gain security in their daily lives and the equality under the law promised them, blacks also had to gain political offices. But in pushing for political power within the Republican party, the freedmen only hastened the flight out of the party of those Southern whites who already believed they were being crushed by taxes to support a propertyless class racially inferior to themselves.

As a result of the defection of Southern whites from the Republican party, the first wave of states to be regained by the Democrats were those where the combined Republican strength of Northern whites and the freedmen was the weakest. These

A Klan Raid. Night raids by the Ku Klux Klan were part of a terroristic campaign to deprive the freedmen of political and economic independence. (The Bettmann Archive)

states—Tennessee, North Carolina, and Georgia—were all back under white Democratic control by 1871. Elsewhere, the Republican loss of native white support stripped away the thin buffer of community protection that had shielded the freedmen from the worst excesses of white landlords determined to regain control over their labor supply.

The excesses were most vicious in the upcountry counties in which the Ku Klux Klan and a host of other paramilitary organizations flourished. The Klan, the best known of these groups, tended to operate as the military arm of local Democratic clubs and as a terroristic weapon of labor discipline on behalf of local planters. The targets of violence could be any active Republicans, but the freedmen were usually singled out, both as voters and as workers. The violence was a savage testimonial to the early successes of political reconstruction. Unwilling to offer the freedmen any meaningful rights or privileges that could wean them from the Republicans, and infuriated by the victories won by the freedmen in securing the best possible labor arrangements for themselves as renters, the planters resorted to violence to regain the control they had lost after emancipation. In the South Carolina upcountry, the major goals were to prevent the freedmen from renting land and to force them into surrendering part of their wages to help pay the land tax. If these goals were not met for 1871, warned George D. Tillman, one of the leaders of the white vigilantes, "We have but one other resource left—the Ku Kluxer's power—the assassin's privilege."[27]

Like all successful guerrilla movements, the Klan had community support in the countryside. Particularly in racially balanced areas in which common whites were losing their land the fastest—that is, in counties in which white farm tenancy rose most rapidly after the war—the planters could count on embittered white farmers to carry out the cabin burnings, whippings, and murders. Where the size of the economic "pie" was shrinking the most, nearly all whites had a common interest in assuring that the portion left over for the freedmen would be as small as possible. It was no wonder that the poorer whites followed the lead of the men with the land.

By the mid-1870s, the North was barraged with reports of violence, political instability, and impending financial ruin in the Southern states still under Republican rule. Crippled from within by Democratic tactics that combined economic pressure, social ostracism, and terror with calls for tax relief and a return to "good government," the Republican governments were weakened from without by the Panic of 1873. Northern capital that had flowed South dried up when a major industrial depression set in and lasted until 1878. Tottering railroad projects, heavily promoted by Republican state leaders in the South, collapsed. Most of the Northern planters who had survived the labor disorganization and poor crops of 1866 and 1867 now permanently left the South. The depression also wiped out the Republican majority in the North. The Democratic party, having already eliminated the Republicans' two-thirds majority in Congress by 1870, regained control of Congress in 1874 for the first time since the late 1850s. Political reconstruction in the South had always been critically dependent on Northern support exercised through Republican majorities in Congress. That majority had passed the Enforcement Acts of 1870 and 1871, which provided the freedmen with some protection against Klan violence, notably in the South Carolina upcountry. Without that Republican majority, and with the Supreme Court ruling in 1873 that major portions of the Enforcement Acts were unconstitutional, even that protection was now gone.

What is known as the Compromise of 1877 traditionally marks the end of congressional Reconstruction. The Republicans, in return for Democratic support of the claim of Rutherford B. Hayes to the presidency in the disputed election of 1876—one in which two rival sets of electoral votes were cast in South Carolina, Louisiana, and Florida—agreed to remove the last federal troops from the South. To use the political language of the victorious Southern Democrats, South Carolina, Florida, and Louisiana were finally "redeemed." In a mutually advantageous bargain, the Republicans received the presidency and the Southern Democrats got white home rule in racial matters.

Ordered Liberty and the End of Reconstruction

With the formal end of political reconstruction in 1877, a crisis of disorder that had existed in the minds of the Northern middle class since the 1850s came to its natural conclusion. From its birth, the Republican party focused on the South the themes of social disorder and loss of self-mastery that the middle class so feared, both in others and in themselves. Secession seemingly confirmed the worst to be expected from the Slave Power. Secession then led to the Civil War, because the Northern middle class refused to let the South depart in peace. Equated with anarchy and a breakdown of all civilized restraints on individual action, secession had to be denied. Otherwise, Northerners told themselves, all forms of socially rebellious behavior would go unpunished. The rallying cry of the Union was "ordered liberty"; unless fused with stable institutional structures, the greatest of which was the Union itself, liberty would be just another name for individual license.

As long as it believed that ordered liberty was threatened by Southern disloyalty, the Northern middle class was willing, even eager, to sanction the measures needed to force loyalty upon the South. This belief held, in varying degrees of intensity, from secession through the passage of the Fifteenth Amendment. But once a new and biracial loyal majority had been created in the South, the Union was deemed safe. Thereafter, during the course of congressional Reconstruction, the disruptive threat to ordered liberty was increasingly identified not with the former rebels, but with the former slaves. The freedmen, after all, were the very propertyless masses whom republican ideology had always warned against entrusting with political power. Northerners quickly concluded that the difficulties of the Republican governments in the South were the inevitable result of separating property from political office.

If the traditional republican fear of the ignorant mob seizing power predisposed the North to accept exaggerated Democratic charges of corruption in the Republican South, the bourgeois definition of freedom that had emerged in the nineteenth century left the Northern middle class unsympathetic to the demands of the Southern poor for economic independence. The freedmen and the poorer white farmers defined freedom in its original republican form of the eighteenth century: the ability to lead a life of self-sufficiency based upon the ownership of property. In contrast, control of self, not economic independence, was the essence of bourgeois freedom. That control, when affixed to the fundamental right of equality before the law, guaranteed an individual's chance to acquire property in the marketplace. The bourgeois definition of freedom was also posited on a clean break between public power and the private economy. Any governmental interference with property rights was regarded as a potential loss of liberty for the individual who had proved his moral worth by accumulating property. Although often violated on behalf of capital, particularly in promotional schemes such as the granting of public land to the transcontinental railroads, this belief in *laissez faire* ("hands off") economics assured that the federal government would play no economic role in political reconstruction. Federal aid to the economy of the prostrate South was not even considered.

The Republicans thus offered as the climax of reconstruction the constitutional principle of equality before the law. The Southern poor accurately saw that this was only the beginning. But when these poor agrarians pushed for a democratic linkage between political and economic reconstruction in the South, they soon became a political liability to the Republican party in the North. Lincoln's party of political antislaveryism was rapidly being transformed into Grant's party of corporate capitalism. Whether for blacks or whites, Northern Republicans could hardly push a program of economic democracy in the South. By so doing they would have run the real risk of worsening class tensions in the industrial North and of alienating their business support within the party.

Limits of class and capitalism, not just of race, aborted the democratic promise of reconstruction. Class divided the Southern Republicans from within and from their larger base of support in the North. Consistent with its retreat from Northern working-class reform in the 1870s, the Republican party also retreated from Southern agrarian reform. The immigrant factory worker and the black field hand were both feared by the Northern middle class in the 1870s as part of the faceless mob of poor who wanted to storm the ramparts of republican order and individual property rights. The Slave Power, the first great enemy of middle-class liberalism, had been vanquished. Concerns over impending chaos and tyranny that had been projected onto Southern planters during the secession crisis were now associated with black reconstruction and labor unrest. Southern whites were given a free hand to deal with the blacks. The Northern middle class, jolted to attention by the great rail strike of 1877, turned its attention to defending liberal capitalism from the challenge of labor. Northern workers, not Confederate soldiers, were now thought to be the major enemies of republicanism.

SUGGESTED READING

Historians have differed sharply in their interpretations of Reconstruction. The dominant view in the first half of the twentieth century, one best represented in William A. Dunning, *Reconstruction, Political, and Economic, 1865–1877* (1907), emphasized Republican vindictiveness, black misrule, and white grievances in the postwar South. A minority view, associated with Charles and Mary Beard, *The Rise of American Civilization* (1927), George F. Milton, *The Age of Hate* (1930), and Howard K. Beale, *The Critical Year* (1930), interpreted Reconstruction as the political expression of the economic interests of the newly triumphant Northern industrialists. Almost a lone voice in combining a class analysis with belief in a genuine Northern interest in the needs of the freedmen was W. E. B. Dubois, *Black Reconstruction* (1935), a neglected classic in American historiography. Interpretations changed significantly in the midst of the civil rights movement of the 1960s, and Radical Reconstruction was cast in a much more favorable light. The best summaries of this scholarship are John Hope Franklin, *Reconstruction after the Civil War* (1961), and Kenneth M. Stampp, *The Era of Reconstruction* (1964). Recent work has stressed class more than race as a motivating factor in Reconstruction and is well-represented in Eric Foner, *Politics and Ideology in the Age of the Civil War* (1980), and *Nothing But Freedom* (1983).

James Sefton, *Andrew Johnson and the Uses of Constitutional Power* (1979), and Albert Castel, *The Presidency of Andrew Johnson* (1979), are the latest studies on Johnson, but their approach to Johnsonian Reconstruction should be balanced with that found in Eric L. McKitrick, *Andrew Johnson and Reconstruction* (1960), and John H. and La Wanda C. Cox, *Politics, Principle, and Prejudice* (1963). On Lincoln's program of reconstruction, one that Johnson claimed to be following, see William B. Hesseltine, *Lincoln's Plan of Reconstruction* (1960); Herman Belz, *Reconstructing the Union* (1969); and Peyton McCrary, *Abraham Lincoln and Reconstruction* (1978). The best account of the clash between Johnson and Congress is in William R. Brock, *An American Crisis* (1963). For the constitutional issues involved in this clash and shifts in legal thought generated by the war, see Harold M. Hyman, *A More Perfect Union* (1973), and Philip S. Paludan, *A Convenant with Death* (1975). Conditions and attitudes in the South under Johnsonian Reconstruction are examined in: Michael Perman, *Reunion without Compromise* (1973); Dan T. Carter, *When the War Was Over* (1985); and Thomas Wagstaff, "Call Your Old Master—'Master': Southern Political Leadership and Negro Labor During Presidential Reconstruction," LH 10 (1969).

Michael Les Benedict, *A Compromise of Principle: Congressional Republicans and Reconstruction, 1863–1869* (1974), is the most carefully detailed study of the evolution of Republican policy, which culminated in what became known as Radical Reconstruction. Also by Benedict, "The Rout of Radicalism: Republicans and the Election of 1867," CWH 18 (1972), is excellent for showing the very real limits that the Northern electorate placed on radical reforms. The standard accounts on the politics of the great postwar constitutional amendments are Joseph B. James, *The Framing of the Fourteenth Amendment* (1956), and William Gillette, *The Right to Vote: Politics and Passage of the Fifteenth Amendment* (1965). The fullest treatment of Republican policy toward the South in the 1870s is William Gillette, *Retreat from Reconstruction, 1867–1879* (1979).

The needs and aspirations that blacks brought to Reconstruction were shaped by the over-powering reality of slavery, and John W. Blassingame, *The Slave Community* (rev. ed., 1979), is the best starting point for understanding how the slaves were able to fashion a collective sense of identity. Although employing a quite different perspective, Eugene D. Genovese, *Roll, Jordan, Roll* (1974), also studies the process of black self-definition under slavery. The strength of black family ties is the central theme of Herbert G. Gutman, *The Black Family in Slavery and Freedom, 1750–1925* (1976). Albert J. Raboteau, *Slave Religion: The "Invisible Institution" in the Antebellum South* (1978), shows how Afro-Christianity was at the core of the cultural expression of the slaves as a people, and Clarence E. Walker, *A Rock in the Weary Land: The African Methodist Episcopal Church During Civil War and Reconstruction* (1982), looks at the institutional history of one of the major black denominations. William F. Mesner, *Freedom and the Ideology of Free Labor: Louisiana, 1862–1865* (1978), emphasizes the conservative motiva-tions of Northern educational efforts in behalf of Southern blacks and also demonstrates how blacks used the threat of a labor strike to win educational concessions from the Union army for their families. On the demand of the freedmen for education and the Northern white response, see also James M. McPherson, *The Abolitionist Legacy* (1976); Ronald E. Butchart, *Northern Schools, Southern Blacks, and Reconstruction* (1980); Jacqueline Jones, *Soldiers of Light and Love: Northern Teachers and Georgia Blacks, 1865–1873* (1980); and Robert C. Morris, *Reading, 'Riting, and Reconstruction: The Education of Freedmen in the South, 1861–1870* (1982).

The failure of a series of halting federal proposals on land distribution for the freedmen is treated in La Wanda Cox, "The Promise of Land for the Freedman," MVHR 45 (1958). The black desire for land is discussed more fully in Edward Magdol, *A Right to the Land* (1977), and Claude F. Oubre, *Forty Acres and a Mule: The Freedmen's Bureau and Black Land Ownership* (1978). On the rapid shift from wage labor to sharecropping in the postwar South, see Ralph Schlomowitz, "The Origins of Southern Sharecropping," AGH 53 (1979). Important works that establish the black initiative in this process are: Peter Kolchin, *First Freedom: The Response of Alabama's Blacks to Emancipation and Reconstruction* (1974); Ronald L. F. Davis, *Good and Faithful Labor: From Slavery to Sharecropping in the Natchez District, 1860–1890* (1982); and Michael Wayne, *The Reshaping of Plantation Society: The Natchez District, 1860–1880* (1983). Particularly valuable on the black political role in Reconstruction are: Vernon Lane Wharton, *The Negro in Mississippi, 1865–1890* (1947); Joel Williamson, *After Slavery: The Negro in South Carolina During Reconstruction, 1861–1877* (1965); Thomas Holt, *Black Over White: Negro Political Leadership in South Carolina During Reconstruction* (1977); and Howard N. Rabinowitz, ed., *Southern Black Leaders in the Reconstruction Era* (1982).

Many of the Northern white Republicans in the South came out of the Freedmen's Bureau, the best sources on which are George R. Bentley, *A History of the Freedmen's Bureau* (1955), and William S. McFeely, *Yankee Stepfather: General O. O. Howard and the Freedmen* (1968). Richard N. Current, "Carpetbaggers Reconsidered," in David Pinkney and Theodore Rapp, eds., *A Festschrift for Frederick B. Artz* (1964), is an excellent revisionist survey of the work on the so-called carpetbaggers. Richard L. Hume, "Carpetbaggers in the Reconstruction South," JAH 64 (1977), and Peter Kolchin, "Scalawags, Carpetbaggers, and Reconstruction," JSH 45 (1979), provide a quantitative framework for understanding who these Republicans were and why their political influence was especially strong in certain Southern states. For a very thorough account of their role in one state, see William C. Harris, *The Day of the Carpetbagger: Republican Reconstruction in Mississippi* (1979). Mark W. Summers, *Railroads, Reconstruc-tion, and the Gospel of Prosperity* (1984), describes the politics of railroads in the postwar South and the efforts of Yankees to spread their version of progress. For the abortive attempts of Yankees to establish themselves in cotton planting, see Lawrence N. Powell, *New Masters: Northern Planters during the Civil War and Reconstruction* (1980).

Much of the literature on Southern white Republicans is reviewed in Otto H. Olsen,

"Reconsidering the Scalawags," CWH 12 (1966). Two important recent studies are James Alex Baggett, "Origins of Upper South Scalawag Leadership," CWH 29 (1983), and Armistead L. Robinson, "Beyond the Realm of Social Consensus: New Meanings of Reconstruction for American History," JAH 68 (1981). The fullest account of these Republicans, as well as the politics of Reconstruction in the South, is Michael Perman, *The Road to Redemption* (1984). The most complete state study is Sarah Woolfolk Wiggins, *The Scalawag in Alabama Politics, 1865–1881* (1977). Gordon B. McKinney, *Southern Mountain Republicans, 1865–1900* (1978), deals with the most persistently loyal of all Southern white Republicans, and Otto H. Olsen, ed., *Reconstruction and Redemption in the South* (1980), provides a state-by-state approach to the history of the party in the South during Reconstruction.

On the role of violence and white vigilantism in ending Reconstruction, see Allen W. Trelease, *White Terror* (1971), and George C. Rable, *But There Was No Peace* (1984). J. C. A. Stagg, "The Problem of Klan Violence: the South Carolina Up-Country, 1868–1871," JAS 8 (1974), offers the most persuasive economic analysis of this violence. The best account of the political maneuverings that formally ended Reconstruction in 1877 is C. Vann Woodward, *Reunion and Reaction* (1956).

For political developments outside the reconstructed South, see Richard O. Curry, ed., *Radicalism, Racism, and Party Realignment: The Border States During Reconstruction* (1969), and James C. Mohr, ed., *Radical Republicans in the North* (1976). Two solid studies of Northern states are Felice A. Bonadio, *North of Reconstruction: Ohio Politics, 1865–1870* (1970), and James C. Mohr, *The Radical Republicans and Reform in New York during Reconstruction* (1973). David Montgomery, *Beyond Equality: Labor and the Radical Republicans, 1862–1872* (1967), is the crucial work in establishing the disillusionment of Northern labor by the 1870s with the middle-class ideology and policies of the Republican party.

NOTES

1. Quoted in Paul D. Escott, *After Secession: Jefferson Davis and the Failure of Confederate Nationalism* (Baton Rouge: Louisiana State University Press, 1978), p. 251.
2. Cited by Frank J. Wetta in a review of Cheryl H. Beneke and Carol D. Summers, eds., *War Fever Cured: The Civil War Diary of Private Joel R. Chambers, 1864–1865* (Memphis: Citizen's Education Council, Inc., 1980) in *Civil War History* 29 (1983): 79.
3. John R. Brumgardt, ed., *Civil War Nurse: The Diary and Letters of Hannah Ropes* (Knoxville: The University of Tennessee Press, 1980), p. 74.
4. Christopher Chancellor, ed., *An Englishman in the American Civil War: The Diaries of Henry Yates Thompson, 1863* (New York: New York University Press, 1971), p. 68.
5. Quoted in Rush Welter, *The Mind of America, 1820–1860* (New York: Columbia University Press, 1975), p. 389.
6. Quoted in James E. Sefton, *Andrew Johnson and the Uses of Constitutional Power* (Boston: Little, Brown, 1980), p. 41.
7. Rachel Sherman Thorndike, ed., *The Sherman Letters: Correspondence between General and Senator Sherman from 1837 to 1891* (New York: Da Capo Press, 1969), p. 254.
8. Quoted in Stephen Skowronek, *Building a New American State: The Expansion of National Administrative Capacities, 1877–1920* (New York: Cambridge University Press, 1982), p. 30.
9. Quoted in Eric L. McKitrick, *Andrew Johnson and Reconstruction* (Chicago: University of Chicago Press, 1960), p. 78.
10. Quoted in Eric Foner, *Politics and Ideology in the Age of the Civil War* (New York: Oxford University Press, 1980), p. 135.
11. Quoted in La Wanda and John H. Cox, "Johnson and the Negro," in Kenneth M. Stampp and Leon F. Litwack, eds., *Reconstruction: An Anthology of Revisionist Writings* (Baton Rouge: Louisiana State University Press, 1969), p. 72.
12. Quoted in David Montgomery, *Beyond Equality: Labor and the Radical Republicans, 1862–1872* (New York: Alfred A. Knopf, 1967), p. 72.
13. For the wording of this very short amendment, see Allen W. Trelease, *Reconstruction: The Great Experiment* (New York: Harper Torchbooks, 1971), p. 214.

14. Quoted in James M. McPherson, *Ordeal By Fire: The Civil War and Reconstruction* (New York: Alfred A. Knopf, 1982), p. 546.
15. Quoted in W. E. B. Du Bois, *Black Reconstruction in America, 1860–1880* (New York: Meridian Books, 1964), p. 299.
16. Both quotes are in Thomas Wagstaff, "Call Your Old Master—'Master': Southern Political Leaders and Negro Labor During Presidential Reconstruction," *Labor History* 10 (1969): 327.
17. Quoted in Foner, op. cit., p. 98.
18. Quoted in Clarence L. Mohr, "Before Sherman: Georgia Blacks and the Union War Effort, 1861–1864," *The Journal of Southern History* 45 (1979): 339.
19. Quoted in William F. Messner, "Black Education in Louisiana, 1863–1865," *Civil War History* 22 (1976): 45, 57.
20. Ibid., p. 59.
21. Quoted in Eric Foner, *Nothing But Freedom: Emancipation and its Legacy* (Baton Rouge: Louisiana State University Press, 1983), p. 56.
22. Quoted in Wagstaff, op. cit., p. 325.
23. Quoted in Peter Kolchin, *First Freedom: The Responses of Alabama's Blacks to Emancipation and Reconstruction* (Westport, Conn.: Greenwood Press, 1972), p. 42.
24. Quoted in Roger L. Ransom and Richard Sutch, *One Kind of Freedom: The Economic Consequences of Emancipation* (New York: Cambridge University Press, 1977), p. 67.
25. Quoted in Richard Paul Fuke, "Hugh Lennox Bond and Radical Republican Ideology," *The Journal of Southern History* 45 (1979): 380–381.
26. Quoted in Otto H. Olsen, "Reconsidering the Scalawags," *Civil War History* 12 (1966): 314.
27. Quoted in J. C. A. Stagg, "The Problem of Klan Violence: The South Carolina Up-Country, 1868–1871," *Journal of American Studies* 8 (1974): 316.

Part III

GILDED AGE AMERICA

8

The Economic Reordering of America

The social and economic map of America was redrawn in the generation after the Civil War. This chapter examines the main components of that process: the mass movement to the trans-Mississippi West, the development of new class relations in the South, the fusion of industrialization, urbanization, and immigration in the North, and the rise of corporations geared to the productive and distributive needs of a managerial economy.

All these components were part of a national experience in which marketplace involvement was no longer a matter of individual choice for most Americans. This was as true in the agricultural West and South as it was in the industrial Northeast. The market was the key to the social reordering of post–Civil War America. Nowhere was this more evident than in the settlement and exploitation of the trans-Mississippi West.

The West and Its Migrants

The West into which Americans moved after the Civil War inspired awe. The following description came from a woman on the Oregon Trail:[1]

> Above us was the bright dome of a heaven so free from all earthly smoke and vapor, so clear and transparent, that the stars seemed closer and shone with an exceeding brilliancy. The air was filled with a balmy sweetness, and yet so limpid and clear that even in the starlight we could catch glimpses of the shimmering trees in the distant river.

This was the Big Sky country across the Mississippi, a land of limitless vistas in which undulating prairies seemingly swayed like ocean swells breaking against patches of cottonwood as the shimmering grasses rolled on towards the Rockies. The cramped and tangled woodlands of the East were here replaced by enormous expanses of plains and skies bathed in unfiltered light. An abundance of wildlife—antelope, deer, prairie chickens, quail, and an immense number of buffalo, grazing upwind in herds of up to 100,000—moved through the vastness of earth and light.

The development of the West, the conversion of nature into natural resources, had its origins in the decisions made by millions of Easterners. What the trans-Appalachian West was to the farmers of Jacksonian America, the trans-Mississippi West was to the sons and daughters of these farmers. The West meant land, the foundations of an economic independence that was fast slipping away in the East. Table 8.1, a measure-

Table 8.1   Net Migration by Decade in the U.S., 1870–1900
           (in thousands)

Two features of the demographic history of the late nineteenth-century United States stand out: (1) The persistent outflow of the native-born population in the East and its movement to the West was more than counterbalanced by a massive influx of the foreign-born into the East. (2) The sharp reversal in the 1890s of the prior pattern, in which the West attracted far more total migrants than the East, marked the end of the agrarian frontier in the West and its overshadowing by the urban-industrial complex in the East.

	TOTAL	NATIVE WHITES	FOREIGN-BORN	BLACKS
East				
1870–1880	+ 54.2	− 963.9	+ 1078.8	− 61.0
1880–1890	+ 1268.4	− 1039.0	+ 2378.5	− 70.5
1890–1900	+ 1714.3	− 354.6	+ 2149.1	− 80.6
West				
1870–1880	+ 1636.6	+ 964.2	+ 612.5	+ 60.8
1880–1890	+ 2153.7	+ 1040.1	+ 1043.7	+ 70.8
1890–1900	+ 974.2	+ 354.3	+ 539.8	+ 80.5

Source: Compiled from *Historical Statistics*, Series C-25–75.

ment of net migration flows with the Mississippi as the dividing line between the East and West, reveals the strong pull of land availability in the West. In the last three decades of the nineteenth century, the West drew off 2½ million of the native-born in the East. During these same years, the establishment of 2½ million new farms doubled the number of American farms. As we would expect, growth was most explosive in the West, which accounted for 86 percent of all additions to farm land between 1870 and 1900.

Population patterns of settlement, growth, maturation, and outflow that had first appeared east of the Appalachians by the late eighteenth century had been repeated by 1870 for the Jacksonian frontier of the trans-Appalachian West. In the 1870s and 1880s, the largest stream of native-born migrants to the trans-Mississippi West, 46 percent of the total, flowed out of the states of the Old Northwest. Land that a generation earlier had been cheap and abundant was now divided into farms and priced beyond the reach of most of the sons of the pioneering generation, so they moved further west.

Often the sons accompanied their families West. As Hamlin Garland said of his father, Richard, the meaning of "all that was fine and hopeful and buoyant in American life"[2] was the anticipation of finding that perfect farm somewhere to the West. As nearly as any one individual could, Richard Garland lived the restlessness of an entire generation of Northern farmers as they shifted and regrouped during the middle years of the nineteenth century. Born into a Maine farm family, he clerked for Amos Lawrence in Boston, went west with his parents on the Erie Canal in 1840, worked as a lumberjack and raftsman in the forests of the upper Midwest, cleared a 160-acre farm in Wisconsin, marched off to fight for the Union as soon as the farm was paid for in

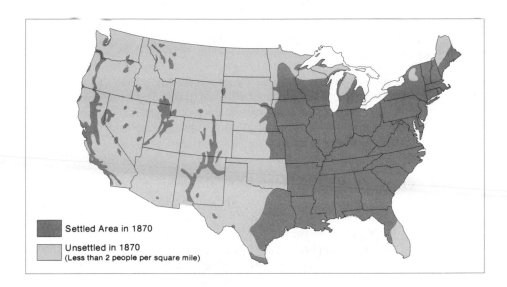

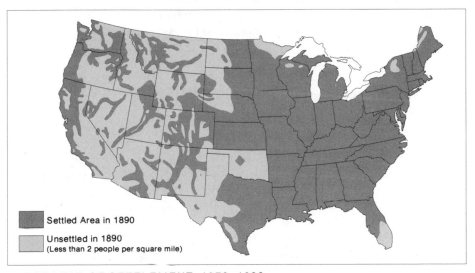

THE SPREAD OF SETTLEMENT, 1870–1890

In the generation after the Civil War, Americans settled the last great expanse of cheap, fertile land in the trans-Mississippi West. The agricultural frontier that had drawn Americans westward since the eighteenth century was about to close.

1863, returned home, sold the farm, and moved with family and kin to Minnesota, then to Iowa, and finally to South Dakota.

When the Garlands left for the Dakota Territory in the late 1870s, the open Iowa prairie they had settled a few years earlier was already taking on the cultivated air of Eastern prosperity. The land was fenced and plowed, the livestock was in pasture, corn and wheat were ripening where mild meadows had bloomed, and maturing groves of maples were shading and softening the bleakness of the homesteads. Much had been gained, but much had been lost. "And yet with all these growing signs of prosperity," recalled Hamlin Garland,

> I realized that something sweet and splendid was dying out of the prairie. The whistling pigeons, the wailing plover, the migrating ducks and geese, the soaring cranes, the shadowy wolves, the wary foxes, all the untamed things were passing, vanishing with the blue-joint grass, the dainty wild rose and the tiger-lily's flaming torch.[3]

With the completion of settlement in the 1870s, or, more precisely, the end of the cycle of a rapid influx of population onto virgin land, Iowa quickly became a large exporter of its native rural population. Most of the migrants moved into the Middle Border—the Dakotas, Nebraska, and Kansas. They followed the railroad and the lure of free government land to homestead. They were in the vanguard of the last great farming frontier, the high plains. The horizon here was endless and the land was utterly flat. For Garland, 'Its lonely unplowed sweep gave me the satisfying sensation of being at last among the men who held the outposts, sentinels for the marching millions who were approaching from the east."[4]

As the Garlands moved through successive frontiers, the market worked to their advantage. The cash from the sale of the previous farm financed the purchase of the new one, the sale of which, after land prices had risen in the wake of an influx of settlers, provided the capital for the next move. The typical migrants who joined the Garlands in the Dakotas, however, were not farmers before they left their old communities. Only about one-third of the native stock settlers on the Dakota frontier had been farmers before they migrated. Another one-third had been farm workers and day laborers when they pulled up stakes further east.

The rise in farm tenancy, especially in the Midwest, pushed many of the settlers into the high plains. Tenancy rates in the Midwest—that is, the percentage of farm operators who did not own land—rose from 15 to 20 percent at mid-century to 25 to 35 percent by the end of the century. Tenancy was highest where land was most expensive—in the more fertile districts best suited to the market sale of grain crops. The lure of nearly free land in the West simultaneously pulled many out of the East. In return for a nominal fee and the occupancy of the land for five years, the Homestead Act of 1862 provided individuals with 160 acres of the public domain. The chance to establish a family homestead was a powerful attraction for most of the native-born migrants, men who had acquired no land as they worked at a succession of odd jobs in gradually moving westward through the Midwest.

Similar push-pull factors were also operating in a trans-Atlantic context after the Civil War. Rising population pressure on limited agricultural resources in Europe broke down the traditional rural economy. Landlords, anxious to consolidate production into larger and more efficient units, forced the peasants off their small strips of land. Faced with a choice in Europe of migrating into cities or struggling for survival on small and dwindling plots of land, millions of peasants chose instead to migrate to America. They reached European ports on the same railroads that distributed the mass-produced goods that undermined village economies, and they left for America on the same steamboats that had brought the flood of American grain that disrupted peasant agriculture. Both within Europe and between Europe and America, cheaper, faster networks of transportation were accelerating the market flows of goods and labor across political boundaries. Most of the immigrants went into American cities. Nonetheless, between 1870 and 1900, some 2.2 million of the foreign-born moved into the trans-Mississippi West, a landed frontier that no longer existed in Europe.

Like the native-born, many of the immigrants worked their way west as lumberjacks, miners, and construction hands on the railroads. Nearly half of the foreign-born who settled in the Dakotas after earlier stops in the Northeast and Midwest had worked as laborers. A large group of Germans who moved to North Dakota in the mid-1870s had originally been recruited to America as miners in southern Wisconsin. When the mines played out and their labor was no longer needed, they collectively decided to head west and homestead. In responding to available economic opportunities, the Germans typically worked at industrial jobs in the corridor of cities along the eastern and southern rim of the Great Lakes, turned to tenant farming when they reached the prairies of the Midwest, and claimed their own homesteads when they arrived in the Middle Border.

In their search for, as one of them phrased it, something "better than working for another,"[5] these homesteading immigrants relied on chain networks of relations and friends for mutual assistance and information in moving. These same family-centered networks, not the aimless wanderings of uprooted individuals, channeled the migratory flows of most of the immigrants. The Germans, German-Russians, Canadians, and Scandinavians who moved into the high plains followed the paths of their ethnic kinsmen and village neighbors who had preceded them. When the brothers, Osten and Henrik Boe, left Norway for America in 1864, they knew where they were headed. An eight-week Atlantic voyage carried them to Quebec City in Canada. Packed first in a canal boat and then the steerage accommodations of immigrant box-cars, they then traveled to Milwaukee, the jumping-off point for rail and wagon transportation to the Norwegian settlement of Decorah in Iowa. There, Osten and Henrik found lodgings in the households of friends from their home district in Norway. They paid for their lodgings with their labor and earned a bit of cash by hiring out for day work. After a year of this initial indoctrination to America, they walked 150 miles to the small Norwegian-American town of Northfield, Minnesota. Here, Henrik stayed. Osten soon pushed on another 250 miles to the north and west, and in 1868 filed a homestead claim on rich prairie soil at the eastern edge of the Red River Valley of the North.

Within a generation, this valley on the border between Minnesota and North Dakota had the largest concentration of Norwegians outside of Norway. Sod houses gave way to log cabins and then to large frame dwellings. Lutheran services in a neighbor's granary moved into wooden chapels. Threshing machines replaced the scythe for the harvest, and grain elevators along the sidings of the Great Northern and Pacific railroad eliminated the necessity of fifty-mile wagon treks over a roadless prairie to the nearest grist mill. All the while, supplied with information from the letters of earlier migrants and the reports in immigrant newspapers, the Norwegians kept coming. The debt-ridden farms of Norway, a country second only to Ireland in the percentage of its population lost to America, had grown too small to support the traditional agricultural lifestyle of a rural family economy. With a sadness streaked with resentment, the peasants left. A peasant ballad captured the sense of hurt:[6]

> Farewell, then, Mother Norway, now I must leave thee!
> Because thou fostered me,
> I must give thee many thanks.
> All too sparing were thee in providing food
> For the throng of thy laborers,
> Though thou givest more than enough
> To thy well-schooled sons.

Most of the migrants went directly to communities of Norwegian settlers along the Minnesota-Iowa border. Acting as feeder colonies, these communities absorbed new-comers from Norway and sent out families to the Red River Valley. In a migratory chain from fjords to prairies, the Norwegians moved along geographic pathways of ethnicity in their search for the stability and dignity of land ownership.

Other ethnic groups followed similar pathways to the West. Kinship bonds and information networks resulted in spatially distinct clusterings of nationalities and local European loyalties. German-Russians transplanted virtually entire villages from the Russian steppes to the Dakota plains. They also sorted themselves out by their religious ties. Their Dakota hamlets were either "Katholisch," "Evangelisch," or "Mennoni-ten." The Swedes entered the upper Midwest in such discrete patterns that the village, kin, and church linkages of individual parishes were recreated. Nearly half of all who left the parish of Rättvik, for example, eventually settled as a close-knit community in Isanti County, Minnesota.

This specificity of settlement also reflected market design. The railroads, notably the transcontinental lines of the West, received 158 million acres from the federal and state governments between 1850 and 1871. It was clearly in the best interests of the railroads to make these construction subsidies of land as productive as soon as possi-ble. Future revenues depended on local freight rates that could be paid only by farmers producing crops to be marketed. Immediate profit was secondary to securing actual settlers for the land grants. The railroads spent millions on advertising, sent immigra-tion agents into European villages, ran display booths at county fairs in the East and Midwest, and offered special excursion rates for groups interested in purchasing their land.

The railroads, along with state and territorial immigration bureaus, succeeded in placing the immigrants where they wanted them. The natural tendency of settlers to seek out an area closely resembling the soil and climate of the one they were leaving was reinforced by the desire of those bidding for settlers to put migrants where their agricultural skills promised a rapid and successful introduction of cash-crop farming. The German-Russians, for example, because of their prior experience with wheat farming in semiarid grasslands, were funneled into the Dakotas. Scandinavians, accus-tomed to grain agriculture in a cold northern climate, were encouraged to move into the upper Midwest. Those with nonagricultural skills, such as German and Cornish min-ers, were imported from the East to work the mineral deposits owned by the railroads. Once the initial settlements were established, letters sent home by the first migrants promoted and directed future migrations of kin and friends.

Although the settlers in the trans-Mississippi West arranged themselves in distinct cultural patterns, the market quickly proved to be a great assimilative force. The immigrants had little choice but to adapt to the American system of land tenure and the productive potential of their new environment. The communal traditions of peasant agriculture that divided up village plots and shared labor for the ploughing, sowing, and harvesting were discarded. More arable land meant a greater emphasis on food crops and less on livestock. The common pressure to grow a marketable crop in order to pay off land bought on credit and to finance improvements and machinery resulted in belts of economic specialization—corn and hogs in the Midwest, wheat in the Middle Border, and cotton and tobacco in Texas. In less than a generation, immigrant and native-born farmers in any given area had the same crop mix and used the same methods of production. The children of the pioneering generations, regardless of their parents' place of birth, found greater attractions in the towns and cities than the family farm. They abandoned the loneliness and drudgery of farm life to join an urban workforce now fed by the agricultural surpluses their parents had wrested from the raw prairie.

The West and Its Dispossessed

The trans-Atlantic market forces that pushed people out of old communities and pulled them to the fresh lands of the West were part of a larger process of industrialization that accelerated earlier patterns of white dispossession of Indian land and resources. Settlers were hurried into the heavily promoted West on bands of steel that sliced across the north-south migratory paths of the great buffalo herds that were food and shelter to the Plains Indians. The railroads, the quintessential fusion of iron and steam in the age of industrial capitalism, brought in the settlers so that crops and mineral resources could be taken out and shipped to an emerging national market laced together by other railroads. Farmers, miners, lumberjacks, and townspeople followed where the rails led. Barriers of time and space that had delayed or prolonged the exploitation of pre–Civil War frontiers were hurdled in the onward rush of rattling steel, flying sparks, and billowing steam. Barriers of Indian resistance were disposed of just as quickly.

Above all, the railroads made the West accessible. As stressed by President Ulysses S. Grant in his annual message of 1869, the same year that the first transcontinental railroad was completed: "The building of railroads, and the access thereby given to all the agricultural and mineral regions of the country, is rapidly bringing civilized settlements into contact with all the tribes of Indians."[7] Another Union war hero, General Sherman, bluntly summarized the consequences: "We must fight the Indians, and force them to collect in agreed-on limits far away from the continental roads."[8] In the decade after the Civil War, 200 battles were fought, and numerous other small engagements were left unrecorded. The warfare was touched off by relentless white pressure. As Colonel Henry B. Carrington, a veteran of many of the battles, explained in 1880: "From 1865 until the present time, there has not been a border campaign which did not have its impulse in the aggressions of a white man."[9]

As in earlier Indian-white conflicts, the root cause of the Plains warfare was a struggle over resources—land, water, and minerals. It was not that the Indians did not yield these resources to whites in treaties; they did. But it was never enough for the whites. Once having migrated to a new area that was not then desired by whites, or having been forcibly removed to land intentionally set aside for them, the Indians soon discovered that white settlers and demands for yet more resources quickly engulfed the tribes even in their new locations. "What is it they want of us at this time?" asked Tatanka Yotanka, known to the whites as Sitting Bull, in 1889. "They want us to give up another chunk of our tribal land. This is not the first time or the last time. They will try to gain possession of the last piece of ground we possess." As for the white promises made in earlier treaties, he noted that "we are dying off in expectation of getting things promised us."[10]

Sitting Bull's people, the Teton Sioux, were at the center of the confrontations with the white military after the Civil War. Originally from woodlands and marshes to the east of the headwaters of the Mississippi, the Sioux were pushed onto the northern prairies in the eighteenth century by stronger tribes armed with guns. After acquiring guns themselves in trade with the French, the Sioux then learned the use of the horse from the Plains Indians. The horse, introduced to the New World by the Spanish, made possible a vastly extended buffalo hunt, the transport of bulky tribal possessions, and a daring, highly mobile form of warfare. The Sioux melded two facets of the white man's culture, the gun and the horse, into a uniquely Indian culture of warrior-hunters. By the early nineteenth century, they were the most powerful race on the northern plains.

The Sioux, and other strong tribes, such as the Cheyenne, Arapaho, Blackfeet, Kiowa, and Comanche, stood in the way of the penetration of the West by the transcontinental railroads. Legally, the tribes had every right to hunt in and move across the land of the railroads. "According to existing treaties with Indians," noted General Sherman in 1867, "they have a right to wander and hunt across all the railroads towards the West." Congress simply ignored these legal rights in the Railroad Enabling Act of 1866. As an inducement for construction, the act granted the railroads alternate sections of public land in a forty-mile swath on either side of the projected rights of way. Reservation land suddenly became the property of the railroads. The rub was that this land was legally not part of the public domain in the first place. One federal treaty after another had guaranteed the Indians permanent possession and ownership of land that was legally theirs in return for massive concessions of tribal lands in the east. The treaties mattered little. "Whether right or wrong," Sherman laconically concluded, "those roads will be built, and everybody knows that Congress, after granting the charters and fixing the routes, cannot now back out and surrender the country to a few bands of roving Indians."[11]

The army's foremost responsibility was to make certain that the railroads were built. The army cleared Indians away from construction sites, forced them onto new reservations, and hunted them down if they wandered off the reservations. In a strategy that owed much to the precepts of total war practiced by Union forces during the Civil War, the Western command under Sherman targeted the resource base and entire tribal population as military objectives. The army preferred to attack in winter campaigns designed to hit the Indians when their ponies were weak, the mobility of the warriors was low, and women and children were huddled in winter encampments. Sweeping columns of cavalry moved across the plains in arcs of several hundred miles and then converged on the scattered winter camps. Their orders were simple—kill all the warriors and ponies, destroy all the food supplies, and round up the starving survivors for relocation on a reservation.

By 1868 the Southern Cheyenne, the Commanche, the Kiowa, and the Arapaho had been forced to reservations south of the Arkansas River. They made a last ditch effort to preserve the vestiges of their independence in the Red River War of 1874–1875. Infuriated by the wanton slaughter of buffalo on *their* reservations by white hunters, the southern Plains tribes drove the hunters off. The army responded with another series of winter campaigns. The slaughter of a hundred Cheyenne fugitives on the banks of the Sappa River in Kansas, and the exile to Florida of the Indian resistance leaders, signaled the final destruction of native independence on the southern plains.

Shortly thereafter, the Powder River War of 1876–1877 broke Indian resistance on the northern plains. The Sioux and the Northern Cheyenne had fought the army to a standstill in the first campaigns after the Civil War. The tribes agreed to leave the Platte River Valley, the site of early railroad construction, and move to new reservations west of the upper Missouri. In return their prime hunting areas in the Powder River and Bighorn country of Wyoming and Montana, and the sacred center of the Sioux universe, the *Pa Sapa* in the Black Hills of South Dakota, were specifically recognized as unceded territory under exclusive Indian control. In a treaty of 1868, the federal government guaranteed Indian possession of this territory for "as long as the grass should grow and the rivers flow."[12] The guarantee held good for about five years. Surveyors for the Northern Pacific, the second major transcontinental railroad, determined that the best route west ran through the middle of Sioux hunting grounds in the valleys of the Powder and Yellowstone Rivers. Meanwhile, reports of gold in the Black Hills set off a stampede into the holy Sioux area previously shunned by whites. The Sioux and Cheyenne fought to defend what they had just been told was theirs forever.

In the ensuing war, Lieutenant Colonel George Custer, by rashly isolating his 7th Cavalry beyond the reach of the supporting columns of the rest of the army, found an immortality that he could have secured in no other way. For all the attention riveted on Custer's Massacre at the Little Bighorn in July 1876, however, the war was a crushing defeat for the northern tribes. The sensationalized national publicity of their victory at the Little Bighorn ensured that efforts to hunt them down and drive them back to the reservations would be unrelenting. Within a year, Sioux military power was broken, and new treaties had been signed for the previously unceded land.

Although small bands of Apaches continued to wage guerrilla warfare in the mountains of the Southwest through the 1880s, the era of plains warfare was over by 1880. The major tribes were all broken, and the remnants herded onto reservations. The choice had been one of death or captivity. Whites now offered what they called civilization and the hope of acquiring material goods, but most of the Indian survivors saw little in this that they wanted to embrace. Red Cloud, one of the greatest of the Sioux warriors, never fought the whites after he agreed to the treaty of 1868. He remained at peace but he wanted nothing to do with the whites. To act like the whites, he counseled his people, meant:[13]

> You must begin anew and put away the wisdom of your fathers. You must lay up food and forget the hungry. When your house is built, your storeroom filled, then look around for a neighbor whom you can take advantage of and seize all he has.

The bitterness of Red Cloud was more than understandable. All the Indians had known was the greed of the whites.

With the bitterness came an overwhelming sense of despair. To be a Plains Indian and to live through the arrival of white settlement was to be part of a world that was continuously being torn apart by shattering cycles of death, disease, and dislocation. It was a world that the prowess of the warrior was powerless to protect. To be sure, the Plains Indians were more than a match for the U.S. army in separate, open battles. They were better horsemen, had tougher, faster mounts, and fought with more determination than undertrained U.S. troops demoralized by low pay and annual desertion rates in excess of 10 percent. But individual exploits of courage in battle were no match for the sheer persistence of the enemy. In a prolonged war of attrition, the army gradually reduced the Plains Indians to impoverishment. Each raid on a village destroyed a particular group's food supplies and the hand-crafted possessions that represented the work of a generation. Horses, the basis of Indian wealth, were singled out for slaughter. A single army raid in the Texas Panhandle in 1874 destroyed 1,400 horses and mules.

Nor could Indian warriors block the steady advance of the railroads. Francis A. Walker, Commissioner of Indian Affairs, was quite close to the mark when he predicted in 1872 that another two years' extension of the Northern Pacific "will of itself completely solve the great Sioux problem, and leave the ninety thousand Indians ranging between the two transcontinental lines as incapable of resisting the Government as are the Indians of New York or Massachusetts."[14] The railroads provided rapid transport for the troops, passage for settlers who soon clamored for the protection of the troops, and markets for the buffalo hunters. The buffalo was the foundation for the material life of the Plains Indians. Its flesh furnished food that, when dried and mixed with fat and berries, was transportable in the form of pemmican; its dried dung (buffalo chips) was fuel; its hide provided shelter when stretched over wooden poles for tents; its fur produced robes and blankets for protection against the prairie winters; and its bones, when carved and shaped, were utensils. Before the arrival of the railroads, there were some eleven to thirteen million buffalo in the West. By the early 1880s there were almost none.

Commercialism and military policy all but exterminated the buffalo in the fifteen years after the Civil War. In 1872 the tanning industry perfected a process that converted buffalo hides into high-grade leather. The market for hides now exploded. White hunters killed an estimated three million buffalo between 1872 and 1874. The hides were smelly and bulky, but the railroads enabled huge quantities to be shipped to eastern markets. Technology also made the actual killing easier and cheaper. Rather than working up a sweat by chasing down the herds, the hunters, now armed with lethal, new rifles, could practice the still hunt. Hunters crouched downwind of the herd, mounted their telescopic-sighted rifles on portable stands, zeroed in on one animal, and then picked off others of the curious beasts as they congregated to watch the death agonies of the mortally wounded members of the herd. Using this technique, a professional could kill over one hundred bison in less than an hour without ever moving from his original location. Joining the professionals were eastern and foreign tourists, the "sportsmen" who slaughtered in the thousands in order to bring home a few trophies, and the white settlers, who could earn a couple of hundred dollars for a few weeks' work. Instead of cutting and hauling timber for a supplemental income, as they did in the East, homesteaders in the West shot and skinned buffalo. It was profitable work as long as the buffalo were plentiful: their hides went for $2.50, their tongues for 25¢.

Buffalo Hides Stacked for Shipment. Taken in Dodge City, Kansas, in 1874, this photograph conveys the enormity of the slaughter of the buffalo herds. About half a million hides were shipped out of southwestern Kansas on the Atchison, Topeka, and Santa Fe Railroad between 1872 and 1874. (The Granger Collection)

The carnage was over quickly. By the mid-1870s, stretches of the southern plains, as described by Colonel Richard Dodge, were "foul with sickening stench, and the vast plain . . . was a dead, solitary, putrid desert."[15] Similar scenes were reported for the northern plains by the early 1880s. The army had done little of the killing, but then again it did not have to. The economic warfare practiced by the army in its winter raids on Indian property had its counterpart in the destruction of the buffalo by civilians. The attitude of General Philip Sheridan was typical: "Let them kill, skin, and sell until the buffalo is exterminated, as it is the only way to bring about lasting peace and allow civilization to advance."[16] It was easier to force starving Indians onto reservations when their food supply was being wiped out, and easier yet to keep them there once that supply was completely gone from the plains. Except for a few hundred survivors, all that was left of the magnificent herds by the 1880s were bleached bones. Even the bones had a market. They were shipped east for processing into glue and fertilizer.

As the buffalo died off, so did the native Americans. Far more died of disease than in battle. Accompanying the first whites were disease-spawning organisms against which the Indians had no immunity. Smallpox in 1837 halved the population of the Plains Indians, and an outbreak of cholera in 1849–1850 was almost as deadly. Particularly hard hit at first were the smaller, more sedentary tribes. Fragments of these tribes then merged with similarly weakened tribes until another bout of disease and attacks by whites or more powerful tribes broke them apart again into ever-dwindling numbers. The Mandans of Dakota, for example, joined with the Arikara and Hidatsi after the epidemic of 1837. After new epidemics and a series of Sioux raids, the three tribes had shrunk to a single village by 1862. Soon, the larger, more mobile tribes were affected as well. The Comanches, the military equivalent on the southern plains of the proud Sioux on the northern, numbered but 1,600 when they were sent to the

Medicine Lodge reservation in 1867. More than half of the tribe had died of smallpox and cholera in 1849. After the disease cycles had run their course by the end of the nineteenth century, the pre-Columbian native population of North America had been reduced to perhaps only one twenty-fifth of its original size.

In the fever of a loved one, the smoke of the burning lodges and tribal possessions, and the stench of the rotting ponies and buffalo, the Indians could see and feel the death of their world and its values. Solace for many came in the form of whiskey—the favorite item of the white Indian traders, because they could always control their profit margins by watering down their product. Alcoholism, as an epidemic disease in its own right, killed off thousands. In just five years, from 1869 to 1874, 25 percent of the Blackfeet are estimated to have died from alcoholism.

Army officers later wrote of their Indian adversaries that "Savage warfare was never more beautiful than in you."[17] But by 1890 the Plains Indians no longer evoked any images of glory. Now they appeared both helpless and doomed. As if in one supplication of anguish, a song rose up from the plains in that year:[18]

> He!   When I met him approaching—
> He!   When I met him approaching—
> My children, my children—
> I then saw the multitude plainly.
> I then saw the multitude plainly.

This was one stanza from the song of the Ghost Dance. In the winter of 1889, after a decade of reservation life in which they were forced to subsist on government doles and watch as their religious and political culture was ridiculed and undermined by missionary teachers and government bureaucrats, the despair of the Plains Indians gave birth to a messianic religion. Wovoka, a Nevada Paiute, emerged as the prophet who preached deliverance. His creed was a nonviolent one that combined Christian themes of the Apocalypse and the Resurrection with the traditional Sun Dance ceremonies of the Plains Indians. In a message of cultural revitalization, he urged the Indians to live in peace among each other and to seek divine guidance and personal visions in the Ghost Dance. Soon, the messiah, the "He" of the song, would approach from across the plains at the head of the ghostly multitude of slain warriors and vanished game returning to claim their homeland. The whites would be destroyed in an earthquake, and the Indians and their land would be reborn. The land and its inhabitants would again be fused in a sacred circle.

Misunderstood and feared by the Indian agents on the reservations, if for no other reason than it represented an aspect of Indian life beyond their control, the religion of the Ghost Dance provoked a military response. White authorities were particularly concerned about the Sioux. The tribe was known to be angry over their most recent loss of land, a cession of eleven million acres in 1889, and Sitting Bull, though old and weak, was still a respected leader who could command a loyal following. Prodded on by hysterical talk of a general Indian uprising, the army was sent in when the Sioux refused to abandon the Ghost Dance. On December 15, 1889, Sitting Bull was killed when his followers resisted his arrest by reservation police. His son, Crow Foot, was then shot. These two deaths were a prelude to the horror at Wounded Knee Creek on December 29.

About 350 Miniconjou Sioux, two-thirds of whom were women and children,

The Scene After the Massacre at Wounded Knee. This painting effectively conveys the utter desolation of the Sioux camp following the battle. The almost defenseless Sioux were helpless against the Army's superior weapons, which included artillery. (The Bettmann Archive)

were being militarily escorted back to the reservation at Pine Ridge, South Dakota. These Sioux had already been on their way back to the reservation when the army intercepted them. Frightened and virtually defenseless, the Indians raised a white flag of surrender. On December 28 they were surrounded by U.S. troops. At dawn the next day, while the Ghost Dancers were being disarmed, a shot rang out, probably from the rifle of a young brave. Artillery previously sighted on the encampment from the encircling hills then opened fire.

When the guns grew silent, and the troops stopped their pursuit of the fleeing Indians, 200 to 250 Sioux were dead. Black Elk, who rode out from the reservation, described what he saw:[19]

> Dead and wounded children and little babies [were] scattered all along where they had been trying to run away. . . . Sometimes they were in heaps because they had huddled together, and some were scattered all along. Sometimes bunches of them had been killed and torn to pieces where the wagon guns hit them. I saw a little baby trying to suck its mother, but she was bloody and dead.

After souvenir hunters had stripped the bodies of what they wanted, the frozen corpses were dumped into a hastily dug trench on New Year's Day, 1890. The destruction of the plains Indians was surely complete.

Table 8.2 Net Migration By Decade in the Southeast, 1870–1900
         (in thousands)

More and more Southerners became mired in agrarian poverty after the Civil War. As a result, the South's population losses from out-migration grew progressively greater. Southern blacks were also trying to escape racial controls that were becoming tighter and more vicious.

	TOTAL	NATIVE WHITES	FOREIGN-BORN	BLACKS
Decade				
1870–1880	− 244.4	− 175.7	− 36.6	− 105.5
1880–1890	− 364.6	− 316.2	+ 84.6	− 132.6
1890–1900	− 461.9	− 298.0	+ 60.9	− 224.9

Source: Compiled from *Historical Statistics*, Series C-25–75.
Note: As defined here, the Southeast included the former slave states east of the Mississippi.

The Other Reconstruction of the South

Unlike the trans-Mississippi West, the post–Civil War South inspired no sense of awe or ever-renewable hope. Instead, frustration was the dominant mood. Many a common white would have confirmed one North Carolinian's recollection of his neighborhood in the 1880s: "I'm tellin' you, all this part of the country was in a hell of a mess. Goddam if it didn't look like every son-of-a-gun and his brother would starve to death tryin' to get started again."[20] Times were tight, and they always seemed to be getting tighter. The demographic response, as shown in Table 8.2, was a consistent outflow of population.

Most of the departing whites were hard-pressed farmers who headed due west into Texas and, by the 1890s, Oklahoma. Blacks resettled in the West as well. In the first large-scale migration of blacks out of the South, 6,000 freedmen, known as the exodusters, left the lower Mississippi Valley for Kansas in 1879. Increasingly, however, blacks looked towards nonagricultural jobs in the Northeast. By the end of the nineteenth century, two-thirds of the black flow out of the South went to the North, not the West. Unable to hold onto its native-born, the postwar South also lagged far behind other regions in attracting immigrants. Whereas the slave South of 1860 was home to 9.5 percent of the nation's foreign-born whites, the free South of 1900 held only 5.5 percent of the foreign-born.

Although the net migration losses in the South were small compared to the mass migration during and after World War II, their persistence decade after decade was as good an indicator as any of the poverty and lack of opportunity that plagued the South after the Civil War. As indicated in Table 8.3, the South's relative share of per-capita national income plunged after the Civil War. The absolute decline was over by the 1870s, and from 1880 to 1900 per-capita income rose from $85 to $116. Nonetheless, the South was unable to close the income gap between itself and the rest of the nation. In 1900 Southern per-capita income was still barely half of the U.S. average.

The Southern economy had experienced three shocks in the Civil War decade. The first was the sheer physical destruction of the war itself. Nonslave property losses

Table 8.3   Relative Regional Shares of National Per-Capita Income, 1860–1900
   (U.S. = 100)

Compared to the rest of the nation, per-capita income in the South plunged because of the economic losses and disruptions of the Civil War and then remained stagnant for the rest of the nineteenth century.

	1860	1880	1900
Region			
Northeast	139	141	137
North Central	68	98	103
South	72	51	51
West	—	190	163

Source: Adopted from Douglas C. North, *Growth and Welfare in the American Past: A New Economic History* (Englewood Cliffs, N.J.: Prentice-Hall, 1966), Table 11, p. 94.

amounted to about $1.1 billion, or 40 percent of the 1860 total. The transportation and manufacturing sectors were restored to or exceeded 1860 levels by 1870, but the rest of the economy was not pulled along. Manufacturing produced a very small fraction of the regional income of the South and employed less than 10 percent of its workforce. The agricultural heart of the economy, commodity crop production, did not quickly return to prewar levels. As measured by the per-capita output of crops in the lower South, agricultural production had regained only 60 percent of its 1859 levels by the 1870s and about 75 percent by the end of the century. Moreover, rates of per-capita growth in commodity production steadily fell until a stagnant level of 0.3 percent was reached in the 1890s. Basic to this dismal performance were the long-range consequences of the two other blows to the Southern economy in the 1860s—the end of slavery and a decisive slowdown in the rise of the international demand for cotton.

From the perspective of the slaveowners, emancipation meant the uncompensated loss of an economic investment with a market value in 1860 of $1.6 billion. In the heartland of the former Confederacy—South Carolina, Georgia, Alabama, Mississippi, and Louisiana—this loss represented 46 percent of the total wealth in 1860. However, from the perspective of the slaves, and the Southern economy as a whole, emancipation was not an absolute capital loss. Rather, in economic terms, freedom gave back to the former slaves the ownership of the capitalized labor that had been embodied in their persons as slave property. The freed population now owned its own labor and the right to any capital that its labor could produce. Self-ownership meant, above all else, that the freedmen refused to work as if they were still slaves. Because they were free, blacks could now limit their labor participation. The number of hours worked by black women and children declined by about 50 percent and those of the men by 20 percent. By assuming much greater control over their living and working conditions than was possible under slavery, blacks reduced their per-capita labor by between 28 percent and 37 percent. Because about 70 percent of prewar Southern labor had been supplied by blacks, this postwar reduction in hours worked was by itself a fundamental factor in the fall of physical productivity.

Of the same order of magnitude in terms of depressing Southern income was the slackening off in the world demand for cotton. This demand had grown at an average annual rate of 5 percent in the thirty years before the Civil War. In the same time span after the war the annual rate was down to 1.3 percent. The nineteenth-century boom in cotton textiles was over and demand was stagnant. Yet, the South, as it regained market shares lost during the war, produced more bales each year. The two million bales produced in 1866 had tripled by 1880 and quadrupled by 1890. It was a buyer's market, and prices steadily fell. By the 1880s, the purchasing power of a bale was half that of the late 1860s. As for the impact on the Southern economy, had cotton demand continued to expand at the prewar rate, the per-capita income of the South in 1880 would have been one-third higher.

The above factors—war damage, the withdrawal of black labor, and less favorable demand conditions for cotton—were all beyond the control of individual planters. Together, these shocks virtually guaranteed the sharp decline of the Southern economy after the war. However, the persistence of Southern poverty and regional backwardness was to a great extent the result of policies pursued by planters.

Throughout the Civil War decade, the planters maintained their disproportionate share of the South's landed property. In 1870 the wealthiest 5 percent of Southerners owned 40 percent of the land, and the top 20 percent close to 75 percent. Neither the membership nor landed power of the planter class had changed as a result of the war. What had changed, of course, were the relations of this class to its prewar labor supply, the slaves. The fact of black freedom defined the central problem of the postwar planters: how to ensure that a formerly bound labor force would continue to work the planter's land in the production of those agricultural staples in which the South had a competitive advantage in world markets.

Southern planters were able to block their former slaves from abandoning staple production and shifting into a peasant-type agriculture geared to the production of food. Concessions to black demands had to be made, but the planters owned the essential means of production—tools, draft animals, and, above all, the land. Once the threat of congressional Reconstruction was over by 1877, the planters then combined these economic advantages with their control of politics and the legal system to fashion a political economy shaped to serve their own class interests. Everyone knew how class control was maintained. As a black cropper aptly summarized it: "De landlord is landlord, de politicians is landlord, de judge is landlord, de shurf is landlord, ever-'body is landlord, en we ain' got nothin!!"[21] The regional consequences were a Southern economy that lacked the flexibility and incentives to move away from an overreliance on a few cash crops. Between 1860 and 1900, the Southern population grew twice as fast as the amount of land brought under cultivation did. Without massive outmigration or economic diversification within the South, the bulk of the population remained tied to the land and locked into a system of production that condemned them to poverty and indebtedness.

Sharecropping was the new social form of organizing labor and agricultural production in the postwar South. When it initially appeared in the late 1860s, sharecropping represented a defeat for the planters. Out of a desire for both economic efficiency and social control, the planters had tried to maintain large, centralized units of production with the gang labor of their former slaves. As we saw in Chapter 7, the effort failed because of the resistance of the freedmen. Although most freedmen did not become independent farmers, they did succeed in breaking up the old plantations into

Table 8.4 Distribution of Farm Size in the Cotton South, 1860–1870

Although planters did not lose ownership of their land after the Civil War, the desire of the freedmen to work their own plots of land resulted in the breaking up of large plantation units into smaller farm units.

	PERCENTAGE OF FARMS		PERCENTAGE OF IMPROVED ACREAGE	
	1860	1870	1860	1870
Improved Acres				
3–49	36.9	60.9	7.4	20.2
50–99	24.2	19.8	12.0	19.6
100–499	32.0	17.2	47.6	49.1
500 +	6.9	2.1	33.0	11.0

Source: Adapted from Roger L. Ransom and Richard Sutch, *One Kind of Freedom: The Economic Consequences of Emancipation* (New York: Cambridge University Press, 1977), Table 4.5, p. 71.

much smaller units of production. As shown in Table 8.4, the size of Southern farms shrank quickly after the war. By 1880 less than 10 percent of Southern land was worked by gang labor on large plots.

The planters were right. The reduction in farm size did result in a loss of efficiency. The crop output per manhour of the former slaves declined about 30 percent between 1860 and 1880. Nonetheless, the freedmen were decidedly better off. Because they were no longer slaves, blacks could now claim that portion of their output beyond mere subsistence, which formerly had been expropriated by the masters. They were able to keep a lot more of what they produced. By one recent estimate, black farmers in 1879 kept 56 percent of their output, whereas as slaves on large plantations in 1859 they were provided with only 22 percent of their output in the form of subsistence. Thus, despite the drop in Southern output after the war, blacks improved their economic position. Per-capita income for black farmers in 1879 was 30 percent higher than the "income" they had received as subsistence on the plantations in 1859.

Whether measured by an increase in leisure time or a material rise in standards of living, sharecropping meant sizable gains for the freedmen. Nonetheless, planters were quick to see how the economic logic of sharecropping favored them in the long run. Because their wealth was now fixed in their land, not their labor, they pursued an economic strategy of increasing labor intensity so as to squeeze the greatest value out of an acre. The strategy worked: In 1860 the ratio of blacks to every 100 improved acres on the large plantations had been just 11:1; in 1880 the ratio was 27:1. What the shift in these ratios indicates was a concerted effort to increase the productivity of the land by putting more labor to work on it.

This pronounced switch in the economic incentives of wealthholders was central to the major structural changes in Southern agriculture associated with sharecropping. It was in the economic self-interest of the landlords to keep rented plots of land as small as possible in order to increase labor intensity. Thus, the average size of Southern farms fell by 59 percent from 1860 to 1900. In turn, small farms were highly correlated with rental and sharecropping arrangements. In the cotton South, three-fourths of all sharecropped farms in 1890 and two-thirds of all rented farms, were under 50 acres. In contrast, only 14 percent of farms operated by their owners were that small.

A large drop in food production also accompanied the decline in farm size. Per-capita production of food crops fell by 50 percent in the cotton South in the generation after the Civil War. Cotton yielded a cash return per acre two or three times that of any other crop, and the smaller the plot the greater was the concentration in cotton production. In an agrarian economy in which an estimated 55 percent to 75 percent of all farmers were dependent on credit to get through the crop year, there was probably little choice but to plant cotton, the only cash crop in most areas of the South. Particularly for croppers and renters, whose plots of land were too small to allow for both the food crops needed for self-sufficiency and the cash crop needed to pay off debts, cotton was the only choice.

By the late nineteenth century, the indebtedness of croppers and tenants had become proverbial. The key mechanism here was the crop-lien system. Crop liens were a form of agricultural credit. Defeat in the Civil War had wiped out Southern capital reserves, and working capital remained very scarce for the rest of the century. Those who had capital to lend were thus in a commanding position. Because slaves were no longer available as collateral, the only form of security that lenders would accept was a lien on the cotton crop. Cotton was nonperishable, easily stored, and readily marketable at fairly predictable prices. Gaining access to credit and winning control over the cotton crop consequently were the fundamental issues in the political economy of the postwar South. Planters, merchants, and laborers all struggled to win political power in order to shape that economy in their own best interests. Until the end of congressional Reconstruction, no clear-cut victor had emerged. After 1877, however, there was little doubt that the laborers were the losers.

The collapse of congressional Reconstruction removed the protection of labor liens that the freedmen had secured under the Republican state governments. Merchants were also losers. The Democratic or redeemer legislatures extended what had always been the landlord's superior lien for recovering rent due on his land to also include the value of any supplies advanced by the landlord. Merchants, placed at a competitive disadvantage in the black belts, then expanded their credit operations in the hill country, where they had a monopoly on servicing white farmers. There, merchants did not have to assume the financial risk of losing their crop collateral while waiting in line until the planters' claims on first rent and then supplies were met. At the end of the line were the sharecroppers.

By the 1880s, nearly all the Southern states legally defined croppers as wage laborers. Under the law a mere employee of the landlord, the cropper had no control over the land he worked and no legal claim on the crop he produced. In sharp distinction to a share tenant, who paid the landlord a specified share of the crop as rent, the sharecropper paid no rent. He was a wage employee, not a renter. And he was only entitled to those wages, usually in the form of one-half the crop produced, that *might be left over* after the planters and merchants had disposed of the crop and taken their shares. In effect, the law placed all the financial risk upon the cropper. The cotton he produced represented an interest-free loan to the landlord that would be paid back only if the landlord's financial needs were first met.

In practice there was usually little, if any, net share wages left over for the cropper. Debt repayments on advances for the planting year consumed most of the income of croppers, as well as that of many tenants. These repayments went to merchants and merchant-planters who monopolized local sources of credit. About two-thirds of all the rural towns in the cotton belt were served by just one or two general stores. Merchants were thus in a position to convert their near monopoly over credit, something that most farmers had to have, into a more generalized monopolistic power of control. In return for furnishing credit, the merchant demanded and got the exclusive right to furnish all the farmer's supplies and to market his cotton. Apart from locking in his market, the merchant gained the higher profit margins of selling to farmers on credit. The merchant's capital, ultimately of Northern origin, cost him around 10 percent per year. This cost was more than covered by charging credit customers 30 percent more for food purchases than cash customers and by levying a yearly carrying charge of 50 percent to 60 percent on all debts outstanding. Because the security for these mounting debts was the cotton crop, the merchant had a double incentive to encourage, if not actually legally coerce, his debtors to plant as much cotton as possible. Cotton production was a prerequisite for receiving an advance in the first place and for carrying debts over from one year to the next. And the greater the concentration on cotton, the greater was the likelihood that the farmer would rely on the merchant year after year for expensive food supplies.

Once it took hold, the crop-lien system snared farmers in an endless cycle of debt. Year after year, Southern farmers bought dear, sold cheap, and wound up in debt to the furnishing merchant. As its production doubled from 1870 to 1890 in the face of stagnant demand, cotton dropped by half in price. In the same two decades, the cost of the farmer's supplies declined by only 20 percent.

In addition to these unfavorable market conditions, a web of legal sanctions limited the chances of escaping the system or starting anew. By the end of the nineteenth century, Southern courts had ruled that a tenant or cropper forfeited any share in a crop that he voluntarily abandoned, permitted unpaid liens on a previous year's crop to be applied against next year's, extended protection for lenders to cover a borrower's personal property in the form of a chattel mortgage, and provided criminal penalties for enticing away any laborer already under contract. Croppers who tried to beat the system by selling crops they had raised before their creditors got their share were jailed for grand larceny.

The crop liens had to be renegotiated every year, but croppers and tenants had little choice but to sign them if they wanted to survive economically and feed their families. Farm-to-farm turnover of labor still occurred, but it amounted to little more than a recycling of frustrations for those trapped by debt and lack of opportunities. The threat of any significant mobility, especially for blacks, was met with imprisonment for debt, whippings, and lynchings. Over 100 blacks were killed in one Southern county as part of a campaign to stop the migration to Kansas in the late 1870s. When legal and market coercions failed, planters fell back on their monopoly of violence to keep blacks tied to the land as a source of cheap, exploitable labor.

The spread of tenancy and cropping, as seen in Table 8.5, accelerated in the late nineteenth-century South. By 1900, 74 percent of all black farm operators in the South, and 35 percent of all white operators, were tenants or croppers. This racial unbalance also characterized those at the very bottom of the agrarian economy. Blacks were twice as likely as whites to be farm laborers hiring out for day wages. Blacks were obviously bunched on the bottom rungs of an agricultural ladder of opportunity that moved

Table 8.5   Rise of Southern Tenancy and Cropping, 1880–1900
          (in thousands)

Especially during the depression decade of the 1890s, a growing number of Southern farmers lost their land and became tenants and croppers.

	1880	1890	1900
Number of Farms	1531	1836	2620
Tenants/Croppers	554	706	1231
Percentage of Tenants/Croppers	36	38	47

Source: Compiled from *Historical Statistics,* Series K-109–153.

upward from laborer to cropper and from tenant to owner. In most cases, overt and legal racial discrimination was not needed to keep blacks at the bottom. For example, wages for unskilled labor were comparable for both races. It would be absurd, however, to deny that racism was not a major factor in perpetuating black poverty. Wages may have been roughly equal for both races, but access to better paying jobs was not. In the cotton South of 1890, the percentage of male blacks in basically menial jobs (agricultural labor and low-skilled nonfarm occupations) was twice that of whites—61 percent to 31 percent. The racial discrimination that did not appear in wage scales had already occurred.

Slavery, an institution that Southern whites defended on racial grounds, left blacks with little of the training, education, and economic assets needed to compete successfully in the postwar South. More importantly, these black disadvantages and inequalities persisted after emancipation. Whites consistently and, when necessary, violently opposed black initiatives in achieving literacy, acquiring or renting land, and marketing the artisan skills they had learned as slaves. For whites without capital, such as the antebellum tenant in North Carolina who fought for the Confederacy because he would "rather git killed than have all these niggers freed and claimin' they as good as I is,"[22] the overriding objective was the preservation of a self-respect made possible only by consigning blacks to a position of inferiority. For whites with capital and land, the goal was more one of economic self-interest. By limiting black access to land, education, and the trades, they assured themselves a cheap and tractable labor supply for commercial agriculture. And because blacks comprised close to half the workforce in the lower South, their presence provided a reserve army of labor that could be used by management to discipline white labor and hold down the wages of both races.

Nate Shaw, an Alabama farmer born in 1885, left a memorable account of growing up black in the rural poverty of the South at the turn of the century. His former-slave father, Hayes, moved around and worked at a variety of odd jobs after the war. He was able at first to accumulate a bit of cash, but he never did establish himself as an independent farmer. Although Nate blamed his father for not buying some pine land when it was cheap in the 1870s, he also recognized that whites used their control of the economy to grind down black initiative. In Nate's words, his father

> had money but—whenever the colored man prospered too fast in this country under the old rulins, they worked every figure to cut you down, cut your britches off you. So, it might have been to his way of thinkin that it weren't no use in climbin too fast; weren't no use in climbin slow, neither, if they was goin to take everything you worked for when you got too high.[23]

Nate watched and learned as his father was "cleaned up twice." The first time Shaw was tricked by Lloyd Albee, his furnishing agent. Albee gave Shaw oral permission to sell a cow owned by Albee and mortgaged to Shaw. After the sale was completed and Shaw brought him his money, Albee immediately sued Shaw for selling mortgaged property without a written release. The purpose of the ruse was to force Shaw to leave his landlord and work on Albee's land. When Shaw refused to move, he was jailed by Albee who then "done come to the house and taken everything my daddy had in the way of stock and farm tools."[24] A few years later, another white creditor hauled away Shaw's horse, wagon, and fattening hog when a cotton crop reduced by drought was insufficient to cover the advance.

Toughened and embittered by what had happened to his father, Nate was determined to avoid what he called living like a slave—that is, being in a position where "he had to take what the white people gived to get along." After years of cropping for halves with nothing to show for it, Nate bought a mule in 1910. It took his savings of four years from weaving baskets and cutting wood for whites, and a last minute $20 loan from his father-in-law, for Nate to come up with the $100 purchase price. The mule was worth it. Now, as Nate put it, "I could rent me a little land and go to work and run my own affairs." The ownership of the mule made the difference. A landless farmer who could offer a landlord only his labor and that of his family was such a poor credit risk that a cropping arrangement was the best that could be hoped for. A farmer with a mule had the essential asset he needed to bargain for a fixed-rental tenancy, which gave him much more control over his farming operation. In Nate's words: "I commenced makin a heavier crop, makin a better crop, handlin my own affairs. Paid cash rent and made a profit from my farmin: I come up from the bottom then."[25]

The Nate Shaws and others persevered. Some, like Nate, struggled to acquire the minimal means of production, achieve economic self-sufficiency, and accumulate some property. Others, like Nate's brother, Peter, consciously lowered their material expectations so as to avoid the pain and humiliation of having whites take their gains away from them by manipulating the system. "He made up his mind," Nate said of Peter, "That he weren't goin to have anything and after that, why, nothing could hurt him."[26] By severely limiting his economic dealings with whites, and accepting a hard, plain life, Peter won a sense of personal freedom in a system designed to deprive him of any autonomy.

Nearly all blacks turned to family and kin to absorb some of the blows of poverty. Distinctive patterns of household composition set apart rural blacks from their white counterparts. At both the beginning of the family cycle, when newlyweds first set up their households, and at the end, when the children were grown and departed, rural blacks were more likely than whites to have aged relatives and unemployed outsiders living with them. In the absence of public institutions to provide for the homeless, unemployed, and dependent elderly, the black household assumed a caretaking role for its friends and relatives.

In the face of white opposition, black accomplishments in the first generation of freedom were nothing short of remarkable. The major economic advances, those that were a direct result of emancipation itself, were largely won by 1880, but gains continued to be made in a number of areas: For every 100 blacks in 1860, only two were enrolled in school; by 1880 that number had risen to 34. Black literacy rose from 20 percent in 1870 to over 70 percent by 1910. Although cropping and tenancy were still the norm in 1900, one-quarter of black farmers had become successful enough to

A Southern Black Family, ca. 1900. Rural black families in the postwar South were large, and they performed a caretaking function by taking in neighboring kin who were unable to provide for themselves. (The Bettmann Archive)

own the land they worked. Their holdings were small, and blacks were rarely able to obtain the capital needed for farm improvements. Still, the economic distance covered since 1870 was considerable: starting from a position where they held virtually no land, blacks advanced to the ownership of 38 percent of the South's farms in 1900.

As blacks were coming up from the bottom, many white farmers were coming down from a secure position in the middle of the Southern economy. Before the Civil War, about 80 percent of all white farmers owned their land. The bulk of these farmers, especially in the upcountry, were nonslaveholders who conceded the market production of cotton to planters. No more than 10 percent of the South's cotton in 1860 was produced by white farmers. By the mid-1870s, that percentage was up to 40 percent, and at the end of the century it was over 60 percent. In the same period, from 1860 to 1900, the percentage of whites who no longer owned their farms increased by 80 percent. More than one-third were croppers or tenants in 1900. The market involvement that had been avoided before the war became after the war an economic trap in which thousands of white farmers lost their land and their independence.

The yeomanry first fell into the trap in the period just after the close of the war. They both pushed themselves in and were pulled in by others. Because of wartime shortages, cotton prices were extraordinarily high in the mid-1860s. Cotton that fetched a price of 11¢ per pound in 1860 went for 84¢ in 1865. It was all the more tempting for a small farmer to try to take advantage of these prices because of his wartime debts and losses. Loans to the Confederacy were now worthless, along with its currency, and heavy war taxes and the plundering of both armies had destroyed much of the wealth of the yeomanry, most notably their livestock. Many of the yeomanry therefore gambled on surrendering self-sufficiency for a concentration on cotton and the possibility of a market windfall.

Had cotton prices remained high, the gamble might have paid off. Instead, they broke in the late 1860s and fell steadily through the 1870s. They hit 10¢ a pound in

1879, traded at that range in the 1880s, and collapsed at 5¢ in the mid-1890s. Long before then, however, many farmers had become entangled in the crop-lien system. The same debts that first drove the yeomanry into the cotton market after the war also necessitated an advance from a furnishing agent. One bad crop year, and both 1866 and 1868 saw widespread failures in cotton production, was all it took for the farmer's initial advance to become a perpetual debt. Then, the only chance to ever get out of debt was to plant cotton year after year. What was economically rational for any given farmer was economically irrational for farmers as a group. Individuals, by producing more cotton, depressed the prices all farmers received. Falling prices forced more and more farmers into dependency on a credit advance. If the farmer had land as collateral, a mortgage on the farm was added to the lien on the crops. Typical of the consequences was the story of S. R. Simonton's account with the firm of T. R. Patrick. Simonton, a white farmer in South Carolina, opened his account in 1887. In the first year, he was debited over $900 for expenditures while he was earning credits of just over $300. He signed a note to carry the unpaid balance of $600 and then, for the next seven years, sank more deeply into debt. His debt reached $1600 by 1894 and was settled by a foreclosure on his farm mortgage. Simonton was reduced to tenancy.

The economic dependency that resulted in Simonton's loss of his farm was foreshadowed for other Southern farmers in the reversal that occurred between 1860 and 1880 in the antebellum relationship between crop mix and farm size in the South. Because the yeomanry traditionally stressed food production first, the ratio of cotton to corn, in proportion to farm size in 1860, was low. The opposite was true in 1880, especially on rented and sharecropped farms. As a result, small farmers lost a foundation critical to their independence—self-sufficiency in foodstuffs. Over 60 percent of all farms in the cotton South of 1880 failed to produce enough grain to meet the consumption needs of family members. And, as a region, the South had shifted from being a net exporter of food to a net importer.

Per-capita production of livestock, down by one-half since 1860, was also markedly lower in 1880. Southern farmers were unable to rebuild their herds after the war and, again, the economic incentives of the crop-lien system help explain the food deficiencies. It was often cheaper for Southern landlords and merchants to import grain and meat from the Midwest than to purchase them locally. Railroads and the telegraph made it economically feasible both to shift cotton markets into the interior of the South and to import food from outside the South. Just as it was in the economic interest of Southern merchants to make their client farmers dependent upon them for their food, so also was it advantageous for Northern creditors to make their client merchants in the South dependent upon them for the food with which to stock their stores. Feeder-lot meat, hogs fed on Midwestern corn, followed the southerly flow of Northern capital. Meanwhile, a concerted political effort led by black-belt planters was closing off the open range of the South.

Farmers and stockowners in the prewar South, in marked contrast to the North, did not have to fence in their livestock on their private property. Instead, the burden and costs of fencing was on the farmer who had to fence in his crops. This arrangement reflected the economic value of livestock, which in 1860 was roughly equal to the combined value of all Southern crops. It also revealed the limits to the political power of the planters. Anyone's private land, even that of a wealthy planter, was legally a quasi-public grazing and roaming area for the hogs and cattle of the common whites.

The planters were in effect furnishing free economic resources that their poorer neighbors were using. In addition to virtually eliminating any costs in raising livestock, the open range also provided tariff-free corridors through which the livestock could be moved to market in long trail drives. Profits in livestock raising were high, and they were also a bonus. Common whites did not need the profits to survive economically and to enjoy a diet that contained one-third more animal protein than a modern American one. Outsiders called them lazy, but perhaps these detractors were envious. With their wealth literally wandering unattended in the woods, common whites could afford plenty of leisure time, and they could take the market or leave it.

Starting with a series of county option laws in 1866, by which a majority of the local electorate could vote to restrict livestock, the range was gradually closed after the war. The pattern of enclosure spread from the black belts to the upcountry, where farmers in some of the hill counties managed to keep the range open until well into the twentieth century. The enclosure movement reached its height in the 1880s and 1890s. As with so many other issues in the South's political economy that remained contested during political reconstruction, the planters won their greatest victories only after they had overturned congressional Reconstruction.

The new fencing laws were crucial in destroying the lifestyle of antebellum common whites and in driving them into the market under terms of dependency. The days of free foraging for livestock and long trial drives over private land were over. The laws also ensured that most former slaves would be denied the basis for a subsistence economy under their own control. At the end of the war many freedmen, such as Hayes Shaw, raised and hunted all the meat their families needed. Said Nate Shaw, ''That's all he done—raised meat to eat and what he didn't raise he got in the woods.''[27] The closing of the range, strict new laws against trespassing on private property, new licensing provisions for hunting and fishing, and criminal statutes, such as Mississippi's ''Pig Law'' of 1876, which made the theft of a hog or cow a grand larceny, were all part of a political campaign to eliminate sources of autonomy for the poor of both races.

The legislation had its desired effect. In its most blatant form, a black jailed for stealing a pig could be put to work in a chain gang on a public road or rented out to private industry under the convict-lease system. Labor, whether public or private, could hardly be cheaper. In a larger context, and regardless of race, the poor lost economic control over their lives and became wage laborers working on someone else's land to produce a cash crop already committed to yet another someone else.

Some of the poor were driven completely off the land. As a result, Southern industrialists now had access to a cheap and predictable source of labor. Beginning in the late 1870s, economically desperate families of whites in the Carolina and Georgia piedmont signed up for work in the textile factories. Slavery was gone, but the binding constraints of debt, combined with legislation that came close to manufacturing poverty, furnished an effective substitute for coercing market labor from both races.

Thus the South, despite its apparent divergence from national development because of its legacy of defeat and poverty, fully shared in what contemporary Northerners were calling the great social question of post–Civil War America: the problem of capital versus labor. Disguised in the South by the overwhelmingly agrarian character of its economy, the problem was much more obvious in the factories and cities of the North.

Table 8.6 Population Increase by Size of Place, 1860–1900
(in thousands)

In the decades after the Civil War, large cities with a population greater than 250,000 were growing seven times faster than rural America.

	POPULATION		PERCENTAGE
	1860	*1900*	OF CHANGE
Size of Place			
250,000+	1,646	10,935	+564
2,500–249,999	4,570	19,223	+321
Rural	25,227	45,835	+82

Source: Compiled from *Historical Statistics*, Series A-57–72.

The North's Fusion of City, Factory, and Immigrant

The village and farm gave way to the city and factory. Much of U.S. history in the generation after the Civil War is encompassed in that generalization. The last federal census that registered a majority of the workforce in agriculture occurred in 1870. From then through 1900, the percentage of agricultural workers steadily declined, from 53 percent to 37 percent. As Americans left the farms, they joined migrants from abroad in the burgeoning cities. Between 1860 and 1900, the percentage of urbanized Americans, defined as those living in a place with a population of 2,500 and over, doubled—from 20 percent to 40 percent. The relative pace of urbanization was actually higher in the antebellum decades, but in terms of sheer numbers, postwar urbanization was much greater. Americans were massing together in compact areas on an unprecedented scale. Many cities doubled in population every decade and, as seen in Table 8.6, growth was greatest in the largest cities.

There is no necessary connection between urbanization and industrialization. Large cities, in the U.S. and elsewhere, clearly predated industrialization. In 1860 only 10 of America's 93 cities with a population greater than 10,000 had any sizable industrial sector. However, after the Civil War, these two processes—one concerned with the massing of population and the other with the massing of the production and consumption of manufactured goods—became linked. Each reinforced the other in such a way as to accelerate the growth of both. By 1900 about 90 percent of America's industrial output came out of urban factories.

Technological innovations were indispensable to this linkage of urbanization and industrialization. Before American cities could mushroom in size, the physical constraints of the antebellum walking city had to be overcome. In the absence of mass transit—that is, a system of moving people according to a schedule along a set route at a standardized fee—the size of cities was bounded by the distance that people could walk to and from work, a radius of roughly two miles. The invention that first allowed cities to spread outward was the horse-drawn omnibus. Little more than a stagecoach adapted to urban use, the omnibus was introduced in Manhattan in 1827. By mid-century, horse railways, coaches pulled along rails, were competing with the omnibus in major Eastern cities.

Both of these were gradually replaced after the war by new forms of mass transit. The key to the change was the shift from animate to inanimate power. Cable cars pulled by underground wires attached by pulleys to a steam engine made their first appearance in San Francisco in 1873; the most extensive use of cable cars was in Chicago during the 1880s. A major technological breakthrough came in 1886, when electric power was first applied to urban transport. Trolley cars, vehicles powered by electricity drawn from overhead wires, ushered in the age of the electric railways. Made possible by the development of massive electric dynamos capable of generating the continuous power needed to propel several cars along the same track, the trolleys quickly multiplied on electrified networks throughout urban America. From 1,260 miles in 1890, less than 20 percent of all street railway mileage, electrified track jumped to 22,000 miles in 1902, 99 percent of the total. In response to this sequential development of mass transit, cities expanded as commuting distances steadily increased. Boston, for example, enlarged its settlement radius from two miles in 1850 to ten by 1900. In order to maintain administrative control, as well as to add to their tax bases, cities annexed the growing residential areas that pushed outward from the original downtown cores.

The steam engines and electric generators that permitted the horizontal expansion of cities also pulled industry into an urban setting. As we saw in Chapter 1, reliance on water power limited the choices for manufacturing sites to places near a source of falling water. Antebellum industry was thus decentralized in factory towns built along the banks of rivers. With the rise in steam power after 1850, the manufacturing pattern became one of increasing concentration. The transition in power sources occurred between 1850 and 1870. As a result of a seven-fold increase in steam horsepower used in manufacturing during these two decades, water was finally displaced as the prime motive power in American industry. The cities were the obvious sites for the industrial concentration that was now possible.

As places with centralized access to capital, labor, and transportation, cities had inherent advantages over the countryside in attracting manufacturing that now relied on coal-fired steam to drive its machinery. The rivers and railroads that had accounted for the commercial prosperity of the cities fed their manufacturing success by hauling in fuel and raw materials and hauling out finished goods. Eastern cities tended to specialize in the production of consumer staples and heavy industrial items, Midwestern cities in the processing of agricultural goods, and those in the West in the extraction and refining of mineral and lumber resources.

Steam power created the nineteenth-century urban factory with which we are most familiar—the rectangular, multistoried, brick fortress. Gloomy, noisy, and poorly ventilated, the factory's primary function was to house machinery; but it also contained, for ten to twelve hours a day, six days a week, the keepers of the machines, an industrial work force drawn increasingly from immigrants. Innovations in industrial technology were concentrating machines and immigrants in the inner city just as innovations in transportation technology were dispersing the middle and business classes in a series of residential rings around the inner city. The city, the factory, and the immigrant became linked together in a common process of industrialization.

The cities grew in tandem with a pace of immigration that surged after the Civil War. An average of four million immigrants a decade entered the U.S. from 1870 to 1900, a rate that was twice as great as the decennial average of two million from 1840 to 1870. Most of the immigrants settled in the cities. By 1890, when only 26 percent of native-stock Americans lived in cities, 62 percent of the foreign-born were urbanized. First- and second-generation immigrants, 80 percent of the population in New York and Chicago in 1900, were to a great extent the urban Americans.

Cities and immigrants had a mutual attraction for each other. As they continually expanded through annexation, cities created a voracious demand for labor. The entire range of municipal services—streets, sewers, schools, hospitals, and transportation systems—had to be built virtually from scratch. These projects involved primarily hand labor, and needed hundreds of thousands of manual workers. Meanwhile, industrial concentration in the cities was also multiplying opportunities for unskilled labor. If nothing else, immigrants did have labor in abundance to offer in urban markets.

In contrast to antebellum immigration, which can be characterized as a folk migration, postwar immigration was a labor migration. The change was from a movement of families to one of unattached adults. About 70 percent of all the English, Scandinavians, and Germans who arrived in the 1840s and 1850s came over in family groups. For every adult male who traveled alone, one migrated in a family unit. By the 1880s, this even ratio in continental migration had shifted drastically. Among the English, for example, it then stood at 8:1 in favor of unattached males. The greater speed, safety, and cheapness of trans-Atlantic travel on steamships by the 1880s also made possible a good deal more remigration. Measured against the pre–Civil War figures, the percentage of immigrants who subsequently returned to their homeland doubled—to 25 percent—in the thirty years after the war. Many of these returners were part of a floating pool of trans-Atlantic laborers who responded to seasonal shifts in wage rates on the continent and in America. Their search for jobs and good wages carried them first from their local villages to a European city and then across the Atlantic and back again in a cycle tied to wage conditions.

This continual movement reflected a lack of skills and the need to take temporary jobs. In another distinguishing characteristic of postwar immigration, the skill level of the immigrants was markedly lower than that of earlier immigrants. At mid-century, only 15 percent of immigrants were classified on arrival as laborers and servants. By 1880 that figure rose to 27 percent and by 1910 to 60 percent. Increasingly, there was a hard edge of desperation in the motives behind migrating to America. "My father had left," recalled Harry Roskolenko, "because he got tired of being a conscript soldier and of being beaten, scarred, and humiliated."[28] Like most of the one-and-a-half million Russian and eastern European Jews who came to America from 1870 to 1914, the father, Barnett, was fleeing poverty, military conscription, and pogroms, organized and murderous persecutions of Jews. Streaming into America with the Jews were millions of Catholic peasants from southern and eastern Europe. The political reunification of Italy in 1859–1860, and Turkish defeats in the Russo-Turkish War of 1877, removed earlier restraints on emigration from Italy and the Balkans. At the same time, nations in northern and western Europe, concerned over possible labor shortages for their own programs of heavy industrialization, and anxious to retain their conscript population as Europe became locked into a set of military alliances, placed restrictions on emigration.

The result was a dramatic change in immigration flows to America. Northern and western Europeans comprised over 90 percent of total antebellum immigration, declined to 68 percent in 1880, and then fell sharply to 19 percent by 1910. More than

Table 8.7   Net Migration By Decade in the Northeast, 1870–1900
          (in thousands)

More native whites left the industrializing Northeast than entered between 1870 and 1900.
The mass arrival of immigrants from Europe and a much smaller flow of blacks from the
South account for the increase in the population of the Northeast.

	PERCENTAGE OF INCREASE OR DECREASE			
	Native Whites	*Foreign-Born*	*Blacks*	*Total*
Decade				
1870–80	− 788.2	+ 1042.2	+ 44.5	+ 298.6
1880–90	− 722.8	+ 2293.9	+ 62.1	+ 1633.0
1890–00	− 56.6	+ 2088.2	+ 144.3	+ 2176.2

Source: Compiled from *Historical Statistics*, Series C-25–75.

Note: As defined here, the Northeast includes the former free states east of the Mississippi.

compensating for this falloff was the concomitant rise in Italians, Slavs, Jews, and
Balkan peoples. The huge increase in southern and eastern Europeans came after 1880.
From less than 10 percent of the total in 1880 their numbers swelled twenty times over,
to 70 percent of all immigrants by 1910. The half-brother of the wife of Barnett
Roskolenko spoke for nearly all of them when he wrote his American relatives at the
turn of the century: "He wants to come to America," said Barnett. "He has four sons
and a wife and they are hungry. . . ."[29] Much more so than the relatively better-off
northern and western Europeans, this new wave of immigrants saw opportunity in the
day labor and unskilled industrial employment that America offered. As a Chicago
Pole reported to his mother in Poland, "Nowhere is life a delight, misery everywhere,
in America it is no good either, but still better than in our country."[30]

     The immigrant flow followed the jobs. These jobs were concentrated in the ur-
banized industrial centers in the Northeast and Midwest, the home regions for close to
90 percent of the foreign-born in 1890. Wherever possible, the native-born shunned the
jobs grasped by the immigrants. As seen in Table 8.7, native whites were leaving the
industrializing East for land in the West after the Civil War. But because even more
immigrants and blacks were arriving to take their places, the Northeast still had net
gains in population from migration. The net gain rose sharply in the 1890s when an
agricultural depression shut off the Western safety valve for the native stock.

     Despite the attempts to preserve a frontier-rural pattern of life, the major avenue of
mobility in post–Civil War America ran from the farm to the city. For every urban
dweller who moved to a farm between 1860 and 1900, twenty farmers moved to a city.
During these four decades, both the urban population and nonfarm jobs were growing
over four times faster than the rural population and the farm labor force. Farms were
still productive; indeed, they were *too* productive. The man-hours needed to produce a
bushel of wheat, for example, declined from 35 to 15 between 1840 and 1900. Sons
and daughters whose labor had been replaced by combines and reapers headed for the
cities in a migration that excelled in numbers even the flow from Europe. Once in the
cities, however, the native-born succeeded in avoiding the dirty, dangerous work of

common labor and factory jobs. By 1900 America's industrial workforce was composed of immigrants and their children.

"Not every foreigner is a workingman, but in the cities, at least, it may almost be said that every workingman is a foreigner."[31] This observation in 1887 by Samuel Lane Loomis, a minister, accurately captured the importance of the immigrant to both the city and the factory. The foreign-born and their offspring composed two-thirds of the population in the large industrial cities of 1900, and they contributed just as disproportionately to the major industries, which relied chiefly on unskilled labor. Although barely 25 percent of the total male population, Americans of foreign and mixed parentage accounted for over 80 percent of the male workforce in textiles and 70 percent in metal manufacturing in 1907. The specific nationality of the workforce in heavy industry changed with each new wave of immigrants. Newcomers were typically assigned the lowest-paying and most physically demanding jobs. An elite of skilled workers, usually native-born and Protestant, remained at the top of the labor hierarchy, but at the bottom and in the middle ranks, ethnic turnover was rapid.

Despite all the turnover, a decided bunching of ethnic groups in certain types of work occurred. In the Boston of 1890, two-thirds of the Irish held manual laboring jobs, whereas one-half of the Germans and Canadians were in skilled jobs. In the early 1900s, 70 percent of the Slovaks went into coal mining. Over 60 percent of the Poles were in manufacturing and mining, as opposed to less than 30 percent of the South Italians. About one-half of all Serbs and one-third of all South Italians, but fewer than 10 percent of the Poles, were general laborers. Greeks were grouped in the personal-service trades and Jews in the ready-made clothing industry. Within individual industries, the same occupational concentration developed. The jobs of stillman helper, still cleaner, and fireman in the Indiana oil refineries, for example, were held almost exclusively by Croatians.

Ethnic stereotyping accounted for some of this bunching effect. Eastern Europeans—Poles, Slovaks, and Serbs—were typecast as physically strong but stupid and plodding and hence were favored for heavy industrial and mining jobs. Because of their presumed affinity for sunshine and the outdoors, Italians were considered particularly well-suited for street labor and construction gangs. It was thought that factory work, such as textiles and shoes, that required quick, repetitive movements made the most efficient use of Jews and southern Europeans who were allegedly more nimble and dexterous than the Slavs.

More fundamental than the crude system of ethnic classification in channeling immigrants into certain kinds of jobs was the actual way in which immigrants acquired jobs. Late-nineteenth-century labor markets were informal—that is, there were few organized means of recruitment, whether by companies or private agencies. What operated in its place was an informal system of family and kin networks that directed relatives and friends to jobs. The plant foreman had the responsibility for hiring, and the individuals he selected were sent to him and recommended by the men and women already working at the plant. In this way an initial ethnic beachhead in a given factory or line of work fed upon itself. The new job seekers were usually late arrivals in the same chain migration that had brought over the first ethnic wave of factory workers.

The specificity of ethnic settlement that we have already noted in the West also characterized immigrant neighborhoods in the Eastern cities. Representative in this regard were the Italians of Rochester, New York. Three-fourths of them came from particular provinces within three regions of southern Italy. A different chain operated for Kansas City, Missouri. Here, two-thirds of the Italians came from Sicily. For all the immigrant groups, the early arrivals attracted kin and village neighbors from Europe, provided them with temporary lodgings, and found them jobs by recommending the newcomers to their own foremen and managers. This recruitment of labor through bonds of ethnicity and kinship delivered millions of unskilled immigrants to the factory gates. Inside those gates, the growing demand was precisely for that semiskilled and unskilled labor that the immigrants could offer. The spread of machinery continually diluted craft skills and, especially after 1880, management subdivided much of the work process into a series of tasks that required no special skill. Just as was true of the immigrant and the city, the immigrant and the factory were mutually drawn to each other.

The immigrants largely fixed themselves in the factories. In turn, the location of a given factory, itself tied down to the source of steam power, greatly influenced where the immigrant workforce in that factory would live in the city. Most factories were within, or on the fringes of, the central business districts. These were also the areas that had the greatest supply of cheap housing, run-down tenements in which living accommodations were available by the room. Here was living space, and it was barely more than that, for the immigrants. Too poor to afford detached dwellings, and anxious to save money, either to bring back to Europe with them or to finance the passage to America of relatives, they were packed into the tenements. Drawn to the central city by affordable rents and factory jobs, the immigrants sorted themselves out in enclaves that clustered around the factories where they worked. Most Philadelphia workers in 1880, for example, lived within a mile of the factory in which they were employed; they had little choice. Urban transportation was available, but it was too costly relative to the low factory wages. Thus only 17 percent of the Philadelphia workers in 1880 commuted to their jobs on the horsecars; most walked. Because factory affiliation was more important than ethnicity in determining one's neighbors, scattered ethnic clusters in industrial areas, not large ethnic ghettoes, were the usual result.

The Industrial Revolution and Labor

Out of this mass of people, machinery, and factories came America's industrial revolution. Virtually any set of statistics confirms what was happening. From 1870 to 1900, the capital invested in manufacturing increased sixfold; overall manufacturing production, the horsepower output of power equipment in manufacturing, and railroad mileage all quadrupled; and the number of workers in manufacturing, mining, construction, and transportation nearly tripled. The quantum jump in steel production from 19,000 tons in 1867 to ten million in 1900 was the single best indicator of America's surge to industrial supremacy. Steel literally provided the structural underpinnings for the massive industrial growth.

Steel replaced iron and wood as the main component in American machinery and durable goods in the last third of the nineteenth century. The superiority of steel over wrought iron had been known for centuries. Steel was harder and had much greater tensile strength (the capability of withstanding forces tending to tear it apart). Not until the 1850s, however, was a process discovered that permitted steel to be produced in large quantities. Named the Bessemer process after its English inventor, Henry Bes-

The Bessemer Process in Operation. Bessemer converters, such as these in a mill in 1896, revolutionized the production of steel from pig iron. Steel, a rare and costly commodity in 1850, was cheap and plentiful by 1900 and had become the basic structural material in the industrialization of America. (Library of Congress)

semer, the new technology was quite simple in concept: rather than heating the surfaces of small batches of pig iron in order to burn off the carbon impurities that caused brittleness, air was forced through molten pig iron in large containers. As the iron oxidized or reacted with the air, enough heat was generated to keep the mixture liquid and to burn off the carbon. When conversion from iron to steel was completed, the white-hot mixture was poured into a series of rollers that squeezed and shaped it into rails and other finished forms. Large-volume, low-cost production was now feasible. Steel that would have taken a day or more to produce using the old process could be manufactured within a half-hour using the Bessemer process.

The technological revolution in the making of steel opened up vast markets for rails, beams, plate, tubing, nails, and wire. By the late 1880s, the market for nails alone was double the total output of steel in the early 1870s. Steel became a basic building material for other industries. It carried the weight of the massive locomotive engines, supported bridges and buildings, stamped out machine parts, encircled the prairies in barbed wire, and connected the communications system of telephones and telegraphs with strings of wire. The market breakthroughs followed the sharp drop in steel prices that set in by the mid-1870s. Steel used in rails fell from $100 a ton in 1873 to $50 in 1875, the year that Andrew Carnegie's Bessemer process plant, the Edgar Thompson works, began production. Steel continued to fall in price until it was going for $12 a ton in the late 1890s. Railroads and other consumers could now afford to use steel for its strength and versatility. The 100,000 miles of track already in place were relaid in steel, and an additional 100,000 miles of steel track were laid during the 1880s. The 2.5 million tons of structural steel being sold annually by 1900 tapped a construction market for girders and plates that was nonexistent a generation earlier. Steel, in conjunction with the development of steam power and electricity, changed the physical face of America. The changes could be seen in the soaring span of the Brooklyn Bridge, finished in the late 1870s with a center section constructed entirely of steel, and in the vertical thrusts of the city skyscrapers that started to climb upward in the 1880s and 1890s around their skeletons of steel.

In steel, as well as in other industries, the physical setting in which production occurred and the size of the work force employed there also changed. As late as 1870, the typical American manufacturing establishment was a small, family-owned shop employing, on the average, eight workers. Outside of textiles and some heavy industries, the use of power machinery was rare and the factory as a distinct architectural form hardly existed. A labor force in a given factory as large as the 400 to 500 who worked in the McCormick agricultural-equipment plant in Chicago was a decided exception. By 1900 over 1500 factories had payrolls of more than 500 workers each. The massing of labor in a fixed factory setting was the general rule everywhere. Measured by the average size of their labor force per plant, eleven of the sixteen largest industries more than doubled in size from 1870 to 1900.

The consolidation of labor, machinery, and capital proceeded as a unit. Heavily capitalized and mechanized firms with more than fifty workers accounted for 77 percent of the new manufacturing jobs created in Philadelphia from 1850 to 1880. Commenting on the industrial figures in the census of 1880, Carroll D. Wright, the first U.S. Commissioner of Labor, detected a trend that seemed to be irreversible:[32]

> In nearly all industries where the terms of the definition of a factory can apply, that is, where raw materials can be converted into finished goods by consecutive, harmonious processes carried along by a central power, the factory system had been adopted. . . . Most of these industries have been brought under the factory system during the past thirty years.

By the end of the century, factories, as distinct from what were now listed in the census as "hand and neighborhood industries," averaged 22 workers per plant and employed 88 percent of all manufacturing labor.

The growth of factories resulted from a series of related innovations in production, transportation, and distribution. In steel, as in textiles a generation earlier, the key innovation was the technological removal of bottlenecks at the point of production. What spinning machinery was to textiles, the Bessemer process was to steel. In meat packing, on the other hand, the breakthrough that led to large factories came from the distribution end. There was no sense in massing workers for high-volume production when the perishable nature of their finished products limited marketing to the immediate area. The logic changed when mechanical energy in the form of the refrigerator rail car tremendously enlarged markets for dressed beef and pork. The first refrigerated shipment left Chicago for Boston in the late 1860s. Central to the business strategies of Philip Armour and Gustavus Swift in their bid for market dominance, the refrigerator car was the key to large-scale production in the meat industry. Armour's Chicago plant, the largest slaughtering and packing factory in the nation, employed over 6,000 workers in 1900, and Swift's the second largest, over 4,000.

The most direct cause of factory growth was the intensified pace of mechanization. Horsepower *per* worker increased by 8 percent in the 1870s, 13 percent in the 1880s, and 35 percent in the 1890s. Not only did more and more machinery that was bulkier and larger require more physical space, but the size of the work force needed to operate and maintain that machinery also had to expand. In order to recoup the heavy fixed costs incurred in putting in new machinery—interest charges on borrowed capital and annual depreciation of the equipment—businessmen wanted to keep the machinery running as continuously as possible. They could easily recruit labor in the cities to tend the machines because factory work increasingly demanded no particular skills.

The machinery reduced skilled levels by subdividing the work process into a series of specialized, repetitive tasks. By the 1870s, for example, few workers were any longer making whole shoes. Beginning in the 1850s, manufacturers built large factories linked up to steam power to drive sewing machines. The McKay stitching machine, introduced in 1862, stitched together the inner, upper, and outer soles in one direct step. From one pair of shoes per hour by the manual method of stitching, production jumped to 80 pair per hour. Labor became so segmented that, as one observer explained in the 1870s, a single shoe "passes through the hands of fifty workmen, each of whom is trained only to make a part."[33]

Nowhere were skills more devalued than in the packing industry. By 1900 the skills that remained from the handicraft methods of the individual butcher were highly specialized ones. Stickers were responsible for the most important one: they had to be able to wield a stiletto with the precision of a surgeon in order to kill up to 500 hogs an hour without damaging the meat. Nearly all the other jobs in the plant involved one unskilled task in an assemblyline of production. Dangling from overhead conveyors and moving through two lines of workers, hog carcasses were at the center of production. In his novel *The Jungle*, Upton Sinclair described the single, frantic task of each man on the line.[34]

One scraped the outside of a leg; another scraped the inside of the same leg. One with a swift stroke cut the throat. . . . Another made a slit down the body; a second opened the body wider; a third with a saw cut the breastbone; a fourth loosened the entrails; a fifth pulled them out [others, just as specifically, cleaned, trimmed, and washed] and for every yard there was a man, working as if a demon were after him.

The industrial trend toward an undifferentiated mass of semiskilled laborers was a general one. In 1895 the economist David Wells noted that "the people who work in the modern factory are, as a rule, taught to do one thing—to perform one and generally a simple operation." Accompanying the loss of skills was a loss in the control of workers over the actual process of production. "The individual no longer works as independently as formerly," Wells concluded, "but as a private in the ranks, obeying orders, keeping step, as it were, to the tap of the drum, and having nothing to say as to the plan of his work, of its final completion, or of its ultimate use and distribution."[35]

Political and cultural motives, as well as economic ones, dictated the introduction of new machinery into the factories. To be sure, machinery raised the productivity of labor by reducing its per-unit cost through the substitution of the semiskilled for the skilled. Equally important, however, was the power that machinery gave management to restructure the social relations of production in such a way as to divest workers of control over their own labor.

Most obviously, machinery permitted an intensification of work. The pace and rhythm at which the machinery operated became the standard used to determine the speed of human labor. When asked by a Congressional Commission on Capital and Labor in 1890 whether machinery had lightened the load of workers, labor leader Samuel Gompers answered, "No. . . . As a matter of fact, the velocity with which machinery is now run calls forth the expenditure of nearly all the physical and mental force which the wage-earner can give to industry."[36] Moreover, the efficient use of machinery required the rigid disciplining of labor through forced adherence to fixed schedules of time and duties. In place of the cycles of heavy work followed by leisurely breaks for conversation and pints of beer that characterized the work practices of independent artisans in their own shops came the smooth rhythms of steady work output synchronized with the machines. From the perspective of capital, the machines offered a weapon with which to impose order on an unruly work force. Andrew Ure, an ideologue of early English industrialization, accurately predicted "that when capital enlists science with her service, the refractory hand of labor will always be taught docility."[37]

The results of a strike in 1886 at the McCormick Harvesting Machine Company in Chicago illustrate this disciplining process. The skilled iron molders had organized the key union at McCormick. After the molders won a strike in 1885, in large measure because they could limit production during peak demands in the spring, McCormick retaliated by investing $500,000 in pneumatic molding machinery, a new and unproven technology. In an effort to protect their jobs, the molders struck again. This time they lost. Leverage was on the side of management, because they could now hire unorganized and unskilled workers to run the new machines, which eliminated the need for the skills of the molders. All 91 molders were fired. For the long-run objective of gaining greater control over production, McCormick sacrificed short-term profits. The new casting machinery broke down frequently, production costs rose, and profits were held down for several years.

Mechanization separated workers from ownership of the means of production, their tools, and transformed the skilled and the unskilled into a common mold of semiskilled operatives. Nonetheless, as long as labor retained the ability to both plan and perform work, the power of capital was limited. William Haywood, the leader of the militant International Workers of the World in the early twentieth century, tersely summarized management's problem: "The manager's brains are under the workman's cap."[38] In more abstract language, Henry Ford, speaking for the other side in the struggle between capital and labor, argued:[39]

> The early factory system was uneconomical. . . . Mere massing of men and tools was not enough; the profit motive, which dominated enterprise, was not enough. There remained the scientific motive which grew eventually into what is called mass production.

Ford's "scientific motive," for all its intended air of detached neutrality, represented the drive of capital to deprive labor of its subjective, thinking role in production. What became known as scientific management was neither neutral nor inevitable. It, like machinery, was a means to the end of greater control by capital over labor. Scientific management aimed at so integrating the worker with the machinery that work itself became an interchangeable cog in a continuous flow of production that was determined by management.

Frederick W. Taylor developed the basic principles of scientific management, or

Taylorism, in the last quarter of the nineteenth century. Taylor showed management how to intervene directly in the process of production, both in planning what would be produced and in supervising how it was produced. These two areas, planning and supervision, were the basis of the workers' control.

In the first phase of American industrialization, one that was coming to an end by the 1870s, manufacturers transferred traditional craft techniques of production into the factories. Because most production rested on knowledge that only the workers possessed—that is, unwritten knowledge they passed down in an oral tradition from father to son and master to apprentice in their craft organizations—manufacturers had to rely on the existing techniques of skilled labor. By so doing, manufacturers initially gained real cost advantages. With the major exception of the textile industry, in which machinery was introduced early in the absence of entrenched craft traditions, most factories, until the 1880s, were collections of shops organized by the workers according to their particular crafts. Because skilled workers supplied much of the equipment, trained and disciplined their helpers, and controlled the actual work, manufacturers were able to minimize expenses for machinery and labor supervision. Of course, manufacturers also incurred the fundamental disadvantage of being dependent upon their labor force for the rate and quantity of production.

In industries that relied on craft skills, the workers arranged among themselves what the stint, or output quota, would be in their shops. When paid by piece rates, as many of the craftsmen were, workers quite rationally tried to limit production in times of increasing wages. To step up production would have been contrary to their self-interests, because management would have reacted by slashing the piece rates or laying off workers in an effort to hold down labor costs. Skilled labor also determined, not subject to negotiation with management, the work rules in their shops. The pace of work, when and how it was to be performed, and the expected standards of quality were all matters for labor alone to decide. As long as skilled artisans controlled the shops within the factories, the growth in the labor supply was the most direct cause of the rise in industrial output. Thus employment gains accounted for 60 percent to 90 percent of the growth in manufacturing production between 1840 and 1870. Manufacturers were producing more, not because they were able to squeeze more productivity out of each worker, but because they employed more workers. Taylor wanted to change that. But, in order to raise output per worker, he needed to find a way to gain for capital what it always had lacked: knowledge of the work process.

Taylor's solution went to the core of the matter. He proposed the enforced separation of the thinking and doing of work. The first step involved elaborate time and motion studies of labor on the job. By precisely analyzing the separate parts in the work process, management would learn what labor had known all along—how the job was done. The second step entailed, in Taylor's phrase, the removal of all "possible brain work"[40] from the shop, concentrating it instead in centralized departments of supervision and planning. By making job techniques the exclusive concern of management, Taylor created a need for the scientific expert to do the thinking formerly done by the skilled worker. In the final step, management was in a position to tell the workers all they needed to know for the execution of any given job order. Management could now achieve greater labor efficiency through its enforced systematization of the entire work process. The planning of work belonged to capital, its execution to labor.

The implications of Taylorism for labor were chilling. At the dawn of the factory

age in the 1830s the Reverend William Channing of Boston had sensed those implications when he spoke to the more humanistic, preindustrial view of labor:[41]

> I do not look on a human being as a machine, made to be kept in action by a foreign
> force, to accomplish an unvarying succession of motions, to do a fixed amount of work,
> and then to fall to pieces at death

Half a century later, Taylor disagreed. He candidly admitted that the full potential of
his ideas

> will not have been realized until almost all of the machines in the shop are run by men
> who are of smaller calibre and attainments, and who are therefore cheaper than those
> required under the old system.[42]

The logic of Taylor's system aimed at making human labor and machine automation
one and the same.

Taylor was a prophet without much of a following in the last two decades of the
nineteenth century. Industrial management did not apply his ideas in any consistent
way until the early twentieth century, for several reasons:

1. The active opposition of craft workers and the dead weight of shop customs
   comprised one set of barriers.
2. There was no need to resort to Taylorism in any planned campaign because the
   abundance of cheap immigrant labor and intensified mechanization combined to
   simplify and reorganize work processes to the advantage of capital. Output per
   worker, which remained constant during the 1860s, increased by 8 percent in the
   1870s, 17 percent in the 1880s, and 21 percent in the 1890s.
3. Most important, Taylorism made economic sense only when the scale of production became large enough that the eventual savings of scientific management
   covered its costs. The reorganization of work flows, redesigning of factory space,
   standardization of tools, centralization of hiring and training by management, and
   the development of research departments all involved capital expenses that typically only the high-volume production of a large company could pay back with
   greater profits.

Control of work processes within the factory by capital had to await the evolution
of a new form of business organization capable of expanding production fast enough to
capture sizable market shares outside the factory. By 1900 that new business enterprise, the corporation, had established its domination. Its emergence was one of the
quietest, but most profound, revolutions of the nineteenth century.

The Revolutionary Nature of the Corporation

The corporate revolution that gathered momentum in the last part of the nineteenth
century has been so complete that it is easy to forget that it ever occurred in the first
place. The essence of that revolution was the transfer of a set of individual rights and
immunities associated with a certain kind of private property, the land and tools of a
farmer, to a radically different kind of private property, the business corporation. In the
process the corporation acquired the freedom from external regulation and controls that
was originally the hallmark of republican freedom in Jefferson's America.

This ideological transfer was successful despite the fact that it rested upon a profound contradiction. The political liberties of a farmer or artisan in 1815 were grounded in a political economy in which the means of production were still widely distributed, at least among adult white males. Individual economic independence—that is, the ownership, use, and enjoyment of productive property—was the indispensable foundation for freedom from the controls of other persons or governmental agencies. Political and economic autonomy were inseparable, and each reinforced the tendency of the other to produce a society that was politically free because economic power was decentralized. The rights and privileges of a corporation in 1900, however, buttressed a political economy in which the very emergence of the corporation had contributed to the concentration of economic power. By the Jeffersonian definition of property, most Americans were no longer economically free. They were economically servile because they were dependent on someone else, on a wage or salary, for their livelihood. As they lost access to productive property, they also became increasingly subjected to the hierarchical, nondemocratic controls of the internal organization of the corporation. Reinforcing this economic dependency were the very political privileges that the corporations had secured, privileges that originally were intended to reinforce the economic independence of the individual. Quite a reversal had occurred: individual rights designed to prevent concentrations of economic and political power from arising were turned inside out in their intent when they were transformed into corporate rights of concentrated power.

At the roots of this reversal were changing legal definitions and public perceptions of corporations in the antebellum period. Until the early nineteenth century, corporations were defined under law, as they had been since the Middle Ages, as public bodies entrusted with certain privileges in the pursuit of the public good. Thus, the most common corporation in colonial America was a municipality. Most of the others received their charters in return for religious, charitable, or educational services. The prevailing assumption was as set forth by Judge Spencer Roane of Virginia in 1809:[43]

> With respect to acts of incorporation, they ought never to be passed, but in consideration of services to be rendered to the public. . . . It may be often convenient for a set of associated individuals, to have the privileges of a corporation bestowed upon them; but if their object is merely *private* or selfish; if it is detrimental to, or not promotive of the public good, they have no adequate claim upon the legislature for the privileges.

Even as Roane was arguing the above, however, the corporation was gradually being detached from its public moorings.

As late as 1780, only seven businesses had incorporated: by 1801 the states had chartered over 300 more. Two-thirds of these incorporations were in the field of transportation, and this remained the antebellum pattern. In Pennsylvania 64 percent of the 2,333 business incorporations between 1790 and 1860 were for turnpikes, canals, and railroads; another 25 percent were in banking, manufacturing, and insurance.

Private and public considerations reinforced each other in these antebellum incorporations. They were conceived of as quasi-public agencies that merged private capital and governmental controls in the pursuit of the public welfare. The states assumed an active entrepreneurial role—in sharp contrast to the commonly held modern-day assumption that they exhibited a laissez-faire attitude toward economic development. They bought corporate stock, guaranteed corporate debt, and often managed the transportation projects in what were known as mixed enterprises. Private investors simultaneously received a variety of privileges in the state charters—monopoly rights of way, tax exemptions, limited liability, the right to raise capital by issuing securities, the right of eminent domain—that is, the taking of private land for public purposes—and freedom from what were called nuisance actions, prosecutions for interfering with the legal rights of others by causing damage or inconvenience. This last right was particularly important for the builders of mills and toll roads and bridges. The very nature of their businesses interfered with the free flow of goods and people on rivers and roads.

The states justified these grants of privileged power on the grounds that they were necessary for the promotion of the general welfare, a public good that now included the rapid development of local economies. Because capital was still scarce and unlikely to be attracted to high-risk, long-range projects in transportation, state officials persuasively argued that entrepreneurs should be positively encouraged, by the conferral of legal privileges, to form corporations. By exploiting economic opportunities faster and more thoroughly than family partnerships, these officials felt that corporations would soon raise living standards in local communities. In other words, the social utility of the benevolent functions of the earlier, eighteenth-century corporations was now applied to the developmental functions of the later, nineteenth-century corporation.

Essential to the freer and wider use of incorporation were shifts in legal doctrine that encouraged capital accumulation, economic growth, and risk taking by entrepreneurs. One major shift was toward a more dynamic, promotional use of property. Under the common-law concepts of the eighteenth century—concepts transplanted from England and traditionally applied to a relatively static agrarian economy—the law protected the landowner in the full use and enjoyment of his or her property. Central to this definition of property was the belief that individual liberty rested upon complete control over private property. Therefore, landowners were entitled to sue for damage if their property was flooded when millowners built dams to store the water needed to drive machinery. Early industrialization was contingent on water power, and the spread of factories along river banks set up a clear conflict with property owners on the rivers. By the 1820s, the courts were allowing mill owners to escape damages from the farmers whose land they were flooding. The presumed greater good of industrial development for the entire society, reasoned the judges, took precedence over the absolute right of individual enjoyment of property. One class of property owners, though representing private interests, was permitted to inflict damages upon another class in the name of the public good. Property was now viewed as an instrument in the service of economic growth and not as a guaranteed security for individual autonomy.

The courts also substituted market values for older notions of equality under contract law. Until the market revolution of the nineteenth century, the legal enforceability of contracts depended on what was considered to be their intrinsic fairness. In the premarket economy, goods and services were believed to have an inherent, objective value that was based on their use and need. Tradition and community needs established the standard of a just price, a value that was legally enforceable because it was morally fair. The interests of the entire community, and not the profits of individual entrepreneurs, were paramount. Contracts, private agreements enforceable by public power, had to meet a test of moral equity. The traditional view, as summarized in 1825 by Gulian C. Verplanck, a legal writer, held that "all bargains are made under the idea of giving and receiving equivalents in value."[44]

As the market emerged as the dominant institution in antebellum America, a new view of contracts became dominant. Fluctuating prices, speculative commercial ventures, and the rise in future trading on agricultural commodities all led to the belief that prices and values were inherently subjective. Prices changed, they were anticipated, and they were set by the daily market factors of supply and demand. Community standards of value were no longer legally binding, because they no longer made any objective sense in a rapidly changing market economy. Anxious to free themselves from older notions of accountability that limited risk-taking, entrepreneurs launched a successful effort to redefine the legal enforceability of a contract. The will of the parties, regardless of any inequalities in skill, experience, or knowledge, made a contract binding. Law and morality were driven apart.

While these legal changes were occurring, antebellum businessmen began to turn to a doctrine of corporate egalitarianism. Under this doctrine, corporations lost what formerly had been their inherently public nature. Instead they were viewed as a convenient legal device that could be used by private businessmen in the pursuit of ordinary business activities. As set forth by Chief Justice Roger Taney in the celebrated *Charles River Bridge* case of 1837, the role of public power was now largely limited to enshrining the principle of equal competition among all corporate comers. In the case at hand, Taney freed a newer corporation, the Warren Bridge, from the monopolistic claims of an older corporation, the Charles River Bridge, the profits of which dropped after it lost business to its new competitor. Taney's decision divested corporations of any implied charter privileges that could result in a monopolistic brake on the economic progress of the community at large. In so doing, Taney also identified the corporate charter as a private contract that carried no responsibilities to the public that could be set by custom or tradition. The corporation lost its public character and assumed its modern form as a private license to compete.

Corporations disciplined the economic energy that legal change helped unleash. Despite the increase in corporate charters, many Americans continued to reject the market interpretation of society that business corporations embodied and that the law reflected and shaped. In particular, corporations remained unpopular because of their privileges and monopolistic rights. In a classic indictment penned in 1820, Daniel Raymond, a lawyer, argued that corporations

> are always created for the benefit of the rich, and never for the poor. The poor have no money to vest in them, and can, therefore, derive no advantage from such corporations. The rich have money, and not being satisfied with the power which money itself gives them, in their private individual capacities, they seek for an artificial combination, or amalgamation of their power, that its force may be augmented.[45]

Anticorporate sentiment pervaded much of the ideological appeal of the Democrats, the party that represented most of the voters hurt by market change. Jackson warned in his farewell presidential address of 1837 that the "agricultural, the mechanical, and the laboring classes have little or no share in the direction of the great moneyed corporations. . . ."[46] For antebellum Democrats, such as Peter D. Vroom of New Jersey, the corporate threat to republican liberties was unmistakable because "it is the danger of associated wealth, with special privileges, and without personal liability."[47]

Democratic anticorporatism was real and persistent. Its effectiveness, however, was weakened by conflicting responses to the corporations. Some Democrats wanted to

Table 8.8   Pattern of Growth in Iron and Steel

The number of iron and steel firms declined by nearly 20 percent between 1870 and 1900, the size of the labor force per firm quadrupled, output increased eleven times over, and capitalization was six times as great.

	1870	1900
Number of Firms	808	669
Labor Force	78,000	272,000
Output in Tons	3,200,000	29,500,000
Capital Invested	$121,000,000	$590,000,000

Source: Adopted from *The Economic Transformation of America*, Second Edition, by Robert L. Heilbroner and Aaron Singer, p. 175. Reprinted with permission of Harcourt Brace Jovanovich, Inc.

eliminate them, others to regulate them, and still others to open up incorporation to all comers so that corporate advantages previously conferred only in special legislative acts would lose their aristocratic overtones and become democratized. Beginning in the 1830s, the Whigs, with some Democratic support, passed general incorporation laws that set up uniform provisions for incorporation. No longer was a special act of the legislature required for each corporation.

The legal foundation for the corporate revolution was in place by the mid-nineteenth century. Still, antebellum corporations were almost exclusively limited to the fields of transportation, banking, and textiles. The full potential of the corporation would not be realized until markets expanded in size after the Civil War.

The Industrial Revolution and the Corporation

American business underwent a revolution in size and power in the generation after the Civil War. The trend, as shown in Table 8.8 for the iron and steel industry, was toward bigness and centralization. Coordinating this trend was a simultaneous move towards incorporation. Before the 1880s, incorporated manufacturing concerns were rare. Out of 161 manufacturing firms in Pittsburgh in 1860, not one was incorporated. As late as 1878, fewer than 5 percent of the companies in Massachusetts were. Then, beginning with an onrush in the 1880s, the pace of the administrative revolution dramatically quickened. By 1900 the vast bulk of the nation's manufacturing output poured out of corporations, and 70 percent of all industrial labor worked for corporations.

The connection between incorporation and market expansion was a direct one. Until the 1850s, American businesses were typically small, family-operated concerns in which a single entrepreneur, working perhaps with a few partners, made all the economic decisions. In these proprietorships and partnerships, ownership and management were one and the same. These small, highly personalized, and unincorporated business organizations were quite adequate to meet the needs of a decentralized and localized economy. Markets were widely scattered, goods were produced and purchased in small quantities, and independent wholesalers handled their distribution. Village merchants stocked goods no more technologically complex than scythes and axes. Then, compressed into a thirty-year period from the 1850s to the 1880s, a whole series of technological breakthroughs paved the way for mass production, markets, and distribution. The application of steam to transportation in the railroad, electricity to communications in the telegraph, and coal to production in the steel furnace vastly increased the speed and expanded the volume of both manufacturing and distribution. Starting in the 1880s, the multi-unit corporations emerged to integrate the new forms of mass production and mass distribution.

Technological innovations created a radically different business environment that placed traditional, unincorporated firms competing with corporations at a crippling disadvantage. Limited life and unlimited liability characterized the traditional business, whether a sole proprietorship or a partnership. Limited life simply meant that the enterprise legally ended with the death of the owner or one of the partners. Unlimited liability meant that each owner or partner was personally liable for any debts incurred by the firm. The financial risk was not limited to one's actual contribution to the firm. Any creditor could sue any partner for full recovery of any debts owed. This impermanence and high risk severely limited the ability of the unincorporated enterprise to attract capital. For the most part, the personal savings of owners, partners, and kin provided the capital.

In the antebellum economy, before economies of scale had emerged, such restricted amounts of capital did not greatly hamper an individual firm's chances to compete. There was no particular advantage in building a larger plant. On one hand, there was no national market in which to sell the additional production. On the other hand, the technology did not exist that would lower the per-unit cost of production as output increased. This was no longer the case by the 1880s; sheer size in many industries was now a decided economic advantage, and manufacturers with access to large pools of capital for business expansion had the best chance to survive and prosper. Increasingly, they turned to incorporation for the financial and organizational resources they needed.

The corporation, a legal body or *corpus* of persons that has been granted a charter conferring special privileges and rights for the pursuit of the common ends that the corporation was formed to achieve, offered politically conferred privileges that were very attractive to manufacturers after the Civil War:

1. Unlike the proprietorship or partnership, the corporation was permanent. Although it had all the legal rights of a person, the corporation did not die with its founders. Barring bankruptcy, it survived as long as its charter was not revoked.
2. Investors in a corporation had the right of limited liability. Established by a Massachusetts statute in 1830, this right limited financial risk to the extent of one's investment. Personal wealth was immune from corporate creditors.
3. Corporations had the right to issue bonds and shares of stock. Its unlimited life, limited liability, and financial flexibility enabled corporations to tap much greater sources of long-term capital than the business forms it replaced.
4. Of equal importance, the separation of personal ownership and company management that was now possible gave the corporation the organizational means of coordinating the growing scale and complexity of business activities. As the corporation grew, a new class of professional managers arose to administer and control daily operations.

The railroads provided the prototype for the modern American corporation. It was here that the corporate advantages in raising capital and organizing a huge enterprise were first realized on a large scale in private business. The amount of capital that had to be secured, and the scope of activities that had to be managed, were unprecedented. A systematic flow of information and control was necessary to supervise first thousands, then tens of thousands, of workers with varied skills strung out over thousands of miles of track in the twenty-four-hour movement of goods and people. More comparable to the administrative needs of a large army than those of a family-run business, the special demands of running a railroad called for a militarylike organization to evaluate, coordinate, and enforce decisions. The result was the modern corporation, with its bureaucratic and hierarchical chains of command flowing downward and outward from central offices. The railroads pioneered in subdividing operations into functional departments for greater efficiency and control. By the 1880s, the major corporate divisions included finance, production, purchasing, and marketing. The railroads were the first businesses to develop staff and line distinctions by corporate division. Their size, integrated multi-units, and administrative hierarchy moved the railroads beyond entrepreneurial capitalism and into the era of managerial capitalism.

In addition to providing a model for future corporate development, the railroads also created the enlarged markets that encouraged more manufacturers to turn to incorporation. In particular, the railroads established a direct link between producers of consumer goods and consumers in the rapidly growing cities. By the 1870s, it was possible for New York City, as a Treasury Department official noted, to get "certain products of Illinois and Iowa at rates little in advance of the rates upon the same commodity from local points within 100 miles of that city."[48] Now that the railroads had nearly eliminated the economic barrier of distance, business success rested on the ability to combine mass production with mass distribution. The first business leaders to respond to the challenge were those who built large-scale enterprises in the consumer-goods industries.

This first wave of corporate organizers—a Gustavus Swift in dressed meat, James B. Duke in tobacco, Cyrus McCormick in agricultural equipment, or William Clark in sewing machines—were all radical innovators in marketing strategies. They had to be because their products were either perishable or new and could not be mass distributed through traditional wholesale outlets. Swift, for example, had to do more than just deliver chilled beef in refrigerated cars to Eastern cities. He had to build an elaborate marketing and distribution network of branch houses in each city with the responsibility of storing the meat and selling it through local retailers. He had to spend money on advertising to convince consumers that his nonlocal meat was healthy and on legal fees to combat the boycotts of local butchers who were losing market shares to Swift. Then, once his branch houses were established, he needed the foresight to expand his sources of supply by building new packing houses close to the cattle frontier and by buying into the stockyards. Swift and four other packers who followed his marketing lead dominated the national sale and distribution of dressed meat by the 1890s. The genius of James B. Duke was in advertising. His firm installed a new cigarette-rolling machine in 1881 that turned out 100,000 cigarettes a day. Threatened with the overproduction of a product that still had but limited sales, Duke bypassed local commission merchants, targeted the urban market with aggressive advertising geared to the industry's first crush-proof box, and developed his own national sales organization. In 1890 Duke was the power behind the merger of the four largest tobacco producers into the American Tobacco Company.

A variant of the same marketing theme held for those products, such as agricultural machinery and sewing machines, that required special credit and servicing arrangements because of their cost and technological complexity. Both McCormick and Clark created new channels of distribution that they organized into agencies, or exclusive sales territories. Supported by the companies' engineering and credit divisions, the commissioned agents and salaried personnel in each agency handled demonstrations, sales, financing, and repairs. In 1909, as a result of their marketing networks, McCormick, by then known as International Harvester, and the Singer Sewing Machine Company ranked fourth and twelfth in assets among America's industrial corporations.

The post-Civil War revolution in business organization was a cause of, as well as a result of, market expansion. However much the railroads removed physical barriers to the formation of a national market, that market could not be fully realized until the legal barriers imposed by the states against interstate commerce were also removed. When the Chicago packers and aggressive retailers, like I. M. Singer & Company, reached out in the 1870s to forge direct ties between national manufacturers and local consumers, they had to challenge state laws designed to keep them out. Passed to protect merchants and manufacturers from out-of-state competition, the laws mandated special licensing, taxation, and inspection fees for goods that were not produced or distributed by locally owned firms. The laws functioned as protective tariffs and were meant to save local jobs. Despite the apparent likelihood that these laws violated the commerce clause of the Constitution, which vested Congress with the authority to regulate interstate commerce, they were commonplace and were not effectively challenged until the 1870s. Then, a series of Supreme Court decisions between 1875 and 1890 overturned most of these restrictive laws.

The rise of national business firms explains the timing. These firms, led by the large packers and the Singer Company, had the financial resources to wage protracted legal battles and the compelling self-interest to force entry into a national market that they insisted should be legally defined as a free-trade unit. A constitutional revolution accompanied the marketing one. For the first time, American companies won the right to compete on equal terms with local businessmen in interstate markets. They were granted that right despite the absence of any congressional regulations over those interstate activities that the states were now prohibited from regulating in the interests of their citizens. In effect, the Supreme Court had legally dissolved the territorial and protectionist units of the states into one common market.

Commodity prices fell steadily after the Civil War. They dropped by 35 percent in the 1870s, 18 percent in the 1880s, and another 17 percent in the first half of the 1890s before recovery set in from the depression of that decade. This unrelenting downward pressure was largely the result of the massive increase in supply made possible by technological advancements in production and by the spread of the factory system. Supply grew faster than demand. Particularly in an industry like oil refining, in which economies of scale pushed down the price of refined oil from 36¢ a gallon in 1863 to 8¢ in 1885, business success was reduced to the basic proposition of combining or perishing. John D. Rockefeller became a millionaire because he learned that lesson very early in his business career. The key to Rockefeller's monopolistic strategy was the underselling of his rivals. He did so by building his own pipelines to carry his oil to market. This in turn gave him the leverage to pressure the railroads to grant him rebates, or discounts, for hauling his oil. After a decade of using such tactics to take business away from his competitors, most of whom he then bought out at his price, Rockefeller controlled 80 percent of the nation's refining in 1880.

Other business leaders found it difficult to follow Rockefeller's lead. With their huge fixed costs in expensive plant equipment, and hence the need to keep production running even if at a loss, manufacturers continually expanded production. Ruinous price wars resulted as industrialists fought for markets "Competition is industrial war,"[49] one of them lamented in 1901. Before New Jersey amended its corporate statutes in 1889 to permit one corporation to hold stock in another and thus gain control of it, there was no legal way to escape this war. The usual method by which businessmen tried to avoid the pricing discipline of free-market competition was through the formation of pools. These voluntary agreements on prices and production between companies in a given industry, however, invariably broke down. The temptation to grab market shares by raising production when prices dropped was just too great. Moreover, the pools, construed by the courts as contracts in restraint of trade, were not legally binding and could not be enforced.

Once New Jersey showed the way in 1889, a legal way to avoid competition was available. Corporations could now buy out other corporations. New industrial giants quickly emerged with control over prices and production that formerly had been exercised by a host of small firms. After the first great wave of mergers peaked around the turn of the twentieth century, 300 corporations controlled 40 percent of the nation's manufacturing.

The corporate order emerged victorious in a debate that was as much cultural as it was economic. The issue was not just one of profits to be earned but of the values by which America was to be defined and structured. Because the middle class held the balance of power between the main contestants in the debate—capital and labor—the next chapter will concentrate on that class and the cultural gulf that now separated it from labor. For both cultural and economic reasons, the middle class would side with capital when the debate over the corporation reached a political climax in the 1890s.

SUGGESTED READING

Walter Prescott Webb, *The Great Plains* (1931), is a classic on the settlement of the trans-Mississippi West, and an excellent survey can be found in John A. Hawgood, *America's Western Frontier* (1967). Two works with more of a cultural focus are Henry Nash Smith, *Virgin Land: The American West as Symbol and Myth* (1950), and J. B. Jackson, *American Space: The Centennial Years, 1864–1876* (1972). Gene M. Greesley, *West by East: The American West in the Gilded Age* (1972), stresses the economic ambitions of the settlers. Railroad land policy and the boomer literature that attracted settlers are covered in Robert G. Athearn, *Union Pacific Country* (1971), and David M. Emmons, *Garden in the Grasslands* (1971). For the role of towns and cities, see Robert J. Dykstra, *The Cattle Towns* (1968), and John W. Reps, *Cities of the American West* (1979). Frederick Turner, *Beyond Geography: The Western Spirit Against the Wilderness* (1980), is a moving account of the spirtual price exacted in the transformation of the West.

The demography of settlement on the Dakota frontier is carefully reconstructed in John C. Hudson, "Migration to an American Frontier," *AAAG* 66 (1976). For the role of women, see Julie Roy Jeffrey, *Frontier Women: The Trans-Mississippi West, 1840–1880* (1979); Glenda Riley, *Frontierswomen: The Iowa Experience* (1981); Joanna L. Strathon, *Pioneer Women: Voices from the Kansas Frontier* (1981); and Lillian Schlissel, *Women's Diaries of the Westward*

Journey (1982). The immigrant experience can be followed in: John C. Rice, "The Role of Culture and Community in Frontier Prairie Farming," JHG 3 (1977); Robert Ostergren, "A Community Transplanted: The Formative Experience of a Swedish Immigrant Community in the Upper-Middle-West," JHG 5 (1979); and Ingrid Semmingsen, *Norway to America* (1978), translated by Einar Haugen.

The standard account on the military subjugation of the Plains Indians is Robert M. Utley, *Frontier Regulars: The United States Army and the Indian, 1866–1891* (1973), a work now supplemented by Paul Andrew Hutton, *Phil Sheridan and His Army* (1985). For a sharp moral critique of army policy and the white attitudes that it expressed, see Dee Brown, *Bury My Heart at Wounded Knee* (1970), and Diane Vári, "A Monstrous Wrong Without Guilt," RAH 3 (1975). Thomas C. Leonard, "Red, White and the Army Blue: Empathy and Anger in the American West," AQ 26 (1974), shows that many army officers found much to admire in Indian culture. For the role of business interests in the destruction of that culture, see H. Craig Miner, *The Corporation and the Indian* (1976). The rise of the Sioux to dominance on the Great Plains is traced in Richard White, "The Winning of the West: The Expansion of the Western Sioux in the Eighteenth and Nineteenth Centuries," JAH 65 (1978). For two of the other major tribes, see William T. Hagan, *United States–Comanche Relations* (1976), and Donald E. Worcester, *The Apaches* (1979).

The fullest treatment of the economic reconstruction of the postwar South is R. L. Ransom and Richard Sutch, *One Kind of Freedom: The Economic Consequences of Emancipation* (1977). Stephen J. De Canio, *Agriculture in the Postbellum South* (1974), and Robert Higgs, *Competition and Coercion: Blacks in the American Economy, 1865–1914* (1977), are also major studies, and they reach quite different conclusions from those of Ransom and Sutch. Robert Gallman and Ralph V. Anderson, "Slaves as Fixed Capital: Slave Labor and Southern Economic Development," JAH 64 (1977), present a succinct analysis based upon the elimination of slavery as a capital investment. Roger W. Shugg, *Origins of Class Struggle in Louisiana* (1939); Jonathan M. Winer, *Social Origins of the New South* (1978); and Jay R. Mandle, *The Roots of Black Poverty* (1978), are important works that argue for the persistence of planter control after the Civil War. For a penetrating review of much of this literature, see Harold D. Woodman, "Sequel to Slavery: The New History Views the Postbellum South," JSH 43 (1977).

The tightening restrictions on black labor are explained in Pete Daniel, "The Metamorphosis of Slavery, 1865–1900," JAH 66 (1979), and Theodore Rosengarten, *All God's Dangers: The Life of Nate Shaw* (1975), is a striking oral history of how one black coped with those restrictions. The closing of the open range and the deteriorating position of the yeomanry is covered in J. Crawford King, Jr., "The Closing of the Southern Range," JSH 48 (1982), and Forrest McDonald and Grady McWhiney, "The South from Self-Sufficiency to Peonage: An Interpretation," AHR 85 (1980). For the role of law as a coercive instrument in controlling agricultural labor, see Harold D. Woodman, "Post–Civil War Southern Agriculture and the Law," AGH 53 (1979), and Wayne K. Durrill, "Producing Poverty: Local Government and Economic Development in a New South County, 1874–1884," JAH 71 (1985). The rhetoric and symbolism employed by the Southern industrialists and town promoters who would benefit from access to cheap labor are discussed in Paul W. Gaston, *The New South Creed: A Study in Southern Mythmaking* (1970). For the conditions of the Southern textile workers, see David Carlton, *Mill and Town in South Carolina, 1880–1920* (1982).

For the growth of cities in the Gilded Age, see Blake McKelvey, *The Urbanization of America, 1860–1915* (1963). Adna F. Weber, *The Growth of Cities in the Nineteenth Century* (1899), is an old but still valuable source for placing American urbanization in a comparative context. The best work on linking urban growth to transportation changes for one metropolitan region is Sam B. Warner, Jr., *Streetcar Suburbs: The Process of Growth in Boston, 1870–1900* (1962). Also helpful on urban transportation is Charles W. Cheape, *Moving the Masses: Urban Public Transit in New York, and Philadelphia, 1880–1912* (1980). The connection between urbanization and industrialization is discussed in Beverly Duncan and Stanley Lieberson, *Metropolis and Region in Transition* (1970). David Ward, *Cities and Immigrants: A Geography of Change in 19th Century America* (1971), is unrivalled for demonstrating the close relationship between urbanization and immigration. A challenging, but illuminating, study that ties all these themes together is Oliver Zunz, *The Changing Face of Inequality: Urbanization, Industrial Development, and Immigrants in Detroit, 1880–1920* (1982). For works that show the cultural adaptations to city life, see Roger Lane, *Violent Death in the City* (1979), and Gunther Barth, *City People: The Rise of Modern City Culture in Nineteenth-Century America* (1980).

Despite its misleading title, Charlotte Erickson, "Emigration from the British Isles to the U.S.A. in 1831," PS 35 (1981), is an excellent source on the late-nineteenth-century shift in immigration from families to single adult males. The other switch, the ethnic one from northern and western to southern and eastern Europe as the major source of immigrants, is covered in: Philip Taylor, *The Distant Magnet* (1970); Leonard Dinnerstein and David Reimers, *Ethnic Americans* (1975); and Alan M. Kraut, *The Huddled Masses: The Immigrant in American Society, 1880–1921* (1982). For an impressionistic synthesis of the immigrant experience, see Oscar Handlin, *The Uprooted* (1951), and for information on individual ethnic groups, Stephan Thernstrom, ed., *The Harvard Encyclopedia of American Ethnic Groups* (1980). Among the best monographs are: John B. Duff, *The Irish in the United States* (1971); Humbert Nelli, *The Italians of Chicago, 1880–1920;* Josef Barton, *Peasants and Strangers: Italians, Rumanians, and Slovaks in an American City* (1975); Irving Howe, *The World of Our Fathers: The Journey of the East European Jews to America and the Life They Made and Found* (1976); and Virginia Yans-McLaughlin, *Family and Community: Italian Immigrants in Buffalo, 1880–1930* (1977). On the work choices made by immigrants and how these affected where they settled, see Caroline Golab, *Immigrant Destinations* (1977). The ways in which ethnic groups found factory jobs for their kin and recent arrivals are discussed in John Bodnar, "Immigration, Kinship, and the Rise of Working-Class Realism in Industrial America," JSOH 14 (1980). The essays in Herbert G. Gutman, *Work, Culture, and Society in Industrializing America* (1976), brilliantly analyze the cultural resistance of immigrants to industrialization.

The best combination of detail and readability on America's industrial revolution is Edward C. Kirkland, *Industry Comes of Age: Business, Labor, and Public Policy, 1880–1897* (1961). Excellent, briefer accounts can be found in Glenn Porter, *The Rise of Big Business, 1860–1910* (1973), and Stuart Bruchey, *Growth of the Modern American Economy* (1975). Phillip S. Bagwell and G. F. Mingay, *Britain and America: A Study of Economic Change, 1850–1939* (1970), is helpful for its comparative framework. On the pace and importance of technological change, see Siegfried Giedion, *Mechanization Takes Command* (1969), and Elting E. Morrison, *From Know-How to Nowhere: The Development of American Technology* (1974). Peter Temin, *Iron and Steel in the 19th Century* (1964), and George R. Taylor and Irene Neu, *The American Railroad Network, 1861–1890,* trace developments in two basic industries.

Harry Braverman, *Labor and Monopoly Capital* (1974), is a powerful critique of how work and the lives of workers changed under industrialization. Similar themes, though from a broader cultural and intellectual perspective, are discussed in Daniel T. Rodgers, *The Work Ethic in Industrial America, 1850–1920* (1978), and James B. Gilbert, *Work without Salvation* (1977). On the emergence of the large factory and the subsequent erosion of the workers' independence, see Daniel Nelson, *Managers and Workers: Origins of the New Factory System in the United States, 1880–1920* (1975). David Montgomery, *Workers' Control in America* (1979), analyzes the efforts of craft workers to maintain their control. David M. Gordon, et al., *Segmented Work, Divided Laborers* (1982), emphasizes the self-interest of management in devaluing the skills of workers. For the McCormick strike of 1885, see R. Ozanne, *A Century of Labor-Management Relations at McCormick and International Harvester* (1967). A good source on Taylorism is Daniel Nelson, *Frederick W. Taylor and the Rise of Scientific Management* (1980). The imposition of managerial controls is also a central theme of Dan Clawson, *Bureaucracy and the Labor Process: The Transformation of U.S. Industry, 1860–1920* (1980).

For the early history of the American corporation, see J. S. Davis, *Essays in the Earlier History of American Corporations* (2 vols., 1917), and Ronald E. Seavoy, *The Origins of the American Business Corporation, 1783–1855* (1982). The quasi-public nature of the first business corporations and the active role of state governments in promoting them are explained in Louis Hartz, *Economic Policy and Democratic Thought: Pennsylvania, 1776–1860* (1954), and Oscar Handlin and Mary F. Handlin, *Commonwealth: A Study of the Role of Government in the American Economy* (1969). James W. Hurst, *Law and the Conditions of Freedom in the Nineteenth Century United States* (1956), explores how positive, developmental conceptions of the law were used to release individual energy in the nineteenth century, and Morton J. Horwitz, *The Transformation of American Law, 1780–1860* (1977), is the best source on how the common law changed to accommodate and promote market change. Tony Allen Freyer, *Forums of Order: The Federal Courts and Business in American History* (1979), shows how the federal judiciary fostered economic development across state lines.

The late-nineteenth-century managerial revolution in business administration that accompanied the industrial revolution in production is set forth in Alfred D. Chandler, Jr., *The Visible Hand: The Managerial Revolution in American Business* (1977). The reasons American businessmen took an early lead in this revolution are explored in Alfred D. Chandler, Jr., and Herman Daems, *Managerial Hierarchies: Comparative Perspectives on the Rise of the Modern Industrial Enterprise* (1980). For the post–Civil War expansion in markets, see Glenn Porter and H. C. Livesay, *Merchants and Manufacturers: Studies in the Changing Structure of 19th Century Marketing* (1971). Charles W. McCurdy, "American Law and the Marketing Structure of the Large Corporation, 1875–1890," JEH 38 (1978), outlines the legal strategies used by corporate leaders to overcome local and constitutional barriers to a national market. Matthew Josephson, *The Robber Barons* (1934), remains the classic denunciation of American business leaders in the Gilded Age. Much more favorable are the sketches offered in Jonathan Hughes, *The Vital Few* (1976), and major biographies such as Allan Nevins, *Study in Power: John D. Rockefeller, Industrialist and Philanthropist* (2 vols., 1953), and Joseph Wall, *Andrew Carnegie* (1970).

NOTES

1. Quoted in Sandra L. Myers, *Westering Women and the Frontier Experience, 1800–1915* (Albuquerque: University of New Mexico Press, 1982), p. 29.
2. Hamlin Garland, *A Son of the Middle Border* (New York: The Macmillan Company, 1925), p. 63.
3. Ibid., pp. 187–188.
4. Ibid., p. 246.
5. Charlotte Erickson, *Invisible Immigrants: The Adaptation of English and Scottish Immigrants in Nineteenth-Century America* (Coral Gables, Fla.: University of Miami Press, 1972), p. 221.
6. The ballad is from the account of Eugene Boe, "Pioneers to Eternity: Norwegians on the Prairie," in Thomas C. Wheeler, ed., *The Immigrant Experience: The Anguish of Becoming American* (Baltimore: Penguin Books, 1972), p. 55.
7. Quoted in Ronald T. Takaki, *Iron Cages: Race and Culture in 19th Century America* (New York: Alfred A. Knopf, 1979), p. 171.
8. Rachel Sherman Thorndike, ed., *The Sherman Letters: Correspondence between General and Senator Sherman from 1837 to 1891* (New York: Da Capo Press, 1969), p. 291.
9. Quoted in Thomas C. Leonard, "Red, White and the Army Blue: Empathy and Anger in the American West," *American Quarterly* 26 (1974): 183.
10. Virgil J. Vogel, ed., *This Country Was Ours: A Documentary History of the American Indian* (New York: Harper & Row, 1972), p. 181.
11. Thorndike, op. cit., p. 296.
12. Quoted in Peter N. Carroll and David W. Noble, *The Free and the Unfree: A New History of the United States* (Baltimore: Penguin Books, 1977), p. 234.
13. Quoted in William Brandon, *The Last Americans: The Indian in American Culture* (New York: McGraw-Hill, 1974), p. 382.
14. Quoted in Wilcomb E. Washburn, *The Indian in America* (New York: Harper Colophon Books, 1975), p. 208.

15. Quoted in Frederick Turner, *Beyond Geography: The Western Spirit Against the Wilderness* (New York: The Viking Press, 1980), p. 268.
16. Quoted in Carroll and Noble, op. cit., p. 233.
17. Quoted in Leonard, op. cit., p. 179.
18. Quoted in Turner, op cit., p. 289.
19. Ibid., p. 294.
20. Tom E. Terrill and Jerrold Hirsch, eds., *Such as Us: Southern Voices of the Thirties* (Chapel Hill: University of North Carolina Press, 1978), p. 46.
21. Ibid., p. 56.
22. Ibid., p. 61.
23. Theodore Rosengarten, *All God's Dangers: The Life of Nate Shaw* (New York: Avon Books, 1975), p. 28. Most of the names and places in this remarkable oral history were changed in order to protect individual privacy.
24. Ibid., p. 32.
25. Ibid., pp. 34, 120, 124.
26. Ibid., p. xxi.
27. Ibid., p. 14.
28. Harry Roskolenko, "America, The Thief: A Jewish Search for Freedom," in Wheeler, op. cit., p. 157.
29. Ibid., p. 165.
30. Quoted in Jerzy Jedlicki, "Land of Hope, Land of Despair: Polish Scholarship and American Immigration," *Reviews in American History* 3 (1975): 93, 94.
31. Quoted in Herbert G. Gutman, *Work, Culture, and Society in Industrializing America: Essays in American Working-Class and Social History* (New York: Vintage Books, 1977), p. 40.
32. Quoted in Edward Chase Kirkland, *Industry Comes of Age: Business, Labor and Public Policy, 1860–1897* (Chicago: Quadrangle Books, 1967), p. 171.
33. John T. Cumbler, ed., *A Moral Response to Industrialism: The Lectures of Reverend Cook in Lynn, Massachusetts* (Albany: State University of New York Press, 1982), p. 37.
34. Quoted in Siegfried Giedion, *Mechanization Takes Command* (New York: The Norton Library, 1969), p. 229.
35. Quoted in Mary McDougall Gordon, "Patriots and Christians: A Reassessment of Nineteenth-Century School Reformers," *Journal of Social History* 11 (1979): 118.
36. Quoted in Robert L. Heilbroner, *The Economic Transformation of America* (New York: Harcourt Brace Jovanovich, 1977), p. 42.
37. Quoted in Jeff Henderson and Robin Cohen, "Capital and the Work Ethic," *Monthly Review* 31 (1979): 15.
38. Quoted in David Montgomery, *Workers' Control in America: Studies in the History of Work, Technology, and Labor Struggles* (New York: Cambridge University Press, 1979), p. 9.
39. Quoted in Gordon, op cit., p. 131.
40. The phrase is cited in Harry Braverman, *Labor and Monopoly Capital: The Degradation of Work in the Twentieth Century* (New York: Monthly Review Press, 1974), p. 113.
41. Quoted in Giedion, op. cit., p. 127.
42. Quoted in Braverman, op cit., p. 118.
43. Quoted in Morton J. Horwitz, *The Transformation of American Law, 1780–1860* (Cambridge: Harvard University Press, 1977), p. 112.
44. Ibid., p. 182.
45. Quoted in George Rogers Taylor, *The Transportation Revolution, 1815–1860* (New York: Harper Torchbooks, 1968), p. 242.
46. Davis, *Antebellum American Culture*, op. cit., p. 193.
47. Quoted in Rush Welter, *The Mind of America, 1820–1860* (New York: Columbia University Press, 1975), p. 80.
48. Quoted in Albro Martin, "The Troubled Subject of Railroad Regulation in the Gilded Age—A Reappraisal," *Journal of American History* 61 (1974): 346.
49. Quoted in Heilbroner, op. cit., p. 107.

9

Social Change and Cultural Conflict

What was the cultural meaning of the social reordering brought about by the economic revolution in Gilded-Age America? How was America to be ordered, and who would define what was meant by order? Who had the power to define what America meant? These questions set the cultural agenda for America in the late nineteenth century, and there was no single set of answers.

The most official and respectable answers were part of a white, middle-class, and largely male-defined program of cultural reform and uplift. However, the various subordinated groups that were to be uplifted yet kept in their proper place—nonwhites and women, as well as immigrants and workers—persisted in finding community in their own cultural groups and living by their own values. The result was the ongoing cultural tension and conflict that this chapter will examine. Despite combining older notions of biological determinism based on race, gender, and age with newer reform ideas rooted in a professionalized ethic of efficiency and expertise, the middle class was continually frustrated in its effort to remake America in its own cultural image.

Color and Social Space

Color provided the most obvious and visible point of demarcation of the social and cultural ordering of America. In an extension of the same ordering device that had evolved in antebellum America, the white majority continued to relegate nonwhite minorities to specially defined positions of inferiority. The resulting hierarchy—one reinforced by law, military force, and popular prejudices—clearly served economic needs. Whites wanted and convinced themselves that they needed the land of the Indians and the labor of blacks, Chinese, and Mexicans. By proclaiming their cultural superiority over all these nonwhite groups, whites legitimated their economic exploitation of them.

In the perceptions of nineteenth-century whites, however, the core issue was civilization, not greed. To be civilized was to live by the Protestant work ethic. Self-control harnessed acquisitiveness in the engine of progress, and without it, neither property nor salvation could be acquired. The whites considered the nonwhites sensual, lazy, barbaric, primitive, and savage. Perhaps because they projected onto others what they repressed in themselves, most whites found virtually all nonwhites deficient in self-control and hence uncivilized. By converting colored minorities into something less than civilized, the Protestant white majority in the Gilded Age both justified the segregation of social and economic space by race and provided themselves with a rationale for their cultural imperialism of uplift and reform.

After the Civil War, Indians were to be separated and secluded from the main-stream of white society, much like the inmates of antebellum asylums, so that they could learn to be civilized. Thus, although the army, railroad officials, and white settlers each had their own reasons for wanting the Plains Indians isolated on reserva-tions, reformers saw the reservations as a way to assimilate Indians into white society. As conceived by the reformers, a group almost exclusively Eastern, urban, and middle class, the reservation was a giant reformatory. As one of them put it, the purpose was "first to tame, next to train, and then to teach"[1] the Indian inmates.

Because they spoke for a class that was so certain of its claim to represent divine will and human betterment, the reformers were contemptuous of Indian culture. With missionary zeal, they agreed with the Commissioner of Indian Affairs who said of the Indians in 1881: "To allow them to drag along in their old superstitions, laziness and filth, when we have the power to elevate them in the scale of humanity, would be a lasting disgrace to our government."[2] Thus, Indian culture was not a way of life to be appreciated but an obstacle to be removed. On the reservation, the hunt was replaced by the government dole, the size of which was manipulated to reward "good" Indians and punish "bad" ones. Schools, first those staffed on the reservations by Eastern missionaries and then off-reservation boarding schools in the East, taught Indian chil-dren to be ashamed of the religion, customs, and values of their parents.

Within a decade, the reformers became impatient with the reservation as a socializing agent. By the mid-1880s, white fears of the savage Indian had given way to concerns over the problem of the idle Indian. Although the Indians had been tamed, reformatory discipline hardly seemed to have made them any more fit for white civili-zation. The reservation itself was now seen as part of the problem. "Reforming a drunkard by keeping him in a saloon," tellingly argued one reformer, "would be quite as sensible as our method of trying to civilize and Americanize our Indians by keeping them separated in tribes on prison reservations excluded from all contact with our civilization."[3]

Having already depersonalized the Indians into children in need of white guid-ance, the reformers now substituted the marketplace for the reservation as the school in which the Indians would be forced to grow up as responsible citizens. Given the middle-class assumptions on which it was based, the rationale for the substitution was compelling. Because American civilization rested on private property, individualism, and acquisitiveness, Indians would be forever on the outside looking in until they acquired property as individuals. Once provided with their own plots of land freed from the shackles of tribal life and the enervating security of property held in common, the Indians would finally have, the reformers were convinced, the self-incentive to advance themselves. In a word, the Indians were to be made selfish. One of their friends put it best:[4]

> We need to *awaken in him wants*. In his dull savagery he must be touched by the wings of the divine angel of discontent. . . . Discontent with the tepee and the starving rations of the Indian camp in winter is needed to get the Indian out of the blanket and into trousers—and trousers with a pocket in them, and with a *pocket that aches to be filled with dollars!*

The General Allotment Act of 1887, known as the Dawes Act, was a victory for those reformers who were weary of a gradualist approach to civilizing the Indians. In the pointed phrase of Theodore Roosevelt, the act was "a mighty pulverizing engine to break up the tribal mass." The act authorized the President (at his discretion, not that of the Indians) to allot reservation lands to individual Indians. Each family head was to receive 160 acres. Citizenship was conferred on those Indians, born in the United States, who either took up allotted land or separated themselves from their tribes and "adopted the habits of civilized life." With the approval of the affected tribe, land left over on the reservations after the allotments were distributed was to be made available for sale to whites. The proceeds of such sales were to be placed in a federally adminis- tered trust fund for the "education and civilization"[5] of the tribe.

The Dawes Act was a classic example of brokerage politics. There was something in it for each of the key interest groups. The act specifically reaffirmed the authority of Congress to grant railroads rights-of-way through reservations, expedited the prying loose of land for white settlers, and held out the promise to Eastern humanitarians of a rapid transformation of Indians into model citizens anxious to improve themselves. As for the tribes, Senator Henry Teller of Colorado came closest to predicting the results. He denounced allotments as a policy "to despoil the Indians of their lands and to make them vagabonds on the face of the earth."[6]

The 138 million acres of land held by the tribes in 1887 shrank by 40 percent in the next decade. Before the allotment policy was ended by Congress in 1934, the Indians lost 60 percent of the acreage they had had when the Dawes Act was passed. Most of the loss, some 60 million acres, was sold by the federal government as "surplus." Another 27 million acres represented land allotted to individual Indians that was subsequently acquired by whites. Contrary to the expectations of the reformers, the ownership of land was not some elixir that converted Indians into a red version of Jefferson's independent yeomanry. Many of the Plains Indians lacked agricultural skills, 160-acre plots were inefficient in the semi-arid West, and whites with the capital and legal knowledge needed to exploit the land for its farming, grazing, and mineral potential were constantly on the lookout for land bargains. Because it was assumed by whites that the Indians would either continue to die off at an alarming rate or be absorbed into white society, no lands were set aside for the future use of the tribes. When the Indian population unexpectedly expanded in the twentieth century, it did so on a declining land base; as a result, Indian poverty became chronic.

The reformers had surely intended something better. They were appalled, with good reason, by the conditions on the reservations in the 1880s. Whooping cough, influenza, and measles carried off the children, alcohol poisoned the adults, and all were usually fed a sludge-like mixture of meat, flour, and offal steamed in large vats and scooped out in pails. The reformers really did care, but their human vision was so limited that in the end their caring hardly mattered. The goal was always to change, not understand, the Indians. What made an Indian an Indian was to be destroyed. "Kill the Indian in him, and save the man"[7] declared Richard H. Pratt, one of the reformers.

Intent on remaking the Indians in the bourgeois image of Protestant piety and entrepreneurial drive, the reformers were oblivious to such vital needs of the tribes as political self-determination and economic self-sufficiency. These needs, recognition of which would have acknowledged that there was an Indian culture worthy of the name, were never on the agenda of reform. Thus it was no wonder that the allotment policy, the reformers' greatest achievement, worsened the condition of most Indians. The reformers, in assuming that they knew what was best for the Indians, succeeded only in giving them the worst both culturally and economically—the loss of their land and the erosion of their communal existence.

The Chinese, in contrast to the Indians, never formed a large enough mass in the Gilded Age to require the "pulverizing engine" of congressional legislation to break them up. Instead, when the numbers of Chinese reached a point at which the racial purity of the republic seemed threatened and the livelihood of white workers undermined, Congress reacted by prohibiting the immigration of Chinese laborers and declaring that Chinese already resident in the United States were ineligible for citizenship. Beginning in 1882, a series of exclusion acts barred Chinese entry until 1943.

The number of Chinese in the United States increased from 7,500 in 1850 to 105,000 in 1880. They were almost ideal immigrant laborers for a booming industrial economy. They worked hard for wages lower than most whites would accept. Over 90 percent were males with no families to support. Because their goal was to earn money quickly and return to China, where their American wages would finance a marriage and purchase some village property, they were temporary laborers willing to endure low pay and dangerous working conditions. Nearly half of them soon returned to China. Unlike white ethnics from Europe, Chinese immigrants could not vote. Highly mobile and with no political power, they posed no threat to capital's control over labor.

The advantages of cheap Chinese labor were most evident in the building of the transcontinental railroads and the industrial development of California. Work crews for the Central Pacific, which pushed eastward from the West Coast, were almost exclusively Chinese. Employing Chinese rather than European labor saved the railroad over $5 million in labor costs between 1866 and 1869. Similar savings were available for manufacturers in California, where the Chinese comprised close to half of the industrial work force in the 1870s. After some Chinese were brought east in 1870 to break a shoemakers' strike in North Adams, Massachusetts, some businessmen dared to hope that they had found the ultimate weapon with which to control labor. "If for no other purpose than the breaking up of the incipient steps towards labor combinations and 'Trade Unions'," wrote a friend of capital in *Scribner's Monthly*, "the advent of Chinese labor should be hailed with warm welcome. . . ."[8]

Rather than being welcomed, Chinese labor was excluded in 1882. Labor bitterly opposed Chinese immigration, but popular prejudices played a larger role in the exclusionary movement. Because of their color, and hence their visibility as nonwhites, the Chinese were, from the beginning, denied equal civil rights. The California Supreme Court put it bluntly in an 1854 case:[9]

> Held, that the words, Indian, Negro, Black, and White are generic terms, designating races. That, therefore, Chinese and all other people not white, are included in the [state] prohibition from being witnesses against whites.

In 1887 the U.S. Supreme Court ruled that the Civil Rights legislation of the Reconstruction period did not apply to the Chinese immigrants. Although, if anything, the Chinese assimilated too easily into the economy, they relied on their own clan structures to enforce their ethical and business codes. This, in turn, reinforced white suspicions that the Chinese rejected assimilation into American society.

Most important in the drive to stop additional Chinese immigration were white perceptions that the Chinese already here were only the vanguard of countless millions

The Anti-Chinese Wall. As shown in this 1882 cartoon with its crude racial and ethnic stereotypes, Congress responded to a variety of economic and cultural pressures in its exclusionary policy against the Chinese. At the same time, the wall of trade restrictions erected by the Chinese was starting to come down. (The Bettmann Archive)

to follow. If a yellow wave ever swept over America, whites of all classes feared that the Chinese might do to them what the whites had already done to the Indians. Candidly expressing this fear, Frank Pixley of San Francisco told a congressional committee on Chinese immigration in 1876:[10]

> The Yellow races are to be confined to what the Almighty originally gave them and as they are not a favored people, they are not to be permitted to steal from us what we have robbed the American savage of.

The success of the exclusionary movement ensured that the permission was not granted.

The productive labor of black Americans, like that of the Chinese, made them valuable to white America. Unlike the Chinese, however, blacks could not be branded as alien outsiders whose very presence in America was subject to government decree. However much vitiated by white opposition in the South and the consensus on white racial superiority in the nation, the great Civil War amendments—the Thirteenth, Fourteenth, and Fifteenth—suggested a commitment to civil equality and full assimilation that minimally recognized that blacks were Americans. Moreover, the blacks were the labor mainstay of the Southern regional economy. Consequently, blacks were segregated there rather than excluded—a physical separation of the races that simultaneously catered to white fears of social disorder and their need for black labor.

Although not formalized into law until the 1890s, segregation as a *de facto* pattern of racial separation emerged in the South soon after the Civil War. Southern whites were obsessed with the need to exert racial control after slavery was destroyed and wanted to exclude the freed population from all public facilities and institutions.

Counterbalancing the white majority were Republican politicians anxious to extend tangible benefits to blacks, their main political supporters, and blacks themselves, who demanded access to the public facilities from which they had been barred in the antebellum years and during the brief reign of the Johnson governments from 1865 to 1867. Measured against what it replaced—total exclusion—segregation represented a positive shift in social relations for the freed population. The black goal was equality of access, but political reality dictated that if blacks were to have any access to such facilities as hospitals and schools, those institutions would have to be segregated.

Separate black and white worlds emerged most sharply in Southern urban centers. It was here in the relatively unstructured and anonymous environment of the cities that white racial fears of losing control were most intense. Blacks belonged in the countryside, whites told themselves, where their labor would not compete with white artisans and their behavior could be personally monitored as in the days of slavery. But the freedmen refused to stay in their assigned places. The black population of Southern cities of over 4,000 almost doubled in the 1860s, whereas that of whites increased by only 13 percent. Blacks migrated to the cities in response to the greater educational and employment opportunities there. Federal army garrisons and the town offices of the Freedman's Bureau also offered them military and legal protection not available in the outlying plantation districts.

In housing, as in other areas of social interaction, urban whites charted the path for future segregation throughout the South. Antebellum residential patterns in Southern cities were relatively integrated by race. Live-in slave residences, usually in the back of the master's house, free black enclaves, and barracks for industrial slaves dispersed the black population among the whites in the cities. In contrast, the postwar cities had clearly defined racial neighborhoods. Poverty and the exclusionary selling practices of white homeowners and real estate developers limited the residential choices of most blacks to lots on the outskirts, where farms and estates were subdivided to meet the demand for cheap housing. By 1890 a black ring of shantytowns, lacking even the rudiments of municipal street, sanitation, and water services, encircled the predominately white core of Southern cities. Within that core, black residences were largely invisible to the casual visitor. Concentrated in alleys and side streets, and often ending in cul-de-sacs, black housing was sealed off from that of whites.

Apart from housing, which represented a clear deterioration in the black position after the war, the segregated access of blacks to social services and welfare facilities was an improvement over their prior exclusion. During congressional Reconstruction schools, hospitals, and orphanages were opened up to blacks for the first time. The freedmen were allowed to form their own militia units and fire companies. Nevertheless, access was separate but never equal. This was all the more true after white Democrats regained power in the 1870s. Under the Democrats, the outlines of Jim Crow began to solidify. Municipal codes governing access by race to public and private spaces multiplied, and the inequalities between white and black facilities, especially in schooling, widened. Thrown back upon their own churches, fraternal orders, and kinship ties, blacks redoubled their efforts at promoting racial solidarity and networks of self-help. Ironically, by so doing, they unintentionally strengthened the white case for yet more forced segregation.

Economic discrimination reinforced social segregation. Jobs in the marketplace, much like places in the social arena, were reserved for the exclusive use of whites.

Whites almost totally monopolized skilled labor and supervisory positions in the post-war South. Tacit agreements between employers and white labor, as well as the general white consensus that blacks should be field laborers, policed a rigid color line between the skilled and the unskilled. By 1880 fewer than one-third of the former slave artisans were able to practice their skills. Only about 30 percent of all employed black males in the lower South in 1890 worked outside agriculture, and, of these, three in four were servants, common laborers, and factory hands. Blacks retained their places in the antebellum industries, such as tobacco processing, and provided, like the immigrants in the North, the muscle of unskilled labor in the new industries of coal mining and iron foundries. But in the textile towns, which were touted as the hallmark of the New South in the 1880s, blacks were almost totally excluded. Poor whites in the Piedmont South held the textile jobs.

Economic discrimination created a reserve army of surplus labor in the South that could be used to weaken and discipline labor in general. All Southern labor paid the price for the job-reservation system. Although whites earned a bit more than blacks for the same job, the race issue effectively divided and subjugated the entire work force. The Southern wage scale for unskilled agricultural and industrial labor, the common lot of most workers, was 25 percent to 30 percent lower than the Northern average.

"In all things that are purely social we can be as separate as the fingers, yet one as the hand in all things essential to mutual progress."[11] By proclaiming in a famous speech the accommodationist policy implicit in this phrase, Booker T. Washington, President of Tuskegee Normal and Industrial Institute in Alabama, emerged as the leader of Afro-Americans in the 1890s. Washington's speech at the Atlanta Exposition in 1895 was just what the white South wanted to hear. In the midst of a national depression, violent labor unrest, and a campaign in the South to disfranchise blacks and codify Jim Crow, Washington soothed the fears of both the racial and economic paternalists. Blacks would have to raise themselves, he counseled, through education, hard work, self-help, and thrift—in short, a black version of the bourgeois work ethic. Blacks should denounce "social equality" as "folly" and aspire only to a "man's chance in the commercial world."[12]

Southern whites interpreted Washington's philosophy, for all its positive stress on black initiative and economic development, as a call for black forebearance and submission in a South in which the whites made the rules that discriminated against blacks. Northern whites agreed. Washington became the power broker between Northern philanthropists and Southern black colleges and, through his connections with Northern Republicans, he soon controlled black political patronage in the South. Praised by his admirers as a pragmatic leader shrewd enough to avoid antagonizing whites, and attacked by a minority of black critics in the North as a fawning accommodationist who refused to condemn white racism publicly, Washington had to accept the reality of unflexible white power.

Washington's leadership reflected the limited options open to blacks at the end of the nineteenth century. Options in the North were little more promising than those in the South. In Northern cities, 70 percent to 80 percent of black males were employed in menial, unskilled jobs. The black employment picture contrasted sharply with that of the Irish and Germans (see Table 9.1). The freed population was no more unprepared for the urban economy than were the European immigrants. As shown in Table 9.2, the skill levels of the first generation of Atlanta freedmen in 1880 were quite comparable to

Table 9.1 Occupational Structure of Males Age 18 and Over in Philadelphia, 1880
(in percentages)

Compared to two major immigrant groups, the Irish and Germans, blacks were overwhelmingly bunched in low-paying, unskilled jobs.

	BLACK	IRISH	GERMAN
High White-Collar	1.1	1.6	1.6
Low White-Collar	4.4	13.4	17.5
Skilled	13.7	31.5	59.7
Unskilled	79.2	50.1	15.3
Other	1.6	3.5	5.9

Source: Adapted from Hershberg, op. cit., Table 5, p. 443.

those of first-generation Irish-Americans in 1850. Nor had the black family been destroyed by slavery. In the rural South and urban North of the postwar period, the percentage of black families headed by both parents was only slightly lower than that of whites. Blacks had the economic and cultural resources to move upward in Northern cities. Exclusionary economic practices by whites explain why they did not.

Denied jobs in department stores, factories, and the public sector, and shunned by most of the trade unions, urban blacks were trapped at the bottom. Unlike the Europeans' experience, black job opportunities did not improve with the length of their residence in a given area. In the Boston of 1870, black males born in Massachusetts were barely better off than the former slaves who had recently arrived from the South. Among the former, 77 percent were domestics and common laborers, and among the latter, 84 percent. Ten years later, this gap had narrowed to 2 percent, and differences in rates of property ownership were just as minimal. Racial discrimination in the job market overshadowed any potential economic advantage of long-term residence for blacks in Boston.

Table 9.2 Occupational Comparison of Males Age 17 and Over
(in percentages)

The economic skills that the freedmen brought to American cities were quite similar to those of first-generation immigrants. By the second generation, however, the occupational gap would widen, because blacks were not allowed to compete for the better, higher-paying jobs that were open to the American-born sons of the immigrants.

	ATLANTA BLACKS, 1880	BOSTON IRISH, 1850
Unskilled	54.6	59.5
Semiskilled	13.1	14.8
Skilled	25.9	16.6
Nonmanual	4.1	7.6
Other	2.3	1.6

Source: Adapted from William Harris, "Work and the Family in Black Atlanta, 1880," *Journal of Social History* 9 (1976): Table 2, p. 321.

Although they composed less than 2 percent of the North's population as late as 1900, blacks alone of the immigrant newcomers to Northern cities were residentially segregated. With the exception of some of the 25 percent minority in the black middle class of skilled laborers and small businessmen who found housing in white middle-class districts, the majority of blacks lived in specific sections of the city. Consisting of enclaves on a few blocks or in alleys, and often designated by whites with racial epithets, the black neighborhoods were scattered throughout the run-down districts of the inner city. By World War I, the more concentrated of these enclaves began to solidify into ghettos, a process of drawing segregated boundaries in which white real-estate brokers, bankers, politicians, and property owners all played a part. Chicago's black ghetto, already taking shape in the 1890s, was the first in a large Northern city.

Blacks worked out their strategies for survival in the least desirable parts of the city in which they were confined. These strategies were formed in the interaction between the black family economy and the urban industrial economy. The central fact confronting urban blacks was the wall of white restrictions around job opportunities. The lack of secure and decent-paying jobs, particularly for husbands, usually made blacks the poorest urban group and created an income gap that had to be closed if black families were to survive.

One way to close that gap was by taking in boarders and subtenants, even if it meant additional pressure on living space that was already too cramped. One-third of black families in Philadelphia in 1880 augmented their income this way. That proportion was twice as high as that for other urban families, immigrant or native. Another way to add to the family income was by finding wage work for others in the household besides the husband. Whereas immigrant families accomplished this by pulling their children out of school at an early age and sending them out to work in the factories, this option was largely ruled out for blacks. Textiles and other industries did not hire black children. Consequently, black children stayed in school longer than immigrant children, and it was the black wife who earned wages. About 20 percent of black married women took in work within the home or worked outside the home as seamstresses or domestics. This percentage was five times greater than the 4 percent of other wives, native or immigrant, who did so.

The black family held together, but the strains on it were tremendous. Most indicative of those strains was the high percentage of black families with children headed by females. That figure was 30 percent in Philadelphia in 1880, a percentage that contrasted with 17 percent for the Irish, 6 percent for the Germans, and 14 percent for native whites. Poverty, not any intrinsic weakness in black culture after slavery, accounted for most of this disparity. The chances of a father being absent increased for all family groups as wealth decreased, and black families were the poorest. Compounding this poverty was a frightfully high rate of black mortality (see Table 9.3) that carried off more males than females in an urban environment in which black women were already normally in the majority because they could more easily find work. Once widowed, a black woman had a very slim chance of ever remarrying. She went to work and raised her children with the help of kin.

The experience of Mexican-Americans was an amalgam of what happened to the Indians, Chinese, and blacks. Like the Indians, the Mexican-Americans lost their lands to white America. The major losses came in the Mexican War of the 1840s. Like the Chinese, Mexican immigrants fleeing poverty in their homeland were a cheap pool of

Table 9.3   Life Expectancy at Birth in 1900
                (in years)

As was true half a century earlier when most blacks were still enslaved (see Table 2.1), the life expectancy of blacks in 1900 was still much shorter than that of white Americans.

	MALE	FEMALE
Black	32.5	33.5
White	46.6	48.7

Source: Historical Statistics, Series B-107–115.

labor for white businesses in the West. The economy of the Southwest was extractive and labor intensive, and it was Chicanos, working for wages 75 percent lower than those for whites, who provided much of the labor in the mines and on the ranches that furnished raw materials to the industrializing East. Like the blacks, Mexican-Americans were subjected to Jim Crow legislation and dehumanizing racial stereotypes. The society of the Southwest was as racially stratified along a brown-white axis as was that of the South with its black-white division.

Already accustomed to viewing nonwhites in the United States as their inferiors, white Americans thus readily accepted the message of cultural imperialism that was implicit in the entertainment at the great turn-of-the-century expositions and industrial fairs. In these celebrations of American progress, the colored races—Indians, Africans, and Asians—each had their specific booths and encampments. On display in their native dress, they were there to satisfy the curiosity of whites and to titillate but not frighten. In their assigned slots of safe subordination, they also served as a model for how white Americans conceived of nonwhites.

Gender and Social Space

The bourgeois cult of domesticity, a product of Jacksonian America, continued to set the proper standards for the position of women in the Gilded Age. As we saw in Chapter 2, this fusion of the ideologies of class and gender was part of a larger biological ordering of America, in which whites and men stood above nonwhites and women. Nonwhites supposedly could be civilized only if subordinated and taught self-control by whites. In turn, white males could remain civilized only if their wives were subordinated in the domestic sphere, in which they would restrain their husbands with nurturing love and teach their children the virtues of self-control.

The cultural ideal of the Victorian lady prescribed many roles for the respectable woman. She was to be an exemplar of Christian love, procreator of children, consumer of fashions, helpmate to her husband, and custodian of all that was precious and pure. All the while, she was told by the best medical advice that her physical health depended on her having children, and that any strenuous or competitive activity outside the home, be it in recreation, business, or education, would upset her delicate sensibilities. Wealthier and more leisured than her Jacksonian predecessor, the Victorian lady both anchored the moral rectitude of the home in a sea of unsettling social change and displayed the wealth that her husband earned in an economy that resulted from that change. Almost reduced to a caricature, her popular image remains fixed as that of a prim and proper lady of fashion bound up in a tightly laced corset.

As a social type, the Victorian lady did exist in Gilded Age America, especially in the upper echelons of urban white society, in which the money for a fashionable lifestyle was plentiful. Themes of domesticity, passivity, and restraint, notably in sexual matters, saturated middle-class magazines and the sentimentalized, family-centered evangelicalism popularized by Henry Ward Beecher. Still, the actual lives of most middle-class women fell short of the cultural ideal, and these women were moving even further away from it during the Gilded Age. By limiting the size of their families, attending school longer and at higher levels, and entering the labor market, these women were beginning to define a quite different culture for themselves.

Three fundamental trends registered the changes in the lives of Victorian women:

1. The fertility rate continued its nineteenth-century decline. The average white family had only half as many children in 1900 (three to four), as it had had in 1800 (seven to eight).
2. Women made significant strides in education. Only three antebellum colleges admitted women; Oberlin became the first, in 1837, followed by Antioch in 1852 and the Elmira Female College in 1855. After the war, a host of private women's colleges were founded, and gender barriers had fallen in most of the state universities. Correspondingly, the number of women who earned bachelor's degrees quadrupled between 1870 and 1900. Only 20 percent of bachelor's degrees in 1900 went to women, but the gender gap was closing. At the high-school level the gap had already closed. Farm or factory work was often more attractive or necessary for male teenagers than high school, and throughout the Gilded Age 60 percent of high-school graduates were female.
3. Most at variance with cultural strictures on staying in the home, women's participation in the wage labor force rose sharply. Nearly all women worked, but those who received pay for their efforts tripled in the last third of the nineteenth century. In 1900 a woman stood a 50 percent greater chance of being a wage earner than in 1870. During those thirty years, the percentage of employed women rose from 14 percent to 21 percent.

All of these trends were interrelated. The link between women's education and the declining birth rate was most strikingly confirmed by the fact that 75 percent of the women who graduated from college before 1900 never married. This was at a time when fewer than 10 percent of other American women remained single throughout their lives. This first generation of women college graduates chose professional careers and reform work rather than marriage. For the far greater number of women who never went to college, the linkage of urbanization and industrialization created both opportunities and constraints that motivated them to delay marriage and have smaller families.

The city was more of a safety valve for the daughters of American farmers than for their sons. As American agriculture became increasingly commercialized and specialized in the Gilded Age, farm work was defined more and more as a male job. The rise in farm productivity and the spread of catalogue sales of factory-made merchandise simultaneously reduced the demand for women's labor on subsistence tasks. As a result, the sex ratio of the rural labor force became more skewed in favor of males, and farm daughters began leaving home before their brothers. This selective outmigration produced a pronounced rural-urban sexual imbalance by 1900. In rural areas, there were 109 white males for every 100 females. In the cities, despite their attraction for single immigrant males, the proportions were reversed. Native-born women went to the cities in search of a greater range of paid work than was available to them in the countryside.

Once in the cities, farm daughters competed for work with black, immigrant, and white native-born women already there. A racial and ethnic job hierarchy emerged that roughly coincided with the skill levels of the competing groups. Black women worked most commonly as maids, seamstresses, and laundresses—jobs that were outside the industrial economy though subsidized by its profits. This labor, a commercialization of the housewife's work, created leisure time for the wives of affluent husbands. Immigrant women were most likely to work at semiskilled factory jobs and were chiefly responsible for the increase in women's share of manufacturing employment—from 14 percent in 1870 to 19 percent in 1900. Whereas immigrant women were on the production line, native-born white women tended to be at the administrative or sales end of the business revolution. The cultural advantage of not being black or ethnic, combined with the marketable skills of literacy, good English, and an education beyond the common-school level, gave these women an entry into the corporate office and department store. From 5 percent of the clerical work force in 1880, women jumped to 18 percent in 1890 and 27 percent in 1900.

Although fertility varied by class in the cities, birth rates as a whole were markedly lower than in rural areas (see Table 9.4). These lower rates reflected the adaptations of urban populations to an economic environment that altered the importance of literacy and the former agrarian roles of women and children in such a way as to encourage smaller families and later marriages. The urban economy, in contrast to the rural, created a range of economic activities that placed a premium on literacy and education. White, single, and native-born women responded to these opportunities by moving into office work and sales. About 90 percent of these women eventually married, but at a later age than rural women did. When they did raise a family, they kept it small. Children, except for those of immigrant families, who were desperately dependent upon their labor for additional income, were more of an economic burden

Table 9.4 Urban and Rural Fertility in 1900
   (children under 5 per 1,000 women, 15–44)

Urban and rural Americans had markedly different fertility patterns, because the economic environment of a large city provided an incentive to have fewer children. Urban black fertility was so low because most manufacturers would not hire black children, and hence the economic cost of having children was greater for black families than for those of immigrants.

	URBAN[a]	SMALL TOWN & RURAL[b]
White	368	552
Black	239	596

Source: Adapted from Herman Lantz and Lewellyn Hendrix, "Fertility and the Black Family in the Nineteenth Century: A Re-Examination of the Past," *Journal of Family History* 3 (1978): Table 2, p. 255.

[a] Defined as cities with a population of 25,000 and over.
[b] Outside cities with a population of 25,000 and over.

than an asset in the city. The middle class had fewer children than the working class and kept them in school longer.

For all the changes in the lives of Victorian women that apparently violated the official cultural codes of conduct, the cult of domesticity was not overturned. It bent, but it never snapped. Victorian conceptions of womenhood easily accommodated many of the changes. More schooling for women meshed nicely with the emphasis on the educative role of the mother in the family. It was also accepted as a practical preparation for the charitable and religious activities that middle-class women had engaged in since the Jacksonian period. The trend toward smaller families could be viewed as a confirmation of the extraordinarily positive value middle-class Victorians placed on the virtues of sexual restraint.

Sharp increases in divorce rates and the entry of middle-class women into clerical work posed, on the surface, more immediate threats to Victorian standards of the respectable married woman within her domestic sphere. However, the five-fold increase in divorce rates between 1870 and 1930 might well have strengthened the institution of marriage and guarded women's place within it. In the eighteenth and early nineteenth centuries, about 20 percent of all marriages were ended within the first fifteen years by the death of one of the spouses, and half were terminated by death within thirty years. When life expectancies rose significantly in the late nineteenth century, divorce began to provide a voluntary means of achieving the marital variety that formerly had been forced on widows and widowers by the death of a spouse. Divorce also served as an outlet for tensions that were no longer cut short by the early death of one of the partners. Divorce did not mean a renunciation of marriage by women. By far the greatest increase in reasons cited by husbands as grounds for a divorce between the 1870s and the early twentieth century was in the category of cruelty, a term nearly synonymous with a wife's refusal to be submissive and meek.

Victorians rarely approved of divorce, but they learned to tolerate it. A similar, somewhat condescending, attitude prevailed toward female workers drawn from the middle class. In transgressing the domestic code by leaving home to take up a job, most middle-class women were trying to live up to that code and were hoping to eventually improve their culturally sanctioned position within the home. This apparent contradiction grew out of the domestic ideology itself: Middle-class daughters from economically marginal or declining families could best meet their domestic obligations by working outside the home. Their incomes enabled their families to maintain or improve their middle-class status and often helped subsidize a brother's education.

At least two-thirds of the female clerks in federal offices in Washington came out of professional or white-collar families. Most were young, single, and native-born. About one-quarter were widows. Recent financial reverses in their families, often triggered by the death of a male breadwinner, were common motivational factors in their decisions to work. Class considerations of status kept them out of factory and domestic work, but clerical jobs were at least quasi-respectable. A similar pattern held for the native-born majority of department-store workers. Most of these young women came from a lower-middle-class background, lived at home with their parents, and surrendered their wages to the family economy.

For nearly all of these women, work was not a substitute for marriage. Forced to take service positions at pay that was half that of males for the same jobs, they left the labor market in their mid-twenties to marry. The traditional household offered them their only real chance to maintain middle-class living standards. Once married, they rarely returned to a wage job. Thus, whereas less than 3 percent of white married women of native stock worked for wages by the turn of the century, about one-third of their single counterparts did. (Economic need would not force women to combine marriage with paid work until the twentieth century. In a startling switch, the percentage of married women in the female labor force soared from 14 percent in 1900 to 62 percent by 1970.)

The very kinds of work open to women in the Gilded Age also illustrated how underlying conceptions of gender continued to structure the economic participation of women. In 1870 about nine in ten women employed outside of agriculture were domestic servants or factory operatives in the apparel industry. By 1900 that figure was around seven in ten. That is, throughout these three decades most employed women continued to work at jobs that were a commercialized extension of their traditional unpaid household labor of cleaning, sewing, and weaving. As evidenced by the two in ten working women who had nonmanual, white-collar jobs by 1900, economic opportunities did broaden. These newer jobs, however, were as much defined by gender as was that most feminized of the older jobs, domestic labor. A teacher, librarian, or nurse was just as likely to be a woman as was a domestic servant in 1900. Over three-fourths of all these jobs were held by women. The same feminization occurred in certain kinds of office work, notably among typists, stenographers, and telephone operators, and in the sales staffs of department stores.

Characteristic of the professional and clerical jobs available to women was a close connection between the labor needs of public and private employers and gender conceptions of the special attributes of women. The feminized professions—nursing, teaching, librarianship, and, toward the end of the Gilded Age, social work—were in rapidly growing job areas that called for relatively close, personalized ties between the expert and client. Not only did women, because of their sex, appear to embody best the nurturing values of patience and caring that were needed, they also offered the cheap and abundant labor that would hold down costs in these expanding service areas. In a circular pattern of cause and effect, an oversupply of women in the few professions open to them led to low wages, which were in turn reinforced by the low status associated with jobs identified as women's work. Employers justified wages barely above the subsistence level by citing the nearly universal assumption that women worked only as a temporary expedient while they waited for marriage and support from their husbands. Within each of the service professions, women were relegated to the lowest-paying jobs with the least amount of authority. School superintendents, head librarians, agency directors, and doctors and hospital administrators were overwhelmingly male.

Gender was also used to organize hierarchies of pay and power within the business bureaucracies that began to take shape in the 1880s. Women were taking over clerical work, formerly a male-dominated occupation that was rapidly losing status. Prior to the corporate revolution of the late nineteenth century, the clerk was an ambitious young man (often the son or nephew of the owner of the company) who stood closer to management than to factory labor in terms of status and pay. With perseverance and a bit of luck, he could reasonably expect to rise to the top of the small firm or partnership that employed him. Upward advancement and possible ownership became much less likely when the administrative demands placed upon businesses multiplied with the

Women Typists, 1897. As shown here in a scene from the audit division of the Metropolitan Life Insurance Company, typing work in American business was very quickly classified as a woman's job. (Courtesy of Metropolitan Life Insurance Company)

increased scope of economic activity. To meet this demand, clerical jobs of recording and communicating information exploded from 77,000 in 1870 to 682,000 in 1900. The typical clerk now was most likely to be just a cog in a bureaucratic machine who was subjected to the same simplification of tasks and repetitive routine as was the factory laborer.

The adoption of a new business technology in the 1880s, the typewriter, accelerated what amounted to a trivialization of office work. It was no coincidence that from the start most typists were women. Typing required, it was assumed, the purported greater nimbleness of women, who by their nature were willing to work at the passive task of copying and making neat and clean information controlled and dictated by men. Expected by male management to have no ambitions for a career of their own, and hence unlikely to be dissatisfied if their jobs offered no prospect of advancement, women became the semiskilled equivalent in the office of the immigrants in the factory. Working at the rapid-turnover, low-paying jobs reserved for them at the bottom of their respective job hierarchies, each group helped push native-born males upward into positions of better pay and more power.

Sales work in stores, which hardly existed as an occupational category before 1870, was early on pegged as a job for women. The sale of consumer goods by women to women seemed to be a natural fit for the owners of department stores who introduced mass retailing in American cities after 1870. Managers utilized women's familiarity with domestic items as a positive asset to be polished in sales techniques. Female clerks were urged to rely on their womanly patience in dealing with customers and to treat them as they would guests in their own home. In short, the bonds of sisterhood that had developed between women in their separate spheres of domesticity were commercialized in the service of sales. In return, female sales personnel were offered greater opportunities to move into middle management than prevailed in most of the white-collar occupations that had become feminized.

For all the changes in family size, education, and work that indicated that Victorian women were gradually acquiring more autonomy in their daily lives, the gender line between the public male and private female spheres remained as a distinct limitation on women's autonomy. The one issue that most directly threatened to erase that line was woman's suffrage. Popular resistance (including that of some women) to the vote for women clearly showed that most Americans were still not prepared to recognize women as self-governing individuals.

Women reformers stepped outside the mainstream of nineteenth-century American culture in their struggle to win the vote. Suffrage directly raised the issue of the individual right of every woman to self-assertion. Because it was feared that such independence would overturn women's subordination within the family, suffrage was blocked in the nineteenth century. The most bitter defeat came with the passage of the Fourteenth and Fifteenth Amendments. The former put the word *male* into the Constitution for the first time, and the latter retreated from natural-rights philosophy when it limited federal authority over voting qualifications in the states to the categories of race, color, and previous condition of servitude. As a result of this defeat, the suffragist ranks split. The more militant faction, led by Elizabeth Cady Stanton and Susan B. Anthony, felt they had been betrayed by male abolitionists and Republicans, their former allies in the cause of antislavery. Stanton and Anthony formed the National Woman Suffrage Association in 1869, an organization exclusively for women and controlled exclusively by women.

As an essential first step in breaking down the gender barriers between the public and private spheres, the suffragists in the Gilded Age correctly argued that women needed to be armed with the vote in order to meet men as equals in the public arena. Nonetheless, the cultural power of the notion of separate spheres was resilient enough to deflect such a frontal assault. The suffragists eventually won the vote at the end of the World War I only by shifting their rationale for demanding it. In the early twentieth century, they abandoned the earlier appeal based on the universal grounds of natural rights. Instead, they turned to gender-based arguments that stressed the special contributions that women could make as housewives and mothers to such public issues as housing and welfare. As was true throughout the Gilded Age, woman's place was still deemed to be within the home.

Age and Social Space

American society in the nineteenth century was much less conscious of specific age boundaries and categories than it is today. Until quite late in the century, Americans did not conceive of childhood, adolescence, middle age, and old age as distinct life stages defined by exclusive forms of behavior and regulated by fixed rules and schedules. For most nineteenth-century Americans, each of these stages haphazardly blended into the next, and the specialized institutions and legal arrangements that today segregate the population by age had just begun to evolve in the Gilded Age. The beginning, however, clearly presaged what has become one of the central features of modern American society—the use of age as an ordering device.

The transition from childhood to adulthood was more casual and less standardized a century ago. Among male youth, precise chronological age did not count so much in determining one's status as did physical strength and maturity. Adolescence was prolonged and unstructured. Sometime before the age of puberty, young males and females began to contribute to their own support. Farm work for both, and apprenticeships and clerical jobs for males, gave them employment and left them only semidependent on their parents and other adults. While working sporadically at temporary jobs, adolescents made loose, changing commitments to living at home and attending school. The males in particular were constantly shifting back and forth between the independence of adulthood and the dependence of childhood.

During the Gilded Age, a distinct urban version of the above rural pattern of adolescence emerged. Most urban families faced a constant struggle for economic security, and the children had a responsibility to provide a margin of material comfort for the family. Beginning in their early teens and continuing for about seven years, young men and women were expected to earn wages to supplement the family income. While these family obligations were being fulfilled, the adolescents usually stayed in their parents' home, picked up some schooling, and delayed marriage. After leaving home in their early twenties, the young further postponed marriage until an average age of 26. Concerned with economic security, they worked until they had some cash reserves to support a family of their own. The actual establishment of a separate household frequently did not occur until the couple were in their early thirties. For a few years, couples tended to board or live with parents as a means of easing the financial strains of heading their own household. As with rural youth, education, work, and residence were intermixed in a flexible timetable for the urban young. Specific boundaries of age did not sharply separate youth from adulthood.

In the late nineteenth century, adults began to draw such age boundaries. Prior to the 1890s, the word *adolescent* was rarely used, and when it was, it referred to early adulthood, the period just after one left their teens. As popularized in the turn-of-the-century writings of psychologist G. Stanley Hall, adolescence was now pushed back into the teens and was identified with a particular state of physical and mental stress brought on by the mere fact of one's chronological age. In Hall's dramatic language, this "stormy period" consisted of a struggle for supremacy between "the very worst and best impulses in the human soul."[13] Hall's ideas added the weight of apparent scientific evidence to the efforts of adults since the mid-nineteenth century to control and regulate the young in age-segregated settings. If, in fact, adolescents were naturally awkward, vulnerable, and unstable, it followed that they should be closely watched and supervised in controlled environments that isolated them from loose and dangerous contacts with the adult world at large.

In the Gilded Age, adult concerns were focused on urban males in the 14-to-18 age group, especially those who were the sons of immigrants. The urban and Protestant middle classes, those who could afford to forego the income of their children's labor, wanted to keep working-class youth as well in the schools past the age of fourteen, at which most of them left to go to work. Motivated by a desire both to prevent the exploitation of child labor and to extend lessons in self-control for as long as possible, these adults pushed for stiffer attendance laws. They also supported the addition of new, age-graded layers to the educational system. Such layers permitted the minority of male teachers to concentrate on disciplining the older students who would now be retained in high school. By the 1890s, these reforms were taking hold. High-school enrollments ballooned from 203,000 to 519,000 during that decade. By the end of the century, a hierarchy of preschool, elementary, junior high, and high schools was being formed that routed the young through discrete age brackets of education.

The middle class did not neglect the presumed needs of their own children. These Protestant adults took the lead in founding and promoting national organizations aimed at instilling Christian character in middle-class youth. A common motivation behind these organizations, the largest of which were Christian Endeavor, the Epsworth League, the junior branches of the Young Men's Christian Association, and, in the early twentieth century, the Boy Scouts of America, was the adult belief that the leisure time of adolescents had to be supervised for their own good. Evangelical teaching and planned physical activities were combined in a youth ethic of Christian self-improvement that was intended to train both the body and the soul. Without such an ethic, the sponsoring adults feared the corruption of their children during that leisure time, which had become more conspicuous as youth worked less and attended school more. In their anxieties, adults saw youth yielding to the sensual temptations of the city, growing soft and bored while their education was prolonged, or, in the case of urban youngsters, running around with street gangs once school was out. In small-town America, where these youth organizations enjoyed their greatest growth, adolescents were constantly leaving for the cities. The Protestant middle class tried to slow this outflow and steel their youth against the enticements of the metropolis by isolating them in a protective network of church-related social activities.

Contrary to the dominant youth organizations of antebellum America, fire gangs and volunteer militia, those of the late Gilded Age were set up and tightly run by adults. Male adolescents still came together in their own groups of spontaneous and boisterous camaraderie, but those of the middle class were increasingly funneled into an adult-controlled group regulated by a strict sense of Christian decorum. The purpose of the new organizations, as defined by adults, was to train youth in those correct precepts of behavior that the youth, because of their age, could not grasp without adult supervision.

Old age, the other end of the biological spectrum, also began to acquire a special social significance in the late Gilded Age. As indicated in Table 9.5, a general aging of the population set in by the second half of the nineteenth century, in response to declining mortality rates. Until this aging and the onset of industrial capitalism, the old

Table 9.5 The Aging of the Population

Although the pace accelerated even further in the twentieth century, the overall aging of the American population first became apparent in the late nineteenth century.

	MEDIAN AGE OF POPULATION	OLD[a] AS PERCENTAGE OF TOTAL POPULATION
1850	18.9	4.1
1900	22.9	6.3
1970	28.1	14.1

Source: Historical Statistics, Series A-119–134, 143–157.
[a]Age 60 and over.

were not arbitrarily separated from those who were younger. No sharp boundaries in working or living arrangements set the elderly apart from the middle aged. By the end of the century, however, had emerged the rationale and first programs for the segregation of the elderly that are characteristic of America today.

In the nineteenth century, the elderly worked as long as they were physically able. In 1890, for example, 73 percent of the male population over age 65 was still working. Today, when a retirement age exists that automatically marks off the aged from younger groups, only about one in four male workers over 65 holds full-time employment. In the absence of private pension plans or programs of public aid, nineteenth-century workers had little choice but to support themselves throughout old age. Less than 2 percent of the elderly were ever placed in almshouses in the nineteenth century. A Massachusetts survey in 1910 revealed that close to 80 percent of those age 65 and over received no form of public relief or assistance, and most of those who did were drawing military pensions.

The rural family economy was adapted to an urban setting in order to meet the exigencies of old age. In both instances, the elderly relied on the assistance of family and kin, but in the city their homes substituted for their farms as a safety net. Wage income could be lost at any time because of illness, layoffs, and wage cuts, or physical incapacities. Ownership of a house was crucial to survival strategies, because it enabled the elderly to exchange what their house had to offer, meals and space to live, for part of the income of kin or strangers. The children comprised the first lifeline of support. Although urban children typically left home at the age of 22 or 23, at least one tended to remain or return later to assist their parents in their old age. Childless parents, or those whose children had left permanently, compensated by taking in boarders and lodgers. These paying co-residents were a means of support in old age that was especially critical for widows.

By no means should the lives of the elderly in the Gilded Age be sentimentalized. Compared to today, their existence was less secure and more unstable. Their financial condition was usually precarious at best, and they were constrained from turning to what very little public aid was available, for fear of being stigmatized as paupers. Still, they did have the consolation of knowing that they would live out their lives among family and relatives. Although the economic security of the elderly has improved since 1900, their family status has declined. In the late nineteenth century, fewer than 1 percent of ever-married Americans age 65 and over lived alone or in an institution for the elderly. By 1970 the old were much more segregated from the general population. One in four aged men and one in three women were institutionalized or living by themselves.

Nothing was more significant in the development of the aged as a segregated class than the creation of retirement as a separate stage of life. A consensus slowly emerged after the Civil War that wage work should be reserved for the young and able-bodied. Older workers, it was argued, should voluntarily agree to leave the work force. If voluntarism failed, then workers should be forced to retire at a predetermined age. Aged workers, 4.7 percent of the employed labor force in 1900, were overrepresented in agriculture, 6.1 percent, and the professions, 5.5 percent, fields in which self-employment was still high. Within the industrial sector, the old more than held their own in traditional crafts that had not yet been revolutionized by machine technology. The old were least likely to be employed in the fast-growing industries of trade, transportation, and metallurgy, in which the machine and the corporation were trans-forming work. As the variations in employment patterns suggest, the technological and administrative revolution in business was bypassing the old. Youth and energy, not age and experience, were more compatible with the corporate stress on speeding up work and making it more efficient.

The drive to separate the aged from work was part of a larger cultural shift in perceptions of the old during the Gilded Age. There were many reasons for this shift:

1. At the most fundamental level, the transition from an agrarian to an industrial social order eroded the economic power that the aged had traditionally mono-polized because of their control over the family's landed property, the source of the next generation's livelihood. With that power came respect, if not always affection. When social progress became identified, as it did in the Gilded Age, with endless technological change that opened up new ways of producing goods and making money, the experience of the old was discounted as an outmoded drag on moving ahead.

2. At the same time, as mortality rates were falling, survival to old age became less and less exceptional. The family burden of having to care for elderly parents, and possible resentment over that burden, increased.

3. The old quite simply were becoming expendable in an industrial economy that could not provide full employment. Throughout the Gilded Age there was a labor surplus that contracted and expanded with the economic cycles of growth and depression. In the long depression of the 1890s, unemployment stood at about 15 percent. Older workers were under constant pressure to move aside for younger ones.

For the health experts, retirement was a medically sound prescription for helping the aged save what was believed to be the little vital energy that was left to them. For social reformers, retirement was a sensible and humane solution to the industrial problem of surplus labor. And, for corporate management, mandatory retirement plans under company control were a helpful tool in disciplining an unruly labor force.

The railroads were the pioneering industries in adopting pension systems that mandated retirement at a prescribed age. The Baltimore and Ohio Railroad instituted the first plan in 1884. The pension plans evolved as part of a management strategy to create a more docile and controllable work force. On one hand, the railroads faced powerful and entrenched unions, as witnessed by the wave of rail strikes of 1877. On the other hand, their labor force was highly unstable; a majority of new employees sought a transfer within six months. What was needed, explained J. N. A. Griswald, Chairman of the Chicago, Burlington, and Quincy Railroad, were company-directed welfare plans that would

> show the men that while we will not submit to their dictation we still have their interests
> at heart and are desirous of making them understand that the interests of the corporation
> and their own are mutual.[14]

Retirement plans met this management need. Central to these plans was a require-ment that an employee had to work continuously for the company for a certain number of years, usually at least twenty, before he could qualify for his pension. Secondly, retirement was mandated at a set age. Quite frequently, the plans also included provisions for a maximum hiring age. If a worker were hired at too late an age, he would lack the time to qualify for a pension and would have less incentive to stay on. Fully controlled by management, including the payments into the retirement fund, the pensions were a check against labor activism. They discouraged job hopping for higher wages, and behavior or demands unapproved by management could lead to a loss of all pension rights.

The twelve pension plans that were in place by 1900 provided a model that was widely copied by the 1920s. As tangible evidence of how the needs of the corporate economy helped redefine perceptions of the old, they were a clear portent of the future. Beginning in the Gilded Age, older workers were assumed, by virtue of their age alone, to be inefficient. Undeterred by the lack of any actual evidence that correlated age with efficiency, the proponents of scientific management continued to redesign work so as to eliminate the need for any prior skills. In this conception of work, one in which the experience of age was clearly minimized, labor was depersonalized to the point at which an older worker was synonymous with a used-up piece of machinery. To remove that machinery, as noted by one efficiency expert in 1909, was good for the health of the company:[15]

> When he has reached the age of retirement he gives way to a junior as one day gives way to another. There was nothing worth preserving, and the elimination of the temporary head produces a desirable wiggle of life all the way down the line.

A circle was closed. The same logic of an industrial economy that seemed to dictate that the young should be segregated in schools and adult-led groups to make them fit for work also seemed to dictate that the old should be segregated out of work when they were no longer fit for it.

The New Order of Professionalism

Race, gender, and age all provided variants on the same theme of using biology for a natural ordering of society. This ordering had the effect of reserving competition in the marketplace and the conferral of power in the society as a whole to adult white males. Even so, competition was fierce within this favored group, and the old rules, based on accumulating and handing down landed property, no longer applied to most of the competitors. The possession of a unique skill, not land, was the key to success for middle-class Americans. In adopting what one historian has dubbed the culture of professionalism, this class forged a new set of rules that ordered competition within its ranks and promised status and power to its winners.

White males, among whom competition for wealth and status was keenest, those in the age bracket 15–44, comprised a growing demographic bulge in the nineteenth century. In 1800, when the median age of white males was 15.7, this age group comprised 40 percent of all white males. As birth rates fell and the extraordinarily young population of the early nineteenth century grew up, this cohort increased to 45 percent of the total by 1870. Further enlarged by the mass arrival of young immigrant males, it reached 48 percent in 1900. It then slowly fell back to 41 percent by 1970 as white males age 45 and over became the fastest-growing age group.

One set of competitive pressures on white males resulted from their tendency to crowd each other out at a steadily increasing rate in the nineteenth century. The other

Table 9.6   Employment Patterns, 1870–1900
          (in thousands)

The white-collar middle class was the fastest-growing occupational category in the Gilded Age. Jobs in the agricultural sector, the bedrock of the early-nineteenth-century economy, expanded the least.

	1870	1900	PERCENTAGE OF CHANGE
Educational and Professional Service	330	1150	+248
Trade, Finance, and Real Estate	830	2760	+232
Transportation and Public Utilities	640	2100	+228
Manufacturing, Mining, and Construction	3180	8760	+175
Agriculture	6850	10710	+56
Others	1490	3590	+141

Source: Historical Statistics, Series D-152–166.

set was economic. Their chances of acquiring land or economic independence declined over time. By mid-century, 59 percent of adult free males owned no real estate, and, as of 1870, two out of three Americans in the workforce were neither employers nor self-employed. If a young man wanted to get ahead after the Civil War and stay out of factory work, he generally had two choices: he could either commit himself at an early age to professional training or accept nonmanual work in an office that offered neither entrepreneurial independence nor the security of land ownership. The occupational demands growing the fastest in the late nineteenth century, as shown in Table 9.6, were in the service sector of the economy. Most striking was the surging growth in the new middle class of salaried and nonpropertied workers. This class multiplied eight times over from 1870 to 1910, and its proportion of the middle class as a whole rose from one-third to two-thirds. At its core was an army of office workers. By the end of the Gilded Age, the typical member of the middle class was no longer a small businessman or farmer but a salaried employee in a corporation.

The new middle class was a product in the service sector of the same progressive division of labor that was creating a new working class of semiskilled operatives in the manufacturing sector. The chief distinction between the two was the superior status and pay attached to nonmanual labor. Within the labor hierarchy, domestic jobs, those where the amount of personal supervision was greatest, were at the bottom. Next came factory jobs, which were apt to be dirty and dangerous, and at the top were white-collar positions, those associated with a clean, healthy environment and a more creative approach to work. As to pay, clerical salaries in 1900 averaged twice as much as the $400 to $500 in annual wages for industrial workers in transportation and manufacturing.

Still, by the precorporate standards of the old middle class, most members of the new middle class were failures. They lacked both land and independence. The new class of professionals, managers, and clerks, however, gradually redefined the fundamental terms by which American society measured status and achievement. Property in the traditional, republican sense of landed security now took on myriad meanings related to a good salary and the accumulation of material goods. Individualism shifted in meaning from economic independence to upward career mobility in a business organization or professional association. Indeed, the new middle class claimed that their careers embodied the very essence of American individualism. Without the advantages of prior wealth or privileges, they had democratically earned esteem and recognition by mastering a skill in public demand.

In its most general sense, the culture of professionalism gave an amorphous group ranging from wealthy, self-employed professionals to struggling, employed clerks an outlook on life that met their need for self-discipline in a fluid society in which opportunities had to be self-created. That outlook held out the advancement of a career in place of the stability of land. By staying in school to learn skills that could be applied to steady promotion in a career that rewarded individual merit, young men were told they would gain a competitive edge that would result in continuous self-improvement. Their career status, based on earned achievement, would be higher than that of an inherited position. Their occupation would be honorific, because only its members had mastered the specialized knowledge that set them apart from the general public. These experts would then make that knowledge available to their clients through codes of professional conduct.

The culture of professionalism can also be understood as the social equivalent of the specialization and interdependence that came to characterize the economy after the Civil War. In this sense, it had a variety of meanings, each as precise as the rules and regulations that the separate professions codified in the self-governing organizations they founded in the Gilded Age. Groups aspiring to professional status rushed to form national associations. Social work in 1874, librarianship in 1876, and law in 1878 were among the more than 200 learned societies founded in the 1870s and 1880s. Older professional organizations, such as the American Medical Association (1847), the American Association for the Advancement of Science (1848), and the American Social Science Association (1865) split up into dozens of specialized units.

Like the corporations, the professional associations were a response to the heightened complexity and rapidity of change in American society during the late nineteenth century. Success, whether in the marketplace of goods or services, demanded specialization and the strength of a formal organization that would bring together like-minded specialists. Corporations combined economic specialization and control over monetary capital in their bid to protect themselves from competition by reserving niches in the economy for themselves. In a similar manner, the professional associations combined occupational specialization and control over cultural capital—that is, the status and power conferred by a professional degree and affiliation—in an effort to carve out a social space in which they alone could market a particular skill. Corporations generated their capital through current earnings, borrowing, and public offerings of stock. The professions created theirs through the certification process of higher education.

During the Gilded Age, higher education assumed a new importance in American life. From their colonial origins through the mid-nineteenth century, American colleges had remained small church-affiliated schools whose purpose was to train ministers, mold character, and pass on a fixed, classical body of thought. After the Civil War, and largely in response to the demands of a growing middle class for a more practical, specialized curriculum, colleges changed dramatically. They tended to break free from religious denominations, and they grew in size as enrollments increased fivefold between 1870 and 1900. Enrollments, though still but 4 percent of the 18-to-21-year-olds in 1900, had grown more than twice as fast as the population as a whole. By offering new, elective fields of study in such popular areas as engineering, the colleges began to serve as vehicles of social mobility for farm youth who were turning to nonfarm jobs. The most striking change was the transformation of some colleges into the German-modeled university—a research center for professional and graduate training in which the goal was the creation, and not just the transmission, of knowledge. It was the university that formed the critical institutional basis for the culture of professionalism.

At the most obvious level, the university was the training ground for future professionals. Formal education now replaced much looser antebellum patterns that had intermixed some schooling with the on-the-job training of an apprentice to his master. The number of professional schools in law, medicine, pharmacy, dentistry, and veterinary science doubled in the last quarter of the nineteenth century. Enrollments grew even more spectacularly; in dentistry, for example, the number of students increased 968 percent from 1878 to 1899, in law 249 percent, and in medicine 142 percent. At the same time, specialized schools in engineering started to take over the training functions formerly handled in the shop culture of craftsmen. By 1900 public health, social work, and urban affairs were among the newer professions that used ties to the university to enhance the credentials of their members.

The practical training required to earn a professional degree was often overshadowed by the enhanced cultural power such a degree gave to its holder. The degree was a symbol of certification, an attainment of rank in a society that recognized no formal ranks among legal equals. It authenticated the holder's right to lay claim to a specialized body of objective knowledge that was beyond the reach of the lay public. As such, it was equivalent to a license to practice a craft and enjoy the rights, privileges, and remunerations of a special guild that legitimately could demand deference from those who came to it for services. In order to ensure that their credentials of expertise were not misused or devalued through too easy availability, each of the professions formed their own national association to regulate themselves from within. These societies set standards of competence, lobbied for strict admission standards for entry into professional training, and pressured legislatures for licensing arrangements that eliminated unwanted competition.

Colleges and universities offered more than a launching pad for careers. They held out a new source of authority that promised to explain and coordinate the bewildering processes of change in American life. That authority was knowledge, a specialized set of ideas certified by the universities to be neutral, objective, and nonpartisan. Deemed to be free of the narrow-mindedness of the small town and the special pleadings of the politician, such knowledge was hailed as an impartial guide for charting America through the complexities of urbanization and industrialization. Thus, equipped with its unique power to confer authority in the form of knowledge, the university was poised by the 1890s for its modern alliance with the nation-state. What was billed as the expertise and impartiality of the former was joined with the political and financial resources of the latter in the effort of the Progressives in the early twentieth century to find an institutional basis for the reordering of America.

The influence of the university, and of the values of the professionalism that it institutionally housed, rested on a self-proclaimed search for rational principles and universal standards. As value-free as this search appeared to be, it actually reflected and reinforced the gender values of American culture. Gender differences, as we have seen, structured the participation of women in the professions. The male champions of professionalism readily accepted these differences. In 1879, Charles William Eliot, the president of Harvard, advised: "To discover and cultivate the special aptitudes of women, as distinguished from those of men, should be the incessant effort of the managers of colleges for women."[16]

Far from posing a threat to the career ambitions of male professionals, this advice enhanced them. The "special aptitudes" of women disqualified them from professions associated with intellectual rigor and mental toughness, such as law, engineering, and architecture. These same aptitudes made them uniquely fit as professionals to care for the young, the sick, and the poor. The feminization of teaching, nursing, and social work created a division of labor within the professions of education, medicine, and urban administration that reserved for males the prestige of research and the power of supervisory positions. In 1900, women accounted for 94 percent of the nurses but only 6 percent of the physicians. The male doctors, like males in all the professions, were overwhelmingly white, Protestant, and native-born.

Thus, despite what appear to be fundamental differences between them, the biological and professional orderings of Gilded Age America were part of the same cultural process that put white males on top of a vertical series of rankings. The nurturing role of women as professionals, one that socialized the young and treated the ill and misfits, helped keep them there.

Professionalism and Reform

Reform and professionalism came together late in the Gilded Age. Both embodied that innate sense of virtue that defined the middle class in the nineteenth century. Both sought the same goal of a society naturally made virtuous and orderly by the elimination of waste, laziness, and inefficiency. And both viewed the city, with its immigrant masses, as the prime source of corruption and disorder in America. Writing in 1898 for the New York Association for the Improvement of the Conditions of the Poor, William Tolman explained why the city was such a threat:[17]

At the present time the social instinct, tending toward congestion in the urban centers, the influx of foreign elements, the nonassimilation or resistance of Americanizing influences, new industrial conditions, the failure or indifference of the church to its social mission, make the modern city a storm center.

The mission of the professionalized reformers was to guide and direct that "social instinct" so as to make the cities and their foreign hosts fit for liberty. They tried to do so by imposing their own definitions of morality and efficiency on the urban masses. Success, they told themselves, would result in a reformation of individual character evidenced by the willingness of the reformed to adapt themselves to disciplined work habits regulated from within.

Urban reformers after the Civil War certainly recognized the reality of class divisions, but they, like most Americans, continued to deny their permanence. The dominant explanation of poverty remained moralistic and individualistic. The poor were the weak, the tired, and, above all, the lazy. Because the middle-class ideology of liberal capitalism presupposed equality of opportunity, the poor had to be held personally responsible for their poverty. As long as poverty was considered the product of a flawed character, its solution was largely a matter of moral uplift. Such an interpretation not only held out hope for eradicating poverty but also defined the role of the reformer as a morally superior individual from the outside who had the right, indeed the duty, to intervene in the lives of the poor. Apart from offering sympathy, guidance, and stern lectures on the virtues of sobriety, thrift, and hard work, the reformers' prime duty in the Gilded Age was to provide a scientific basis for distinguishing between the worthy poor and the unworthy poor.

The need for such a distinction resulted from the rise in unemployment during the nineteenth century. Throughout the colonial and early national periods, the poor who received public assistance were primarily the unemployables, not the unemployed. They were the sick, the disabled, and widows with children. Unemployment in the modern sense was rare because the employables could find plenty of work in an unmechanized rural economy, either as independent producers on their own land or as laborers on the land of others. This gradually changed under first commercial and then industrial capitalism. Pushed off the land by demographic pressures and agricultural mechanization, and pulled into cities and factories, in which they could sell their labor power, growing numbers of Americans found themselves in a labor pool that was consistently larger than the supply of steady jobs. Unemployment averaged 10 percent in the depression decades of the 1870s and 1890s, and even in relatively prosperous times, about one-third of the male workers were unemployed for three to four months out of the year. Work, even when it was available, by no means guaranteed subsistence for a family. The average wages of a male industrial worker usually provided no more than 60 percent of the subsistence needs of his family. Thus, as a direct consequence of the shift from an agrarian to an industrial economy, a new class of the unemployed and the underemployed joined the traditional class of the unemployables in the ranks of the poor.

It was in the self-interest of capital—the owners of the businesses and the providers of the jobs—to separate these two classes in terms of access to public relief or private charity. If denied access to aid, the unemployed poor would be driven by the sheer need of survival to accept virtually any job that might come along, at virtually any wage. By insisting, contrary to all evidence, that jobs were always available for all who wanted them, the business community and their reform allies were able to stigmatize the unemployed poor as the unworthy poor. In practice, this meant that anyone who was physically capable of subsistence labor was assumed to be morally unfit for public assistance. To assume otherwise, it was argued, meant perpetuating poverty by rewarding the shiftless with public subsidies. Such a parasitic class, if not screened out by relief agencies, would morally and economically debilitate the entire community.

Much of the impetus for the professionalization of urban reform in the Gilded Age came out of this perceived need to protect local communities by screening out the unworthy poor. Private groups, who by 1880 had banded together into the Charity Organization Movement, and state boards of charities assumed a protective role over both the poor and the public. Reformers, though still stressing the redemptive power of moral exhortation, increasingly placed their faith in what they called "scientific charity." Thus, the Charity Organization Movement took pride in its centralization of charity work, gathering and assessing data on applicants, monitoring of the behavior of the poor through the use of friendly visitors, and efficient dispensing of aid according to official guidelines.

The local branches of the Charity Organization Movement acted as a central clearinghouse for information on all the poor in their communities. Church benevolent organizations referred applicants to them, and the Overseers of the Poor agreed to accept their recommendations on ferreting out the alleged unworthy. Convinced that most applicants were in no real need of aid and squandered what they did receive on alcohol, the male directors of the local charities instructed their female volunteers, the actual visitors in the homes of the poor, to make relief "conditional upon *good conduct and progress*." These men felt that what had to be eradicated was not poverty but rather a misplaced charity that produced pauperism, a degraded state of dependency that threatened to become inheritable. The poor were taught that the mere asking for relief endangered the stability of their families. In 1892, the directors of a Massachusetts Charity asked rhetorically, "If he knew that his home must be broken up or its inmates sent to the almshouse, would it not have some deterrent effect upon him?"[18]

Despite the label "scientific," charity in the Gilded Age was more an amalgam of Christian philanthropy and class control than an objective evaluation and treatment of the poor. This was especially true in the smaller industrial cities, in which the factory owners ran the relief programs and their wives and daughters served as volunteers. Here, the industrialists, the source of the low wages and substandard housing that created the structural underpinnings for poverty, used work relief to organize and control a surplus pool of laborers whose very presence helped discipline their factory hands. In return for meals and lodging, the transient poor were forced to work in the mill towns of New England. The men chopped wood and the women cleaned laundry in town projects operated by the local charities. After passing what amounted to a work test in these relief programs, they were kept on for possible work in the mills and added to the labor glut, which reduced the bargaining power of the workers.

At its best, scientific charity was not very caring. In 1886 a poet, John Boyle O'Reilly, wrote:[19]

> The organized charity scimped and iced
> In the name of a cautious, statistical Christ.

In these words O'Reilly captured the ambivalence, if not the hostility, of the poor toward their purported benefactors. In part to bridge that gulf, and even more so to find a calling that would justify their higher education, the first generation of college-trained women established the Social Settlement House movement in the late 1880s. By the turn of the century, there were close to one hundred settlement houses in the urban slums. The best known was Hull House in Chicago, founded by Jane Addams and Ellen Starr in 1889.

The settlement houses were therapeutic for both the volunteers who staffed them and the poor clientele these volunteers served. Speaking for a class of educated women prone, like herself, to neurotic aliments of nervous despair when frustrated by the lack of professional leadership open to them, Jane Addams explained that moving into the slums was "more for the benefit of the people who do it than for the other class. . . . Nervous people do not crave rest but activity of a certain kind."[20] Because of this intense personal need to define themselves by caring for others, the settlement workers

were empathetic to the problems of the poor. They assumed, unlike the charity workers, that poor families were fundamentally normal, healthy, and honest. Their programs—neighborhood centers for education and recreation, social research to uncover
the facts that lay behind poverty, and social action to alleviate the worst conditions of
the poor through legislation—were all based on a respect for the working-class and
immigrant cultures they encountered. This respect was heightened by the searing
experience of living in the slums when the depression of the 1890s descended. This
experience, more than anything else, convinced the settlement workers that the root
causes of poverty were environmental, rather than genetic or moral. From that conviction sprang much of the reform legislation of the Progressive era.

By denying that moral shortcomings accounted for poverty, the settlement workers undermined the central tenet of nineteenth-century charity work. The environmental explanation of poverty, one publicized by settlement workers in careful, empirical
research, opened up two possibilities: The first, best exemplified in the settlement work
of Jane Addams in Chicago and Robert A. Woods in Boston, looked toward democratic forms of community organizing. Knowing from first-hand involvement how
working-class communities actually coped with poverty and joblessness, Addams and
Woods argued that the urban poor, if assisted by outside experts, had the resources
within their own neighborhoods to shape a better life for themselves. This approach,
though predicated on the need for outside intervention in the form of experts who
would document the facts of poverty and lobby for political solutions to urban ills,
stressed the capacity of the poor for self-organization. That capacity was downgraded
by those who responded to the second possibility presented by the environmental
concept of poverty. A bureaucracy of social workers emerged in the late nineteenth
century that relied on professionalism to resurrect in a new guise the old moral
superiority of the outsider working with the poor. Whereas Addams and Woods had
tried to blend expertise with neighborliness, most social workers emphasized only the
expertise they brought to the poor.

By the 1890s, charity volunteers were gradually being replaced by salaried social
workers—the permanent, professional representatives of the propertied classes among
the urban poor. The authority of these representatives now rested not on morality but
on the presumed superiority of a knowledge certified by the academic credentials of a
college education. If, to use a favorite metaphor of the settlement movement, urban
slums were a great social laboratory, then the professional social workers were the
researchers who could explain the complex interdependency of the urban world. Concerned more with how poverty functioned in a social setting than with its causes, and
taught that a professional had to establish emotional distance from a client, the social
workers became dispassionate experts at treating the symptoms of poverty. They often
cared deeply for their clients, but instead of neighborhood autonomy and participatory
democracy, they preferred administrative solutions imposed from the outside. For all
their work during the early twentieth century in promoting urban parks, municipal
hospitals, and reform legislation to protect women and children in the labor market,
social workers were for many of the poor just another external force telling them how
to run their lives.

In 1896 Mary Richmond, a charity reformer, correctly predicted that the role of
professionalized social work would be "to stand between the charitable Scylla of an
old fogy conservatism and the charitable Charybdis of . . . socialism."[21] The same

generalization applied to the professionalization of public education in the Gilded Age. The gains made in public education between 1870 and 1898 were impressive. Enrollments in public schools more than doubled, from 7 million to 15 million. Measured as a percentage of youth between the ages of five and eighteen, school attendance during this period rose from 61 percent to 71 percent. At mid-century, only 47 percent of all funds for schooling went to public education; by the end of the century, 79 percent did. No single group or agency forced public education on the taxpayers. Americans clearly wanted education for their children, and they taxed themselves to support it. Nonetheless, and despite continued hopes that public education would contribute to a more open, egalitarian society, the language and aims of school reform became more and more repressive after the Civil War.

Themes of control, order, and discipline were invoked in a determined effort to protect what in 1880 the school board of Portland, Oregon, called "the right of preservation of a body politic." What threatened the "body politic"? In the wake of the strikes of 1877, William T. Harris, the U.S. Commissioner of Education, voiced the fears of most school reformers when he warned of class warfare "if the systematic vagrancy of the ignorant, vicious, and criminal classes should continue to increase." He concluded that "Capital, therefore, should weigh the cost of the mob and the tramp against the cost of universal and sufficient education."[22] Much as the recognition of class conflict had produced the professional social worker in the role of a specialist mediating between the propertied and the poor, so also did the social consequences of industrial capitalism produce the professional school administrator in the role of a specialist trained to use education as a mechanism for social harmony.

The greatest demand for school reform in the Gilded Age came from the middle and upper classes in urban areas and in rapidly growing industrial regions with heavy influxes of immigrant workers. Antebellum ideals of a harmonious community in which education nurtured the moral individuality of the child, ideals frequently lost in the conformist design of even antebellum schools, now seemed dangerously outmoded. Labor unrest and ethnic diversity, both represented by the immigrant, registered the real and potential conflict within cities and industrializing communities. Only the schools, argued a Pennsylvania school administrator in the 1890s, could stay the development of

> an irresponsible and vicious proletariat [and] drive out of our borders, out into the shadows of oblivion . . . those special monstrosities, libels on men and beasts—the nihilists and communists, the scum of civilized life.[23]

If the schools were to stabilize an unsettled society, then the authority and power of the state had to be enlisted in the campaign for the proper socialization of youth. Urbanization and the spread of industrial capitalism resulted in new living and working conditions that seemingly mocked the traditional constraints of Protestant, village America. Families could no longer be entrusted with their civic duty of raising up good citizens because so many parents were now immigrants. Their foreign birth meant, in the eyes of most reformers, that they were completely ignorant of the respect for work and civilized restraints of the native-born. Their children, said a Boston school committee member in 1889, were raised in "homes of vice and crime. In their blood are generations of inequity. . . ."[24] Precisely because immigrant parents were beyond the reach of civilizing influences, the state had to intervene and instill a respect for law and order in their children. "If the parent will not or cannot educate, the State must."[25] This was the rationalizing principle laid down in the *Pennsylvania School Journal* in 1893.

State intervention in the form of compulsory-attendance laws was the critical coercive element in a far-reaching program of Americanization in public education during the Gilded Age. The number of states with such laws doubled, from sixteen to thirty-one, between 1885 and 1900. Most urban schools were already overcrowded by 1885, but stricter laws were needed to catch the truants, predominately the children of poor, immigrant families. Although ignored in many communities, these laws undoubtedly contributed to the rise in the average number of days attended by each pupil (age 5 to 17), from 44.7 in 1870 to 71.8 by 1900. Often challenged on the grounds that they interfered with the natural right of parents to govern their children, the attendance laws were upheld by the courts. In a typical ruling, the Supreme Court of Indiana stated in 1901 that "The natural rights of a parent to the custody and control of his infant child are subordinate to the power of the State, and may be restricted and regulated by municipal laws."[26]

Enrolling more youth in schools for longer periods of time was the first step in the Americanization program. Intended specifically for immigrant children, and more generally for all children of the working class, Americanization was a catchall label for the forced homogenization of the urban masses into a common mold defined by the success models of middle-class culture. Both fears of social anarchy and hopes for social equality motivated the Americanizers. Unable to penetrate or understand what they saw as clannish colonies of immigrants in city wards, sealed off from the better classes and harboring in their ignorance destructive notions of socialism, reformers and the middle class demanded that the public schools assume the civilizing mission of teaching the foreign-born how to be Americans.

Industriousness and loyalty, not the development of intelligence per se, were the main goals in the schools. "A citizen who is merely intelligent," explained a school superintendent in 1906,

> may be either useless or dangerous to the State. He must be industrious also. To labor is duty, the common lot of humanity and a blessing to the world. One had better not exist than to live to be merely a blank in the world's work. The public schools must therefore develop workers.[27]

Along with the self-restraint, concentration, and orderly patterns of behavior that youth presumably needed in order to take their place as productive workers in an industrial economy, loyalty to state, society, and the rights of private property were inculcated for the preservation of social order. The power of the state became both the means and the end of public education. "Nothing less than the State can check the prevalence of revolutionary ideas and the assailment of social and proprietary rights," insisted J.E. Seaman of the National Education Association in 1885. It followed, in a conclusion that would have been repugnant to most Americans earlier in the century, that the "first steps of the State should be to get possession of the minds of men; get control of their ideas."[28] The loyalty of disciplined citizens to the state became the essence of the Americanism that the schools were expected to produce.

The immigrants were not led like sheep into the schools. For all their stress on control and regimentation, the schools were free, and a free education was a priceless gift to many of the immigrants. It was, recalled a Russian Jew, what "American opportunity" was all about, "the treasure that no thief could touch, not even misfortune or poverty."[29] Many immigrant groups, especially the Germans, fought for the right to have instruction in their native tongue, and Catholics often turned to parochial schools for the protection of their cultural and religious heritage, but on the whole, the immigrants did not oppose the expansion and consolidation of public education in the Gilded Age. English, after all, was the language of business and professions, and ambitious immigrants well understood its value to their children. This willingness of immigrants to accept Americanization for their children helped to defuse campaigns for school centralization that were filled with the language of ethnic and class conflict. It also eased the tasks of the new educational experts in their political efforts to win public acceptance for their roles as the engineers of educational efficiency.

Professional school administrators presented themselves as the equivalent in education of the corporate leaders in the economy. Just as corporations were successful because they were led by men who recognized that the unprecedented scale of market activity necessitated large combinations broken down into specialized functions controlled by an internal hierarchy, so also an efficient educational system had to be based on combination and specialization. The campaign for administrative centralization was over in most states by 1900. The broad authority of superintendents over consolidated school districts replaced the voluntarism and decentralization that had characterized the smaller school districts of the 1870s. Local autonomy was more democratic, but it was successfully attacked for failing to promote the efficiency that the superintendents claimed to deliver.

After promoting the idea that the schools had to be run like businesses, the superintendents cited their professional expertise as the only legitimate basis for implementing the authority of the state in an efficient system of education. Only professionals, not lay members sitting on local schools boards, had the qualifications to hire and evaluate teachers, set standards of performance, or define the content of educational policy. They would bring to the schools what allegedly was most needed, "a supervision that can keep a constant eye upon every teacher, every study, every class, every pupil." This was the efficient system, noted a Pennsylvania superintendent in 1880, that "they have on railroads, and in manufacturing establishments, and our system of schools will be comparatively weak until it can have the benefit of it."[30] In winning the struggle for control of the schools, the administrators carved out a career for themselves. As paid agents of the state, they were the professionals who institutionalized the campaign for Americanization.

Culture, Work, and Leisure

In his immensely popular tract of 1885, *Our Country: Its Possible Future and Its Present Crisis,* Josiah Strong, a Congregationalist minister, warned that the class divisions of industrial capitalism were hardening into an impassible gulf. A social explosion was possible at any time. "We are preparing conditions which make possible a Reign of Terror that would begger the scenes of the French Revolution."[31] Out of this terrifying middle-class vision came the special urgency of reform in the Gilded Age. It generated the massive commitment of the middle class in the 1880s to such antebellum reforms as temperance and Sabbatarian legislation, and by the 1890s it was expressed in the concern of the professionals with using expert knowledge for an ordering of American society. Nonetheless, the reformers—the native-born and Protestant middle classes—remained frustrated in their efforts to restrain, educate, and elevate the working classes. Popularly referred to as the "dangerous classes," they seemed to remain just that—sullen, alienated, uncontrollable, and always on the brink of revolt.

The reforming impulse of the middle class and the continued resistance of the working class to being "reformed" were both rooted in quite different cultural responses to the material conditions that shaped each as a class. Both faced the same problem of coping with a sense of dislocating change. Neither had the security of landed property to be handed down from generation to generation; but the middle class, through its ownership and control of capital, had access to a material security unattainable for the vast majority of the working class, and from it flowed cultural strategies for survival that only reinforced the belief of the middle class that industrial workers and the urban poor were uncivilized and in need of reform.

In the late 1870s, state investigating committees began to document the prevalence of poverty among industrial wage earners. After hearing testimony from workers at the Harmony Cotton Mills in Cohoes, New York, a State Assembly Committee concluded that "very few families are enabled to save money, while a majority of them barely manage to make both ends meet at the close of the year."[32] In Massachusetts, as of 1883, the average workman who headed a family earned $559. That was well under the average expenses of $754 for a working-class family. The economy was producing plenty of wealth, but it was very unequally distributed. Thus in the Boston of 1890, the poorest 60 percent of all families owned less than 5 percent of the total wealth.

Because their wages were so low, the working classes had little, if any, economic cushion for protection against those threats that were largely a function of their class position. Far more so than the middle class, industrial workers were likely to suffer from death or injuries in job accidents, poor health, and technological layoffs. Much industrial work was brutal and dangerous. Steel mills, for example, were fiery cauldrons of smoking gases, molten iron, and flying shreds of metal. Among newly arrived immigrants who were hired at Carnegie's South works in Pittsburgh between 1907 and 1910, nearly one in four were killed or injured in the mills. Nationwide, at the turn of the century about 35,000 workers were killed annually in industrial accidents, and another 500,000 were injured. There was no workmen's compensation and no disability insurance.

Mortality rates in the cities were higher than in rural areas, and within the cities, they were highest in working-class neighborhoods. It was here that the crowded conditions and often contaminated food and water supplies that made the cities so unhealthy were the worst. At least 80 percent of the urban working class could afford housing only in multifamily tenements. The packed tenements of 1900 resulted in population densities in the central wards of New York and Chicago that were among the highest in the world. Diseases spread by close contact in a polluted environment—such as tuberculosis, pneumonia, and typhoid—were major killers. Before an antitoxin was developed in the 1880s, diphtheria was also virulent. A disease that attacks the mucous lining of the throat and other air passages, and one that was unknown before the industrial revolution, diphtheria was most likely triggered by air pollution. Not surprisingly, Pittsburgh had the highest urban rate of diphtheria deaths in 1890.

Because most Gilded Age cities provided municipal services only in proportion to the ability of neighborhood residents to pay for them, the distribution of road, water, and sewer facilities followed along class lines. Property owners had to pay individually for the installation of services, and consequently working-class neighborhoods either did without or suffered from inferior services. This in turn exacerbated problems of public health. Backyard cesspools overflowed, outdoor privies had to be shared by many families, flies bred in the horse manure that piled up on unpaved streets, and the water that had to be laboriously hauled into the house in buckets from an outside pump was frequently contaminated. The water supply for the South Side of Pittsburgh, a working-class district, was drawn out of the Monongahela River just below the point where raw sewerage and industrial refuge poured into it. Able to afford cleaner water, the middle and upper classes of the city had far fewer deaths from typhoid.

Unhealthy conditions in their local neighborhoods lowered the recovery rate of industrial workers suffering from occupational diseases. Respiratory ailments, for example, were commonplace among textile operatives. The cotton fibers they inhaled for ten hours a day irritated and damaged their lungs. They worked in poorly ventilated factories that were kept moist with hot steam because the cotton warp had to be damp for its efficient processing by the machines. The workers paid the price for this efficiency with high incidences of pneumonia. Sweaty and exhausted when they left for home, their resistance was continually weakened by the extreme temperature variations and polluted air that they lived with daily on their jobs.

Layoffs and irregular employment when new machinery was introduced were another threat that was disproportionately borne by working-class families. By maximizing production, industrial technology created a corresponding need for enlarged business bureaucracies capable of administering and marketing the greater flow of goods. This need, largely clerical in nature, was met by the middle class. But the same technology cheapened the skills of workers and, in certain industries, suddenly produced a glut of workers whose skills were no longer needed. This was the position confronting Thomas O'Donnell, a mule spinner (a skilled textile worker who operated a type of spinning machinery called a mule), when the textile manufacturers of Fall River, Massachusetts, replaced the mules with ring spinning frames in 1879. In testimony at labor hearings in the U.S. Senate, he reported earnings in 1882 of $133. He had been able to find work at $1.50 per day for only three months out of the year. He, his wife, and two children survived by scavenging for wood, coal, and food. The children were kept out of school during the winter months because the parents had no money to buy them shoes. When asked by a senator why he did not pull up stakes and homestead in the West, where all he would need was a cash outlay of $1,500 to get started, O'Donnell reminded the senator that the working poor rarely had any cash. "Well, I never saw over a $20 bill, and that is when I have been getting a month's pay at once. If someone would give me $1,500 I will go. . . ."[33]

The West was not a viable option for Eastern labor. Instead, working-class families, regardless of ethnicity or race, committed themselves to a collective economy in which the labor of children was an integral part of a strategy for survival and security. This economy, and the role of children in it, sharply differentiated working-class from middle-class families.

Because any income the children could earn would help raise the family above the poverty line by adding to the barely subsistence wage of the father, working-class parents lacked the incentives of middle-class ones to limit fertility. Quite the opposite.

Table 9.7   Fertility in Three Massachusetts Towns by Occupation Level of Husband, 1880

Although many factors affected fertility, the class position of the father, as approximated by his occupation, was perhaps the most important. In particular, working-class families in the Gilded Age needed the wage income from their children in order to survive economically.

	OCCUPATION		
	High	*Middle*	*Low*
Age Group			
20–24	556	674	692
25–29	684	988	937
30–34	793	712	914
35–39	607	814	659
40–44	160	329	484
45–49	116	111	179
20–49	449	617	680

Source: Adapted from Tamara K. Hareven and Maris A. Vinovskis, "Patterns of Childbearing in Late Nineteenth-Century America: The Determinants of Marital Fertility in Five Massachusetts Towns in 1880," in Hareven and Vinovskis, eds., *Family and Population in Nineteenth-Century America* (Princeton University Press, 1978), Table 2-16, p. 107.
Note: Figures are for number of children ages 0–4 per 1000 married women ages 20–49.

"When the French Canadians first came to Manchester, having many children was the only way they could survive,"[34] remembered Alice Lacasse, one of twelve children in a French-Canadian family that worked at the Amoskeag Mills in Manchester, New Hampshire. Thus, as was the case in the antebellum period, fertility was highest in those families in which the income and occupational status of the father were lowest. The pattern for the Massachusetts towns of Lawrence, Lynn, and Salem is shown in Table 9.7.

More children meant more family income. Children were expected to make an economic contribution from a very early age. They started by taking to the streets and becoming experts in hukstering or street selling. They also learned the art of scavenging, the sorting through of garbage and trash to find something that had cash value on the street. Some working-class children went to work in factories before the age of ten, but most delayed factory labor until they left school around the age of fourteen. The importance of their labor to their families varied according to the skill levels, and hence income, of their fathers. In the textile city of Lowell, Massachusetts, 90 percent of families headed by an unskilled father depended on the wage earnings of their children in the 1870s. That figure dropped to 44 percent if the father was skilled. Throughout the late nineteenth century, the working class as a whole relied on their children for 20 percent to 25 percent of the total family income. In most cases, the children's wages were essential for economic survival.

By 1910 over 90 percent of the male industrial workforce was foreign-born or the sons of the foreign-born. Basic to this fusion of ethnicity and the working class was the adaptation of a family economy rooted in peasant traditions to the one that took shape in a radically different industrial setting. Most of the immigrants came from agrarian societies in which children had a high economic value and the status of women was

Child Labor in the Mines. These "breaker boys" in the Pennsylvania mines inhaled coal dust for twelve to fourteen hours a day while bent over conveyer belts of coal. Their job was to pick out the slate from the coal. The 25¢ a day they earned was turned over to their parents. (George Eastman House)

directly tied to childbearing. This cultural legacy of pronatalism helps explain why, in all classes, the immigrants had higher fertility than the native-born. More particularly, for the vast majority of immigrants this pronatalism was reinforced by the job opportunities for children opened up by America's industrial revolution. By having large families and sending their children into the factories to work alongside kin, first-generation immigrants were able to gain some measure of control over their very uncertain economic environment.

After ten years or so, when the threat of dire poverty was not quite as immediate, and on into the second generation, working-class children and young adults continued to work in factories to help pay the premium on their parents' old-age insurance, a mortgage on a rent-free home. Ownership of a house meant a source of income in old age and the security that came with that income. After twenty to thirty years of extraordinary underconsumption and overwork for the family as a whole, the goal was achieved. Chicago was typical. In the 1880s only 7 percent of the workers in the city owned their own homes. By 1930 Chicago's foreign-born, its working class, had the highest percentage of home ownership in the city, 42 percent. Only 19 percent of the families headed by the native-born owned their homes.

Within the limits of their class position, immigrant workers actively created their own environment. They relied on their own traditions and their own definitions of success. The middle-class ideology of success was worse than useless. By grounding material success in moral self-worth, it implicitly condemned most workers as the naturally poor who lacked diligence and thrift. The rapid upward mobility of the self-made man, central to middle-class notions of success, was beyond the reach of all but a handful of the working class in the Gilded Age. Even in a very prosperous town like Warren, Pennsylvania, in which the discovery of oil touched off a prolonged boom after the Civil War, movement out of the working class was quite limited. Fewer than 10 percent of the manual workers in Warren moved upward into white-collar positions during the last third of the nineteenth century, and most of those were at the clerical level. Mobility patterns elsewhere, based on the small minority of unskilled laborers who stayed put long enough to be traced through decennial censuses, show that the most typical occupational mobility in the working class was from unskilled to semi-skilled in the course of one generation.

Success for the working class meant a steady job, providing for the family, support for kin, the security of a house, and some measure of independence and control in their work. Success was critically important to the working class, but it was normally not based on individual advancement. Family cohesion and responsibilities to kin took precedence over personal ambition. The Irish of New York, most of whom were common laborers, sent $30 million in savings back to Ireland between 1851 and 1880. The remittances, the total of thousands of small individual deposits at savings banks, paid the trans-Atlantic passage of relatives and helped others in Ireland to subsist. Sons and daughters deprived themselves of skills they needed to advance economically when they left school for the dead-end jobs that contributed to the family economy and their parents' purchase of a house. The fathers in the mills and mines criticized fellow workers who looked out only for themselves as a threat to the cooperative unity that labor needed in demanding its rights from management. Such workers, in the eyes of the majority, were as greedy and selfish as the successful manufacturers who made it to the top by refusing to pay their laborers a living wage.

In rejecting middle-class notions of success and the rise of the self-made man, the working class also rejected much of the tenor and programs of the middle-class reformers. What reformers saw as a well-meaning effort to help workers improve their lives, the working class saw as regimentation condescendingly imposed by outsiders who trumpeted their moral superiority. These different perceptions did not represent misunderstandings, but rather a clash of world views, in which barriers of social and ideological distance were widened more than they were narrowed.

Virtually everything about working-class life was foreign and alien to middle-class tastes and experience. The world of the factory was unknown to the middle class, and apparently they preferred it that way. "The American public does not like to read about the life of toil," noted novelist William Deans Howells in 1891. He added that if writers dealt with realistic themes "of how mill hands, or miners, or farmers, or iron-puddlers really live," then the public would soon let them know that it "did not care to meet such vulgar and commonplace people."[35] Workers bitterly complained of being enslaved to machines in an endless cycle of toil and monotony. The middle class praised the same machinery for its power to reduce economic inefficiency and lighten the work load in the middle-class home. Starting in the 1870s, iceboxes, toilets, and sewing and washing machines made middle-class domestic life more pleasant. But the benefits did not extend to the workers. Such durable goods were too expensive for their family budgets.

In order to spread the work around, eventually increase wages, and enjoy more time of their own, industrial workers campaigned throughout the Gilded Age for a reduction in their long and numbing shifts of ten to twelve hours per day. The eight-hour movement, which, to labor, was a demand for human dignity and moral self-improvement, was opposed by employers and the middle class as a license to unleash dangerous passions. Middle-class spokesmen such as the minister Jonathan Baxter Harrison insisted that "more than eight hours' labor per day is necessary, in order to keep down and utilize the forces of the animal nature and passions."[36] When industrial work was being monopolized by immigrants, those whose civility and self-control the middle class automatically suspected, Harrison's moralistic argument carried all the more weight.

Deep class divisions also characterized the cultural realms of home and leisure. Reformers were shocked by the living arrangements of the working class. Rather than seeing the remarkable extent to which even slum families were able to maintain their integrity, they focused instead on what struck them as the desecration of that central bourgeois institution, the home. Working-class conceptions of motherhood, childhood, and domestic space seemed the very antithesis of what the middle class valued in the enshrinement of private domesticity as a refuge from the public world. In the middle-class home of Victorian America, space was ordered and controlled, and every family function had its proper place. The parlor, for example, served to screen visitors and regulate their access to the more private parts of the house. Here, as well, the family displayed its material status by carefully arranging "store-bought" goods and furnishings. In contrast, the working-class home or tenement was incredibly small, cramped, and unkempt. To the reformers, it appeared that everything and everybody were promiscuously jumbled together. There was no room for privacy or moral nurturing. Mothers, rather than keeping their children at home and treating them as moral innocents to be protected from the outside world, permitted them to roam the streets and encouraged them to earn some income.

The reformers were right in that working-class parents did treat their children as if

Mulberry Street, Lower East Side, New York City, 1890. In contrast to the upper and middle classes, much of the social and economic life of the working class took place in the public arena of the city streets. (Library of Congress)

they were little adults. Where they were wrong was in assuming that such a conception of children necessarily represented a moral failing on the part of these parents, particularly the mother. In the working class, parental responsibilities and ways of expressing care for children were in fact quite different than those in the middle class. Under no illusion that their children were likely to become professionals or entrepreneurs, working-class parents realized that it was in the best interests of their children to be exposed at an early age to the burdens of work. In addition, their children had to acquire the tough combative skills of the street if they were to survive in the unforgiving economic environment that would confront them as adults. The only help they could expect would be from kin and neighbors, the same ethnic and community ties that reformers interpreted as a thick shell of ignorance and clannishness that prevented their good intentions from taking effect.

Increasingly, the reformers keyed their efforts to controlling the leisure time of the working class. From its inception in the nineteenth century, the evangelicalized middle class had sharply criticized the rowdiness, hard drinking, and spontaneity that defined so much of the workers' culture. "Blue Monday" was a colloquialism for the decided tendency of workers to take an extra day to recover from a weekend of defying the Protestant ethic. The rush of industrialization after the Civil War greatly intensified middle-class concerns. Many now felt that the very nature of industrial work was stripping workers of any meaningful culture at all. "When the operation of the machine tends to relieve the operative of all thought," reasoned industrialist Edward Atkinson, "the man or woman who tends it risks becoming a machine, well oiled and cared for, but incapable of independent life."[37] In the past, Atkinson reasoned, work and culture were united because workers had to draw on all their faculties in an ongoing process of mental stimulation and physical achievement. In ignoring the possibility that industrial work could be restructured so as to give workers greater autonomy and creativity, Atkinson concluded that henceforth workers could find any sense of cultural worth only through leisure. At the turn of the century, Andrew Carnegie succinctly made the same point when he proclaimed that "how [a man] spends his hours of recreation is really the key to his progress in all the virtues."[38]

Most workers would have agreed with the central insight of Atkinson and Carnegie: industrialization separated work from culture by divorcing work from thought. Where workers strongly disagreed was in their insistence that they, not the business and middle classes, had the right to determine their own culture and their own leisure habits.

Because the coming of the factory both created a sharp division between work and play and severely restricted the free hours available for leisure, workers were all the more determined to control their own recreational time and space. Working-class recreation was mostly noncommercialized. It had to be. Even including the use of tobacco and liquor as recreation, the average working-class family in the 1880s had less than 2 percent of its budget available for entertainment. Even attending a professional baseball game was prohibitively expensive. Workers devoted their leisure time to free lectures and reading rooms in union halls, ethnic festivals, group sports in open spaces, Sunday parades and picnics, boisterous July Fourth celebrations, and, for the males, socializing in beer-gardens and saloons. Organized around either craft or ethnic lines in specific neighborhoods, working-class recreation sustained a sense of community, and it valued, above all, freedom from outside regimentation and control.

The leisure habits of the working class were neither restrained nor refined enough for those reformers who made it clear that they wanted to use culture as an instrument of class control. "Capital must protect itself by organized activities for a new object— the education of the people,"[39] cautioned the Reverend Harrison in his *Certain Dangerous Tendencies in American Life* of 1880. This class bias of the reformers was often obvious. In Pittsburgh in the late 1880s, it took the form of arresting milk dealers and bakers for selling their goods on Sunday in violation of Sabbatarian laws, but permitting industrial corporations, such as railroads, to continue their operations on the Sabbath. In most cities, the moral crusaders had enough political power to enact statutes restricting behavior on Sundays, the one day that workers could call their own. These laws, however, rarely reflected a community consensus. Resisted by Catholics and workers, who had their own Sunday traditions they wanted to uphold, the laws could be enforced only on a selective basis for political reasons. The Protestant drive for moral hegemony reduced respect for the law and, as a byproduct, contributed to the corruption of the urban police.

Local prohibition laws had the same effect in those cities in which they were passed. To the reformers, the saloon symbolized the subversion of those disciplined ambitions and inner controls that defined the civilized American. The saloon was, they believed, the cesspool from which flowed poverty, venereal disease, prostitution, gambling, crime, and all the vices of passion to which the working class was especially susceptible. There were a lot of saloons, and they were quite popular with male workers. By the 1890s, brewing companies battling for market shares had increased the number of saloons in urban, working-class neighborhoods to where there was one per fifty adult males. The connection between some saloons and vice was real, but there is no evidence that most saloons were not just what most workers found them to be, informal social clubs in which working men could meet, play cards, read newspapers, have a beer, and relax among friends. The saloons also offered a welcome and needed escape from the rigid discipline of the factory and the stifling overcrowding of the tenements.

Public-health reformers revealed a similar class bias. These reformers came out of the upper and middle classes, as did the more openly moral crusaders in temperance, and they believed that disease was literally caused by the stench and noxious odors that fouled the air in the poorer sections of the city. They associated disease with those they labeled the filthy and irresponsible poor, and they came close to blaming these poor for the very existence of urban diseases. Not until the 1890s did reformers begin to connect diseases with specific pathogens that were communicable by human contact regardless of class. Up to then, physicians supported the urban middle classes in their refusal to report cases of tuberculosis to public health boards and their opposition to being subjected to the inconvenience of a quarantine. Because the middle class believed disease was bred in and carried out of the urban slums, they felt that only the poor who lived there should be quarantined or forcibly removed to hospitals.

In addition to isolating the diseased poor, the public-health movement in the Gilded Age stressed sanitation. The goal was to remove disease-producing garbage by cleaning the streets and creating new systems of water and sewerage treatment. The problem of garbage was certainly a staggering one. The streets were clogged with refuse. During the 1880s, the movement of ships in New York's lower harbor was often blocked because so much trash was dumped into it. By 1900 American cities were generating two to three times more garbage per capita than European cities. The major source, however, was not working-class poverty but middle-class affluence. Better-off urbanites threw away far more than did the working poor they condemned for making the city filthy.

This class interpretation of urban wastes was a useful political weapon in the street-paving campaigns of the 1880s and 1890s. The campaigns pitted a middle-class concept of the street as an artery of transportation between the suburbs and the inner city against the working-class concept that valued the street as a source of social and recreational space. Middle-class children in the suburbs could play in the backyards or on the porches of their parents' home. Working-class children in the city had to use the streets. There, they mingled with local vendors who sold goods in pushcarts that otherwise would have been unavailable to the working poor whose mobility in the city was constrained by the high cost of public transportation. Despite the objections of the working class, who feared that the increase in steam and electric-powered traffic would disrupt the community use of the streets and endanger their children, the streets were paved. By claiming, with some justification, that paved streets would be cleaner, the public-health reformers successfully argued that the real beneficiaries of the new street-car lines would be the working poor.

Urban parks, museums, playgrounds, and libraries represented more subtle means of using culture for political purposes. All were intended to promote social harmony and mute class resentments. The great landscape architect, Frederick Law Olmsted, designed his urban parks to provide a common meeting ground where all classes could come together to enjoy nature and breathe pure air. More specifically, he felt they would provide a wholesome, moral environment that would spiritually elevate the discontented poor. After observing visitors in 1870 at his most famous project, Central Park in New York, he wrote that there could be little doubt that the park "exercises a distinctly harmonizing and refining influence upon the most unfortunate and most lawless classes of the city— an influence favorable to courtesy, self-control, and temperance."[40]

Museums were designed to serve the same purpose but in a more indirect way. Antebellum museums collected all sorts of objects and were meant to attract all classes. Those of the Gilded Age, built with the money of the new rich who were anxious to establish their social credentials and good taste, were citadels of high culture. They housed expensive European masterpieces and embodied a trickle-down theory of cultural diffusion. They were not intended for the direct benefit of immigrants and the working class. Most museums were closed after business hours and on Sundays, the only times most workers could visit them. Instead, it was expected that the propertied classes would visit them and thereby be exposed to the higher values that would make them more worthy of leading and instructing the lower classes. On the other hand, neighborhood playgrounds and library extension services were meant to have a direct impact on working-class children. Supervised play and morally sound books would harness the wasteful, and often destructive, energies of these children into lessons of cleanliness and socially responsible behavior.

The reformers surely tried, and they did help to humanize living conditions in the cities, but the working class seemingly remained stubbornly unappreciative. The high culture of their social betters was not their culture. Most urban parks were too far away from the factory districts for easy access by the working class. Well-meaning reformers too often acted like moral censors. And, most important, as long as workers remained bound to their jobs from dawn to dusk, middle-class campaigns for self-improvement through leisure fell on deaf ears. What most concerned workers were the inequalities of an economic system that left 40 percent of all industrial workers below the poverty line of a $500 annual income and another 45 percent barely above it. The classes remained far apart. Writing in an 1895 issue of *Forum* magazine, William Hale related his social impressions of the textile city of Fall River, Massachusetts. He found class relations between owners and operatives to be divided by feelings "of mutual suspicion, hatred and war."[41]

Middle-class programs of cultural uplift did not close the gap that Hale described. If anything united the classes, it most often was their capacity to live apart from each other. The one great exception was American politics. Here, classes came together in massive electoral alliances orchestrated by the party professionals. Gilded Age politics simultaneously reflected and deflected the class and ethnic conflicts that so concerned the middle class. The next two chapters will examine how it did so.

SUGGESTED READING

The cultural history and social tension of the Gilded Age are brought together in two fine surveys: Walter T. K. Nugent, *From Centennial to World War: American Society, 1876–1917* (1976), and Alan Trachtenberg, *The Incorporation of America: Culture and Society in the Gilded Age* (1982). Robert Wiebe, *The Search for Order* (1968), is a major work that presents a provocative thesis on the spread of bureaucratic thought and values. T. J. Jackson Lears, *No Place of Grace: Antimodernism and the Transformation of American Culture, 1880–1920* (1981), is especially illuminating on cultural tensions in the upper and middle classes. Also helpful on cultural themes are: Howard Mumford Jones, *The Age of Energy: Varieties of American Experience* (1970); Daniel Walker Howe, ed., *Victorian America* (1976); and E. Reid Badger, *The Great American Fair: The World's Columbian Exposition and American Culture* (1979).

Ralph K. Andrist, *The Long Death: The Last Days of the Plains Indians* (1964), is a very readable account that is sensitive to the plight of the Indians. Francis Paul Prucha, *American Indian Policy in Crisis: Christian Reformers and the Indians, 1865–1900* (1976), explains the perspective of the white missionaries. Helen M. Bannan, "The Idea of Civilization and American Indian Policy Reformers in the 1880s," JAC 1 (1978), concisely summarizes white notions of civilization. For the government bureaucrats, see Edmund Jefferson Danziger, Jr., *Indians and Bureaucrats* (1974), and, on the Dawes Act, Francis Paul Prucha, ed., *The Dawes Act and the Allotment of Indian Lands* (1973). Frederic E. Howe, *A Final Promise: The Campaign to Assimilate the Indians, 1880–1920* (1984), is the best study of efforts after 1880 to change the reservation system for the alleged good of the Indians.

Stanford M. Lyman, *Chinese Americans* (1974), is a useful survey, and Gunter Barth, *Bitter Strength: A History of the Chinese in the United States, 1850–1870* (1964), concentrates on the mid-nineteenth century. An excellent history of white attitudes is Stuart C. Miller, *The Unwelcome Immigrant: The American Image of the Chinese, 1785–1882* (1969), and the fears of white labor are highlighted in Alexander Saxton, *The Indispensable Enemy: Labor and the Anti-Chinese Movement in California* (1971). For one of the worst episodes of anti-Chinese violence in the Rocky Mountain mining camps, see Paul Crane and Alfred Larson, "The Chinese Massacre," AW 12 (1940). The fruitless efforts of some white planters in the South to replace emancipated blacks with Chinese laborers are discussed in Lucy M. Cohen, *Chinese in the Post–Civil War South: A People without a History* (1984).

The classic study on Southern race relations after the Civil War is C. Vann Woodward, *The Strange Career of Jim Crow* (1966). A recent major work is Joel Williamson, *The Crucible of Race* (1984). Howard N. Rabinowitz, *Race Relations in the Urban South, 1865–1900* (1978), argues persuasively that segregation, when measured against what it replaced, represented a gain for the social position of Southern blacks. Two other important works are Roger A. Fischer, *The Segregation Struggle in Louisiana* (1974), and Joseph H. Cartwright, *The Triumph of Jim Crow: Tennessee Race Relations in the 1880s* (1976). Comparative approaches are offered in John W. Cell, *The Highest Stage of White Supremacy: The Origins of Segregation in South Africa and the American South* (1982), and, in a work that is not as tightly argued, George M. Fredrickson, *White Supremacy: A Comparative Study in American and South African History* (1981). The rural poverty of blacks in the postwar South and the family strategies they used to cope with that poverty are carefully discussed in Crandall A. Shiflett, *Patronage in the Tobacco South: Louisa County, Virginia, 1860–1900* (1982). Nell Irvin Painter, *Exodusters: Black Migration to Kansas after Reconstruction* (1977), relates black efforts to make a fresh start outside the South. On the economic skills of the first generation of freedmen, see John W. Blassingame, *Black New Orleans, 1860–1880* (1973), and William Harris, "Work and the Family in Black Atlanta, 1880," JSOH 9 (1976). Elizabeth Pleck, *Black Migration and Poverty: Boston, 1865–1900* (1979), shows how white prejudice in the North prevented migrating blacks from utilizing those skills. David A. Gerber, *Black Ohio and the Color Line, 1860–1915* (1977), is a solid study of white racial attitudes in the North. For the nineteenth-century origins of the twentieth-century black ghettos, see David M. Katzman, *Before the Ghetto: Black Detroit in the Nineteenth Century* (1973); Kenneth L. Kusmer, *A Ghetto Takes Shape: Black Cleveland, 1870–1930* (1976); and Thomas Lee Philpott, *The Slum and the Ghetto: Neighborhood Deterioration and Middle-Class Reform, Chicago, 1880–1930* (1978). August Meier, *Negro Thought in America: Racial Ideologies in the Age of Booker T. Washington, 1880–1915* (1963), is a fine survey of the black response to white attitudes. An outstanding study of the best-known black leader of this generation is Louis R. Harlan, *Booker T. Washington: The Making of a Black Leader, 1865–1901* (1972).

A good history of the Southwest for this period is Howard R. Lamar, *The Far Southwest, 1846–1912* (1966). For the Mexican-American, or Chicano, viewpoint of what happened to them under the Anglos, see Cary McWilliams, *North From Mexico: The Spanish-Speaking People in the United States* (1948); Rodolfo Acuña, *Occupied America: The Chicano Struggle for Liberation* (1972); and Robert J. Rosenbaum, *Mexicano Resistance in the Southwest* (1981). Among the best treatments of the economic discrimination suffered by the Mexican Americans are: Alvin R. Sunseri, *Seeds of Discontent: New Mexico in the Aftermath of the American Conquest, 1846–1861* (1979); Roxanne Dunbar Ortiz, *Roots of Resistance: Land Tenure in New Mexico, 1680–1980* (1980); and Richard Griswold del Castillo, *The Los Angeles Barrio, 1850–1890* (1979).

Lois Banner, *Women in Modern America* (1974), Sheila Rothman, *Woman's Proper Place: A History of Changing Ideals and Practices, 1870 to the Present* (1978), and Margaret Gibbons Wilson, *The American Woman in Transition: The Urban Influence, 1870–1920* (1979), provide a good introduction to women's history in the Gilded Age. An overview and analysis of the continuing decline in the birth rate can be found in Stewart E. Tolnay, et al., "Own-Child Estimates of U.S. White Fertility, 1886–99," HM 15 (1982). The special health problems that resulted in the fertility of black women dropping more sharply than that of whites are discussed in Phillips Cutright and Edward Shorter, "The Effects of Health on the Completed Fertility of Nonwhite and White U.S. Women Born From 1867 Through 1935," JSOH 13 (1979). The markedly lower fertility of both races in the cities as opposed to rural areas is shown in Herman Lantz and Lewellyn Hendrix, "Fertility and the Black Family in the Nineteenth Century," JFH 3 (1978). For the entry of women into higher education and the impact of that experience on their lives, see Roberta Frankfurt, *Collegiate Women: Domesticity and Career in Turn-of-the-Century*

America (1977), and Barbara Miller Solomon, *In the Company of Educated Women: A History of Women and Higher Education in America* (1985). Elaine Tyler May, *Great Expectations: Marriage and Divorce in Post-Victorian America* (1980), and Robert L. Griswold, *Family and Divorce in California, 1850–1890* (1982), are the best discussions of divorce in the late nineteenth century.

Alice Kessler-Harris, *Out to Work: A History of Wage-Earning Women in the United States* (1982), is easily the best survey of women's participation in the wage labor force. For an overview of the demographic and economic trends that resulted in the migration of rural women into the cities, see Bengt Akarro, "Agriculture and Women's Work," JFH 4 (1979). On the clerical work of predominately white middle-class women, see Cindy S. Aron, " 'To Barter Their Souls for Gold': Female Clerks in Federal Government Offices, 1862–1890," JAH 67 (1981), and Janice Weiss, "Educating for Clerical Work: The Nineteenth-Century Private Commercial School," JSOH 14 (1981). Women as office workers and sales personnel are superbly covered in Margery W. Davies, *Women's Place Is at the Typewriter* (1982), and Susan Porter Benson, " 'The Customers Ain't God': The Work Culture of Department-Store Saleswomen, 1890–1940," in Michael H. Frisch and Daniel J. Walkowitz, eds., *Working-Class America* (1983). For the role of women as industrial workers, see Daniel J. Walkowitz, "Working-Class Women in the Gilded Age," JSOH 5 (1972); Judith A. McGaw, "A Good Place to Work: Industrial Workers and Occupational Choice," JIH 10 (1979); and Susan Levine, *Labor's True Women: Carpet Weavers, Industrialization, and Labor Reform in the Gilded Age* (1984). The most common job for a woman, especially a black, was that of a domestic, and David M. Katzman, *Seven Days a Week* (1978), Daniel E. Sutherland, *Americans and Their Servants* (1981), and Faye E. Dudden, *Serving Women: Household Service in Nineteenth-Century America* (1983), provide good surveys on domestic service. For women at the other end of the occupational spectrum, see Barbara J. Harris, *Beyond Her Sphere: Women and the Professions in American History* (1979), and for a specific group, Dee Garrison, *Apostles of Culture: The Public Librarian and American Society, 1876–1920* (1979). Joan Jacobs Brumberg and Nancy Tomes, "Women in the Professions," RAH 10 (1982), offer a penetrating analysis of the persistence and function of gender distinctions in the professions. For stimulating and contrasting interpretations of women and reform in the Gilded Age, see: Jill Conway, "Women Reformers and American Culture, 1870–1930," JSOH 5 (1972); Karen J. Blair, *The Clubwoman as Feminist* (1980); Gwendolyn Wright, *Moralism and the Model Home* (1980); William Leach, *True Love and Perfect Union* (1980); and Mari Jo Buhle, *Women and American Socialism* (1981). Ruth Bordin, *Women and Temperance: The Quest for Power and Liberty, 1873–1900*, 1980 focuses on the most popular reform issue among women. The struggle for political equality and the vote can be followed in: Eleanor Flexner, *Century of Struggle: The Women's Rights Movement in the United States* (1959); Aileen Kraditor, *The Ideas of the Woman Suffrage Movement, 1908–1920* (1965); and Alan P. Grimes, *The Puritan Ethic and Woman Suffrage* (1967).

The increasing age consciousness of the late nineteenth century, the way in which age was used to structure experiences and career opportunities, can be broadly traced in Joseph F. Kett, *Rites of Passage: Adolescence in America, 1790 to the Present* (1977); David Hackett Fischer, *Growing Old in America* (1977); W. Andrew Achenbaum, *Old Age in the New Land* (1978); and Carole Haber, *Beyond Sixty-Five: The Dilemma of Old Age in America's Past* (1983). A good synthesis of current work on the late nineteenth century is Howard P. Chudacoff, "The Life Course of Women: Age and Age Consciousness, 1865–1915," JFH 5 (1980). For studies focusing youth in the Gilded Age, see David I. Macleod, *Building Character in the American Boy: The Boy Scouts, YMCA, and Their Forerunners, 1870–1920* (1983), and the statistical data on the transition to adulthood in John Modell, et al., "Social Change and Transitions to Adulthood in Historical Perspective," in Theodore Hershberg, ed., *Philadelphia: Work, Space, Family, and Group Experience in the Nineteenth Century* (1981). For the elderly, see Howard P. Chudacoff and Tamara K. Hareven, "From the Empty Nest to Family Dissolution: Life Course Transitions in Old Age," JFH 4 (1979). Carole Haber, "Mandatory Retirement in 19th-Century America: The Conceptual Basis for a New Work Cycle," JSOH 12 (1978), argues for a connection between mandatory retirement programs and the evolution of corporate capitalism.

Burton J. Bledstein, *The Culture of Professionalism* (1976), is a provocative overview of the nineteenth century that sees professionalism as the specific creation of an upwardly mobile middle class. For the explosive growth in office and retail work, see the tables in Albe M. Edwards, *Comparative Occupation Statistics for the United States, 1870 to 1940* (1943). Richard Sennett, *Families against the City: Middle Class Homes of Industrial Chicago, 1872–1890* (1970), offers a psychological and sociological interpretation of middle-class reactions to urbanization. Samuel P. Hays, *The Response to Industrialism, 1885–1914* (1957), was the first major work that highlighted the importance of professional associations in assessing the response to the heightened competition of a nationalized economy. For the impact of professionalization on higher education and the very definition of knowledge, see Mary O. Furner, *Advocacy and Objectivity: A Crisis in the Professionalization of American Social Science, 1865–1905* (1975); Thomas L. Haskell, *The Emergence of Professional Social Science* (1977); and Alexandra Oleson and John Voss, eds., *The Organization of Knowledge in Modern America* (1979). The essays in Konrad H. Jarausch, ed., *The Transformation of Higher Learning, 1860–1930* (1983), show that the institutional revolution in American institutions was part of a larger process occurring throughout Western nations. Shifts in undergraduate majors and values in the U.S. are explained in Joseph R. De Martini, "Student Culture as a Change Asset in American Higher Education," JSOH 9 (1976).

June Axinn and Herman Levin, *Social Welfare: A History of the American Response to Need* (2nd edition, 1982), is the best survey of reform efforts directed at the poor. Especially helpful for the Gilded Age and the functional relationship of poor relief to industrial capitalism, are Marvin E. Gettleman, "Philanthropy as social control in late nineteenth-century America," *Societas* 5 (1975), and John T. Cumbler, "The Politics of Charity: Gender and Class in Late 19th Century Charity Policy," JSOH 14 (1980). Allen F. Davis, *Spearheads of Reform: The Social Settlements and the Progressive Movement* (1967), and Andrew J. Polsky, "Welfare Policy: Why the Past Has No Future," *democracy* 3 (1983), are excellent on social reformers in the cities. For the restructuring of public education, see Marvin Lazerson, *Origins of the Urban School: Public Education in Massachusetts, 1870–1915* (1971); William A. Bullough, *Cities and Schools in the Gilded Age* (1974); and David B. Tyack, *The One Best System: A History of American Urban Education* (1974). William Issel, "Americanization, Acculturation and Social Control: School Reform Ideology in Industrial Pennsylvania, 1880–1910," JSOH 12 (1979), presents the most sustained argument for linking the rise of educational experts to fears over controlling the industrial immigrants.

For the living conditions of the working classes and the extent of poverty, see Philip R. Silvia, Jr., "The Positions of Workers in a Textile Community: Fall River in the Early 1880s," LH 16 (1975); Susan J. Kleinberg, "Technology and Women's Work: The Lives of Working Class Women in Pittsburgh, 1890–1900," LH 17 (1976); Eudice Glassberg, "Work, Wages, and the Cost of Living: Ethnic Differences and the Poverty Line, Philadelphia, 1880," PH 66 (1979); and Peter R. Shergold, *Working-Class Life: The 'American Standard' in Comparative Perspective, 1899–1913* (1982). The reliance on child labor and the subsequent need for a large family are explained in Frances H. Early, "The French-Canadian Family Economy and Standard-of-Living in Lowell, Massachusetts, 1870," JFH 7 (1982), and Jerry Wilcox and Hilda H. Golden, "Prolific Immigrants and Dwindling Natives?: Fertility Patterns in Western Massachusetts, 1850 and 1880," JFH 7 (1982). Allan Pred, "Production, Family, and Free-Time Projects," JHG 7 (1981), shows how industrialization radically changed the internal organization of working-class families. Working-class culture as a whole is superbly handled in John Bodnar, *Immigrants and Industrialization: Ethnicity in an American Mill Town, 1870–1940* (1977), and John T. Cumbler, *Working-Class Community in Industrial America* (1979). Jon M. Kingsdale,

"The 'Poor Man's Club': Social Functions of the Urban Working-Class Saloon," AQ 25 (1973), examines the key role of the saloon in that culture, and Norman H. Clark, *Deliver Us from Evil: An Interpretation of American Prohibition* (1976), offers a compelling interpretation of the middle-class drive to destroy the saloon. On the working-class quest for home ownership, see David Hogan, "Education and the Making of the Chicago Working Class, 1880–1930," HEQ 18 (1978).

For differing class conceptions of success, see James A. Henretta, "The Study of Social Mobility: Ideological Assumptions and Conceptual Bias," LH 18 (1977), and Susan J. Kleinberg, "Success and the Working Class," JAC 2 (1979). Just how and why the working-class mother differed from the middle-class ideal is set forth in Christine Stansell, "Women, Children, and the Uses of the Streets: Class and Gender Conflict in New York City, 1850–1860," FS 8 (1982). For the clash between the working classes and middle-class reformers over leisure time, see Roy Rosenzweig, *Eight Hours for What We Will: Workers and Leisure in an Industrial City, 1870–1920* (1983), and Francis G. Couvares, *The Remaking of Pittsburgh: Class and Culture in an Industrializing City, 1877–1919* (1984). As shown in John F. Kasson, *Amusing the Millions* (1978), much of the rigidity of middle-class attitudes toward leisure softened with the development of a mass, consumerized culture around the turn of the century. Class divisions over public health and the use of the streets are covered in Judith Walzer Leavitt, *The Healthiest City: Milwaukee and the Politics of Health Reform* (1982), and Clay McShane, "Transforming the Use of Urban Space: A Look at the Revolution in Street Pavement, 1880–1924," JUH 5 (1979). Jean B. Quandt, "Religion and Social Thought: The Secularization of Postmillennialism," AQ 25 (1973), and Helen Lefkowitz Horowitz, *Culture and the City: Cultural Philanthropy in Chicago from the 1880s to 1917* (1976), analyze the combination of moral uplift, social control, and faith in technological progress that motivated the reform efforts of the upper and middle classes.

NOTES

1. Quoted in Helen M. Bannan, "The Idea of Civilization and American Indian Policy Reformers in the 1880s," *Journal of American Culture* 1 (1978): 789.
2. Quoted in Richard Hofstadter and Michael Wallace, eds., *American Violence: A Documentary History* (New York: Vintage Books, 1971), p. 278.
3. Quoted in Bannan, op. cit., p. 789.
4. Quoted in Frederick Turner, *Beyond Geography: The Western Spirit Against the Wilderness* (New York: The Viking Press, 1980), p. 287.
5. Virgil J. Vogel, ed., *This Country Was Ours: A Documentary History of the American Indian* (New York: Harper & Row, 1972), p. 179.
6. Quoted in Wilcomb E. Washburn, *The Indian in America* (New York: Harper Colophon Books, 1975), p. 245.
7. Quoted in Bannan, op. cit., p. 793.
8. Quoted in Ronald T. Takaki, *Iron Cages: Race and Culture in 19th-Century America* (New York: Alfred A. Knopf, 1979), p. 240.
9. Ibid., p. 220.
10. Quoted in Richard Drinnon, *Facing West: The Metaphysics of Indian-Hating and Empire-Building* (New York: New American Library, 1980), pp. 220–221.
11. Cited in Melvin Drimmer, ed., *Black History: A Reappraisal* (Garden City: N.Y.: Doubleday & Co., 1968), p. 337.
12. Quoted in Takaki, op. cit., p. 213.
13. Quoted in David I. Macleod, "Act Your Age: Boyhood, Adolescence and the Rise of the Boy Scouts of America," *Journal of Social History* 16 (1982): 8.
14. Quoted in Carole Haber, "Mandatory Retirement in 19th-Century America: The Conceptual Basis for a New Work Cycle," *Journal of Social History* 12 (1978): 82.
15. Ibid., p. 87.
16. Quoted in Burton J. Bledstein, *The Culture of Professionalism: The Middle Class and the Development of Higher Education in America* (New York: W. W. Norton, 1976), p. 120.

17. Quoted in Marvin E. Gettleman, "Philanthropy as social control in late nineteenth-century America: some hypotheses and data on the rise of social work," *Societas* 5 (1975): 50.
18. These quotations are from the 1889 and 1892 annual reports of the Associated Charities of Fall River, Massachusetts, as cited in John T. Cumbler, "The Politics of Charity: Gender and Class in Late 19th Century Charity Policy," *Journal of Social History* 14 (1980): 103, 105.
19. Quoted in June Axinn and Herman Levin, *Social Welfare: A History of the American Response to Need* (New York: Harper & Row, 1982), p. 104.
20. Quoted in Jill Conway, "Women Reformers and American Culture, 1870–1930," *Journal of Social History* 5 (1972): 171.
21. Quoted in Gettleman, op. cit., p. 59.
22. Quoted in David B. Tyack, *The One Best System: A History of American Urban Education* (Cambridge: Harvard University Press, 1974), pp. 75, 74.
23. Quoted in William Issel, "Americanization, Acculturation and Social Control: School Reform Ideology in Industrial Pennsylvania, 1880–1910," *Journal of Social History* 12 (1979): 572.
24. Quoted in Tyack, op. cit., p. 75.
25. Quoted in Issel, op. cit., p. 578.
26. Cited in Robert H. Bremner, ed., *Children and Youth in America: A Documentary History*, Vol. II: 1866–1932, Part 8 (Cambridge: Harvard University Press, 1971), p. 1422.
27. Quoted in Issel, op. cit., p. 574.
28. J. E. Seaman, "High Schools and the State," *The Journal of Proceedings and Addresses of the National Educational Association* (New York, 1886), cited in Bremner, op. cit., pp. 1387–1388.
29. Mary Antin, *The Promised Land* (Boston, 1912), cited in ibid., p. 1318.
30. Quoted in Issel, op. cit., p. 584.
31. David Brion Davis, ed., *The Fear of Conspiracy: Images of Un-American Subversion from the Revolution to the Present* (Ithaca: Cornell Paperbacks, 1972), p. 175.
32. Quoted in Daniel Walkowitz, "Working-Class Women in the Gilded Age: Factory, Community and Family Life among Cohoes, New York, Cotton Workers," *Journal of Social History* 5 (1972): 465.
33. Quoted in Philip T. Silvia, Jr., "The Position of Workers in a Textile Community: Fall River in the Early 1880s," *Labor History* 16 (1975): 235.
34. An oral-history interview cited in Tamara K. Hareven and Randolph Langenback, *Amoskeag: Life and Work in an American Factory-City* (New York: Pantheon Books, 1978), p. 256.
35. Quoted in Daniel T. Rodgers, *The Work Ethic in Industrial America, 1850–1920* (Chicago: The University of Chicago Press, 1978), pp. 68–69.
36. Jonathan Baxter Harrison, *Certain Dangerous Tendencies in American Life* (Boston, 1880), cited in Alan Trachtenberg, ed, *Democratic Vistas, 1860–1880* (New York: George Braziller, 1970), p. 180.
37. Quoted in Trachtenberg, op. cit., p. 19.
38. Quoted in Francis G. Couvares, "The Triumph of Commerce: Class Culture and Mass Culture in Pittsburgh," in Michael H. Frisch and Daniel J. Walkowitz, eds., *Working-Class America: Essays on Labor, Community, and American Society* (Urbana, Ill.: University of Illinois Press, 1983), p. 136.
39. Harrison, cited in Trachtenberg, op. cit., p. 18.
40. Quoted in Stanley L. Schultz, "Pioneer of the Crabgrass Frontier," *Reviews in American History* 2 (1974): 342.
41. Quoted in John T. Cumbler, "Transatlantic Working-Class Institutions," *Journal of Historical Geography* 6 (1980): 288.

10

Gilded Age Politics

The politics of the Gilded Age easily lends itself to caricature. Ever since Twain and Warner coined the phrase "the Gilded Age," political life from the end of congressional Reconstruction in the 1870s to the beginnings of Progressivism in 1900 has conjured up an image of shallow, glittering materialism. Politics was seemingly dominated not by statesmen, but by confidence men, fat businessmen, and venal politicians who all conspired to be first in line to feast at a great barbecue of government favors and subsidies. The best that E. L. Godkin, editor of the liberal journal *The Nation* and a persistent critic of the party system, could say of congressmen in 1874 was that "we underrate their honesty, but we overrate their intelligence."[1] One is reminded of the famous quip of Henry Adams, another patrician critic of the contemporary political scene, that all that was needed to disprove Darwin's theory of evolution was a study of the evolution of the presidency from Washington through Grant.

As in all caricatures, there is an element of truth in this one. Republicans and Democrats regularly accused each other of buying votes and shepherding repeat voters from one critical election district to another. In the absence of any tradition of professional service and the funds or administrative staff to manage federal programs, such as the land-grant legislation for the railroads, policy was usually just a synonym for the pursuit of private gain through public subsidies. At all levels of government, the line between public service and private gain was often so blurred as to be meaningless.

The corruption was undeniable, but its extent can easily be exaggerated. What was usually depicted as corruption was in fact an informal alliance of businessmen and politicians that was brought about by public demands for rapid economic growth and generous distribution of benefits. Rather than a wholesale decline in political morality in the wake of the Civil War, a quantum jump in demands placed on governmental structures without the administrative capacity to police those demands produced the great free-for-all at the public trough. As it was, much that we decry as corruption in the Gilded Age has been sanitized in the twentieth century under the labels of lobbying activities and retainers for services rendered.

Especially if we avoid the temptation to read back twentieth-century issues and notions of governmental responsibilities, politics in the Gilded Age can be approached on its own terms of intricately organized mass loyalties to the two major parties. Popular interest in politics was at an all-time high in the late nineteenth century. Nearly

80 percent of the electorate regularly voted in national elections. Partisan loyalties were powerful, very evenly balanced, and all but immovable. The high turnouts, partisan balance, and intense loyalties set apart Gilded Age politics as a distinct party system. This chapter will focus on that system—the limited role of the presidency within it, the forces that shaped it, the economic and cultural issues it debated, and the dissident groups that unsuccessfully tried to change it in the 1870s and 1880s.

The Presidency in the Gilded Age

In tacit recognition of their relatively minor role, most of us have forgotten or never learned the names and sequence of the presidents in the Gilded Age. If we remember them at all, it is usually for the colorful anecdotes and slogans that their antics and personalities inspired. The Blaine-Cleveland election of 1884, for example, gave us a memorable piece of political doggerel. The Republicans leaked the story that Cleveland was the father of an illegitimate child, and Cleveland, a man of scrupulous personal integrity, admitted that yes, he well might be the father of a child born to the widow Mrs. Marcia Halperin. There were several likely candidates for the fatherly role, but Cleveland assumed the moral and financial responsibility. Now the Republicans could chant:[2]

> Ma, Ma, where's my Pa?
> Going to the White House, ha! ha! ha![2]

Cleveland at least had the virtue of a certain charisma in the personality he projected to the public. The Republican presidents, Rutherford B. Hayes (1876–1880) and Benjamin Harrison (1888–1892) by contrast were lampooned for their chilly dourness. Hayes, a teetotaler, infuriated official Washington by banning alcohol from the White House. His wife was known as "Lemonade Lucy," and a state dinner was now, according to Congressman James A. Garfield of Ohio, a "wet down with coffee and cold water." As for Harrison, those about to meet him for the first time were warned that his handshake was "like a wilted petunia." Talking with Harrison was "like talking to a hitching post,"[3] noted one senator.

This image of Gilded Age presidents as apt material for witticisms but hardly makers of policy is not altogether inaccurate. None of them in fact was in a position to exercise forceful, positive leadership. Grant, with his untarnished prestige in 1868 as the architect of Union victory, was a partial exception, but the massive scandals of his two terms sullied that prestige and confirmed the ingrained suspicions of former Whigs and Republicans that the presidency was more a source of corruption than of inspiration. What was said of Chester Arthur—he had "done well . . . by not doing anything bad"[4]—pretty much summarized what Americans expected of their presidents after Grant's first term. As for the presidents themselves, Grover Cleveland voiced the feelings of all of them when he anticipated that his first term would be "a dreadful self-inflicted penance for the good of my country."[5]

What Cleveland so dreaded went to the heart of the Gilded Age conception of the presidency. The chief responsibility of the president was to immerse himself in the intricacies of the daily workings of his party by distributing the rewards of patronage in the cause of party unity. Patronage was the lifeblood of the parties. By awarding offices to loyal party workers and assessing them part of their salaries for party needs, the parties simultaneously financed themselves and created internal bonds of al legiance. As the head of patronage distribution, the president had to act as a partisan leader, not a policymaker, and that role was all-consuming. The stream of office seekers never seemed to stop. "Once or twice I felt like crying out in the agony of my soul against the greed for office and its consumption of my time,"[6] fairly shrieked President Garfield in his diary for June 1881.

The president was both the major dispenser of patronage and its major captive. He owed his presidential nomination to patronage concessions he had made to the leaders of the state political machines who in turn lined up their delegates behind him. The national parties were primarily coalitions of these state organizations, and the national committees maintained no continuity between presidential campaigns. State leaders jealously guarded their independence and there was no centralized, bureaucratic structure that could entice or force them to defer to presidential authority.

A leader among men, but scarcely a ruler over them, every president was frustrated by the demands of patronage on his time and energy. He had no time to formulate policy, no one expected him to, and he lacked a staff to help him do so. After Congress appropriated money in 1901 for an expansion of the executive staff, it still numbered no more than a dozen persons, including telegraphers and doorkeepers. The party system of the Gilded Age cast its presidents in a rigid, partisan mold and gave them little room or reason to maneuver.

The Gilded Age Party System

What most directly shaped this party system was the impact of the Civil War and Reconstruction on party ideologies and loyalties rooted in the Jacksonian era and the realignment of the 1850s. The Republican conception of a strong, reformist government, one that was galvanized by the need to win the war and define the position of former slaves after the war, provoked a sharp Democratic response, which ideologically polarized the parties around the issue of centralized authority versus states' rights. After the polarizing issues of black rights and Reconstruction faded by the mid-1870s, both parties avoided headlong ideological strife. Organizational loyalties, not reform causes, became the staple of politics. Chastened by the memory of how ideological crusades had exploded into the Civil War and Reconstruction, the voters had no desire for a politics of intensity. Instead, they responded to political rhetoric that constantly appealed to Civil War loyalties.

After the war, as during it, Northern Democrats called upon the party faithful to protect local rights of self-governance from the tyrannical centralization and fanatical zeal of the Republicans. Meanwhile, the Republicans resorted to a technique known as waving the bloody shirt. Benjamin Butler, a Union general and Massachusetts congressman, once literally did wave such a shirt during a political speech in 1866. It came from the back of a white Ohioan who had been beaten in Mississippi for his pro-Republican politics. Other Republicans were not as dramatic as Butler, but the figurative use of the bloody shirt was a staple of Republican oratory. It was a way of reminding the voters that the Republicans were the party that had saved the Union and stood by to protect all its true friends from unrepentant Southerners. The equivalent in

"Boys in Blue." Throughout the Gilded Age the Republicans drew upon their Civil War record for political campaigning. Shown here are Union veterans at the head of a parade for the Republican presidential candidate in 1876, Rutherford B. Hayes. (The Granger Collection)

the South was the Democratic appeal to white supremacy, a reminder to Southern whites that although the war had been lost, the greater battle of saving the South from the degradation of black rule could be safely entrusted only to the Democratic party.

Without a doubt, some politicians cynically manipulated the loyalties and hatreds that were a legacy of the war and its ultimate political settlement. By mobilizing these highly charged emotions, they were able to avoid or neutralize the divisive postwar issues of class and economic adjustment. In the South, appeals to racism split the single class of tenants and croppers into antagonistic groups of blacks and whites that could be played off against each other. During an economic downturn in the North, as Hayes explained to James G. Blaine in the campaign of 1876, a Republican appeal to "the dread of a solid South, rebel rule, etc., etc. . . . leads people away from 'hard times', which is our deadliest foe."[7]

The politicians could afford such cynicism because they so well understood the popular feelings that were anything but irrelevant to the voters. A veteran aptly summarized what the war experience meant: "There had grown up between the boys an attachment for each other they never had nor ever will have for any other body of men."[8] When the war was over, that attachment took the form of an institutionalized and partisan fraternity. In the North the veterans organized the Grand Army of the Republic. Still 400,000 strong in 1890, the G.A.R. was a social club, a lobby for veterans' benefits, and an indispensable adjunct to the Republican party. In the South the United Confederate Veterans provided a living embodiment of what Southern whites refused to believe had died at Appomattox. The cult of the lost cause assumed the mythical dimensions of a civil religion and offered a substitute for the bond of community shattered by wartime deaths and postwar poverty. Adherence to the cult, and observance of its ritualistic ceremonies in days of fasting, praying, and dedicating war memorials, assured Southern whites they were still a noble and virtuous people who revered the memory of departed Christian heroes.

By the mid–1870s, the politically mobilized loyalties of the war years balanced the two major parties in a virtual dead heat. In the South, congressional Reconstruction was about finished, and the Democrats were the ruling party. In the North, the Democrats made a strong comeback when a depression hit the economy in 1873 and the Republican majority was splintered by the emergence of new issues such as labor reform, prohibition, and corruption in the Grant administration. The postwar dominance of the Republicans was over.

The Republicans failed, in every presidential election from 1876 through 1892, either to win a majority of the popular vote or even to gain a plurality of the counties in the nation as a whole. In three of these five presidential elections, the margin of victory was less than 1 percent (see Table 10.1). One of the closest was the Garfield-Hancock election of 1880, which Garfield carried with a plurality of four-tenths of 1 percent. This was the trend-setting national election in the Gilded Age, because Democratic white conservatives had regained full power in the South for the first time since

Table 10.1 Presidential Elections, 1876–1892

Extremely close party competition in presidential elections was one of the most striking characteristics of Gilded Age politics. In the elections of 1876 and 1888, the eventual winners in the electoral college—Hayes and Harrison—came out second best in the popular vote.

YEAR	CANDIDATE	PARTY	PERCENTAGE OF POPULAR VOTE
1876	Hayes	Republican	48.0
	Tilden	Democratic	51.0
1880	Garfield	Republican	48.5
	Hancock	Democratic	48.1
	Weaver	Greenback-Labor	3.4
1884	Cleveland	Democratic	48.5
	Blaine	Republican	48.2
	Butler	Greenback-Labor	1.8
	St. John	Prohibition	1.5
1888	Harrison	Republican	47.9
	Cleveland	Democratic	48.6
	Fisk	Prohibition	2.2
	Streeter	Union Labor	1.3
1892	Cleveland	Democratic	46.1
	Harrison	Republican	43.0
	Weaver	Populist	8.5
	Bidwell	Prohibition	2.2

Source: Adapted from George Brown Tindall, *America: A Narrative History*, Vol. 2 (New York: W. W. Norton & Co., 1984), pp. A33, A34. Reprinted by permission of the publisher.

the end of the war. Free to vote in 1880 as they had shot in the war, Southern whites ironically voted for someone they *did* shoot at during the war, Winfield Scott Hancock, a Union general at Gettysburg and the Democratic presidential nominee. Hancock carried every Southern state. Because Garfield likewise won every state but New Jersey in the Northeast and Midwest, Hancock lost.

The stalemate in presidential politics was repeated in Congress. After 1874, the Democrats usually had a slight edge in the House, and the Republicans in the Senate. Consequently, neither party controlled both Congress and the presidency for any extended period of time. In sixteen of the twenty-two years from 1874 to 1896, a different party held one or the other. A ruling national party, able to command the majorities needed to overcome the checks and balances of federalism, was simply out of the question.

Because access to the spoils of patronage took precedence over any concept of actually ruling while in office, winning an election provided most of its own rewards. The states that were the key to doing so in a presidential campaign comprised an evenly balanced belt of six that stretched from Connecticut in the east to Illinois in the west. These swing states in the North were characterized by either a large urban vote that tended to be Democratic, as in Connecticut, New York, and New Jersey, or a Southern-born rural electorate, as in the lower halves of Ohio, Indiana, and Illinois. Confronted with a solidly Democratic South, the Republicans needed New York and all three of these midwestern states to win a presidential election. Their standard strategy was to pick their presidential nominee from Ohio or Indiana and their vice-president from New York. The Democrats, knowing that a Southern candidate would unite the entire North against them, reversed the sequence. Their presidential choices usually came from New York and their vice-presidential ones from the Midwest.

The same care that was paid to maximizing the chances for victory by geographically tuning the ticket was also lavished on the voters, almost to a man. The parties, not public authorities or independent agencies, maintained lists of registered voters, printed the ballots, and conducted pre-election polls that were accurate to within a few votes of the total. The parties were the source of virtually all political information and, in the absence of anything like today's mass media, they dramatized the issues for the voters. Newspapers were party papers, and independent journals of opinion reached but a small and highly educated audience in the Northeast. In addition to informing the electorate, the parties also entertained it. Before the rise of spectator sports, movies, radio, and television, an elaborately staged political rally was second only to the coming of the circus as a form of mass entertainment in rural, small-town America. Politics as pageant was the great national game.

The actual election campaigns were run with a military degree of precision and discipline. Up-to-date canvasses by party workers identified areas in need of extra support, and financial aid and oratorical flourishes were adjusted accordingly. Because party regularity was so high and allegiances so balanced, elections turned on which of the parties got out the greatest percentage of its normal vote. Accordingly, the parties were extremely cautious in introducing new issues that might break up their voting coalitions. There was little to be gained and much to be lost by straying from tried-and-true party appeals in an effort to win support from independents. The uncommitted or floating vote, especially in comparison to modern American politics, was insignificant. Two-thirds of the voters always voted a straight party ticket, and another 10 to 15 percent normally did. The party professionals did their job and so did the voters. Between 1876 and 1896, an average of 79 percent of the voters cast a ballot in each of the presidential elections, and 63 percent voted in the off-year elections. How extraordinarily high these rates were can be gauged by the figures for American politics in the 1970s and early 1980s. Barely half (the better-educated and wealthier half) turned out for a presidential contest, and just over a third in congressional and state elections.

The Party Issues

Clearly, Gilded Age culture placed a high value on political participation for males. It did so not only because of the sectional fusions of Civil War patriotism and party loyalty, but also because politics were very decentralized and hence quite sensitive to local issues of most immediate concern to the voters. On the surface at least, these issues were primarily racial and ethnocultural in nature. In the South there was the never-ending demand for the perpetuation of racial home rule by local white majorities. Elsewhere prohibition, Sabbatarian legislation, and struggles for control of the public school system pitted pietistic Protestants and the native-born against Catholics and the immigrants.

Partisan cleavages were closely related to ethnoreligious conflicts. Predominately in the Republican camp were the evangelical Protestants—Methodists, Presbyterians, and Christian Disciples of Christ—who turned to the power of the state to sanctify the society around them according to their notions of right behavior. Mostly in the Democratic camp were the liturgical groups—Lutherans, Regular Baptists, and Roman Catholics—who stressed right belief as the key to salvation and who entrusted only the governing bodies of their own churches with the regulation of morality. Thus, the major parties split along lines of both sectionalism and those of kinship, religion, and ethnic identity. The Republicans can be summarized as mostly the party of Northern Protestants imbued with a concept of an active, socially responsive government. Their heartland was New England and its cultural colonies of Yankeeism in the Midwest. They were the party of Protestant morality and middle-class respectability. The Democrats were typically the party of Catholic immigrants in the Northern cities and of whites in the South and lower Midwest. They valued a government dedicated to majority rule on the local level and rejected the positive liberalism of the Republicans as an undemocratic interference with their own moral codes and community mores.

The party managers had every reason to cater on the local level to the cultural sensibilities of their respective coalitions. By so doing they increased the likelihood of holding together their voting coalitions. As voting patterns in state legislatures reveal, party lines held firmly on such issues as prohibition, school language laws, and Sunday closings. In contrast, different party configurations emerged on each economic issue. Even more so than before industrialization, cultural appeals were effective in building party unity, because they gave voters a way of establishing some sense of personal autonomy and control in the disorienting environment produced by rapid socioeconomic change.

The cultural divisions between the parties did not reflect a competing set of religious values per se, but rather the interaction of those values with memories of the Civil War and factors of class and social status. Although the South was a stronghold of evangelical Protestantism, most Southern whites were Democrats. In the North issues of banning alcohol, controlling the schools, and preserving the Sabbath simultaneously spoke to the millennial hopes of Republicans as evangelicals and to the class fears of Republicans as businessmen and propertyholders. Evangelical cultural norms were, as we saw in Chapter 9, used for purposes of class control, and most of the evangelicals were in the middle class. In Illinois in the late 1870s, to cite one study of eight townships, 76 percent of the nonfarming pietists held jobs of middle or upper status. Fewer than half, 47 percent, of the liturgicals did. Northern evangelicalism, with its stress on individual initiative and social betterment, reinforced and reflected the behavioral patterns of the economically successful in commercial agriculture and white-collar occupations. Northern Democrats, in the reverse of this linkage of economic and religious status, were disproportionately both liturgicals and the economically unsuccessful who were concentrated in subsistence farming and unskilled jobs.

Catholics were overwhelmingly Democratic, but there was nothing in Catholic theology that precluded a strong stand by the Church in favor of the public regulation of morals. Where Catholics were dominant in nineteenth-century Europe, the Church took just such a "pietistic" stance. In Gilded Age America the Catholics were a minority suspected of being un-American, and the Church fought off cultural legislation that it feared was designed to absorb Catholics into the Protestant mainstream. Most Catholics were also unskilled laborers. They saw that for the Protestant reformers an issue such as prohibition was, as the Reverend Joseph Cook expressed it, essential to "the great problem of the right management of cities,"[9] and they knew that they were the ones to be managed.

Variations in ethnicity, religion, and class were all intertwined in the United States. For that reason, status politics based on ethnic and religious rankings emerged out of, not in spite of, the class divisions of industrialism. Immigrants and Catholics were disproportionately the workers, and the efforts of capital to regulate labor inevitably followed the cultural fault plane of Protestant native versus Catholic immigrant. Splintered into ethnic and religious subgroups, workers struggled to assert, in the cultural politics of their local neighborhoods, the control and independence that capital denied them in the factory routinization and discipline of labor. In the Southern version of this process, Democratic planters and merchants offered poor white farmers the security of a superior racial status as a replacement for the economic security those farmers lost when only the planters and merchants made profits from the falling price of cotton.

It was in the interest of the parties to keep cultural issues localized in state politics. If nationalized, the ethnic and religious conflicts would have torn apart the party coalitions. This was especially true for the Republicans. Their followers usually took the offensive in the cultural battles, and Republican leaders were always trying to keep a rein on the loathings of rural Protestantism in an effort to hold on to the party share of the ethnic and labor vote. Thus, whereas it was to the advantage of the Democrats to stress limited government and strict constitutionalism as a way of assuring white cultural minorities that the party would protect them from the Republicans, the strength of the Republicans was in portraying themselves as the loyal party of the Union and prosperity. Issues related to these themes were the staple of Republican platforms in national politics.

One of these issues was black civil rights. For Republicans, the freedom and citizenship of the former slaves were intimately linked to the great cause of the Union, and they continued to assume the moral high ground of espousing black equality before the law. Much of this espousal was largely rhetorical, however. The end of congressional Reconstruction and its potential for a biracial democracy in the South removed any political leverage Afro-Americans might have exerted on Republicans to enforce black rights of citizenship. Blacks in the North were simply too few in numbers to require the serious attention of the party, and those in the South were largely abandoned by the party after 1876. The Republicans maintained a party organization in the South, but it was increasingly lily-white.

In what was correctly perceived by contemporaries as the last gasp of the social idealism of the 1860s, Republicans did push a major civil rights bill through Congress in 1875. The original version of the bill provided for broad federal guaranties of desegregation in schools, juries, churches, cemeteries, and all public accommodations. The version that passed was limited just to public accommodations. Still, it would have offered meaningful protection for black rights, had the courts decided to interpret it that way; they did not.

As climaxed in the Civil Rights Cases of 1883, the courts practically invalidated the Civil Rights Act of 1875, and the intent of the Fourteenth Amendment, as well. Federal protection of civil rights was held to extend only to the impairment of those rights through the actions of states, not individuals. The doctrine of laissez-faire, which the courts applied to the economy, was extended to race relations. Just as individuals had to take their chances in the marketplace, so also blacks had to in their dealings with whites. The judges said they had no more right to interfere in the contractual obligations between freely consenting adults than they did to regulate the racial arrangements that presumably represented voluntary agreements between blacks and whites. But, in a double standard that became most obvious in the *Plessy* v. *Ferguson* case of 1896, the Supreme Court treated the respective rights of corporations and of blacks quite differently. After consistently restricting, in the 1880s and 1890s, the legal authority of states to regulate corporations and, in the process, converting the due-process clause of the Fourteenth Amendment into a shield for the rights of a corporation as a legal citizen, the Supreme Court decided in *Plessy* v. *Ferguson* that the states *did* have such legal authority to regulate race relations. Segregationalist laws imposed by the states were constitutional, according to a majority on the Court, if equal facilities were made available to both races. There was more than enough room for Jim Crow in that legal loophole.

Aside from the Civil Rights Act of 1875, the only other major effort by Gilded Age Republicans on behalf of black rights was a bill that never passed Congress, the Federal Elections Bill of 1890. Although aimed specifically at voting frauds in the South, where violence and intimidation deprived blacks of their suffrage rights, the bill was national in scope. It created mechanisms for the federal supervision of elections wherever fraud was alleged. This national coverage foredoomed the bill. Labor leaders and Democratic city bosses, smelling a Republican plot to use election inspectors to undermine the immigrant vote, joined a united front of Southern whites in blocking what quickly became known as the Force Bill.

What was left of the party's idealism failed to produce a positive record by the Republicans on black civil rights. Nonetheless, the party retained a firm hold on the black vote. Blacks could hardly turn to the more overtly racist Democrats, the party that had opposed even the Thirteenth Amendment freeing the slaves. Until the depression of the 1930s converted blacks from Lincoln's party of freedom to Roosevelt's party of economic assistance, blacks were integrated into the Republican party through segregated local machines. Black politicians served as a liaison between the party's white leaders and the mass of black voters. Before the development of ghettos in the twentieth century provided an independent power base for black politicians, they remained economically and politically dependent on whites. Men of moderate means and bourgeois standards, they were drawn from the small black middle class of professionals, shopkeepers, and artisans who catered to a predominately white clientele. They saw themselves as a model for the black community and, as long as they did not transgress the barriers of proper racial etiquette, they were valued by white Republicans as an example of how blacks could achieve social mobility through individual merit.

Social mobility for individuals was also the keynote of the Republican position on the one economic issue that most clearly differentiated them from Democrats at the national level, the tariff. During the Gilded Age, more words were uttered and ink spilled on the tariff than on any other issue. The shortest and economically most accurate statement was made by Hancock during the 1880 campaign when he said that "The tariff question is a local question."[10] Tariff schedules were immensely complicated affairs that were negotiated in logrolling sessions between spokesmen for

Republicans on the Tariff. This Republican cartoon of 1888 depicts a standard refrain of the party: lowering the tariff would wreck American industry and destroy factory jobs by inundating the economy with a flood of cheap foreign imports manufactured by pauperized labor. (Culver Pictures, Inc.)

particular industries and localities. But Hancock was only half right; as presented to the voters by the Republicans, the tariff was more than just a local economic issue. It was also an indispensable political tool with which to harmonize the interests of capital and labor without upsetting the tenets of liberal capitalism. Protective tariffs were the linchpin of the Republican appeal to labor, and the one issue the Republicans were convinced could deliver them a national constituency that cut across class lines. The Republicans held out such high hopes for the protective tariff because it alone seemed to offer the best of all possible worlds—profits for manufacturers and high wages and individual advancement for ambitious workers.

The Republicans, as had their Whig predecessors, started from the premise that American manufacturers suffered the disadvantage of having to compete against foreign manufacturers, notably the British, whose labor costs were much lower. They concluded that in an economic environment of free trade, American manufacturers could survive and prosper only if they likewise reduced production costs by driving the wages of American labor down to the level of mere subsistence. America, like England, would then have a pauperized working class. Unlike England, however, American workers had the vote and, it was feared, would use their political power to force fundamental changes in the organization of the economy. Francis Bowen, in an argument for tariff protection in 1863, reasoned:[11]

> The class of laborers, who must always form the majority in any community, and who, with us, also have the control in politics, will not be satisfied without organic changes in the laws, which will endanger at once our political and social system.

Thus the goals of the Republican protectionists were both social stability and economic prosperity. A high tariff, by assuring American manufacturers control of the home market, would guarantee a continuation of the comparatively high wages that gave labor a stake in the existing order and the incentive and material rewards with which to rise into the entrepreneurial class. The same high wages would underwrite the prosperity of the American farmer by increasing the purchasing power of labor for American foodstuffs. Manufacturers, freed of the necessity of cutting wages to meet foreign competition, would compete among themselves by turning to labor-saving and more efficient machinery. Eventually, competition at home would reduce the prices of manufactured goods, and the entire economy would benefit.

During the Civil War, the Republicans doubled the tariff rates. The large jump was possible because, aside from the absence of Southern congressmen who would have opposed it, the Republicans could cite the need for wartime revenue to help finance the war and the hardships of Union manufacturers who were burdened with wartime taxes that cut into their profits. After the war, the business taxes were removed but the high tariff remained. Despite persistent demands by the Democrats for downward revisions, and some tinkering with the rates, tariff duties as a percentage of the value of the imported goods subject to the tariff stayed at 40 to 50 percent throughout the late nineteenth century.

The Democrats, consistent with their ideological traditions and the needs of the major economic interests in their party, carried the banner for a low tariff. As opposed to the Republicans, who represented the major manufacturing interests of the Northeast and Midwest, the economic leadership of the Democrats came from planters in the South and importing merchants in the East, and both these groups felt they were hurt

Democrats on the Tariff. This Democratic cartoon of 1886 ridicules the Republican bugaboo of free trade by depicting a factory owner made wealthy by a protective tariff magnanimously, but hypocritically, defending his workers from the exaggerated threat of a lower tariff. (The New York Public Library)

by high tariffs. Since the days of Jackson, the Democrats had insisted that protective tariffs were class legislation that fostered monopolies and violated the concept of equal rights. One class of the citizenry, manufacturers, received special privileges, from which they alone derived benefits and which other classes had to pay for in higher prices for manufacturered items. Typical of the Democratic position was President Cleveland's denunciation in 1887 of the protective tariff as a "vicious, inequitable, and illogical source of unnecessary taxation."[12] In the political economy of the Democrats, all producers should be subjected equally to the discipline of the market. It was unfair that farmers, who sold their products in an unprotected market, should be forced by governmental action to subsidize the profits of manufacturers favored with a protected market. As for labor, any benefits they might receive from higher wages would be more than offset by the higher costs they had to pay as customers.

The other economic issue that was a focal point of national party debate was the currency. The problem, for many Americans, was that there was not enough of it. After spurting during the Civil War, the nation's money supply fell sharply just after the war, was stagnant in the 1870s, and then grew slowly in the 1880s and 1890s. In per-capita terms, the currency in circulation outside the Treasury was still lower in 1900, about $27, than it had been in 1865, about $30. Meanwhile, prices were falling throughout the period. The wholesale price index of all commodities declined by 18 percent in the last half of the 1860s and by 33 percent in the 1870s, 19 percent in the 1880s, and 7 percent in the 1890s. Because production was growing much faster than the supply of money, prices fell. Those groups whose economic position suffered from falling prices—farmers and small businessmen pressed by debt, workers trying to set up cooperative ventures in production, and entrepreneurs anxious for easier credit—

sought relief in an inflationary expansion of the currency. Conversely, those who were benefiting from deflation—the more established and efficient businessmen and cred itors in general—fought to hold the line against monetary expansion.

The sheer size of the greatly magnified financial role of the federal government as a direct result of the Civil War virtually guaranteed that monetary policy would be a major political issue. The war left the government with a national debt that had ballooned from $65 million in 1860, or $2.06 per capita, to $2.7 billion in 1865, or $75.01 per capita. Most of this debt was in the form of interest-bearing bonds, the sale of which had met 74 percent of the war costs in the Union. The bonds in turn were linked to the new banking system created by the National Banking Acts of 1863 and 1864. Private banks, in return for investing at least one-third of their capital in U.S. bonds, received a national charter and the right to issue national banknotes up to 90 percent of the market value of the bonds they left on deposit with the Treasury. In 1865 a prohibitive tax of 10 percent on state banknotes drove them out of circulation and forced more banks into the system of federally chartered ones.

Greenbacks, another new form of national currency created during the Civil War, comprised a much smaller proportion of the national debt in 1865 than the bonds did. About $450 million of these non-interest-bearing Treasury notes were issued during the war. They were legal tender but not redeemable in specie. The greenbacks were issued only because of the government's immediate and compelling need for cash with which to meet its obligations. To vote against them was to vote against the Union.

Both major parties agreed after the war that national honor, economic stability, and moral honesty required a rapid retirement of federal debt and a quick return to money convertible into specie. Nineteenth-century republicanism condemned government debt as a corrupting source of unearned wealth and assumed that paper money not backed up by specie had no intrinsic value and hence was immoral. Thus, neither party permitted the new currencies spawned by the pressures of the wartime emergency to keep pace with demographic and economic expansion after the war. The maximum amount of national bank notes was limited to $300 million until 1875. However, even when the limit was lifted, the notes were still tied to federal bonds, and those bonds were steadily being retired, or paid back, by the Treasury. When government bonds in private hands decreased from $2.3 billion in 1866 to $0.6 billion in 1893, the volume of national banknotes correspondingly fell. By 1879 greenbacks were made redeemable in gold, and the amount in circulation was gradually reduced.

Because there were decided winners and losers as a result of these fiscally conservative policies, currency became a raging political issue. The most obvious winners were the holders of federal bonds. They had purchased the bonds with greenbacks depreciated by inflation during the war and were paid back in gold after the war. On top of the interest they received, they were the beneficiaries of unearned income that represented the difference between the purchasing power of dollars they loaned the government during an inflationary period and of those dollars returned to them by the government in a deflationary period. This same bonus applied to all groups who had loaned out money during the war. Debtors had to pay back their creditors in dollars worth more than the dollars they had received.

On top of these creditor-debtor divisions, a sectional split of East versus West developed over the currency question. The price of wheat, the major Western crop, fell by half from the mid-1860s to the mid-1870s and by another half in the next twenty years. Farmers who had gone into debt to purchase their land or expand production were caught in a vise, in which they had to produce more and more to pay back less and less. Many of them wanted the currency to be expanded, not contracted, and they wanted it in the flexible form that had become known as the people's money during the Civil War, greenbacks that were not necessarily secured by gold. Such a currency, they felt, would help lift prices for agricultural commodities and enable them to escape from their economic trap.

A final major division pitted labor against the bankers. Many trade unionists blamed the depressions of the postwar years on an inflexible and inadequate currency that was manipulated by bankers in order to keep interest rates, and hence their profits, artificially high. Working through the National Labor Union in the late 1860s, the trade unionists demanded an enlarged and flexible currency of greenbacks that would be interconvertible with low-interest government bonds. They argued that such a currency would break the monopoly of the bankers, release the nation's productive energy, and bring full employment to all the producing classes. Bankers and most businessmen responded that only faith in the sound money doctrines of the federal government kept the depressions from getting any worse.

The very complexity of these divisions tended to prevent the currency question from becoming a partisan issue that divided Republicans from Democrats. The political divisions over currency largely occurred within the parties, not between them, and they fell along an axis that increasingly became a sectionalized one of the East versus West. This was all the more true when Western silver interests entered the debate in the mid-1870s with a demand for a large increase in the coinage of silver. When necessary, the fiscal conservatives who dominated both parties compromised with the silver inflationists. The Bland-Allison Act of 1878 and the Sherman Silver Purchase Act of 1890 committed the Treasury to monetize some silver but not enough to reverse the downward drift in commodity prices.

These compromises defused the potential for full-scale party revolts, but dissident farm and labor groups continued to be attracted to greenback doctrines of a people's currency that would expand or contract as economic conditions warranted. These groups, along with the prohibitionists, periodically bolted the major parties for their own independent parties. Ironically, the only dissidents who had much of an impact on the politics of the Gilded Age were those who were fewest in number and most poorly equipped for party battles, the patrician reformers who attacked the patronage system. Much to the dismay of the party professionals, civil service reform joined the tariff and currency as a major national issue.

The Party Dissenters

The Republicans had major party defections in 1872 and 1884. Those in 1872 were more permanent bolters, because many of them were returning to their original political home in the Democratic party. From its birth in the mid-1850s through Grant's first administration the Republicans had drawn together former Whigs and a smaller number of Democrats in a grand coalition against the threat of the slave South to the free labor principles of equality under the law. As long as the Confederacy existed and as long as it appeared that the North would not have the opportunity after the war to enforce fairly the terms of its victory, that coalition held together. It broke up among party leaders soon after Grant's election in 1868 when it appeared that the war-related issues had been resolved. The Liberal Republican movement of 1872 was the political expression of that breakup.

Two postwar developments came together in the Liberal Republicans. The first related to an ideological and power shift within the Republican party. Republican state leaders quickly discovered after the war that reforming idealism and party strength did not mix. When divorced from the unifying causes of antislavery and the Union, such idealism exposed the Republicans to effective Democratic counterattacks, especially on the issue of the Republican call for black suffrage. Consequently, Republicans began to downplay ideological issues of public policy and concentrated instead on federal patronage and business support as props for the institutional strength of the party. In reaction to what then emerged as a business-party alliance of subsidies and mutual favors, those Republicans who had entered the party from the ranks of the antimonopoly Democrats became increasingly disillusioned. Their resentment was summarized by Johann Stallo, a Cincinnati lawyer who issued the call in 1872 for Ohio Liberals to organize against the Grant Republicans. He denounced the party for

of late being wickedly and fraudulently used by those who have assumed control of its forces . . . to lay the foundations of a permanent subjection of labor to capital, of the freedom of commerce to monopoly, of honest industry to dishonest speculation, of powerless individuals to powerful corporations, of impotent States to an omnipotent Central Government.[13]

Joining these former Democrats in defecting from the regular Republicans in 1872 was a smaller group of former Whigs, founders of the party, such as Charles Sumner of Massachusetts, who felt that the idealism of Lincoln's party had been perverted by the crass materialism of Grant's party.

In a second postwar development, many of those men, regardless of their former party ties, who had favored the Republicans as a bulwark of decency and civilized order against the onslaughts of the Slave Power, drew back in 1872 out of a fear that the party had pushed too hard and too fast in its reconstruction program for the South. There was a general sense among these bolters that Southern whites were being treated too harshly. Since they also believed that Southern blacks had been given the vote before they had proved their moral fitness for suffrage, the bolters sympathized with what they saw as a South struggling to free itself of barbarism and corruption.

A small but highly visible group of Liberal Republicans were known as the Genteel Reformers. Most were men of independent wealth from old New England stock who lived in Boston or New York. What most set them apart as a group was their extraordinarily high level of education and commitment to professionalism. At a time when fewer than 3 percent of Americans went to college, about 80 percent of the Genteel Reformers had a college education. Concentrated in the leadership positions of law, medicine, academics, and publishing, they were in the vanguard of the movement for the professionalization of American public life. Their professional expertise, they believed, offered the essential antidote to the social disharmony and political corruption that they felt was making a mockery of the republic.

These reformers were scornful of the new industrial elite, which was too crass and irresponsible for their tastes. Despite this alienation from Gilded Age businessmen, the patrician reformers blamed the ills of American society not on industrial capitalism but on the excesses of political democracy, which aggravated those ills by breeding incompetence and corruption. The root of the problem, as Godkin said of the electorate in New York City, was that too many voters were "unendowed with the self restraint and discrimination of men bred to the responsibilities of citizenship."[14] The Genteel Reformers and members of their educated class viewed themselves, of course, as just such responsible men. They wanted to play a prominent role in American politics, or at least set standards of efficiency and merit for it, and were frustrated when the professional politicians said no.

The Liberal Republican party of 1872 was more of a patchwork effort to beat Grant that was dominated by Democrats than a unified ideological movement among Republicans. Reformers were overshadowed by politicians disgruntled with having been pushed aside by the Stalwarts, those Republicans most loyal to Grant and in favor of a Radical policy in the South. Although the party called for tariff reduction, civil service reform, and sectional reconciliation in its platform, its presidential nominee, Horace Greeley, was best known for his stands on protectionism and antislaveryism. Greeley had been the ardently Republican editor of the *New York Tribune* in the 1850s and 1860s. His recent break with the Grant administration for its alleged subversion of self-government in the South made him potentially attractive to a Democratic party anxious to establish a new image as a party willing to accept the results of the war and to work for sectional peace. The Democrats did officially support Greeley, but it made little difference. Unpopular with Southern Democrats because of his antislavery background and with Northern Republicans because he was a party renegade, he suffered the worst defeat of any major presidential candidate between 1828 and 1904. He carried only six Southern and border states.

As a political movement, Liberal Republicanism did not survive the rout of 1872. As a somewhat petulant pressure group, the Genteel Reformers persisted. In 1884 they broke party ranks a second time and backed Cleveland, the Democrat, for the presidency. With more than their usual air of self-righteousness, they were deeply offended by their party's nomination of James G. Blaine, the most popular Republican of his day but one whose name was publicly linked to a railroad scandal. The patricians interpreted his nomination, in Godkin's words, as "the final sign that the corrupt element in the party had gotten control of the organization [and] had to be resisted just as you would resist a bunch of thieves."[15]

The patricians doubted the honesty of the party regulars, who in turn doubted the manliness of the patricians. The rigid cultural polarities of the Gilded Age defined politics as an exclusively masculine sphere of virility and aggressiveness in which real men, like real soldiers, remained loyal to their party organizations. Once party competition had become deadlocked by the mid-1870s, any party defector was savagely attacked for his disloyalty. About the mildest label attached to the patrician dissenters was Mugwump, a pompous term of derision supposedly derived from an old Indian word for captain. More to the point were characterizations of the bolters as the "third sex" in politics, "political hermaphrodites," "carpet-knights," and those whose meaning of love was akin to "the eunuch's admiration for the ram." Needless to say, Blaine was now championed by the Republican regulars as that "thoroughbred stallion."[16]

After the pundits had had their day, Blaine lost to Cleveland in an election that was so close that any number of groups could claim credit for tipping the balance to the Democrats. The Mugwumps were certain that they deserved the credit, but their claim was beside the point. They had already won a far more significant victory by playing a key role in the passage of the first major legislation that led to civil service reform, the Pendleton Act of 1883.

By zeroing in on patronage, the Mugwumps exposed the Achilles' heel of the party system. At stake were not only jobs and campaign funds but also the main mechanism by which party leaders exercised some control over local factions and established the basis for a national coalition. For all its abuses, and they were legion, especially if your party was out of power, patronage did personally link party officials to the mass electorate. In New York City, for example, about one-eighth of the voters held some kind of political office in the 1870s. These party jobs were basic to building the decentralized ethnic alliances at the heart of urban politics. The patronage system fostered localism, provided jobs for immigrants, and catered to their sensibilities in a very direct, personalized way. It represented everything that the Mugwumps most decried in American politics. From their perspective, it intensified partisanship at the expense of a disinterested concern for the public good; it bred incompetence and parochialism by shunning expertise and centralized authority; and it made a mockery of honest government by giving political jobs to the ignorant rabble of the ethnic hordes rather than to men of talent and education, such as themselves.

The Mugwumps had two indispensable allies in their attacks on the spoils system, urban merchants and the Presidents. The former complained that their businesses were hampered by the inefficiency of party hacks in the customhouses and post offices. The Presidents resented constant patronage battles with the Senate, and all of them would have seconded what Garfield confided in his diary: "In some way the civil service must be regulated by law, or the president can never devote his time to administration."[17] Further adding to the pressure for change was the steady, and seemingly irreversible, increase in the number of federal employees. From 51,000 in 1871, it grew to 100,000 in 1881, and 240,000 in 1901. Even the party professionals found it hard to rebut the central point that Carl Schurz, one of the more persistent reformers, repeatedly made. It is "self-evident," said Schurz,

> that as the functions of government grow in extent, importance and complexity, the necessity grows of their being administered not only with honesty, but also with trained ability and knowledge.[18]

The assassination of President Garfield in 1881 by a disappointed office-seeker sparked public interest in the issue of patronage reform. Republicans and Democrats, anxious not to have the reformers upset the even political balance by throwing their full weight behind one party or the other, agreed to reform in 1883. The Pendleton Act set up a classified list of certain federal jobs and applied the principle of tenure with merit to them. Future applicants for a classified job had to pass a competence examination administered by a Civil Service Commission. Presidents were given broad discretionary powers to add to the classified list as they saw fit. Although not foreseen at the time, this provision practically guaranteed a rapid expansion of jobs immune from the spoils system. Control of the presidency switched back and forth every four years for the next twelve, and each outgoing President protected his appointees by placing their positions on the classified list. The classified list grew from 14,000 in 1884, or 10 percent of the civilian employees of the federal government, to 86,000, or half of the employees, by the time McKinley became president in 1896.

The Genteel Reformers, for all the epithets of silly and effeminate sentimentality hurled against them, had the last laugh. They proved to be the hard-nosed realists. They had successfully pushed for the one reform that permitted the modern bureaucratic state to emerge. Without the merit system and tenure in office for federal employees, and the consequent weakening of party government, the edifice of the administrative state of the twentieth century could never have been erected. It would have lacked the expertise that was the basis of its claim to responsibility for administering the lives and businesses of the citizenry.

The civil service reformers sought a secular millennium of efficiency. The Prohibitionists, another band of party dissenters spun off primarily from Republican ranks, sought a religious millennium of salvation. The banning of alcohol, not the enshrinement of experts, was to be their path to the promised land of social harmony. Whereas the Genteel Reformers, chastened by the debacle of 1872, avoided third-party action, the Prohibitionists seemed to glorify in it. Starting in 1872, they ran a presidential candidate in every national election, and by the late 1880s could count on a regular vote of close to 250,000, or 2 percent of the electorate.

The small national vote of the Prohibitionists is a misleading indicator of the appeal and political impact of the movement they championed. In the pietistic farm communities and small towns of the Midwest, prohibition was often *the* issue in local politics. A majority of Republicans throughout the North agreed with the goals of the Prohibitionists but refused to weaken Lincoln's party of the Union by casting their ballot for a single-issue candidate. In the South prohibition gained a wide following among a white middle class anxious to keep alcohol out of the hands of blacks in the fields and whites in the mills. A battery of local option devices and regulatory legislation, including a legal stipulation in all the states by 1902 that lessons in the evils of alcohol be included as a regular part of the public school curriculum, attested to the pervasive appeal of the drys.

The Prohibition party was a stilted label for what its followers experienced as a crusade to usher in the Kingdom of Christ. The head of the Women's Christian Temperance Union, Francis Willard, asked that the party be judged by only one standard: "What is the relation of this party, this platform, this candidate to the setting up of Christ's kingdom on the earth?"[19] Those who answered Willard's call were, with the exception of the Swedes, overwhelmingly old stock, middle-class pietists from the towns and farm villages of the rural heartland. Many of them had identified the millennium with Union victory in the war and the death of slavery, and the war itself was explained as a divinely authored drama of judgment and redemption. Yet, something had clearly gone wrong. The South refused to be remade in the Yankee image of piety, and the North was treated to the sordid spectacle of wholesale corruption that peaked in the second Grant administration. And, looming like a dark shadow that threatened to blot out the light of Christian purity, was the city.

"Think of cities and large towns under the control of the organizations whose sole business is to make criminals and paupers,"[20] warned one dry crusader from Iowa. Those organizations were pictured as an amalgam of the collusionary interests of immigrants, city politicians, and liquor dealers. Nothing was too vile to be attributed to them. The only defense was an attack on the source of the city's evils—the flow of alcohol that released individuals from the self-restraints of a Christian conscience. The Prohibitionists could not recreate in the city the cloistered atmosphere of small-town gossip that, when reinforced by the manipulation of economic rewards and punishments, policed the drinkers in their local communities. But they were confident that they could force a moral homogenization on the city by which abstinence from drink would be the test of both Americanism and Christianity. The Slave Power was dead. It was now time to destroy Demon Run, the next great conspiracy that Satan had devised to delay the coming of the Christian commonwealth.

Prohibition was part of the broader social-purity crusade of the Gilded Age. Usually dated from the 1872 founding of the New York Society for the Suppression of Vice, this crusade was a more generalized expression of the same Protestant and middle-class concern with regulating behavior that motivated the Prohibitionists. Its enemies were the same—immigrants, city bosses, Catholics, and that generalized lower class whose baser instincts were unleashed by the impersonality of the factory and urban crowd. Unable to accept the very existence of a pluralistic society in which different cultural groups compromised between themselves in a mutual ethic of give-and-take, these crusaders, like the Prohibitionists, tried to convert their own religious values into standards of social behavior binding on all.

The best-known example of purity legislation was the Comstock Act of 1873, which banned obscene literature, including information on birth control, from the U.S. mails. What was obscene, the federal and state courts agreed, was whatever the local community felt threatened public morals. The regulation of sex extended to the formation of White Cross societies, which were designed to help young men resist their sexual urges. In a number of other areas—prostitution, gambling, public entertainments, Sunday activities, and the use of tobacco and drugs—a host of local and state statutes were aimed at cleansing society by saving its sinners from themselves. Undeterred by the constant refrain of their critics that it was self-contradictory to claim to be seeking a society of morally autonomous individuals by passing legislation that forced those individuals to act in a certain way, the purity crusaders pushed for ever-more-coercive legislation. More so than the Prohibitionists, these crusaders worked through, not outside, the Republican party. As the self-proclaimed party of decency and respectability, the Republicans absorbed and channeled the purity impulse.

The third major group of party dissenters—farm and labor coalitions—chipped away at both the Democratic and Republican vote. Still, the extent of the threat can easily be exaggerated. What is most striking about these dissidents is their record of failure. As opposed to the Genteel Reformers, who could point to the Pendleton Act, or the Prohibitionists, who dried out most of the South and Midwest, the farm-labor bolters were most noted for a confusing assortment of third-party names and a string of national candidates even more obscure than typical Gilded Age politicos.

The party labels of these dissidents constantly changed. There were the National Labor Reformers of 1872, the Independent Nationalists of 1876, the Greenback Laborers of 1878, the Antimonopolists and Union Laborers of the 1880s, and a slew of combinations on the local level that used the word *socialist* in their party titles. This very flux indicated the lack of a unifying basis on which farmers and workers could define just what they wanted out of dissident political action. What made the continuing effort to find such a basis all the more frustrating was the belief of the reformers that an agrarian-labor alliance was a natural one. Join hands, said a labor reformer to the Workingmen's Party of Chicago in 1874,

with the farmers, the laborers of the country, your natural allies, in one common, united effort to free this country from the shackles of monopoly. . . . Aid them in their brave warfare with your common enemy, hydraheaded monopoly.[21]

In actuality this alliance, as shown by the failure of the Greenback movement in the late 1870s, was anything but natural. A minority of Southern and Western farmers were attracted to Greenbackism in the hope that a government-managed system of banking and currency would inflate agricultural prices. At the same time, a minority of industrial workers, primarily those who were seeking to escape the dependency of factory labor by setting up cooperative ventures for producing and distributing goods, valued Greenbackism more for its potential to bring down the cost of credit by destroying the usurious power of private bankers. These two goals were not necessarily incompatible, but tensions between them were inherent. Inflationary benefits for wheat and cotton farmers meant that workers would pay higher prices for food and clothing. Moreover, until a devastating agricultural depression hit in the late 1880s, most farmers viewed themselves as producer-entrepreneurs, not as workers. The high cost of credit did not concern them so much as did the low price of their agricultural production. Unlike many workers, they had no basic quarrel with an industrial system in which labor was treated as just another factor of production.

For a brief period that lasted about as long as the economic pain from the depression of the 1870s was still acute, the Greenbackers were able to reconcile their farmer-labor tensions and enjoy some limited victories. Fourteen Greenbackers were elected to Congress in 1878, and the party's presidential candidate in 1880, James B. Weaver of Iowa, polled 309,000 votes, or 3½ percent of the national total. But even this success was shallow and short-lived. All the Greenback congressmen elected in 1878 had run on fusion tickets that were subsidized by whichever of the major parties felt it had the most to gain by using a Greenbacker to defeat the candidate of the other party. The return of better times in the early 1880s, an upturn in the supply of currency, and higher agricultural prices deflated the appeal of Greenback doctrines. No longer forced together by hard times, the labor and agrarian wings of the party went their separate ways. The Antimonopoly party picked up the vote of Greenback workers and the Union Labor party that of farmers in the South and West. Neither of these parties attracted much more than 1 percent of the national vote.

The farm-labor dissidents were hopelessly divided from within and exploited from without. Splintered into warring sects of ideological combatants and manipulated by both Republicans and Democrats, they were further vulnerable to the charges in the South of upsetting racial harmony and in the North of disturbing class harmony. It would be easy enough to dismiss them as losers were it not for the fact that they introduced a long list of issues that became political orthodoxy in the next generation. Their party platforms called for a graduated income tax, protective legislation for labor, government regulation of railroad rates, suffrage for women, and most notably, a flexible money supply managed by the government. Perhaps these dissidents were ahead of their times and other Americans were behind. It is more likely, however, that as time passed, more and more Americans joined them in feeling a need for some governmental controls over unregulated industrial capitalism.

Workers and Politics

Of all the defeats incurred by the critics of the value structure and power relations of the ruling economic order in Gilded Age America, none is so puzzling in retrospect as the failure of labor to mount an effective political response to the rise of the factory and the corporation The spread of industrial capitalism constituted a social and economic revolution in which labor was the major loser. And no one had to inform Gilded Age workers of that basic fact. The opening to the preamble of the constitution of the Knights of Labor, the largest labor organization formed during the Gilded Age, read as follows:[22]

> The recent alarming developments and aggression of aggregated wealth, which, unless checked, will invariably lead to the pauperization and helpless degradation of the toiling masses, render it imperative, if we desire to enjoy the blessings of life, that a check should be placed upon its power and upon unjust accumulation, and a system adopted which will secure to the laborer the fruits of his toil.

The first stated objective of the Knights was to make "industrial and moral worth, not wealth, the true standard of individual and national greatness."[23] That objective, along with the overall vision of a cooperative commonwealth of producers, was never attained. Moreover, contrary to workers in other industrialized nations in the Western world, American labor fell short of even building a permanent political vehicle of their own to bring about the changes they desired. Why was American labor the major exception? Why did the social vision of the Knights and other working-class reformers never take hold?

Part of the answer to these questions dates back to antebellum America. The working class developed in the social and political context of industrializing eastern cities in the half-century between the War of 1812 and the Civil War. The most salient social feature that shaped its development was the separation of work and residence. This separation was characteristic of industrial labor throughout the Western world. Only when combined with the one politically unique feature of American labor—the fact that it had the suffrage from the beginning of its class formation and hence was always part of the formal political process—did this social division between production and residence set up the conditions out of which evolved a particularly American language of politics and a distinct spatial location for electoral behavior.

Compared to England and the rest of industrializing Europe, workers in America did not combine issues of work and community in a class movement against the exclusionary power of a strong nation-state. Political power in the U.S. did not radiate downward through a legalized aristocracy and an official bureaucracy but outward and upward from a multiplicity of local communities. The widespread suffrage of the late eighteenth century became nearly universal for adult white males by the Jacksonian period. At the same time, and despite sporadic efforts to do so, individual states lacked the power to prevent workers from organizing on their own behalf. The reverse was true in Europe. There, a class-conscious politics developed out of the struggle of workers against the state power that denied them, as a class, the suffrage and the right to join trade unions. Following the lines of least resistance, American workers divided their consciousness as a class at precisely the point at which the strong resistance of the state unified the class consciousness of European workers. Whereas American workers politically experienced industrialization as an invasion of their local turf by immigrants competing against them for social space in a status politics of ethnicity and cultural recognition, European workers experienced it as a class struggle for liberation against the tyranny of the state.

American artisans in the older eastern cities did organize a series of workingmen's parties in the 1820s and 1830s. Broadly reformist in nature, these parties argued that the republican ideal of the citizen worker could be realized only through an extension of the principles of equal rights. At the top of their list of reforms were free public education, the abolition of imprisonment for debt, and the ten-hour day for labor. These workers' parties were short-lived. The depression of 1837–1843 forced labor to concentrate on its economic survival, and the major parties coopted the leading issues of the labor reformers. The most fundamental reason for their failure, however, was the emergence of two institutions that more successfully met the immediate needs of labor. These institutions separately organized workers at the site of their work and at their place of residence. One was the trade union, and the other was the urban component of the mass-based political parties.

In the workplace, trade unions that had been devastated following the panic of 1837 were rebuilt in the late 1840s and 1850s. By stressing bread-and-butter issues of wages and working conditions, they secured immediate benefits and some protection to those workers whose skills still gave them some bargaining power with employers. Although they organized across ethnic lines in the same trades, they excluded common laborers and avoided political action beyond the work environment.

Meanwhile, the decentralized urban machines of the party system were politically organizing labor, not as workers but as members of a particular city neighborhood and ethnic group. Here, as was true of the trade unions, workers won immediate gains. Urban politics amounted to a contest between competing neighborhoods for access to municipal services. Ward bosses, tied into a citywide network of patronage, dispensed those services at the level of the individual neighborhoods. Political participation in party clubs and gangs was necessary if workers were to have any control over public schools and the police and to gain their share of construction contracts. Party jobs also provided a ladder of upward social mobility that was especially valuable to ethnics who had to compete in urban economies dominated by old-line Yankee families. In turn, the mobilization of the workers was essential if the politicians were to achieve their overriding goal of winning elections. It was a political system that delivered for both leaders and followers. In the process, it relegated class to the domain of the workplace.

As the politics of the working class split into the class concerns of the factory and the ethnic ones of the neighborhood, cultural allegiances were also divided from within. Expressed as a cultural phenomenon—that is, a given set of beliefs and behavioral patterns—the class consciousness of native-born workers had fragmented into three broad categories by the 1850s. In a pattern that roughly paralleled the diversity of work settings, the loyalties of the working class lined up for or against the new industrial morality.

Those in the outdoor trades and artisan shops least affected by mechanization and the division of labor clung to the spontaneous and relaxed values of a preindustrial culture. Their daily lives were not compartmentalized into work and leisure. They continued to enjoy self-governance on the job and worked and played in unabashed bouts of self-indulgence that they casually intermixed. They rejected the temperance, disciplined individualism, and devotion to work for its own sake that were the hallmarks of the new code of industrial behavior. Those who accepted this new code worked in environments being transformed by the spread of commercial and industrial capitalism. Where the transformation was most complete—as with wage laborers in a factory setting, or, conversely, small businessmen who had risen from the ranks of the artisans—individuals tended to embrace evangelicalism and its accompanying message of a spiritual unity between all classes. On the other hand, workers caught in the middle of the transformation were more likely to be free thinkers or radical evangelicals who called upon fellow workers to engage in collective action to realize the equal rights and self-improvement to which they were entitled as republican citizens.

The cultural divisions within labor were more complex than the above sketch would indicate, and they would be intensified by the mass arrival of the Catholic immigrants; but the core split was undeniable. The individualized values of thrift, frugality, and self-help associated with the new industrial morality divided labor against itself at least as much as the collective traditions of the past united it against capital.

Thus, before the massive industrialization of the Gilded Age, the salient political weaknesses of the American working class were clearly fixed. Still, these weaknesses did not eliminate the possibility that a vibrant, working-class politics might emerge. As late as the 1880s, the European working class looked to their American counterparts to take the lead in the struggle against industrial capitalism. Class tensions rose after the Civil War as sectional ones subsided. In particular, Northern labor interpreted the refusal of the Republican party to support the movement for an eight-hour day as final proof that the victorious crusade against slavery was not going to be extended against wage slavery.

The 1880s witnessed an apparent breakthrough by labor. Membership in the Knights of Labor exploded from 18,000 in 1881 to 110,000 by 1885. It may have peaked as high as 800,000 in 1886. As part of what contemporaries called the Great Upheaval of labor in the mid-1880s, labor candidates backed by the Knights won scores of local elections in towns and cities across the nation. Founded as a secret society of Philadelphia garment cutters in the late 1860s, the Knights survived the depression of the 1870s and burst into political prominence in the 1880s when they organized the first mass union in American history. Much of the appeal of the Knights rested on their ability to give a community expression to the traditional tenets of America's republican heritage. At the center of that heritage was the belief that political liberty was inseparable from economic independence. By focusing upon the emerging corporate order as a radical threat to that independence, the Knights successfully portrayed themselves as the conservative protectors of American republicanism.

The Knights offered all workers, regardless of sex, race, or skill, an alternative culture to the reigning one based on individualism and competition. They accepted industrialization but not the wage system. They wanted to replace that system with worker-owned cooperatives in which the wealth produced by labor would be distributed equitably. The basic organizational unit of the Knights, the local assembly, was much more than just a trade union or political interest group. Combining the functions of fraternal lodges, social clubs, mutual-aid societies, and religious brotherhoods, the local assemblies embodied the Knights' vision of a shared, active citizenship. For all of the Knights, the dignity of labor was at the core of that vision and, for many of the Protestant members, that dignity was upheld by their belief in a perfectionist Christianity. In the social Christianity of the Knights, God would eventually redress economic injustice. Change had to come, said a leader of the Knights, because in the sight of God and God's angels the wrongs of the toiling millions on earth are a curse and a crime, and that as God is mercy and God is love, in His own good time the toiler will be free.[24]

Aside from being the only major union that sought the participation of women (as well as blacks), the Knights also supported women's suffrage and equal rights for women as wage laborers. Such stands were often unpopular, but they were central to the Knights' insistence that all individuals had to have responsibility for their own sovereignty. The need for that responsibility was most critical in the realm of politics. The restoration and protection of the economic independence that was being lost entailed both an effort to create workers' cooperatives and an ongoing commitment to political action.

During the Great Upheaval in 1885–1886, the Knights successfully organized third parties in over 200 towns and cities. In this heady atmosphere of what appeared to be a snowballing working-class movement, labor editor John Swinton could be excused for proclaiming in 1887 that

there will soon be but two parties in the field, one composed of honest workingmen, lovers of justice and equality; the other . . . composed of kid-gloved, silk-stockinged, aristocratic capitalists and their contemptible toadies.[25]

Swinton could not have been more wrong. The only two strong parties in the field remained the Democrats and Republicans. As the political situation dictated, they either absorbed or deflected working-class concerns, but in no instance did they permit labor to have an independent policy-making role. As for the Knights, they collapsed as quickly as they had grown. Membership fell by half in 1887, and by 1890 the Knights were dead as a mass movement. What had happened to the Knights and to the political offensive, limited as it was, that they had mounted?

A determined counterattack launched by business provides some of the answers. If the aristocrats of business wore kid-gloves, those same gloves clothed a fist of iron. Strikes in the late 1880s and 1890s were repeatedly smashed by lockouts and the intervention of a national guard subsidized and promoted by business interests. Renamed the National Guard in the 1880s, the state militias were expanded and rearmed after the rail strikes of 1877.

Slashed wages and increased workloads had triggered a mass uprising by labor in all the major rail centers outside New England and the South in 1877. Violence flared when rail strikers sacked and burned company property, and only a fortuitous shift in the wind prevented Pittsburgh from going up in flames along with the rolling stock of the Pennsylvania Railroad. To aid the local police, the state militias were called out, but discipline frequently broke down and many of the men, drawn from the working class themselves, openly sympathized with the strikers. Order was restored only by bringing in the U.S. Army and federal marshals. Businessmen and a badly frightened middle class drew the appropriate lesson. As summarized by General Hancock: "This 'thing' will appear again—and at that time it will be necessary that the States should have a well organized militia of pride and power, that it be used promptly."[26]

In the last quarter of the nineteenth century, state troops were called out about 700 times to quell civil disturbances, most of which were related to disputes between capital and labor. The state militias became largely a middle-class institution that was strongest in the cities. Separated from the strikers by the distance of both class and geography, the militia soldiers were now an effective antilabor weapon when deployed in the industrial towns and rail junctions of the interior. It was no wonder that one worker, writing in the *Journal of the Knights of Labor*, accused the National Guard of being "a standing army and a menace to liberty. . . . Its promoters, supporters and patrons are the plutocrats, the corporations, syndicates and trusts."[27]

In addition to the force used against labor, a number of other factors plagued the political organization of workers as a class. While ethnic divisions within the workforce deepened during the Gilded Age, manufacturers were replacing skilled positions, held by the native-born and the earlier immigrants from the British Isles, with the semiskilled labor of the later immigrants from Southeastern Europe. Economic bitterness over lost and downgraded jobs acquired ethnic overtones and spilled over into the political disunity of labor as a whole. Meanwhile, different kinds and levels of mobility were siphoning off the potential for a pervasive sense of working-class consciousness.

The economic system was slowly but steadily delivering higher real wages to the workers. As shown in Table 10.2, the decline in the consumer price index after the Civil War converted the downward to flat trend in the annual wages of workers to a steady increase in real wages. This increase made it possible for second-generation immigrant workers to begin to achieve property mobility through the ownership of a home. Others experienced occupational mobility, either through a more skilled job or through a party job with the local urban machine. Most young workers were very mobile geographically as they moved around in search of a steady job. All these kinds of mobility made it difficult to organize workers in the factory, let alone into their own political movement.

These factors certainly played a role in the demise of the Knights, but they were not necessarily the decisive ones, because each of them had the potential to be turned to the political advantage of labor. The resorting to military force, for example, was more

Table 10.2   Wages of Nonfarm Employees and Prices, 1860–1900

Persistent deflation after the Civil War was the major factor in the slow but steady increase in the purchasing power of American workers in the late nineteenth century. For example, although annual wages dropped by 6 percent from the early 1870s to the late 1890s, real wages measured in constant dollars rose by 34 percent.

	ANNUAL WAGES	REAL WAGES	CONSUMER PRICE INDEX
1860–64	416	419	106.1
1865–69	495	347	143.2
1870–74	472	397	116.4
1875–79	393	394	99.7
1880–84	420	436	96.7
1885–89	460	503	91.3
1890–94	463	512	90.4
1895–99	446	532	83.8

Source: Compiled from *Historical Statistics*, Series D-735–738.

Note: Wages and prices are shown in five-year averages. Real wages are expressed in 1914 dollars, and the price index is set at 100 for 1914.

a sign of the weakness of capital than of its strength. The need to fall back upon it indicated that the political power of the new manufacturing class was not yet dominant in local communities. The escalation of violence against labor was more likely to radicalize workers than to subdue them, and it carried the additional risk of alienating the middle classes from the corporations. Ethnicity could cut both ways, as well. To be sure, it provided a basis for nonclass appeals to discrete blocs of working-class voters, and it exacerbated tensions over job competition, but it could also galvanize a sense of class solidarity. The United Mine Workers became a powerful force for change in the anthracite fields of eastern Pennsylvania when they learned to organize each ethnic group into a separate local. In the coal strikes of the late 1890s English, Welsh, German, Slavic, and Italian miners were all involved, and it was the newer immigrants who took the lead. Coming out of rural societies in which class lines were often deep and bitter, many of the immigrants adapted collective traditions of agrarian resistance to their industrial environment in America. Labor surveys in New Jersey and Illinois in the late 1880s, for example, revealed that a much higher proportion of foreign-born workers were organized into trade unions than native-born labor.

Upward mobility for workers was real, but in the Gilded Age it proceeded with glacial slowness. To the extent that it did occur, it heightened the frustrations of the majority that was held back by what workers denounced as the unfair advantages of capital. Although the purchasing power of labor slowly rose in the late nineteenth century, the only study that systematically compares the living standards of manual workers in the United States (Pittsburgh) and Europe (Birmingham, England) shows no significant differences. What advantages were enjoyed by American workers accrued almost entirely to the skilled minority. And those advantages were counterbalanced by fewer social services, longer, more intense hours on the job, and a greater chance of suffering a job-related injury. The bulk of American workers had every reason to organize politically against low wages and harsh working conditions.

Thus, however narrow it might have been, the Knights did confront a political environment in which an opening existed for independent party action by workers. The Knights failed to widen that opening, indeed helped to shut it, because their conception of state power was so limited by their artisan republicanism. The Knights were elected as, and viewed themselves as, fellow citizens, not class-conscious workers. As traditional republicans, they were just as likely to view the power of the state as a threat to republican independence as they were the corporation. They conceived of governmental power as an unnatural impediment to be removed from the back of labor, rather than as a positive force to be organized on behalf of labor. Consequently, aside from the vague goal of liberating the state from the monopolists and returning it to its rightful guardian, the citizens, the Knights ventured into politics without any specific political program. They expected that the citizenry, once freed from unjust laws stacked in favor of capital, would spontaneously reform society around community associations of self-governing producers.

Corporate businessmen, despite all the talk of laissez faire, had learned to use the state for their own ends through land-grant legislation, protective tariffs, unrestricted immigration, and liberal laws of incorporation. Perhaps because their immediate economic setting was more localized than that of corporate leaders who were putting together companies on a national scale, nineteenth-century labor never learned that lesson. Some expansion of public-service jobs, control of the police, and, in a few areas, municipal ownership of utilities was about the sum total of the Knights' actual political agenda. Thus, the Knights were in the anomalous position of being politicians without a political program. Largely because of that anomaly, they quickly lost what little political power they once had. They had little positive to offer that could not be promised by one of the major parties.

At the same time as the political weaknesses of the Knights were being exposed, two events in 1886 touched off the plunge in the Knights' membership. The first was a bombing at Haymarket Square in Chicago. On May 4, a day after four workers were killed in a clash with police during a strike against the McCormick Harvester Company, a bomb exploded at a labor rally held in support of the strikers and the eight-hour day. One policeman was killed by the bomb and several others subsequently died of wounds received when the police fired indiscriminately into the crowd of unarmed workers. Although the identity of the bomb-thrower was never established, eight anarchists (mostly German-Americans who called for the overthrow of the wage system, with violence if necessary) were arrested and tried on a vague conspiracy law. On the basis of what they had said, not what they did, four of them were executed in 1887. "The bomb," as John Swinton noted, "was a godsend to the enemies of the labor movement."[28] After Haymarket, the middle class equated organized labor with violence and anarchy, and a wave of labor repression crippled the organizational efforts of the Knights.

On the same day that the bomb exploded in Chicago, the Knights admitted defeat in their strike against Jay Gould's Texas-Pacific Railroad. This defeat was at least as damaging to the Knights as the antilabor uproar over the Haymarket affair. A victory over the same Gould railroads in 1885 had been the catalyst that attracted about half a million new members to the Knights. The defeat in 1886 reversed that flow into a stampede out of the Knights.

Both the victory over Gould in 1885 and the Knights' high rate of success in local strikes until 1886 were based on the Knights' ability to forge a community consensus around the issues of antimonopoly and local autonomy. These issues spoke directly to the desire of local citizens to control their own lives in their own communities. To the extent that the corporation could be portrayed as a threat to that community control, citizens of all classes would unite against it. They often did so because distant centers of power beyond the control of local communities were increasingly making decisions that directly affected the economic livelihoods of individuals in those communities. The modest, but very real, local monopolies of craftsmen and producers of all sorts were inundated by the mass-produced goods imported from outside by the railroads. Especially in smaller towns not yet rigidly segregated by residence and class, preindustrial elites, struggling businessmen, and the clergy often supported workers in their strikes against an outside economic power. Most of the community believed, as the speakers at a strike rally in Sedalia, Missouri, expressed it in 1886, "that unless they stood up for their rights as free men of a free land . . . they would never be able to secure justice from monopolies. . . ."[29]

By 1886 community support was on the verge of shifting away from the Knights. Even before the Haymarket hysteria erupted, the Knights found themselves cast in the second strike against Gould as the outside conspirators who threatened local independence. The huge and sudden growth of the Knights in 1885 had necessitated some steps towards a centralized administration for the union. The flood of newcomers also demanded immediate economic benefits that only a disciplined, national organization had any chance of delivering. The Knights never built such an organization, but what limited centralization they did achieve often deprived them of community support because it called for loyalty to an organization which could not claim to speak for the local community. By the same token, outside sources of centralized authority threatened that equality of fraternal decision making that initially had drawn workers to the Knights. Torn between conflicting demands that resulted from their trying to be too many things to too many workers, the Knights quickly fell apart as a coherent labor movement.

The failure of the Knights, both at the voting booth and the workplace, confirmed that the separation of work and residence that characterized the political participation of workers by the mid-nineteenth century would extend into the twentieth century as well. Even when the Knights were at their peak, most workers voted for the consensus politics of the two major parties. As the Knights collapsed, the skilled minority of labor—the male craftsmen of old immigrant stock—turned to the "pure and simple" trade unionism of the American Federation of Labor under the leadership of Samuel Gompers. Unlike the Knights, the A.F.L. avoided direct political action and any demands for a "radical change in the existing industrial system."[30] Instead, Gompers urged workers to accept their place in that system and push for a greater share of its material rewards through bargaining and a disciplined use of the strike. Skilled labor did make real gains under Gompers. Still, until the mass organizing drives of the late 1930s, around 90 percent of all industrial workers remained outside of the unions. They, along with the social reformist stance of the Knights, had been abandoned by the A.F.L.

The Genteel Reformers, Prohibitionists, farmer-labor third parties, and the Knights had all failed to break the Gilded Age stalemate of what has been called the politics of dead center. Until the Populists burst upon the scene in the early 1890s, the extraparty dissidents never totaled much more than 3 percent of the vote in a presidential election. The vast majority of voters remained evenly divided between the two major parties, the leaders of whom had learned that organizational strength and traditional appeals to ingrained party loyalties were the keys to political victory and access to federal patronage.

SUGGESTED READING

There are several excellent introductions to Gilded Age politics. H. Wayne Morgan, *From Hayes to McKinley: National Party Politics, 1877–1896* (1971), provides the fullest political narrative, and Morton Keller, *Affairs of State: Public Life in Nineteenth Century America* (1977), is most successful at integrating public issues into a political framework. Colorful and highly readable, but not always reliable, is Matthew Josephson, *The Politicos, 1865–1896* (1938). Robert Kelley, *The Transatlantic Persuasion: The Liberal-Democratic Mind in the Age of Gladstone* (1969), focuses on the common intellectual and cultural roots of political liberalism in the United States and England. For an innovative institutional study, see David Rothman, *Politics and Power: The United States Senate, 1869–1901* (1966).

John A. Garraty, *The New Commonwealth, 1877–1890* (1968), has a fine discussion of the Gilded Age presidents and the conditions that limited their effective power. For a similar analysis, as well as the best description of the organizational workings of the party system, see Robert D. Marcus, *Grand Old Party: Political Structure in the Gilded Age, 1880–1896* (1971). Leonard D. White, *The Republican Era, 1869–1901* (1958), is the best source for understanding the centrality of patronage to party politics, and Mary R. Dearing, *Veterans in Politics* (1952), has useful material on the political role of the Grand Army of the Republic. Charles Reagan Wilson, *Baptized in Blood: The Religion of the Lost Cause, 1865–1920* (1980), shows how memories of the Civil War permeated Southern white culture. For outstanding regional studies of political developments, see C. Vann Woodward, *The Origins of the New South, 1877–1913* (1951); Horace S. Merrill, *Bourbon Democracy in the Midwest, 1865–1896* (1967); and Ballard C. Campbell, *Representative Democracy: Public Policy and Midwestern Legislatures in the Late Nineteenth Century* (1980). John C. Teaford, *The Unheralded Triumph: City Government in America, 1870–1900,* (1984), effectively rebuts the traditional view that American cities were badly misgoverned in the Gilded Age, and C. K. Yearley, *The Money Machines: The Breakdown and Reform of Governmental and Party Finance in the North, 1860–1920* (1970), looks at the neglected issue of taxation and how it affected party politics at the state and municipal level.

Voting behavior in the Gilded Age and the ethnocultural values that divided the parties have been most carefully studied in Melvyn Hammarberg, *The Indiana Voter: The Historical Dynamics of Party Allegiance During the 1870s* (1977), and two works by Paul Kleppner, *The Cross of Culture: A Social Analysis of Midwestern Politics, 1850–1900* (1970), and *The Third Electoral System, 1853–1892* (1979). For a critique of the emphasis on religious and ethnic determinants of partisanship, see Allan J. Lichtman, "Political Realignment and 'Ethnocultural' Voting in Late Nineteenth Century America," JSOH 16 (1983). Party attitudes toward black Americans are covered in Stanley P. Hirshon, *Farewell to the Bloody Shirt: Northern Republicans and the Southern Negro, 1877–1893* (1962); Vincent P. DeSantis, *Republicans Face the Southern Question: The New Departure Years, 1877–1897* (1959); and Lawrence Grossman, *The Democratic Party and the Negro: Northern and National Politics, 1868–1892* (1976). Two excellent sources for the political role of blacks in the respective sections are David Gerber, "A Politics of Limited Options: Northern Black Politics and the Problem of Change and Continuity in Race Relations Historiography," JSOH 14 (1980), and Eric Anderson, *Race and Politics in North Carolina, 1872–1901* (1981). James L. Huston, "A Political Response to Industrialism: The Republican Embrace of Protectionist Labor Doctrines," JAH 70 (1983), clearly sets forth the Republican position on the tariff and the Democratic rejoinder. The tariff issue in the Gilded Age is detailed in Tom E. Terrell, *The Tariff, Politics, and American Foreign Policy, 1884–1901* (1973). For the magnitude and consequences of the Civil War debt in the nation's money markets, see Jeffrey G. Williamson, "Watersheds and Turning Points: Conjectures on the Long-Term Impact of Civil War Financing," JEH 34 (1974). The political, class, and cultural issues raised by the refunding of this debt and the whole currency issue are explained in three major works: Robert P. Sharkey, *Money, Class, and Party* (1959); Irwin Unger, *The Greenback Era* (1964); and Walter T. K. Nugent, *The Money Question During Reconstruction* (1967). The first stirrings of the future silver crusade are traced in Allen Weinstein, *Prelude to Populism: Origins of the Silver Issue, 1867–1878* (1970). For the broad consensus in the major parties on distributing economic resources with few political restrictions, see Wallace Farnham, "The Weakened Spring of Government," AHR 68 (1963), and Richard L. McCormick, "The Party Period and Public Policy," JAH 65 (1979).

In addition to an old monograph, E. D. Ross, *The Liberal Republican Movement* (1919), the Republican bolters of 1872 can best be approached in Michael E. McGeer, "The Meaning of Liberal Republicanism: The Case of Ohio," CWH 28 (1982). For the Genteel Reformers, known as the Mugwumps after 1884, see John G. Sproat, *The Best Men: Liberal Reformers in the Gilded Age* (1968); John Tomsich, *A Genteel Endeavor: American Culture and Politics in the Gilded Age* (1971); and Gerald W. McFarland, *Mugwumps, Morals, and Politics, 1884–1920* (1975). Geoffrey Blodgett, "The Mugwump Reputation: 1870 to the Present," JAH 66

(1980), is particularly helpful on the masculine rituals and symbolism of nineteenth-century politics that the Mugwumps were accused of violating. Ari Hoogenboom, *Outlawing the Spoils: A History of the Civil Service Reform Movement, 1865–1883* (1963), is a solid account of patronage reform, which should be supplemented with the analysis in Stephen Skowronek, *Building a New American State: The Expansion of National Administrative Capacities, 1877–1920* (1982). The best discussion of the Prohibition Party and its local sources of support is in Richard J. Jensen, *The Winning of the Midwest: Social and Political Conflicts, 1888–1896* (1971). David J. Pivar, *Purity Crusade: Sexuality, Morality and Social Control, 1868–1900* (1973), and James C. Mohr, *Abortion in America* (1978), deal with the increasingly restrictive demands of the crusaders for social purity and moral homogenization. Nativist fears over the immigrant as a moral threat are examined in John Higham, *Strangers in the Land* (1955). The farm and labor dissidents have yet to be investigated in a comprehensive study. The best overall treatment is Chester McArthur Destler, *American Radicalism, 1865–1901* (1966). Helpful as well are: Howard Quint, *The Forging of American Socialism* (1953); Theodore Saloutos, *Farmer Movements in the South, 1865–1933* (1960); and Roy V. Scott, *The Agrarian Movement in Illinois, 1880–1896* (1962). For the three best-known dissenters from Gilded Age politics and business policies, see John L. Thomas, *Alternative America: Henry George, Edward Bellamy, Henry Demarest Lloyd and the Adversary Tradition* (1983).

For an introduction to the new cultural approach to labor history and the old issue of labor's role in American politics, see David Brody, "The Old Labor History and the New: In Search of an American Working Class," LH 20 (1979); Mike Davis, "Why the U.S. Working Class Is Different," NLR 123 (1980); and David Montgomery, "To Study the People: The American Working Class," LH 21 (1980). The political implications for American labor of the division between work and neighborhood are most systematically set out in Ira Katznelson, *City Trenches: Urban Politics and the Patterning of Class in the United States* (1981). Antebellum tensions between labor and management are assessed in David Grimsted, "Ante-bellum Labor: Violence, Strike, and Communal Arbitration," JSOH 19 (1985), and Sean Wilentz, *Chants Democratic: New York City and the Rise of the American Working Class, 1790–1865* (1984), has a brilliant discussion of how the tradition of artisan republicanism shaped the response of workers to the initial stages of industrialization. In addition to Wilentz, Walter Hugins, *Jacksonian Democracy and the Working Class* (1960), and Edward Pessen, *Most Uncommon Jacksonians: Radical Leaders of the Early Labor Movement* (1967), are helpful for understanding the workingmen's parties of the Jacksonian era. The success of urban political machines in organizing workers by ethnicity and neighborhood can be seen in Amy Bridges, *A City in the Republic: Antebellum New York and the Origins of Machine Politics* (1984), and, for the late nineteenth century, John M. Allswang, *Bosses, Machines, and Urban Voters* (1977). For the cultural cross-pressures and competing value systems of individualism and communalism that divided labor from within, see Alan Dawley and Paul Faler, "Working-Class Culture and Politics in the Industrial Revolution: Sources of Loyalism and Rebellion," JSOH 9 (1976).

The best general surveys of labor in the Gilded Age are Melvyn Dubofsky, *Industrialism and the American Worker, 1865–1920* (1975), and Irwin Yellowitz, *Industrialization and the American Labor Movement, 1850–1900* (1977). For the spectacular rise of the Knights of Labor and their critique of the industrial system, see Leon Fink, *Workingmen's Democracy: The Knights of Labor and American Politics* (1983). Melton A. McLaurin, *The Knights of Labor in the South* (1970), looks at the movement in the region in which it had its most limited successes. For the rail strike of 1877 and the labor upheaval that it provoked, see Robert V. Bruce, *1877: Year of Violence* (1970), Philip S. Foner, *The Great Labor Uprising of 1877* (1977), and David T. Burbank, *Reign of the Rabble: The St. Louis General Strike of 1877* (1966). The subsequent mobilization of the militia as an antilabor force is traced out in Robert Reinders, "Militia and Public Order in Nineteenth-Century America," JAS 11 (1977), and Sidney L. Harring, *Policing a Class Society: The Experience of American Cities, 1865–1915* (1983), makes a strong case for the use of urban police departments by industrialists to control the protest of workers. For an informative statistical analysis of the upsurge of strike activity in the Gilded Age, see Sari Bennett and Carville Earle, "The Geography of Strikes in the United States, 1881–1894," JIH 13 (1982). Michael A. Gordon, "The Labor Boycott in New York City, 1880–1886," LH 16 (1975), shows how the labor tactic of the boycott drew on the traditions of Irish agrarian radicalism. For the variety of local conditions that shaped worker protest in different industrial settings, see Daniel Walkowitz, *Worker City, Company Town: Iron and Cotton Worker Protest in Troy and Cohoes, New York, 1855–1884* (1978).

A good example of the argument that ethnic divisions and the resistance of immigrants to reformist politics crippled an effective labor response to industrialism is Gerald Rosenblaum, *Immigrant Workers: Their Impact on American Labor Radicalism* (1973). For evidence to the contrary, see Harold W. Aurand, *From the Molly Maguires to the United Mine Workers* (1971), and the stunning opening essay in Herbert G. Gutman, *Work, Culture, and Society in Industrializing America* (1977). Stephen Thernstrom, *Poverty and Progress: Social Mobility in a Nineteenth-Century City* (1964), is the pioneering study of mobility among the American workers. Of the many works that it spawned, Clyde and Sally Griffin, *Natives and Newcomers: The Ordering of Opportunity in Mid-Nineteenth Century Poughkeepsie* (1978), is the most imaginatively conceived; and A. Gordon Darrock, "Migrants in the Nineteenth Century: Fugitives or Families in Motion," JFH 6 (1981), is the most successful at placing high rates of geographic mobility in the context of a working-class culture. Henry David, *The History of the Haymarket Affair* (1936), and Paul Avrich, *The Haymarket Tragedy* (1984), are excellent on the bombing incident that turned so much of the middle class against the labor movement. For a superb analysis of the strike against the Gould rail system in 1886 and its disastrous consequences for the Knights in a local community, see Michael J. Cassity, "Modernization and Social Crisis: The Knights of Labor and a Midwest Community, 1885–1886," JAH 66 (1979). Leon Fink, "The Uses of Political Power: Toward a Theory of the Labor Movement in the Era of the Knights of Labor," in Michael H. Frisch and Daniel J. Walkowitz, eds., *Working-Class America* (1983), explores the issue of whether the workers' sense of republican citizenship hindered their ability to develop a positive political program for using state power on their own behalf, and David R. Roediger, " 'Not Only the Ruling Classes to Overcome, But Also the So-Called Mob': Class, Skill, and Community in the St. Louis General Strike of 1877," JSOH 19 (1985), suggests that the republicanism of the native-born, skilled workers aligned them more closely with the interests of the middle class than those of the immigrant, unskilled workers. On the philosophical and organizational differences between the Knights and the A.F.L., see Gerald N. Grob, *Workers and Utopia: A Study of Ideological Conflict in the American Labor Movement, 1865–1900* (1981).

NOTES

1. William M. Armstrong, ed., *The Gilded Age Letters of E. L. Godkin* (Albany: State University of New York Press, 1974), p. 207.
2. Cited in H. Wayne Morgan, *From Hayes to McKinley: National Party Politics, 1877–1896* (Syracuse: Syracuse University Press, 1969), p. 215.
3. The quotes are from Paul F. Boller, Jr., *Presidential Anecdotes* (Baltimore: Penguin Books, 1982), pp. 165, 183, 185.
4. Quoted in Morton Keller, *Affairs of State: Public Life in Late Nineteenth Century America* (Cambridge: Belknap Press, 1977), p. 441.
5. Quoted in Leonard D. White, *The Republican Era: A Study in Administrative History, 1867–1901* (New York: The Free Press, 1965), p. 105.
6. Ibid., p. 94.
7. Quoted in John A. Garraty, *The New Commonwealth, 1877–1890* (New York: Harper Torchbooks, 1968), p. 241.

8. Quoted in Wilson Carey McWilliams, *The Idea of Fraternity in America* (Berkeley: University of California Press, 1973), p. 377.
9. John T. Cumbler, ed., *A Moral Response to Industrialism: The Lectures of Reverend Cook in Lynn, Massachusetts* (Albany: State University of New York Press, 1982), p. 101.
10. Quoted in Morgan, op. cit., p. 117.
11. Quoted in James L. Huston, "A Political Response to Industrialism: The Republican Embrace of Protectionist Labor Doctrines," *Journal of American History* 70 (1983): 43.
12. Cleveland's annual message to Congress, 1887, cited in William Nisbet Chambers, *The Democrats in American Politics* (New York: An Anvil Original, 1972), p. 167.
13. Quoted in Michael E. McGeer, "The Meaning of Liberal Republicanism: The Case of Ohio," *Civil War History* 28 (1982): 313.
14. Armstrong, op. cit., p. 403.
15. Ibid., p. 316.
16. The quotations are cited in Geoffrey Blodgett, "The Mugwump Reputation, 1870 to the Present," *Journal of American History* 66 (1980): 883, 884.
17. Quoted in Morgan, op. cit., p. 162.
18. Quoted in Stephen Skowronek, *Building a New American State: The Expansion of National Administrative Capacities, 1877–1920* (New York: Cambridge University Press), p. 49.
19. Quoted in Richard J. Jensen, *The Winning of the Midwest: Social and Political Conflict, 1888–1896* (Chicago: University of Chicago Press, 1971), p. 191.
20. Ibid., p. 183.
21. Quoted in Chester McArthur Destler, *American Radicalism, 1865–1901* (Chicago: Quadrangle Paperback, 1966), pp. 27–28.
22. Paul F. Boller, Jr. and Ronald Story, eds., *A More Perfect Union: Documents in U.S. History,* Vol. II (Boston: Houghton Mifflin, 1984), p. 73.
23. Ibid., p. 73.
24. Charles Litchman, quoted in Herbert G. Gutman, *Work, Culture, and Society in Industrializing America: Essays in American Working-Class and Social History* (New York: Vintage Books, 1977), p. 111.
25. Quoted in Leon Fink, "The Uses of Political Power: Toward a Theory of the Labor Movement in the Era of the Knights of Labor," in Michael H. Frisch and Daniel J. Walkowitz, eds., *Working-Class America: Essays on Labor, Community, and American Society* (Urbana, Ill.: University of Illinois Press, 1983), p. 114.
26. Quoted in Robert Reinders, "Militia and Public Order in Nineteenth-Century America," *American Studies* 11 (1977): 94.
27. Ibid., p. 99.
28. Quoted in Alan Trachtenberg, *The Incorporation of America: Culture and Society in the Gilded Age* (New York: Hill and Wang, 1982), p. 90.
29. Quoted in Michael J. Cassity, "Modernization and Social Crisis: The Knights of Labor and a Midwest Community, 1885–1886," *Journal of American History* 66 (1977): 47.
30. The quote is part of a resolution by 1884 General Assembly of the Knights, cited in Melvyn Dubofsky, *Industrialism and the American Worker, 1865–1920* (New York: Thomas Y. Crowell, 1975), p. 55.

11

Renewed Crisis and Its Resolution

Frozen in place since the mid-1870s, the political equilibrium of partisan loyalties between Republicans and Democrats held as long as the Civil War was still the central, life-defining event for a majority of the electorate. By the late 1880s, however, the passage of time was starting to erode the equilibrium that the party dissidents had barely disturbed. The generation that had fought the war was beginning to die off, and the veterans, now in their fifties, were being replaced by a newer, younger, and more urbanized electorate who had experienced the war only through the stories of their parents and neighbors. Meanwhile, a bloc of six Western states—North Dakota, South Dakota, Montana, and Washington in 1888 and Idaho and Wyoming in 1890—entered the Union more concerned with fighting for a higher price for wheat or silver than with refighting the Civil War.

This was the backdrop for the breakdown of the Gilded Age party system in the 1890s. Although the first signs of change appeared in the late 1880s, the critical phase of the new alignment occurred between 1893 and 1896 in the midst of a national depression. This realignment was part of a larger process by which the social and economic transformation of the 1870s and 1880s caught up with America's political culture in the 1890s. Agrarian protest, industrial depression, and a crisis of confidence in the nation's future combined in the 1890s to produce sharply polarized tensions rivaled earlier only by the sectional antagonisms of the 1850s. The result was a decade in which for the last time the fundamental meaning of America was open to a public debate fueled by a mass political movement from below.

That movement took the name of Populism. It forced out into open debate the fundamental question of whether the corporate revolution of the Gilded Age could be brought under democratic control and made compatible with traditional republican definitions of freedom and independence. One of the Populists, Henry Demarest Lloyd, phrased the issue this way at a Chicago rally in 1894: "Government exists only by the consent of the governed. Business, property, capital, are also governments and must also rest on the consent of the governed."[1]

Middle-class, metropolitan Americans decisively turned back the Populist revolt, and the ultimate winners in the political turmoil of the 1890s turned out to be the leaders of one of the established parties, the Republicans. The defeat of the Populists and the victory of the Republicans at the expense of both the Populists and the

395

Democrats will provide the organizing themes in this final chapter on American politics between 1885 and 1896. The story begins in the mid-1880s with the first Cleveland administration, at a time when the Gilded Age party system still appeared unshakable.

Cleveland, Harrison, and Cleveland Again

Until well into Cleveland's first term (1885–1889), national politics fit the normal Gilded Age pattern of appeals to Civil War loyalties. As the first Democrat to occupy the White House since the war, the leader of a party whose power base was in the states that had formed the Confederacy, and a noncombatant during the war, Cleveland was a ready-made target for partisan attacks from the Republican veterans in the GAR. He made himself more of a target by vetoing the Dependent Pension Bill of 1887 and a whole series of private pension bills for Union soldiers. As a result of the lobbying efforts of the GAR, one-fourth of the federal budget by the mid-1880s was devoted to pensions for Union veterans, and Cleveland was convinced that any more benefits would be just a fraudulent waste of the taxpayers' money. Out of political naiveté, he then further rekindled the passions of the war by endorsing the suggestion of the Adjutant General that Confederate battle flags captured during the war be returned to the South as a sign of national reconciliation. No other issue received as much newspaper attention in the summer of 1887 as the battle over the flags. Assailed by the GAR for ignoring the heroism and sacrifices that the captured flags symbolized, Cleveland quietly backed down. The Civil War was, and always would be, a winning issue for the Republicans in national politics.

Hoping to find an equivalent winning issue for his party and a popular cause that could secure his reelection, Cleveland dramatically shifted the grounds of political debate in his annual message to Congress in December 1887. With language that echoed with the fervor of Jackson's denunciation of the Money Power in the Bank Veto of 1832, Cleveland blasted the tariff protectionists for lusting after "immense profits instead of moderately profitable returns" and darkly hinted that they had "an organized combination all along the line to maintain their advantage. . . ."[2] By his figures, fewer than one in six American workers were employed in protected industries. Only the monopolists profited from the high tariffs, he charged, but a majority of all consumers would benefit from significant downward revisions.

Quite uncharacteristically for a Gilded Age President, Cleveland had focused national attention on a contemporary economic issue. Yet the result was not tariff reform but a presidential election in 1888 that was very characteristic of the politics of the Gilded Age. Cleveland lacked the political skill, and his Democratic party the votes, to make any headway against the entrenched special interests that talk of tariff reform always immediately mobilized. Although the Harrison-Cleveland election had a more specific focus in the tariff than earlier Gilded Age elections, it typically was so evenly balanced that the result turned on superior party organization and last-minute shifts by a relative handful of voters. Cleveland won more popular votes than Harrison, but his Republican opponent, by a margin of 233 to 168, won the vote that really counted—the one in the electoral college.

The Republicans now used the tariff as a springboard to make the first session of the 51st Congress in 1890 the most productive of any in the Gilded Age. They did so in part because they were finally in a position to act. For the first time since 1875, they controlled the presidency and both houses of Congress. Just as importantly, they felt compelled to act. The elections of 1889 went poorly for the party. Throughout the 1880s, the Democrats had made steady gains in the normally safe Republican regions of New England and the upper Midwest. When the Republicans lost the governorships of Ohio and, for the first time ever, Iowa, in 1889, the Democratic momentum in the North was seemingly on the verge of producing a Republican rout. Immigrants with no Civil War loyalties and a new generation of post–Civil War voters were tipping the balance of electoral power toward the Democratic party. Anxious to reverse their losses, the Republicans turned to their strong suit as the champions of positive governmental assistance in the promotion of economic prosperity.

Picking up the gauntlet thrown down by Cleveland in 1887, the Republicans led off with the tariff. The McKinley Tariff of 1890 raised the average duties on manufactured items to a level just under 50 percent. Along with this higher tariff came three other significant pieces of legislation in 1890. The Disability Pension Act doubled the number of Union pensioners and raised outlays on payments from $89 million to $175 million within three years. The Sherman Antitrust Act (largely unenforced until the administration of Theodore Roosevelt) relied on common-law precedent to declare illegal "Every contract, combination in the form of trust or otherwise, or conspiracy, in restraint of trade or commerce among the several States, or with foreign nations."[3] And the Sherman Silver Purchase Act, also named after the Republican senator from Ohio, mandated the Treasury to purchase 4½ million ounces of silver per month. Payment was to be made by issuing new paper money that would be redeemable in either gold or silver.

The key to this legislative package was the McKinley Tariff. Upward revisions of the tariff collided with the political problem of the treasury surplus. For a long continuous stretch from 1866 to 1893, the Treasury took in more each year than it spent. The annual surplus was over $100 million in the 1880s, and agrarian critics accused the federal government of locking up money that an expanding economy needed to stop the deflationary price spiral. Much of the surplus was used to reduce the huge bonded debt incurred during the Civil War. But in paring back the debt from $2.8 billion in 1866 to $1 billion by 1891, the Treasury bid up the price of federal bonds in the open market. High tariffs, by apparently adding to the federal surplus, were thus vulnerable to the political charge that they further enriched those who were already rich—industrialists and bondholders. Consequently, the McKinley Tariff had to be accompanied by lavish pork-barrel legislation to soak up the surplus. The disability Pension Act fitted the need perfectly. Further reductions were achieved by stepping up spending on public improvements and by putting sugar, a popular item in the consumers' budget, on the free list in the tariff schedules. American sugar producers were compensated through the direct payment of federal subsidies.

Because the McKinley Tariff obviously favored the manufacturers of the Northeast and Midwest, Western farming interests, whose votes were necessary for its passage, could be induced to support the tariff only through the concessions made in the Sherman Silver Purchase Act. By nudging the federal government toward the monetarization of silver, the act held out the hope of inflation to Western farmers desperate for relief from falling prices for their crops. Finally, the Sherman Antitrust Act, with its sweeping, though vague, indictment of monopolistic businesses, catered to a mounting public demand for protection from market changes that deprived individuals of economic independence. It also neatly offset, at least temporarily, the pro-business charges that the Democrats hurled at the Republicans.

All in all, it was a program of which the Republicans thought they could be proud. They had actually lived up to their campaign pledges of 1888. The tariff was higher, taxes were lower, the surplus was on the way down, farmers received some relief, and businessmen were about to be enjoined to honor fair competition. Yet, as soon as the election returns of 1890 were in, it was clear that the Republicans had blundered. In the congressional elections of that year, the Republicans suffered the worst defeat of any party since the Democrats were swamped in the wake of the unpopular Kansas-Nebraska Act of 1854.

For all its artful balance, the Republican program came across to the voters as a clumsy free-for-all in which private groups ransacked the public treasury in proportion to their financial stake in the Republican party. The Democrats successfully depicted the Republicans as the party of fiscal extravagance responsible for the "Billion-Dollar Congress." Nonetheless, Democratic gains in 1890 owed even more to the voter reaction against the cultural offensive that the Republicans had launched in the late 1880s. At the national level, the Republicans had responded to the waning of Civil War loyalties with a lavish dispersal of the public monies that had accumulated as a surplus in the revolutionized economy of the Gilded Age. At the local and state levels, the Republicans responded not with cash but with righteousness. The war was fading as a mobilizing device for party allegiances, but the Republicans fell back on their war vision of a transformed Protestant republic as they struggled to contain the social consequences of economic change after the war.

Shaken by the labor upheavals of the mid-1880s, local Republicans stepped up their efforts to regulate the behavior of the ethnic minorities. Particularly in the Midwest, the Republicans committed themselves to prohibition and the compulsory use of English as the official language of instruction in all schools, private as well as public. When also linked to legislation against child labor and the vesting in school boards of final authority over educational policies traditionally reserved for parents, these Republican efforts struck directly at the economic and cultural self-interests of immigrant workers. As the party professionals predicted, the Democrats were handed a winning issue in 1890. They scored especially heavily among German Lutherans in the Midwest. Campaigning as the party of fiscal conservatism and individual conscience, the Democrats politically punished the Republicans for their burst of activism in economic and cultural affairs.

In 1890, and more noticeably in 1892, the Republicans were also punished for not being more active in the one area in which the electorate was demanding significant change: the farm economy. By 1890 farmers were on the verge of a political revolt. Their share of national production had declined in value from 26 percent to 21 percent during the 1880s, and their plight worsened in the 1890s. Wheat and cotton fell nearly 50 percent in price between 1888 and 1894. This market collapse, on top of drought conditions in the Plains states after 1887 and a heavy burden of debt for farm mortgages in the Middle Border and for store credit in the South, was the catalyst for the formation of a new agrarian party, the Populists. After sending eight representatives and two senators to the 52nd Congress elected in 1890, the Populists built a national organization for the presidential election of 1892. For a new third party, their showing was impressive. They polled over one million votes, about 8 percent of the total, and by carrying the normally Republican states of Kansas, Colorado, Nevada, and Idaho, became the first third party in the Gilded Age to break into the electoral college.

Although the appeal of Populism was strongest among poor farmers in the cotton South, most Southern whites were initially loath to disturb the politics of white supremacy by abandoning the Democrats for a new party. Until 1892, Southern recruits to the Populist party came predominately from a white minority of Republican hill farmers. In the Middle Border and Rocky Mountain states, areas normally in the Republican fold, the Populists did not have to combat the politics of race, and they had greater success in organizing independently from the two major parties. Thus, it was the Republicans, not the Democrats, who were politically hurt the most by the Populists in 1892.

Cleveland, despite winning only 46 percent of the national vote, won the presidency in 1892 by the largest popular margin since Grant overwhelmed Greeley in 1872. The Democrats carried all the swing states in the North and retained the solid South. Aside from the formerly Republican states they won outright, the Populists also deprived the Republicans of Illinois, Wisconsin, and California. The surprising strength of the Populists had an ironic result. Thanks to the Populists, the Democrats had won by such a wide margin that they were lulled into ignoring the agrarian insurgents in the South and West. In turn, this refusal to deal with the agrarian unrest was reinforced by the fiscal conservatism of the Eastern bankers, financiers, and importers who comprised Cleveland's closest confidants and circle of social friends. Nor did the Democratic city bosses in the North, whose perspective on politics had no wider focus than the distribution of party spoils to their ward followers, see any need to take up the cause of the farmers.

Despite their dismay over their party's showing, shrewd Republican observers saw room for optimism. They sensed that the Democrats were in for a fall. With a combination of class snobbery and political acumen that befitted his role as a constructive conservative, Orville Platt, a Republican senator from Connecticut, offered the most perceptive post-mortem on the election:[4]

> Socialists, anarchists, communists, hoodlums, as well as farmers, laborers, and people of small means, and the discontented everywhere, expect now that all their ideas whether reasonable or wild, are to be carried out in practical legislation by the Democratic party.

Because he granted that the source of much of this discontent "has foundation in the conduct of the capitalistic classes," Platt saw no way that the Democrats could accommodate what he felt were the unreasonable hopes of those who had voted them into power. After all, the "Democratic party has as much wealth and as much aggressive capitalistic influence in it as the Republican party." Platt anticipated a political crisis which would pit the "aristocracy" of the Democrats against its "proletariat."

The Democrats and Depression

The crisis exploded a few months after Cleveland assumed the presidency for the second time. In May 1893, the stock market crashed. The failure of the Philadelphia and Reading Railroad a few days before Harrison left office began a run on bank reserves that reached the point of financial panic when the National Cordage Company went under in May. Despite calling in their loans and thus drying up credit,

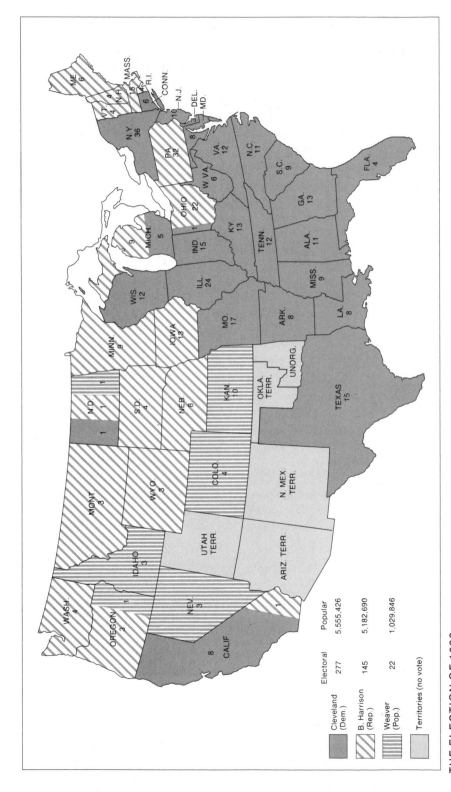

THE ELECTION OF 1892

The combination of the solidly Democratic South and key swing states in the North, such as New York, Connecticut, and Indiana, gave the Democrats a convincing victory in the election of 1892 without any significant support west of the Mississippi. The Populists, in a portent of the party's fusion in 1896 with the Democrats on the silver issue, won their electoral majorities mostly in the silver states of the West.

	Electoral	Popular
Cleveland (Dem.)	277	5,555,426
B. Harrison (Rep.)	145	5,182,690
Weaver (Pop.)	22	1,029,846
Territories (no vote)		

ME. 6
N.H. 4
VT. 4
MASS. 15
R.I. 4
CONN. 6
N.Y. 36
N.J. 10
PA. 32
DEL. 3
MD. 8
W. VA. 6
VA. 12
N.C. 11
OHIO 22
MICH. 9
WIS. 12
IND. 15
KY. 13
TENN. 12
S.C. 9
GA. 13
ALA. 11
FLA. 4
MINN. 9
IOWA 13
ILL. 24
MO. 17
ARK. 8
MISS. 9
LA. 8
N.D. 1
S.D. 4
NEB. 8
KAN. 10
OKLA. TERR.
UNORG.
TEXAS 15
MONT. 3
WYO. 3
COLO. 4
N. MEX. TERR.
UTAH TERR.
IDAHO 3
ARIZ. TERR.
WASH. 4
OREGON 3
NEV. 3
CALIF. 8

hundreds of banks suspended specie payments. "Never before," declared the *Commercial and Financial Chronicle* in August, "has there been such a sudden and striking cessation of industrial activity."[5] The economic wreckage and social pain were extraordinary. Before the year was out, 500 banks and 16,000 businesses had failed. At the trough of the depression in 1894, nearly four million workers had lost their jobs. Unemployment shot up from 3 percent in 1892 to 18 percent by 1894. Because the average length of unemployment was three to four months, an unemployment rate of 18 percent meant that over half of the work force at any given time in the mid-1890s was looking for a job. While doing so, they had only soup kitchens and the aid of kin to fall back upon as an economic lifeline.

The economic crisis of the 1890s differed from earlier ones only in its length and severity. Unemployment, for example, which had peaked at 7 percent in the downturn of the late 1850s and at 13 percent in the depression of the 1870s, now approached 20 percent. As more and more Americans, decade after decade, left the security of self-employment and became dependent on an employer for their livelihood, each succeeding economic slump exposed more of them to the vagaries of the market.

As was true in 1819, 1837, 1857, and 1873, the depression of the 1890s was triggered by a financial panic. In repetitive business cycles of boom and bust that were common in the capitalist world's economy, the U.S. economy lurched through the nineteenth century in rhythm with the expansion or contraction of the expected rate of profit. At the beginning of a cycle, the productivity of capital was high. Demand for goods and services, a function of demographic trends and technological innovations, rose, and demand for labor grew correspondingly. This demand was met by flows of migration from the American and European countrysides into American cities. More jobs and a rising level of wages in turn reinforced an increasing demand for transportation facilities, durable goods, and construction of homes and factories. The boom was self-perpetuating until the saturation point of the profit rate in capital investments was reached. At that point, investors with capital at risk tried to bail out while they still could. When enough of them tried to do so at the same time, the result was a financial panic. In the ensuing depression, bloated inventories and speculative capital ventures were liquidated for whatever they would bring. In an industrial economy, that meant factory closings and a loss of jobs.

This was the economic stage that had been reached by the 1890s. A long, expansionary phase in the capitalist world economy that had begun in the 1820s entered a period of increasing stagnation in the 1870s and bottomed out in a world recession between 1893 and 1897. In the 1890s, the American economy collapsed under the weight of overcapacity when the decline in agricultural purchasing power widened the gap in what was already a grossly uneven distribution of national income. As of 1890, about half of all American families owned only negligible amounts of property or none at all. The total income of all these families was less than that of the wealthiest 1 percent of American families, a group who owned more property than the other 99 percent combined. There was a lack of purchasing power to hold up the economy, and in its free fall, the railroads fell the fastest, because they were overbuilt and undercapitalized. In the first year of the depression, 156 of them went bankrupt. By 1897 more than one-fourth of the nation's rail mileage was in the hands of receivers and was being recombined into new units at a handsome profit by the large banking houses of New York City.

With a dedication born of certainty, Cleveland attacked what he felt was the single greatest cause of the depression—the Sherman Silver Purchase Act of 1890 and its implicit undermining of the gold standard. There was just enough truth in Cleveland's claim to convince him, as well as Eastern conservatives, that it was the whole truth. About $400 million in foreign capital flowed out of the U.S. between 1890 and 1896, and the loss of this capital and the bank reserves that it supported pushed many shaky American businesses over the edge into bankruptcy. Foreign investors were worried about the safety of their American holdings and, when the Panic of 1893 hit, they unloaded those holdings and converted them into gold. Speculators were likewise selling dollars for gold. Finally, the price of silver on the open market had dropped to the point at which it was now profitable to present silver certificates to the Treasury to be exchanged for gold under the terms of the Sherman Act. The result of all these financial maneuverings was, of course, a huge drain on the government's gold reserves. In order to stem that drain and restore confidence in the dollar, Cleveland called Congress into special session in the summer of 1893 and won a bitter struggle to repeal the Sherman Act.

Still, gold continued to flow out. The Cleveland administration eventually stopped the loss by arranging for bond issues that were syndicated through New York bankers and that brought in $300 million in gold. The bankers made a tidy profit (the amount of which J. P. Morgan, the leading syndicator, always refused to divulge), and Cleveland saved the gold standard. It was hard to find any other winners. Contrary to Cleveland's belief, a firm commitment to a gold dollar did not lift the nation out of the depression. Weak purchasing power by farmers, combined with industrial overcapacity, sent the economy reeling again in 1895.

While the Cleveland administration was conveying the impression that it cared more for the profits of bankers than the plight of the average citizen, disputes between capital and labor were becoming increasingly raw and ugly. In 1894 the American Railway Union, led by Eugene V. Debs, took on the Pullman Company of Chicago in the most publicized strike of a year that saw 750,000 workers go out on strike. The Pullman strike was touched off by wage cuts of 25 to 40 percent, the laying off of more than half the work force after the depression began, and the one-sided paternalism of management, under which rent for workers' housing in the company town of Pullman and prices at the company store stayed up while wages plummeted.

After more than holding its own during the first ten days of the strike, the American Railway Union was smashed when the Cleveland administration intervened in the strike with federal troops. The twenty-four railroad companies operating out of Chicago had pursued a clever and successful strategy. They banded together into a General Managers Association and imported strikebreakers whom they ordered to attach mail cars to the Pullman trains. They thereby created a bogus issue—workers' interference with the delivery of the U.S. mail—and used that as a pretext to secure a federal order dispatching troops to Chicago. The strike was crushed, and Debs was sent to prison for defying a federal injunction ordering him to send his men back to work. A trade unionist and a moderate when he went to prison, he was a socialist when he was released.

Labor abandoned the Cleveland Democrats after Pullman. Many farmers were already in open political rebellion. They denounced the Cleveland administration as the head of an evil conspiracy that banned silver and labor unions, milked the people, and

The Army and Striking Workers in Pullman, 1894. This sketch shows the violence that broke out after Cleveland ordered federal troops into the Pullman strike. Convinced that Cleveland, a Democrat, had unfairly intervened on the side of capital, many American workers switched to the Republicans in the elections of 1894. (The Granger Collection)

spoke only for the trusts. In their repeal of the Silver Purchase Act and single-minded devotion to the gold standard, the Cleveland Democrats had declared war on the agrarian program for inflationary relief from depressed farm prices. The impact of their financial politics was deflationary. The nation's stock of money barely grew at all between 1890 and 1896, and the squeeze on farmers, between fixed costs and low income, grew tighter.

A battered and hopelessly divided Democratic party was an easy prey for the Republicans in the congressional elections of 1894. Virtually every significant element of the party, with the exception of the fiscal conservatives in its Eastern wing, now known as goldbugs, felt used and betrayed by the administration. Even many businessmen, otherwise sympathetic with Cleveland for his stand on gold, broke with the administration when Cleveland took up the battle once again for a lower tariff. The result, the Wilson-Gorman Tariff of 1894, was marginally lower than the McKinley Tariff, but the House version was saddled with so many rate-raising amendments in the Senate that Cleveland regretted ever bringing up the issue in the first place. In disgust, he permitted the tariff bill to become law without his signature.

The voters registered a much more pervasive disgust over the whole thrust of Cleveland's policies when they went to the polls in 1894. The Democrats lost 113 congressional seats, and in twenty-four states they were completely shut out of any representation in the House. The big gainers in 1894 were the Republicans. Indeed, they had registered the greatest single gain of any party in the history of congressional elections. Measured against the Democratic rout, the Populists, who had increased their share of the popular vote by 42 percent over their total in 1892, now seemed poised to become a major party. For the first time as a separate party, they had begun to pry apart the "solid South." The propertied classes in both major parties looked nervously toward the presidential election of 1896. "The Chicago labor riots and the growth of 'populism' have frightened people a good deal,"[6] noted E. L. Godkin, editor of *The Nation,* in late 1894. He was among the many Eastern conservatives who expected the worst.

From Alliancemen to Populists

The Populist movement that Godkin so dreaded developed out of a series of farmers' alliances in the 1880s. The largest of these was the Southern Farmers' Alliance. From its origins on the Texas farming frontier in the 1870s, the Southern Alliance swept back into the cotton South and fanned northward into the wheat country. Falling cotton prices and increases in tenantry and cropping were the main reasons for its growth. At its peak in 1890, the Alliance enlisted 850,000 members, about one-quarter of the adult male population in the rural South.

A genuine mass movement organized from the bottom up, the Southern Alliance set as its goal a revolution in the credit arrangements for Southern agriculture. The indispensable first step toward that goal was the self-education of the people in the workings of the economic system that entrapped so many of them. Through meetings in the thousands of suballiances, speeches by cadres of lecturers, and editorials and debates in a network of Alliance newspapers, the Southern rural masses did educate themselves. In so doing, they also joined a community. They rushed to the Alliance with the fervor of going to a revival. Evangelical and secular traditions in the Southern backcountry of mutual assistance and communalism flowed together in a powerful sense of brotherhood and sisterhood. "You cannot imagine what a kindred feeling has sprung up among us,"[7] reported a member from a North Carolina suballiance in 1888.

Out of this movement culture came the organizational strength and shared sense of purpose that were essential for the launching of Alliance cooperatives in marketing and purchasing. The cooperatives were a large-scale experiment in agrarian self-help. By pooling their resources and cooperating in the bulk buying of their supplies and the selling of their cotton, farmers tried to build an economic solidarity that would raise cotton prices and thus free themselves from the near-monopolistic power of the local furnishing merchant.

In 1889 the Southern Alliance scored its greatest victory. The cartel that controlled the importing and sale of jute, the coarse fiber used for cotton bagging, announced a sudden price increase in jute of 40 percent. By organizing, through its suballiances, a boycott of jute and a switch to cotton as a substitute for the bagging, the Alliance defeated the jute thrust. In part because of the enthusiasm generated by this victory, the number of Alliance cooperatives grew spectacularly in the late 1880s and reached a peak of about 450 in early 1891. From then on the number quickly dropped.

The Alliance cooperatives, like those of the Knights, were short-lived because of managerial inexperience, the opposition of local business interests, and, above all, the lack of operating capital. In order to gain access to credit, the Southern Alliance called for a radical restructuring of national credit arrangements that would mobilize capital resources on behalf of the farming poor. Their plan was known as the subtreasury system. Under its provisions, the federal government would build warehouses, or subtreasuries, in which farmers could store nonperishable crops as collateral for low-interest loans in the form of greenbacks. Presumably, farm prices would rise. The greenbacks would inflate the currency, and farmers would no longer be forced by financial pressure to unload their crops during the annual harvest glut.

The subtreasury system was a controversial and complicated plan, and there were several versions of it. Yet, as evidenced by conservative variations of it in the twentieth-century farm programs of the federal government, it was by no means unworkable. And it had the undeniable advantages of creating a mechanism for a more flexible national currency that would vary with economic need, of meeting the pressing need of Southern farmers for short-term credit at a reasonable cost, and of enhancing the leverage of farmers in marketing their major staples. It met bitter opposition because it threatened existing power relations, not only in the financing, shipping, and marketing of agricultural commodities, but also in the supplying of the nation's currency by private bankers. All those whose power was threatened, from bankers in the East to planters and merchants in the South, joined with the *New York Times* in denouncing the plan as "one of the wildest and most fantastic projects ever seriously proposed by sober man."[8]

The subtreasury plan originated in the Southern Alliance. It was quickly amended through provisions for loans based upon land to meet the needs of farmers in the Middle Border (Kansas, Nebraska, and the Dakotas) for long-term credit to cope with their burden of farm mortgages. These were the debt-ridden farmers who flowed into the Northern Alliance in the late 1880s. About 40 percent of the farms in the North Central states were mortgaged in 1890, and the percentage of Alliance farmers with a mortgage debt was much higher. In an 1890 survey of 2,000 Alliance members, the Topeka *Advocate* found that 83 percent of them were carrying a mortgage. In Marshall County, South Dakota, one of the last areas settled in the boom of the 1880s, the Alliance attracted only 29 percent of the landed farmers who were free of debt but 58 percent of those with debts greater than $1,000.

The typical Alliance member in the South was a middling farmer slowly being ground under by debt, while the recently upwardly mobile farmer who was suddenly faced with losing everything dominated the membership of the Northern Alliance. Common to both by the late 1880s was the realization that they had to gain political power in order to further their interests and to reclaim control of the government from what they believed was a conspiracy of Eastern capitalists. Out of that realization came the Populist movement.

The Appeal of Populism

To hundreds of thousands of rural Americans, Populism was simultaneously a cultural movement and a political party that appealed to their hopes for a better life and enhanced personal dignity. To its critics, centered in the Eastern circles of propertied respectability, Populism amounted to the cockeyed and dangerous rantings of a rural mob of economic losers who were at best irresponsible country bumpkins and at worst hayseed anarchists. It was the dual character of Populism—its cultural rejection of what America had become and its political program for what it could be—that gave Populism its dynamism and terrified its opponents.

Populism appealed to only certain kinds of farmers, and but a minority of farmers ever became Populists. Those that did shared several characteristics:

1. They tended to be heavily dependent on a single crop—wheat in the Middle Border, which stretched southward from the Dakotas into the Texas pandhandle, and cotton in a belt of the lower South that extended westward from the Carolina piedmont into central Texas.
2. They were burdened by heavy debts—farm mortgages in the plains states and the crop-lien system in the South.
3. They lived in the most economically, socially, and geographically isolated areas of the farm economy.
4. They were relative newcomers to a market economy in which they had little choice but to become dependent on the impersonal logic of a cash calculus for their success or failure.

The anger and alienation that found a political expression in Populism fed upon this combination of economic distress, social isolation, and recent exposure to commercialized agriculture. The Populists were the newest, the most financially exposed, and the least successful entries in a market economy that they felt had betrayed them.

These characteristics differentiated the Populists from the majority of American farmers. In the Midwest (that is, the states of the Old Northwest), the Northeast, and much of the Upper South, farmers were able to cushion themselves against the market forces that enmeshed the Populists in poverty and enraged dependency. Outside the wheat and cotton belts, farmers were much more likely to own their land, to be free of major debts, and to practice a diversified agriculture geared to specialized and growing urban markets. Unable to compete against Western farmers in cereal production, Eastern farmers took marginal land out of production, worked the remainder more intensively, and increasingly switched to dairy products and perishable fruits, which they shipped by rail for overnight delivery to nearby cities. As the center of wheat production moved across the Mississippi, Midwestern farmers began to rely on a hog-corn agriculture as the basis for steady profits. Low grain prices, which were disastrous for a farmer in North Dakota growing only grain, simply lowered the cost of livestock production for a farmer in Illinois raising both grain and hogs. Therefore, watching closely the ratio between hog and corn prices, they either sold their corn when the price was high or fed it to their hogs to be converted into pork when the price was low.

These farmers were businessmen, and they identified themselves as such. They were at least a generation removed from even a semblance of self-sufficiency, and they readily acknowledged that in their lives the uncertainties of the market had replaced the greater security of only limited market involvement. Recognizing that the day of the independent yeoman was past, the *Minnesota Farmer* noted in 1879:[9]

> The farmer has become a purchaser—buys all that he wears, buys much that he eats, buys oftentimes his fuel and lights. To meet these demands, he has occasion to study the markets, to find out what people want in exchange for the things he must purchase.

The Populists were also purchasers of fixed wants, but unlike Eastern and Midwestern farmers, they were not in a position to adjust successfully to market conditions. In the lower South, for example, acreage steadily shifted out of corn into cotton between 1868 and 1890. Yet during this same period, the price of corn relative to cotton had risen to the antebellum levels, in which a bushel of corn was worth six to eight times what a pound of cotton was worth. Had Southern farmers been free to follow the logic of the market, they would have been planting more corn and returning to the safety-first strategy they had been practicing before the Civil War of providing for the food needs of their families before gambling on cotton. Yet, cotton became an ever-more-tyrannical king. Cotton declined in price year after year because of an overproduction that can best be explained as the consequence of the political and economic power wielded by planters and merchants through the crop-lien system. Those being squeezed the hardest by this system were the rank and file of Southern Populism.

Despite Populist rhetoric about the monopolistic power of Eastern moneylenders who forced unwanted and artificially expensive mortgages on Western farmers, there was no equivalent of the crop-lien system that would have forced farmers in the West to grow wheat. Rather, the overproduction of wheat, as had happened earlier with cotton in the South, steadily eroded the prices received for the crop, until the bottom was reached in the 1890s. Wheat production doubled from the early 1870s to the mid-1890s, and the price per bushel fell from $1.20 to about half that. Apparently, Populist farmers in the Middle Border should have had no one but themselves to blame for not cutting back on production.

Likewise, Populist charges of being economically exploited by railroads, middle-men, mortgage companies, and other agents of the Money Power in the East seem to be overblown. Long-standing agricultural problems of credit, transportation, and marketing were resolved after 1870. Credit was more easily available than before the Civil War, and interest rates for short-term mortgages of four to five years were generally falling. Rates fell because of competition among mortgage companies, which pooled Eastern capital to service Western markets. On the other hand, Western farmers still had to pay more for credit than their Eastern counterparts. In 1890, when the average farm mortgage in the East was at 5½ percent and the one in the West at 8 percent, the Western debtor was paying 45 percent more in interest charges. Part of this 45 percent difference represented price gouging by Eastern moneylenders, but most of it reflected the greater risks inherent in lending to a farmer in the West, who had to battle drought and low prices for his cash crops. The risks were indeed great. Most of the mortgage companies that dealt with Western farmers went bankrupt between 1888 and 1894.

With regard to transportation and marketing, as well as to credit, Western farmers during the Gilded Age were better served than their antebellum predecessors. Farm goods could be moved far greater distances at much cheaper prices after the war than before. The expansion of railroads into the trans-Mississippi West was so rapid, and competition between rail lines so keen, that freightage rates on hauling Western grain fell, though erratically, in the last quarter of the nineteenth century. Meanwhile, the finished goods that the railroads were importing into the West were generally declining in price slightly faster than the agricultural goods being exported out of the West. These two trends often reversed themselves, but after 1870 the terms of trade for Western farmers—the difference between what they received and what they paid in prices—gradually improved. Yet, the railroads were singled out, along with allegedly monopolistic Eastern capitalists, for Populist condemnation. According to the National

Farmers' Alliance in 1889, a seedbed for future Populists, "There are two classes of men who seem above the reach of adverse financial fortune, moneylenders and railroad owners."[10] With an unforeseen irony, the Alliance had pinpointed the two major holders of Eastern capital who were especially hard hit by the depression of the 1890s.

This fact suggests that contemporary conservatives were correct in dismissing the Western Populists as a cranky, irrational bunch of market losers; and had the anger of these Populists been focused on the level of prices per se, that dismissal would be warranted. In fact, however, what most angered these farmers was their utter dependence on prices in the first place. Economic survival on the Great Plains, to say nothing of prosperity, required that farmers commit themselves to a commercialized form of agriculture in which individual success or failure was measured by the movement of prices and the decisions of outsiders, over which farmers had no control. This sense of being a dependent pawn in an impersonal system of supply and demand fed the cultural side of Western Populism, while the economic misery that was the fate of the latecomers to Plains agriculture in the mid-1880s fed its economic side and transformed cultural protest into a political party.

The Great Plains were the last great agricultural frontier. Yet the conditions under which they could be farmed precluded the realization of the traditional goals of independence and security that migrants had brought to earlier frontiers. Of the farms established under the Homestead Act, two-thirds had failed by 1900. The rate of failure was so high because the settlers were so much more at the mercy of the physical environment and market conditions than farmers in the East or Midwest.

Alone in vast stretches of a treeless landscape, the pioneering families in the Middle Border had to contend with periodic invasions of crop-destroying insects and punishing extremes in temperatures and moisture. The wood and water that could almost be taken for granted further east were scarce and expensive. A balanced agriculture that allowed farmers in other areas to become more self-sufficient was out of the question, because only a narrow range of crops could be grown in the semiarid plains. These crops, and most notably wheat, required the use of expensive agricultural machinery in order to work the heavy soil when its moisture content was high enough to warrant putting in a crop. Even then, crop yields per acre tended to be low because of the lack of moisture. A commercially viable farm therefore had to be an extensive operation, one that was larger than the 160 acres of land that could be claimed free under the Homestead Act. Because most migrants brought little capital with them (the expenses of moving used up most of their savings), and because the capital costs of converting the raw land of a homestead tract into a farm were at least $1,000 on the plains, the migrants had to go into debt if they wanted to become farmers.

Thus from the very beginning, farmers in the Middle Border had to assume a degree of market risk that was still relatively uncommon among the rest of the nation's farmers. As late as 1872, only 40 percent of American farm produce was sold in nonlocal markets. This percentage was always much higher in the Great Plains. Crops had to be exported, both to pay off the debts incurred in growing them and to pay for the consumer goods that this sparsely populated region could not provide for its isolated farmers.

Contrary to earlier generations of American farmers, who had more freedom to choose if and when they wanted to engage in commercial agriculture, farmers in the Middle Border had little real choice but to produce marketable surpluses. For the former, profits from market sales were a welcome bonus; for the latter, such profits were an absolute necessity if they wanted to remain farmers. Similarly, farmers on the plains had less freedom in choosing the economic agents for their marketing activity. As a consequence of their isolation, they were frequently dependent upon just one railroad, one banker, one operator of a grain elevator, and one supplier of store goods. These were the market intermediaries whom the Populists denounced as monopolizers and conspirators. Given the inordinate power that these intermediaries wielded over the economic lives of the farmers, such a personalization of market forces was not at all irrational.

When service was disrupted or the farmers felt they had been treated unfairly, they responded with an anger that sheer dependency intensified into rage. In 1884 rail officials told wheat growers in an isolated corner of the Dakota Territory that they could stop raising wheat if they refused to deliver their grain to the elevators of Charles Pillsbury, a large Minneapolis miller. The farmers reacted by forcibly seizing rail cars and loading their own wheat. When the same railroad, the St. Paul, Minneapolis and Manitoba, shifted its cars to construction work in Montana in 1887, farmers along the Canada–North Dakota border were denied their only outlet for marketing their wheat. In petitions to the Interstate Commerce Commission, a federal agency that had just been created, the farmers drew on republican antimonopolism to express their sense of injustice. They saw themselves as members of an "industrious community" that was being "skinned and guffed" by a "ring or conspiracy" that was seeking monopolistic control over the shipping, storage, sale, and price of wheat. They wanted to be independent farmers, but the railroad wanted to reduce every pioneer to the status "of a laborer working upon starvation wages solely as their vassal, and to swell the dividends upon their watered stock." In addition to explaining the nature of the threat to their independence, the republicanism of these petitioners also pointed the way to a solution, one that did not reject economic change but sought to democratize it:[11]

> If individuals are to be set above us—I refer now to the heads of corporations—who are to set a price upon our products . . . under a free government those individuals should be such as we ourselves may select.

When the threat or reality of economic ruin merged with this political effort to overcome abject dependency, Western Populism was born. The crucial years were the late 1880s. Until then, rainfall patterns and the terms of trade generally favored farmers in the Middle Border. This was especially true for those who arrived first in the early 1870s. Their land steadily appreciated in value, and the returns from their crops were high in proportion to the original cost of their land. Unencumbered by heavy debts, this first wave of settlers was able to withstand the crash that wrecked the hopes of the larger wave that arrived in the 1880s.

The demographic side of the boom and bust cycle in the wheat country is shown in Table 11.1. Hundreds of thousands of those who came in the mid-1880s stayed just long enough to be wiped out, pack up what little they had left, and head back east. At the height of the exodus, a Kansas editor observed: "In one season eighteen thousand prairie schooners passed east over the Mississippi River bridge at Omaha—never to return."[12] These aspiring farmers could not have arrived at a worse time. They caught the agricultural cycle at its peak and rode it to its bottom.

By the early 1880s, a generalized sense that free or cheap land was about to run

Table 11.1   Net Population Flows in the Plains States, 1880–1900
(in thousands)

The demographic patterns of boom (1880s) and bust (1890s) in the Plains states were triggered by economic and climatic cycles that first favored and then devastated the chances of a farmer profitably growing wheat in this semiarid region.

	1880–1890	1890–1900
Dakotas	+243.4	+64.1
Nebraska	+362.5	−153.9
Kansas	+159.7	−149.8
Total	+765.6	−239.6

Source: Compiled from *Historical Statistics,* Series C-25–75.

out, in combination with bumper crops, good prices, and a decade of above-average rainfall, sent migrants pouring into the higher, drier sections of the Middle Border. The best of the homesteading acreage was gone. Plenty of privately owned land was available, but it cost two to three times what it had a decade earlier, and a speculative frenzy in 1886–1887 further inflated land prices. The newcomers had to assume a much heavier debt than their predecessors. And just when they did, a drastic decline in rainfall and wheat prices shattered any chance they had of repaying that debt. The drought began in the summer of 1887 and barely let up for a decade.

As the drought withered wheat crops in the Middle Border, large crops in the more humid Midwest and in the new fields opened up abroad by the spread of railroads, continued to flood the market with wheat. Between 1881 and 1894, the price of wheat fell by 59 percent. It was this combination—high debt, low wheat prices, and pinched production on their own farms—that made commercial agriculture a nightmare for those wheat farmers who entered the marketplace in the 1880s. These were the farmers who organized Populism in the wheatlands. At Omaha, Nebraska, on July 4, 1892, they joined farmers who had come out of the Southern Alliance and representatives of a host of reform organizations in formally launching the new third party.

Like so much of Populism, the Omaha convention blended the spiritual bonding of a camp meeting with a hardheaded presentation of economic issues. From the first sentence of the preamble to the party platform—"We meet in the midst of a nation brought to the verge of moral, political, and material ruin"—through the reading of the platform by Ignatius Donnelly, the convention moved toward an emotional climax. An Eastern journalist reported that with the adoption of the platform,

> cheers and yells . . . rose like a tornado from four thousand throats and raged without cessation for thirty-four minutes, during which women shrieked and wept, men embraced and kissed their neighbors, locked arms [and] leaped upon tables and chairs in the ecstasy of their delirium.[13]

To Easterners all this was enthusiasm run beserk. To the participants it was the collective joy of a people who had found the self-confidence to reclaim their government from the Money Power, which had made a sham of the political parties.

Unabashedly, the platform spoke of "the love of the whole people for each other and for the nation" as the only basis on which the republic could "endure as a free government."[14] Such was the language of a cooperative vision of America in which

Harvest Hands in the Wheat Country, 1890. The desolation of this scene evokes the blighted hopes for agricultural independence that fueled so much of the appeal of Populism. The artist has here placed the migrant harvest hands at a temporary encampment in the midst of the market forces—the railroad, grain elevator, and farm machinery—that were transforming agriculture in the wheat states into a big business. (Library of Congress)

power rested in the hands of small and equal producers not yet culturally isolated from each other by the competitive pressures of an economic individualism that destroyed communalism and promised greater material rewards in return. The Populists saw little of these rewards in their own lives. Their way of life, and the economic independence that was its cornerstone, was under siege, and the Populists dramatized that siege as a vast conspiracy to impoverish the producing masses. The language was exaggerated, but the core truth remained. Economic power, power held by men and institutions and not by shadowy market forces, had outstripped the ability of the people to control it through democratic means. The balance could be redressed, insisted the Populists, only through a radical restructuring of governmental authority over the economy.

Land, transportation, and currency were the three focal points of these restructuring demands by the Populists. The Omaha Platform called for government ownership of the railroads and the telephone and telegraph systems on the grounds that all of these were a "public necessity" essential for the exchange of goods and information. Invoking the Greenback ideology, the Populists sought to abolish the national banking system, set up postal savings banks run by the government, and replace national bank notes with the legal-tender treasury notes provided for in the subtreasury plan. The expectation was that these greenbacks, plus the unrestricted coinage of silver, another Populist demand, would dramatically raise the per-capita circulation of money, inflate farm prices, and promote economic growth. As for land, the Populists wanted the government to forbid alien ownership and to reclaim all that was held by corporations and railroads "in excess of their actual needs."[15] In an effort to democratize what was seen as a corrupt and issueless political system, the Populist proposed the popular election of U.S. Senators (until the 17th Amendment passed in 1913, senators were appointed by their state legislatures) and the initiative and referendum, devices by which the people could initiate legislation and decide on issues presented to them. And, in an appeal to urban labor, the platform called for a graduated income tax, an eight-hour day for government work, limits on immigration, and an end to the use of private armies of strike-breaking detectives by industrial companies.

It was a bold program, and to Easterners and most Americans of property, a shocking one. In one coordinated plan of reform the Populists had attacked the ethical basis of corporate capitalism and the financial mechanisms and government subsidies through which the suppliers of credit and owners of production exercised their power. The Omaha Platform pitted a collective ideal of public power against the reality of the private power that was leading America into the corporate age. Now the Populists had to build the voting support to transform that ideal into a new political reality.

From Populists to "Popocrats"

The Populists never did create a majority coalition of voters, or even come close to it. The political numbers necessary for the enactment of their program just were not there. As noted earlier, Populism had little appeal to farmers outside the debt-ridden regions of the cotton South and the wheat belts of the Middle Border. The Populist presidential candidate in 1892, Jamas B. Weaver, was a native son of the Midwest and a Union veteran who had served as a colonel in an Iowa regiment. Yet, he drew less than 5 percent of the vote in the Midwest, even in his home state of Iowa, which had sent him to Congress as a Greenbacker.

Working through the Patrons of Husbandry, or, as it was commonly known, the Grange, Midwestern farmers had supported protest movements in the 1870s. In particular, they pushed for the state regulation of railroad rates. But this protest, one that was strongly backed by local mercantile interests, stopped far short of an open political rebellion. Merchants and shippers at interior points throughout the Midwest turned to regulation in an effort to even out the price differentials between the rates charged by the railroads for long and short hauls. Rates for long, continuous hauls were much cheaper and worked to the competitive advantage of rival businessmen in terminal-market cities. The so-called Granger laws were passed, which gave regulatory powers to state agencies in the Midwest. After the Supreme Court ruled in 1886 that these state powers violated the federal regulation of interstate commerce, Congress created the Interstate Commerce Commission in 1887 to exercise those powers denied to the states. Thus by the 1890s, the prime issue behind farm protest in the Midwest had been removed. Just as importantly, land values were rising and farm debt was falling. Economically secure and relatively prosperous, the established farmers of the Midwest had little reason to find Populism attractive.

Unable to win farm converts north of the Ohio and east of the Mississippi, the Populists also ran into the problem of holding on to their original agrarian supporters. These men and their families did not leave Populism for another party; they simply left. Many, perhaps most, of the economically distressed farmers who gave Populism its initial electoral victories in the Middle Border moved on after the crash of the late 1880s. About 180,000 people left Kansas alone between 1887 and 1891. Nebraska and

Kansas experienced a net loss of 300,000 in population during the 1890s. The loss was greatest in those recently settled western counties of high indebtedness in which the appeal of Populism was strongest.

A minority party even in the countryside, the Populists obviously needed to forge a coalition with urban labor if they ever wanted to become a major party. If ever the two were going to come together, 1894 was surely the year. Armies of the unemployed were traveling the rails in search of work, others were marching on Washington to demand relief in the form of public work projects, and still more were taxing the relief services of private charities and municipal governments to the breaking point. The depression was at its worst, and workers seemingly had every reason to abandon the party system that had failed them. Yet, although the Populists redoubled their efforts for an alliance, labor repeatedly rejected them. With the exception of some support from the shoeworkers in Massachusetts, coal miners in the Midwest, and immigrant labor in Milwaukee, Populist-labor tickets ran very poorly in 1894. Industrial workers in Eastern and Midwestern cities turned away from the Democrats with a vengeance, but they turned toward the Republicans, not the Populists.

The Republicans offered labor sound-money doctrines, instead of the Populist threat of inflation. They also offered something that the Populists could not— creditability as a governing party. The Republicans' proven record on tariff protection, promotion of economic growth, and governmental spending—the very issues that had worked to the party's disadvantage in 1890—were now quite appealing to labor. For those issues of union recognition and job benefits that were of most immediate concern to labor, working-class leaders relied not on direct political action but on trade unions. After slumping during the mid-1890s, union membership more than quadrupled between 1897 and 1902. Though comprising less than 15 percent of the workers in nonfarm enterprises by 1905, unionized labor mobilized the critical leadership among workers that the Populists had been unable to tap. Meanwhile, issues of ethnic recognition and neighborhood services continued to define the political agenda for labor in the urban wards in which they lived. From the perspective of this agenda, Populism not only had little meaningful to offer to urban labor, but its uniform ethic of evangelical moralism also posed a distinct threat to the diversity of immigrant and working-class cultures.

In the language, as well as the purpose, of their politics, the Populists and labor fundamentally differed. The Populists' political language was that of the working-men's parties from the preindustrial Jacksonian era. Their world was divided into just two classes, the nonproducers who manipulated the money supply for their own enrichment, and the producers whose wealth was siphoned off by the nonproducers. This ideology identified their main economic enemies, bankers and shippers, and provided the analytical insights that the Populists developed into their most original idea, the subtreasury plan. But this producer-nonproducer ideology of small-scale capitalism, which was so relevant to the needs of Populist farmers, was tangential to the needs of labor.

The exploitation that workers endured was that of the industrial wage-labor system, in which the worker was just a factor of production who had to sell his labor on a daily basis in order to survive. "An empty stomach can make no contracts,"[16] reasoned one labor reformer in an attack on the alleged equality of labor's bargaining position under industrial capitalism. Precisely because the Populists identified themselves as independent producers who owned or aspired to the ownership of property, labor rejected the claim of the Populists that they were the party of all the workers. Labor defined work, as it had to under the factory system, as wage labor. Using this political vocabulary, labor viewed the Populists as well-intentioned employers whose interests of necessity diverged from those of employees.

In the absence of any labor support to speak of, and with a shrinking base of minority rural support, the Populists had to resort to the only tactic that permitted them to stay alive politically. They fused with one of the major parties—the Democrats in the Middle Border and the Republicans in the cotton South. This was how the Populists came to power in Kansas and North Carolina, two states that illustrate how fusion took hold where real two-party competition had been weak. Although fusion gave the Populists access to offices, it also carried the inevitable risk of a loss of the party's own organization and ideology. This risk was all the greater when Populist politicians gave in to the temptation to water down party doctrine in an effort to attract the greatest number of voters. Haunted by their knowledge of the ineffectiveness of third parties throughout the Gilded Age, and goaded on by a public image that depicted them as political quacks who were too ignorant to be entrusted with real power, Populist leaders committed the party to one final fusion in 1896. This one was with the Bryan Democrats, and the road to fusion was paved with free silver.

The cause of silver, like the tariff, seemed to generate more rhetoric than reason. Americans in the 1890s saw in silver and gold the respective symbols for the change or stability they wanted in the social order around them, and they attached passionate importance to the one they preferred. For the lobby of silver-mine owners, however, the issue was not one of passion but of profits.

In 1873 Congress put the U.S. on the gold standard by dropping provisions for the coinage of silver. Later denounced by many silverites as "the crime of '73," a treacherous act by a conspiracy of the gold forces who wanted to contract the nation's money supply, the decision in 1873 was simply a recognition of rather mundane market forces. Mine owners were not bringing their silver to be minted into coins. Silver was then scarce relative to gold and was worth more in the open market than in a minted coin where, by law, its weight had been fixed at sixteen times that of the gold in a gold dollar. Very soon after 1873, however, new deposits of silver were opened up in the Rocky Mountains, and production boomed. The market price of silver, a commodity just like wheat or cotton, fell, and by the mid-1890s its market value was only about half what it was worth if used in the limited number of silver dollars authorized to be minted by the Bland-Allison Act and the Sherman Silver Purchase Act. The producers of the metal clearly had every economic incentive to lobby for the "free and unlimited" coinage of silver.

As revealed by the phenomenal success of William H. Harvey's silver tract of 1894, *Coin's Financial School,* the cause of silver became a great popular panacea that promised to lead debtors out of their misery by inflating prices. The American Bimetallic League, a lobby funded by the silver producers, fanned the enthusiasm by stepping up its activities to win votes for silver. Pro-silver and anti-Cleveland Democrats controlled the party's convention at Chicago in 1896 and made silver the touchstone of party regularity. William Jennings Bryan, a two-term congressman from Nebraska who had lost his seat in the Republican landslide of 1894, captured the nomination with a perfectly timed speech. Silver was to be the salvation of his "producing masses,'' and to those who demanded a gold standard, Bryan replied: "You shall not press upon the brow of labor this crown of thorns, you shall not crucify mankind upon a cross of gold.''[17] With these words Bryan concluded his Chicago oration. No revivalist could have more electrified an audience.

At their national convention in St. Louis two weeks later, the Populists made an agonizing decision. They nominated their own vice-presidential candidate, Thomas Watson of Georgia, but supported Bryan for the Presidency. The Populist leaders carried the day for fusion by arguing that this was their chance, probably their only one, to achieve the status of a major party and unite the forces of reform. Moreover, free silver, part of the Omaha Platform, had been the party's most popular issue. It also was the overriding issue in the one area in which the Populists were the majority party, the silver-producing states of the West. Still, the fact remained, Henry Demarest Lloyd pointed out, that ''silver was only the most trifling installment of reform, and many [Populists]—a great many—did not conceal their belief that it was no reform at all.''[18]

The fusionists stressed that the Democratic platform of 1896 also called for tax-free state banks to replace the national banks, stricter governmental controls over the railroads, and a constitutional amendment in favor of an income tax that the Supreme Court had recently struck down. Nonetheless, what the platform added up to was a pale replica of the Omaha demands, with little of their substance. The Democrats barely touched upon the power relationships that the Populists wanted to change. Thus, the risks of fusion were momentous. By staking their all on silver, the Populists might well lose not just an election but also their reform drive and their party. It soon became apparent that when the ''Popocrats'' were born, Populism died.

The Election of 1896 and Its Aftermath

The election of 1896 was the most significant one since that of 1860. Like all critical elections, it marked both an end and a beginning. What most obviously ended with the election was the existence of Populism as a cohesive political and cultural force. What most clearly began was an era of Republican hegemony in national affairs that would last, save for the two Wilson administrations, until 1930.

Fusion with the Bryan forces confused and demoralized the rank-and-file Populists, especially in the South. They had sacrificed for Populism in the belief that it offered them a real governing alternative. Now all the sacrifices boiled down to supporting a non-Populist who could talk only about silver and who refused even to accept officially the nomination of the Populist Party. A week after Bryan's defeat at the hands of the Republican nominee, William McKinley, Tom Watson of Georgia wrote what in effect was an epitaph for the Populists. ''The sentiment is still there, the votes are still there, but confidence is gone, and the party organization is almost gone.''[19]

The decline of Populism in the Middle Border was slower and less traumatic than in the South. Populists often dominated coalitions with Democrats for the next decade, and when fusion ran its course, the two-party system in the wheat states was more competitive and responsive to economic issues than it had been before the Populist challenge. Meanwhile, an upturn in farm prosperity and the continued outmigration of the most economically distressed farmers drained Populism of its inflationary appeal and its potential voting support.

Poor European harvests in the late 1890s, combined with a price inflation triggered by new gold production in South Africa, Alaska, and Australia, drove up the price of wheat and other farm staples. As the Populists had predicted, currency inflation brought back prosperity. The irony, of course, was that gold, the bankers' money, received the credit and not silver or greenbacks, the people's money. Better farm prices, however, did not reverse the trend toward higher rates of farm tenancy. The agrarian poor moved on to another frontier, the wheatlands of Canada. About one million Americans migrated to Canada between 1898 and 1914, and most of them moved directly north from the Middle Border. Many of them carried their agrarian radicalism north. Strong agrarian parties of democratic socialists emerged on the Canadian prairies, and echoes of them, and of the Populism from which they sprang, were to be found in the Non-Partisan Leagues of Dakota farmers during World War I.

The fusion of 1896, a tactical decision to Western Populists, was an act of betrayal to Southern Populists. With scant exaggeration, a Southerner at the St. Louis convention in 1896 explained to a fellow Populist from the West:[20]

> The feeling of the Democracy against us is one of murderous hate. I have been shot at many times. Grand juries will not indict our assailants. Courts give us no protection.

To many Southern whites the Populists might as well have been criminals, for they had committed the cultural treason of defying white supremacy. The Southern Populists were not racial egalitarians, and they certainly did not push for social equality between the races. The Southern Alliance was a white organization not open to blacks, and many Alliancemen depended on landless blacks, who were likely to be in the Colored Farmers' Alliance, to pick their cotton crop. Nonetheless, Southern Populists did recognize the potential equality and importance of blacks in political terms, and they based their strategy as a party on one fundamental insight: poor white and black farmers had to join forces politically if they were ever to break the economic stranglehold of the planters and merchants who controlled the land, the credit, and the crops. Thus, the logic of attempting to build a class alliance across racial lines was compelling.

In making that attempt the Populists directly challenged the class power of the planters and merchants, which was exercised through their domination of the Southern Democratic party. Because one of the cornerstones of that power was the division of the Southern rural poor along the lines of race, the Populist challenge inevitably raised issues of race as well as of class. The two were interlocked, as they had been ever since whites fastened slavery upon the South. As Watson told the Georgia farmers of both races:[21]

> You are kept apart that you may be separately fleeced of your earnings. You are made to hate each other because upon that hatred is rested the keystone of the arch of financial despotism which enslaves you both.

A Democratic planter could hate Watson as a "communist," an "anarchist," or a "Negro lover." All the venomous labels amounted to the same thing.

Demoralized and disgusted by the fusion of 1896, Southern Populists quickly abandoned the party. Only in Texas, and to a lesser extent in Alabama and Georgia, did the party still have any base of support by 1898. The demise of Southern Populism was part of a fundamental restructuring of Southern politics that would hold until the civil rights revolution of the 1960s. In tacit recognition that Watson had been right in asserting that issues of class could unite the agrarian poor of both races into a voting majority that would threaten the existing economic and political centers of power within the South, Democratic party leaders pushed through election laws in the turn-of-the-century South that disfranchised their opponents. Legal and constitutional restrictions in the form of poll taxes, literacy tests, and complicated registration requirements drastically shrank the size of the electorate. The dimensions of that change can be seen by comparing the 62 percent of the potential Southern electorate who voted in the presidential election of 1888 to the 30 percent who did so in the election of 1908. Blacks were almost totally disenfranchised, and the white electorate, most notably the poorer classes of tenants and mill hands, was reduced by one-third to one-half.

Favored by the wealthy and well-educated Democratic elites of the black belts, and aimed at poor whites as well as blacks, this political counterrevolution from above eliminated any possibility that a real two-party system might develop in the South. The consistent 20 to 25 percent of the voters who had supported opposition parties during the 1880s and 1890s were legally removed as a political force. The Democratic opposition was reduced to 10 percent of the electorate after 1900. This counterrevolution also rechanneled the frustration and rage of Southern Populists from economic relations of dependency to social relations of white supremacy.

The postslavery generation of blacks was now legally assigned a fixed and inferior position in Southern society, and all white males were pledged to keep blacks in their proper place. For blacks, the most horrifying penalty for not staying on their side of the color line was a lynching. A wave of sadistic lynchings of blacks swept the South in the 1890s and early 1900s. Although the lynch mobs usually came from lower-class whites, their actions were condoned and often encouraged by upper-class whites. Blacks, in the most direct and horrible way imaginable, were forced to pay the price for the intense white fears of economic dependency and vulnerability and the cultural shame of having failed to provide for their families. For a brief moment, white Populists had viewed blacks as political allies in a biracial alliance. After that moment passed, blacks became the scapegoats for the shattered hopes of Southern Populism. Among the most vicious of the race baiters after 1900 was Tom Watson.

As Populism died in 1896, a long period of Republican dominance began. Although Bryan retained a personal following in the West, the Democratic party was reduced to little more than a regional party of the South and an ethnic party of Irish Catholics. The fall of the Populists and the rise of the Republicans were related. Populism was the last mass-based political movement that challenged the ethical basis of the emerging corporate order, and its defeat was measured by the decisiveness with which the nation turned to the Republicans, the political expression of that corporate order.

McKinley's victory over Bryan in 1896 confirmed the Republican breakthrough that had occurred in the congressional elections of 1894. The politics of dead center was over, and the Republicans were now the normal majority party in national elections. McKinley's margin of victory, 4.4 percent of the total Republican-Democratic vote, was the greatest since Grant had defeated the inept Greeley in 1872. The Republicans were on top, and they would stay there until the next major depression in the 1930s, because they had won the battle to capture the massive urban-industrial electorate that had formed during the Gilded Age. Bryan swept most of the rural South and

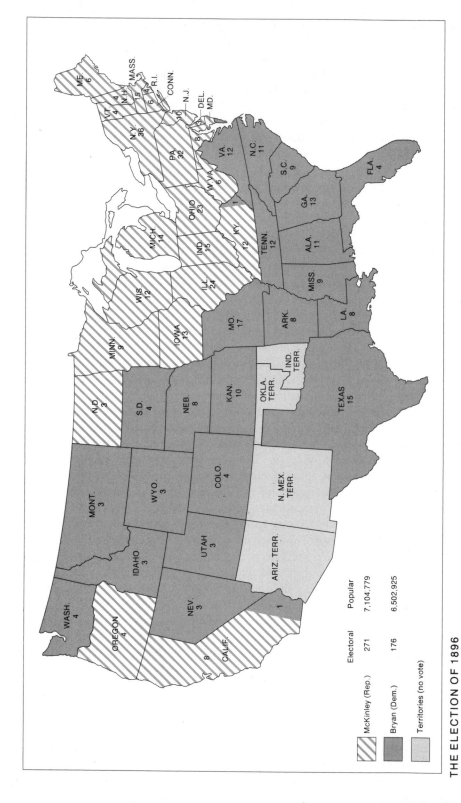

THE ELECTION OF 1896

Electoral sweeps in the urbanized, industrial Northeast and the corn/hog states of the Midwest accounted for the Republican triumph in 1896. A comparison with the election map on p. 400 shows how quickly the Democrats had been transformed into the party of agrarian discontent in the West. What won the election, however, were the additional two million votes that the Republicans picked up over their showing in 1892.

	Electoral	Popular
McKinley (Rep.)	271	7,104,779
Bryan (Dem.)	176	6,502,925
Territories (no vote)		

West but failed to take a single state north of the Ohio and east of the Mississippi rivers. He carried only five of the seventy largest cities outside the South. In the metropolitan centers of the Northeast and Midwest, about 400,000 former Democrats, or 7 percent of Cleveland's support in 1892, switched to the Republicans.

The simple fact that a Democratic administration presided over a devastating depression had much to do with the appeal of the Republicans to city dwellers and factory workers. The Democratic party's chances in 1896 were further damaged when Bryan projected himself to Eastern voters as a single-issue, rural candidate who could talk only about free silver in the biblical language of a revivalist. Yet, the Republicans also seized every opportunity the Democrats handed them, and they revealed a sophisticated awareness of how best to respond to shifts in the concerns and composition of the electorate. Deemphasizing the now-faded memories of the Civil War and moralistic and divisive issues, such as prohibition, the Republicans presented themselves as pragmatic moderates. The gold standard, the protective tariff, and fiscal responsibility were the themes that the McKinley forces artfully tailored to the concerns of businessmen, workers, and consumers. All the while, in a marked departure from the regimental, "hoopla" campaigning style of the 1880s, which featured parades, rallies, and a calling to the colors of the party faithful, the Republicans ran a low-keyed campaign of persuasion aimed specifically at winning new converts to the party. It worked brilliantly. More than two-thirds of the new voters in the election of 1896 voted for McKinley.

When the election was over, and Bryan had been defeated, Americans of property heaved a collective sigh of relief. The republic itself had been at stake, or at least that was the belief of spokesmen for Eastern capital and culture. To them, Bryan was not just another politician; he was an economic radical who had an angry and dangerous mob at his back. The editor of the Philadelphia *Press* warned that the leaders of the Democratic party that had nominated Bryan "incarnate a spirit of Communism and Anarchy which is new to America on any large scale. . . ."[22] The Catholic hierarchy

The Urban Middle Class, 1880s. Members of the urbanized middle class that turned decisively to the Republicans in the 1890s are shown enjoying an afternoon at the zoo. These city-dwellers had the leisure time to enjoy the amenities of urban life and the income to purchase new consumer products, such as the portable camera held by the young man wearing the bowler. They embraced the Republicans as the party of respectability and prosperity. (The Brooklyn Museum)

The Sacrilegious Candidate. This was the dominant image of Bryan in the East—a dangerous religious demagogue and economic radical who had to be defeated before he destroyed civilized order. (The Granger Collection)

and conservative Protestant ministers for once had a common cause that united them—the defeat of Bryan, the blasphemous anarchist. The Reverend Cortland Myers, a Baptist minister, saw a Democratic platform in 1896 that "was made in hell," and Archbishop John Ireland told Catholics:[23]

> The war of class against class is upon us, the war of the proletariat against the propertyholder. No other meaning than this can be given to the appeals to the "common people," to the "laborer," to the "poor and downtrodden," and to the denunciations against "plutocrats" and "corporations" and "money grabbers" and "bankers."

Bryan, the son of a Baptist minister and the husband of the daughter of a well-to-do storekeeper, was anything but a radical. He reiterated that by carefully disassociating himself from the Populist Platform. A mediocre lawyer, he found his calling in politics and never deviated from his belief that he was the authentic voice of the people. His people were the same as Jackson's, the real producers who wanted only a fair and equal chance to get ahead. "When you come before us and tell us that we are to disturb your business interests," he told the gold Democrats at Chicago, "we reply that you have disturbed our business interests by your course."[24] This was the cry of the frustrated propertyholder, not the alienated radical. Middle-class to the core and the very personification of evangelical values, Bryan was about as conservative in 1896 as any American could be.

What, then, was at stake in 1896? If Bryan was not an anarchist, why, apart from the obvious partisan advantage to the Republicans in depicting him as such, was he widely believed to be one? Above all, why did his defeat in the midst of the collapse of Populism leave Americans with the sense that a watershed had been passed, that a corner had been turned and there was no looking back?

The Passage of a Century

Henry Adams, a scion of the famous Adams family of presidents and public servants, provided a useful framework for answering these questions in his classic autobiography. Adams recalled the 1890s as that decade when "the majority at last declared itself, once for all, in favor of the capitalistic system with all its necessary machinery." Until then, in Adams's view, nineteenth-century Americans "had hesitated . . . between two forces." One represented limited production in household and small-scale enterprises and the other a much greater production organized and controlled through the mass application of energy and capital. He believed that the former fostered individualism, but the latter, concerned only with mass and efficiency, hammered out a "new American," one who was the "servant of the power-house."[25] Now, after the 1890s, there was no turning back.

Adams's mechanical metaphors were too rigid and deterministic to capture the human choices involved in historical change, but they did capture a central truth of the 1890s, and it was the same one that his contemporaries expressed in their lurid imagery of a Republican conspiracy of Wall Street versus a Democratic conspiracy of anarchists. Americans realized that they were at a crossroads in the 1890s, and they engaged in the last great mass debate over what America meant and how power within it was to be distributed. What was at stake was not the republic itself, but competing visions of the republic. Each of these visions could legitimately claim to be grounded in a common revolutionary heritage of republicanism, but each had followed a different current in the social passage of republicanism in the nineteenth century. These currents had so diverged by the 1890s that Americans stood upon opposite banks of that republican passage and denounced as heretical the vision of those on the other side.

The core value of early-nineteenth-century republicanism was freedom from degrading dependency upon others in personalized hierarchies of social control. The possession of property was the means of achieving that freedom. Property as a means to independence was thus the material base for political freedom and personal security. On this, all nineteenth-century Americans agreed. But the meaning of property, and the republican freedoms derived from it, changed as a market revolution transformed the social relations of production throughout the century.

One set of these relations, the older and preindustrial one, persisted in the localized and independent household economies of farmers and artisans on the periphery of the market. These Americans, an overwhelming proportion of the free population in 1815, clung to the precapitalist definition of property as something that was tangible and static. Property was part of the productive assets of nature and, above all, it was land. This form of property made possible, in Jefferson's phrase in the Declaration of Independence, "the pursuit of happiness," and its management and control ensured the independence of the family unit in the present and its perpetuation into the future. By providing the family with security, and freeing it from dependency on the corrupting favors of others, landed property (or its equivalent, artisan ownership of the means of production) made possible the virtuous citizenry without which Americans believed the republic would quickly degenerate into anarchy or despotism. This citizenry was independent but not isolated from each other. An ethic of mutual obligation, rooted economically in local exchanges of good and services and expressed politically as the need for the virtuous to protect the community from tyrannical outsiders, bound individuals together in neighborhoods of reciprocal responsibilities.

Another set of social relations organically developed out of this older one and shaped the material context for a shift away from the self-reliance of classical republicanism to the acquisitive individualism of the liberal capitalism of the nineteenth century. Simultaneously a product and an initiator of the social changes we label as commercial and industrial capitalism, this set comprised the market relations of capital and wage labor, employer and employee. Annual increases in per-capita real product of 1.1 percent in the first half of the nineteenth century and 1.6 percent in the second half attested to the dynamic pace of economic growth. A new middle class evolved by learning how to substitute education and marketable skills for landed property as a basis for social advancement. More and more farmers benefited from a steady rise in the value of their land and expanding markets for their crops. They increased output by reinvesting capital in their land and, like all good businessmen, paying close attention to matters of detail and the efficient budgeting of their time.

Other, poorer farmers, in an effort to preserve the independence of the family economy, put their daughters out to work for merchant capitalists and sent their children into the early factories. Immigrants, most of whom never had a family farm to pass on, valued industrial jobs and steady wages as a means of preserving family stability. In the case of either the poorer farmers or the immigrants, conservative motivations resulted in radical change over time. In adjusting to change, Americans were constantly propelling it forward. By the end of the nineteenth century, society was stratified along class lines rather than the earlier age rankings of Americans within patriarchal families, which were centers of both production and consumption. Production had been taken out of the home, and dependency upon a national and international market had gradually replaced reliance upon neighborhood networks of exchange.

Central to these social transformations of the nineteenth century was a new definition of property that was much more abstract and speculative than the traditional one. Property now referred primarily not to land but to wealth. And more and more of the wealth was held not by individuals but by corporations. As illustrated by the case of farmers' land being flooded to provide water power for manufacturers, the acquisition of wealth often took precedence over older property rights. Property as wealth placed one in relationship, not to nature, but to a monetary scale of value by which one's status could be quantified and measured against others. Individual self-interest, not mutual obligation, was increasingly seen as the prime regulator for society as a whole. In responding rationally to market opportunities, individuals would naturally stabilize society through a competitive balance in which all were free to earn and consume more. Any resulting inequalities in the marketplace, because they were based on free and equal competition, were natural ones and could hardly be criticized for being morally unfair.

Throughout the nineteenth century, there was constant friction between these older and newer sets of social relations and values. This friction provided the underlying rationale for the partisan division of the electorate into the Whig-Republican camp on the one hand and the Democratic on the other. Although the fit was not an exact one, it registered the general attitude of the respective major parties toward market change. The Democrats, representing marginal farmers and laborers, were consistently the party of localism, which critiqued the market economy from a tradition of equal rights and antimonopoly. The Republicans were the party of nationalism and economic development, which spoke for a broadening middle-class constituency in favor of more market change.

This division, contained within the value structure of a free labor economy, was overshadowed at the end of the antebellum period by the more fundamental struggle between the social visions of free labor and slave labor. The Civil War broke out when a majority in each section felt they would lose their republican independence if the social system of the other section spread through the nation or into the territories. When the debate over the spread of the market reemerged in the 1870s, virtually all the participants were now involved in a market economy. On one side were farmers, industrial workers, and small businessmen who felt victimized by an economy that was depriving them of their autonomy. On the other side were the commercially successful farmers, the managers of corporate capitalism, and the salaried middle class whose economic opportunities expanded with every increase in the scale of business activity.

The successive shocks of first an agricultural and then an industrial depression transformed this debate into a full-scale cultural collision in the 1890s. The collision, however, for all the passion on both sides, produced no structural change in the political economy. Despite similar visions of America as a cooperative common-wealth, Populist farmers and urban workers never came together in a common political front. When it came down to a choice between Populism and corporate capitalism, the middle class, and those who hoped to join it, overwhelmingly chose the latter. Alienated by a Populist ideology that seemed to both attack and cherish property rights, the middle class dismissed Populism as the ignorance of the hopelessly confused.

In fact, Populist ideology, and the shadow of it in the Bryan Democratic party was contradictory. Although it emphatically was not socialistic, it did call for public own-ership of key economic services. It did so in the belief that the property rights of small producers were threatened by the corporate control of transportation, finance, and communications. The confusion was obvious: the Populists were both for and against capitalism. More precisely, they used the ethical standards of an older definition of property to attack the newer corporate forms of property that had arisen out of the rights of preindustrial property. But the Populists could not have it both ways. They could not reject on moral grounds certain kinds of corporate capitalism without also rejecting the entire value system of private property and capital accumulation that served as the ethical basis for that corporate capitalism. Because most Americans now believed that the whole purpose of liberty was to protect property rights, whether individual or corporate, they interpreted the Populist program on collective ownership of some forms of property as an attack upon all property ownership. Too conservative for Socialists and some workers, the Populists were too radical for just about everybody else.

The political decision of 1896 confirmed a cultural one that had been made long before. That cultural decision had been made in countless different places at different times throughout the nineteenth century. Over time the republicanism of the farmers and artisans of 1815 no longer expressed the lived experience of most Americans. A new market definition of republicanism evolved that equated it with economic growth and control over capital in a social setting of freely competing individuals. In its modern version, we identify the political health of the republic with the economic size of the Gross National Product.

This market definition of republicanism was the social creation of the beneficiaries of rapid economic growth in the nineteenth century. The most powerful of these Americans came from the preindustrial elites who turned to the private corporation after 1815 for a collective basis with which to consolidate and expand their cultural and economic leadership. They used the corporate form of organization not just for business, but for private colleges, reform societies, and professional fraternities. Consequently, the antebellum social elites never lost control of the industrial revolution in the second half of the century. The corporate leaders of 1896 were drawn almost exclusively from the most respectable and long-established American families of native-born Protestants. Many of them were the sons of the Protestant laymen who had fashioned the nation's first bureaucratic organizations, the sectarian associations of evangelical reform. Even more so than their fathers, these men fused industrial prosperity, entrepreneurial republicanism, and Protestant Christianity into a single set of values.

Beneath this elite in 1896, and sharing their values, were the moderately successful in a native-born middle class that had grown continuously throughout the nineteenth century. Out of this class came the community leaders who persisted in the same towns decade after decade and who dominated the membership of the local business and social organizations that spoke in a unified voice for the entrepreneurial ambitions of the community. The lower ranks of this class were growing the fastest. They were the salaried white-collar workers who staffed the offices of the business corporations. Although denied much economic independence by their dependence on hierarchical chains of command in which they pursued their careers at the bottom or middle of the corporate ladder, they accepted these controls over their lives as a necessary tradeoff for greater material benefits. And, if their avid readership of the Horatio Alger literature is a reliable guide, this new middle class aspired to little more than a secure corporate niche. The heroes of Alger's stories did not find economic independence or great wealth. Instead, through a stroke of luck, they found a personal benefactor who looked after them and secured them a good white-collar job.

A similar longing for security was met by the new genre of utopian literature in the late nineteenth century. Edward Bellamy's 1888 novel, *Looking Backward,* set the standard. These novels offered their middle-class readers futuristic images of stable and socially homogeneous communities in which technocratic elites ruled in the name of the people in order to assure a standardized abundance for all. Thus, even in their ambivalence about the pace of technological and social change, the middle class was prone to look to experts, not to the people, as the regulators of social harmony. The same tendency, as we saw earlier, characterized middle-class professionalism and reform in the Gilded Age.

The upper echelons of the middle class and the elites at the top were the source of America's political, economic, and cultural leadership in the late nineteenth century. Their right to rule was challenged by the dissidents in the 1890s, the decade in which it appeared that all the underdogs in American society might band together and politically defeat their alleged betters. Oliver Wendell Holmes, soon to be a justice on the

Supreme Court, expressed the class fears of those on top when he identified the depression year of 1893 as the time when "a vague terror went over the earth and the word socialism began to be heard."[26] To combat that terror, and the threat of socialism that they saw in the Bryan Democrats, the business elites threw all their cultural and economic resources behind the McKinley campaign. America's leadership classes were rarely so united. They presented a solid phalanx of respectability and money that successfully portrayed Bryan as a cultural anarchist, if not an economic one. Voters made up their own minds, but it was hard not to vote for McKinley and the gold standard when the cultural and economic weight of the nation equated both with civilization and prosperity.

When the campaign of 1896 was over, more than an election had been won. The right of certain kinds of Americans, those with a disproportionate share of the corporate and cultural power, to speak and rule for all Americans was reaffirmed. Ever since 1896, their definition of America has rarely been an issue for public debate and has largely been taken for granted. It has been a definition that has encouraged Americans to substitute the pleasures of mass consumption for participation in public life. We consume more private goods today, but barely half of us who are eligible to vote bother to do so in national elections.

The size of the active electorate has shrunk for many reasons, but surely two of the most fundamental ones date from the Republican victory in 1896. Starting in the late 1890s, Republican-dominated legislatures passed antifusion laws aimed against the Populists and third parties in general. These laws made it much more difficult for third parties to put together a mixed slate of candidates in combination with one of the major parties. The Australian secret ballot, introduced in the 1890s, also offered an opportunity to curb third parties. Official ballots were now prepared by the states, not by the political parties, and dissident citizens could no longer just call themselves a party and print their own ballots. By manipulating the definition of a party in terms of a minimum percentage of the votes cast in the preceding election or of a certain number of signatures on a petition for inclusions on the ballot, Republican legislatures outside the South succeeded in denying potential third parties access to the ballot. After having held the balance of power in a majority of the non-Southern states from the mid-1880s through the early 1890s, third parties were now largely eliminated as an alternative political voice to the rule of the two major parties.

While independent political action from the bottom was being limited after 1896, governmental controls from the top were being expanded. McKinley's successor, Theodore Roosevelt, provided the initial leadership for the gradual expansion of the federal bureaucracy through a series of executive agencies that were based on the same organizational models of expert knowledge and centralized authority that were developed by businessmen in their corporations and middle-class professionals in their reform associations. Thus problems of increasing scale and complexity in the economic, social, and political spheres of American life in the twentieth century all pointed to the same response—the concentration of authority and prestige in the hands of the few who were at the top of a hierarchical command structure. Because the federal agencies were staffed by nonelected experts, who presumably knew what was best for their clients, the people, voters have quite rationally concluded that their electoral participation counts less and less in the decisions that affect their lives.

The voice for an alternative definition of America, the cooperative vision of the reform unionism of the Knights and the agrarian radicalism of the Populists, was politically silenced in the late nineteenth century, but it still speaks to our needs in the late twentieth century. It will do so as long as American republicanism faces the dilemma of reconciling the facts of economic inequality with a tradition of political egalitarianism. Walt Whitman best expressed what that tradition was all about when he wrote in 1867:[27]

> The mission of government . . . is not authority alone, nor even of law, nor . . . the rule of the best men . . . but, higher than the highest arbitrary rule, to train communities through all their grades, beginning with individuals and ending there again, to rule themselves.

The realization of that mission still eludes us today.

SUGGESTED READING

Alexander B. Callow, Jr., *From Hayes to McKinley* (1969), and Vincent P. De Santis, *The Shaping of Modern America, 1877–1916* (1973), provide good treatments of the 1890s, and Harold U. Faulkner, *Politics, Reform and Expansion* (1959), is the most thorough monograph. R. Hal Williams, *Years of Decision: American Politics in the 1890s* (1978), is a concise survey. For national politics in the Cleveland-Hayes years of the late 1880s, see Allan Nevins, *Grover Cleveland* (1932); Horace S. Merrill, *Bourbon Leader: Grover Cleveland and the Democratic Party* (1957); and Harry J. Sievers, *Benjamin Harrison*, Vols. 2 and 3 (1968). The standard account of the election of 1892 is George Harmon Knoles, *The Presidential Campaign and Election of 1892* (1942).

For the depression of 1893, see Reindigs Fels, *American Business Cycles, 1865–1917* (1959); Charles Hoffman, *The Depression of the Nineties* (1970); and Robert Higgs, *The Transformation of the American Economy, 1865–1914* (1971). Lucid discussions of the cyclical nature of the nineteenth-century economy that are especially useful for the nonspecialist can be found in Douglas C. North, *Growth and Welfare in the American Past* (1966), and Robert L. Heilbroner, *The Economic Transformation of America* (1977). The social misery caused by the depression can be gauged in Robert H. Bremner, *From the Depths: The Discovery of Poverty in America* (1956). J. Rogers Hollingsworth, *The Whirligig of Politics: The Democracy of Cleveland and Bryan* (1963), is excellent on the political reaction of the Cleveland administration to the depression. Nick Salvatore, *Eugene V. Debs: Citizen and Socialist* (1982), has a superb account of the Pullman strike and its impact on Debs. For the backlash of the voters against the Democrats' handling of the depression, see the discussion on the 1890s in Walter Dean Burnham, *Critical Elections and the Mainsprings of American Politics* (1970). Richard Jensen, *The Winning of the Midwest: Social and Political Conflict, 1888–1896* (1971), and Samuel T. McSeveney, *The Politics of Depression: Political Behavior in the Northeast, 1893–1896* (1972), are superb regional studies that detail the switch to the Republicans. For the policy changes brought about by this realignment in a key Northern state, see Richard L. McCormick, *From Realignment to Reform: Political Change in New York State, 1893–1910* (1981).

Fred A. Shannon, *The Farmer's Last Frontier* (1945), and Gilbert C. Fite, *The Farmer's Frontier, 1865–1900* (1963), are excellent surveys of the economic conditions that spawned agrarian protest. Lawrence Goodwyn, *Democratic Promise: The Populist Movement in America* (1976), is a major work that places the Southern Alliance and its cooperative experience at the heart of the Populist movement. Also helpful on the Southern Alliance are Robert McMath, *Populist Vanguard: A History of the Southern Farmers Alliance* (1975), and, from a more sociological perspective, Michael Schwartz, *Radical Protest and Social Structures: The Southern Farmers' Alliance and Cotton Tenancy* (1976), and Donna A. Barnes, *Farmers in Rebellion:*

The Rise and Fall of the Southern Farmers Alliance and People's Party in Texas (1984). For a very precise look at the grassroots membership of the Alliance in a South Dakota county, see John Dibbern, "Who Were the Populists?," AGH 56 (1982).

Although it slights the South, John D. Hicks, *The Populist Movement* (1931), remains the standard account for the Populists. In addition to Hicks and Goodwyn, works that should be consulted are: Stanley B. Parsons, *The Populist Context: Rural versus Urban Power on a Great Plains Frontier* (1973); Bruce Palmer, "*Man Over Money": The Southern Populist Critique of American Capitalism* (1980); and James Turner, "Understanding the Populists," JAH 67 (1980). Among a host of state studies, the following stand out: Gene O. Clanton, *Kansas Populism: Ideas and Men* (1969); James E. Wright, *The Politics of Populism: Dissent in Colorado* (1974); Robert W. Cherney, *Populism, Progressivism, and the Transformation of Nebraska Politics, 1885–1915* (1981); Alex M. Arnett, *The Populist Movement in Georgia* (1922); and Sheldon Hackney, *From Populism to Progressivism in Alabama* (1969). The classic indictment of the Populists as agrarian reactionaries who had no economically rational basis for attacking railroads and banks will be found in Richard Hofstadter, *The Age of Reform* (1954). The counter argument is best represented in Norman Pollack, *The Populist Response to Industrial America* (1966). The issue of interest rates on farm mortgages is most carefully taken up in Allan G. Bogue, *Money at Interest: The Farm Mortgage on the Middle Border* (1955). By arguing that the rise in farm tenancy in the Midwest represented a healthy market response to the commercialization of agriculture and a first step towards the acquisition of a farm, Donald L. Winters, *Farmers without Farms: Agricultural Tenancy in Nineteenth-Century Iowa* (1978), implicitly denies a connection between tenancy and political protest. For the older view that identifies tenancy and migrant farm labor with a decline in agricultural opportunity, see La Wanda F. Cox, "The American Agricultural Wage Earner, 1865–1900," AGH 22 (1948). Anne Mayhew, "A Reappraisal of the Causes of Farm Protest in the United States, 1870–1900," JEH 32 (1974), links the political anger of the Populists with their forced dependency upon a market system over which they had no control. A similar argument, coupled with an insistence on the reformist and cooperative response of the Populists to the corporate power of industrial capitalism, is in Alan Trachtenberg, *The Incorporation of America: Culture and Society in the Gilded Age* (1982).

The spread of a business mentality among farmers in the dairy and corn-hog belts of the Midwest, a mentality that made it unlikely that they would embrace Populism, is explained in Adam Ward Rome, "American Farmers as Entrepreneurs, 1870–1900," AGH 56 (1982). The connection between crop systems in the Midwest and the geographic boundaries of Populism is shown in Benton H. Wilcox, "An Historical Definition of Northwestern Radicalism," MVHR 26 (1929). George H. Miller, *Railroads and the Granger Laws* (1971), convincingly argues that the so-called Granger Laws of the 1870s, which regulated railroad rates, were secured by a coalition of shippers, merchants, and farmers who were acting out of economic self-interest, a view that replaced the earlier interpretation found in Solon J. Buck, *The Granger Movement* (1913), which stressed the antimonopolism of farmers in the passage of the laws. On the failure of the Populists to forge an alliance with urban labor, see Norman Pollack, *The Populist Response to Industrial America* (1966), and Chester McArthur Destler, *Henry Demarest Lloyd and the Empire of Reform* (1963). The larger question of the failure of American labor to pursue more radical politics in the 1890s or thereafter is addressed in William M. Dick, *Labor and Socialism in America: The Gompers Era* (1972); John H. M. Laslett and Seymour Martin Lipset, eds., *Failure of a Dream? Essays in the History of American Socialism* (1974); and Aileen S. Kraditor, *The Radical Persuasion, 1890–1917* (1981). Walter T. K. Nugent, "Money, Politics, and Society," in H. Wayne Morgan, ed., *The Gilded Age* (1970), is a lucid guide through the intricacies of the currency question. Richard Hofstadter's introduction to William H. Harvey, *Coin's Financial School* (1894; reprinted in 1963), explains the popularity of the silver issue in the 1890s.

On the fusion of the Populists with the Democrats and the election of 1896, see Stanley L. Jones, *The Presidential Election of 1896* (1964); Paul W. Glad, *McKinley, Bryan, and the People* (1964); and Robert F. Durden, *The Climax of Populism: The Election of 1896* (1965). Paolo E. Coletta, *William Jennings Bryan: Political Evangelist, 1860–1908* (1964); Louis W. Koenig, *Bryan: A Political Biography of William Jennings Bryan* (1971); and H. Wayne Morgan, *William McKinley and His America* (1963), are excellent biographies of the major figures in the campaign. For the demographic conditions that contributed heavily to the failure of Populism in the Middle Border, see James C. Malin, "The Turnover of Farm Population in Kansas," KHQ 4 (1935). Paul F. Sharp, "When Our West Moved North," AHR 55 (1950), discusses the migration to Canada. The rapid collapse of Southern Populism after 1896 can be followed in C. Vann Woodward, *Tom Watson, Agrarian Rebel* (1938). J. Morgan Kousser, *The Shaping of Southern Politics: Suffrage Restriction and the Establishment of the One-Party South, 1880–1910* (1974), documents the success of conservative white elites in sharply limiting the size of the Southern electorate by the early twentieth century. For two contrasting views of the attitudes and policies of Southern white Populists towards blacks, see William F. Holmes, "The Demise of the Colored Farmers Alliance," JSH 4 (1975), and Lawrence Goodwyn, "Populist Dreams and Negro Rights: East Texas as a Case Study," AHR 75 (1971), a much more favorable appraisal.

The best analysis of the election of 1896 as a cultural battle over who had the right to hold power and speak for America is in Lawrence Goodwyn, *Democratic Promise* (1976). Walter Dean Burnham, "The System of 1896: An Analysis," in Paul Kleppner, et al., *The Evolution of American Electoral Systems* (1981), is an important source for the argument that the Republican victory was a triumph for industrial and financial elites anxious to restrain a mass electorate with unpredictable tendencies that could upset the emerging corporate order. Peter H. Argersinger, "A Place on the Ballot: Fusion Politics and Antifusion Laws," AHR 85 (1980), shows how the Australian ballot and antifusion laws very quickly defused the threat that third parties had earlier posed for the major parties. For the adjustment of nineteenth-century republicanism to corporate power in the early twentieth century, see R. Jeffrey Lustig, *Corporate Liberalism: The Origins of Modern American Political Theory, 1890–1920* (1982).

For two concise overviews of the development of the nineteenth-century middle class and its values, see Gregory H. Singleton, "Essay Review—'Mere Middle-Class Institutions': Urban Protestantism in Nineteenth-Century America," JSOH 6 (1973), and Ronald E. Butchart, "Education and Culture in the Trans-Mississippi West: An Interpretation," JAC 3 (1980). The importance of bureaucratic organization for the religious reformers of this class is stressed in Gregory H. Singleton, "Protestant Voluntary Organizations and the Shaping of Victorian America," Daniel Walker Howe, ed., *Victorian America* (1976); Ronald Story, *The Forging of an Aristocracy: Harvard and the Boston Upper Class, 1800–1870* (1980), and Peter Dobkin Hall, *The Organization of American Culture, 1700–1900* (1982), both show how the corporation was used by the upper middle class as an instrument of social and cultural power throughout the nineteenth century. Meanwhile, as can be seen in Frances W. Gregory and Irene D. Neu, "The American Industrial Elite in the 1870s: Their Social Origins," in William E. Miller, ed., *Men in Business: Essays in the History of Entrepreneurship* (1952), and John N. Ingham, *The Iron Barons: A Social Analysis of an American Urban Elite, 1874–1965* (1978), the antebellum social elite retained its economic power into the age of industrial capitalism. For the tension, if not contradiction, that developed in the nineteenth century between corporate economic power and democratic political participation in the government, see Robert A. Dahl, "On Removing Certain Impediments to Democracy in the United States," *Dissent,* Summer (1978). Daniel Horowitz, "Consumption and Its Discontents: Simon N. Patten, Thorstein Veblen, and George Gunton," JAH 67 (1980), analyzes how intellectuals in the Gilded Age reacted to this tension by beginning to argue that mass consumption itself was a sign of a healthy democracy. The result in the early twentieth century, as shown in William L. O'Neill, *The Progressive Years: America*

Comes of Age (1975), was a political system that favored economic efficiency and growth over democratic equality and participation.

NOTES

1. Quoted in Chester McArthur Destler, *American Radicalism, 1865–1901* (Chicago: Quadrangle Paperback, 1966), p. 218.
2. Quoted in William Nisbet Chambers, *The Democrats in American Politics* (New York: An Anvil Original, 1972), p. 169.
3. Cited in Harold U. Faulkner, *Politics, Reform and Expansion, 1890–1900* (New York: Harper Torchbooks, 1963), p. 100.
4. Quoted in Robert D. Marcus, *Grand Old Party: Political Structure in the Gilded Age, 1880–1896* (New York: Oxford University Press, 1971), pp. 192–193.
5. Quoted in Faulkner, op. cit., p. 141.
6. William M. Armstrong, ed., *The Gilded Age Letters of E. L. Godkin* (Albany: State University of New York Press, 1974), p. 459.
7. Quoted in Robert C. McMath, Jr., *Populist Vanguard: A History of the Southern Farmers' Alliance* (New York: The Norton Library, 1977), p. 64.
8. New York *Times,* Dec. 12, 1890, cited in John D. Hicks, *The Populist Revolt* (Lincoln, Neb.: University of Nebraska Press, 1961), p. 441.
9. Cited in Adam Ward Rome, "American Farmers as Entrepreneurs, 1870–1900," *Agricultural History* 56 (1982): 38.
10. Quoted in Allan G. Bogue, *Money at Interest: The Farm Mortgage on the Middle Border* (Lincoln, Neb.: Bison Book, 1969), p. 262.
11. Quoted in Leonard Rapport, "The Interstate Commerce Commission Formal Case Files: A Source for Local History," *Prologue: Journal of the National Archives* 15 (1983): 232, 234.
12. Quoted in Faulkner, op. cit., p. 54.
13. Ibid., pp. 129–130.
14. "Omaha Platform," in Hicks, op. cit., p. 441.
15. Ibid., p. 443.
16. Quoted in David Montgomery, *Beyond Equality: Labor and the Radical Republicans, 1862–1872* (New York: Alfred A. Knopf, 1967), p. 252.
17. Quoted in Chambers, op. cit., p. 174.
18. Quoted in Norman Pollack, *The Populist Response to Industrial America* (New York: The Norton Library, 1966), p. 104.
19. Quoted in Lawrence Goodwyn, *Democratic Promise: The Populist Movement in America* (New York: Oxford University Press, 1976), p. 494.
20. Quoted in C. Vann Woodward, *Tom Watson: Agrarian Rebel* (New York: Oxford University Press paperback, 1963), p. 223.
21. Ibid., p. 220.
22. Quoted in J. Robert Hollingsworth, *The Whirligig of Politics: The Democracy of Cleveland and Bryan* (Chicago: The University of Chicago Press, 1963), p. 67.
23. Quoted in Richard J. Jensen, *The Winning of the Midwest: Social and Political Conflict, 1888–1896* (Chicago: University of Chicago Press, 1971), p. 285.
24. Quoted in Chambers, op. cit., p. 170.
25. Henry Adams, *The Education of Henry Adams* (New York: The Modern Library, 1931), pp. 344, 466.
26. Quoted in Geoffrey Blodgett, "The New Political History of the 1890s," *Reviews in American History* 1 (1973): 236.
27. Walt Whitman, "Democracy," in Alan Trachtenberg, ed., *Democratic Vistas, 1860–1880* (New York: George Braziller, 1970), pp. 355–356.

Index

Abolitionism: and egalitarianism, 167; and market revolution, 167; as a career, 171; and Southern secession, 200–202. *See also* Antislavery

Abolitionists: and Texas annexation, 161; critique of slavery and South, 167, 172, 184; doctrine of immediatism, 167–68; on racial equality, 168, 170; role as agitators, 168–69; radicalism of, 170; Garrisonian wing, 170; support for, 171; in Civil War, 220, 222; image of blacks under slavery, 241

Abortions, 93

Adams, Charles Francis, 173–74

Adams, Henry, 363, 421

Adams, John Quincy, 148; and election of 1824, 133–34; as president, 134–36; and election of 1828, 137; on Slave Power, 172

Adams-Onis Treaty, 132, 134, 162

Addams, Jane, 343–44

Adolescence: prolonged in nineteenth century, 217–18; early nineteenth-century attitudes toward, 333; emergence as a separate stage in life, 332–34

Adolescents: and early factory labor, 38; and apprenticeship, 106. *See also* Youth

Africa, and colonization of free blacks, 73, 143

African slave trade, 9, 142; prohibited, 132; move to reopen, 205; effects of closing on U.S. slaves, 247

Africans, 326

Afro-Americans: *see* Blacks; Slaves

Age: preindustrial attitudes toward, 332; as a social ordering device, 332–37

Aging (of population), 334–35

Agrarian revolt of 1890s, 2, 3, 5, 395, 398–99, 402–405. *See also* Populism and Populist party

Agricultural society: in colonial period, 9; and family-centered independence, 9, 14; and republicanism, 10, 18, 126; demographic pattern of, 11–12, 17; and rural exchange networks, 20, 36

Agricultural workforce, decline in, 11, 293

Agriculture: colonial, 13; on frontier, 19–20, 28; in Jacksonian and pre–Civil War periods, 20–25, 35–36, 44–45; mechanization of, 24–25, 46–47, 296; in pre–Civil War South, 25–30, 45–48; in Confederacy, 224–25; in Civil War North, 227; in post–Civil War South, 250–52, 256, 259–60, 283–93; in trans-Mississippi West, 269–75; and depression of the Gilded Age, 398, 401, 403–405, 409–10; and return of prosperity in late 1890s, 415–16

Aiken, D. Wyatt, 251

Alabama: settlement of, 16; pre–Civil War society and economy, 24, 27, 30, 132, 202, 204; Indian removal, 59–60; election of 1828, 137; secession, 209; Civil War, 225; economic losses of Civil War, 254, 283; Populists, 416

Alabama Territory, 25

Alaska, 416

Albany, New York, 21

Albany Regency, 138, 146

Albee, Lloyd, 219

Liberalism (*continued*)
class, 240; and Reconstruction, 245, 248–49
Liberal Republican party, 377–78
Liberator, The, 168
Liberia, 71, 73
Liberty party, 170–74
Librarianship: defined as women's work, 330; and professionalization, 339
Life expectancy: contrast of, between whites and blacks, 71, 326; rise of, 329, 336
Lincoln, Abraham: free-labor ideology, 88, 158; election of 1860, 189–90, 236; on slavery as a moral issue, 197; in secession crisis, 210–12; on issues of Civil War, 212; call for troops, 212–13; and emancipation, 220–22, 226; enlistment of black soldiers, 222, 226; election of 1864, 227, 237; wartime Reconstruction, 239; assassination, 237
Literacy: in pre–1815 period, 106; in mid-nineteenth century, 113; and slaves, 252; and freedmen, 288–89; and job opportunities for white women, 328
Little Bighorn, battle of, 277
Livestock: improved quality in pre–Civil War North, 23, 37; poor quality in pre–Civil War South, 46–48; Southern losses in Civil War, 256, 290; and closing of the open range, 291–92
Lloyd, Henry Demarest, 395, 415
Localism: and Democratic party, 226, 365, 423; and patronage, 379
Looking Backward, 424
Loomis, Samuel Lane, 297
Louisiana: slavery, 132, 247; secession, 209; in Reconstruction, 239, 253, 255, 260; freedmen schools, 248; economic losses of emancipation, 283
Louisiana Purchase, 10, 18, 67, 126
Louisiana Territory, 132
Lowell, Massachusetts, 39, 350
Lumpkin, Wilson, 170
Lutherans: and republicanism, 122; in trans-Mississippi West, 273; in Gilded Age politics, 369, 398
Lynchings (of blacks), 287, 417
Lynn, Massachusetts, 34, 350

Madison, James, 64, 132; rationale for a large republic, 124; Jeffersonian Republican party, 124; as president, 130; states' rights, 142
Maine: prohibition, 105; Missouri Compromise, 133
Managerial capitalism, 310
Manchester, New Hampshire, 350
Mandans, 279
Manliness, and political culture of Gilded Age, 378
Mann, Horace, 88, 106–108, 112
Manufacturers: origins of, 33–35; evangelicalism, 102; temperance, 105; abolitionism, 171; in post–Civil War South, 292; scientific management, 302–304; legal creation of a national market, 311; protective tariff, 373–74; switch to unskilled labor, 387
Manufacturing: as threat to republican liberties, 10; pre–Civil War, 10–11, 24, 31–42, 47–49, 129; and pre–Civil War urbanization, 42–45; relative absence in pre–Civil War South, 46–48; in post–Civil War South, 283; growth in productivity, 303–304; and corporations, 308; and women, 328, 330. *See also* Factories; Industrialization
Market economy: interaction with republicanism, 1, 261, 421–25; limited in colonial period, 9; pre–Civil War politics, 150–52, 157–59, 162, 174, 178–79, 182; abolitionist critique of slavery, 167; declining birthrates, 176; integration of pre–Civil War Northern economy, 182; fears over change, 198, 398; Reconstruction and freedmen, 246; trans-Atlantic nature of, 272–73, 375; changing conceptions of corporations, 306–307; reforming the Indians, 318–19; culture of professionalism, 339; Populism, 406, 408–10. *See also* Agriculture; Corporations; Industrialization; Manufacturing
Marriage: changing conceptions of, 81; slavery and, 247, 249; delaying of, 327–28; divorce, 329; urban family economy, 373
Marriage, patterns of: in rural society, 11–13, 36; free blacks, 68; Philadelphia gentry, 81; urban and rural, in 1900, 327–28

Wells, David, 301
Welsh, 34–35, 388
West (pre–Civil War): settlement of, 3, 10, 14–31, 59, 269; agricultural exports to East, 35–36; in politics, 129–30, 174, 176; Panic of 1819, 121; debts to East, 135; repudiation of state bonds, 163; and Mexican War, 165–66; and a unified Northern market, 182. *See also* Old Northwest; Old Southwest
West (post–Civil War): settlement of, 269–75, 296; agriculture in, 272–75; economic exploitation of, 275; and blacks, 282, 287; manufacturing, 294; and working class, 349; in politics, 375–76, 397, 382; and election of 1896, 419. *See also* Middle Border
West Indies, and slave imports, 132
Wheat: as a commercial crop, 23; and agricultural mechanization, 24–25; labor demands of, 29, 296; in Upper South, 47, 66; post–Civil War fall in price, 375–76, 398; role in Populism, 406–407, 408–10, 415–16
Whig party, 4, 123, 139, 376; formation of, 145–48; in 1840s, 159–62, 164; in 1850s, 172, 174, 176; in secession and Civil War, 197, 200; Reconstruction, 239, 255; ideology of, 149–52, 157–58, 162, 422; and corporations, 308
Whig party (English), 122
White, Reverend Elipha, 107
White-collar jobs, growth of, 424
White males, privileges of, 56–57, 73
Whitman, Walt, 426
Whitney, Eli, 25
Willard, Francis, 380
Williams, James M., 218
Wilmot, David, 164
Wilmot Proviso, 164, 166, 173
Wilson-Gorman Tariff (1894), 403
Wilson, Woodrow, 415
Wisconsin: wealth holdings and age, 17; and Black Hawk's War, 62; increase in free states, 201; black suffrage, 240; mobility of farmers, 270; and Germans, 273; election of 1892, 399
Women: and biological determinism, 3, 56–57; in Revolutionary era, 74–75; in westward migration, 14–15; in household production, 36–37; jobs in wage econ-

omy, 38–41, 80, 325, 327–31; and dominance of churches, 77; declining birthrates, 75–77, 327–29; rising status as mothers, 77–78, 109; as key to social order, 79–82; in reform movements, 82, 102–104, 329, 343–44; abortions, 93; evangelicalism, 103; lack of property rights, 105; abolitionism, 169; in pre–Civil War South, 207–208, commitment to Civil War, 223, 237; in slave families, 247–49; cultural ideal of the lady, 326–27; education of, 327; demand for suffrage, 332; and Knights of Labor, 386. *See also* Cult of Domesticity; Gender roles; Marriage
Women's Christian Temperance Union, 380
Women's-rights movement, 80–81, 332
Woods, Robert A., 344
Wool cloth, and household production, 37
Worcester v. *Georgia* (1832), 60
Work: preindustrial conceptions and patterns of, 23, 28, 36–37, 76, 103–104; amount of, under slavery, 30; lengthened in nineteenth century, 48; intensified by industrial machinery, 49, 301–302; redefined in market society, 76–77, 114, 167; conceptions of, in pre–Civil War South, 66, 114; separation from residence, 81, 158, 383–84, 390; and planter attitudes regarding blacks, 246; comparison under slavery and sharecropping, 250–51; attitude of freedmen toward, 283; and scientific management, 303–304; associated with youth, 336–37; dangers of, under industrial capitalism, 348; as wage labor, 414
Working class: viewed as threat to social order, 4–5, 261–62, 317; as targets of social reform, 6, 348, 353–57; birthrates, 76, 93; attitudes toward women, 76; emergence of, 88, 92, 111; and immigrants, 92, 297, 352; and evangelicalism, 99, 102; and temperance, 105; attitudes toward schooling, 109, 178; and Democratic party, 151, 157; in Confederacy, 225; attitudes toward children, 328–29, 333; and social settlement workers, 344; living and working conditions of, 348–49; family economy of, 349–51; culture of, 352–57; in Gilded Age politics, 370, 381–82; unique development of, in U.S.,